Enterprise JavaBeans 3.0

FIFTH EDITION

Enterprise JavaBeans™ 3.0

Bill Burke and Richard Monson-Haefel

O'REILLY®

Beijing · Cambridge · Farnham · Köln · Paris · Sebastopol · Taipei · Tokyo

Enterprise JavaBeans™ 3.0, Fifth Edition
by Bill Burke and Richard Monson-Haefel

Published by O'Reilly Media, Inc., 1005 Gravenstein Highway North, Sebastopol, CA 95472.

O'Reilly books may be purchased for educational, business, or sales promotional use. Online editions are also available for most titles (*safari.oreilly.com*). For more information, contact our corporate/institutional sales department: (800) 998-9938 or *corporate@oreilly.com*.

Editor: Mike Loukides
Production Editor: Colleen Gorman
Copyeditor: Audrey Doyle
Proofreaders: Matt Hutchinson and Rachel Monaghan
Indexer: Julie Hawks
Cover Designer: Hanna Dyer
Interior Designer: David Futato
Illustrators: Robert Romano and Jessamyn Read

Printing History:

June 1999:	First Edition.
March 2000:	Second Edition.
September 2001:	Third Edition.
June 2004:	Fourth Edition.
May 2006:	Fifth Edition.

RepKover™ This book uses RepKover™, a durable and flexible lay-flat binding.

ISBN: 0-596-00978-X
[M]

For my girls: Monica, Molly, Abby, and Winnie

—Bill Burke

For my wife and best friend,
Hollie

—Richard Monson-Haefel

Table of Contents

Part II. The JBoss Workbook

Part III. Appendix

Foreword

Enterprise JavaBeans™ is the core component technology of the Java Enterprise Edition platform. It is an enterprise infrastructure designed to provide developers with the automatic management of many of the services essential to enterprise applications. The EJB container—the immediate environment of enterprise bean components and the provider of managed services to them—is at the center of this architecture.

However, to use this managed environment in earlier versions of EJB, developers had to write to APIs that focused more on the EJB container's requirements than on the business logic of enterprise applications. Consequently, EJB development was unnecessarily complex. For example:

- Implementation of various EJB interfaces led to a lot of boilerplate code for methods that were required by the interface, but not needed by the application.
- An XML deployment descriptor was required to integrate the application with its environment and with container services. Access to the components' environment was clumsy and nonintuitive.
- The design of container-managed persistence made domain object modeling unnecessarily complex and heavyweight. While container-managed persistence was originally conceived as an ease-of-use facility, in practice, it was awkward and limiting.

The purpose of the EJB 3.0 release was to refocus EJB on simplifying the developer's tasks—and to fix all of these problems, and more.

One of the first steps in this process was evaluating the sources of complexity in the earlier EJB releases. This involved examining criticisms of EJB; understanding which EJB design patterns were really antipatterns; identifying APIs that were clumsy to use, were nonintuitive to newcomers to the technology, or could be dispensed with entirely; and recognizing other aspects of the technology that were obstacles to ease of use.

The preliminary list of what needed to be fixed together with a proposal for how the task could be approached formed the basis of JSR 220, the Java Community Process specification request with which I launched EJB 3.0. Starting with the initial list of the APIs that needed improvement, the EJB 3.0 Expert Group undertook the process of brainstorming on better, simpler constructs. Bill Burke, the chief architect of the JBoss application server and author of this book, was one of the key participants in this effort.

The Expert Group's work has resulted in a major simplification and improvement. All of the key EJB APIs are easier to use, and the configuration-by-exception approach of EJB 3.0 allows developers to rely on expected default behaviors. The XML deployment descriptor has become unnecessary, except for addressing more advanced cases.

The Java language metadata facility, newly added to Java SE, aided us in making these simplifications. EJB 3.0 uses metadata annotations to express within Java code the dependencies of EJB components upon container services, and thus to avoid the need to provide a deployment descriptor. Further, EJB 3.0 provides default values for metadata so that in general, this metadata can be sparse.

By using metadata annotations to designate environment dependencies and life cycle callbacks, EJB 3.0 has also been able to eliminate the requirement for the bean class to implement to the EnterpriseBean interfaces. A bean class can now selectively specify what it needs, and can implement only needed methods rather than unnecessary boilerplate code.

We were able to eliminate the earlier EJBHome factory patterns as well by requiring smarter interpositioning on the part of the container (transparently to the application) in creating references to components and their instances at the time of lookup or injection. Session beans can now be programmed as ordinary Java classes with ordinary business interfaces, rather than as heavyweight components.

These and other changes have greatly simplified the developer view. Further, they leave the underlying EJB architecture fundamentally unchanged, providing a migration path to EJB 3.0.

The simplification of container-managed persistence provided a greater challenge. We began the effort here with the same steps as the simplification of session beans and message-driven beans: elimination of unneeded interfaces, use of annotations for configuration information, and so on. It soon became clear, however, that EJB persistence needed a more radical transformation. Further, the success of lighter-weight object/relational mapping technologies such as Hibernate gave clear guidance to the direction that this transformation should take.

As described in this book, the resulting Java Persistence API replaces container-managed persistence with a lighter-weight, Plain Old Java Object (POJO) persistence layer. This layer provides extensive support for domain object modeling, including inheritance and polymorphism; numerous enhancements to the EJB QL query language to provide rich query capabilities; and a specification for portable object/relational mapping through use of annotations or an XML descriptor. Persistent entities are now instances of ordinary (but managed) Java classes. As such, they can be created with `new` and passed to other application tiers as ordinary Java objects. The managed persistence contexts provided by the Java Persistence API provide particular leverage within EJB 3.0 environments, and enable the easy modeling of extended client "conversations."

Because of the scope of this work, EJB 3.0 has greatly simplified enterprise application development, and many of the features it has introduced have been incorporated elsewhere in the Java EE platform. Beyond this, the Java Persistence API has been expanded to support use "outside the container" in Java SE environments.

Bill Burke's contributions to EJB 3.0 and the Java Persistence API have been numerous and far reaching. As chief architect for the JBoss application server, he brought to the EJB 3.0 Expert Group key insights on container innovations, extensive experience with the Hibernate object/relational persistence technology, and a broad perspective on the needs of developers and their use of the EJB technology in real-world applications. In this new edition of *Enterprise JavaBeans*, based on the earlier work by Richard Monson-Haefel, Bill Burke shares these insights together with his in-depth perspective on how these new, simplified EJB 3.0 APIs transform the enterprise Java landscape for application developers.

—Linda DeMichiel
EJB 3.0 Architect and Specification Lead
Sun Microsystems
Santa Clara, California

Preface

Author's Note

In the spring of 2000, I left my CORBA development job at Iona and went to a small startup that was building an e-marketing portal. Coming from a CORBA background to an Enterprise JavaBeans™ project was a bit alien to me. I remember thinking, "Why does the server side need a component model?" I quickly learned that declarative transaction, security, and persistence metadata played a crucial role in developing business applications.

Like many startups at that time, we ran into funding problems at the end of 2000. We were about to go into beta with our first customers when our problems were compounded when our application server vendor revoked our demo license and demanded payment. We had to find a free solution fast, and that was when I stumbled into the open source application server, JBoss.

It didn't take very long to convert to JBoss, but I found that JBoss 2.0 was a bit raw in some areas. I had an extensive background in writing middleware under the tutelage of Steve Vinoski at Iona, so it wasn't too difficult to jump into the codebase. I immediately began fixing bugs here and there, submitting patches to the JBoss mail list. After a few months of contributing, I received a strange email:

```
what do you do in real life
```

The email was from JBoss's founder, Marc Fleury. Let me tell you, JBoss was the first open source project I had ever contributed to, and receiving an email from the founder himself was almost like receiving a message from God. OK, maybe I'm exaggerating a bit here. It was more like receiving a coded message from Morpheus in the movie *The Matrix*. I responded to Marc's email, saying I worked for a struggling startup and that I had written middleware at my previous job at Iona. I got a one-sentence response from Marc:

```
do you want to take the red pill
```

I was hooked. I replied yes, and my journey down the rabbit hole began. I became a CVS committer and first worked on entity bean synchronization. Later that year, I helped Sacha Labourey on JBoss's first clustering implementation. The rest is history.

Back in 2002, Richard Monson-Haefel, the original author of the EJB book series, contacted Marc about contributing a JBoss workbook. Marc wasn't interested, so he introduced Richard to Sacha Labourey and me, and we wrote the workbook that O'Reilly published with its book, *Enterprise JavaBeans*, Fourth Edition. When Richard retired from writing last year, I guess my work was good enough that O'Reilly offered me the opportunity to update the series to the latest EJB 3.0 specification.

Who Should Read This Book

This book explains and demonstrates the fundamentals of the EJB 3.0 and Java Persistence programming models. Although EJB makes application development much simpler, it is still a complex technology that requires a great deal of time and study to master. This book provides a straightforward, no-nonsense explanation of the underlying technology, Java™ classes and interfaces, the component model, and the runtime behavior of EJB. It does not include material on previous versions of the specification, however.

Although this book focuses on the fundamentals, it's not a "dummies" book. EJB is an extremely complex and ambitious enterprise technology. While using EJB may be fairly simple, the amount of work required to understand and master EJB is significant. Before reading this book, you should be fluent in the Java language and have some practical experience developing business solutions. Experience with distributed object systems is not a must, but you will need some experience with JDBC (or at least an understanding of the basics) to follow the examples in this book. If you are unfamiliar with the Java language, I recommend *Learning Java*; this book was formerly *Exploring Java* (both from O'Reilly). If you are unfamiliar with JDBC, I recommend *Database Programming with JDBC and Java* (O'Reilly). If you need a stronger background in distributed computing, I recommend *Java Distributed Computing* (O'Reilly).

How This Book Is Organized

This book is organized into two parts: the technical manuscript, followed by the JBoss workbook. The technical manuscript explains what EJB is, how it works, and when to use it. The JBoss workbook provides step-by-step instructions for installing, configuring, and running the examples from the manuscript on the JBoss 4.0 Application Server.

Part I: The EJB 3.0 Standard

Part 1 was adapted from Richard Monson-Haefel's fourth edition of this book by yours truly, Bill Burke. Linda DeMichiel, the EJB 3.0 specification lead, wrote the foreword to this book. Jason T. Greene adapted Chapters 18 and 19. Here is a summary of the content of the technical manuscript chapters:

Chapter 1, *Introduction*
: This chapter defines component transaction monitors and explains how they form the underlying technology of the EJB component model.

Chapter 2, *Architectural Overview*
: This chapter defines the architecture of the EJB component model and examines the differences between the three basic types of enterprise beans: entity beans, session beans, and message-driven beans.

Chapter 3, *Resource Management and Primary Services*
: This chapter explains how the EJB-compliant server manages an enterprise bean at runtime.

Chapter 4, *Developing Your First Beans*
: This chapter walks you through the development of some simple enterprise and entity beans.

Chapter 5, *Persistence: EntityManager*
: This chapter explains how entity beans interact with the new entity manager service.

Chapter 6, *Mapping Persistent Objects*
: This chapter defines the basic relational database mapping provided by the Java Persistence specification.

Chapter 7, *Entity Relationships*
: This chapter picks up where Chapter 6 left off, expanding your understanding of persistence and complex bean-to-bean relationships.

Chapter 8, *Entity Inheritance*
: This chapter discusses entity bean inheritance and how an object hierarchy can be mapped to a relational database.

Chapter 9, *Queries and EJB QL*
: This chapter addresses the Enterprise JavaBeans Query Language (EJB QL), which is used to query entity beans and to locate specific entity beans in Java Persistence.

Chapter 10, *Entity Callbacks and Listeners*
: This chapter covers the life cycle of an entity bean and how you can write classes that can intercept entity life cycle events.

Chapter 11, *Session Beans*
: This chapter shows how to develop stateless and stateful session beans.

Chapter 12, *Message-Driven Beans*
: This chapter shows how to develop message-driven beans.

Chapter 13, *Timer Service*
: This chapter shows how to use the Timer Service in EJB 3.0.

Chapter 14, *The JNDI ENC and Injection*
: This chapter explains the JNDI ENC as well as the new injection annotations and their XML equivalents.

Chapter 15, *Interceptors*
: This chapter discusses EJB interceptors and how you can use them to extend the behavior of your EJB container.

Chapter 16, *Transactions*
: This chapter provides an in-depth explanation of transactions and describes the transactional model defined by EJB.

Chapter 17, *Security*
: This chapter walks you through the basics of EJB security.

Chapter 18, *EJB 3.0: Web Services Standards*
: This chapter explains the XML, SOAP, WSLD, and UDDI web services standards.

Chapter 19, *EJB 3.0 and Web Services*
: This chapter discusses how the JAX-RPC API supports web services in EJB.

Chapter 20, *Java EE*
: This chapter provides an overview of Java EE 5 and explains how EJB 3.0 fits into this new platform.

Chapter 21, *EJB Design in the Real World*
: This chapter provides some basic design strategies that can simplify your EJB development efforts and make your EJB system more efficient.

Part II: The JBoss Workbook

The JBoss workbook shows how to execute examples from those chapters in the book that include at least one significant example. You'll want to read the introduction to the workbook to set up JBoss and configure it for the examples. After that, just go to the workbook chapter that matches the chapter you're reading. For example, if you are reading Chapter 6 on mapping persistent objects, use the "Exercises for Chapter 6" chapter of the workbook to develop and run the examples on JBoss.

Software and Versions

This book covers EJB 3.0 and Java Persistence 1.0. It uses Java language features from the Java SE 5 platform, including JDBC. Because the focus of this book is on developing vendor-independent EJB components and solutions, I have stayed away from proprietary extensions and vendor-dependent idioms. You can use any EJB-compliant server with this book, but you should be familiar with your server's specific installation, deployment, and runtime-management procedures to work with the examples. A workbook for the JBoss Application Server is included at the end of this book to help you get started.

Conventions Used in This Book

The following typographical conventions are used in this book:

Italic
: Used for filenames and pathnames, hostnames, domain names, URLs, and email addresses. *Italic* is also used for new terms where they are defined.

`Constant width`
: Used for code examples and fragments, XML elements and tags, and SQL commands, table names, and column names. `Constant width` is also used for class, variable, and method names and for Java keywords used within the text.

`Constant width bold`
: Used for emphasis in some code examples.

`Constant width italic`
: Used to indicate text that is replaceable. For example, in *`BeanName`*`PK`, you would replace *`BeanName`* with a specific bean name.

Indicates a tip, suggestion, or general note.

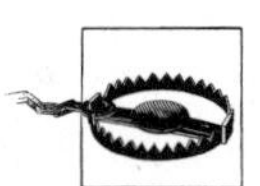

Indicates a warning or caution.

An Enterprise JavaBean consists of many parts; it's not a single object, but a collection of objects and interfaces. To refer to an enterprise bean as a whole, we use its business name in roman type, followed by the acronym EJB. For example, we will refer to the TravelAgent EJB when we want to talk about the enterprise bean in general and the Customer entity when we want to talk about entity beans. If we put the name in a constant-width font, we are referring explicitly to the bean's interface or class; thus, `TravelAgentRemote` is the remote interface that defines the business methods of the TravelAgent EJB.

Using Code Examples

This book is here to help you get your job done. In general, you may use the code in this book in your programs and documentation. You do not need to contact us for permission unless you're reproducing a significant portion of the code. For example, writing a program that uses several chunks of code from this book does not require permission. Selling or distributing a CD-ROM of examples from O'Reilly books does require permission. Answering a question by citing this book and quoting example code does not require permission. Incorporating a significant amount of example code from this book into your product's documentation does require permission.

We appreciate, but do not require, attribution. An attribution usually includes the title, author, publisher, and ISBN. For example: "*Enterprise JavaBeans 3.0*, Fifth Edition, by Bill Burke and Richard Monson-Haefel. Copyright 2006 O'Reilly Media, Inc., 0-596-00978-X."

If you feel your use of code examples falls outside fair use or the permission given above, feel free to contact us at *permissions@oreilly.com*.

Safari® Enabled

When you see a Safari® enabled icon on the cover of your favorite technology book, that means the book is available online through the O'Reilly Network Safari Bookshelf.

Safari offers a solution that's better than e-books. It's a virtual library that lets you easily search thousands of top tech books, cut and paste code samples, download chapters, and find quick answers when you need the most accurate, current information. Try it for free at *http://safari.oreilly.com*.

Comments and Questions

Please address comments and questions concerning this book to the publisher:

O'Reilly Media, Inc.
1005 Gravenstein Highway North
Sebastopol, CA 95472
800-998-9938 (in the United States or Canada)
707-829-0515 (international or local)
707-829-0104 (fax)

There is a web page for this book, which lists errata, examples, and any additional information. You can access this page at:

http://www.oreilly.com/catalog/entjbeans5

To comment on or ask technical questions about this book, send email to:

bookquestions@oreilly.com

For more information about books, conferences, software, Resource Centers, and the O'Reilly Network, see the O'Reilly web site at:

http://www.oreilly.com

Acknowledgments

Many individuals share the credit for this book's development and delivery. Michael Loukides, the editor, and his team were pivotal to the success of every edition of this book. Without his team's experience, craft, and guidance, this book would not have been possible. I want to thank Jason T. Greene for taking over the web services chapters. I had no desire to learn JAX-WS beyond the `@WebService` annotation. Without the earlier work of Richard Monson-Haefel, this book would not have been possible. It amazes me how the structure of this book could last five editions, and it is a testament to Richard's writing capabilities. I also want to thank Richard for passing the baton to me on this series. It has been a great opportunity for me and for JBoss Inc.

Many expert technical reviewers helped ensure that the material was technically accurate and true to the spirit of EJB and Java Persistence. Of special note are Emmanuel Bernard, who sits with Gavin King and me on the EJB 3.0 Expert Group as JBoss's representatives, as well as John Mazzitelli, who was the only reviewer to read every single chapter. Richard Monson-Haefel was also instrumental in providing feedback. Other reviewers to thank are Scott Stark, Kabir Kahn, and Vimal Kansal.

Many JBoss folks deserve a lot of credit for releasing a top-notch implementation of EJB 3.0 on which I could base the JBoss workbook. To my team of Bill DeCoste and Kabir Kahn: you guys do a great job. To the Hibernate team: Emmanuel, thanks for bailing me out on so many occasions; Gavin, thanks for putting up with my yelling, whining, and complaining late into the evening. Thanks to Marc Fleury, who made all of this happen.

Thanks also to Linda DeMichiel, the EJB 3.0 specification lead. Not only did she write the foreword to this book, but she also had to put up with an extraordinary amount of JCP politics to get this specification finished. She also took a lot of heated complaining from Gavin King and me. The success of the EJB 3.0 specification is a testament to her patience and ability.

I want to thank my mother for staying up late at night to edit my English papers in high school decades ago. I haven't forgotten, Mom! Finally, I want to thank my wife, Monica, for putting up with this grumpy old troll. Her love and support are all I need in life.

PART I

The EJB 3.0 Standard

CHAPTER 1
Introduction

This book is about Enterprise JavaBeans 3.0, the latest version of the Enterprise JavaBeans specification, and its counterpart, the new Java Persistence specification. Just as the Java platform has revolutionized the way we think about software development, the Enterprise JavaBeans (EJB) and Java Persistence specifications have revolutionized the way we think about developing mission-critical enterprise software. They combine server-side components with distributed object technologies, asynchronous messaging, web services, and persistence to greatly simplify the task of application development. It automatically takes into account many of the requirements of business systems, including security, resource pooling, concurrency, and transactional integrity.

This book shows you how to use Enterprise JavaBeans and Java Persistence to develop scalable, portable business systems. But before we can start talking about EJB itself, we'll need a brief introduction to the technologies addressed by EJB and Java Persistence, such as component models, distributed objects, asynchronous messaging, and web services. In Chapter 2, we'll learn about the overall architecture that EJB and Persistence provide. In Chapters 3 and 4, we'll look at how these APIs are integrated together in a Java enterprise environment. The rest of the book is devoted to developing enterprise and entity beans for an imaginary business, and discussing advanced issues.

It is assumed that you're already familiar with Java; if you're not, *Learning Java* (O'Reilly) is an excellent introduction, as is *Head First Java* (O'Reilly). This book also assumes that you're conversant in the JDBC API, or at least in SQL. If you're not familiar with JDBC, see *Database Programming with JDBC and Java* (O'Reilly).

One of Java's most important features is platform independence. Since it was first released, Java has been marketed as "write once, run anywhere." While the hype has gotten a little heavy-handed at times, code written with Sun's Java programming language is remarkably platform-independent. EJB and Java Persistence aren't just platform-independent; they are also implementation-independent. If you've worked with JDBC, you know a little about what this means. Not only can the JDBC API run on a

Windows machine or on a Unix machine, it can also access relational databases of many different vendors (DB2, Oracle, MySQL, MS SQL Server, etc.) by using different JDBC drivers. You don't have to code to a particular database implementation; just change JDBC drivers, and you change databases.* It's the same with EJB and Java Persistence. Ideally, an EJB component (an enterprise bean) or a Java Persistence object (an entity bean) can run in any application server that implements these specifications.† This means that you can develop and deploy your EJB business system in one server, such as BEA's WebLogic, and later move it to a different EJB server, such as Pramati, Sybase's EAServer, or IBM's WebSphere, or to an open source project such as JBoss, Apache Geronimo, or JOnAS. Implementation independence means that your business components do not depend on the brand of server, which gives you many more options before, during, and after development and deployment.

Server-Side Components

Object-oriented languages such as Java, C++, C#, Python, and Ruby are used to write software that is flexible, extensible, and reusable—the three axioms of object-oriented development. In business systems, object-oriented languages are used to improve development of GUIs, to simplify access to data, and to encapsulate the business logic. The encapsulation of business logic into business objects is a fairly recent focus in the information-technology industry. Business is fluid, which means that a business's products, processes, and objectives evolve over time. If the software that models the business can be encapsulated into business objects, it becomes flexible, extensible, and reusable, and therefore evolves as the business evolves.

A server-side component model may define an architecture for developing *distributed business objects* that combines the accessibility of distributed object systems with the fluidity of objectified business logic. Server-side component models are used on middle-tier application servers, which manage the components at runtime and make them available to remote clients. They provide a baseline of functionality that makes it easy to develop distributed business objects and assemble them into business solutions.

Server-side components can also be used to model other aspects of a business system, such as presentation and routing. A Java servlet, for example, is a server-side component that generates HTML and XML data for the presentation layer of a web application (Struts and JSF components are also examples of this type of server-side component). EJB message-driven beans, discussed later in this book, are server-side components that can be used to consume and process asynchronous messages.

* In some cases, differences in a database vendor's support for SQL may require customization of SQL statements used in development.

† Provided that the bean components and EJB servers comply with the specification, and no proprietary functionality is used in development.

Server-side components, like other components, can be bought and sold as independent pieces of executable software. They conform to a standard component model and can be executed without direct modification in a server that supports that component model. Server-side component models often support attribute-based programming, which allows the runtime behavior of the component to be modified when it is deployed, without having to change the programming code in the component. Depending on the component model, the server administrator can declare a server-side component's transactional, security, and even persistence behavior by setting these attributes to specific values.

As an organization's services, products, and operating procedures evolve, server-side components can be reassembled, modified, and extended so that the business system reflects those changes. Imagine a business system as a collection of server-side components that model concepts such as customers, products, reservations, and warehouses. Each component is like a Lego™ block that can be combined with other components to build a business solution. Products can be stored in the warehouse or delivered to a customer; a customer can make a reservation or purchase a product. You can assemble components, take them apart, use them in different combinations, and change their definitions. A business system based on server-side components is fluid because it is objectified, and it is accessible because the components can be distributed.

Enterprise JavaBeans Defined

Sun Microsystems' definition of the Enterprise JavaBeans architecture is as follows:

> The Enterprise JavaBeans architecture is a component architecture for the development and deployment of component-based distributed business applications. Applications written using the Enterprise JavaBeans architecture are scalable, transactional, and multi-user secure. These applications may be written once, and then deployed on any server platform that supports the Enterprise JavaBeans specification.*

That's a mouthful, but it's not atypical of how Sun defines many of its Java technologies—have you ever read the definition of the Java language itself? It's about twice as long. This book offers a shorter definition of EJB:

> Enterprise JavaBeans is a standard server-side component model for distributed business applications.

This means the EJB specification offers a standard model for building server-side components that represent business processes (purchasing, inventory, and so on). Once you have built a set of components that fit the requirements of your business, you can combine them to create business applications. On top of that, as "distributed" components, they don't all have to reside on the same server. Components can

* Sun Microsystems' *Enterprise JavaBeans Specification, v3.0*, Copyright© 2002 by Sun Microsystems, Inc.

reside wherever it's most convenient: a TravelAgent component can "live" near the reservation database, or a Purchase business-process component can live near the user interface. You can do whatever's necessary to minimize latency, share the processing load, or maximize reliability.

Persistence and Entity Beans

Persistence is a higher-level abstraction above JDBC. The persistence layer maps objects to database storage so that they can be queried, loaded, updated, or removed without having to go through a verbose API such as JDBC. In older versions of EJB, persistence was part of the EJB platform. Starting with EJB 3.0, persistence has been spun off to its own specification, called the Java Persistence API.

The Java Persistence API defines a way to map regular, plain *old* Java objects (sometimes referred to as POJOs) to a database. These plain Java objects are called entity beans. Entity beans are like any other Java class, except that they have been mapped, using Java Persistence metadata, to a database. Therefore, they may be inserted and loaded from a database without the developer writing any JDBC connection code or reading from result sets. The Java Persistence API also defines a query language that has features that parallel those in SQL, but is tailored to work with Java objects rather than a raw relational schema.

In the EJB 2.1 specification, entity beans were very "heavyweight" and dependent on the application server and the entire Java EE runtime environment. In Java Persistence, entity beans are regular Java objects that are managed by a persistence service. Unlike their EJB 2.1 counterparts, entities in Java Persistence are not required to implement any special spec-defined interfaces or classes. Another weakness of the older specification was that it left individual vendors to decide how an object should be mapped to a particular database representation. This made EJB 2.1 entity beans mostly nonportable between vendors. The new Java Persistence specification defines a complete object to relational mapping (ORM) so that entity beans can be ported easily from vendor to vendor. Furthermore, because entity beans are now plain Java objects, they are not just portable between application servers; they can be used in regular Java applications outside of an application server and can even be used to transfer data between a client and a server. This makes designs simpler and more compact.

Asynchronous Messaging

In addition to supporting RMI-based distributed business objects, Enterprise JavaBeans supports asynchronous messaging. An asynchronous messaging system allows two or more applications to exchange information in the form of messages. A message, in this case, is a self-contained package of business data and network routing headers. The business data contained in a message can be anything—depending on the business scenario—and usually contains information about some business transaction. In enterprise systems, messages inform an application of some event or occurrence in another system.

Asynchronous messages may be transmitted from one application to another on a network using message-oriented middleware (MOM). MOM products ensure that messages are properly distributed among applications. In addition, MOM usually provides fault-tolerance, load-balancing, scalability, and transactional support for enterprises that need to reliably exchange large quantities of messages. MOM vendors use different message formats and network protocols for exchanging messages, but the basic semantics are the same. An API is used to create a message, give it a payload (application data), assign it routing information, and then send the message. The same API is used to receive messages produced by other applications.

In modern enterprise-messaging systems, applications exchange messages through virtual channels called *destinations*. When you send a message, it's addressed to a destination, not to a specific application. Any application that subscribes to or registers an interest in that destination may receive that message. In this way, the applications that receive messages and those that send messages are decoupled. Senders and receivers are not bound to each other in any way and may send and receive messages as they see fit.

Enterprise JavaBeans integrates the functionality of MOM into its component model. This integration extends the EJB platform so that it supports both RMI and asynchronous messaging. EJB 3.0 supports asynchronous messaging through the Java Message Service (JMS) and a new component called the message-driven bean. In addition to JMS, message-driven beans can support other synchronous and asynchronous messaging systems.

Java Message Service

Each MOM vendor implements its own networking protocols, routing, and administration facilities, but the basic semantics of the developer API provided by different MOMs are the same. It's this similarity in APIs that makes the Java Message Service (JMS) possible.

JMS is a vendor-agnostic Java API that can be used with many different MOM vendors. JMS is very similar to JDBC in that an application developer can reuse the same API to access many different systems. If a vendor provides a compliant service provider for JMS, the JMS API can be used to send messages to and receive messages from that vendor. For example, you can use the same JMS API to send messages with Progress's SonicMQ as with IBM's MQSeries.

Message-Driven Beans and JCA 1.5

Enterprise JavaBeans 2.0 introduced a new kind of component, called a *message-driven bean*, which is a kind of standard JMS bean. It can receive and send asynchronous JMS messages, and can easily interact with other EJBs.

EJB 2.1 extended the programming model of the message-driven bean beyond JMS to any messaging system. While EJB vendors must continue to support JMS-based message-driven beans (JMS-MDBs), other types of messaging systems are also allowed. It's likely that vendors will develop new message-driven bean types to support all kinds of protocols, including SMTP for email, SNMP for device control, peer-to-peer protocols (e.g., BEEP and Jabber), and many other open and proprietary messaging systems. In addition, the message-driven bean has become an elegant option for serving connections to legacy transaction processing systems like CICS, IMS, openUTM, and others.

The expansion of message-driven beans in EJB 2.1 to other protocols was made possible by the new Java EE Connector Architecture (JCA 1.5), which defines a portable programming model for interfacing with enterprise information systems. The use of JCA in Java EE is analogous to the use of USB in computer hardware. A computer that supports USB can interface with just about any USB-compliant device. Similarly, an EJB 3.0 container that supports JCA 1.5 can interface with any JCA 1.5-compliant resource. For example, if Vendor XYZ creates a new message-driven bean component for its proprietary messaging system based on JCA 1.5, that component will be portable across all EJB 2.1 and higher-compliant servers. Figure 1-1 illustrates how a JCA connector for a messaging system integrates with EJB.

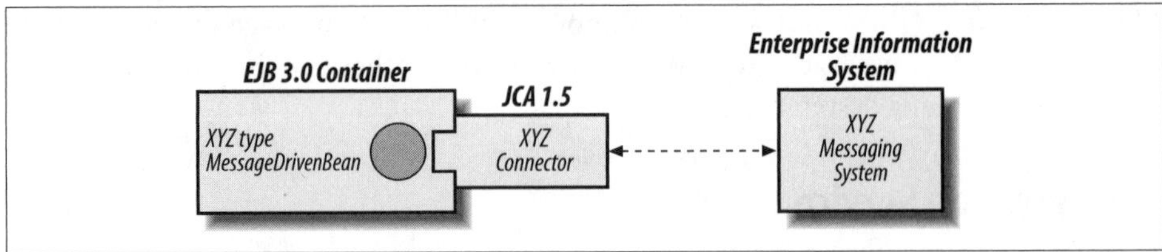

Figure 1-1. EJB 3.0 message-driven beans and JCA 1.5

Message-driven beans in EJB 3.0 allow other applications to send messages that can be captured and processed by the EJB application. This feature allows EJB applications to better integrate with legacy and other proprietary systems.

Web Services

Web services represent the latest wave in distributed computing. Although the term *web services* is bandied about quite a bit, arriving at a concrete definition is difficult because web services is, at the highest level, not specific to any particular technology or platform. It's often defined in fairly abstract terms, like "a substrate for building distributed applications using software running on different operating systems and devices"* or "self-contained, self-describing, modular applications that can be published, located, and invoked across the Web."† Of course, these quotes are taken out of context, but that's the essential point: you need some kind of context to define web services. Here's my definition of web services that has meaning in the context of Java EE, EJB, .NET, and most other web services platforms:

> Web services are network applications that use SOAP and WSDL to exchange information in the form of XML documents.

To understand this definition, you need to understand SOAP and WSDL. Here are brief definitions of these terms:

SOAP 1.1
: Simple Object Access Protocol (SOAP) is an XML grammar, developed by Microsoft, IBM, and others, that is currently under the auspices of the W3C. It's an application protocol used in both RPC and asynchronous messaging. SOAP is very flexible and extensible and, unlike its predecessors (DCE RPC, CORBA IIOP, Java RMI-JRMP, and DCOM), it's been endorsed and adopted by just about every major vendor. (If you're not familiar with XML, see *Java and XML* or *XML in a Nutshell*, both from O'Reilly.)

WSDL 1.1
: The Web Service Description Language (WSDL) is another XML grammar, developed by Microsoft and IBM under the auspices of the W3C. It is an XML-based Interface Definition Language (IDL) that can be used to describe web services, including the kind of message format expected, the Internet protocol used, and the Internet address of the web service.

Web services are truly platform-independent. Although Java RMI and CORBA IIOP also claim to be platform-independent, in fact these older technologies require their own platforms. To use Java RMI, you need a Java virtual machine and the Java programming language; a program written in Visual Basic or C++ can't interact with a Java program using RMI. CORBA IIOP is also restrictive, because the IIOP protocol usually requires an elaborate infrastructure like a CORBA ORB, which limits developers to those few vendors that support CORBA or to the Java environment (which includes built-in support for CORBA IIOP).

Web services, on the other hand, are not tied to a specific platform like the JVM or to a technology infrastructure like CORBA because they focus on the protocols used

* Tim Ewald, "The Web Services Idea," July 12, 2002, Microsoft.com (*http://msdn.microsoft.com/webservices/understanding/readme/default.asp*).

† Doug Tidwell, "Web services—the Web's next revolution," November 29, 2000, IBM.com (*http://www-105.ibm.com/developerworks/education.nsf/webservices-onlinecourse-bytitle/BA84142372686CFB862569A400601C18?OpenDocument*).

to exchange messages—SOAP and WSDL—and not on the implementation that supports those protocols. In other words, you can build web services on any platform using any programming language any way you please.

EJB 3.0 allows enterprise beans to be exposed as web services so that their methods can be invoked by other J2EE applications as well as applications written in other programming languages on a variety of platforms. Web services in EJB 3.0 support both RPC-style and document-style messaging. Support for web services is based on a web service API: JAX-WS. Web services and the use of JAX-WS are covered in detail in Chapters 18 and 19.

Titan Cruises: An Imaginary Business

To make things easier and more fun, we discuss all the concepts in this book in the context of an imaginary business, a cruise line called Titan Cruises. A cruise line makes a particularly interesting example because it incorporates several different businesses: it has ship cabins that are similar to hotel rooms; it serves meals like a restaurant does; it offers various recreational opportunities; and it needs to interact with other travel businesses.

This type of business is a good candidate for a distributed object system because many of the system's users are geographically dispersed. Commercial travel agents, for example, who need to book passage on Titan ships need to access the reservation system. Supporting many—possibly hundreds—of travel agents requires a robust transactional system to ensure agents have access and reservations are completed properly.

Throughout this book, we will build a fairly simple slice of Titan's EJB system that focuses on the process of making a reservation for a cruise. This exercise will give us an opportunity to develop Ship, Cabin, TravelAgent, ProcessPayment, and other enterprise and entity beans. In the process, you will need to create relational database tables for persisting data used in the example. It is assumed that you are familiar with relational database management systems and that you can create tables according to the SQL statements provided.

What's Next?

To develop business objects using EJB and Java Persistence, you have to understand the life cycles and architectures of EJB components and entity bean objects. This means understanding the concepts of how EJB components are managed and made available as distributed objects. Developing an understanding of the EJB and Java Persistence architectures, and how they fit into the larger Java EE environment, is the focus of the next two chapters.

CHAPTER 2

Architectural Overview

To use Enterprise JavaBeans and Java Persistence effectively, you need to understand their architectures. This chapter explores the core of the EJB and Java Persistence architectures: how enterprise beans are distributed as business objects and how they interact with Java Persistence. Chapter 3 explores the services and resource-management techniques supported by EJB.

In order to be truly versatile, the EJB component design had to be smart. For application developers, assembling enterprise beans requires little or no expertise in the complex system-level issues that often plague three-tier development efforts. While EJB makes the process easier for application developers, it also provides EJB server developers with a great deal of flexibility in how they support the EJB specification.

Java Persistence also makes it fairly easy for developers to write objects that can be persisted to a relational database. Writing a persistent entity bean can be as easy as using a few strategically placed annotations with little to no information about the database. Although it is easy to prototype entity beans, the specification is rich enough to provide facilities for more complex database mappings.

The Entity Bean

Entity beans in the Java Persistence 1.0 specification are available only as plain old Java objects (POJOs), and are mapped to tables in a relational database. Unlike other EJB types, entities can be allocated, serialized, and sent across the network like any other POJO.

A good rule of thumb is that entity beans model business concepts that can be expressed as nouns. For example, an entity bean might represent a customer, a piece of equipment, an item in inventory, or even a place. In other words, entity beans model real-world objects; these objects are usually persistent records in some kind of database. Our hypothetical cruise line will need entity beans that represent cabins, customers, ships, etc.

A good way to understand the design of entity beans is to look at how you'd go about implementing one. To implement an entity bean, you need to define a bean class and decide what field you will use as the identifier (primary key) of that bean class:

Primary key
: The primary key is something that provides a pointer into the database. It gives the entity bean class's identity both in memory as an object and in the database as a row in a table. The primary key can be a class or a primitive type.

Bean class
: The entity bean class may contain business logic but is usually just the object representation of persistence storage. In general, only business logic like validation should be placed in the entity bean class. The bean class is a POJO that does not have to implement any interface or even be serializable. It must be tagged with the `@javax.persistence.Entity` annotation and have at least one field or getter method that is designated as the primary key of the entity bean class in the database. This is usually done with the `@javax.persistence.Id` annotation. Entities have other annotations available to define a full object-relational database mapping as well.

In Java Persistence, entity beans are not components like their EJB 2.1 counterparts are. Application code works directly with the entity bean classes and does not interact with the entity through a component interface, as you would with an EJB session bean. So how is an entity queried? How is it stored? Is some magic involved? No. To interact with entity beans, Java Persistence provides a new service called the `EntityManager`. All access to an entity goes through this service. It provides a query API and life cycle methods for the entity. No magic. No bytecode manipulation. No special proxies. Just plain Java.

Unlike older versions of the EJB specification, in Java Persistence, entity beans and the `EntityManager` do not require an application server to be used. You can use Java Persistence in unit tests and standalone Java applications like you would any other Java library. However, the EJB 3.0 specification does provide additional tight integration with Java Persistence to make it easier to manage persistence services. Other than allowing you to write less code, this integration has additional features that are not available in Java Persistence.

The Entity Bean Class

Before we get any further, let's decide on some naming conventions for our entity beans. When we speak about an entity bean, we will call it by its common business name followed by the word *entity*. For example, an entity bean that is developed to model a cabin on a ship will be called the Cabin entity.

Entity beans are different from EJB session beans in that they are POJOs. They do not have a remote or local interface and can be accessed only as POJOs. Later on, we'll see how to interact with an entity bean using the `EntityManager` service, but for now, we'll just take a peek at how to implement this bean type. To define an entity bean, all we'll need to do is define the bean class and annotate it:

```
import javax.persistence.* ;

@Entity
@Table(name="CABIN")
public class Cabin {
    private int id;
    private String name;
    private int deckLevel;

    @Id
    @GeneratedValue
    @Column(name="CABIN_ID")
    public int getId( ) { return id; }

    public void setId(int pk) { this.id = pk; }

    @Column(name="CABIN_NAME")
    public String getName( ) { return name; }

    public void setName(String str) { this.name = str; }

    @Column(name="CABIN_DECK_LEVEL")
    public int getDeckLevel( ) { return deckLevel; }

    public void setDeckLevel(int level) { this.deckLevel = level; }
}
```

Unlike EJB 2.1, in which entity beans were implemented as abstract classes, Java Persistence entity beans are real objects. They don't implement any particular EJB interface. They have fields that represent the persistent state and *setter* and *getter* methods to access those fields. The bean classes are annotated with `@javax.persistence.Entity`. Java Persistence defines a relatively complete object-to-relational database mapping (ORM). This is what the rest of the annotations in the bean class are doing. The `@javax.persistence.Table` annotation specifies the database table to which the entity will be mapped. The `@javax.persistence.Column` is attached to the *getter* methods of the persistent properties of the entity bean. It defines which column the property is mapped to in the entity bean's relational table. Finally, the `@javax.persistence.Id` specifies the primary key's property, and the `@javax.persistence.GeneratedValue` specifies that the container or the database will automatically generate the ID when instances of the Cabin entity are created within the database.

That's all we need to do to define an entity. We'll see later in this chapter how to create/access entity beans through the `EntityManager` service.

XML Deployment Descriptors and JAR Files

Once you have written your entity bean classes, you need to be able to deploy them in your environment. Entity beans are grouped into a finite set of classes called a *persistence unit*. There is an `EntityManager` service that manages a persistence unit, and it must be identified so that it can be referenced in application code. Also, each persistence unit must be associated to a particular database so that the persistence provider knows where, how, and with what kind of database it is interacting. This information is stored in an XML deployment descriptor named *persistence.xml* and is a required artifact.

Annotations allow developers to specify database-mapping metadata directly in the bean class file. Although this is a very simple way to define this information, whether annotations should be used in development is a much-heated debate in the Java community. Many feel that database mappings are configuration metadata that should be defined separate from the entity bean class. To facilitate this requirement, the Java Persistence specification allows you to define the bean to database mappings in an additional XML deployment descriptor called a mapping file. This XML mapping file can be used instead of bean class annotations. If bean class annotations already exist, then this mapping file can either override these annotations or provide additional metadata. XML mapping files always take precedence over any bean class annotations.

Once you have defined your XML deployment descriptors and entity bean classes, you must package them all in a Java Archive (JAR) file. The JAR file is used as both a library at runtime and a holder for deployment information. Whether you are using persistence in an application server or within a standalone Java application, the persistence provider will examine the JAR file to determine how to deploy one or more persistence units into your environment.

The Enterprise Bean Component

Enterprise JavaBeans server-side components come in two fundamentally different types: *session beans* and *message-driven beans*. Session beans are server-side components that can be accessed using a variety of distributed object protocols. Message-driven beans process messages asynchronously from systems like the JMS, legacy systems, and web services. All EJB servers must at least support a JMS-based message-driven bean, but they may also support other types of message-driven beans.

Session beans are extensions of the client application that manage processes or tasks. A Ship entity bean provides methods for doing things directly to a ship, but it doesn't say anything about the context under which those actions are taken. Booking passengers on the ship requires that we use a Ship entity, but it also requires a lot of things that have nothing to do with the ship itself: we'll need to know about passengers, ticket rates, schedules, and so on. A session bean is responsible for this kind of coordination. Session beans tend to manage particular kinds of activities, such as the act of making a reservation. They have a lot to do with the relationships between different entity beans. A TravelAgent session bean, for example, might use a Cruise, a Cabin, and a Customer—all entity beans—to make a reservation.

Similarly, message-driven beans coordinate tasks involving other session and entity beans. Message-driven beans and session beans differ primarily in how they are accessed. While a session bean provides a remote interface that defines which methods can be invoked, a message-driven bean subscribes to or listens for messages. It responds by processing the message and managing the actions that other beans take. For example, a ReservationProcessor message-driven bean would receive asynchronous messages—perhaps from a legacy reservation system—from which it would coordinate the interactions of the Cruise, Cabin, and Customer beans to make a reservation.

The activity that a session or message-driven bean represents is fundamentally transient: you start making a reservation, you do a bunch of work, and then it's finished. The session and message-driven beans do not represent things in the database. Obviously, session and message-driven beans have lots of side effects on the database; in the process of making a reservation, you might create a new Reservation by assigning a Customer to a particular Cabin on a particular Ship. All of these changes would be reflected in the database by actions on the respective entity beans. Session and message-driven beans like TravelAgent and ReservationProcessor, which are responsible for making a reservation on a cruise, can even access a database directly and perform reads, updates, and deletes to data. But there's no TravelAgent or ReservationProcessor record in the database—once the bean has made the reservation, it waits to process another.

What makes the distinction between the different types of beans difficult to understand is that it's extremely flexible. The relevant distinction for Enterprise JavaBeans and Java Persistence is that an entity bean has persistent state; session and message-driven beans model interactions but do not have a persistent state.

Classes and Interfaces

A good way to understand the design of enterprise beans is to look at how you'd go about implementing one. To implement session and message-driven enterprise beans, you need to define their component interfaces, and a bean class:

Remote interface
: The remote interface defines a session bean's business methods, which can be accessed from applications outside the EJB container: the business methods a bean presents to the outside world to do its work. The remote interface is a plain Java interface. It is tagged with the `@javax.ejb.Remote` annotation to identify that it is a remote interface.

Local interface

The local interface defines a session bean's business methods that can be used by other beans in the same EJB container: the business methods a bean presents to other beans running in the same JVM. It allows beans to interact without the overhead of a distributed object protocol, which improves their performance. The local interface is a plain Java interface. It is tagged with the `@javax.ejb.Local` annotation to identify that it is a local interface.

Endpoint interface

The endpoint interface defines business methods that can be accessed from applications outside the EJB container via SOAP. The endpoint interface is based on Java API for XML-RPC (JAX-RPC) and is designed to adhere to the SOAP and WSDL standards. The endpoint interface is a plain Java interface that is annotated with the `@javax.jws.WebService` annotation.

Message interface

Message-driven beans implement the message interface, which defines the methods by which messaging systems, such as the JMS, can deliver messages to the bean.

Bean class

The session bean class contains business logic and must have at least one remote, local, or endpoint interface. It usually implements these interfaces, but it is not required to. A bean class may also have more than one interface of a given type. The EJB container usually determines whether a session bean is remote and/or local by the interfaces it implements. The session bean class must also be tagged with the `@javax.ejb.Stateful` or `@javax.ejb.Stateless` annotation so that the EJB container knows what session bean type it is.

A message-driven bean implements one or more message delivery methods (e.g., `onMessage()`) defined in a message interface. The container calls these methods when a new message arrives. The message-driven bean class must also be tagged with the `@javax.ejb.MessageDriven` annotation. EJB 3.0 containers must support JMS-based message-driven beans, which implement the `javax.jms.MessageListener` interface. EJB also supports message-driven beans that process messages from other types of messaging systems with their own message interfaces.

Local interfaces provide a way for session beans in the same container to interact efficiently. Calls to methods in the local interface don't involve a distributed object protocol. A session bean isn't required to provide a local interface if it will only ever interact with remote or web service clients. Likewise, a session bean doesn't need to provide a remote or an endpoint interface if you know it will be called only by session beans in the same container. You can provide any combination of local, remote, and endpoint interfaces.

Clients of a session bean never interact with the session bean class directly (this includes clients that are themselves session beans). Instead, clients must always use the methods of the session bean's component interfaces to do their work. When they go through the component interfaces, the clients are actually interacting with proxies or stubs that are generated automatically by the container. Although local interfaces do not involve a distributed object protocol, they still represent a proxy or stub to the bean class. This is because, although no network is involved, the proxy or stub will still allow the container to monitor the interactions between the bean and its client, thus allowing the container to apply security and engage in transactions as appropriate.

It's important to note that message-driven beans don't support remote, local, or endpoint component interfaces, but they may become the clients of other session beans and interact with those beans through their component interfaces. The session beans with which the message-driven bean interacts may be located in the same container, in which case the message-driven bean uses their local component interfaces; or, they may be located in a different address space and EJB container, in which case the remote or endpoint component interfaces are used.

There are also many interactions between an enterprise bean and its container. (Many people use the terms *container* and *server* interchangeably, which is understandable because the difference between the terms isn't clearly defined.) The container is responsible for creating new instances of beans, making sure they are stored properly by the server, and so on. Tools provided by the container's vendor do a tremendous amount of work behind the scenes. At least one tool takes care of creating the mapping between entity beans and records in the database. Other tools generate code based on the component interfaces and the bean class itself. The generated code does things like create the bean, store it in the database, and so on.

Naming conventions

Before going on, let's establish some conventions. When we speak about an enterprise bean as a whole—its component interfaces, bean class, and so forth—we will call it by its common business name followed by the acronym *EJB*. For example, an enterprise bean that is developed to process credit card payments will be called the ProcessPayment EJB. Notice that we don't use a constant-width font for "ProcessPayment," because we are referring to all the parts of the bean (the component interfaces, bean class, etc.) as a whole, not just to one particular part, such as the remote interface or bean class. The term *enterprise bean* or *bean* denotes any kind of bean, including session and message-driven beans. *Session bean* denotes a session-type enterprise bean; *message-driven bean* denotes a message-driven–type enterprise bean. The acronym *MDB* is frequently used in place of the term *message-driven bean*.

We also use suffixes to distinguish between local, remote, and endpoint component interfaces. When we are talking about the remote interface of a TravelAgent session bean, we will combine the common business name with the word *Remote*. For example, the remote interface for the TravelAgent EJB is called the `TravelAgentRemote` interface. The local interface for the TravelAgent EJB would be the `TravelAgentLocal` interface. The endpoint interface for the TravelAgent EJB-based web service would be `TravelAgentWS` (WS stands for web service). The bean class is always the common business name followed by the word *Bean*. For example, the TravelAgent EJB's bean class would be named `TravelAgentBean`.

These naming conventions are used for clarity; they are not prescriptive or even recommended for use in production. Once you understand the differences between the component interfaces and the different types of beans, you can use any naming strategy you wish.

The remote interface

Having introduced the machinery, let's look at how to build a very simple stateless session bean with a remote component interface. In this section, we examine the Calculator EJB, a session bean that exposes basic calculator functions as a service. Let's start with its remote interface.

We'll define the remote interface for the Calculator bean using the `CalculatorRemote` interface, which defines arithmetic operations. Remote interfaces are denoted by the `@javax.ejb.Remote` annotation:

```
import javax.ejb.Remote;

@Remote
public interface CalculatorRemote {
    public int add(int x, int y);
    public int subtract(int x, int y);
}
```

You'll notice that even though this is the remote interface of the EJB, there is no reference to Java RMI interfaces or APIs. This is a big change in the EJB 3.0 specification compared to older versions. The EJB specification requires at least Java RMI-IIOP as an underlying network transport protocol, but all references to RMI have been removed to facilitate plugging in any other protocol that your container vendor wants to provide. Java RMI-IIOP will be discussed in more detail in the next chapter.

The bean class

Now let's look at an actual stateless session bean class. Here's the code for the `CalculatorBean` class; it's a sparse implementation, but it shows how the pieces fit together:

```
import javax.ejb.*;

@Stateless
public class CalculatorBean implements CalculatorRemote {
    public int add(int x, int y) {
        return x + y;
    }
```

```
    public int subtract(int x, int y) {
        return x - y;
    }
}
```

The CalculatorBean class is required to implement at least one remote or local interface and to be annotated with @javax.ejb.Stateless. Those familiar with earlier EJB specifications will notice that session beans do not have to implement an EJB-specific interface or any of the callback notifications. This is one of the ease-of-use mandates of the EJB 3.0 specification where EJBs must be as close to plain Java objects as possible. That's not to say the specification has removed callback notifications, but rather that they can be added on an as-needed basis. We'll discuss callback notifications in Chapter 11.

What about message-driven beans?

Message-driven beans also have a bean class that implements a message interface; they don't implement remote, local, or endpoint interfaces. This bean class is annotated using the @javax.ejb.MessageDriven annotation. The kind of message delivery methods implemented by the MDB depends on the type of messaging service it supports. For example, a JMS-based MDB, which all EJB containers must support, must implement the onMessage( ) method, which is called every time a new asynchronous JMS message is delivered.

Message-driven beans don't have a primary key, for the same reason that session beans don't. They are not persistent, so there is no need for a key to the database. Message-driven beans are covered in detail in Chapter 12.

Annotations, Deployment Descriptors, and JAR Files

The interfaces and classes we have discussed don't address how beans are managed at runtime. We didn't talk about how beans interact with security, transactions, naming, and other services common to distributed object systems. These types of primary services are handled automatically by the EJB container; but that begs the question, "How does the EJB container know how to handle security, transactions, and so on?" The EJB container gets this kind of runtime information from intuitive defaults, annotations, and/or XML deployment descriptors.

To simplify development of EJBs, the new EJB 3.0 specification defines a set of intuitive defaults so that developers do not have to add the syntactical sugar of an annotation or write an XML deployment descriptor. For instance, the default transaction property is REQUIRED. The default security semantics are UNCHECKED. These defaults allow the developer to focus on writing business logic instead of focusing on unneeded metadata.

When a default is not enough, you can use explicit Java annotations. Annotations allow EJB developers to specify metadata like security, transactions, and database mappings directly in the bean class file. Annotations alleviate some of the reliance on specific EJB tools because the metadata for EJB is expressed as annotations rather than just XML. Most integrated development environments (IDEs) support automatic code completion, and EJB annotations just become another element that an IDE can code-complete.

Annotations are by far the easiest way to define EJB metadata. Sometimes, though, you will want to override an annotation on a per-deployment basis. Furthermore, some in the Java community do not like annotations at all. To solve both of these issues, the EJB specification has the notion of an XML *deployment descriptor*. Deployment descriptors allow you to customize an EJB's runtime behavior without having to change the software itself and recompile anything. Deployment descriptors are also similar to the property sheets used in Visual Basic and PowerBuilder. Where property sheets allow us to describe the runtime attributes of visual widgets (background color, font size, etc.), deployment descriptors allow us to describe runtime attributes of server-side components (security, transactional context, etc.).

When a bean class and its interfaces have been defined, a deployment descriptor for the bean may be created and populated with data about the bean as an override or alternative to any annotations used. IDEs that support the development of Enterprise JavaBeans often allow developers to set up the deployment descriptors they need using visual utilities like property sheets. After the developer has set all of the bean's properties, the deployment descriptor is saved to a file. Once the deployment descriptor is completed and saved to a file, the bean can be packaged in a JAR file for deployment.

The choice between annotations and XML deployment descriptor comes down to personal taste. Some developers like to see EJB metadata embedded in the bean class and interface. They think an XML file is just too verbose. Annotations can also act like documentation. By looking at a class or interface source file, you know the exact semantics of what a particular EJB will be. On the other hand, others view this metadata as intrusive and want to code their business logic as plain Java, with no reference to EJB whatsoever. They also want to be able to change this metadata without modifying code. This could be really important if the EJB metadata needs to be different on a per-deployment basis. Since annotation metadata can be overridden partially or entirely by an XML deployment descriptor, there really is no need for this debate. Developers can rapidly prototype EJBs using annotations, and then, if needed, the metadata can be overridden within XML. The introductory examples in the early chapters of this book rely entirely on annotations to explain themselves. Chapter 11 will walk through how you can use XML as an alternative to annotations when defining session or message-driven beans.

JAR files are Zip files that package Java classes and other resources that are ready to be used in some type of application. JARs are used for packaging applets, Java applications, JavaBeans, web applications (servlets and JSPs), and Enterprise JavaBeans. A

JAR file containing one or more enterprise beans includes the bean classes, component interfaces, and supporting classes for each bean. It also may contain a deployment descriptor if the bean developer has decided to use XML to define a bean's metadata. When a bean is deployed, the JAR file's location is given to the container's deployment tools.

When the container opens the JAR file, it looks for classes that are annotated as EJBs and/or reads the deployment descriptor (if one has been defined) to learn about the bean and how it should be managed at runtime. From the annotations and/or the deployment descriptor, the deployment tools know what kinds of beans are in the JAR file (session or message-driven), how they should be managed in transactions, who has access to the beans at runtime, and other information. The person deploying the bean can alter some of these settings, such as transactional and security access attributes, to customize the bean for a particular application.

The EJB Container

Session beans declare component interfaces that their clients use to access them. (Entity and message-driven beans are a very different kind of animal.) In EJB 3.0, clients outside the container system always use the enterprise bean's remote component interfaces. Clients outside the container system have the option of accessing stateless session beans as web services as well. Clients within the same Java EE system (i.e., enterprise beans, servlets, and JSPs) can use local component interfaces if they are running within the same virtual machine. This section explains how session bean component interfaces are connected to instances of the bean class at runtime.

Now that you have a basic understanding of some of an enterprise bean's parts (component interfaces, bean class, annotations, and deployment descriptor), it's time to talk more precisely about how these parts come together inside an EJB container system. Since the author of this book is a lead developer on the JBoss open source Java EE application server, you'll get some pretty good insight on how EJB containers are architected. Specifically, we'll talk about how JBoss' EJB container implements the component interface of a session bean so that clients—either applications outside the container or other co-located enterprise beans—can interact with and invoke methods on the bean class.

The three pieces you need in order to understand this architecture are the proxy stub, the container, and the bean instance itself. You will probably never deal with the internal architecture of your EJB container because the purpose of middleware is to alleviate these concerns so that you can focus on writing business logic. This practice is useful, though, because it represents a separation of responsibilities along areas of expertise. As an application developer, you are intimately familiar with how your business environment works and needs to be modeled, so you will focus on creating the applications and beans that describe your business. System-level developers, the people who write EJB servers, don't understand your business, but they do understand how to develop containers and support distributed objects. It makes sense for system-level developers to apply their skills to the mechanics of managing distributed objects but to leave the business logic to you, the application developer. Let's talk briefly about the proxy, the EJB container, and the bean instance so that you can get a general understanding of the internal architecture of EJB.

The proxy stub, EJB container, and bean instance

This chapter has said a lot about a bean's remote and local interfaces. When your business logic interacts with a session bean, it is not working directly with instances of the bean class; it is working through the bean's remote or local interface. When you invoke methods on the remote or local interface, the object instance you are using is something called a *proxy stub*. This proxy stub implements the remote or local interface of the session bean and is responsible for sending your session bean method invocation over the network to your remote EJB container or routing the request to an EJB container that is local in the JVM. The proxy stub can be generated by a precompiler, such as RMI's *rmic*. Or, as in the case of JBoss, it is dynamically generated at deployment time using the `java.lang.reflect.Proxy` facilities that come with the JDK.

The proxy stub routes the method invocation to the EJB container on the server (or in the server if it is a local interface). It is the EJB container's job to manage bean class instances as well as security and transaction demarcation. The EJB container has knowledge of the metadata defined as annotations on the bean class or as elements in the XML deployment descriptor. Based on this metadata, it will start a transaction and perform authentication and authorization tasks. It also is responsible for managing the life cycle of the bean instance and routing the request from the proxy to the real bean class instance.

After the EJB container has managed the life cycle of the bean instance, started any transactions, and performed its security checks, it routes the invocation to an actual bean instance.

Using Enterprise and Entity Beans

Let's look at how a client would use an enterprise bean to do something useful. In this example, we'll create a TravelAgent session bean that creates a reservation for a remote client. This TravelAgent EJB will interact with various entity and other session bean types.

Modeling Taskflow with Session Beans

Entity beans are useful for representing data and describing business concepts that can be expressed as nouns, but they're not very good at representing a process or a task. A Ship bean provides methods and behavior for doing things directly to a ship, but it does not define the context under which these actions are taken. We don't want business logic in the client application—that's why we went to a multitier architecture in the first place. Similarly, we don't want this kind of logic in our entity beans that represent ships and cabins. Booking passengers on a ship or scheduling a ship for a cruise is a type of activity or function of the business, not of the Ship or Cabin bean, and is therefore expressed in terms of a process or task.

Session beans act as agents that manage business processes or tasks for the client; they're the appropriate place for business logic. A session bean is not persistent; nothing in a session bean maps directly into a database or is stored between sessions. Session beans work with entity beans, data, and other resources to control *taskflow*. Taskflow is the essence of any business system, because it expresses how entities interact to model the actual business. Session beans control tasks and resources but do not themselves represent data.

The term *taskflow* was coined specifically for this book. It's derived from the term *workflow*, which is frequently used to describe the management of business processes that may span several days with lots of human intervention. In contrast to workflow, taskflow is used in this book to describe the interactions of beans within a single transaction that takes only a few seconds to execute.

The following code demonstrates how a session bean designed to make cruise-line reservations might control the taskflow of other entity and session beans. Imagine that a piece of client software, in this case a user interface, obtains a remote reference to a TravelAgent session bean. Using the information entered into text fields by the user, the client application books a passenger on a cruise:

```
// Get the credit card number from the text field.
String creditCard = textField1.getText( );
int cabinID = Integer.parseInt(textField2.getText( ));
int cruiseID = Integer.parseInt(textField3.getText( ));

Customer customer = new Customer(name, address, phone);

// Create a new TravelAgent session, passing in a reference to a
// customer entity bean.
TravelAgentRemote travelAgent = ...; // Use JNDI to get a reference
travelAgent.setCustomer(customer);
// Set cabin and cruise IDs.
travelAgent.setCabinID(cabinID);
travelAgent.setCruiseID(cruiseID);

// Using the card number and price, book passage.
// This method returns a Reservation object.
Reservation res = travelAgent.bookPassage(creditCard, price);
```

We start by getting a remote reference to the TravelAgent EJB's remote interface. We need a remote reference rather than a local interface because the client is an application located outside the EJB container. It's not shown in the example, but references to remote session beans are obtained using JNDI. JNDI is a powerful API for locating resources, such as remote objects, on networks. JNDI lookups are covered in subsequent chapters.

The rest of the client code interacts with the TravelAgent EJB to set the Customer, Cabin, and Cruise beans for the reservation desired. It then books the ticket by calling the `bookPassage( )` method. It gets back a `Reservation` instance so that it can display it to its GUI to provide a receipt for the customer.

This is a fairly coarse-grained abstraction of the process of booking a passenger: most of the details are hidden from the client. Hiding the fine-grained details of taskflow is important because it provides the system with flexibility as it evolves: we know that we will always want to book passengers, but the process for booking a passenger may change.

Coarse-grained and *fine-grained* are terms that are sometimes used to describe the level of detail exposed by the public interface of a component. A fine-grained component is one that exposes a lot of detail about how the component functions via its public interfaces. Components that provide a public interface but do not expose the details of its operation are called coarse-grained. When dealing with remote clients, coarse-grained interfaces are usually preferred because they are more flexible—the client doesn't have to be aware of all the nitty-gritty details of how the component works.

The following listing shows some of the code for the `TravelAgentBean`. The `bookPassage( )` method works with four entity beans, the Customer, Cabin, Cruise, and Reservation entities, and another session bean, the ProcessPayment EJB. The ProcessPayment EJB provides several methods for making a payment, including by check, cash, and credit card. In this case, we use the ProcessPayment bean to make a credit card payment. Once payment has been made, the Reservation created is detached automatically from persistence storage and is returned to the client.

```
@Stateful
public class TravelAgentBean implements TravelAgentRemote {
    @PersistenceContext private EntityManager entityManager;
    @EJB private ProcessPaymentRemote process;

    private Customer customer;
    private Cruise cruise;
    private Cabin cabin;

    public void setCustomer(Customer cust) {
        entityManager.create(cust);
        customer = cust;
    }
    public void setCabinID(int id) {
       cabin = entityManager.find(Cabin.class, id);
```

```
    }
    public void setCruiseID(int id) {
       cruise = entityManager.find(Cruise.class, id);
    }

    public Reservation bookPassage(String card, double price)
        throws IncompleteConversationalState {
        if (customer == null ||cruise == null ||cabin == null){
            throw new IncompleteConversationalState( );
        }
        try {

            Reservation reservation =
                new Reservation(customer,cruise,cabin,price,new Date( ));

            entityManager.persist(reservation);

            process.byCredit(customer,card,price);


            return reservation;
        }catch(Exception e){
            throw new EJBException(e);
        }
    }

}
```

There are a few things going on within this TravelAgent EJB. References to the EntityManager service and the ProcessPayment EJB are injected directly into the TravelAgent by the EJB container. The EJB container knows how to do this by the @javax.persistence.PersistenceContext and @javax.ejb.EJB annotations on the private fields of the session bean. We'll talk more about injection in Chapter 11 and we'll provide complete details in Chapter 14. Notice that the Customer entity is allocated on the client, passed to the server, and then created by the EntityManager. The setCabinID( ) and setCruiseID( )methods use the EntityManager to locate those beans in persistent storage. The bookPassage( ) method allocates a Reservation entity, inserts the reservation in the database by calling EntityManager.persist( ), and then bills the customer's credit card by invoking on the ProcessPayment EJB. Finally, when the bookPassage( ) method completes (and along with it, the transaction), the Reservation entity becomes unmanaged and detached from the EntityManager. It is returned as a plain Java object to the client.

This example leaves out some details, but it demonstrates the difference in purpose between a session bean and an entity bean. Entity beans represent the behavior and data of a business object, and session beans model the taskflow. The client application uses the TravelAgent EJB to perform a task using other beans. For example, the TravelAgent EJB uses a ProcessPayment EJB and a Reservation EJB in the process of booking passage. The ProcessPayment EJB processes the credit card, and the Reservation

EJB records the actual reservation in the system. Session beans can also be used to read, update, and delete data that can't be adequately captured in an entity bean. Session beans don't represent records or data in the database, but they can access data.

Session beans allow clients to perform tasks without being concerned with the details that make up those tasks. A developer can update the session bean, possibly changing the taskflow, without affecting the client code. In addition, if the session bean is properly defined, other clients that perform the same tasks can reuse it. The ProcessPayment session bean, for example, can be used in many areas besides reservations, including retail and wholesale sales. For example, the ship's gift shop could use the ProcessPayment EJB to process purchases. As a client of the ProcessPayment EJB, the TravelAgent EJB doesn't care how ProcessPayment works; it's only interested in the ProcessPayment EJB's coarse-grained interface, which validates and records charges.

Moving taskflow logic into a session bean also simplifies the client application and reduces network traffic. Excessive network traffic is a common problem for distributed object systems: it can overwhelm the server and clog the network, hurting response time and performance. Session beans, if used properly, can reduce network traffic by limiting the number of requests needed to perform a task. The user of session beans keeps the interaction between the beans involved in a taskflow on the server. One method invocation on the client application results in many method invocations on the server, but the network sees only the traffic produced by the client's call to the session bean. In the TravelAgent EJB, the client invokes `bookPassage( )`; in turn, `bookPassage( )` makes several method invocations on other enterprise beans. Furthermore, the TravelAgent bean may be in the same container as the other beans, and therefore can use the local interfaces, further reducing network traffic. For the network cost of one method invocation, the client gets several method invocations.

Stateful and statelessl session beans

Session beans can be either *stateful* or *stateless*. Stateful session beans maintain *conversational state* when used by a client. Conversational state is not written to a database; it's information that is kept in memory while a client carries on a conversation with an enterprise bean, and it is lost when the conversation ends or the EJB container crashes. For example, a client making a reservation through the TravelAgent bean may call the methods that set cabin and cruise IDs. These IDs are part of the session's conversational state, and they affect the behavior of subsequent method calls, such as the call to `bookPassage( )` that makes the actual reservation. Conversational state is kept only as long as the client application is actively using the bean. Once the client shuts down or releases the TravelAgent EJB, the conversational state is lost forever. Stateful session beans are not shared among clients; they are dedicated to the same client for the life of the enterprise bean.

Stateless session beans do not maintain any conversational state. Each method is completely independent and uses only data passed in its parameters. The ProcessPayment EJB is a perfect example of a stateless session bean: it doesn't need to maintain any conversational state from one method invocation to the next. All the information needed to make a payment is passed into the `byCredit( )` method. Stateless session beans provide better performance and consume fewer resources than entity and stateful session beans because a few stateless session bean instances can serve hundreds and possibly thousands of clients. Chapter 11 talks more about stateless session beans.

Message-Driven Beans

Message-driven beans are integration points for other applications interested in working with EJB applications. Java applications or legacy systems that need to access EJB applications can send messages to message-driven beans via JMS. These beans process those messages and perform the required tasks using other entity and session beans. EJB 3.0 is not limited to JMS-based message-driven beans: message-driven beans can support any messaging system that implements the correct JCA 1.5 contracts. However, support for JMS-based message-driven beans (JMS-MDBs) in EJB 3.0 is mandatory, so JMS-MDBs are the type of message-driven bean addressed in this section.

In many ways, JMS-MDBs fulfill the same role as stateless session beans: they manage the taskflow of entity and session beans. The task is initiated by an asynchronous message sent by an application using JMS. Unlike session beans, which respond to business methods invoked on their component interfaces, a JMS-MDB responds to messages delivered through its `onMessage( )` method. Since the messages are asynchronous, the client that sends them doesn't expect a reply. The messaging client simply sends the message and forgets about it.

As an example, we can recast the TravelAgent EJB developed earlier as the ReservationProcessor JMS message-driven bean:

```
@MessageDriven
public class ReservationProcessorBean implements javax.jms.MessageListener {
    @PersistenceContext private EntityManager entityManager;
    @EJB private ProcessPaymentRemote process;

    public void onMessage(Message message) {
        try {
            MapMessage reservationMsg = (MapMessage)message;

            Customer customer = (Customer)reservationMsg.getObject("Customer");
            int cruisePk = reservationMsg.getInt("CruiseID");
            int cabinPk = reservationMsg. getInt("CabinID");
            double price = reservationMsg.getDouble("Price");
```

```
                String card = reservationMsg.getString("card");
                entityManager.persist(customer);

                Cruise cruise = entityManager.find(Cruise.class, cruisePK);
                Cabin cabin = entityManager.find(Cabin.class, cruisePK);

                Reservation reservation =
                    new Reservation(customer,cruise,cabin,price,new Date( ));

                entityManager.create(reservation);

                process.byCredit(customer,card,price);

            } catch(Exception e) {
                throw new EJBException(e);
            }
        }
    }
```

All the information about the reservation is obtained from the message delivered to the MDB. JMS messages can take many forms; the `javax.jms.MapMessage` used in this example carries name-value pairs. Once the information is gathered from the message and the enterprise bean references are obtained, the reservation is processed in the same way as it was in the session bean. The only difference is that the `Reservation` object isn't returned to the sender of the message; message-driven beans don't have to respond to the sender.

Regardless of the messaging system, message-driven beans do not maintain any conversational state. Each new message is independent of the previous messages. The message-driven bean is explained in detail in Chapter 12.

The Bean-Container Contract

The environment that surrounds the beans on the EJB server is often called the *container*. The container is more a concept than a physical construct. It acts as an intermediary between the bean and the EJB server. It manages the EJB objects and helps these constructs manage bean resources and provide services such as transactions, security, concurrency, and naming at runtime. The distinction between the container and the server is not clearly defined, but the EJB specification defines the component model in terms of the container's responsibilities, so we will follow that convention here.

Enterprise bean components interact with the EJB container through a well-defined component model. All EJB types register for various life cycle events that the EJB container emits. They register for these events by annotating a method within their bean class that is interested in the specific event. At runtime, the container invokes these annotated methods on the bean instance when relevant events occur. For example, after the container allocates and injects referenced services into an EJB instance, it will call a method annotated with `@javax.annotation.PostConstruct` on the EJB's bean class if one is provided. This call gives the bean instance an opportunity to do any additional initialization before the EJB services any request. Other callback methods can be used by the bean class in a similar fashion. EJB defines when these various callback methods are invoked and what can be done within their contexts.

In EJB 3.0, your code does not have to implement empty callback methods like it does in older versions of the EJB specification. You write code only for those events that you are interested in. Beans that implement callback methods usually access resources that aren't managed by the EJB system. Enterprise beans that wrap legacy systems often fall into this category.

`javax.ejb.EJBContext` is an interface that is implemented by the container and is also part of the bean-container contract. Session beans use a subclass called `javax.ejb.SessionContext`. Message-driven beans use the subclass `javax.ejb.MessageDrivenContext`. These `EJBContext` types provide the bean with information about its environment: its container, the client using the enterprise bean, and the bean itself. The bean can use this information while processing requests from clients and callback methods from the container.

An enterprise bean's interface with the container also includes a JNDI namespace, called the *environment-naming context*, which the bean can use to look up the resources it needs (including other beans). The JNDI environment-naming context and the `EJBContext` (and its subclasses) are described in more detail in Chapters 11, 12, and 14.

Summary

This chapter covered a lot of ground in describing the basic architecture of an EJB and Java Persistence system. At this point, you should understand that beans are business object components. Session beans have remote and local interfaces that define the public business methods of the bean. Message-driven and entity beans do not have component interfaces. Entity beans are plain Java objects. The bean class is where the state and behavior of the bean are implemented.

There are three basic kinds of beans: entity, session, and message-driven. Entity beans are persistent and represent a person, place, or thing. Session beans are extensions of the client and embody a process or a taskflow that defines how other beans interact. Session beans are not persistent: they receive their state from the client and live only as long as the client needs them. Message-driven beans are integration points that allow other applications to interact with EJB applications using JMS or some other JCA 1.5–compliant resource. Message-driven beans, like stateless session beans, are not persistent and do not maintain conversational state.

The EJB proxy stub is a conceptual construct that delegates method invocations to session beans from the client and helps the container manage the enterprise bean at runtime. The clients of session beans do not interact with the instances of the session bean class directly. Instead, the client software interacts with the proxy stub. The proxy stub implements the remote and/or local interface and expands the bean class's functionality. Entity beans are created in the same way as any other Java object and are managed by the `EntityManager` service.

Beans interact with their containers through the well-defined bean-container contract. This contract provides callback methods, the `EJBContext`, and the JNDI environment-naming context. The callback methods notify the bean class that it is involved in a life cycle event. The `EJBContext` and JNDI environment-naming context provide the bean instance with information about its environment.

CHAPTER 3

Resource Management and Primary Services

Chapter 2 discussed the basic architecture of Enterprise JavaBeans and Java Persistence, including the relationship between the bean class, the EJB container, and the `EntityManager` service. These artifacts define a common model for distributed server-side components as well as a persistence model that can be used on the server or in standalone applications. But this model isn't enough to make EJB interesting or even particularly useful. EJB servers also manage the resources used by beans, and can manage thousands or even millions of distributed objects simultaneously. They must manage how distributed objects use memory, threads, database connections, processing power, and more. Furthermore, the EJB specification defines interfaces that help developers take advantage of these common practices.

EJB servers support six primary services: concurrency, transaction management, persistence, object distribution, naming, and security. These services provide the kind of infrastructure that is necessary for a successful three-tier system. EJB also supports two additional services: asynchronous messaging and a timer service.

This chapter discusses the resource-management facilities and the primary services that are available to Enterprise JavaBeans.

Resource Management

A large business system with many users can easily have thousands or even millions of objects in use simultaneously. As the number of interactions among these objects increases, concurrency and transactional concerns can degrade the system's response time and frustrate users. EJB servers increase performance by synchronizing object interactions and sharing resources.

There is a relationship between the number of clients and the number of distributed objects that are required to service them. Not surprisingly, the larger the client population, the more distributed objects are needed. At some point, the increase in clients affects performance and diminishes throughput. EJB explicitly supports two mechanisms that make it easier to manage large numbers of beans at runtime: instance pooling and activation. In addition, EJB supports the use of the Java EE Connector Architecture (Java EE Connectors) for managing resource connections. As the number of distributed objects and clients increases, the number of resource connections also increases. Java EE Connectors work with the EJB container to manage connections to databases, enterprise messaging, ERP, legacy systems, and other types of resources.

Instance Pooling

The concept of pooling resources is not new. It's common to pool database connections so that the business objects in the system can share database access. This trick reduces the number of database connections needed, which reduces resource consumption and increases throughput. The Java EE Connector Architecture (JCA) is frequently the mechanism employed by EJB containers when pooling connections to databases and other resources, and is covered a little later. Most EJB containers also apply resource pooling to server-side components; this technique is called *instance pooling*. Instance pooling reduces the number of component instances—and therefore resources—needed to service client requests.

As you already know, clients of session beans interact with the beans through the remote and local interfaces implemented by EJB objects. Client applications never have direct access to an actual session bean class instance. Similarly, JMS clients never interact with JMS-based message-driven beans (JMS-MDBs) directly. They send messages that are routed to the EJB container system. The EJB container then delivers these messages to the proper message-driven instance.

Instance pooling is possible because clients never access beans directly. Therefore, there's no fundamental reason to keep a separate copy of each enterprise bean for each client. The server can keep a much smaller number of enterprise beans around to do the work, reusing each enterprise bean instance to service different requests. Although this sounds like a resource drain, when done correctly, it greatly reduces the resources required to service all the client requests.

The stateless session bean life cycle

To understand how instance pooling works, let's examine the life cycle of a stateless session bean. Stateless beans exist in one of three states:

No state
: When a bean instance is in this state, it has not yet been instantiated. We identify this state to provide a beginning and an end for the life cycle of a bean instance.

Pooled state

When an instance is in this state, it has been instantiated by the container but has not yet been associated with an EJB request.

Ready state

When a bean instance is in this state, it has been associated with an EJB request and is ready to respond to business method invocations.

Because a stateless session bean does not maintain any state between method invocations, every method invocation operates independently, performing its task without relying on instance variables. This means that any stateless session instance can service requests for any EJB object of the proper type. The container can therefore swap bean instances in and out between method invocations.

Each EJB vendor implements instance pooling differently, but all instance-pooling strategies attempt to manage collections of bean instances so that they are quickly accessible at runtime. To set up an instance pool, the EJB container creates several instances of a bean class and then holds on to them until they are needed. As clients make business-method requests, bean instances from the pool are assigned to the EJB requests associated with the clients. After the request is complete, the EJB object doesn't need the instance anymore and it's returned to the instance pool. An EJB server maintains instance pools for every type of stateless session bean deployed. Every instance in an instance pool is *equivalent*—they are all treated equally. Instances are selected arbitrarily from the instance pool and are assigned to EJB requests as needed.

Figure 3-1 illustrates instance swapping between stateless session bean method invocations. In Figure 3-1a, instance A is servicing a business method invocation delegated by EJB object 1. Once instance A has serviced the request, it moves back to the instance pool (Figure 3-1b). When a business method invocation on EJB object 2 is received, instance A is associated with that EJB object for the duration of the operation (Figure 3-1c). While instance A is servicing EJB object 2, another method invocation is received by EJB object 1 from the client and is serviced by instance B (Figure 3-1d).

Using this swapping strategy allows a few stateless session bean instances to serve hundreds of clients, because the amount of time it takes to perform most method invocations is typically much shorter than the pauses between method invocations. When a bean instance is finished servicing a request for an EJB object, it is immediately made available to any other EJB object that needs it. This allows fewer stateless session instances to service more requests, which decreases resource consumption and improves performance.

Soon after the bean instance is placed in the pool, it's given a reference to a `javax.ejb.EJBContext` if the session bean has requested that this context object be injected (see Chapter 14 for more information). The `EJBContext` provides an interface that the

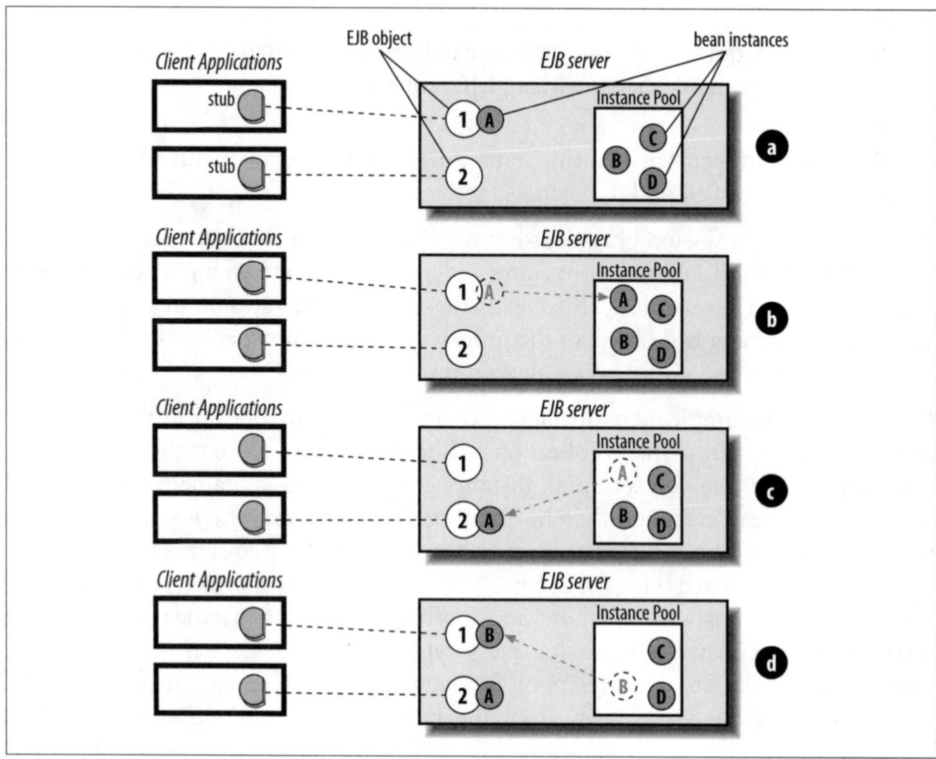

Figure 3-1. Stateless session beans in a swapping strategy

bean can use to communicate with the EJB environment. This `EJBContext` becomes more useful when the bean instance moves to the Ready state.

When a bean instance is servicing a request, the `EJBContext` takes on new meaning. The `EJBContext` provides information about the client that is using the bean. It also provides the instance with access to its own EJB stub proxy, which is useful when the bean needs to pass references to itself or to other enterprise beans. So the `EJBContext` is not a static class; it is an interface to the container.

Stateless session beans are declared "stateless" via the annotation `@javax.ejb.Stateless` or in the deployment descriptor. Once a bean class is deployed as stateless, the container assumes that no conversational state is maintained between method invocations. A stateless bean can have instance variables, but because bean instances can be servicing several different EJB objects, they should not be used to maintain conversational state.

Message-driven beans and instance pooling

Message-driven beans, like stateless session beans, do not maintain state specific to a client request, which makes them excellent candidates for instance pooling.

In most EJB containers, each type of message-driven bean has its own instance pool that services incoming messages. JMS-MDBs subscribe to a specific message destination, which is a kind of address used when sending and receiving messages. When a JMS client sends an asynchronous message to a destination, the message is delivered to the EJB container of the beans that subscribe to the destination. The EJB container determines which JMS-MDB subscribes to that destination and then chooses an instance of that type from the instance pool to process the message. Once the JMS-MDB instance has finished processing the message (when the `onMessage()` method returns), the EJB container returns the instance to its instance pool. Figure 3-2 illustrates how client requests are processed by an EJB container.

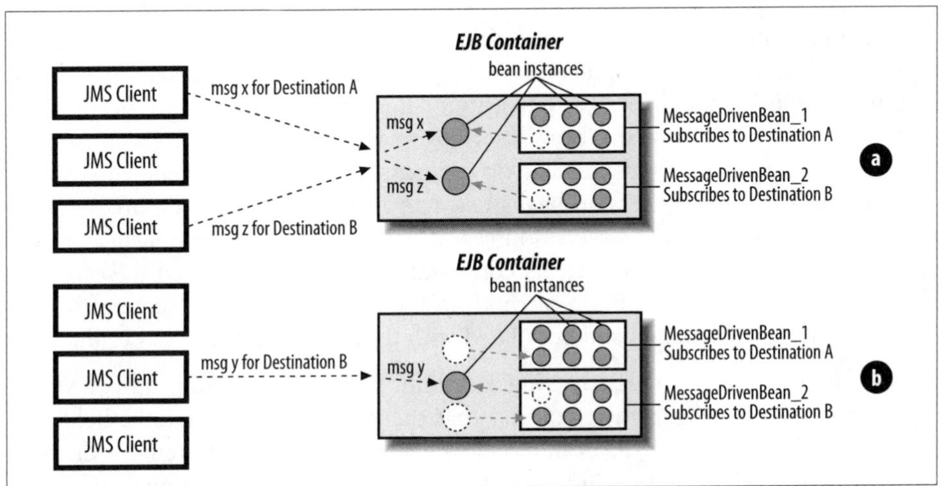

Figure 3-2. JMS-MDB instance pooling

In Figure 3-2a, the top JMS client delivers a message to destination A, and the bottom JMS client delivers a message to destination B. The EJB container chooses an instance of `MessageDrivenBean_1` to process the message intended for destination A and an instance of `MessageDrivenBean_2` to process the message intended for Destination B. The bean instances are removed from the pool and are used to process the messages.

A moment later, in Figure 3-2b, the middle JMS client sends a message to destination B. At this point, the first two messages have already been processed and the container is returning the instances to their respective pools. As the new message comes in, the container chooses a new instance of `MessageDrivenBean_2` to process the message.

JMS-MDBs are always deployed to process messages from a specific destination. In Figure 3-2, instances of `MessageDrivenBean_1` process messages only for destination A, and instances of `MessageDrivenBean_2` process messages only for destination B. Several messages for the same destination can be processed at the same time. If, for example, 100 messages for destination A arrive at the same time, the EJB container simply chooses 100 instances of `MessageDrivenBean_1` to process the incoming messages; each instance is assigned a message.

EJB 2.1 and its successors have expanded the role of message-driven beans beyond JMS so that they can support other messaging services and APIs. This opens up the message-driven bean to just about any kind of resource, including messaging systems other than JMS, ERP systems like SAP, and legacy systems like IMS. Regardless of the type of resource represented by the message-driven bean, the instances of the bean type will be pooled in the same way as the JMS-MDBs.

The Activation Mechanism

Unlike other enterprise beans, stateful session beans maintain state between method invocations. *Conversational state* represents the continuing conversation with the stateful session bean's client. The integrity of this conversational state needs to be maintained for the life of the bean's service to the client. Stateful session beans, unlike stateless session and message-driven beans, do not participate in instance pooling. Instead, stateful session beans use activation to conserve resources. When an EJB server needs to conserve resources, it can evict stateful session beans from memory. When a bean is evicted, its conversational state is serialized to secondary storage. When a client invokes a method on the EJB object, a new stateful session bean instance is instantiated and populated with the state from the initial bean.

Passivation is the act of disassociating a stateful bean instance from its EJB object and saving its state. Passivation requires that the bean instance's state be held relative to its EJB object. After the bean has been passivated, it is safe to remove the bean instance from the EJB object and evict it from memory. Clients are unaware of the deactivation process. Remember that the client uses the bean's remote reference, which is implemented by an EJB stub proxy, and therefore does not directly communicate with the bean instance. As a result, the client's connection to the EJB object can be maintained while the bean is passivated.

Activating a bean is the act of restoring a stateful bean instance's state relative to its EJB object. When a method on the passivated EJB object is invoked, the container automatically creates a new instance and sets its fields equal to the data stored during passivation. The EJB object can then delegate the method invocation to the bean as normal. Figure 3-3 shows activation and passivation of a stateful bean. In Figure 3-3a, the bean is being passivated. The state of instance B is read and held relative to the EJB object it was serving. In Figure 3-3b, the bean has been passivated and its state preserved. Here, the EJB object is not associated with a bean instance. In Figure 3-3c, the bean is being activated. A new instance, instance C, has been instantiated and associated with the EJB object and is in the process of having its state populated with the state held relative to the EJB object.

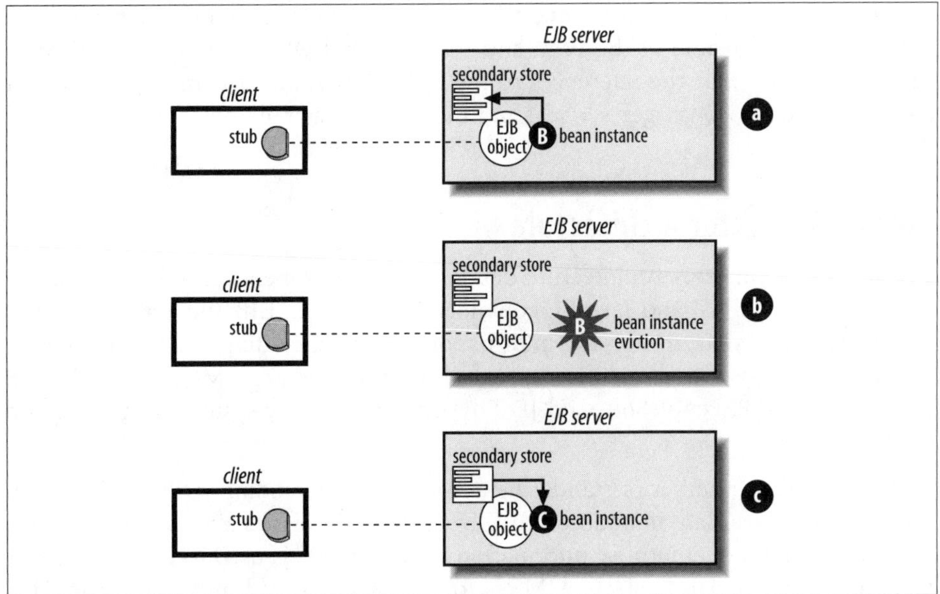

Figure 3-3. The passivation and activation processes

Since a stateful bean class does not have to be serializable, the exact mechanism for activating and passivating stateful beans is up to the vendor. Note that the transient property is not treated as you might expect when activating a passivated bean. In Java serialization, transient fields are always set to the initial value for that field type when the object is deserialized. `Integer`s are set to `0`, `Boolean`s to `false`, object references to `null`, and so on. In EJB, transient fields are not necessarily set back to their initial values but can maintain their original values, or any arbitrary value, after being activated. Take care when using transient fields, since their state following activation is implementation-specific.

The activation process is supported by life cycle callback methods. In EJB 3.0 (unlike in EJB 2.1), life cycle callback methods are added to the stateful bean class when they are needed and are not imposed on the bean class by a session bean interface. Bean developers can hook into life cycle callbacks in their stateful bean classes by annotating methods that are interested in these callbacks. A `@javax.ejb.PostActivate` annotated method is called immediately following the successful activation of a bean instance if it is defined in the bean class. It can be used to reset transient fields to an initial value. A `@javax.ejb.PrePassivate` annotated method is called immediately prior to passivation of the bean instance, again, if the bean developer has defined this method. These two methods are especially helpful if the bean instance maintains connections to resources that need to be closed or freed prior to passivation and reobtained following activation. Because the stateful bean instance is evicted from memory, open connections to resources are not maintained. The exceptions are remote references to other beans and the `SessionContext`, which must be maintained with the serialized state of the bean and reconstructed when the bean is activated. EJB also requires that the references to the JNDI environment context, component interfaces, the `EntityManager` service, and the `UserTransaction` object be maintained through passivation.

Java EE Connector Architecture

The Java EE Connector Architecture defines an interface between Enterprise Information Systems (EISs) and Java EE container systems (i.e., EJB and Servlet containers). EIS is a generic term for any information system, including relational database servers, message-oriented middleware (e.g., MQSeries and SonicMQ), CORBA, ERP systems (e.g., SAP, PeopleSoft, and JD Edwards), and legacy systems (e.g., IMS and CICS).

Java EE defines a number of standard enterprise APIs, including JDBC, JMS, JNDI, Java IDL, and JavaMail, in addition to EJB. Each API provides a vendor-neutral API for a specific kind of enterprise information system. JDBC is used to exchange information with relational databases; JMS is for message-oriented middleware; JNDI is for naming and directory services; JavaMail is for electronic mail systems; and Java IDL is for CORBA. Requiring support for these APIs ensures that the enterprise beans that use them are portable across EJB vendors.

Although the enterprise APIs are vendor-agnostic, the products behind the APIs are always proprietary. When an enterprise bean uses the enterprise APIs, it's the EJB container's responsibility to pool and maintain the EIS connections, enroll the EIS in transactions, propagate security credentials, etc. These tasks often require the EJB container to interact with the underlying EIS in ways not addressed by the generic APIs. In effect, each Java EE vendor had to write proprietary code to manage each brand of EIS. Faced with this situation, Java EE vendors chose which EISs they would support for each standard API. This situation had a significant impact on the brands of EIS an EJB vendor could be expected to support: for example, Vendor A might support JDBC connectivity to Oracle, and Vendor B might support only DB2.

Java EE Connectors 1.5

EJB 2.0 required support for the new Java EE Connector Architecture, which went a long way toward solving this problem. However, it didn't go far enough. In particular, it didn't support the *push* model for messaging, which is needed because several EISs push data to clients, without the clients explicitly making a request—for example, JMS. Both EJB 2.1 and 3.0 require support for Java EE Connector Architecture 1.5, which supports the push model. To support the push model, JCA 1.5 uses the message-driven bean programming model. Specifically, it defines a container/connector interface that allows incoming messages, sent asynchronously from the EIS, to be processed by message-driven beans. For example, Vendor X could develop a Java EE Connector for a *Mail Delivery Agent* (MDA), which is software that delivers Internet email. Vendor X defines a message-listening interface, the `EmailListener`, which can be implemented to create an Email-Message Driven Bean (Email-MDB) for processing email. As the MDA receives email from the Internet, it pushes the email to the EJB container, which delegates each message to an instance of the Email-MDB. The application developer then writes an Email-MDB that is annotated with the `@javax.ejb.MessageDriven` annotation and implements the `com.vendor.EmailListener` interface. Once the Email-MDB is created and deployed, it can process incoming messages.

Primary Services

Many value-added services are available for distributed applications. This book looks at eight value-added services that are called the *primary services* because they are required to complete the Enterprise JavaBeans platform. The primary services include concurrency, transactions, persistence, distributed objects, asynchronous messaging, a timer service, naming, and security. EJB servers automatically manage all of the primary services. This capability relieves application developers from the task of mastering these complicated services. Instead, developers can focus on defining the business logic that describes the system and can leave the system-level concerns to the EJB server. The following sections describe each primary service and explain how they are supported by EJB.

Concurrency

Concurrency is important to all the bean types, but it has different meanings for each type.

Concurrency with session and entity beans

Session beans do not support concurrent access. This limitation makes sense if you consider the nature of stateful and stateless session beans. A stateful bean is an extension of one client and serves only that client. It doesn't make sense to make stateful beans concurrent if they are used only by the clients that created them. Stateless session beans don't need to be concurrent because they don't maintain state that needs to be shared. The scope of the operations performed by a stateless bean is limited to the scope of each method invocation. Because neither stateful nor stateless session beans represent shared data, there is no need for concurrency.

Because EJB servers handle concurrency, a bean's methods do not have to be made thread-safe. In fact, the EJB specification prohibits the use of the `synchronized` keyword. Prohibiting the use of the thread synchronization primitives prevents developers from thinking that they control synchronization and enhances the performance of bean instances at runtime. In addition, the EJB specification explicitly prohibits beans from creating their own threads. In other words, as a bean developer, you cannot create a thread within a bean. The EJB container has to maintain complete control over the bean in order to properly manage concurrency, transactions, and persistence. Allowing the bean developer to create arbitrary threads would compromise the container's ability to track what the bean is doing and would make it impossible for the container to manage the primary services.

Entity beans represent data that is shared and may be accessed concurrently. Entity beans are shared components. In Titan Cruises' EJB system, for example, there are three ships: the *Paradise*, the *Utopia*, and the *Valhalla*. At any given moment, the Ship entity bean that represents the *Utopia* might be accessed by hundreds of clients. To make concurrent access to entity beans possible, the persistence provider needs to protect the data represented by the shared bean while allowing many clients to access the logical entity bean simultaneously.

In the Java Persistence specification, the persistence container protects shared entity data by making a copy of the entity bean instance on a per-transaction basis. Since each transaction has a snapshot of the entity, concurrent multithreaded access is possible. So how does the container protect against stale reads or different transactions trying to update the same entity at the same time? Optimistic concurrency using version fields is one way. Another way is setting the JDBC isolation level to SERIALIZED. Vendor implementations may also provide ways to obtain row locks directly in the database. All of this is discussed in great detail in Chapter 16.

Concurrency with message-driven beans

In message-driven beans, *concurrency* refers to the processing of more than one message at a time. If message-driven beans could process only a single message at a time, they would be practically useless in a real-world application because they couldn't handle heavy message loads. As Figure 3-4 illustrates, if three messages are delivered to a specific destination from three different clients at the same time, three instances of a single JMS-MDB that subscribes or listens to that destination can be used to process the messages simultaneously.

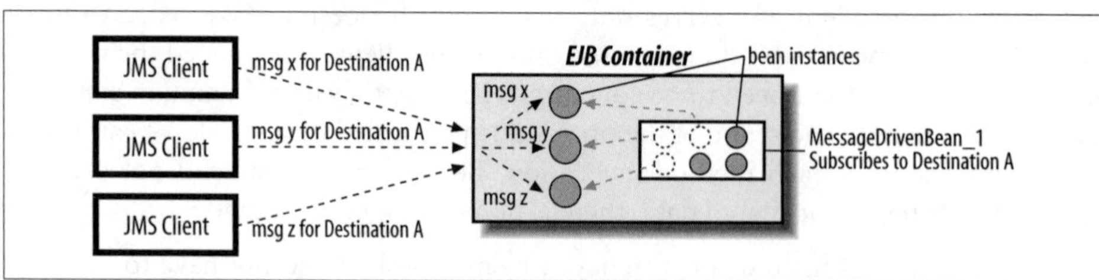

Figure 3-4. Concurrent processing with message-driven beans

Message-driven beans that implement APIs other than JMS benefit from the same concurrency controls as JMS-MDBs. Message-driven beans of all kinds are pooled and used to process incoming messages concurrently so that hundreds, possibly thousands, of messages can be handled simultaneously.*

Transactions

A *transaction* is a unit of work or a set of tasks that are executed together. Transactions are atomic; in other words, all the tasks in a transaction must be completed together for the transaction to be considered a success. In the previous chapter, we used the TravelAgent bean to describe how a session bean controls the interactions of other beans. Here is the bookPassage( ) method described in Chapter 2:

```
public Reservation bookPassage(CreditCardDO card,double price)
    throws IncompleteConversationalState {
     if (customer == null ||cruise == null ||cabin == null){
         throw new IncompleteConversationalState( );
     }
     try {
          Reservation reservation =
             new Reservation(customer,cruise,cabin,price,new Date( ));
          entityManager.persist(reservation);
          process.byCredit(customer,card,price);
          return reservation;
     } catch(Exception e) {
         throw new EJBException(e);
     }
}
```

The bookPassage( ) method consists of two tasks that must be completed together: the creation of a new Reservation entity and the processing of the payment. When the TravelAgent EJB is used to book a passenger, the charges to the passenger's credit card and the creation of the reservation must both be successful. It would be inappropriate for the ProcessPayment EJB to charge the customer's credit card if the creation of a new Reservation entity fails. Likewise, you can't make a reservation if the customer's credit card is not charged. An EJB server monitors the transaction to ensure that all the tasks are completed successfully.

Transactions are managed automatically, so, as a bean developer, you don't need to use any APIs to manage a bean's involvement in a transaction. Simply declaring the transactional attributes at deployment time tells the EJB server how to manage the bean at runtime. EJB does provide a mechanism that allows beans to manage transactions explicitly, if necessary. Setting the transactional attributes during deployment is discussed in Chapter 16, as are explicit management of transactions and other transactional topics.

* In reality, it's very difficult to process anything simultaneously without multiple processors, but conceptually this statement is true. Multiple threads in the same VM or multiple VMs on the same processor (computer chip) imitate simultaneous processing.

Persistence

Entity beans represent the behavior and data associated with real-world people, places, or things. Unlike session and message-driven beans, entity beans are persistent, which means that the state of an entity is saved in a database. Persistence allows entities to be durable so that both their behavior and their data can be accessed at any time without concern that the information will be lost because of a system failure.

Java Persistence

Persistence in EJB 3.0 has been totally revamped and rearchitected within the Java Persistence specification. While the EJB 2.1 model was component-based persistence, the Java Persistence model is a plain Java-based model (often called POJO Persistence). Entities can be created outside the scope of the EJB container. They are allocated as any other Java object using the `new()` operator. An entity can be attached to container management, or detached. Bean instances are attached to persistent storage through the `EntityManager` service. The `EntityManager` service provides methods to create, find, query, remove, and update entity beans. When a bean instance is attached, the container manages the persistent state of the bean and automatically synchronizes the bean with its data source.

An interesting thing about the Java Persistence model is that bean instances can be detached from the EJB container. Bean instances are usually detached from the EJB container when a transaction completes. These detached instances can be sent around the network to remote clients or even saved to disk. Their state can be modified and then reattached to the EJB container by using the `EntityManager.merge()` method. When bean instances are reattached, any changes made to the bean are synchronized with persistent storage. This new persistence model allows EJB developers to throw away the old Data Transfer Object pattern, greatly simplifying application architecture. We'll talk more about this in Chapter 5.

Object-to-relational persistence

Object-to-relational (O/R) persistence involves mapping an entity bean's state to relational database tables and columns. Since relational databases are used in 99 percent of database applications, the EJB 3.0 Expert Group realized that it is better to focus on object-to-relational mapping than to try to create a persistence architecture that is one-size-fits-all. As a result, the Java Persistence specification provides rich relational database mapping with advanced features such as inheritance, multitable mappings, versioning, and expanded EJBQL support. Since O/R mapping is mandated by the specification now, this makes EJB applications *much* more portable between vendors, as there will be a lot less vendor-specific metadata.

Let's give a simple overview of O/R mapping. In Titan's system, `Cabin` models the concept of a ship's cabin. `Cabin` defines three fields: `name`, `deckLevel`, and `id`. The definition of `Cabin` looks like this:

```
@Entity
@Table(name="CABIN")
public class Cabin {
    private int id;
    private String name;
    private int deckLevel;

    @Column(name="NAME")
    public String getName( ) { return name; }
    public void setName(String str) { name = str; }

    @Column(name="DECK_LEVEL")
    public int getDeckLevel( ) { return deckLevel;
    public void setDeckLevel(int level) { deckLevel = level; }

    @Id
    @Column(name="ID")
    public int getId( ) { return id; }
    public void setId(int id) { this.id = id; }

}
```

In this example, the accessor methods represent the entity bean's container-managed fields. With O/R database mapping, the fields of an entity bean correspond to columns in a relational database. Metadata about the O/R mapping is defined in annotations on the access methods (`@Column` and `@Id`) and on the bean class (`@Table`). `Cabin`'s `deckLevel` field, for example, maps to the column labeled `DECK_LEVEL` in a table called `CABIN` in Titan's relational database. Figure 3-5 shows a graphical depiction of this type of mapping.

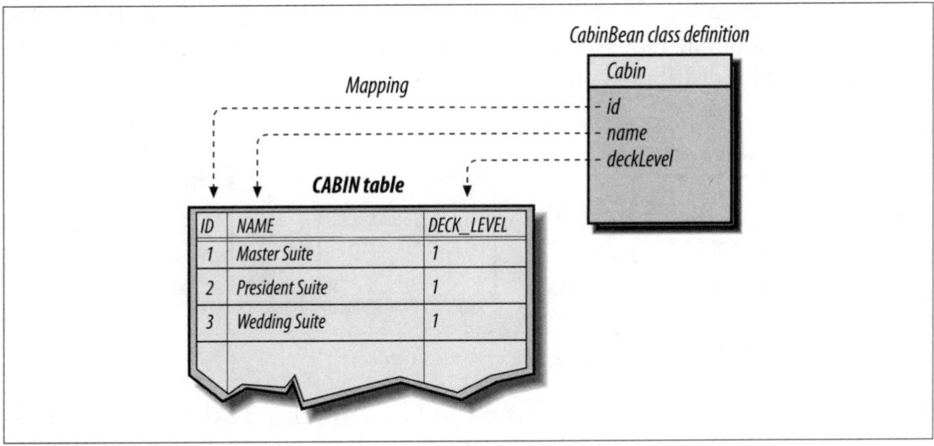

Figure 3-5. O/R mapping of entity beans

Once a bean's fields are mapped to the relational database, the container takes over the responsibility of keeping the state of an entity bean instance consistent with the corresponding tables in the database. This process is called *synchronizing* the state of the bean instance. In the case of `Cabin`, bean instances map one to one to rows in the `CABIN` table of the relational database. When a change is made to a Cabin entity, it is written to the appropriate row in the database. Sometimes, bean types map to more than one table. These are more complicated mappings, often requiring an SQL join and multiple updates, and are discussed in later chapters.

In addition, Java Persistence defines entity bean relationship fields, which allow entity beans to have one-to-one, one-to-many, and many-to-many relationships with other beans. Entity beans can maintain collections of other entity beans or single references. The Java Persistence model is covered in Chapters 5–10.

Distributed Objects

When we discuss the component interfaces and other EJB interfaces and classes used on the client, we are talking about the client's view of the EJB system. The *EJB client view* doesn't include session bean class instances, the EJB container, instance swapping, or any of the other implementation specifics of session beans. As far as a remote client is concerned, a bean is defined by its remote interface or endpoint interface.* Everything else is invisible, including the mechanism used to support distributed objects. As long as the EJB server supports the EJB client view, any distributed object protocol can be used. EJB 3.0 requires that every EJB server support Java RMI-IIOP, but it doesn't limit the protocols an EJB server can support to just Java RMI-IIOP (the Java RMI API using the CORBA IIOP protocol). It also requires support for SOAP 1.2 via the JAX-RPC API.

Regardless of the protocol, the server must support Java clients using the Java EJB client API, which means that the protocol must map to the Java RMI-IIOP or the JAX-RPC programming model. Figure 3-6 illustrates the Java language EJB API supported by different distributed object protocols.

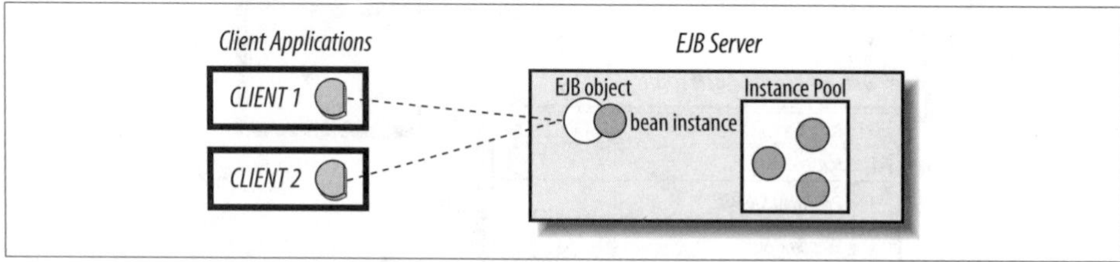

Figure 3-6. Java EJB client view supported by various protocols

EJB also allows servers to support access to beans by clients written in languages other than Java. An example of this capability is the EJB-to-CORBA mapping

* This doesn't include entity beans, though, as entity bean class instances may be detached from container management and sent to a remote client as long as these entity classes implement `java.io.Serializable`.

defined by Sun.[*] This document describes the CORBA Interface Definition Language (IDL) that can be used to access enterprise beans from CORBA clients. A CORBA client can be written in any language, including C++, Smalltalk, Ada, and even COBOL. The mapping also includes details about supporting the Java EJB client view, as well as details about mapping the CORBA naming system to EJB servers and distributed transactions across CORBA objects and beans. Another example is the EJB-to-SOAP mapping based on JAX-RPC. It allows SOAP client applications written in languages such as Visual Basic .NET, C#, and Perl to access stateless session beans. Figure 3-7 illustrates the possibilities for accessing an EJB server from different distributed object clients.

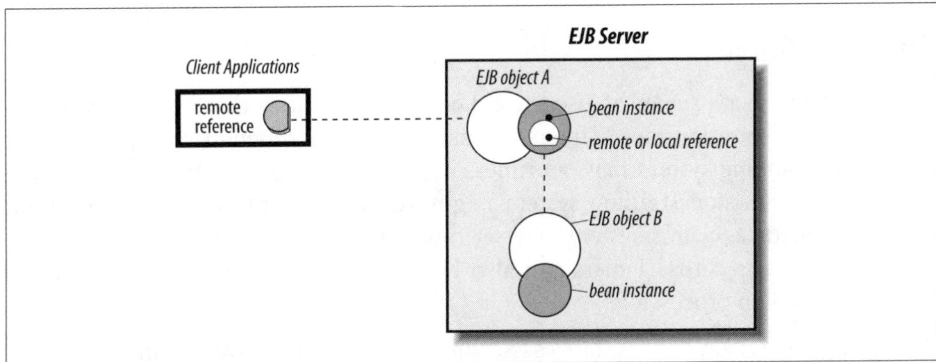

Figure 3-7. EJB accessed from different distributed clients

Asynchronous Enterprise Messaging

Prior to EJB 2.0, asynchronous enterprise messaging was not considered a primary service because it wasn't necessary in order to have a complete EJB platform. However, with the introduction of message-driven beans, asynchronous enterprise messaging with JMS has become so important that it has been elevated to the status of a primary service.

Support for enterprise messaging requires that the EJB container reliably route messages from JMS clients to JMS-MDBs. Reliable routing involves more than the simple delivery semantics associated with email or even the JMS API. With enterprise messaging, messages must be reliably delivered, which means that a failure while delivering the message may require the JMS provider to attempt redelivery.[†] What's more, enterprise messages may be persistent, which means they are stored to disk or

[*] Sun Microsystems' *Enterprise JavaBeans™ to CORBA Mapping, Version 1.1*, by Sanjeev Krishnan. Copyright© 1999 by Sun Microsystems

[†] Most EJB vendors will place a limit on the number of times a message can be redelivered. If redelivery is attempted too many times, the message might be placed in a "dead message" repository, where it can be reviewed by an administrator.

to a database until they can be properly delivered to their intended clients. Persistent messages also must survive system failures; if the EJB server crashes, these messages must still be available for delivery when the server comes back up. Most importantly, enterprise messaging is transactional. That means if a JMS-MDB fails while processing a message, that failure will abort the transaction and will force the EJB container to redeliver the message to another message-driven bean instance.

In addition, message-driven beans, stateless session beans, and entity beans can also send JMS messages. Sending messages can be as important to Enterprise JavaBeans as delivery of messages to JMS-MDB—support for both facilities tends to go hand in hand.

EJB Timer Service

The EJB Timer Service can be used to schedule notifications that are sent to enterprise beans at specific times. Timers are useful in many different applications. For example, a banking system may set timers on mortgage accounts to check for past-due payments. A stock-trading system might allow timers to be set on "buy limit orders." A medical claims system may set timers for automatic fraud audits of individuals' medical records. Timers can also be used in applications like self-auditing systems and batch processing.

Timers can be set on entity, stateless session, and message-driven beans. With session and entity beans, the bean sets the timers itself. For example, when a mortgage loan is created, the entity bean that represents the loan might set a past-due timer when the loan is created and reset the timer whenever a payment is made. Some EJB container systems may support message-driven bean timers, which are configured at deployment time and perform batch processing at regular intervals. The Timer Service is covered in detail in Chapter 13.

Naming

All naming services do essentially the same thing: they provide clients with a mechanism for locating distributed objects or resources. To accomplish this, a naming service must provide two things: object binding and a lookup API. *Object binding* is the association of a distributed object with a natural language name or identifier. The `TravelAgentRemote` object, for example, might be bound to the name "TravelAgent-Remote" or "agent." A binding is really a pointer or an index to a specific distributed object. A *lookup API* provides the client with an interface to the naming system. Simply put, lookup APIs allow clients to connect to a distributed service and request a remote reference to a specific object.

Enterprise JavaBeans mandates the use of JNDI as a lookup API on Java clients. JNDI supports just about any kind of naming and directory service. Although JNDI can become extraordinarily complex, the way it's used in Java EE applications is usually fairly simple. Java client applications can use JNDI to initiate a connection to an EJB server and to locate a specific EJB. The following code shows how the JNDI API might be used to locate and obtain a reference to the `TravelAgentRemote` EJB:

```
javax.naming.Context jndiContext = new javax.naming.InitialContext( );
Object ref = jndiContext.lookup("TravelAgentRemote");
TravelAgentRemote agent = (TravelAgentRemote)
    PortableRemoteObject.narrow(ref, TravelAgentRemote.class);

Reservation res = agent.bookPassage(...);
```

The properties passed into the constructor of `InitialContext` tell the JNDI API where to find the EJB server and what JNDI service provider (driver) to load. The `Context.lookup( )` method tells the JNDI service provider the name of the object to return from the EJB server. In this case, we are looking for the remote interface to the TravelAgent EJB. Once we have the TravelAgent EJB's remote interface, we can begin to invoke methods on the service to do things like book reservations.

There are many different kinds of directory and naming services; EJB vendors can choose the one that best meets their needs, but all vendors must support the CORBA naming service in addition to any other directory services they choose to support.

Security

Enterprise JavaBeans servers can support as many as three kinds of security:

Authentication
: Simply put, authentication validates the identity of the user. The most common kind of authentication is a simple login screen that requires a username and a password. Once users have successfully passed through the authentication system, they are free to use the system. Authentication can also be based on secure ID cards, swipe cards, security certificates, and other forms of identification. While authentication is the primary safeguard against unauthorized access to a system, it is fairly crude because it doesn't police an authorized user's access to resources within the system.

Authorization
: Authorization (a.k.a. access control) applies security policies that regulate what a specific user can and cannot do. Access control ensures that users access only those resources for which they have been given permission. Access control can police a user's access to subsystems, data, and business objects, or it can monitor more general behavior. Certain users, for example, may be allowed to update information while others are allowed only to view the data.

Secure communication
: Communication channels between a client and a server are frequently the focus of security concerns. A channel of communication can be secured by encrypting the communication between the client and the server. When communication is

secured by encryption, the messages passed are encoded so that they cannot be read or manipulated by unauthorized individuals. This normally involves the exchange of cryptographic keys between the client and the server. The keys allow the receiver of the message to decode the message and read it.

We'll talk more about security in Chapter 17.

Primary Services and Interoperability

Interoperability is a vital part of EJB. The specification includes the required support for Java RMI-IIOP for remote method invocation and provides for transaction, naming, and security interoperability. EJB also requires support for JAX-RPC, which itself requires support for SOAP 1.1 and WSDL 1.1; these are the standards of the web services industry.

IIOP

EJB requires vendors to provide an implementation of Java RMI that uses the CORBA 2.3.1 IIOP protocol. The goal of this requirement is that Java EE application servers will be able to interoperate so that Java EE components (enterprise beans, applications, servlets, and JSPs) in one Java EE server can access enterprise beans in a different Java EE server. The Java RMI-IIOP specification standardizes the transfer of parameters, return values, and exceptions, as well as the mapping of interfaces and value objects to the CORBA IDL.

Vendors may support protocols other than Java RMI-IIOP, as long as the semantics of the RMI interfaces adhere to the types allowed in RMI-IIOP. This constraint ensures that a client's view of EJB is consistent, regardless of the protocol used in remote invocations.

Transaction interoperability between containers for two-phase commits is an optional but important feature of EJB. It ensures that transactions started by a Java EE web component propagate to enterprise beans in other containers. The EJB specifications detail how two-phase commits are handled across EJB containers as well as how transactional containers interact with nontransactional containers.

EJB also addresses the need for an interoperable naming service for looking up enterprise beans. It specifies CORBA `CosNaming` as the interoperable naming service, defining how the service must implement the IDL interfaces of beans in the `CosNaming` module and how EJB clients use the service over IIOP.

EJB provides security interoperability by specifying how EJB containers establish trust relationships and how containers exchange security credentials when Java EE components access enterprise beans across containers. EJB containers are required to support the Secure Sockets Layer (SSL 3.0) protocol and the related IETF-standard Transport Layer Security (TLS 1.0) protocol for secure connections between clients and enterprise beans.

While IIOP has been around for a long time and offers interoperability in a number of areas, the truth is it hasn't been very successful. There are a variety of reasons why IIOP has not been the silver bullet it was intended to be, but perhaps the biggest reason is complexity. Although IIOP is platform-independent, it's not trivial for vendors to implement. In addition, there appear to be numerous gaps in the IIOP and other CORBA protocols, which cause interoperability problems when actually deployed in a production environment. It's rare to hear of real-world systems that have successfully deployed interoperating EJB systems based on IIOP. The solution the industry seems to have latched on to is web services, which depend on SOAP and WSDL as the bases for interoperability.

SOAP and WSDL

SOAP (Simple Object Access Protocol) is the primary protocol used by web services today. It's based on XML and can be used for both RPC- and document (asynchronous)-style messaging. The fact that SOAP is based on XML means that it's fairly easy to support. Any platform (operating system, programming language, software application, etc.) that can create HTTP network connections and parse XML can handle the SOAP protocol. This is why SOAP has gained widespread acceptance in a short period of time. More than 70 SOAP toolkits (code libraries) are available today for just about every modern programming environment, including Java, .NET, JavaScript, C, C++, Visual Basic, Delphi, Perl, Python, Ruby, Smalltalk, and others.

WSDL (Web Service Description Language) is the IDL of the web services. A WSDL document is an XML file that describes what web services a company supports, as well as the protocols, message formats, and network addresses of those web services. WSDL documents are highly structured, so they can be used to autogenerate RPC stubs and other software interfaces for communicating with web services. Although WSDL documents are open enough to describe any type of service, they are typically used to describe web services that use the SOAP protocol.

WSDL and SOAP are normally used in combination. They form the building blocks for other interoperability standards covering security, transaction, orchestration, enterprise messaging, and a cornucopia of other topics. There is a lot of overlap among different groups that are developing infrastructure protocols based on SOAP and WSDL, and, as a result, there are a lot of conflicting and immature standards. SOAP and WSDL have a lot of promise, but it's still too soon to say whether web services will solve the interoperability problems that have plagued enterprise computing since the beginning. It's likely that SOAP, WSDL, and the infrastructure protocols based on these standards will go farther than IIOP, DCOM, and other predecessors, but they won't be a silver bullet. Web services are covered in more detail in Chapters 18 and 19.

What's Next?

The first three chapters of this book gave you a foundation on which to develop Enterprise JavaBeans components and applications. While we haven't gone into detail, we've shown you most of the topics that you'll be dealing with. Beginning with Chapter 4, you will develop your own beans and learn how to apply them in EJB applications.

CHAPTER 4

Developing Your First Beans

The primary goal of the EJB 3.0 and Java Persistence specifications was to make it as easy as possible to write and deploy an EJB-based application. Creating an application is as easy as compiling your code, jarring up your classes, and running your application server. This chapter gives an introduction to writing your first entity and session bean. You'll find that getting up and running is fairly simple.

Developing an Entity Bean

Let's start by examining how to create an entity bean. We'll implement the Cabin entity that is part of the Titan Cruises Java EE application. The Cabin entity encapsulates the data and behavior associated with a cruise ship cabin in Titan's business domain. Although you can interact with entity beans outside of an application server, we will later create a TravelAgent session bean to serve as a data access interface for creating and locating cabins.

Cabin: The Bean Class

When developing an entity bean, all we need to define is the bean class. Entities in Java Persistence are plain Java objects that are annotated with O/R mapping metadata. We started to define the Cabin entity in Chapter 2; here, we add two new methods for setting and getting the ship ID and the bed count. The ship ID identifies the ship to which the cabin belongs, and the bed count tells how many people the cabin can accommodate:

```
package com.titan.domain

import javax.persistence.*;

@Entity
@Table(name="CABIN")
public class Cabin implements java.io.Serializable{
```

```
    private int id;
    private String name;
    private int deckLevel;
    private int shipId;
    private int bedCount;

    @Id
    @Column(name="ID")
    public int getId( ) { return id; }
    public void setId(int pk) { id = pk; }

    @Column(name="NAME")
    public String getName( ) { return name; }
    public void setName(String str) {name = str; }

    @Column(name="DECK_LEVEL")
    public int getDeckLevel( ) { return deckLevel; }
    public void setDeckLevel(int level) { deckLevel = level; }

    @Column(name="SHIP_ID")
    public int getShipId( ) { return shipId; }
    public void setShipId(int sid) { shipId = sid; }

    @Column(name="BED_COUNT")
    public int getBedCount( ) { return bedCount; }
    public void setBedCount(int bed) { bedCount = bed; }

}
```

The `Cabin` bean class is annotated with `@javax.persistence.Entity` and `@javax.persistence.Table`. The `@Entity` annotation tells the persistence provider that this is an entity class that is mapped to a database and that can be managed by an `EntityManager` service. The `@Table` annotation tells the EJB container to which database table the bean class should map. The bean class implements `java.io.Serializable`, but it is not required to. Having entity classes implement `Serializable` allows them to be used as the parameters and return values of the remote interface methods of a session bean. This allows you to use the same class for both persistence and data transfer.

`Cabin` also defines four properties: `name`, `deckLevel`, `shipId`, and `bedCount`. *Properties* are attributes of an entity bean that can be accessed by public *set* and *get* methods; they can also be accessed directly through the bean's fields. In this example, we use public *set* and *get* methods. For each property, we define how it maps to the columns in the `CABIN` database table with the `@javax.persistence.Column` annotation. The `getId( )` property is marked as the primary key of the Cabin entity by using the `@javax.persistence.Id` annotation. The primary key denotes the identity of a particular entity bean at runtime and when it is persisted in the database.

Table-mapping annotations like @Table and @Column are not required; if they're omitted, they default to the unqualified name of the class and the property name, respectively. However, primary-key identification is required.

Notice that we have made the Cabin bean class a part of a new package named com.titan.domain. Place all the classes and interfaces associated with each type of bean in a package specific to the bean. Because our beans are for use by Titan Cruises, we placed these packages in the com.titan package hierarchy. We also created directory structures that match package structures. If you are using an IDE that works directly with Java files, create a new directory called *dev* (for development) and create the directory structure shown in Figure 4-1. Copy the Cabin bean class into your IDE and save its definition to the *domain* directory. Compile the Cabin bean class to ensure that its definition is correct. The *Cabin.class* file, generated by the IDE's compiler, should be written to the *domain* directory, the same directory as the *Cabin.java* file. The rest of the Cabin bean's classes will be placed in this same directory. We are done defining the Cabin entity.

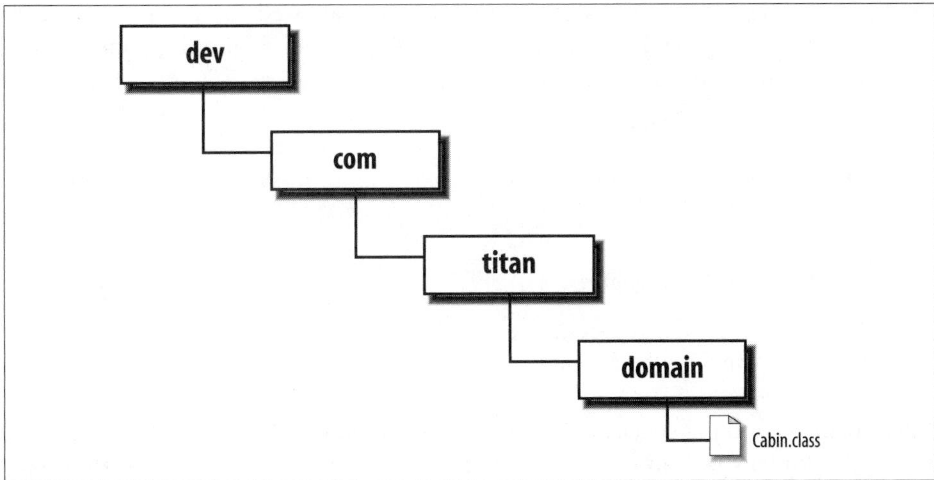

Figure 4-1. dev directory structure

The persistence.xml File

The Java Persistence specification requires a simple XML deployment descriptor file, *persistence.xml*, which configures basic things like the name of the EntityManager service that will be managing the set of entities deployed in a particular deployment package. It also defines what database the EntityManager service will be communicating with and may also specify additional, vendor-specific properties.

```
<persistence>
   <persistence-unit name="titan">
```

```
        <jta-data-source>java:/TitanDB</jta-data-source>
    </persistence-unit>
</persistence
```

The *<name>* element represents the set of classes that are managed by a given `EntityManager`. The `<jta-data-source>` element defines the database that will be used to persist entities in this deployment. This *persistence.xml* file is located in a *META-INF* directory. *persistence.xml* is discussed in detail in Chapter 5.

Developing a Session Bean

Now that our Cabin entity is ready, we need to create a session bean that will act as the interface for interacting with the Cabin entity. This session bean will take on the business process and responsibilities of a travel agent and will be called the TravelAgent EJB.

TravelAgentRemote: The Remote Interface

The first part of creating the TravelAgent EJB is to define its remote interface. This interface specifies what business methods a client is allowed to invoke on the EJB. Clients interact with the TravelAgent's `createCabin( )` and `findCabin( )` methods to manipulate Cabin entities:

```
package com.titan.travelagent;

import javax.ejb.Remote;
import com.titan.domain.Cabin;

@Remote
public interface TravelAgentRemote {

    public void createCabin(Cabin cabin);
    public Cabin findCabin(int id);
}
```

There really is nothing special about the remote interface of the TravelAgent EJB. It looks like a plain Java interface, except that it is annotated with the `@javax.ejb.Remote` annotation. This annotation tells the EJB container that this particular interface is the remote business interface of the TravelAgent EJB. Unlike EJB 2.1, also notice that the business methods do not have to throw `java.rmi.RemoteException`. They can if they want to, but they don't have to.

TravelAgentBean: The Bean Class

Now that we have defined the remote interface to the TravelAgent EJB, we need to implement the bean class that contains the business logic for this session bean. The TravelAgent EJB is defined as a stateless bean. We use the `@javax.ejb.Stateless` annotation to denote this. Although they are not required to, it is good practice for stateless session beans to implement all of their business interfaces so that the client/bean contract can be enforced by the Java compiler. In this case, the business interface is TravelAgentRemote. Here is the complete definition of the TravelAgentBean class:

```
package com.titan.travelagent;

import javax.ejb.Stateless;
import javax.persistence.EntityManager;
import javax.persistence.PersistenceContext;

import com.titan.domain.Cabin;

@Stateless
public class TravelAgentBean implements TravelAgentRemote{
    @PersistenceContext(unitName="titan") private EntityManager manager;

    public void createCabin(Cabin cabin) {
        manager.persist(cabin);
    }

    public Cabin findCabin(int pKey) {
       return manager.find(Cabin.class, pKey);
    }
}
```

A bunch of things are going on in this implementation. First, the TravelAgentBean class uses the @javax.persistence.PersistenceContext annotation to get access to the EntityManager service that it uses to create and find Cabin entities. @PersistenceContext tells the EJB container that it must set the manager field with an EntityManager instance. The EJB container sees that the type of the field is javax.persistence.EntityManager and knows that it must set the field to be a reference to an EntityManager service that references the Titan persistence unit we defined in the *persistence.xml* file. This field will be initialized when the bean instance is instantiated.

The next two methods interact with the EntityManager service to create a Cabin entity within the database and to locate a Cabin entity based on its primary key. The createCabin( ) method invokes EntityManager.persist( ), passing in an instance of the entity that we want to create. After this operation is complete, the Cabin instance is attached to persistence management and is stored in the database. We'll see later on that you create the Cabin instance as you would any other plain Java object. The findCabin( ) method takes as its parameter a primary key of a cabin in the database. It calls the EntityManager.find( ) method, passing the Cabin bean class as a parameter and the actual primary key. The Cabin bean class parameter tells the EntityManager which entity it is trying to find in the database. The findCabin( ) method then returns the found Cabin entity back to the remote client.

titan.jar: The JAR File

The JAR file is a platform-independent file format for compressing, packaging, and delivering several files together. Based on the Zip file format and the zlib compression standards, the JAR (Java Archive) tool was originally developed to make downloads of Java applets more efficient. As a packaging mechanism, however, the JAR file format is a very convenient way to "shrink-wrap" components and other software for delivery to third parties. In EJB development, a JAR file packages all the classes and interfaces associated with a bean. Besides EJB definitions and classes, you are also allowed to package entity beans and their *persistence.xml* deployment descriptor.

Creating the JAR file for deployment is easy. Position yourself in the *dev* directory that is just above the *com/titan* directory tree and execute the following command:

```
C:\dev> jar cf titan.jar com/titan/domain/*.class
                         com/titan/travelagent/*.class
                            META-INF/persistence.xml
```

The c option tells the *jar* utility to create a new JAR file that contains the files indicated in subsequent parameters. It also tells the *jar* utility to stream the resulting JAR file to standard output. The f option tells *jar* to redirect the standard output to a new file named in the second parameter (*titan.jar*). It's important to get the order of the option letters and the command-line parameters to match. You can learn more about the *jar* utility and the `java.util.zip` package in *Java in a Nutshell* or *Learning Java* (both published by O'Reilly).

The *jar* utility creates the file *titan.jar* in the *dev* directory. If you're interested in looking at the contents of the JAR file, you can use any standard Zip application (WinZip, PKZIP, etc.) or the command `jar tvf titan.jar`. Figure 4-2 shows the structure of this Jar file.

Creating a CABIN Table in the Database

One of the primary jobs of a deployment tool is mapping entity beans to databases. In the case of the Cabin entity, we must map its `id`, `name`, `deckLevel`, `shipId`, and `bedCount` fields to some data source. Before proceeding with deployment, you need to set up a database and create a `CABIN` table. You can use the following standard SQL statement to create a `CABIN` table that will be consistent with the examples provided in this chapter:

```
create table CABIN
(
    ID int primary key NOT NULL,
    SHIP_ID int,
    BED_COUNT int,
    NAME char(30),
    DECK_LEVEL int
)
```

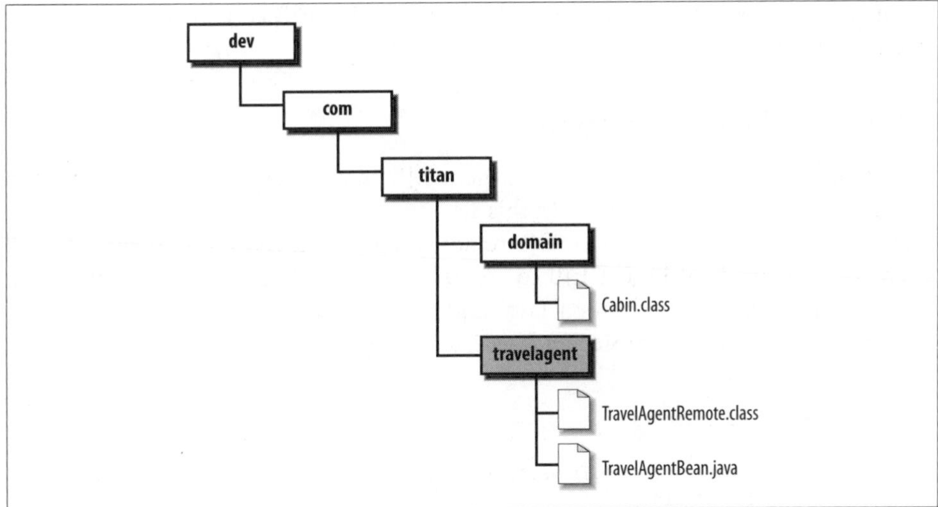

Figure 4-2. titan.jar contents

This statement creates a `CABIN` table that has five columns corresponding to the container-managed fields in the `Cabin` class. Once the table is created and connectivity to the database is confirmed, you can proceed with the deployment process.

Alternatively, most if not all persistence provider implementations will support autogeneration of your database tables. For example, you can configure JBoss to create the tables for each entity bean when the application server boots and deploys its EJBs. Other application servers will have different mechanisms to do this.

Deploying the EJB JAR

Deployment is the process of reading the bean's JAR file, changing or adding properties to the deployment descriptor, mapping the bean to the database, defining access control in the security domain, and generating any vendor-specific classes needed to support the bean in the EJB environment. Some EJB server products require you to use a set of deployment tools to deploy your EJBs to your application server. These tools may provide a graphical user interface or a set of command-line programs.

A deployment tool reads the JAR file and looks for annotated classes as well as any possible XML deployment descriptors so that it can determine which EJBs and entities are being deployed. In a graphical deployment wizard, the metadata of each EJB and entity is presented using a set of property sheets similar to those used in environments such as Visual Basic .NET, PowerBuilder, and JBuilder.

Some EJB servers, like JBoss, do not require any special vendor-generated classes, so there is no need for a deployment tool. JBoss, for instance, just requires you to put your *ejb* JAR in a *deploy/* directory. The application server examines the JAR file at runtime when the server boots up to determine which EJB containers must be created and attached to the runtime.

Creating a Client Application

Now that the Cabin entity and TravelAgent EJBs have been deployed, we want to access them from a remote client. In this section, we create a remote client that connects to the EJB server, locates the EJB remote interface for the TravelAgent EJB, and interacts with the TravelAgent EJB to create and pull Cabin entities from the database. The following code shows a Java application that creates a new Cabin entity, sets its `name`, `deckLevel`, `shipId`, and `bedCount` properties, and then locates it again using its primary key:

```
package com.titan.clients;

import com.titan.travelagent.TravelAgentRemote;
import com.titan.domain.Cabin;

import javax.naming.InitialContext;
import javax.naming.Context;
import javax.naming.NamingException;
import java.util.Properties;
import javax.rmi.PortableRemoteObject;

public class Client {
    public static void main(String [] args) {
        try {
            Context jndiContext = getInitialContext( );
            Object ref = jndiContext.lookup("TravelAgentBean/remote");
            TravelAgentRemote dao = (TravelAgentRemote)
                PortableRemoteObject.narrow(ref,TravelAgentRemote.class);

            Cabin cabin_1 = new Cabin( );
            cabin_1.setId(1);
            cabin_1.setName("Master Suite");
            cabin_1.setDeckLevel(1);
            cabin_1.setShipId(1);
            cabin_1.setBedCount(3);

            dao.createCabin(cabin_1);

            Cabin cabin_2 = dao.findCabin(1);
            System.out.println(cabin_2.getName( ));
            System.out.println(cabin_2.getDeckLevel( ));
            System.out.println(cabin_2.getShipId( ));
            System.out.println(cabin_2.getBedCount( ));

        } catch (javax.naming.NamingException ne){ne.printStackTrace( );}
    }
```

```
        public static Context getInitialContext( )
            throws javax.naming.NamingException {

            Properties p = new Properties( );
            // ... Specify the JNDI properties specific to the vendor.
            return new javax.naming.InitialContext(p);
        }
    }
```

To access an enterprise bean, a client starts by using JNDI to obtain a directory connection to a bean's container. JNDI is an implementation-independent API for directory and naming systems. Every EJB vendor must provide a directory service that is JNDI-compliant. This means that they must provide a JNDI service provider, which is a piece of software analogous to a driver in JDBC. Different service providers connect to different directory services—not unlike JDBC, where different drivers connect to different relational databases. The `getInitialContext( )` method uses JNDI to obtain a network connection to the EJB server.

The code used to obtain a JNDI context depends on which EJB vendor you use. Consult your vendor's documentation to find out how to obtain a JNDI context appropriate to your product. For example, the code used to obtain a JNDI context in WebSphere might look something like the following:

```
public static Context getInitialContext( )
    throws javax.naming.NamingException {

    java.util.Properties properties = new java.util.Properties( );
    properties.put(javax.naming.Context.PROVIDER_URL, "iiop:///");
    properties.put(javax.naming.Context.INITIAL_CONTEXT_FACTORY,
        "com.ibm.ejs.ns.jndi.CNInitialContextFactory");
    return new InitialContext(properties);
}
```

The same method developed for JBoss would be different:

```
public static Context getInitialContext( )
    throws javax.naming.NamingException {

    Properties p = new Properties( );
    p.put(Context.INITIAL_CONTEXT_FACTORY,
        "org.jnp.interfaces.NamingContextFactory");
    p.put(Context.URL_PKG_PREFIXES,
        " org.jboss.naming:org.jnp.interfaces");
    p.put(Context.PROVIDER_URL, "jnp://localhost:1099");
    return new javax.naming.InitialContext(p);
}
```

Once a JNDI connection is established and a context is obtained from the `getInitialContext( )` method, the context can be used to look up the remote interface of the TravelAgent EJB:

```
Object ref = jndiContext.lookup("TravelAgentBean/remote");
```

Throughout this book, we'll use lookup names like "TravelAgentBean/remote" for remote client applications. The actual name you use to do a lookup may be different, depending on the requirements of your vendor. You will need to bind a lookup name to the EJB server's naming service, and some vendors may require a special directory path or provide a default binding.

If you are using a standard Java EE component (Servlet, JSP, EJB, or Java EE Application Client), you will not need to set the properties explicitly when creating a JNDI `InitialContext`, no matter which EJB vendor you are using. That's because the JNDI properties can be configured at deployment time and are applied automatically. A Java EE component would obtain its `InitialContext` as follows:

```
public static Context getInitialContext( )
    throws javax.naming.NamingException {

    return new javax.naming.InitialContext( );
}
```

This is simpler and more portable than configuring JNDI properties for simple Java clients. All Java EE components use the same JNDI naming system that enterprise beans use to look up any service. Specifically, they require that EJB references be bound to the "java:comp/env/ejb/" namespace. For example, for a different Java EE component like a servlet, here's all we need to look up the TravelAgent EJB:

```
Object ref = jndiContext.lookup("java:comp/env/ejb/TravelAgentRemote");
```

At deployment time, you would use the vendor's deployment tools to map that JNDI name to the TravelAgent EJB's remote interface. In later sections, we'll see that special annotations allow you to inject EJB references directly into the bean class. We already saw an example of one of them when the `EntityManager` service was injected into the `TravelAgentBean` class. In this book, Java client applications will need to use explicit parameters for JNDI lookups. As an alternative, you could use a special Java EE component called a Java EE Application Client, but this type of component is outside the scope of this book. For more information about Java EE Application Client components, consult the Java EE 5 specification.

The `Client` application uses the `PortableRemoteObject.narrow( )` method to narrow the `Object ref` to a `TravelAgentRemote` reference:

```
Object ref = jndiContext.lookup("TravelAgentRemote");
CabinHomeRemote home = (TravelAgentRemote)
    PortableRemoteObject.narrow(ref,TravelAgentRemote.class);
```

The `PortableRemoteObject.narrow( )` method was first introduced in EJB 1.1 and continues to be used on remote clients in EJB 3.0. It is needed to support the requirements of RMI over IIOP. Because CORBA supports many different languages, casting is not native to CORBA (some languages don't have casting). Therefore, to get a remote reference to `TravelAgentRemote`, we must explicitly narrow the object returned from `lookup( )`.

The name used to find the TravelAgent EJB's remote interface is set by a vendor-specific default value, a vendor-specific annotation or deployment descriptor, or the deployer using a deployment wizard if one exists for that EJB product. The JNDI name is entirely up to the person deploying the bean; it can be the same as the bean name set in the XML deployment descriptor, or something completely different.

Creating a new Cabin entity

In this example, you finally see how Cabin entities are created. Java's `new( )` operator is used to allocate an instance of the `Cabin` bean class. Nothing magical is happening. The client initializes the properties locally on the `Cabin` bean instance. The `id`, `name`, `deckLevel`, `shipId`, and `bedCount` of the Cabin entity are set:

```
Cabin cabin_1 = new Cabin( );
Cabin_1.setId(1);
cabin_1.setName("Master Suite");
cabin_1.setDeckLevel(1);
cabin_1.setShipId(1);
cabin_1.setBedCount(3);
```

The Cabin entity does not get inserted into the database when you allocate it on the client. The instance must be passed to the TravelAgent EJB where it will be created in the database when the `EntityManager.persist( )` method is called.

Figure 4-3 shows how the relational database table we created should look after this code has been executed. It should contain one record.

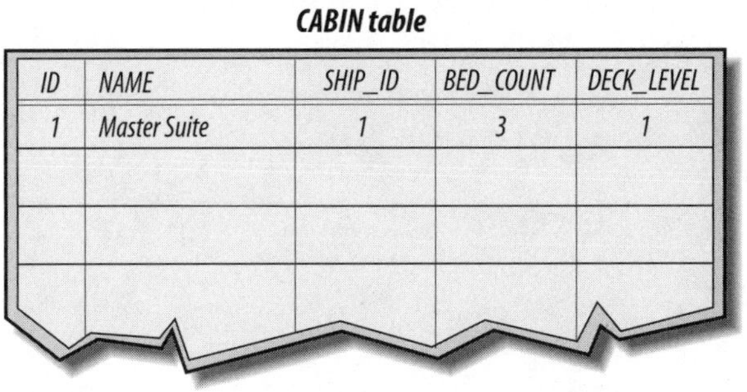

CABIN table

ID	NAME	SHIP_ID	BED_COUNT	DECK_LEVEL
1	Master Suite	1	3	1

Figure 4-3. CABIN table with one cabin record

The client locates Cabin entity beans by passing the primary key to the `Travel-AgentRemote`'s `findCabin( )` method. As you saw before, this session bean interacts with the `EntityManager` service to find the bean in the database. The TravelAgent passes back an instance of a `Cabin` with that primary key. This is possible because we defined the `Cabin` bean class to implement the `java.io.Serializable` interface, which allowed the `Cabin` bean instance to be marshaled across the wire back to the client.

We can now interrogate the Cabin bean instance locally to get the Cabin entity's name, deckLevel, shipId, and bedCount:

```
Cabin cabin_2 = dao.findCabin(1);
System.out.println(cabin_2.getName( ));
System.out.println(cabin_2.getDeckLevel( ));
System.out.println(cabin_2.getShipId( ));
System.out.println(cabin_2.getBedCount( ));
```

We are ready to create and run the Client application. Compile the Client application and deploy the Cabin entity into the container system. Then run the Client application. The output should look something like this:

```
Master Suite
1
1
3
```

Congratulations! You just created and used your first stateless session bean and entity bean. Of course, the Client application doesn't do much, but this is a good first step to learning how to implement EJBs and entities.

CHAPTER 5

Persistence: EntityManager

Persistence is a key piece of the Java EE platform. In older versions of Java EE, the EJB specification was responsible for defining this layer. In Java EE 5, persistence has been spun off into its own specification: Java Persistence 1.0. Persistence provides an ease-of-use abstraction on top of JDBC so that your code can be isolated from database, vendor-specific peculiarities and optimizations. It can also be described as an object-to-relational mapping engine (ORM). This means that the Java Persistence API can automatically map your Java objects to and from a relational database. In addition to object mappings, this service also provides a query language that is very SQL-like but is tailored to work with Java objects rather than a relational schema.

Chapter 4 showed how to create and interact with an entity bean. For those of you familiar with the older EJB 2.x model for entity beans, you may have noticed that entity beans no longer have a `Home` interface. So, how are entity beans created? How are they updated and removed? How can you perform queries and such? All of these persistent actions are now performed through the `javax.persistence.EntityManager` service.

In the new Java Persistence specification, the `EntityManager` is the central service for all persistence actions. Entities are plain Java objects that are allocated just like any other Java object. They do not become persistent until your code explicitly interacts with the `EntityManager` to make them persistent. The `EntityManager` manages the O/R mapping between a fixed set of entity classes and an underlying data source. It provides APIs for creating queries, finding objects, synchronizing objects, and inserting objects into the database. It also can provide caching and manage the interaction between an entity and transactional services in a Java EE environment such as JTA. The `EntityManager` is tightly integrated with Java EE and EJB but is not limited to this environment; it can be used in plain Java programs.

You can use Java Persistence outside of an application server and in plain Java SE programs.

This chapter focuses on the details of the persistence service and how it can be accessed within Java EE and with regular Java programs that run outside of a Java EE environment.

Entities Are POJOs

Entities, in the Java Persistence specification, are plain old Java objects (POJOs). You allocate them with the new( ) operator just as you would any other plain Java object. Instances of an entity bean class do not become persistent until they are associated with an EntityManager. For instance, let's look at a simple example of a Customer entity:

```
import javax.persistence.*;

@Entity
public class Customer {
   private int id;
   private String name;

   @Id @GeneratedValue
   public int getId( ) {
      return id;
   }
   public void setId(int id) {
      this.id = id;
   }

   String getName( ) {
      return name;
   }

   public void setName(String name) {
      this.name = name;
   }
}
```

If we allocate instances of this Customer class, no magic happens when new( ) is invoked. Calling the new operator does not magically interact with some underlying service to create the Customer class in the database:

```
Customer cust = new Customer( );
cust.setName("Bill");
```

Allocated instances of the Customer class remain POJOs until you ask the EntityManager to create the entity in the database.

Managed Versus Unmanaged Entities

Before we can go any deeper into the entity manager service, we need to delve more deeply into the life cycle of entity object instances. An entity bean instance is either managed (a.k.a. attached) by an entity manager or unmanaged (a.k.a. detached). When an entity is attached to an `EntityManager`, the manager tracks state changes to the entity and synchronizes those changes to the database whenever the entity manager decides to flush its state. When an entity is detached, it is unmanaged. Any state changes to an entity that is detached are not tracked by the entity manager.

Persistence Context

A *persistence context* is a set of managed entity object instances. Persistence contexts are managed by an entity manager. The entity manager tracks all entity objects within a persistence context for changes and updates made, and flushes these changes to the database using the flush mode rules discussed later in this chapter. Once a persistence context is closed, all managed entity object instances become detached and are no longer managed. Once an object is detached from a persistence context, it can no longer be managed by an entity manager, and any state changes to this object instance will not be synchronized with the database.

When a persistence context is closed, all managed entity objects become detached and are unmanaged.

There are two types of persistence contexts: transaction-scoped and extended persistence contexts.

Transaction-scoped persistence context

Persistence contexts may live as long as a transaction and be closed when a transaction completes. This is called a *transaction-scoped persistence context*. When the transaction completes, the transaction-scoped persistence context will be destroyed and all managed entity object instances will become detached. Only application server managed persistence contexts can be transaction-scoped. In other words, only EntityManager instances injected with the `@PersistenceContext` annotation or its XML equivalent may be transaction-scoped.

```
@PersistenceContext(unitName="titan")
EntityManager entityManager;

@TransactionAttribute(REQUIRED)
public Customer someMethod( ) {
   Customer cust = entityManager.find(Customer.class, 1);
   cust.setName("new name");
   return cust;
}
```

When someMethod( ) is executed, the EJB container invokes it within the context of a JTA transaction. A customer reference is pulled from the EntityManager, and the setName( ) method is used to change the name of the customer. The Customer instance that the EntityManager returns will remain managed for the duration of the JTA transaction. This means that the change made by calling the setName( ) method will be synchronized with the database when the JTA transaction completes and commits. The Customer instance is returned by someMethod( ). After the JTA transaction completes, the transaction-scoped persistence context is destroyed, and this Customer instance is no longer managed. This means that if setName( ) is called after it becomes detached, no changes will be made to any database.

Extended persistence context

Persistence contexts may also be configured to live longer than a transaction. This is called an *extended persistence context*. Entity object instances that are attached to an extended context remain managed even after a transaction is complete. This feature is extremely useful in situations where you want to have a conversation with your database but not keep a long-running transaction, as transactions hold valuable resources like JDBC connections and database locks. Here's some small pseudocode to illustrate this concept:

```
Customer cust = null;

transaction.begin( );  // start transaction 1
cust = extendedEntityManager.find(Customer.class, 1);
transaction.commit( ); // transaction 1 ends

transaction.begin( ); // start transaction 2
cust.setName("Bill");
extendedEntityManager.flush( );
transaction.commit( ); // cust instance remains managed and changes are flushed
```

In this example, a local variable, cust, is initialized by calling the find( ) method in transaction 1. Unlike a transaction-scoped persistence context, the Customer instance pointed to by this local variable remains managed. This is because persistence context stays alive past the completion of transaction 1. In transaction 2, the customer is updated and the changes are flushed to the database.

Extended persistence contexts may be created and managed by application code. We'll see examples of this later in this chapter. They can also be created and managed by stateful session beans. You can see examples of the integration between stateful session beans and extended persistence contexts in Chapter 11.

Detached entities

Entity instances become unmanaged and detached when a transaction scope or extended persistence context ends. An interesting side effect is that detached entities can be serialized and sent across the network to a remote client. The client can make changes remotely to these serialized object instances and send them back to the server to be merged back and synchronized with the database.

This behavior is very different from the EJB 2.1 entity model, where entities are always managed by the container. In EJB 2.1, applications using entity beans always had a proxy to the entity bean; in EJB 3.0, you work with concrete instances of plain Java classes. For EJB 2.1 developers, this behavior will seem strange at first, since you are used to the container managing every aspect of the entity. You'll find that after you get used to the new EJB 3.0 model, your application code actually shrinks and is easier to manage.

EJB 2.1 code often used the Value Object Pattern (often called Data Transfer Objects). The idea of this pattern was that the entity bean exposed a method that copied its entire state into an object that could be serialized to remote clients (like a Swing application) that needed access to the entity's state:

```
// EJB 2.1 Entity bean class
public class CustomerBean implements javax.ejb.EntityBean {

    CustomerValueObject getCustomerVO( ) {
       return new CustomerValueObject(getFirstName( ), getLastName( ),
                                  getStreet( ), getCity( ), getState, getZip( ));
    }
}
```

It is very expensive to make a remote method call to an entity bean from a client. If the client had to call `getFirstName( )`, `getLastName( )`, etc., to get information about a customer it was displaying, performance would suffer. This is where the Value Object Pattern came in. EJB 3.0 eliminates the need for this pattern because persistent objects become value objects automatically when they are detached from a persistent context.

Packaging a Persistence Unit

An `EntityManager` maps a fixed set of classes to a particular database. This set of classes is called a *persistence unit*. Before you can even think about creating or querying entities with an entity manager, you must learn how to package a persistence unit for use within a Java SE (regular Java application) or Java EE (application server) environment. A persistence unit is defined in a *persistence.xml* file. This file is a required deployment descriptor for the Java Persistence specification. A *persistence.xml* file can define one or more persistence units. This file is located in the *META-INF* directory of:

- A plain JAR file within the classpath of a regular Java SE program.
- An EJB-JAR file. A persistence unit can be included with an EJB deployment.
- A JAR file in the *WEB-INF/lib* directory in a web archive file (*.war*). See Chapter 20 for details on what a WAR file is.

- A JAR file in the root of an enterprise archive (*.ear*). See Chapter 20 for details on what an EAR file is.
- A JAR file in the EAR *lib* directory.

Figure 5-1 shows what the structure of one of these JAR files might look like.

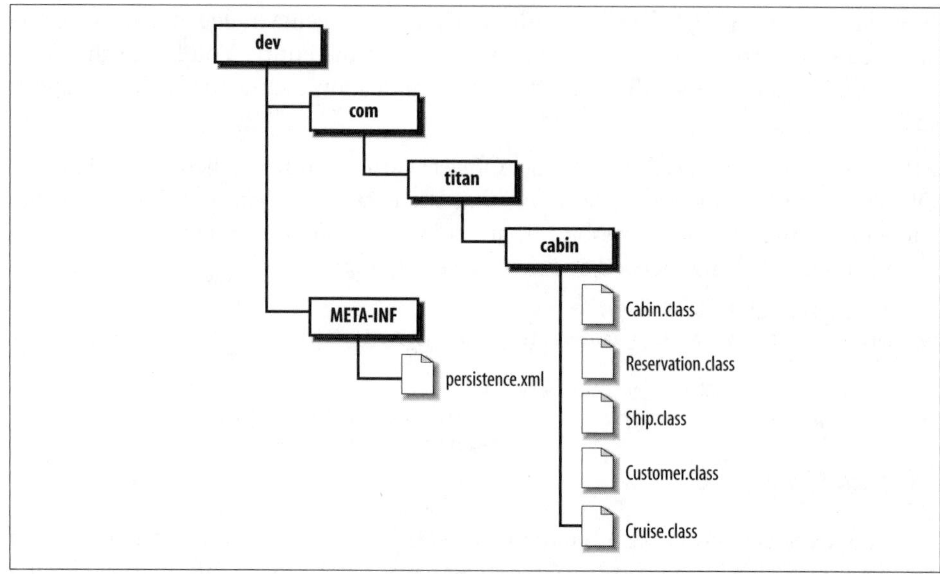

Figure 5-1. titan-persistence.jar

The *persistence.xml* deployment descriptor defines the identities and configuration properties of each persistence unit described within it. Each persistence unit must have an identity, although the empty string is a valid name.

The set of classes that belong to the persistence unit can be specified, or you can opt for the persistence provider to scan the JAR file automatically for the set of classes to deploy as entities. When scanning is used, the persistence provider will look at every class file within the JAR to determine if it is annotated with the `@javax.persistence.Entity` annotation and, if it is, it will add it to the set of entities that must be mapped.

Each persistence unit is tied to one and only one data source. In Java SE environments, vendor-specific configuration must be used to define and configure these data sources. In Java EE environments, specific XML elements define this association.

The root of the *persistence.xml* XML schema is the `<persistence>` element, which contains one or more `<persistence-unit>` elements. Each `<persistence-unit>` has two attributes: `name` (required) and `transaction-type` (optional). The subelements of `<persistence-unit>` are `<description>` (optional), `<provider>` (optional), `<jta-data-source>` (optional), `<non-jta-data-source>` (optional), `<mapping-file>` (optional),

<jar-file> (optional), <class> (optional), <properties> (optional), and <exclude-unlisted-classes> (optional).

Here's an example of a *persistence.xml* file:

```
<persistence>
   <persistence-unit name="titan">
      <jta-data-source>java:/OracleDS</jta-data-source>
      <properties>
         <property name="org.hibernate.hbm2ddl">update</property>
      </properties>
   </persistence-unit>
</persistence>
```

The name attribute defines the name by which the unit will be referenced. This name is used by injection annotations and XML deployment descriptor elements to reference this unit. This attribute is required.

The transaction-type attribute defines whether you want your persistence unit to be managed by and integrated with Java EE transactions (JTA) or you want to use the resource local (RESOURCE_LOCAL) javax.persistence.EntityTransaction API to manage the integrity of your EntityManager instances. This attribute defaults to JTA in Java EE environments and to RESOURCE_LOCAL in SE environments.

The <description> element is really just a comment describing the given persistence unit and is not required.

The <provider> element is the fully qualified name of a class that implements the javax.persistence.PersistenceProvider interface. In Java EE and SE environments, the persistence implementation is pluggable: your vendor provides an appropriate implementation. Usually, you do not have to define this element and can rely on the default value.

If you are using JTA or RESOURCE_LOCAL persistence units, you will probably define a <jta-data-source> or <non-jta-data-source> element, respectively. These elements specify a vendor-specific identity of a particular data source. Usually, this string is the global JNDI name for referencing the data source. If neither is defined, then a vendor-provided default will be used.

The <properties> element defines the set of vendor-specific attributes passed to the persistence provider. They specify configuration that is specific to a vendor implementation. Since there is no registry or JNDI service within Java SE, this is usually how vendors configure data sources, instead of using the <jta-data-source> and <non-jta-data-source> elements.

The JAR file of the persistence unit may also optionally contain a mapping XML deployment descriptor called *orm.xml* in the *META-INF* directory of the deployment. This file is used to define the mapping between the classes contained in the persistence unit and the database to which they map. Additional mapping files can be referenced using the <mapping-file> element. The value of this element is a classpath location and not a hardcoded URL. You can specify as many `<mapping-file>` elements as you wish. Examples of *orm.xml* mapping files are shown throughout Chapters 6–8.

The Persistence Unit Class Set

A persistence unit maps a fixed set of classes to a relational database. By default, if you specify no other metadata within your *persistence.xml* file, the JAR file that contains *persistence.xml* will be scanned from its root for any classes annotated with the `@javax.persistence.Entity` annotation. These classes are added to the set of classes the persistence unit will manage. You can specify additional JARs that you want to be scanned using the `<jar-file>` element. The value of this element is a path relative to the JAR file that contains *persistence.xml*:

```
<persistence>
   <persistence-unit name="titan">
      <jta-data-source>java:/OracleDS</jta-data-source>
      <jar-file>../lib/customer.jar</jar-file>
      <properties>
         <property name="org.hibernate.hbm2ddl">update</property>
      </properties>
   </persistence-unit>
</persistence>
```

Scanning JAR files is guaranteed to work in Java EE environments but is not portable in Java SE applications. In theory, it may not be possible to determine the set of JAR files that must be scanned. In practice, however, this is not the case. All major vendors in the EJB 3.0 Expert Group were polled unofficially and said they would have no problems supporting this feature in SE. Whether you do or do not rely on a JAR scan, classes can be listed explicitly with the `<class>` element:

```
<persistence>
   <persistence-unit name="titan">
      <jta-data-source>java:/OracleDS</jta-data-source>
      <class>com.titan.domain.Cabin</class>
      <class>com.titan.domain.Customer</class>
      <properties>
         <property name="org.hibernate.hbm2ddl">update</property>
      </properties>
   </persistence-unit>
</persistence>
```

The `Cabin` and `Customer` classes listed within the `<class>` elements are added to the persistence unit set along with any other classes scanned in the persistence unit's archive. If you do not want the *persistence.xml*'s JAR file to be scanned, then you can use the `<exclude-unlisted-classes>` element.

```
<persistence>
   <persistence-unit name="titan">
      <jta-data-source>java:/OracleDS</jta-data-source>
      <class>com.titan.domain.Cabin</class>
```

```
        <class>com.titan.domain.Customer</class>
        <exclude-unlisted-classes/>
        <properties>
           <property name="org.hibernate.hbm2ddl">update</property>
        </properties>
     </persistence-unit>
  </persistence>
```

The final set of classes is determined by a union of all of the following metadata:

- Classes annotated with `@Entity` in the *persistence.xml* file's JAR file (unless `<exclude-unlisted-classes>` is specified)
- Classes annotated with `@Entity` that are contained within any JARs listed with any `<jar-file>` elements
- Classes mapped in the *META-INF/orm.xml* file if it exists
- Classes mapped in any XML files referenced with the `<mapping-file>` element
- Classes listed with any `<class>` elements

Usually, you will find that you do not need to use the `<class>`, `<jar-file>`, or `<mapping-file>` element. One case where you may have the need is when the same class is being used and mapped within two or more persistence units.

Obtaining an EntityManager

Now that you have packaged and deployed your persistence units, you need to obtain access to an `EntityManager` so that you can persist, update, remove, and query your entity beans within your databases. In Java SE, entity managers are created using a `javax.persistence.EntityManagerFactory`. Although you can use the factory interface in Java EE, this platform provides some additional features that make it easier and less verbose to manage entity manager instances.

EntityManagerFactory

`EntityManager`s may be created or obtained from an `EntityManagerFactory`. In a Java SE application, you must use an `EntityManagerFactory` to create instances of an `EntityManager`. Using the factory isn't a requirement in Java EE.

```
package javax.persistence;

public interface EntityManagerFactory {
   EntityManager createEntityManager( );
   EntityManager createEntityManager(java.util.Map map);
   void close( );
   boolean isOpen( );
}
```

The `createEntityManager( )` methods return `EntityManager` instances that manage a distinct extended persistence context. You can pass in a `java.util.Map` parameter to override or extend any provider-specific properties you did not declare in your *persistence.xml* file. When you are finished using the EntityManagerFactory, you should close( ) it (unless it is injected; ee'll discuss this later). The isOpen( ) method allows you to check to see if the EntityManagerFactory reference is still valid.

Getting an EntityManagerFactory in Java SE

In Java SE, the javax.persistence.Persistence class is responsible for bootstrapping an EntityManagerFactory:

```
public class Persistence {
   public static EntityManagerFactory createEntityManagerFactory(
           String unitName
   );
   public static EntityManagerFactory createEntityManagerFactory(
           String unitName,
           java.util.Map properties
   );
```

The javax.persistence.Persistence class looks for *persistence.xml* deployment descriptors within your Java classpath. The unitName parameter you pass in will allow the Persistence implementation to locate an EntityManagerFactory that matches the given name. Additionally, you can override or add any vendor-specific properties defined in the <properties> element of the *persistence.xml* file by passing in a java.util.Map as a second parameter:

```
EntityManagerFactory factory = Persistence.createEntityManagerFactory("CRM");
...
factory.close( );
```

In Java SE, it is recommended that you close( ) the EntityManagerFactory. This frees up any resources that are being held by the factory.

Getting an EntityManagerFactory in Java EE

In Java EE, it is a bit easier to get an EntityManagerFactory. It can be injected directly into a field or *setter* method of your EJBs using the @javax.persistence.PersistenceUnit annotation:

```
package javax.persistence;

@Target({METHOD, FIELD, TYPE}) @Retention(RUNTIME)
public @interface PersistenceUnit {
   String name( ) default "";
   String unitName( ) default "";
}
```

The unitName( ) is the identity of the PersistenceUnit. When the PersistenceUnit is used, it not only injects the EntityManagerFactory, it also registers a reference to it within the JNDI ENC of the EJB. (The JNDI ENC is discussed more in Chapters 11 and 14.) The EJB container is responsible for noticing the @PersistenceUnit annotation and injecting the correct factory:

```
import javax.persistence.*;
import javax.ejb.*;

@Stateless
public MyBean implements MyBusinessInterface {

   @PersistenceUnit(unitName="CRM")
   private EntityManagerFactory factory;

   private EntityManagerFactory factory2;

   @PersistenceUnit(unitName="CUSTDB")
   public void setFactory2(EntityManagerFactory f) {
      this.factory2 = f;
   }
```

When an instance of the stateless session bean is created, the EJB container sets the factory field to the persistence unit identified by "CRM". It also calls the setFactory2( ) method with the "CUSTDB" persistence unit.

Unlike in Java SE, an injected EntityManagerFactory is automatically closed by the EJB container when the instance is discarded. In fact, if you call close( ) on an injected EntityManagerFactory, an IllegalStateException is thrown. The @PersistenceUnit annotation and its XML equivalent are covered in more detail in Chapter 14.

Obtaining a Persistence Context

A persistence context can be created by calling the EntityManagerFactory.createEntityManager( ) method. The returned EntityManager instance represents an extended persistence context. If the EntityManagerFactory is JTA-enabled, then you have to explicitly enlist the EntityManager instance within a transaction by calling the EntityManager.joinTransaction( ) method. If you do not enlist the EntityManager within the JTA transaction, then changes you make to your entities are not synchronized with the database.

EntityManager.joinTransaction( ) is required to be invoked only when an EntityManager is created explicitly using an EntityManagerFactory. If you are using EJB container managed persistence contexts, then you do not need to perform this extra step.

Using the EntityManagerFactory API is a bit verbose and can be awkward when you are making nested EJB calls, for instance. Fortunately, EJB and the Java Persistence specification are nicely integrated. An EntityManager can be injected directly into an

EJB using the @javax.persistence.PersistenceContext annotation (or equivalent XML discussed in Chapter 14):

```
package javax.persistence;

public enum PersistenceContextType
{
   TRANSACTION,
   EXTENDED
}

public @interface PersistenceProperty {
   String name( );
   String value( );
}

@Target({METHOD, TYPE, FIELD}) @Retention(RUNTIME)
public @interface PersistenceContext {
   String name( ) default "";
   String unitName( ) default "";
   PersistenceContextType type( ) default TRANSACTION;
   PersistenceProperty[] properties( ) default {};
}
```

The @PersistenceContext annotation works in much the same way as @PersistenceUnit except that an entity manager instance is injected instead of an EntityManagerFactory:

```
@Stateless
public class MySessionBean implements MySessionRemote {
   @PersistenceContext(unitName="titan")
   private EntityManager entityManager;
...
}
```

The unitName( ) attribute identifies the persistence. By default, a transaction-scoped persistence context is injected when using this annotation. You can override this default with the type( ) attribute. When you access this transaction-scoped EntityManager, a persistence context becomes associated with the transaction until it finishes. This means that if you interact with any entity managers within the context of a transaction, no matter if they are different instances that are injected into different beans, the same persistence context will be used. The details of this annotation are discussed in Chapter 14. Persistence context propagation is discussed in Chapter 16.

You must never call close( ) on an injected entity manager. Cleanup is handled by the application server. If you close an entity manager, an IllegalStateException is thrown.

An EXTENDED entity manager can only be injected into a stateful session bean; stateless session and message-driven beans are pooled, and there would be no way to close the persistence context and release any managed entity instances. In order to obtain an extended context, a stateful session bean uses the @javax.persistence.PersistenceContext annotation with a type of EXTENDED:

```
@Stateful
public class MyStatefulBean implements MyStatefulRemote {
   @PersistenceContext(unitName="titan", type=PersistenceContextType.EXTENDED)
   private EntityManager manager;
...
}
```

When this MyStatefulBean is created, a persistence context is also created for the injected manager field. The persistence context has the same life span as the bean. When the stateful session bean is removed, the persistence context is closed. This means that any entity object instances remain attached and managed as long as the stateful session bean is active. Chapter 11 has more details on this subject.

It is strongly suggested that you use the @PersistenceContext annotation or the XML equivalent when using Java Persistence with EJBs. These features were defined to make it easier for developers to interact with entity beans. Entity managers created using EntityManagerFactory are more error-prone because the application developer has to worry about more things. For instance, the developer could forget to close( ) an entity manager and leak resources. Take advantage of the ease-of-use facilities of your EJB container!

Interacting with an EntityManager

Now that you have learned how to deploy and obtain a reference to an entity manager, you are ready to learn the semantics of interacting with it. The EntityManager API has methods to insert and remove entities from a database as well as merge updates from detached entity instances. There is also a rich query API that you can access by creating query objects from certain EntityManager methods:

```
package javax.persistence;

public interface EntityManager {
   public void persist(Object entity);
   public <T> T find(Class <T> entityClass, Object primaryKey);
   public <T> T getReference(Class <T> entityClass, Object primaryKey);
   public <T> T merge(T entity);
   public void remove(Object entity);
   public void lock(Object entity, LockModeType lockMode);

   public void refresh(Object entity);
   public boolean contains(Object entity);
   public void clear( );

   public void joinTransaction( );
   public void flush( );
   public FlushModeType getFlushMode( );
   public void setFlushMode(FlushModeType type);
```

```
    public Query createQuery(String queryString);
    public Query createNamedQuery(String name);
    public Query createNativeQuery(String sqlString);
    public Query createNativeQuery(String sqlString, String resultSetMapping);
    public Query createNativeQuery(String sqlString, Class resultClass);

    public Object getDelegate( );

    public void close( );
    public boolean isOpen( );
}
```

Persisting Entities

Persisting an entity is the act of inserting it within a database. You persist entities that have not yet been created in the database. To create an entity, you first allocate an instance of it, set its properties, and wire up any relationships it might have with other objects. In other words, you initialize an entity bean just as you would any other Java object. Once you have done this, you then interact with the entity manager service by calling the `EntityManager.persist( )` method:

```
Custom cust = new Customer( );
cust.setName("Bill");

entityManager.persist(cust);
```

When this method is called, the entity manager queues the `Customer` for insertion into the database, and the object instance becomes managed. When the actual insertion happens depends on a few variables. If `persist( )` is called within a transaction, the insert may happen immediately, or it may be queued until the end of the transaction, depending on the flush mode (described later in this chapter). You can always force the insertion manually within a transaction by calling the `flush( )` method. You may call `persist( )` outside of a transaction if and only if the entity manager is an `EXTENDED` persistence context. When you call `persist( )` outside of a transaction with an `EXTENDED` persistence context, the insert is queued until the persistence context is associated with a transaction. An injected extended persistence context is automatically associated with a JTA transaction by the EJB container. For other extended contexts created manually with the EntityManagerFactor API, you must call `Entity.Manager.joinTransaction( )` to perform the transaction association.

If the entity has any relationships with other entities, these entities may also be created within the database if you have the appropriate cascade policies set up. Cascading is discussed in detail in Chapter 7. In Chapter 6, we'll also see that Java Persistence can automatically generate a primary key when the `persist( )` method is invoked. So, in the previous example, if you had auto key generation enabled, you could view the generated key after the `persist( )` method completed.

The persist( ) method throws an IllegalArgumentException if its parameter is not an entity type. TransactionRequiredException is thrown if this method is invoked on a transaction-scoped persistence context. However, if the entity manager is an extended persistence context, it is legal to call persist( ) outside of a transaction scope; the insert is queued until the persistence context interacts with a transaction.

Finding Entities

The entity manager provides two mechanisms for locating objects in your database. One way is with simple entity manager methods that locate an entity by its primary key. The other is by creating and executing queries.

find( ) and getReference( )

The EntityManager has two different methods that allow you to find an entity by its primary key:

```
public interface EntityManager {
   <T> T find(Class<T> entityClass, Object primaryKey);
   <T> T getReference(Class<T> entityClass, Object primaryKey);
}
```

Both methods take the entity's class as a parameter, as well as an instance of the entity's primary key. They use Java generics so that you don't have to do any casting. How do these methods differ? The find( ) method returns null if the entity is not found in the database. It also initializes the state based on the lazy-loading policies of each property (lazy loading is discussed in Chapter 6):

```
Customer cust = entityManager.find(Customer.class, 2);
```

In this example, we are locating a Customer with a primary key ID of 2. How does this compile when the find( ) method expects an Object as its second parameter type? Well, Java 5 has a feature called autoboxing that converts primitive types directly into their Object type. So, the constant 2 is converted to a java.lang.Integer:

```
Customer cust = null;
try {
   cust = entityManager.getReference(Customer.class, 2);
} catch (EntityNotFoundException notFound) {
   // recovery logic
}
```

getReference( ) differs from find( ) in that if the entity is not found in the database, this method throws a javax.persistence.EntityNotFoundException and there is no guarantee that the entity's state will be initialized.

Both find( ) and getReference( ) throw an IllegalArgumentException if their parameters are not an entity type. You are allowed to invoke them outside the scope of a transaction. In this case, any object returned is detached if the EntityManager is transaction-scoped but remains managed if it is an extended persistence context.

Queries

Persistent objects can also be located by using EJB QL. Unlike EJB 2.1, there are no *finder* methods, and you must create a Query object by calling the EntityManager's createQuery( ), createNamedQuery( ), or createNativeQuery( ) method:

```
public interface EntityManager {
   Query createQuery(String queryString);
   Query createNamedQuery(String name);
   Query createNativeQuery(String sqlString);
   Query createNativeQuery(String sqlString, Class resultClass);
   Query createNativeQuery(String sqlString, String resultSetMapping);
}
```

Creating and executing an EJB QL query is very analogous to creating and executing a JDBC PreparedStatement:

```
Query query = entityManager.createQuery("from Customer c where id=2");
Customer cust = (Customer)query.getSingleResult( );
```

Queries and EJB QL are discussed in great detail in Chapter 9.

All object instances returned by find( ), getResource( ), or a query remain managed as long as the persistence context in which you accessed them remains active. This means that further calls to find( ) (or whatever) will return the same entity object instance.

Updating Entities

Once you have located an entity bean by calling find( ), calling getReference( ), or creating and executing a query, the entity bean instance remains managed by the persistence context until the context is closed. During this period, you can change the state of the entity bean instance as you would any other object, and the updates will be synchronized automatically (depending on the flush mode) or if you call the flush( ) method directly:

```
@PersistenceContext EntityManager entityManager;

@TransactionAttribute(REQUIRED)
public void updateBedCount(int id, int newCount) {
   Cabin cabin = entityManager.find(Cabin.class, id);

   cabin.setBedCount(newCount);
}
```

In this code, the Cabin entity returned by the find( ) method is still managed by the EntityManager because an active persistence context is still associated with the transaction. This means that you can modify the object instance and the database will be updated automatically when the EntityManager decides to flush changes from memory to your database.

Merging Entities

The Java Persistence spec allows you to merge state changes made to a detached entity back into persistence storage using the entity manager's merge( ) method. Consider a remote Swing client. This client calls a method on our remote TravelAgent session bean to find a cabin in the database:

```
@PersistenceContext EntityManager entityManager;

@TransactionAttribute(REQUIRED)
public Cabin findCabin(int id) {
   return entityManager.find(Cabin.class, id);
}
```

In this example, the persistence context ends when the findCabin( ) method finishes, as it is a single JTA transaction. When a Cabin instance is serialized, it is detached from the entity manager and is sent to the remote Swing client. This Cabin instance is a plain Java object and is no longer associated with any entity manager. You can call the *getter*s and *setter*s on this object just like you can on any other plain Java object. The Swing client makes a few changes to the Cabin instance and sends them back to the server.

```
Cabin cabin = travelAgent.findCabin(1);

cabin.setBedCount(4);

travelAgent.updateCabin(cabin);
```

The TravelAgentBean.updateCabin( ) method takes its cabin parameter and merges it back into the current persistence context of the entity manager by calling the merge( ) operation:

```
@PersistenceContext EntityManager entityManager;

@TransactionAttribute(REQUIRED)
public void updateCabin(Cabin cabin) {
   Cabin copy = entityManager.merge(cabin);
}
```

The changes made by the remote Swing client will now be reflected in persistence storage when the entity manager decides to flush to the database. The following rules apply when merging in the cabin parameter of the updateCabin( ) method:

- If the entity manager isn't already managing a Cabin instance with the same ID, a full copy of the cabin parameter is made and returned from the merge( ) method. This copy is managed by the entity manager, and any additional *setter* methods called on this copy will be synchronized with the database when the EntityManager decides to flush. The cabin parameter remains detached and unmanaged.
- If the entity manager is already managing a Cabin instance with the same primary key, then the contents of the cabin parameter are copied into this managed

object instance. The merge( ) operation will return this managed instance. The cabin parameter remains detached and unmanaged.

The merge( ) method will throw an IllegalArgumentException if its parameter is not an entity type. The TransactionRequiredException is thrown if this method is invoked on a transaction-scoped persistence context. However, if the entity manager is an extended persistence context, it is legal to invoke this method outside of a transaction scope and the update will be queued until the persistence context interacts with a transaction.

Removing Entities

An entity can be removed from the database by calling the EntityManager.remove( ) method. The remove( ) operation does not immediately delete the cabin from the database. When the entity manager decides to flush, based on the flush rules described later in this chapter, an SQL DELETE is executed:

```
@PersistenceContext EntityManager entityManager;

@TransactionAttribute(REQUIRED)
public void removeCabin(int id) {
   Cabin cabin = entityManager.find(Cabin.class, id);
   entityManager.remove(cabin);
}
```

After remove( ) is invoked, the cabin instance will no longer be managed and will become detached. Also, if the entity has any relationships to other entity objects, those may also be removed depending on the cascading rules discussed in Chapter 7. The remove( ) operation can be undone only by re-creating the entity instance using the persist( ) method.

The remove( ) method throws an IllegalArgumentException if its parameter is not an entity type. The TransactionRequiredException is thrown if this method is invoked on a transaction-scoped persistence context. However, if the EntityManager is an extended persistence context, it is legal to invoke this method outside of a transaction scope and the remove will be queued until the persistence context interacts with a transaction.

refresh( )

If you are concerned that a current managed entity is not up-to-date with the database, then you can use the EntityManager.refresh( ) method. The refresh( ) method refreshes the state of the entity from the database, overwriting any changes made to that entity:

```
@PersistenceContext EntityManager entityManager;

@TransactionAttribute(REQUIRED)
```

```
public void removeCabin(int id) {
   Cabin cabin = entityManager.find(Cabin.class, id);
   entityManager.refresh(cabin);
}
```

If the entity bean has any related entities, those entities may also be refreshed, depending on the cascade policy set up in the metadata of the entity mapping.

The `refresh( )` method throws an `IllegalArgumentException` if its parameter is not managed by the current entity manager instance. The `TransactionRequiredException` is thrown if this method is invoked on a transaction-scoped persistence context. However, if the entity manager is an extended persistence context, it is legal to invoke this method outside of a transaction scope. If the object is no longer in the database because another thread or process removed it, then this method will throw an `EntityNotFoundException`.

contains( ) and clear( )

The `contains( )` method takes an entity instance as a parameter. If this particular object instance is currently being managed by the persistence context, it returns `true`. It throws an `IllegalArgumentException` if the parameter is not an entity.

If you need to detach all managed entity instances from a persistence context, you can invoke the `clear( )` method of the `EntityManager`. Be aware that when you call `clear( )` any changes you have made to managed entities are lost. It is wise to call `flush( )` before `clear( )` is invoked so you don't lose your changes.

flush( ) and FlushModeType

When you call `persist( )`, `merge( )`, or `remove( )`, these changes are not synchronized with the database until the entity manager decides to flush. You can force synchronization anytime by calling `flush( )`. By default, flushing automatically happens before a correlated query is executed (inefficient implementations may even flush before *any* query) and at transaction commit time. The exception to this default rule is `find( )`. A flush does not need to happen when `find( )` or `getReference( )` is called because finding by a primary key is not something that would be affected by any updates.

You can control and change this default behavior by using the `javax.persistence.FlushModeType` enumeration:

```
public enum FlushModeType {
   AUTO,
   COMMIT
}
```

`AUTO` is the default behavior described in the preceding code snippet. `COMMIT` means that changes are flushed only when the transaction commits, not before any query.

You can set the FlushModeType by calling the setFlushMode() method on the EntityManager.

Why would you ever want to change the FlushModeType? The default flush behavior makes a lot of sense. If you are doing a query on your database, you want to make sure that any updates you've made within your transaction are flushed so that your query will pick up these changes. If the entity manager didn't flush, then these changes may not be reflected in the query. Obviously, you want to flush changes when a transaction commits.

FlushModeType.COMMIT makes sense for performance reasons. The best way to tune a database application is to remove unnecessary calls to the database. Some vendor implementations will do all required updates with a batch JDBC call. If the updateBeds() method used the default, FlushModeType.AUTO, then an SQL UPDATE would happen when each query executed. Using COMMIT allows the entity manager to execute all updates in one huge batch. Also, an UPDATE usually ends up in the row being write-locked. Using COMMIT limits the amount of time the transaction holds on to this database lock by holding it only for the duration of the JTA commit.

Locking

The EntityManager API supports both read and write locks. Because locking behavior is closely related to the concept of transactions, using the lock() method is discussed in detail in Chapter 16.

getDelegate()

The getDelegate() method allows you to obtain a reference to the underlying persistence provider object that implements the EntityManager interface. Most vendors will have API extensions to the EntityManager interface that can be executed by obtaining and typecasting this delegate object to a provider's proprietary interface. In theory, you should be able to write vendor-independent code, but in practice, most vendors provide a lot of extensions to Java Persistence that you may want to take advantage of in your applications. The getDelegate() method provides one way to access vendor-specific APIs.

Resource Local Transactions

An entity manager's persistence context is usually managed by a JTA transaction in a Java EE environment. When running in a non-Java EE environment, JTA is not available, so the Java Persistence API specification has provided a transaction-like API through the EntityTransaction interface. You can obtain access to an EntityTransaction through the EntityManager.getTransaction() operation:

```
public interface EntityTransaction {
   public void begin( );
   public void commit( );
   public void rollback( );
   public boolean isActive( );
}
```

The begin( ) method throws an IllegalStateException if there is already an active EntityTransaction. The commit( ) and rollback( ) methods throw an IllegalStateException if there is not an active transaction.

It is possible for a vendor implementation to allow the use of the EntityTransaction API within a Java EE environment, but the application developer is encouraged to use JTA.

You cannot use EntityTransactions if the transaction type of your persistence unit is JTA.

Let's take our example from Chapter 4 and convert it to a standalone Java application using the javax.persistence.Persistence API and EntityTransaction:

```
import javax.persistence.*;

public class StandaloneClient {
   public static void main(String[] args) throws Exception {
      EntityManagerFactory factory =
         Persistence.createEntityManagerFactory("titan");
      EntityManager manager = factory.createEntityManager( );
      try {
         createCabin(manager);
         Cabin cabin_2 = manager.find(Cabin.class, 1);
         System.out.println(cabin_2.getName( ));
         System.out.println(cabin_2.getDeckLevel( ));
         System.out.println(cabin_2.getShipId( ));
         System.out.println(cabin_2.getBedCount( ));
      } finally {
         manager.close( );
         factory.close( );
      }
   }

   public static void createCabin(EntityManager manager) {
      Cabin cabin_1 = new Cabin( );
      cabin_1.setId(1);
      cabin_1.setName("Master Suite");
      cabin_1.setDeckLevel(1);
      cabin_1.setShipId(1);
      cabin_1.setBedCount(3);

      EntityTransaction transaction = manager.getTransaction( );
      transaction.begin( );
```

```
            manager.persist(cabin_1);
            transaction.commit( );
        }
    }
```

The first thing we do in this example is to obtain a reference to an EntityManager-Factory that represents our persistence unit. We use the javax.persistence.Persistence class to find our titan persistence unit through the createEntity-ManagerFactory( ) static method described earlier in this chapter. Once a factory is found, we then create an EntityManager with which to interact.

The createCabin( ) method receives an EntityManager as a parameter. In order to be able to insert a new Cabin entity into the database, we need to interact with the entity manager in a transactional unit. Since we are running outside the application server, we cannot use JTA and must instead use the EntityTransaction API to begin and commit a unit of work.

This example is very analogous to how we would perform the same operation using JDBC. With JDBC, we would obtain a java.sql.Connection from a data source, just as we obtained an EntityManager from an EntityManagerFactory. We would then use the java.sql.Connection commit( ) and rollback( ) methods to finish our work, just as we are using the EntityTransaction in our earlier example.

CHAPTER 6

Mapping Persistent Objects

In this chapter, we'll take a thorough look at the process of developing entity beans—specifically, mapping them to a relational database. A good rule of thumb is that entity beans model business concepts that can be expressed as nouns. Although this is a guideline rather than a requirement, it helps determine when a business concept is a candidate for implementation as an entity bean. In grammar school, you learned that nouns are words that describe a person, place, or thing. The concepts of "person" and "place" are fairly obvious: a person entity might represent a customer or passenger, and a place entity might represent a city or port of call. Similarly, entity beans often represent "things:" real-world objects like ships and credit cards, and abstractions such as reservations. Entity beans describe both the state and behavior of real-world objects and allow developers to encapsulate the data and business rules associated with specific concepts; a Customer entity encapsulates the data and business rules associated with a customer, for example. This makes it possible for data associated with a concept to be manipulated consistently and safely.

In Titan's cruise ship business, we can identify hundreds of business concepts that are nouns and, therefore, could conceivably be modeled by entity beans. We've already seen a simple Cabin entity in Chapter 4, and we'll develop Customer and Address entities in this chapter. Titan could clearly use a Cruise entity, a Reservation entity, and many others. Each business concept represents data that needs to be tracked and possibly manipulated.

Entities represent data in the database, so changes to an entity bean result in changes to the database. That's ultimately the purpose of an entity bean: to provide programmers with a simpler mechanism for accessing and changing data. It is much easier to change a customer's name by calling `Customer.setName( )` than by executing an SQL command against the database. In addition, using entity beans provides opportunities for software reuse. Once an entity bean has been defined, its definition can be used throughout Titan's system in a consistent manner. The concept of a customer, for example, is used in many areas of Titan's business, including booking, accounts receivable, and marketing. A Customer entity provides Titan with one complete way of accessing customer information and thus ensures that access to the information is consistent and simple. Representing data as entity beans can make development easier and more cost-effective.

When a new entity is created and persisted into the entity manager service, a new record must be inserted into the database and a bean instance must be associated with that data. As the entity is used and its state changes, these changes must be synchronized with the data in the database: entries must be inserted, updated, and removed. The process of coordinating the data represented by a bean instance with the database is called *persistence*.

The Java Persistence specification gave a complete overhaul to entity beans. CMP 2.1 had a huge weakness in that applications written to that specification were completely nonportable between vendors because there was no object-to-relational (O/R) mapping. O/R mapping was completely left to the vendor's discretion. The next three chapters will focus solely on Java Persistence's object mappings to a relational database. This chapter focuses on basic entity bean mappings to a relational database. Chapter 7 will discus how entities in the Titan Cruises application, like Address, Phone, CreditCard, Cruise, Ship, Cabin, and Reservation, can have complex relationships to one another and how Java Persistence can map these to your database. Chapter 8 introduces persisting inheritance hierarchies. Inheritance was another huge feature that was missing in earlier specifications. Chapter 9 shows you how to interact with entity beans through the greatly expanded Enterprise JavaBeans Query Language (EJB QL).

The Programming Model

Entities are plain Java classes in Java Persistence. You declare and allocate these bean classes just as you would any other plain Java object. You interact with the entity manager service to persist, update, remove, locate, and query for entity beans. The entity manager service is responsible for automatically managing the entity beans' state. This service takes care of enrolling the entity bean in transactions and persisting its state to the database. Chapter 5 discussed the entity manager in great detail.

The Customer Bean

The Customer bean is a simple entity bean that models the concept of a cruise customer or passenger, but its design and use are applicable across many commercial domains. Java Persistence is all about relational databases. This section introduces the Customer entity's design and implementation. This entity will be refactored in many different ways throughout this chapter so that we can show you the multiple ways in which you can map the Customer entity to a relational database.

The Bean Class

The `Customer` bean class is a plain Java object that you map to your relational database. It has fields that hold state and, optionally, it has *getter* and *setter* methods to access this state. It must have, at minimum, a no-argument constructor:

```
package com.titan.domain;

import javax.persistence.*;

@Entity
public class Customer implements java.io.Serializable {
   private long id;
   private String firstName;
   private String lastName;

   @Id
   public long getId( ) { return id; }
   public void setId(long id) { this.id = id; }

   public String getFirstName( ) { return firstName; }
   public void setFirstName(String firstName) { this.firstName = firstName; }

   public String getLastName( ) { return lastName; }
   public void setLastName(String lastName) { this.lastName = lastName; }
}
```

Java Persistence requires only two pieces of metadata when you are creating a persistent class: the `@javax.persistence.Entity` annotation denotes that the class should be mapped to your database, and the `@javax.persistence.Id` annotation marks which property in your class will be used as the primary key. The persistence provider will assume that all other properties in your class will map to a column of the same name and of the same type. The table name will default to the unqualified name of the bean class. Here is the table definition the persistence provider is assuming you are mapping to:

```
create table Customer(
   id long primary key not null,
   firstName VARCHAR(255),
   lastName VARCHAR(255)
);
```

The `@javax.persistence.Entity` annotation tells the persistence provider that your class can be persisted:

```
package javax.persistence;

@Target(TYPE) @Retention(RUNTIME)
public @interface Entity
{
   String name( ) default "";
}
```

The @Entity annotation has one name( ) attribute. This name is used to reference the entity within an EJB QL expression. If you do not provide a value for this attribute, the name defaults to the unqualified name of the bean class.

How you apply the @javax.persistence.Id annotation determines whether you will use the Java bean style for declaring your persistent properties or whether you will use Java fields. If you place the @Id annotation on a *getter* method, as done in this example, then you must apply any other mapping annotations on *getter* and *setter* methods in the class. The provider will also assume that any other *getter* and *setter* methods in your class represent persistent properties and will automatically map them based on their base name and type.

```
@Entity
public class Customer implements java.io.Serializable {
   @Id
   private long id;
   private String firstName;
   private String lastName;

   public long getId( ) { return id; }
   public void setId(long id) { this.id = id; }

   public String getFirstName( ) { return firstName; }
   public void setFirstName(String firstName) { this.firstName = firstName; }

   public String getLastName( ) { return lastName; }
   public void setLastName(String lastName) { this.lastName = lastName; }
}
```

Here, we have placed the @Id annotation on a member field of the class. The persistence provider will also assume that any other member fields of the class are also persistent properties and will automatically map them based on their base name and type. Any mapping annotations must be placed on member fields in this example, not on *getter* or *setter* methods. Here, we are really defining the *access type*—that is, whether our relational mappings are defined on the fields or the methods of a class.

XML Mapping File

If you do not want to use annotations to identify and map your entity beans, you can alternatively use an XML mapping file to declare this metadata. By default, the persistence provider will look in the *META-INF* directory for a file named *orm.xml*, or you can declare the mapping file in the <mapping-file> element in the *persistence.xml* deployment descriptor. Here's how the Customer entity mapping would look in XML:

```
<entity-mappings>
   <entity class="com.titan.domain.Customer" access="PROPERTY">
      <attributes>
         <id name="id"/>
```

```
        </attributes>
    </entity>
</entity-mappings>
```

The mapping file has a top element of <entity-mappings>. The <entity> element defines the entity class and access type: PROPERTY or FIELD. The <id> element is a subelement of the <attributes> element and defines what attribute your primary key is. Like annotated classes, the persistence provider will assume that any other property in your class is a persistent property, and you do not have to explicitly define them.

Basic Relational Mapping

A developer can take two directions when implementing entity beans. Some applications start from a Java object model and derive a database schema from this model. Other applications have an existing database schema from which they have to derive a Java object model.

The Java Persistence specification provides enough flexibility to start from either direction. If you are creating a database schema from a Java object model, most persistence vendors have tools that can autogenerate database schemas based on the annotations or XML metadata you provide in your code. In this scenario, prototyping your application is fast and easy, as you do not have to define much metadata in order for the persistence engine to generate a schema for you. When you want to fine-tune your mappings, the Java Persistence specification has the necessary annotations and XML mappings to do this.

If you have an existing database schema, many vendors have tools that can generate Java entity code directly from it. Sometimes, though, this generated code is not very object-oriented and doesn't map to your database very well. Luckily, the Java Persistence specification provides the necessary mapping capabilities to facilitate this problem.

You will find that your use of annotations and mapping XML will depend on the direction you are coming from. If you are autogenerating your schema from your entity classes, you will probably not have a need for annotations like `@Table` and `@Column`, as you will rely on well-defined specification defaults. If you have an existing schema, you will find that a lot more metadata will need to be specified.

Elementary Schema Mappings

We don't like the default table and column mappings of our original `Customer` entity class. Either we have an existing table we want to map to, or our DBA is forcing some naming conventions on us. Let's actually define the relational table we want to map our Customer entity to and use the `@javax.persistence.Table` and `@javax.`

persistence.Column annotations to apply the mapping. Here's the table definition in SQL:

```
create table CUSTOMER_TABLE
(
    CUST_ID integer primary key not null,
    FIRST_NAME varchar(20) not null
    lastName varchar(255) not null,
);
```

We want to change the table name and the column names of the id and firstName properties. We also want firstName to have a not-null constraint and want to set the VARCHAR length to 20. Let's modify our original Customer entity class and add the mapping annotations:

```
package com.titan.domain;

import javax.persistence.*;

@Entity
@Table(name="CUSTOMER_TABLE")
public class Customer implements java.io.Serializable {
   private long id;
   private String firstName;
   private String lastName;

   @Id
   @Column(name="CUST_ID", nullable=false, columnDefinition="integer")
   public long getId( ) { return id; }
   public void setId(long id) { this.id = id; }

   @Column(name="FIRST_NAME", length=20, nullable=false)
   public String getFirstName( ) { return firstName; }
   public void setFirstName(String firstName) { this.firstName = firstName; }

   public String getLastName( ) { return lastName; }
   public void setLastName(String lastName) { this.lastName = lastName; }
}
```

@Table

The @javax.persistence.Table annotation tells the EntityManager service the relational table your bean class maps to. You do not have to specify this annotation if you do not want to, as, again, the table name defaults to the unqualified class name of the bean. Let's look at the full definition of this annotation:

```
package javax.persistence;

@Target({TYPE}) @Retention(RUNTIME)
public @interface Table
{
   String name( ) default "";
   String catalog( ) default "";
```

```
    String schema() default "";
    UniqueConstraint[] uniqueConstraints() default {};
}
```

The catalog() and schema() attributes are self-explanatory, as they identify the relational catalog and schema the table belongs to:

```
public @interface UniqueConstraint
{
    String[] columnNames();
}
```

The @Table.uniqueConstraints() attribute allows you to specify unique column constraints that should be included in a generated Data Definition Language (DDL). Some vendors have tools that can create DDLs from a set of Entity classes or even provide automatic table generation when a bean is deployed. The UniqueConstraint annotation is useful for defining additional constraints when using these specific vendor features. If you are not using the schema generation tools provided by your vendor, then you will not need to define this piece of metadata.

The @Table and @UniqueConstraint annotations have an XML equivalent in the mapping file schema:

```
<table name="CUSTOMER_TABLE" catalog="TITAN" schema="TITAN">
    <unique-constraint>
        <column-name>SOME_OTHER_ATTRIBUTE</column_name>
    </unique-constraint>
</table>
```

The <table> element is a subelement of <entity>. You can specify as many <unique-constraint> elements as you need to. A unique constraint can contain several columns as well to represent multicolumn unique constraints.

@Column

Using the @Column annotation, we set the id property's column name to be CUST_ID and not nullable, and for its database type to be an integer. For the firstName property, we also changed its column name and set the VARCHAR length it will be mapped to 20.

The @javax.persistence.Column annotation describes how a particular field or property is mapped to a specific column in a table:

```
public @interface Column
{
    String name() default "";
    boolean unique() default false;
    boolean nullable() default true;
    boolean insertable() default true;
    boolean updatable() default true;
    String columnDefinition() default "";
    String table() default "";
```

```
    int length( ) default 255;
    int precision( ) default 0;
    int scale( ) default 0;
}
```

The name( ) attribute obviously specifies the column name. If it is unspecified, the column name defaults to the property or field name. The table( ) attribute is used for multitable mappings, which we'll cover later in this chapter. The rest of the attributes are used when you are autogenerating the schema from vendor-provided tools. If you are mapping to an existing schema, you do not need to define any of these attributes. The unique( ) and nullable( ) attributes define constraints you want placed on the column. You can specify whether you want this column to be included in SQL INSERT or UPDATE by using insertable( ) and updatable( ), respectively. The columnDefinition( ) attribute allows you to define the exact DDL used to define the column type. The length( ) attribute determines the length of a VARCHAR when you have a String property. For numeric properties, you can define the scale( ) and precision( ) attributes.

The @Column annotation has the XML equivalent in the <column> element. This element is a subelement of the attribute mapping types <id>, <basic>, <temporal>, <lob>, and <enumerated> that are described later in this chapter.

```
<basic name="lastName">
   <column name=""
           unique="true"
           nullable="true"
           insertable="true"
           updatable="true"
           column-definition=""
           table=""
           length=""
           precision=""
           scale=""
   />
</basic>
```

The attributes of the <column> element have the same behavior and default values as their annotation counterparts.

XML

Let's take this entire mapping example and see how it maps in XML:

```
<entity-mappings>
   <entity class="com.titan.domain.Customer" access="PROPERTY">
      <table name="CUSTOMER_TABLE"/>
      <attributes>
         <id name="id">
            <column name="CUST_ID"
                    nullable="false"
                    column-definition="integer"/>
```

```
        </id>
        <basic name="firstName">
           <column name="FIRST_NAME"
                   nullable="false"
                   length="20"/>
        </basic>
      </attributes>
   </entity>
</entity-mappings>
```

Primary Keys

A *primary key* is the identity of a given entity bean. Every entity bean must have a primary key, and it must be unique. Primary keys can map to one or more properties and must map to one of the following types: any Java primitive type (including wrappers), `java.lang.String`, or a primary-key class composed of primitives and/or strings. Let's first focus on simple one-property primary keys.

@Id

The `@javax.persistence.Id` annotation identifies one or more properties that make up the primary key for your table:

```
package javax.persistence;

@Target({METHOD, FIELD}) @Retention(RUNTIME)
public @interface Id
{
}
```

You can generate the primary key for your entity beans manually or have the persistence provider do it for you. When you want provider-generated keys, you have to use the `@javax.persistence.GeneratedValue` annotation:

```
package javax.persistence;

@Target({METHOD, FIELD}) @Retention(RUNTIME)
public @interface GeneratedValue
{
   GenerationType strategy( ) default AUTO;
   String generator( ) default "";
}

public enum GenerationType
{
   TABLE, SEQUENCE, IDENTITY, AUTO
}
```

Persistence providers are required to provide key generation for primitive primary keys. You can define the type of primary generator you would like to have using the strategy( ) attribute. The GeneratorType.AUTO strategy is the most commonly used configuration:

```
package com.titan.domain;

import javax.persistence.*;

@Entity
public class Customer implements java.io.Serializable {
   private long id;
   private String firstName;
   private String lastName;

   @Id
   @GeneratedValue
   public long getId( ) { return id; }
   public void setId(long id) { this.id = id; }

   public String getFirstName( ) { return firstName; }
   public void setFirstName(String firstName) { this.firstName = firstName; }

   public String getLastName( ) { return lastName; }
   public void setLastName(String lastName) { this.lastName = lastName; }
}
```

The AUTO strategy tells the persistence provider that you are allowing it to generate the key for you. The IDENTITY strategy uses a special column type, available in many database implementations, for creating primary keys. Let's look at this example in XML:

```
<entity-mappings>
   <entity class="com.titan.domain.Customer" access="PROPERTY">
      <attributes>
         <id name="id">
            <generated-value strategy="AUTO">
         </id>
      </attributes>
   </entity>
</entity-mappings>
```

The <generated-value> element is a subelement of the <id> element. If you want the IDENTITY strategy instead, replace AUTO with IDENTITY.

The TABLE and SEQUENCE types require additional metadata beyond the @GeneratedValue or <generated-value> element. We discuss both of these mappings in the next two sections.

Table Generators

The TABLE strategy designates a user-defined relational table from which the numeric keys will be generated. A relational table with the following logical structure is used:

```
create table GENERATOR_TABLE
(
    PRIMARY_KEY_COLUMN VARCHAR not null,
    VALUE_COLUMN long not null
);
```

The PRIMARY_KEY_COLUMN holds a value that is used to match the primary key you are generating for. The VALUE_COLUMN holds the value of the counter.

To use this strategy, you must have already defined a table generator using the @javax.persistence.TableGenerator annotation. This annotation can be applied to a class or to the method or field of the primary key:

```
package javax.persistence;

@Target({TYPE, METHOD, FIELD}) @Retention(RUNTIME)
public @interface TableGenerator
{
   String name( );
   String table( ) default "";
   String catalog( ) default "";
   String schema( ) default "";
   String pkColumnName( ) default "";
   String valueColumnName( ) default "";
   String pkColumnValue( ) default "";
   int allocationSize( ) default 50;
   UniqueConstraint[] uniqueConstraints( ) default {};
}
```

The name( ) attribute defines the name of the @TableGenerator and is the name referenced in the @Id.generator( ) attribute. The table( ), catalog( ), and schema( ) attributes describe the table definition of the generator table. The pkColumnName( ) attribute is the name of the column that identifies the specific entity primary key you are generating for. The valueColumnName( ) attribute specifies the name of the column that will hold the counter for the generated primary key. pkColumnValue( ) is the value used to match up with the primary key you are generating for. The allocationSize( ) attribute is how much the counter will be incremented when the persistence provider queries the table for a new value. This allows the provider to cache blocks so that it doesn't have to go to the database every time it needs a new ID. If you are autogenerating this table, then you can also define some constraints using the uniqueConstraints( ) attribute.

Let's look at how you would actually use this generator on the Customer entity:

```
package com.titan.domain

import javax.persistence.*;

@Entity
public class Customer implements java.io.Serializable {
   private long id;
```

```
    private String firstName;
    private String lastName;

    @TableGenerator(name="CUST_GENERATOR"
                    table="GENERATOR_TABLE"
                    pkColumnName="PRIMARY_KEY_COLUMN"
                    valueColumnName="VALUE_COLUMN"
                    pkColumnValue="CUST_ID"
                    allocationSize=10)
    @Id
    @GeneratedValue(strategy=GenerationType.TABLE, generator="CUST_GENERATOR")
    public long getId( ) { return id; }
    public void setId(long id) { this.id = id; }

    public String getFirstName( ) { return firstName; }
    public void setFirstName(String firstName) { this.firstName = firstName; }

    public String getLastName( ) { return lastName; }
    public void setLastName(String lastName) { this.lastName = lastName; }
}
```

Now if you allocate and persist( ) a Customer entity, the id property will be autogenerated when the persist( ) operation is called.

Let's look at how this would be defined within XML:

```
<entity-mappings>
   <entity class="com.titan.domain.Customer" access="PROPERTY">
      <table-generator name="CUST_GENERATOR"
                       table="GENERATOR_TABLE"
                       pk-column-name="PRIMARY_KEY_COLUMN"
                       value-column-name="VALUE_COLUMN"
                       pk-column-value="CUST_ID"
                       allocation-size="10"/>
      <attributes>
         <id name="id">
            <generated-value strategy="TABLE" generator="CUST_GENERATOR"/>
         </id>
      </attributes>
   </entity>
</entity-mappings>
```

The <table-generator> element is a subelement of the <entity> element. Its attributes are the exact same as those in the annotation, so they need no further explanation. One thing to note is that with the <generated-value> element, you must specify the generator attribute, just as you would if you were using the @GeneratedValue annotation with this strategy.

Sequence Generators

Some RDBMs, specifically Oracle, have an efficient, built-in structure to generate IDs sequentially. This is the SEQUENCE generator strategy. This generator type is declared via the @javax.persistence.SequenceGenerator:

```
package javax.persistence;

@Target({METHOD, TYPE, FIELD}) @Retention(RUNTIME)
public @interface SequenceGenerator
{
   String name( );
   String sequenceName( ) default "";
   int initialValue( ) default 1;
   int allocationSize( ) default 50;
}
```

The name( ) attribute specifies how this @SequenceGenerator is referenced in @Id annotations. Use the sequenceName( ) attribute to define what sequence table will be used from the database. initialValue( ) is the first value that will be used for a primary key, and allocationSize( ) is how much it will be incremented when it is accessed. Let's again look at applying the SEQUENCE strategy on our Customer entity bean:

```
package com.titan.domain

import javax.persistence.*;

@Entity
@Table(name="CUSTOMER_TABLE")
@SequenceGenerator(name="CUSTOMER_SEQUENCE",
                   sequenceName="CUST_SEQ")
public class Customer implements java.io.Serializable {
   private long id;
   private String firstName;
   private String lastName;

   @Id
   @GeneratedValue(strategy=GenerationType.SEQUENCE, generator="CUSTOMER_SEQUENCE")
   public long getId( ) { return id; }
   public void setId(long id) { this.id = id; }

   public String getFirstName( ) { return firstName; }
   public void setFirstName(String firstName) { this.firstName = firstName; }

   public String getLastName( ) { return lastName; }
   public void setLastName(String lastName) { this.lastName = lastName; }
}
```

This example is a little different from our TABLE strategy example in that the generator is declared on the bean's class instead of directly on the property. TABLE and SEQUENCE generators can be defined in either place. As with the TABLE generation type, the primary key is autogenerated when the EntityManager.persist( ) operation is performed.

Let's look at the XML equivalent for this mapping:

```
<entity-mappings>
   <entity class="com.titan.domain.Customer" access="PROPERTY">
      <sequence-generator name="CUSTOMER_SEQUENCE"
                          sequence-name="CUST_SEQ"
                          initial-value="0"
                          allocation-size="50"/>
      <attributes>
         <id name="id">
            <generated-value strategy="SEQUENCE" generator="CUSTOMER_SEQUENCE"/>
         </id>
      </attributes>
   </entity>
</entity-mappings>
```

The <sequence-generator> element is a subelement of <entity>. Its attributes are the same as the attributes of the @SequenceGenerator annotation. Notice also that the <generated-value> element references the sequence generator defined.

Primary-Key Classes and Composite Keys

Sometimes relational mappings require a primary key to be composed of multiple persistent properties. For instance, let's say that our relational model specified that our Customer entity should be identified by both its last name and its Social Security number instead of an autogenerated numeric key. These are called *composite keys*. The Java Persistence specification provides multiple ways to map this type of model. One is through the @javax.persistence.IdClass annotation; the other is through the @javax.persistence.EmbeddedId annotation.

@IdClass

The first way to define a primary-key class (and, for that matter, composite keys) is to use the @IdClass annotation. Your bean class does not use this primary-key class internally, but it does use it to interact with the entity manager when finding a persisted object through its primary key. @IdClass is a class-level annotation and specifies what primary-key class you should use when interacting with the entity manager.

```
@Target(TYPE)
@Retention(RUNTIME)
public @interface IdClass
{
   Class value( );
}
```

In your bean class, you designate one or more properties that make up your primary key, using the @Id annotation. These properties must map exactly to properties in the

@IdClass. Let's look at changing our Customer bean class to have a composite key made up of last name and Social Security number. First, let's define our primary-key class:

```
package com.titan.domain;

public class CustomerPK implements java.io.Serializable {
   private String lastName;
   private long ssn;

   public CustomerPK( ) {}

   public CustomerPK(String lastName, long ssn)
   {
      this.lastName = lastName;
      this.ssn = ssn;
   }

   public String getLastName( ) { return this.lastName; }
   public void setLastName(String lastName) { this.lastName = lastName; }

   public long getSsn( ) { return ssn; }
   public void setSsn(long ssn) { this.ssn = ssn; }

   public boolean equals(Object obj)
   {
      if (obj == this) return true;
      if (!(obj instanceof CustomerPK)) return false;
      CustomerPK pk = (CustomerPK)obj;
      if (!lastName.equals(pk.lastName)) return false;
      if (ssn != pk.ssn) return false;
      return true;
   }

   public int hashCode( )
   {
      return lastName.hashCode( ) + (int)ssn;
   }
}
```

The primary-key class must meet these requirements:

- It must be serializable.
- It must have a public no-arg constructor.
- It must implement the equals( ) and hashCode( ) methods.

Our Customer bean must have the same exact properties as the CustomerPK class, and these properties are annotated with multiple @Id annotations:

```
package com.titan.domain;

import javax.persistence.*;
```

```
@Entity
@IdClass(CustomerPK.class)
public class Customer implements java.io.Serializable {
   private String firstName;
   private String lastName;
   private long ssn;

   public String getFirstName( ) { return firstName; }
   public void setFirstName(String firstName) { this.firstName = firstName; }

   @Id
   public String getLastName( ) { return lastName; }
   public void setLastName(String lastName) { this.lastName = lastName; }

   @Id
   public long getSsn( ) { return ssn; }
   public void setSsn(long ssn) { this.ssn = ssn; }
}
```

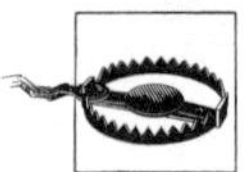

Primary-key autogeneration is not supported for composite keys and primary-key classes. You will have to manually create the key values in code.

Let's now look at the XML mapping equivalent to `@IdClass`:

```
<entity-mappings>
   <entity class="com.titan.domain.Customer" access="PROPERTY">
      <id-class>com.titan.domain.CustomerPK</id-class>
      <attributes>
         <id name="lastName"/>
         <id name="ssn"/>
      </attributes>
   </entity>
</entity-mappings>
```

The `<id-class>` element is a subelement of `<entity>`, and its value is the fully qualified class name of the primary-key class. Notice also that multiple `<id>` elements for each property map to the primary-key class.

The primary-key class is used whenever you are querying for the `Customer`:

```
CustomerPK pk = new CustomerPK("Burke", 9999999);
Customer cust = entityManager.find(Customer.class, pk);
```

Whenever you call an `EntityManager` method like `find( )` or `getReference( )`, you must use the primary key class to identify the entity.

@EmbeddedId

A different way to define primary-key classes and composite keys is to embed the primary-key class directly in your bean class. The `@javax.persistence.EmbeddedId` annotation is used for this purpose in conjunction with the @javax.persistence.Embeddable annotation:

```
package javax.persistence;

public @interface EmbeddedId
{
}

public @interface AttributeOverrides
{
   AttributeOverride[] value( );
}

public @interface AttributeOverride
{
   String name( );

   Column[] column( ) default {};
}

public @interface Embeddable
{
}
```

There are two ways to map the properties of your primary-key class to columns in your table. One is to specify the @Column mappings within the primary-key class source code; the other is to use @AttributeOverrides. Let's look at the former and then the latter.

```
package com.titan.domain;

import javax.persistence.*;

@Embeddable
public class CustomerPK implements java.io.Serializable {
   private String lastName;
   private long ssn;

   public CustomerPK( ) {}

   public CustomerPK(String lastName, long ssn)
   {
      this.lastName = lastName;
      this.ssn = ssn;
   }

   @Column(name="CUSTOMER_LAST_NAME")
   public String getLastName( ) { return this.lastName; }
   public void setLastName(String lastName) { this.lastName = lastName; }

   @Column(name="CUSTOMER_SSN")
```

```
    public long getSsn( ) { return ssn; }
    public void setSsn(long ssn) { this.ssn = ssn; }

    public boolean equals(Object obj)
    {
       if (obj == this) return true;
       if (!(obj instanceof CustomerPK)) return false;
       CustomerPK pk = (CustomerPK)obj;
       if (!lastName.equals(pk.lastName)) return false;
       if (ssn != pk.ssn) return false;
       return true;
    }

    public int hashCode( )
    {
       return lastName.hashCode( ) + (int)ssn;
    }
}
```

We then change our Customer bean class to use the CustomerPK directly, using the @EmbeddedId annotation:

```
package com.titan.domain

import javax.persistence.*;

@Entity
public class Customer implements java.io.Serializable {
   private String firstName;
   private CustomerPK pk;

   public String getFirstName( ) { return firstName; }
   public void setFirstName(String firstName) { this.firstName = firstName; }

   @EmbeddedId
   public PK getPk( ) { return pk; }
   public void setPk(CustomerPK pk) { this.pk = pk; }

}
```

The CustomerPK primary-key class is used whenever you are fetching the Customer using EntityManager APIs:

```
CustomerPK pk = new CustomerPK("Burke", 9999999);
Customer cust = entityManager.find(Customer.class, pk);
```

Whenever you call an EntityManager method like find( ) or getReference( ), you must use the primary-key class to identify the entity.

If you do not want to have the @Column mappings with the primary-key class, or you just want to override them, you can use @AttributeOverrides to declare them directly in your bean class:

```
@Entity
public class Customer implements java.io.Serializable {
```

```
    private String firstName;
    private CustomerPK pk;

    public String getFirstName( ) { return firstName; }
    public void setFirstName(String firstName) { this.firstName = firstName; }

    @EmbeddedId
    @AttributeOverrides({
        @AttributeOverride(name="lastName", column=@Column(name="LAST_NAME"),
        @AttributeOverride(name="ssn", column=@Column(name="SSN"))
    })
    public PK getPk( ) { return pk; }
    public void setPk(CustomerPK pk) { this.pk = pk; }

}
```

The @AttributeOverrides annotation is an array list of @AttributeOverride annotations. The name( ) attribute specifies the property name in the embedded class you are mapping to. The column( ) attribute allows you to describe the column the property maps to.

Let's now look at the XML mapping equivalent to @IdClass:

```
<entity-mappings>
   <embeddable class="com.titan.domain.CustomerPK" access-type="PROPERTY">
      <embeddable-attributes>
         <basic name="lastName">
            <column name="CUSTOMER_LAST_NAME"/>
         </basic>
         <basic name="ssn">
            <column name="CUSTOMER_SSN"/>
         </basic>
      </embeddable-attributes>
   </embeddable>
   <entity class="com.titan.domain.Customer" access="PROPERTY">
      <attributes>
         <embedded-id name="pk">
            <attribute-override name="lastName">
               <column name="LAST_NAME"/>
            </attribute-override>
            <attribute-override name="ssn">
               <column name="SSN"/>
            </attribute-override>
         </embedded_id>
      </attributes>
   </entity>
</entity-mappings>
```

The <embeddable> element is a subelement of <entity-mappings> and describes the embeddable class. The <embeddable-attributes> element identifies the persistent properties of the embeddable class. Within <embeddable-attributes>, you can define <basic>, <lob>, <temporal>, and <enumerated> column mappings. These subelements are optional.

The <embedded-id> element is used within the <attributes> element to identify the embedded primary-key property of the entity. The <attribute-override> element is used to specify any column overrides for the properties of the embedded class.

Property Mappings

So far, we have only shown how to specify column mappings for simple primitive types. There are still a few bits of metadata that you can use to fine-tune your mappings. In this section, you'll learn more annotations for more complex property mappings. Java Persistence has mappings for JDBC `Blob`s and `Clob`s, serializable objects, and embeddable objects, as well as optimistic concurrency with version properties. We will discuss all of these.

@Transient

In our first example of our `Customer` bean class, we showed that the persistence manager would assume that every nontransient property (*getter/setter* or field, depending on your access type) in your bean class is persistent, even if the property does not have any mapping metadata associated with it. This is great for fast prototyping of your persistent objects, especially when your persistence vendor supports autotable generation. However, you may have properties that you don't want to be persistent, and, therefore, this default behavior is inappropriate. For instance, let's take our `@EmbeddedId` example. The interface for that class has you obtaining a `CustomerPK` class instance if you want to view the last name or Social Security number of your customer. It may be nicer to have *getter* methods on the `Customer` bean class that directly provide that level of information. This is where the `@javax.persistence.Transient` annotation comes in:

```
@Entity
public class Customer implements java.io.Serializable {
   private String firstName;
   private CustomerPK pk;

   public String getFirstName( ) { return firstName; }
   public void setFirstName(String firstName) { this.firstName = firstName; }

   @Transient
   public String getLastName( ) { return pk.getLastName( ); }

   @Transient
   public long getSsn( ) { return pk.getSsn( ); }


   @EmbeddedId
   public PK getPk( ) { return pk; }
   public void setPk(CustomerPK pk) { this.pk = pk; }
}
```

When you annotate a property with @javax.persistence.Transient, the persistence manager ignores it and doesn't treat it as persistent. Here is what the XML equivalent looks like:

```
<entity-mappings>
   <embeddable class="com.titan.domain.CustomerPK" access-type="PROPERTY">
      <embeddable-attribute name="lastName">
         <column name="CUSTOMER_LAST_NAME"/>
      </embeddable-attribute>
      <embeddable-attribute name="ssn">
         <column name="CUSTOMER_SSN"/>
      </embeddable-attribute>
   </embeddable>
   <entity class="com.titan.domain.Customer" access="PROPERTY">
      <attributes>
         <embedded-id name="pk"/>
         <transient name="lastName"/>
         <transient name="ssn"/>
      </attributes>
   </entity>
</entity-mappings>
```

The <transient> element is used within an <attribute> declaration to identify @Transient properties.

@Basic and FetchType

The @Basic annotation is the simplest form of mapping for a persistent property. This is the default mapping type for properties which are primitives, primitive wrapper types, java.lang.String, byte[], Byte[], char[], Character[], java.math.BigInteger, java.math.BigDecimal, java.util.Date, java.util.Calendar, java.sql.Date, java.sql.Time, and java.sql.Timestamp. You do not need to tell your persistence manager explicitly that you're mapping a basic property because it can usually figure out how to map it to JDBC using the property's type.

```
public @interface Basic
{
   FetchType fetch( ) default EAGER;
   boolean optional( ) default true;
}

public enum FetchType
{
   LAZY, EAGER
}
```

Usually, you would never annotate your properties with this annotation. However, at times you may need to specify the fetch( ) attribute, which allows you to specify whether a particular property is loaded lazily or eagerly when the persistent object is first fetched from the database. This attribute allows your persistence provider to optimize your access to the database by minimizing the amount of data you load with a query. So, if the fetch() attribute is LAZY, that particular property will not be initialized until you actually access this field. All other mapping annotations have this same attribute. The weird thing about the specification, though, is that the fetch() attribute is just a hint. Even if you mark the property as LAZY for a @Basic type, the persistence provider is still allowed to load the property eagerly. This is due to the fact that this feature requires class-level instrumentation. It should also be noted that lazy loading is neither really useful nor a significant performance optimization. It is best practice to eagerly load basic properties.

The optional() attribute is useful for when the persistence provider is generating the database schema for you. When this attribute is set to true, the property is treated as nullable. Let's take our Customer entity and show how to use the @Basic annotation:

```
package com.titan.domain

import javax.persistence.*;

@Entity
public class Customer implements java.io.Serializable {
   private long id;
   private String firstName;
   private String lastName;

   @Id
   @GeneratedValue
   public long getId( ) { return id; }
   public void setId(long id) { this.id = id; }

   @Basic(fetch=FetchType.LAZY, optional=false)
   public String getFirstName( ) { return firstName; }
   public void setFirstName(String firstName) { this.firstName = firstName; }

   @Basic(fetch=FetchType.LAZY, optional=false)
   public String getLastName( ) { return lastName; }
   public void setLastName(String lastName) { this.lastName = lastName; }
}
```

In this code, we hint that both the firstName and lastName properties are lazily loadable. Also, these properties are not nullable in the database schema.

The @Basic annotation also has an XML equivalent:

```
<entity-mappings>
   <entity class="com.titan.domain.Customer" access="PROPERTY">
      <attributes>
         <id name="id">
            <generated-value/>
         </id>
         <basic name="firstName" fetch="LAZY" optional="false"/>
         <basic name="lastName" fetch="LAZY" optional="false"/>
      </attributes>
   </entity>
</entity-mappings>
```

@Temporal

The `@Temporal` annotation provides additional information to the persistence provider about the mapping of a `java.util.Date` or `java.util.Calendar` property. This annotation allows you to map these object types to a date, a time, or a timestamp field in the database. By default, the persistence provider assumes that the temporal type is a timestamp:

```
package javax.persistence;

public enum TemporalType
{
   DATE,
   TIME,
   TIMESTAMP
}

public @interface Temporal
{
   TemporalType value( ) default TIMESTAMP;
}
```

This annotation can be used in conjunction with the `@Basic` annotation. For example, say we want to add a time-created property to the Customer entity. We would do it as follows:

```
package com.titan.domain;

import javax.persistence.*;

@Entity
public class Customer implements java.io.Serializable {
   private long id;
   private String firstName;
   private String lastName;
   private java.util.Date timeCreated;

   @Id
   @GeneratedValue
   public long getId( ) { return id; }
   public void setId(long id) { this.id = id; }

   public String getFirstName( ) { return firstName; }
   public void setFirstName(String firstName) { this.firstName = firstName; }

   public String getLastName( ) { return lastName; }
   public void setLastName(String lastName) { this.lastName = lastName; }

   @Temporal(TemporalType.TIME)
   public java.util.Date getTimeCreated( ) { return timeCreated; }
   public void setTimeCreated(java.util.Date time) { timeCreated = time; }
}
```

The timeCreated property is stored in the database as a TIME SQL type. Let's look at the XML equivalent:

```
<entity-mappings>
   <entity class="com.titan.domain.Customer" access="PROPERTY">
      <attributes>
         <id name="id">
            <generated-value/>
         </id>
         <basic name="timeCreated"/>
            <temporal>TIME</temporal>
         </basic>
      </attributes>
   </entity>
</entity-mappings>
```

The <temporal> element is used within a <basic> element definition and can have the same values as the enumeration type discussed earlier.

@Lob

Sometimes your persistent properties require a lot of memory. One of your fields may represent an image or the text of a very large document. JDBC has special types for these very large objects. The java.sql.Blob type represents binary data, and java.sql.Clob represents character data. The @javax.persistence.Lob annotation is used to map these large object types. Java Persistence allows you to map some basic types to a @Lob and have the persistence manager handle them internally as either a Blob or a Clob, depending on the type of the property:

```
package javax.persistence;

public @interface Lob
{
}
```

Properties annotated with a @Lob are persisted in a:

- Blob if the Java type is byte[], Byte[], or java.io.Serializable
- Clob if the Java type is char[], Character[], or java.lang.String

The @Lob annotation is usually used in conjunction with the @Basic annotation to hint that the property should be lazily loaded. Let's modify our Customer bean to add a property that represents a JPEG image of that customer:

```
package com.titan.domain;

import javax.persistence.*;
import com.acme.imaging.JPEG;

@Entity
```

```
public class Customer implements java.io.Serializable {
   private long id;
   private String firstName;
   private String lastName;
   private JPEG picture;

   @Id
   @GeneratedValue
   public long getId( ) { return id; }
   public void setId(long id) { this.id = id; }

   public String getFirstName( ) { return firstName; }
   public void setFirstName(String firstName) { this.firstName = firstName; }

   public String getLastName( ) { return lastName; }
   public void setLastName(String lastName) { this.lastName = lastName; }

   @Lob
   @Basic(fetch=FetchType.LAZY)
   public JPEG getPicture( ) { return picture; }
   public void setPicture(JPEG picture) { this.picture = picture; }
}
```

When using @Lob types, it is probably best to mark the fetch type as lazy, since you usually won't access these large objects when interacting with a Customer bean.

Let's look at the XML equivalent to @Lob:

```
<entity-mappings>
   <entity class="com.titan.domain.Customer" access="PROPERTY">
      <attributes>
         <id name="id">
            <generated-value/>
         </id>
         <basic name="picture">
            <lob/>
         </basic>
      </attribute>s
   </entity>
</entity-mappings>
```

The <lob> element is used within a <basic> element and identifies the property as a @Lob type.

@Enumerated

The @Enumerated annotation maps Java enum types to the database. It is used in conjunction with the @Basic annotation and lets you specify additional fetch semantics:

```
package javax.persistence;

public enum EnumType
{
```

```
      ORDINAL,
      STRING
   }

   public @interface Enumerated
   {
      EnumType value( ) default ORDINAL;
   }
```

A Java enum property can be mapped either to the string representation or to the numeric ordinal number of the enum value. For example, let's say we want a Customer entity property that designates the kind of customer that is purchasing a reservation. This could be represented in a Java enum called CustomerType with the enum values UNREGISTERED, REGISTERED, or BIG_SPENDAH. We would do it as follows:

```
package com.titan.domain;

import javax.persistence.*;

public enum CustomerType
{
   UNREGISTERED,
   REGISTERED,
   BIG_SPENDAH
}

@Entity
public class Customer implements java.io.Serializable {
   private long id;
   private String firstName;
   private String lastName;
   private CustomerType customerType;

   @Id
   @GeneratedValue
   public long getId( ) { return id; }
   public void setId(long id) { this.id = id; }

   public String getFirstName( ) { return firstName; }
   public void setFirstName(String firstName) { this.firstName = firstName; }

   public String getLastName( ) { return lastName; }
   public void setLastName(String lastName) { this.lastName = lastName; }

   @Enumerated(EnumType.STRING)
   public CustomerType getCustomerType( ) { return customerType; }
   public void setCustomerType(CustomerType type) { customerType = type; }
}
```

You are not required to use the @Enumerated annotation to map a property. If you omit this annotation, the ORDINAL EnumType value is assumed.

Here's the XML equivalent:

```
<entity-mappings>
   <entity class="com.titan.domain.Customer" access="PROPERTY">
      <attributes>
         <id name="id">
            <generated-value/>
         </id>
         <basic name="customerType">
            <enumerated>STRING</enumerated>
         </basic>
      </attributes>
   </entity>
</entity-mappings>
```

The `<enumerated>` element is used within an `<attribute>` element and can have the `ORDINAL` or `STRING` value.

Multitable Mappings with @SecondaryTable

Sometimes you have to deal with one logical entity that is stored in two different tables. You want one entity bean class to represent your object, but it is mapped into two different tables because you're working with a legacy database model. Java Persistence allows you to map an entity bean class to one or more tables using the `@javax.persistence.SecondaryTable` annotation. For example, let's say our Customer bean has properties that define the address of the `Customer`, but the address data is stored in a separate table. Here's what the tables would look like:

```
create table CUSTOMER_TABLE
(
    CUST_ID integer Primary Key Not Null,
    FIRST_NAME varchar(20) not null,
    LAST_NAME varchar(50) not null
);

create table ADDRESS_TABLE
(
   ADDRESS_ID integer primary key not null,
   STREET varchar(255) not null,
   CITY varchar(255) not null,
   STATE varchar(255) not null
);
```

To use the `@SecondaryTable` annotation, the primary key columns of the `ADDRESS_TABLE` must be joinable with one or more columns in the `CUSTOMER_TABLE`:

```
public @interface SecondaryTable
{
   String name( );
   String catalog( ) default "";
   String schema( ) default "";
```

```
    PrimaryKeyJoinColumn[] pkJoinColumns( ) default {};
    UniqueConstraint[] uniqueConstraints( ) default {};
}

public @interface PrimaryKeyJoinColumn
{
    String name( ) default "";
    String referencedColumnName( ) default "";
    String columnDefinition( ) default "";
}
```

The `@SecondaryTable` annotation looks a lot like the `@Table` annotation, except it additionally has a `pkJoinColumns( )` attribute defined. In the `Customer` bean class, you would define this annotation and specify that the primary key of the `ADDRESS_TABLE` was using the embedded `@PrimaryKeyJoinColumn` annotation. The `name( )` attribute of the `@PrimaryKeyJoinColumn` annotation represents the column in the `ADDRESS_TABLE` that you will use in the join. The `referencedColumnName( )` attribute represents the column name in the `CUSTOMER_TABLE` that is used to join with the `ADDRESS_TABLE`.

```
package com.titan.domain;

import javax.persistence.*;
import com.acme.imaging.JPEG;

@Entity
@Table(name="CUSTOMER_TABLE")
@SecondaryTable(name="ADDRESS_TABLE",
                pkJoinColumns={
                   @PrimaryKeyJoinColumn(name="ADDRESS_ID")})
public class Customer implements java.io.Serializable {
...
```

The `@PrimaryKeyJoinColumn` specifies the column in the `ADDRESS_TABLE` that you will join with the primary key of the `CUSTOMER _TABLE`. In this case, it is `ADDRESS_ID`. We do not need to specify the `referencedColumnName( )` attribute of this annotation because it can default to the Customer entity's primary-key column.

The next step is to map the street, city, and state properties to columns in the `ADDRESS_TABLE`. If you remember the full `@Column` annotation, one of the attributes we did not go over fully is the `table( )` attribute. You use this to map the address properties to your secondary table:

```
package com.titan.domain;

import javax.persistence.*;
import com.acme.imaging.JPEG;

@Entity
@Table(name="CUSTOMER_TABLE")
@SecondaryTable(name="ADDRESS_TABLE",
                pkJoinColumns={
                   @PrimaryKeyJoinColumn(name="ADDRESS_ID")})
```

```
public class Customer implements java.io.Serializable {
   private long id;
   private String firstName;
   private String lastName;
   private String street;
   private String city;
   private String state;
...
   @Column(name="STREET", table="ADDRESS_TABLE")
   public String getStreet( ) { return street; }
   public void setStreet(String street) { this.street = street; }

   @Column(name="CITY", table="ADDRESS_TABLE")
   public String getCity( ) { return city; }
   public void setCity(String city) { this.city = city; }

   @Column(name="STATE", table="ADDRESS_TABLE")
   public String getState( ) { return state; }
   public void setState(String state) { this.state = state; }
...
```

What do you do if you have more than one secondary table? For example, let's say that you want to embed credit card properties, but this information was also stored in another table. In that instance, you would use the `@SecondaryTables` annotation:

```
package com.titan.domain;

import javax.persistence.*;
import com.acme.imaging.JPEG;

@Entity
@Table(name="CUSTOMER_TABLE")
@SecondaryTables({
    @SecondaryTable(name="ADDRESS_TABLE",
            pkJoinColumns={@PrimaryKeyJoinColumn (name="ADDRESS_ID")}),
    @SecondaryTable(name="CREDIT_CARD_TABLE",
            pkJoinColumns={@PrimaryKeyJoinColumn (name="CC_ID")})
})
public class Customer
```

You would then match the properties with their appropriate `@Column.table( )` attributes set.

Let's look at the XML mapping for this multitable mapping:

```
<entity-mappings>
   <entity class="com.titan.domain.Customer" access="PROPERTY">
      <table name="CUSTOMER_TABLE"/>
      <secondary-table name="ADDRESS_TABLE">
         <primary-key-join-column name="ADDRESS_ID"/>
      </secondary-table>
      <secondary-table name="CREDIT_CARD_TABLE">
         <primary-key-join-column name="CC_ID"/>
      </secondary-table>
      <attributes>
```

```
            <id name="id">
               <generated-value/>
            </id>
            <basic name="street">
               <column name="STREET"
                       table="ADDRESS_TABLE"/>
            </basic>
...
         </attributes>
      </entity>
   </entity-mappings>
```

The `<secondary-table>` element can be declared multiple times within an `<entity>` element. The `<primary-key-join-column>` is a subelement of `<secondary-table>` and has the `name`, `referenced-column-name`, and `column-definition` attributes. You use the `<column>` `table` attribute to map the attribute to the secondary table of your choice.

@Embedded Objects

The Java Persistence specification allows you to embed nonentity Java objects within your entity beans and map the properties of this embedded value object to columns within the entity's table. These objects do not have any identity and they are owned exclusively by their containing entity bean class. The rules are very similar to the `@EmbeddedId` primary-key example given earlier in this chapter. We first start out by defining our embedded object:

```
package com.titan.domain;

import javax.persistence.*;

@Embeddable
public class Address implements java.io.Serializable {
   private String street;
   private String city;
   private String state;

   public String getStreet( ) { return street; }
   public void setStreet(String street) { this.street = street; }

   public String getCity( ) { return city; }
   public void setCity(String city) { this.city = city; }

   public String getState( ) { return state; }
   public void setState(String state) { this.state = state; }
}
```

The embedded `Address` class has the `@Column` mappings defined directly within it. Next, let's use the `@javax.persistence.Embedded` annotation within our `Customer` bean class to embed an instance of this `Address` class:

```
package javax.persistence;

public @interface Embedded {}
```

As with @EmbeddedId, the @Embedded annotation can be used in conjunction with the @AttributeOverrides annotation if you want to override the column mappings specified in the embedded class. The following example shows how this overriding is done. If you don't want to override, leave out the @AttributeOverrides.

```
package com.titan.domain;

import javax.persistence.*;

@Entity
@Table(name="CUSTOMER_TABLE")
public class Customer implements java.io.Serializable {
   private long id;
   private String firstName;
   private String lastName;
   private Address address;

...
   @Embedded
   @AttributeOverrides({
      @AttributeOverride(name="street", column=@Column(name="CUST_STREET")),
      @AttributeOverride(name="city", column=@Column(name="CUST_CITY")),
      @AttributeOverride(name="state", column=@Column(name="CUST_STATE"))
   })
   public Address getAddress( ) {
      return address;
   }
...
}
```

In this example, we're mapping the Address class properties to columns in the CUSTOMER_TABLE. If you do not specify the @Embedded annotation and the Address class is serializable, then the persistence provider would assume that this was a @Lob type and serialize it as a byte stream to the column in the CUSTOMER_TABLE.

Let's look at the XML mapping for this:

```
<entity-mappings>
   <embeddable class="com.titan.domain.Address" access-type="PROPERTY"/>
   <entity class="com.titan.domain.Customer" access="PROPERTY">
      <attributes>
         <id name="id"/>
         <embedded name="address">
            <attribute-override name="street">
               <column name="CUST_STREET"/>
            </attribute-override>
            <attribute-override name="city">
               <column name="CUST_CITY"/>
            </attribute-override>
            <attribute-override name="state">
```

```
                <column name="CUST_STATE"/>
            </attribute-override>
         </embedded>
      </attributes>
   </entity>
</entity-mappings>
```

This looks exactly like our `<embedded-id>` mapping, except we are mapping a specific property using the `<embedded>` element. Everything else is the same.

That's about it for basic property mappings. In the next chapter, we'll discuss how to map complex relationships between entity beans.

CHAPTER 7
Entity Relationships

Chapter 6 covered basic persistence mappings, including various ways to define primary keys as well as simple and complex property-type mappings. This chapter develops our Titan Cruises application a bit further by discussing the seven relationships that entity beans can have with each other.

In order to model real-world business concepts, entity beans must be capable of forming complex relationships. If we turned our embedded `Address` object in Chapter 6 into a first-class entity bean, we would have had a one-to-one relationship between our Customer entity and an Address entity. The Address could be queried and cached like any other entity, yet a close relationship would be forged with the Customer entity. Entity beans can also have one-to-many, many-to-one, and many-to-many relationships. For example, the Customer entity may have many phone numbers, but each phone number belongs to only one customer (a one-to-many relationship). A customer may have been on many cruises, and each cruise has many customers (a many-to-many relationship).

The Seven Relationship Types

Seven types of relationships can exist between entity beans. There are four types of cardinality: *one-to-one*, *one-to-many*, *many-to-one*, and *many-to-many*. In addition, each relationship can be either *unidirectional* or *bidirectional*. These options seem to yield eight possibilities, but if you think about it, you'll realize that one-to-many and many-to-one bidirectional relationships are actually the same thing. Thus, there are only seven distinct relationship types. To understand relationships, it helps to think about some simple examples:

One-to-one unidirectional
: The relationship between a customer and an address. You clearly want to be able to look up a customer's address, but you probably don't care about looking up an address's customer.

One-to-one bidirectional
The relationship between a customer and a credit card number. Given a customer, you obviously want to be able to look up his credit card number. Given a credit card number, it is also conceivable that you would want to look up the customer who owns the credit card.

One-to-many unidirectional
The relationship between a customer and a phone number. A customer can have many phone numbers (business, home, cell, etc.). You might need to look up a customer's phone number, but you probably wouldn't use one of those numbers to look up the customer.

One-to-many bidirectional
The relationship between a cruise and a reservation. Given a reservation, you want to be able to look up the cruise for which the reservation was made. And given a particular cruise, you want to be able to look up all reservations. (Note that a many-to-one bidirectional relationship is just another perspective on the same concept.)

Many-to-one unidirectional
The relationship between a cruise and a ship. You want to be able to look up the ship that will be used for a particular cruise, and many cruises share the same ship, though at different times. It's less useful to look up the ship to see which cruises are associated with it, although if you want this capability, you can implement a many-to-one bidirectional relationship.

Many-to-many unidirectional
The relationship between a reservation and a cabin. It's possible to make a reservation for multiple cabins, and you clearly want to be able to look up the cabin assigned to a reservation. However, you're not likely to want to look up the reservation associated with a particular cabin. (If you think you need to do so, implement it as a bidirectional relationship.)

Many-to-many bidirectional
The relationship between a cruise and a customer. A customer can make reservations on many cruises, and each cruise has many customers. You want to be able to look up both the cruises on which a customer has a booking and the customers that will be going on any given cruise.

Note that these relations represent the navigability of your domain model. Using EJB QL, you'll be able to return even unmapped association (for example, return the Cruises made by a given ship even if the association has been mapped as many-to-one unidirectional from Cruise to Ship). Once again, the associations defined in the metadata represent the domain object navigation only.

In this chapter, we will discuss how to specify relationships by applying annotations to your related entity beans. We will also discuss several different common database schemas, and you will learn how to map them to your annotated relationships.

One-to-One Unidirectional Relationship

An example of a one-to-one unidirectional relationship is one between our Customer entity and an Address entity. In this example, each Customer has exactly one Address, and each Address has exactly one Customer. Which bean references which determines the direction of navigation. While the Customer has a reference to the Address, the Address doesn't reference the Customer. The relationship is therefore unidirectional—you can only go from the Customer to the Address, not the other way around through object navigation. In other words, an Address entity has no idea who owns it. Figure 7-1 shows this relationship.

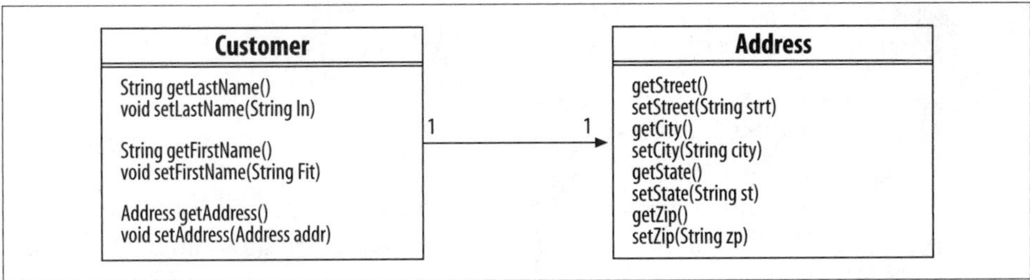

Figure 7-1. One-to-one unidirectional relationship

Relational database schema

As shown in Figure 7-2, one-to-one unidirectional relationships normally use a fairly typical relational database schema in which one table contains a foreign key (pointer) to another table. In this case, the `CUSTOMER` table contains a foreign key to the `ADDRESS` table, but the `ADDRESS` table doesn't contain a foreign key to the `CUSTOMER` table. This allows records in the `ADDRESS` table to be shared by other tables, a scenario explored in the "Many-to-Many Unidirectional Relationship" section, later in this chapter.

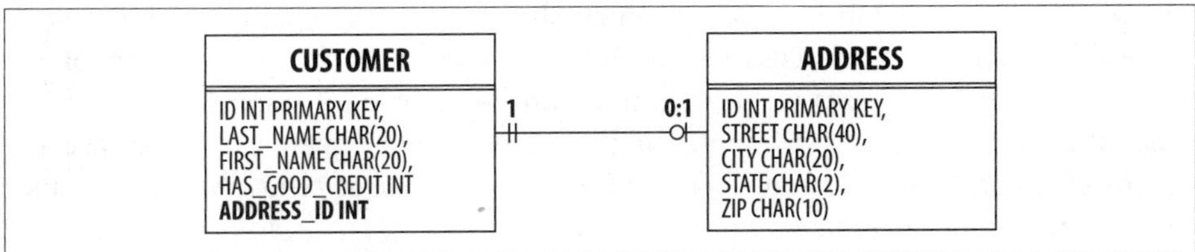

Figure 7-2. One-to-one unidirectional relationship in RDBMS

Programming model

In unidirectional relationships (navigated only one way), one of the entity beans defines a property that lets it get or set the other bean in the relationship. Thus, inside the `Customer` class, you can call the `getAddress( )/setAddress( )` methods to access the Address entity, but there are no methods inside the `Address` class to access the Customer. Let's look at how we would mark up the Customer bean class to implement this one-to-one relationship to Address:

```
package com.titan.domain;

@Entity
public class Customer implements java.io.Serializable {
   ...
   private Address address;

...
   @OneToOne(cascade={CascadeType.ALL})
   @JoinColumn(name="ADDRESS_ID")
   public Address getAddress( ) {
      return homeAddress;
   }
   public void setAddress(Address address) {
      this.homeAddress = address;
   }
```

A one-to-one relationship is specified using the @javax.persistence.OneToOne annotation and is mapped with the @javax.persistence.JoinColumn annotation. Let's first look at the @JoinColumn annotation:

```
public @interface JoinColumn
{
   String name( ) default "";
   String referencedColumnName( ) default "";
   boolean unique( ) default false;
   boolean nullable( ) default true;
   boolean insertable( ) default true;
   boolean updatable( ) default true;
   String columnDefinition( ) default "";
   String table( ) default "";
}
```

The @JoinColumn annotation is pretty much the same as the @Column annotation. It defines the column in the Customer's table that references the primary key of the ADDRESS table in the schema we defined in Figure 7-2. If you are joining on something other than the primary-key column of the ADDRESS table, then you must use the referencedColumnName( ) attribute. This referencedColumnName( ) must be unique, since this is a one-to-one relationship.

If you need to map a one-to-one relationship in which the related entity has a composite primary key, use the @JoinColumns annotation to define multiple foreign-key columns:

```
public @interface @JoinColumns
{
   JoinColumn[] value( );
}
```

Now let's learn about the @OneToOne annotation:

```
public @interface OneToOne
{
   Class targetEntity( ) default void.class;
   CascadeType[] cascade( ) default {};
   FetchType fetch( ) default EAGER;
   boolean optional( ) default true;
   String mappedBy( ) default "";
}
```

The targetEntity( ) attribute represents the entity class you have a relationship to. Usually, you do not have to initialize this attribute, as the persistence provider can figure out the relationship you are setting up from the type of the property.

The fetch( ) attribute works the same as we described in Chapter 6. It allows you to specify whether you want the association to be lazily or eagerly loaded. In Chapter 8, we'll show you how you can eagerly fetch a relationship with EJB QL, even when you have marked the FetchType as LAZY.

The optional( ) attribute specifies whether this relationship can be null. If this is set to false, then a non-null relationship must exist between the two entities.

The cascade( ) attribute is a bit complicated. We'll discuss it later in this chapter, as all relationship types have this attribute.

The mappedBy( ) attribute is for bidirectional relationships and is discussed in the next section.

The XML mapping has the same exact attributes as those for the annotation. Let's take a look:

```
<entity-mappings>
   <entity class="com.titan.domain.Customer" access="PROPERTY">
      <attributes>
         <id name="id">
            <generated-value/>
         </id>
         <one-to-one name="address"
                     targetEntity="com.titan.domain.Address"
                     fetch="LAZY"
                     optional="true">
            <cascade>ALL</cascade>
            <join-column name="ADDRESS_ID"/>
         </one-to-one>
      </attributes>
   </entity>
</entity-mappings>
```

Primary-key join columns

Sometimes the primary keys of the two related entities are used instead of a specific join column. In this case, the primary keys of the related entities are identical, and there is no need for a specific join column. Figure 7-3 shows that there is no specific foreign-key column that maps the relationship, as the tables are joined using the primary key.

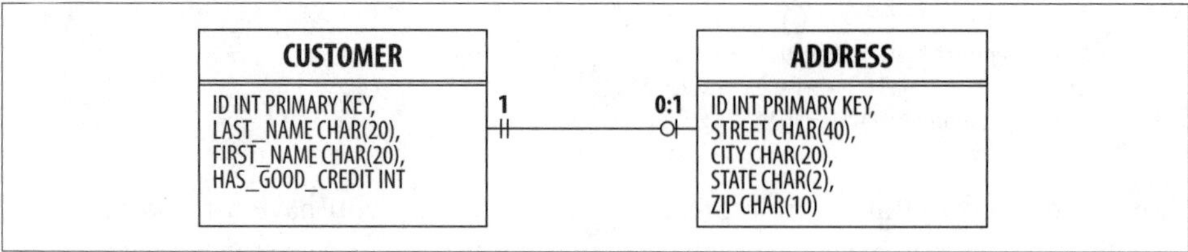

Figure 7-3. Primary-key joins

In this mapping scenario, you are required to use an alternative annotation to describe the mapping—`@javax.persistence.PrimaryKeyJoinColumn`:

```
public @interface PrimaryKeyJoinColumn
{
   String name( ) default "";
   String referencedColumnName( ) default "";
   String columnDefinition( ) default "";
}
```

The `name( )` attribute refers to the primary-key column name of the entity the annotation is applied to. Unless your entity has a composite primary key, you can leave this blank and the persistence provider will figure it out.

The `referencedColumnName( )` is the column to join to on the related entity. If this is left blank, it is assumed that the related entity's primary key will be used.

The `columnDefinition( )` will be used when the persistence provider is generating schema and it will specify the SQL type of the `referencedColumnName( )`.

If the primary-key join in question is of a composite nature, then the `@javax.persistence.PrimaryKeyJoinColumns` annotation is available to you:

```
public @interface PrimaryKeyJoinColumns
{
   PrimaryKeyJoinColumn[] value( );
}
```

So, let's use this annotation to map the Customer/Address entity one-to-one relationship shown in Figure 7-3:

```
package com.titan.domain;

@Entity
public class Customer implements java.io.Serializable {
   ...
   private Address homeAddress;

...
   @OneToOne(cascade={CascadeType.ALL})
```

```
@PrimaryKeyJoinColumn
public Address getAddress( ) {
   return homeAddress;
}
public void setAddress(Address address) {
   this.homeAddress = address;
}
```

Since we're joining on the primary keys of the Customer and Address entities and they are not composite keys, we can simply annotate the address property of `Customer` with the defaulted `@PrimaryKeyJoinColumn` annotation.

One-to-one unidirectional XML mapping

This is what the XML mapping would look like:

```
<entity-mappings>
   <entity class="com.titan.domain.Customer" access="PROPERTY">
      <attributes>
         <id name="id">
            <generated-value/>
         </id>
         <one-to-one name="address"
                     targetEntity="com.titan.domain.Address"
                     fetch="LAZY"
                     optional="true">
            <cascade-all/>
            <primary-key-join-column/>
         </one-to-one>
      </attributes>
   </entity>
</entity-mappings>
```

Default relationship mapping

If your persistence provider supports auto schema generation, you do not need to specify metadata like `@JoinColumn` or `@PrimaryKeyJoinColumn`. Auto schema generation is great when you are doing fast prototypes:

```
package com.titan.domain;

@Entity
public class Customer implements java.io.Serializable {
   ...
   private Address address;

...
   @OneToOne
   public Address getAddress( ) {
      return homeAddress;
   }
   public void setAddress(Address address) {
      this.homeAddress = address;
   }
```

When you do not specify any database mapping for a unidirectional one-to-one relationship, the persistence provider will generate the necessary foreign-key mappings for you. In our Customer/Address relationship example, the following tables would be generated:

```
CREATE TABLE CUSTOMER
(
    ID INT PRIMARY KEY NOT NULL,
    address_id INT,
...
)

ALTER TABLE CUSTOMER ADD CONSTRAINT customerREFaddress
   FOREIGN KEY (address_id) REFERENCES ADDRESS (id);
```

For unidirectional one-to-one relationships, the default mapping creates a foreign-key column named from a combination of the property you are mapping followed by an _ character concatenated with the primary-key column name of the referenced table.

One-to-One Bidirectional Relationship

We can expand our Customer entity to include a reference to a CreditCard entity, which maintains credit card information. The Customer will maintain a reference to its CreditCard, and the CreditCard will maintain a reference back to the Customer—this makes good sense, since a CreditCard should be aware of who owns it. Since each CreditCard has a reference back to one Customer and each Customer references one CreditCard, we have a one-to-one bidirectional relationship.

Relational database schema

The CreditCard has a corresponding `CREDIT_CARD` table, so we need to add a `CREDIT_CARD` foreign key to the `CUSTOMER` table:

```
CREATE TABLE CREDIT_CARD
(
    ID INT PRIMARY KEY NOT NULL,
    EXP_DATE DATE,
    NUMBER CHAR(20),
    NAME CHAR(40),
    ORGANIZATION CHAR(20),
)

CREATE TABLE CUSTOMER
(
    ID INT PRIMARY KEY NOT NULL,
    LAST_NAME CHAR(20),
    FIRST_NAME CHAR(20),
    ADDRESS_ID INT,
    CREDIT_CARD_ID INT
)
```

One-to-one bidirectional relationships may model relational database schemas in the same way as our one-to-one unidirectional relationship, in which one of the tables holds a foreign key that references the other. Remember that in a relational database model, there is no such notion of directionality, so the same database schema will be used for both unidirectional and bidirectional object relationships. Figure 7-4 illustrates how this schema would be implemented for rows in the CUSTOMER and CREDIT_CARD tables.

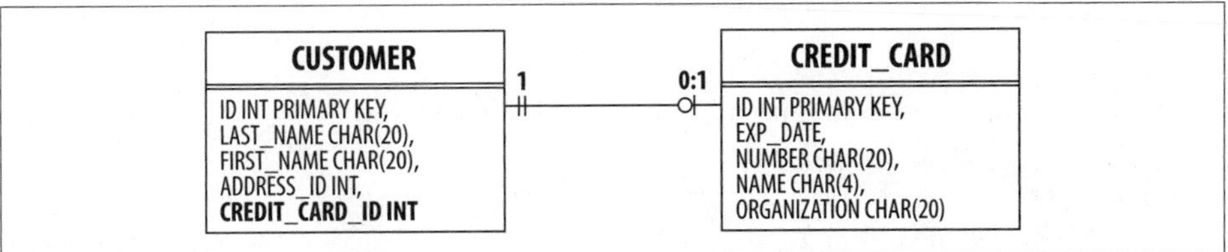

Figure 7-4. One-to-one bidirectional relationship in RDBMS

To model the relationship between the Customer and CreditCard entities, we need to declare a relationship property named customer in the CreditCard bean class:

```
@Entity
public class CreditCard implements java.io.Serializable {
    private int id;
    private Date expiration;
    private String number;
    private String name;
    private String organization;
    private Customer customer;
    ...

    @OneToOne(mappedBy="creditCard")
    public Customer getCustomer( ) {
       return this.customer;
    }
    public void setCustomer(Customer customer) {
       this.customer = customer;
    }

    ...

}
```

The mappedBy( ) attribute is new here. This attribute sets up the bidirectional relationship and tells the persistence manager that the information for mapping this relationship to our tables is specified in the Customer bean class, specifically to the creditCard property of Customer.

We also need to add a relationship property to the Customer bean class for the CreditCard relationship:

```
@Entity
public class Customer implements java.io.Serializable {
```

```
    private CreditCard creditCard;
    ...

    @OneToOne(cascade={CascadeType.ALL})
    @JoinColumn(name="CREDIT_CARD_ID")
    public CreditCard getCreditCard( ) {
       return creditCard;
    public void setCreditCard(CreditCard card) {
       this.creditCard = card;
    }
    ...
}
```

Here is an example for setting up a bidirectional relationship:

```
Customer cust = new Customer( );
CreditCard card = new CreditCard( );
cust.setCreditCard(card);
card.setCustomer(cust);

entityManager.persist(cust);
```

We have the cascade( ) attribute set to ALL. When we discuss cascading operations, you will see that this attribute setting causes the CreditCard creation to be cascaded when the Customer entity is persisted.

There are some peculiarities with bidirectional relationships. With all bidirectional relationship types, including one-to-one, there is always the concept of an *owning* side of the relationship. Although a setCustomer( ) method is available in the CreditCard bean class, it will not cause a change in the persistent relationship if we set it. When we marked the @OneToOne relationship in the CreditCard bean class with the mappedBy( ) attribute, this designated the CreditCard entity as the *inverse* side of the relationship. This means that the Customer entity is the *owning* side of the relationship. If you wanted to associate a CreditCard instance with a different Customer, you would have to call setCreditCard( ) on the old Customer, passing in null, and then call setCreditCard( ) on the new Customer:

```
Customer newCust = em.find(Customer.class, newCustId);
CreditCard card = oldCustomer.getCreditCard( );
oldCustomer.setCreditCard(null);
newCust.setCreditCard(card);
```

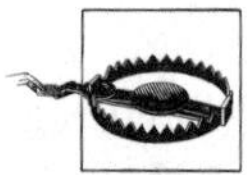

Always wire both sides of a bidirectional relationship when modifying relationships. Entities are like any other Java object that has an association to another object. You have to set the values of both sides of the relationship in memory for the relationship to be updated.

If the customer cancelled his credit card, then you would have to set the Customer's creditCard property to null and remove the CreditCard entity from the database:

```
Customer cust = em.find(Customer.class, id);
em.remove(cust.getCreditCard( ));
cust.setCreditCard(null);
```

Since entity beans are POJOs, it is up to the application developer to manage the relationship, not the persistence provider. This is especially critical when the application deals with detached objects.

One-to-one bidirectional XML mapping

Let's look at the XML for wiring the Customer/CreditCard entity one-to-one bidirectional relationship:

```
<entity-mappings>
   <entity class="com.titan.domain.Customer" access="PROPERTY">
      <attributes>
         <id name="id">
            <generated-value/>
         </id>
         <one-to-one name="creditCard"
                     target-entity="com.titan.domain.CreditCard"
                     fetch="LAZY">
            <cascade-all/>
            <join-column name="CREDIT_CARD_ID"/>
         </one-to-one>
      </attributes>
   </entity>
   <entity class="com.titan.domain.CreditCard" access="PROPERTY">
      <attributes>
         <id name="id">
            <generated-value/>
         </id>
         <one-to-one name="customer"
                     target-entity="com.titan.domain.Customer"
                     mapped-by="creditCard"/>
      </attributes>
   </entity>
</entity-mappings>
```

Default relationship mapping

As we saw previously, you do not need to specify metadata like @JoinColumn if your persistence provider supports auto schema generation:

```
 package com.titan.domain;

@Entity
public class Customer implements java.io.Serializable {
   ...
   private CreditCard creditCard;

...
   @OneToOne
   public CreditCard getCreditCard( ) {
      return homeAddress;
   }
...
}
```

```
@Entity
public class CreditCard implements java.io.Serializable {
...
    private Customer customer;
    ...

    @OneToOne(mappedBy="creditCard")
    public Customer getCustomer( ) {
       return this.customer;
    }
...
}
```

When you do not specify any database mapping for a bidirectional one-to-one relationship, the persistence provider will generate the necessary foreign-key mappings for you. In our Customer/CreditCard relationship example, the following tables would be generated:

```
CREATE TABLE CUSTOMER
(
    ID INT PRIMARY KEY NOT NULL,
    creditCard_id INT,
...
)

ALTER TABLE CUSTOMER ADD CONSTRAINT customerREFcreditcard
   FOREIGN KEY (creditCard_id) REFERENCES CREDITCARD (id);
```

For bidirectional one-to-one relationships, the default mapping creates a foreign-key column named from a combination of the property you are mapping followed by an _ character concatenated with the primary-key column name of the referenced table.

One-to-Many Unidirectional Relationship

Entity beans can also maintain relationships with multiplicity. This means one entity bean can aggregate or contain many other entity beans. For example, a customer may have relationships with many phones, each of which represents a phone number. This is very different from simple one-to-one relationships—or, for that matter, from multiple one-to-one relationships with the same type of bean. One-to-many and many-to-many relationships require the developer to work with a collection of references instead of a single reference when accessing the relationship field.

Relational database schema

To illustrate a one-to-many unidirectional relationship, we will use a new entity bean, the Phone, for which we must define a table, the PHONE table:

```
CREATE TABLE PHONE
(
    ID INT PRIMARY KEY NOT NULL,
    NUMBER CHAR(20),
```

```
    TYPE INT,
    CUSTOMER_ID INT
)
```

One-to-many unidirectional relationships between the CUSTOMER and PHONE tables could be implemented in a variety of ways. For this example, we chose to have the PHONE table include a foreign key to the CUSTOMER table. In practice, a unidirectional one-to-many relationship is usually mapped with a join table.

The table of aggregated data can maintain a column of nonunique foreign keys to the aggregating table. In the case of the Customer and Phone entities, the PHONE table maintains a foreign key to the CUSTOMER table, and one or more PHONE records may contain foreign keys to the same CUSTOMER record. In other words, in the database, the PHONE records point to the CUSTOMER records. In the programming model, however, it is the Customer entity that points to many Phones—two schemas are reversed. How does this work? The container system hides the reverse pointer so that it appears as if the Customer is aware of the Phone, and not the other way around. When you ask the container to return a Collection of Phones (invoking a method on the collection returned from getPhoneNumbers( )), it queries the PHONE table for all the records with a foreign key matching the Customer entity's primary key. The use of reverse pointers in this type of relationship is illustrated in Figure 7-5.

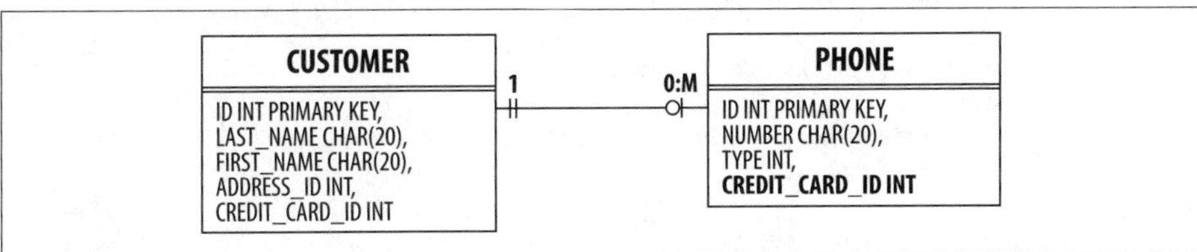

Figure 7-5. One-to-many unidirectional relationship in RDBMS using a foreign key

This database schema illustrates that the structure and relationships of the actual database can differ from the relationships as defined in the programming model. In this case, the tables are set up in reverse, but the persistence manager will manage the beans to meet the specification of the bean developer. When you are dealing with legacy databases (i.e., databases that were established before the EJB application), reverse-pointer scenarios like the one illustrated here are common, so supporting this kind of relationship mapping is important.

Programming model

You declare one-to-many relationships using the @javax.persistence.OneToMany annotation:

```
public @interface OneToMany
{
   Class targetEntity( ) default void.class;
   CascadeType[] cascade( ) default {};
```

```
    FetchType fetch( ) default LAZY;
    String mappedBy( ) default "";
}
```

The attribute definitions are pretty much the same as those for the @OneToOne annotation.

In the programming model, we represent multiplicity by defining a relationship property that can point to many entity beans and annotating it with @OneToMany. To hold this type of data, we'll employ some data structures from the java.util package: Collection, List, Map, and Set. The Collection maintains a homogeneous group of entity object references, which means that it contains many references to one kind of entity bean. The Collection type may contain duplicate references to the same entity bean, and the Set type may not.

For example, a customer may have relationships with several phone numbers (e.g., a home phone, work phone, cell phone, fax, etc.), each represented by a Phone entity. Instead of having a different relationship field for each Phone, the Customer entity keeps all the Phones in a collection-based relationship:

```
@Entity
public class Customer implements java.io.Serializable {
    ...
    private Collection<Phone> phoneNumbers = new ArrayList<Phone>( );
    ...
    @OneToMany(cascade={CascadeType.ALL})
    @JoinColumn(name="CUSTOMER_ID")
    public Collection<Phone> getPhoneNumbers( ) {
       return phoneNumbers;
    }
    public void setPhoneNumbers(Collection<Phone> phones) {
        this.phoneNumbers = phones;
    }
}
```

The @JoinColumn annotation references the CUSTOMER_ID column in the PHONE table. Notice also that we use a Java Generic to templatize the definition of the collection of Phones. Using a Generic is not only good programming practice because it gives a concrete type to your collection, but it also allows the persistence manager to figure out exactly what you are relating the Customer entity to. If you did not use a Generic Collection, then you would have to specify the @OneToMany.targetEntity( ) attribute. Also, since this is a unidirectional relationship, the mappedBy( ) attribute of the @OneToMany annotation did not need to be set. The mappedBy( ) is only used with bidirectional relationships.

The Phone bean class is shown in the next listing. Notice that the Phone doesn't provide a relationship property for the Customer. It's a unidirectional relationship; the Customer entity maintains a relationship with many Phones, but the Phones do not maintain a relationship field back to the Customer. Only the Customer is aware of the relationship.

```
package com.titan.domain;

import javax.persistence.*;

@Entity
public class Phone implements java.io.Serializable {
    private int id ;
    private String number;
    private int type;

    // required default constructor
    public Phone( ) {}

    public Phone(String number, int type) {
       this.number = number;
       this.type = type;
    }

    @Id @GeneratedValue
    public int getId( ) { return id; }
    public void setId(int id) { this.id = id; }

    public String getNumber( ) { return number; }
    public void setNumber(String number) { this.number = number; }

    public int getType( ) { return type; }
    public void setType(int type) { this.type = type; }
}
```

To illustrate how an entity bean uses a collection-based relationship, let's look at some code that interacts with the EntityManager:

```
Customer cust = entityManager.find(Customer.class, pk);
Phone phone = new Phone("617-333-3333", 5);
cust.getPhones( ).add(phone);
```

Since the Customer entity is the owning side of the relationship, the new Phone will automatically be created in the database because the persistence manager will see that its primary key is 0, generate a new ID (GeneratorType is AUTO), and insert it into the database.

If you need to remove a Phone from the relationship, you need to remove the Phone from both the collection and the database:

```
cust.getPhones( ).remove(phone);
entityManager.remove(phone);
```

Removing the Phone from the Customer's collection does not remove the Phone from the database. You have to delete the Phone explicitly; otherwise, it will be orphaned.

One-to-many unidirectional XML mapping

Let's look at the XML mapping for this type of relationship:

```
<entity-mappings>
   <entity class="com.titan.domain.Customer" access="PROPERTY">
      <attributes>
         <id name="id">
            <generated-value/>
         </id>
         <one-to-many name="phones"
                      targetEntity="com.titan.domain.Phone">
            <cascade-all/>
            <join-column name="CUSTOMER_ID"/>
         </one-to-many>
      </attributes>
   </entity>
</entity-mappings>
```

Join table mapping

Another relational database mapping for the Customer/Phone entity relationship could be an association table that maintains two columns with foreign keys pointing to both the CUSTOMER and PHONE records. We could then place a constraint on the PHONE foreign-key column in the association table to ensure that it contains only unique entries (i.e., that every phone has only one customer), while allowing the CUSTOMER foreign-key column to contain duplicates. The advantage of this association table is that it doesn't impose the relationship between the CUSTOMER and PHONE records onto either of the tables. This is the most commonly used mapping when using a unidirectional relationship.

```
create table CUSTOMER_PHONE
(
   CUSTOMER_ID int not null,
   PHONE_ID int not null unique
);
```

To have this type of mapping, we need to change from a @JoinColumn annotation in our Customer bean class to using a @javax.persistence.JoinTable annotation:

```
public @interface JoinTable
{
   String name( ) default "";
   String catalog( ) default "";
   String schema( ) default "";
   JoinColumn[] joinColumns( ) default {};
   JoinColumn[] inverseJoinColumns( ) default {};
   UniqueConstraint[] uniqueConstraints( ) default {};
}
```

The @JoinTable annotation looks pretty much the same as @Table, except it has the additional attributes of joinColumns( ) and inverseJoinColumns( ). The joinColumns( )

attribute should define a foreign key mapping to the primary key of the owning side of the relationship. The `inverseJoinColumns( )` attribute maps the nonowning side. If either side of the relationship had a composite primary key, we would just add more `@JoinColumn` annotations to the array:

```
@Entity
public class Customer implements java.io.Serializable {
    ...
    private Collection<Phone> phoneNumbers;
    ...
    @OneToMany(cascade={CascadeType.ALL})
    @JoinTable(name="CUSTOMER_PHONE"),
               joinColumns={@JoinColumn(name="CUSTOMER_ID")},
               inverseJoinColumns={@JoinColumn(name="PHONE_ID")})
    public Collection<Phone> getPhoneNumbers( ) {
       return phoneNumbers;
    }
    public void setPhoneNumbers(Collection<Phone> phones) {
        this.phoneNumbers = phones;
    }
}
```

With this definition, we're saying that the primary key for `Customer` maps to the `CUSTOMER_ID` join column in the `CUSTOMER_PHONE` table. The primary key of the Phone entity maps to the `PHONE_ID` join column in the `CUSTOMER_PHONE` table. Because the relationship between customers and phones is one-to-many, a unique constraint will be put on the `PHONE_ID` column of the `CUSTOMER_PHONE` table by the persistence provider if it supports and if you've activated DDL generation. As per the definition of the relationship, one customer has many phones, but a phone has only one customer. The unique constraint enforces this.

One-to-many unidirectional join table XML mapping

Let's look at the XML for this type of mapping:

```
<entity-mappings>
   <entity class="com.titan.domain.Customer" access="PROPERTY">
      <attributes>
         <id name="id">
            <generated-value/>
         </id>
         <one-to-many name="phones" targetEntity="com.titan.domain.Phone">
            <cascade-all/>
            <join-table name="CUSTOMER_PHONE">
               <join-column name="CUSTOMER_ID"/>
               <inverse-join-column name="PHONE_ID"/>
            </join-table>
         </one-to-many>
      </attributes>
   </entity>
</entity-mappings>
```

Default relationship mapping

If your persistence provider supports auto schema generation, you do not need to specify metadata like @JoinColumn. Auto schema generation is great when you are doing fast prototypes:

```
package com.titan.domain;

@Entity
public class Customer implements java.io.Serializable {
    ...
    private Collection<Phone> phoneNumbers = new ArrayList<Phone>( );
    ...
    @OneToMany
    public Collection<Phone> getPhoneNumbers( ) {
       return phoneNumbers;
    }
...
}
```

When you do not specify any database mapping for a unidirectional one-to-many relationship, the persistence provider does a default mapping based on the join table mapping discussed earlier in this section. For our Customer/Phone relationship example, the following join table would be generated:

```
CREATE TABLE CUSTOMER_PHONE
(
    CUSTOMER_id INT,
    PHONE_id INT
);
ALTER TABLE CUSTOMER_PHONE ADD CONSTRAINT customer_phone_unique
   UNIQUE (PHONE_id);

ALTER TABLE CUSTOMER_PHONE ADD CONSTRAINT customerREFphone
   FOREIGN KEY (CUSTOMER_id) REFERENCES CUSTOMER (id);

ALTER TABLE CUSTOMER_PHONE ADD CONSTRAINT customerREFphone2
   FOREIGN KEY (PHONE_id) REFERENCES PHONE (id);
```

The name of the join table created is a concatenation of the owning entity's table followed by an _ character followed by the table name of the related entity. The foreign-key columns are a concatenation of each entity's table name followed by an _ followed by the primary-key column name of that entity. A unique constraint is placed on the many side of the relationship. Foreign-key constraints are applied to both columns.

The Cruise, Ship, and Reservation Entities

By now, I imagine that you're bored by all of these phone numbers, credit cards, and addresses. To make things more interesting, we are going to introduce some more entity beans so that we can model the remaining four relationships: many-to-one unidirectional; one-to-many bidirectional; many-to-many bidirectional; and many-to-many unidirectional.

In Titan's reservation system, every customer (a.k.a. passenger) can be booked on one or more cruises. Each booking requires a reservation. A reservation may be for one or more (usually two) passengers. Each cruise requires exactly one ship, but each ship may be used for many cruises throughout the year. Figure 7-6 illustrates these relationships.

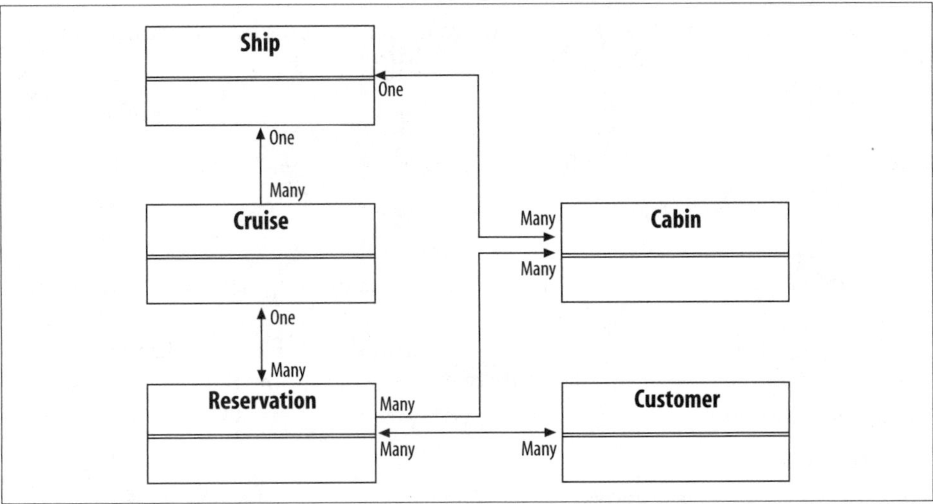

Figure 7-6. Cruise, Ship, Reservation, Cabin, and Customer class diagram

Many-to-One Unidirectional Relationship

Many-to-one unidirectional relationships result when many entity beans reference a single entity bean, but the referenced entity bean is unaware of the relationship. In the Titan Cruises business, for example, the concept of a cruise can be captured by a Cruise entity bean. As shown in Figure 7-6, each Cruise has a many-to-one relationship with a Ship. This relationship is unidirectional: the Cruise entity maintains a relationship with the Ship entity, but the Ship entity does not keep track of the Cruises for which it is used.

Relational database schema

The relational database schema for the Cruise/Ship entity relationship is fairly simple; it requires that the `CRUISE` table maintain a foreign key column for the `SHIP` table, with each row in the `CRUISE` table pointing to a row in the `SHIP` table. The `CRUISE` and `SHIP` tables are defined in the following code snippets; Figure 7-7 shows the relationship between these tables in the database.

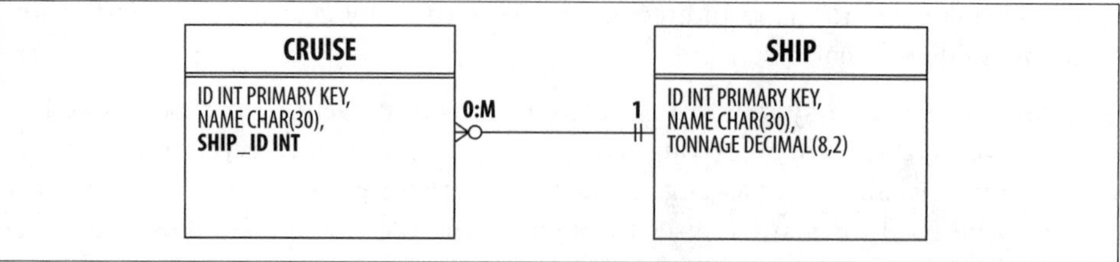

Figure 7-7. Many-to-one unidirectional relationship in RDBMS

An enormous amount of data would be required to describe an ocean liner adequately, but we'll use a simple definition of the SHIP table here:

```
CREATE TABLE SHIP
(
    ID INT PRIMARY KEY NOT NULL,
    NAME CHAR(30),
    TONNAGE DECIMAL (8,2)
)
```

The CRUISE table maintains data on each cruise's name, ship, and other information that is not germane to this discussion. (Other tables, such as RESERVATIONS, SCHEDULES, and CREW, would have relationships with the CRUISE table through association tables.) We'll keep it simple and focus on a definition that is useful for the examples in this book:

```
CREATE TABLE CRUISE
(
    ID INT PRIMARY KEY NOT NULL,
    NAME CHAR(30),
    SHIP_ID INT
)
```

Programming model

Many-to-one relationships are described with the @javax.persistence.ManyToOne annotation:

```
public @interface ManyToOne
{
   Class targetEntity( ) default void.class;
   CascadeType[] cascade( ) default {};
   FetchType fetch( ) default EAGER;
   boolean optional( ) default true;
}
```

The attribute definitions are pretty much the same as those for the @OneToOne annotation.

The programming model is quite simple for our relationship. We add a Ship property to our Cruise entity bean class and annotate it with the @ManyToOne annotation:

```
@Entity
public class Cruise implements java.io.Serializable {
```

```
    private int id;
    private String name;
    private Ship ship;

    // required default constructor
    public Cruise( ) {}

    public Cruise(String name, Ship ship) {
       this.name = name;
       this.ship = ship;
    }

    @Id @GeneratedValue
    public int getId( ) { return id; }
    public void setId(int id) { this.id = id; }

    public String getName( ) { return name; }
    public void setName(String name) { this.name = name; }

    @ManyToOne
    @JoinColumn(name="SHIP_ID")
    public Ship getShip( ) { return ship; }
    public void setShip(Ship ship) { this.ship = ship; }

}
```

Even though we have a convenience constructor that takes a name and a ship, the Java Persistence spec still requires a default no-arg constructor. The `@JoinColumn` annotation specifies that the Cruise entity's table has an additional column called `SHIP_ID` that is a foreign key to the Ship entity's table. If you are using your persistence provider's auto schema generation facilities, you do not need to specify a `@JoinColumn` as the provider has well-known defaults for this.

The relationship between the Cruise and Ship entities is unidirectional, so the `Ship` bean class doesn't define any relationship back to the Cruise, just persistent properties:

```
@Entity
public class Ship implements java.io.Serializable {
    private int id;
    private String name;
    private double tonnage;

    // required default constructor
    public Ship( ) {}

    public Ship(String name,double tonnage) {
        this.name = name;
        this.tonnage = tonnage;
    }

    @Id @GeneratedValue
    public int getId( ) { return id; }
    public void setId(int id) { this.id = id; }
```

```
    public String getName( ) { return name; }
    public void setName(String name) { this.name = name; }
    public double getTonnage( ) { return tonnage ; }
    public void setTonnage(double tonnage) { this.tonnage = tonnage ; }

}
```

All of this should be mundane to you now. The impact of exchanging Ship references between Cruise entities should be equally obvious. As shown previously in Figure 7-7, each Cruise may reference only a single Ship, but each Ship may reference many Cruise entities. If you take Ship A, which is referenced by Cruises 1, 2, and 3, and pass it to Cruise 4, Cruises 1 through 4 will reference Ship A, as shown in Figure 7-8.

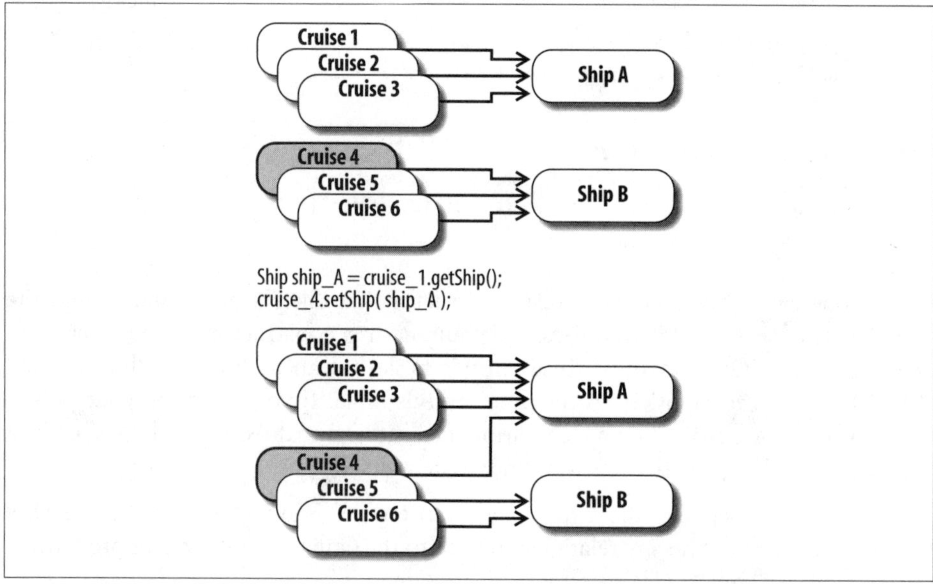

Figure 7-8. Sharing a bean reference in a many-to-one unidirectional relationship

Many-to-one unidirectional XML mapping

Let's look at the XML mapping for this type of relationship:

```
<entity-mappings>
   <entity class="com.titan.domain.Cruise" access="PROPERTY">
      <attributes>
         <id name="id">
            <generated-value/>
         </id>
         <many-to-one name="ship"
                      target-entity="com.titan.domain.Ship"
                      fetch="EAGER">
            <join-column name="SHIP_ID"/>
         </many-to-one>
```

```
        </attributes>
    </entity>
    <entity class="com.titan.domain.Ship" access="PROPERTY">
        <attributes>
            <id name="id">
                <generated-value/>
            </id>
        </attributes>
    </entity>
</entity-mappings>
```

Default relationship mapping

If your persistence provider supports auto schema generation, you do not need to specify metadata like @JoinColumn. Applications can be built very quickly in this manner:

```
@Entity
public class Cruise implements java.io.Serializable {
...

    @ManyToOne
    public Ship getShip( ) { return ship; }
```

The default database mapping for a many-to-one relationship is similar to a unidirectional one-to-one. When you do not specify any database mapping, the persistence provider will generate the necessary foreign-key mappings for you. In our Cruise/Ship relationship example, the following tables would be generated:

```
CREATE TABLE CRUISE
(
    ID INT PRIMARY KEY NOT NULL,
    ship_id INT,
...
)

ALTER TABLE CRUISE ADD CONSTRAINT cruiseREFship
   FOREIGN KEY (ship_id) REFERENCES SHIP (id);
```

For unidirectional many-to-one relationships, the default mapping creates a foreign-key column named from a combination of the property you are mapping followed by an _ character concatenated with the primary-key column name of the referenced table.

One-to-Many Bidirectional Relationship

One-to-many and many-to-one bidirectional relationships sound like they're different, but they're not. A one-to-many bidirectional relationship occurs when one entity bean maintains a collection-based relationship property with another entity bean, and each entity bean referenced in the collection maintains a single reference back to its aggregating bean. For example, in the Titan Cruises system, each Cruise entity maintains a collection of references to all the passenger reservations made for that cruise, and each Reservation maintains a single reference to its Cruise. The relationship is a one-to-many bidirectional relationship from the perspective of the Cruise and a many-to-one bidirectional relationship from the perspective of the Reservation.

Relational database schema

The first table we need is the `RESERVATION` table, which is defined in the following listing. Notice that the `RESERVATION` table contains, among other things, a column that serves as a foreign key to the `CRUISE` table.

```
CREATE TABLE RESERVATION
(
    ID INT PRIMARY KEY NOT NULL,
    AMOUNT_PAID DECIMAL (8,2),
    DATE_RESERVED DATE,
    CRUISE_ID INT
)
```

While the `RESERVATION` table contains a foreign key to the `CRUISE` table, the `CRUISE` table doesn't maintain a foreign key back to the `RESERVATION` table. The persistence manager can determine the relationship between the Cruise and Reservation entities by querying the `RESERVATION` table, so explicit pointers from the `CRUISE` table to the `RESERVATION` table are not required. This illustrates the separation between the entity bean's view of its persistence relationships and the database's actual implementation of those relationships.

The relationship between the `RESERVATION` and `CRUISE` tables is shown in Figure 7-9.

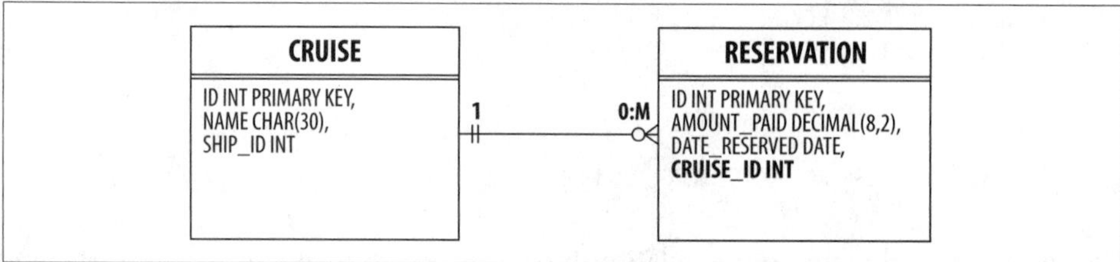

Figure 7-9. One-to-many/many-to-one bidirectional relationship in RDBMS

Programming model

To model the relationship between Cruises and Reservation entities, we first define the `Reservation`, which maintains a relationship field to the `Cruise`:

```
@Entity
public class Reservation implements java.io.Serializable {
    private int id;
    private float amountPaid;
    private Date date;
    private Cruise cruise;
```

```
    public Reservation( ) {}
    public Reservation(Cruise cruise) {
       this.cruise = cruise;
    }

    @Id @GeneratedValue
    public int getId( ) { return id; }
    public void setId(int id) { this.id = id; }

    @Column(name="AMOUNT_PAID")
    public float getAmountPaid( ) { return amountPaid; }
    public void setAmountPaid(float amount) { amountPaid = amount; }

    @Column(name="DATE_RESERVED")
    public Date getDate( ) { return date; }
    public void setDate(Date date) { this.date = date; }

    @ManyToOne
    @JoinColumn(name="CRUISE_ID")
    public Cruise getCruise( ) { return cruise; }
    public void setCruise(Cruise cruise) { this.cruise = cruise ; }
}
```

We need to add a collection-based relationship property to the `Cruise` bean class so that it can reference all the `Reservations` that were created for it:

```
@Entity
public class Cruise implements java.io.Serializable {
    ...
    private Collection<Reservation> reservations = new ArrayList<Reservation>( );
    ...
    @OneToMany(mappedBy="cruise")
    public Collection<Reservation> getReservations( ) { return reservations; }
    public void setReservations(Collection<Reserveration> res) {
       this.reservations = res;
    }
}
```

The interdependency between the Cruise and Reservation entities produces some interesting results. As with one-to-one bidirectional relationships, there must be one owning side of a relationship in a one-to-many bidirectional relationship. Java Persistence currently requires that the many-to-one side always be the owner—in this case, it is the Reservation entity. What does this mean? Well, it requires you to call `Reservation.setCruise( )` whenever you add or remove a `Cruise`'s `Reservations`. If you do not call `Reservation.setCruise( )`, the relationship will not change in the database. This may seem very confusing, but if you obey the cardinal rule of always wiring both sides of a relationship, then you will have no problems.

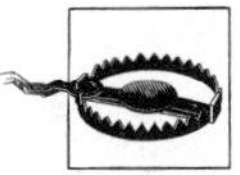

Always wire both sides of a bidirectional relationship in your Java code.

In our Titan Cruises system, Reservation entities never change their Cruises once the relationship is set up. If a customer wants to book a different Cruise, he needs to delete the old reservation and create a new one. So, instead of setting `Reservation.setCruise( )` to `null`, application code would just remove the `Reservation`:

```
entityManager.remove(reservation);
```

Since the Reservation entity is the owning side of the relationship, the `Cruise`'s `reservations` property is updated with the removal the next time it is loaded from the database.

One-to-many bidirectional XML mapping

Let's look at the XML mapping for this type of relationship:

```
<entity-mappings>
   <entity class="com.titan.domain.Cruise" access="PROPERTY">
      <attributes>
         <id name="id">
            <generated-value/>
         </id>
         <one-to-many name="ship"
                      target-entity="com.titan.domain.Reservation"
                      fetch="LAZY"
                      mapped-by="cruise">
         </one-to-many>
      </attributes>
   </entity>
   <entity class="com.titan.domain.Reservation" access="PROPERTY">
      <attributes>
         <id name="id">
            <generated-value/>
         </id>
         <many-to-one name="cruise"
                      target-entity="com.titan.domain.Cruise"
                      fetch="EAGER">
            <join-column name="CRUISE_ID"/>
         </many-to-one>
      </attributes>
   </entity>
</entity-mappings>
```

Default relationship mapping

Like other relationship mapping types, if your persistence provider supports auto schema generation, you do not need to specify metadata like `@JoinColumn`:

```
@Entity
public class Reservation implements java.io.Serializable {
...

    @ManyToOne
    public Cruise getCruise( ) { return cruise; }
```

The default database mapping for a one-to-many bidirectional relationship is similar to a unidirectional many-to-one. When you do not specify any database mapping, the persistence provider will generate the necessary foreign-key mappings for you. In our Reservation/Cruise relationship example, the following tables would be generated:

```
CREATE TABLE RESERVATION
(
    ID INT PRIMARY KEY NOT NULL,
    cruise_id INT,
...
)

ALTER TABLE RESERVATION ADD CONSTRAINT reservationREFcruise
   FOREIGN KEY (cruise_id) REFERENCES CRUISE (id);
```

For bidirectional one-to-many relationships, the default mapping creates a foreign-key column named from a combination of the property you are mapping followed by an _ character concatenated with the primary-key column name of the referenced table.

Many-to-Many Bidirectional Relationship

Many-to-many bidirectional relationships occur when many beans maintain a collection-based relationship property with another bean, and each bean referenced in the collection maintains a collection-based relationship property back to the aggregating beans. For example, in Titan Cruises, every Reservation entity may reference many Customers (a family can make a single reservation), and each Customer can have many reservations (a person may make more than one reservation). In this many-to-many bidirectional relationship, the Customer keeps track of all of its reservations, and each reservation may be for many customers.

Relational database schema

The `RESERVATION` and `CUSTOMER` tables have already been established. To establish a many-to-many bidirectional relationship, we create the `RESERVATION_CUSTOMER` table. This table maintains two foreign key columns: one for the `RESERVATION` table and another for the `CUSTOMER` table:

```
CREATE TABLE RESERVATION_CUSTOMER
(
    RESERVATION_ID INT,
    CUSTOMER_ID INT
)
```

The relationship between the `CUSTOMER`, `RESERVATION`, and `RESERVATION_CUSTOMER` tables is illustrated in Figure 7-10.

Many-to-many bidirectional relationships always require an association table in a normalized relational database.

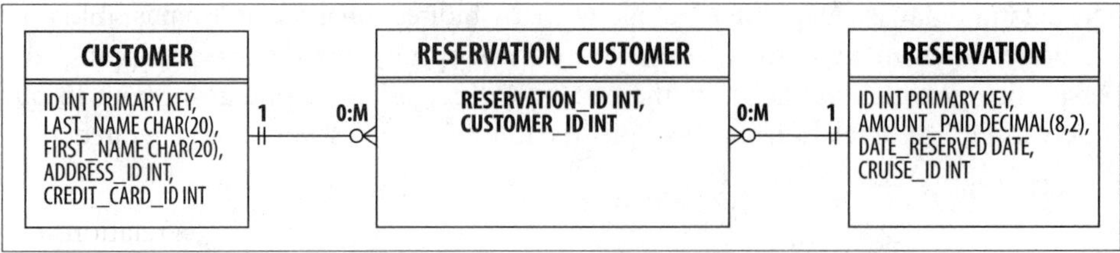

Figure 7-10. Many-to-many bidirectional relationship in RDBMS

Programming model

Many-to-many relationships are logically defined using the `@javax.persistence.ManyToMany` annotation:

```
public @interface ManyToMany
{
   Class targetEntity( ) default void.class;
   CascadeType[] cascade( ) default {};
   FetchType fetch( ) default LAZY;
   String mappedBy( ) default "";
}
```

To model the many-to-many bidirectional relationship between the Customer and Reservation entities, we need to include collection-based relationship properties in both bean classes:

```
@Entity
public class Reservation implements java.io.Serializable {
    ...
    private Set<Customer> customers = new HashSet<Customer>( );
    ...
    @ManyToMany
    @JoinTable(name="RESERVATION_CUSTOMER"),
               joinColumns={@JoinColumn(name="RESERVATION_ID")},
               inverseJoinColumns={@JoinColumn(name="CUSTOMER_ID")})
    public Set<Customer> getCustomers( ) { return customers; }
    public void setCustomers(Set customers);
    ...
}
```

The `customers` relationship is declared as a `java.util.Set`. The `Set` type should contain only unique `Customers` and no duplicates. Duplicate `Customers` would introduce some interesting but undesirable side effects in Titan's reservation system. To maintain a valid passenger count, and to avoid overcharging customers, Titan requires that a customer be booked only once in the same reservation. The `Set` collection type expresses this restriction. The effectiveness of the `Set` collection type depends largely on referential-integrity constraints established in the underlying database.

As with all bidirectional relationships, there has to be an owning side. In this case, it is the Reservation entity. Since the Reservation owns the relationship, its bean class defines the `@JoinTable` mapping. The `joinColumns( )` attribute identifies the foreign-key column in the RESERVATION_CUSTOMER table that references the RESERVATION table. The inverseJoinColumns( ) attribute identifies the foreign key in the RESERVATION_CUSTOMER table that references the CUSTOMER table.

Like with @OneToMany relationships, if you are using your persistence provider's auto schema generation facilities, you do not need to specify a @JoinTable mapping. The Java Persistence specification has a default mapping for @ManyToMany relationships and will create the join table for you.

We have also modified the Customer to allow it to maintain a collection-based relationship with all of its Reservations. The Customer bean class now includes a reservations relationship property:

```
@Entity
public class Customer implements java.io.Serializable {
    ...
    private Collection<Reservation> reservations = new ArrayList<Reservation>( );
    ...
    @ManyToMany(mappedBy="customers")
    public Collection<Reservation> getReservations( ) {
       return reservations;
    }
    public void setReservations(Collection<Reservation> reservations) {
       this.reservations = reservations;
    }
    ...
```

As with one-to-many bidirectional relationships, the mappedBy( ) attribute identifies the property on the Reservation bean class that defines the relationship. This also identifies the Customer entity as the inverse side of the relationship.

As far as modifying and interacting with the relationship properties, the same ownership rules apply as we saw in the one-to-many bidirectional example. The Customer/ Reservation entity relationship is something our Titan Cruises application may want to modify after it is established. The customer may want to add a relative or nanny to the reservation, or remove a friend that is too sick to come on the cruise:

```
Reservation reservation = em.find(Reservation.class, id);
reservation.getCustomers( ).remove(customer);
```

Since the reservation is the owning side of the relationship, you must remove the customer from the Reservation's customers property. If you instead removed the reservation from the Customer's reservations property, there would be no database update because the Customer entity is the inverse side of the relationship.

Many-to-many bidirectional XML mapping

Let's look at the XML mapping for this type of relationship:

```
<entity-mappings>
   <entity class="com.titan.domain.Reservation" access="PROPERTY">
      <attributes>
```

```
            <id name="id">
               <generated-value/>
            </id>
            <many-to-many name="customers"
                          target-entity="com.titan.domain.Customer"
                          fetch="LAZY">
               <join-table name="RESERVATION_CUSTOMER">
                  <join-column name="RESERVATION_ID"/>
                  <inverse-join-column name="CUSTOMER_ID"/>
               </join-table>
            </many-to-many>
         </attributes>
      </entity>
      <entity class="com.titan.domain.Customer" access="PROPERTY">
         <attributes>
            <id name="id">
               <generated-value/>
            </id>
            <many-to-many name="cruise"
                          target-entity="com.titan.domain.Reservation"
                          fetch="LAZY"
                          mapped-by="customers">
            </many-to-many>
         </attributes>
      </entity>
   </entity-mappings>
```

Default Rrelationship mapping

Like the other relationship types, bidirectional many-to-many relationships support auto schema generation with minimal metadata:

```
public class Reservation implements java.io.Serializable {
    ...
    private Set<Customer> customers = new HashSet<Customer>( );
    ...
    @ManyToMany
    public Set<Customer> getCustomers( ) { return customers; }
    public void setCustomers(Set customers);
    ...
}
```

When you do not specify any database mapping for a bidirectional many-to-many relationship, the persistence provider creates the join table mapping for you. For our Reservation/Customer relationship example, the following join table would be generated:

```
CREATE TABLE RESERVATION_CUSTOMER
(
    RESERVATION_id INT,
    CUSTOMER_id INT,
);
ALTER TABLE RESERVATION_CUSTOMER ADD CONSTRAINT reservationREFcustomer
   FOREIGN KEY (RESERVATION_id) REFERENCES RESERVATION (id);
```

```
ALTER TABLE RESERVATION_CUSTOMER ADD CONSTRAINT reservationREFcustomer2
   FOREIGN KEY (CUSTOMER_id) REFERENCES CUSTOMER (id);
```

The name of the join table created is a concatenation of the owning entity's table followed by an _ character followed by the table name of the related entity. The foreign-key columns are a concatenation of each entity's table name followed by an _ followed by the primary-key column name of that entity. Foreign-key constraints are applied to both columns.

Many-to-Many Unidirectional Relationship

Many-to-many unidirectional relationships occur when many beans maintain a collection-based relationship with another bean, but the bean referenced in the `Collection` does not maintain a collection-based relationship back to the aggregating beans. In Titan's reservation system, every Reservation is assigned a Cabin on the Ship. This allows a customer to reserve a specific cabin (e.g., a deluxe suite or a cabin with sentimental significance) on the ship. In this case, each reservation may be for more than one cabin, since each reservation can be for more than one customer. For example, a family might make a reservation for five people for two adjacent cabins (one for the kids and the other for the parents).

While the Reservation entity must keep track of the Cabins it reserves, it's not necessary for the Cabins to track all the Reservations made by all the Cruises. The Reservations reference a collection of Cabin beans, but the Cabin beans do not maintain references back to the Reservations.

Relational database schema

Our first order of business is to declare a `CABIN` table:

```
CREATE TABLE CABIN
(
    ID INT PRIMARY KEY NOT NULL,
    SHIP_ID INT,
    NAME CHAR(10),
    DECK_LEVEL INT,
    BED_COUNT INT
)
```

The `CABIN` table maintains a foreign key to the `SHIP` table. While this relationship is important, we don't discuss it because we covered the one-to-many bidirectional relationship earlier in this chapter. To accommodate the many-to-many unidirectional relationship between the `RESERVATION` and `CABIN` tables, we need a `CABIN_RESERVATION` table:

```
CREATE TABLE CABIN_RESERVATION
(
    RESERVATION_ID INT,
    CABIN_ID INT
)
```

The relationship between the CABIN records and the RESERVATION records through the CABIN_RESERVATION table is illustrated in Figure 7-11.

Figure 7-11. Many-to-many unidirectional relationship in RDBMS

This many-to-many unidirectional relationship looks a lot like the join table mapping for the one-to-many unidirectional Customer/Phone relationship discussed earlier. The big difference is that there are no unique constraints on the CABIN_RESERVATION table: many cabins can have many reservations, and vice versa.

Programming model

To model this relationship, we need to add a collection-based relationship field for Cabin beans to the Reservation:

```
@Entity
public class Reservation implements java.io.Serializable {
    ...
    @ManyToMany
    @JoinTable(name="CABIN_RESERVATION",
               joinColumns={@JoinColumn(name="RESERVATION_ID")},
               inverseJoinColumns={@JoinColumn(name="CABIN_ID")})
    public Set<Cabin> getCabins( ) { return cabins; }
    public void setCabins(Set<Cabin> cabins) { this.cabins = cabins; }
    ...
}
```

In addition, we need to define a Cabin bean. Notice that the Cabin bean doesn't maintain a relationship back to the Reservation. The lack of a relationship field for the Reservation tells us the relationship is unidirectional:

```
@Entity
public class Cabin implements java.io.Serializable {
    private int id;
    private String name;
    private int bedCount;
    private int deckLevel;
    private Ship ship;

    @Id @GeneratedValue
    public int getId( ) { return id; }
    public void setId(int id) { this.id = id; }
    public String getName( ) { return name; }
    public void setName(String name) { this.name = name; }
```

```
    @Column(name="BED_COUNT")
    public int getBedCount( ) { return bedCount; }
    public void setBedCount(int count) { this.bedCount = count; }

    @Column(name="DECK_LEVEL")
    public int getDeckLevel( ) { return deckLevel; }
    public void setDeckLevel(int level) { this.deckLevel = level; }

    @ManyToOne
    @JoinColumn(name="SHIP_ID")
    public Ship getShip( ) { return ship; }
    public void setShip(Ship ship) { this.ship = ship; }
}
```

Although the Cabin bean doesn't define a relationship field for the Reservation, it does define a one-to-many bidirectional relationship for the Ship. The effect of exchanging relationship fields in a many-to-many unidirectional relationship is the same as in a many-to-many bidirectional relationship.

Many-to-many unidirectional XML mapping

Let's look at the XML mapping for this type of relationship:

```
<entity-mappings>
   <entity class="com.titan.domain.Reservation" access="PROPERTY">
      <attributes>
         <id name="id">
            <generated-value/>
         </id>
         <many-to-many name="cabins"
                       target-entity="com.titan.domain.Cabin"
                       fetch="LAZY">
            <join-table name="CABIN_RESERVATION">
               <join-column name="RESERVATION_ID"/>
               <inverse-join-column name="CABIN_ID"/>
            </join-table>
         </many-to-many>
      </attributes>
   </entity>
   <entity class="com.titan.domain.Cabin" access="PROPERTY">
      <attributes>
         <id name="id">
            <generated-value/>
         </id>
         <many-to-one name="ship"
                      target-entity="com.titan.domain.Ship"
                      fetch="LAZY">
            <join-column name="SHIP_ID"/>
         </many-to-one>
      </attributes>
   </entity>
</entity-mappings>
```

Default relationship mapping

If your persistence provider supports auto schema generation, you do not need to specify metadata like @JoinTable:

```
@Entity
public class Reservation implements java.io.Serializable {
    ...
    @ManyToMany
    public Set<Cabin> getCabins( ) { return cabins; }
    public void setCabins(Set<Cabin> cabins) { this.cabins = cabins; }
    ...
}
```

When you do not specify any database mapping for a unidirectional many-to-many relationship, the persistence provider creates the join table mapping for you. For our Reservation/Cabin relationship example, the following join table would be generated:

```
CREATE TABLE RESERVATION_CABIN
(
    RESERVATION_id INT,
    CABIN_id INT,
);
ALTER TABLE RESERVATION_CABIN ADD CONSTRAINT reservationREFcabin
   FOREIGN KEY (RESERVATION_id) REFERENCES RESERVATION (id);

ALTER TABLE RESERVATION_CABIN ADD CONSTRAINT reservationREFcabin2
   FOREIGN KEY (CABIN_id) REFERENCES CABIN (id);
```

The name of the join table created is a concatenation of the owning entity's table followed by an _ character followed by the table name of the related entity. The foreign-key columns are a concatenation of each entity's table name followed by an _ followed by the primary key column name of that entity. Foreign-key constraints are applied to both columns.

Mapping Collection-Based Relationships

The one-to-many and many-to-many examples we've seen so far have used the java.util.Collection and java.util.Set types. The Java Persistence specification also allows you to represent a relationship with a java.util.List or a java.util.Map.

Ordered List-Based Relationship

The java.util.List interface can express collection-based relationships. You do not need any special metadata if you want to use a List rather than a Set or Collection type. (In this case, the List actually gives you a bag semantic, an unordered collection that allows duplicates). A List type can give you the additional ability to order the returned relationship based on a specific set of criteria. This requires the additional metadata that is provided by the @javax.persistence.OrderBy annotation:

```
package javax.persistence;

@Target({METHOD, FIELD}) @Retention(RUNTIME)
public @interface OrderBy
{
   String value( ) default "";
}
```

The value( ) attribute allows you to declare partial EJB QL that specifies how you want the relationship to be ordered when it is fetched from the database. If the value( ) attribute is left empty, the List is sorted in ascending order based on the value of the primary key.

Let's take the Reservation/Customer relationship, which is a many-to-many bidirectional relationship, and have the customers attribute of Reservation return a List that is sorted alphabetically by the Customer entity's last name:

```
@Entity
public class Reservation implements java.io.Serializable {
    ...
    private List<Customer> customers = new ArrayList<Customer>( );
    ...
    @ManyToMany
    @OrderBy("lastName ASC")
    @JoinTable(name="RESERVATION_CUSTOMER"),
               joinColumns={@JoinColumn(name="RESERVATION_ID")},
               inverseJoinColumns={@JoinColumn(name="CUSTOMER_ID")})
    public List<Customer> getCustomers( ) { return customers; }
    public void setCustomers(Set customers);
    ...
}
```

"lastName ASC" tells the persistence provider to sort the Customer's lastName in ascending order. You can use ASC for ascending order and DESC for descending order. You can also specify additional restrictions like @OrderBy('lastname asc, firstname asc"). In this case, the list will be ordered by lastname, and for duplicates last names, it will be ordered by first name.

List XML mapping

Let's look at the XML mapping for this type of relationship:

```
<entity-mappings>
   <entity class="com.titan.domain.Reservation" access="PROPERTY">
      <attributes>
         <id name="id">
            <generated-value/>
         </id>
         <many-to-many name="customers"
                       target-entity="com.titan.domain.Customer"
                       fetch="LAZY">
            <order-by>lastName ASC</order-by>
            <join-table name="RESERVATION_CUSTOMER">
```

```
                <join-column name="RESERVATION_ID"/>
                <inverse-join-column name="CUSTOMER_ID"/>
             </join-table>
          </many-to-many>
       </attributes>
    </entity>
...
</entity-mappings>
```

Map-Based Relationship

The `java.util.Map` interface can be used to express collection-based relationships. In this case, the persistence provider creates a map with the key being a specific property of the related entity and the value being the entity itself. If you use a `java.util.Map`, you must use the `@javax.persistence.MapKey` annotation:

```
package javax.persistence;

@Target({METHOD, FIELD}) @Retention(RUNTIME)
public @interface MapKey
{
   String name( ) default "";
}
```

The `name( )` attribute is the name of the persistent property that you want to represent the key field of the map object. If you leave this blank, it is assumed you are using the primary key of the related entity as the key of the map.

For an example, let's use a map to represent the one-to-many unidirectional Customer/Phone relationship discussed earlier in this chapter:

```
@Entity
public class Customer implements java.io.Serializable {
    ...
    private Map<String, Phone> phoneNumbers = new HashMap<String, Phone>( );
    ...
    @OneToMany(cascade={CascadeType.ALL})
    @JoinColumn(name="CUSTOMER_ID")
    @MapKey(name="number")
    public Map<String, Phone> getPhoneNumbers( ) {
       return phoneNumbers;
    }
    public void setPhoneNumbers(Map<String, Phone> phones) {
        this.phoneNumbers = phones;
    }
}
```

In this example, the `phones` property of `Customer` will return a `java.util.Map` where the key is the `number` property of the Phone entity and the value is, of course, the Phone entity itself. There is no extra column to keep the map key since the map key is borrowed from the Phone entity.

Map XML mapping

Here's what the XML mapping would be for this example:

```
<entity-mappings>
   <entity class="com.titan.domain.Customer" access="PROPERTY">
      <attributes>
         <id name="id">
            <generated-value/>
         </id>
         <one-to-many name="phoneNumbers"
                      target-entity="com.titan.domain.Phone"
                      fetch="LAZY">
            <cascade-all/>
            <map-key name="number"/>
            <join-column name="CUSTOMER_ID"/>
         </one-to-many>
      </attributes>
   </entity>
...
</entity-mappings>
```

Detached Entities and FetchType

In Chapter 5, we discussed how managed entity instances become detached from a persistence context when the persistence context ends. Since these entity instances are no longer managed by any persistence context, they may have uninitialized properties or relationships. If you are returning these detached entities to your clients and basically using them as data transfer objects between the client and server, you need to fully understand the effects of accessing any uninitialized relationships.

When an entity instance becomes detached, its state may not be fully initialized because some of its persistent properties or relationships may be marked as lazily loaded in the mapping metadata. Each relationship annotation has a `fetch()` attribute that specifies whether the relationship property is loaded when the entity is queried. If the `fetch()` attribute is set to `FetchType.LAZY`, then the relationship is not initialized until it is traversed in your code:

```
Customer customer = entityManager.find(Customer.class, id);
customer.getPhoneNumbers().size();
```

Invoking the `size()` method of the `phoneNumbers` collection causes the relationship to be loaded from the database. It is important to note that this lazy initialization does not happen unless the entity bean is being managed by a persistence context. If the entity bean is detached, the specification is not clear on what actions the persistence provider should perform when accessing an unloaded relationship of a detached entity. Most persistence providers throw some kind of lazy instantiation exception when you call the accessor of the relationship or when you try to invoke an operation on the relationship of a detached entity:

```
Cruise detachedCruise = ...;
try
```

```
{
   int numReservations = detachedCruise.getReservations( ).size( );
}
catch (SomeVendorLazyInitializationException ex)
{
}
```

In this code, the application has received an instance of a detached Cruise entity and attempts to access the @OneToMany reservations relationship. Since the fetch( ) attribute of this relationship is LAZY, most vendor implementations will throw a vendor-specific exception. This lazy initialization problem can be overcome in two ways. The obvious way is just to navigate the needed relationships while the entity instance is still managed by a persistence context. The second way is to perform the fetch eagerly when you query the entity. In Chapter 9, you will see that the EJB QL query language has a FETCH JOIN operation that allows you to preinitialize selected relationships when you invoke a query.

How is the persistence provider able to throw an exception when accessing the relationship when the Cruise class is a plain Java class? Although not defined in the specification, the vendor has a few ways to implement this. One is through bytecode manipulation of the Cruise class. In Java EE, the application server is required to provide hooks for bytecode manipulation for persistence providers. In Java SE, the persistence provider may require an additional post-compilation step on your code base. Another way for vendors to implement this is to create a proxy class that inherits from Cruise and that reimplements all the accessor methods to add lazy initialization checking. For collection-based relationships, the persistence provider can just provide its own implementation of the collection and do the lazy check there. Whatever the implementation, make a note to discover what your persistence provider will do in the detached lazy initialization scenario so that your code can take appropriate measures to handle this exception.

Cascading

There is one annotation attribute that we have ignored so far: the cascade( ) attribute of the @OneToOne, @OneToMany, @ManyToOne, and @ManyToMany relationship annotations. This section discusses in detail the behavior that is applied when using the cascade( ) attribute.

When you perform an entity manager operation on an entity bean instance, you can automatically have the same operation performed on any relationship properties the entity may have. This is called *cascading*. For example, if you are persisting a new Customer entity with a new address and phone number, all you have to do is wire the object and the entity manager can automatically create the customer and its related entities, all in one persist( ) method call:

```
Customer cust = new Customer( );
customer.setAddress(new Address( ));
customer.getPhoneNumbers( ).add(new Phone( ));
```

```
// create them all in one entity manager invocation
entityManager.persist(cust);
```

With the Java Persistence specification, cascading can be applied to a variety of entity manager operations, including persist( ), merge( ), remove( ), and refresh( ). This feature is enabled by setting the javax.persistence.CascadeType of the relationship annotation's cascade( ) attribute. The CascadeType is defined as a Java enumeration:

```
public enum CascadeType
{
   ALL, PERSIST, MERGE, REMOVE, REFRESH
}
```

The ALL value represents all of the cascade operations. The remaining values represent individual cascade operations. The cascade( ) attribute is an array of the cascade operations you want applied to your related entities.

Let's look again at the one-to-one unidirectional relationship between the Customer and Address entities we discussed earlier in this chapter. As you can see, it has a CascadeType of both REMOVE and PERSIST:

```
package com.titan.domain;

@Entity
public class Customer implements java.io.Serializable {
   ...
   private Address homeAddress;

...
   @OneToOne(cascade={CascadeType.PERSIST, CascadeType.REMOVE})
   @JoinColumn(name="ADDRESS_ID")
   public Address getAddress( ) {
      return homeAddress;
   }
   public void setAddress(Address address) {
      this.homeAddress = address;
   }
```

Whenever you persist( ) a Customer and the Address entity associated with the Customer is also new, the Address is also persisted. If you remove( ) the Customer, the associated Address entity is also removed from the database. Let's look at this same example expressed in an XML mapping:

```
<entity-mappings>
   <entity class="com.titan.domain.Customer" access="PROPERTY">
      <attributes>
         <id name="id">
            <generated-value/>
         </id>
         <one-to-one name="address"
                     targetEntity="com.titan.domain.Address"
                     fetch="LAZY"
                     optional="true">
            <cascade-persist/>
```

```
            <cascade-remove/>
            <primary-key-join-column/>
         </one-to-one>
      </attributes>
   </entity>
</entity-mappings>
```

The <cascade-persist> and <cascade-remove> elements are declared as subelements of the <one-to-one> element to specify the cascade policy. You can also use <cascade-refresh> and <cascade-merge> as desired. <cascade-all> can be used when you want to apply all cascade types to the relationship.

We'll use this particular Customer/Address relationship example throughout this section to explain the details of cascading.

PERSIST

PERSIST has to deal with the creation of entities within the database. If we had a CascadeType of PERSIST on the Customer side of our one-to-one relationship, you would not have to persist your created Address as well. It would be created for you. The persistence provider will also execute the appropriate SQL INSERT statements in the appropriate order for you:

```
Customer cust = new Customer( );
Address address = new Address( );
cust.setAddress(address);

entityManager.persist(cust);
```

If you did not have a cascade policy of PERSIST, then you would have to call EntityManager.persist( ) on the address object as well.

MERGE

MERGE deals with entity synchronization, meaning inserts and, more importantly, updates. These aren't updates in the traditional sense. If you remember from previous chapters, we mentioned that objects could be detached from persistent management and serialized to a remote client, updates could be performed locally on that remote client, the object instance would be sent back to the server, and the changes would be merged back into the database. Merging is about synchronizing the state of a detached object instance back to persistent storage.

So, back to what MERGE means! MERGE is similar to PERSIST. If you have a cascade policy of MERGE, then you do not have to call EntityManager.merge( ) for the contained related entity:

```
cust.setName("William");
cust.getAddress( ).setCity("Boston");

entityManager.merge(cust);
```

In this example, when the cust variable is merged by the entity manager, the entity manager will cascade the merge to the contained address property and the city will also be updated in the database.

Another interesting thing about MERGE is that if you have added any new entities to a relationship that have not been created in the database, they will be persisted and created when the merge( ) happens:

```
Phone phone = new Phone( );
phone.setNumber("617-666-6666");

cust.getPhoneNumbers( ).add(phone);
entityManager.merge(cust);
```

In this example, we allocate a Phone and add it to a Customer's list of phone numbers. We then call merge( ) with the customer, and, since we have the MERGE CascadeType set on this relationship, the persistence provider will see that it is a new Phone entity and will create it within the database.

Remember that only the graph returned by the merge operation is in managed state, not the one passed as a parameter.

REMOVE

REMOVE is straightforward. In our Customer example, if you delete a Customer entity, its address will be deleted as well. This is exactly the same kind of functionality that is in EJB 2.1 CMP.

```
Customer cust = entityManager.find(Customer.class, 1);
entityManager.remove(cust);
```

REFRESH

REFRESH is similar to MERGE. Unlike merge, though, this only pertains to when EntityManager.refresh( ) is called. Refreshing doesn't update the database with changes in the object instance. Instead, it refreshes the object instance's state from the database. Again, the contained related entities would also be refreshed.

```
Customer cust ...;
entityManager.refresh(cust); // address would be refreshed too
```

So, if changes to the Customer's address were committed by a different transaction, the address property of the cust variable would be updated with these changes. This is useful in practice when an entity bean has some properties that are generated by the database (by triggers, for example). You can refresh the entity to read those generated properties. In this case, be sure to make those generated properties read-only from a persistence provider perspective, i.e., using the @Column(insertable=false, updatable=false).

ALL

`ALL` is a combination of all of the previous policies and is used for the purposes of simplicity.

When to Use Cascading

You don't always want to use cascading for every relationship you have. For instance, you would not want to remove the related Cruise or Customer when removing a Reservation entity from the database because these entities have a life span that is usually longer than the Reservation. You might not want to cascade merges because you may have fetched stale data from the database or simply not filled the relationship in one particular business operation. For performance reasons, you may also not want to refresh all the relationships an entity has because this would cause more round trips to the database. Be aware how your entities will be used before deciding on the cascade type. If you are unsure of their use, then you should turn off cascading entirely. Remember, cascading is simply a convenient tool for reducing the `EntityManager` API calls.

CHAPTER 8

Entity Inheritance

In order to be complete, an object to relational mapping engine must support inheritance hierarchies. The Java Persistence specification supports entity inheritance, polymorphic relationships/associations, and polymorphic queries. These features were completely missing in the older EJB CMP 2.1 specification.

In this chapter, we'll modify our Customer entity that we defined in earlier chapters to make it fit into an inheritance hierarchy. We'll have it extend a base class called `Person` and define an `Employee` class that extends a `Customer` class. Employees will be treated with a special discount when making reservations with Titan Cruises. Figure 8-1 shows this class hierarchy.

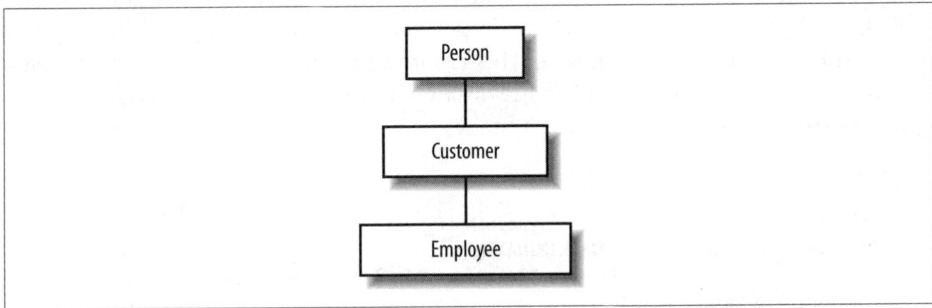

Figure 8-1. Customer class hierarchy

The Java Persistence specification provides three different ways to map an inheritance hierarchy to a relational database:

A single table per class hierarchy
: One table will have all properties of every class in the hierarchy.

A table per concrete class
: Each class will have a table dedicated to it, with all of its properties and the properties of its superclass mapped to this table.

A table per subclass
: Each class will have its own table. Each table will have only the properties that are defined in that particular class. These tables will not have properties of any superclass or subclass.

In this chapter, we'll use these three strategies to map the `Customer` class hierarchy defined in Figure 8-1.

Single Table per Class Hierarchy

In the single table per class hierarchy mapping strategy, one database table represents every class of a given hierarchy. In our example, the Person, Customer, and Employee entities are represented in the same table, as shown in the following code:

```
create table PERSON_HIERARCHY (
   id integer primary key not null,
   firstName varchar(255),
   lastName varchar(255),
   street varchar(255),
   city varchar(255),
   state varchar(255),
   zip varchar(255),
   employeeId integer,
   DISCRIMINATOR varchar(31) not null
);
```

As you can see, all the properties for the `Customer` class hierarchy are held in one table, `PERSON_HIERARCHY`. The single table per class hierarchy mapping also requires an additional discriminator column. This column identifies the type of entity being stored in a particular row of `PERSON_HIERARCHY`. Let's look at how the classes will use annotations to map this inheritance strategy:

```
@Entity
@Table(name="PERSON_HIERARCHY")
@Inheritance(strategy=InheritanceType.SINGLE_TABLE)
@DiscriminatorColumn(name="DISCRIMINATOR",
                     discriminatorType=DiscriminatorType.STRING)
@DiscriminatorValue("PERSON")
public class Person {
   private int id;
   private String firstName;
   private String lastName;

   @Id @GeneratedValue
   public int getId( ) { return id; }
   public void setId(int id) { this.id = id; }

   public String getFirstName( ) { return firstName; }
   public void setFirstName(String first) { this.firstName = first; }
```

```
    public String getLastName( ) { return lastName; }
    public void setLastName(String last) { this.lastName = last; }
}
```

The `@javax.persistence.Inheritance` annotation is used to define the persistence strategy for the inheritance relationship:

```
package javax.persistence;

@Target(TYPE) @Retention(RUNTIME)
public @interface Inheritance {
   InheritanceType strategy( ) default SINGLE_TABLE;
}

public enum InheritanceType {
   SINGLE_TABLE, JOINED, TABLE_PER_CLASS
}
```

The `strategy( )` attribute defines the inheritance mapping that we're using. Since we're using the single table per class hierarchy, the `SINGLE_TABLE` enum is applied. The `@Inheritance` annotation only has to be placed on the root of the class hierarchy, unless you are changing the mapping strategy of a subclass.

```
package javax.persistence;

@Target(TYPE) @Retention(RUNTIME)
public @interface DiscriminatorColumn
   String name( ) default "DTYPE";
   DiscriminatorType discriminatorType( ) default STRING;
   String columnDefinition( ) default "";
   int length( ) default 10;
}
```

Since one table is representing the entire class hierarchy, the persistence provider needs some way to identify which class the row in the database maps to. It determines this by reading the value from the discriminator column. The `@javax.persistence.DiscriminatorColumn` annotation identifies which column in our table will store the discriminator's value. The `name( )` attribute identifies the name of the column, and the `discriminatorType( )` attribute specifies what type the discriminator column will be. It can be a `STRING`, `CHAR`, or `INTEGER`. For our `Customer` class hierarchy mapping, you do not have to specify the `discriminatorType( )`, as it defaults to being a `STRING`. If you're OK with the default column name, you can remove the `@DiscriminatorColumn` entirely.

```
package javax.persistence;

@Target(TYPE) @Retention(RUNTIME)
public @interface DiscriminatorValue {
   String value( )
}
```

The @javax.persistence.DiscriminatorValue annotation defines what value the discriminator column will take for rows that store an instance of a Person class. You can leave this attribute undefined if you want to. In that case, the persistence manager would generate a value for you automatically. This value would be vendor-specific if the DiscriminatorType is CHAR or INTEGER. The entity name is used by default when a type of STRING is specified. It is good practice to specify the value for CHAR and INTEGER values.

The rest of the class hierarchy is quite easy. The only specific inheritance metadata you have to specify is the discriminator's value, if you want a value other than the default:

```
@Entity
@DiscriminatorValue("CUST")
public class Customer extends Person {
   private String street;
   private String city;
   private String state;
   private String zip;

   public String getStreet( ) { return street; }
   public void setStreet(String street) { this.street = street; }
...
}


// use the default discriminator value
@Entity
public class Employee extends Customer {
   private int employeeId;

   public int getEmployeeId( ) { return employeeId; }
   public void setEmployeeId(int id) { employeeId = id; }
}
```

So, in this example, the Customer entity sets the discriminator column value to be CUST, using the @DiscriminatorValue annotation. For the Employee entity, the discriminator column's value defaults to Employee, which is the entity name of the Employee bean class.

Now that you have a good understanding of this mapping type, let's look at how we would map this using XML rather than annotations:

```
<entity-mappings>
   <entity class="com.titan.domain.Person">
      <inheritance strategy="SINGLE_TABLE"/>
      <discriminator-column name="DISCRIMINATOR"
                            discriminator-type="STRING"/>
      <discriminator-value>PERSON</discriminator-value>
      <attributes>
         <id>
```

```
            <generated-value/>
         </id>
      </attributes>
   </entity>
   <entity class="com.titan.domain.Customer">
      <discriminator-value>CUST</discriminator-value>
   </entity>
   <entity class="com.titan.domain.Employee"/>
</entity-mappings>
```

Advantages

The SINGLE_TABLE mapping strategy is the simplest to implement and performs better than all the inheritance strategies. There is only one table to administer and deal with. The persistence engine does not have to do any complex joins, unions, or subselects when loading the entity or when traversing a polymorphic relationship, because all data is stored in one table.

Disadvantages

One huge disadvantage of this approach is that all columns of subclass properties must be nullable. So, if you need or want to have any NOT NULL constraints defined on these columns, you cannot do so. Also, because subclass property columns may be unused, the SINGLE_TABLE strategy is not normalized.

Table per Concrete Class

In the table per concrete class strategy, a database table is defined for each concrete class in the hierarchy. Each table has columns representing its properties, and all properties of any superclasses.

```
create table Person (
   id integer primary key not null,
   firstName varchar(255),
   lastName varchar(255),
);

create table Customer (
   id integer primary key not null,
   firstName varchar(255),
   lastName varchar(255),
   street varchar(255),
   city varchar(255),
   state varchar(255),
   zip varchar(255),
);
```

```
create table Employee (
   id integer primary key not null,
   firstName varchar(255),
   lastName varchar(255),
   street varchar(255),
   city varchar(255),
   state varchar(255),
   zip varchar(255),
   employeeId integer,
);
```

One major difference between this strategy and the SINGLE_TABLE strategy is that no discriminator column is needed in the database schema. Also notice that each table contains every persistent property in the hierarchy. Let's now look at how we map this strategy with annotations:

```
@Entity
@Inheritance(strategy=InheritanceType.TABLE_PER_CLASS)
public class Person {
...
}

@Entity
public class Customer extends Person {
...
}

@Entity
public class Employee extends Customer {
...
}
```

Notice that the only inheritance metadata required is the InheritanceType, and this is needed on only the base Person class.

Let's look at the XML mapping for this strategy type:

```
<entity-mappings>
   <entity class="com.titan.domain.Person">
      <inheritance strategy="TABLE_PER_CLASS"/>
      <attributes>
         <id>
            <generated-value/>
         </id>
      </attributes>
   </entity>
   <entity class="com.titan.domain.Customer"/>
   <entity class="com.titan.domain.Employee"/>
</entity-mappings>
```

Like their annotation counterparts, the metadata you have to describe is pretty sparse if you rely on default attribute mappings. All we need is the <inheritance> element defined with TABLE_PER_CLASS in the root of the class hierarchy.

Advantages

The advantage to this approach over the SINGLE_TABLE strategy is that you can define constraints on subclass properties. Another plus is that it might be easier to map a legacy, preexisting schema using this strategy.

Disadvantages

This strategy is not normalized, as it has redundant columns in each of its tables for each of the base class's properties. Also, to support this type of mapping, the persistence manager has to do some funky things. One way it could be implemented is for the container to use multiple queries when loading an entity or polymorphic relationship. This is a huge performance hit because the container has to do multiple round trips to the database. Another way a container could implement this strategy is to use SQL UNIONs. This still would not be as fast as the SINGLE_TABLE strategy, but it would perform much better than a multiselect implementation. The downside to an SQL UNION is that not all relational databases support this SQL feature. It is probably not wise to pick this strategy when developing your entity beans, unless you absolutely have to.

Table per Subclass

In the table per subclass mapping, each subclass has its own table, but this table contains only the properties that are defined on that particular class. In other words, it is similar to the TABLE_PER_CLASS strategy, except the schema is normalized. This is also called the JOINED strategy.

```
create table Person (
   id integer primary key not null,
   firstName varchar(255),
   lastName varchar(255),
);

create table Customer (
   id integer primary key not null,
   street varchar(255),
   city varchar(255),
   state varchar(255),
   zip varchar(255),
);

create table Employee (
   EMP_PK integer primary key not null,
   employeeId integer
);
```

When the persistence manager loads an entity that is a subclass or traverses a polymorphic relationship, it does an SQL join on all the tables in the hierarchy. In this mapping, there must be a column in each table that can be used to join each table. In our example, the EMPLOYEE, CUSTOMER, and PERSON tables share the same primary-key values. The annotation mapping is quite simple:

```
@Entity
@Inheritance(strategy=InheritanceType.JOINED)
public class Person {
...
}

@Entity
public class Customer extends Person {
...
}

@Entity
@PrimaryKeyJoinColumn(name="EMP_PK")
public class Employee extends Customer {
...
}
```

The persistence manager needs to know which columns in each table will be used to perform a join when loading an entity with a JOINED inheritance strategy. The @javax.persistence.PrimaryKeyJoinColumn annotation can be used to describe this metadata:

```
package javax.persistence;

@Target({TYPE, METHOD, FIELD})
public @interface PrimaryKeyJoinColumn
   String name( ) default "";
   String referencedColumnName( ) default "";
   String columnDefinition( ) default "";
}
```

The name( ) attribute refers to the column you will perform a join on that is contained in the current table. It defaults to the primary-key column of the superclass's table. The referencedColumnName( ) is the column that will be used to perform the join from the superclass's table. It can be any column in the superclass's table, but it defaults to its primary key. If the primary-key column names are identical between the base and subclasses, then this annotation is not needed. For instance, the Customer entity does not need the @PrimaryKeyJoinColumn annotation. The Employee class has a different primary-key column name than the tables of its superclasses, so the @PrimaryKeyJoinColumn annotation is required. If class hierarchy uses a composite key, there is a @javax.persistence.PrimaryKeyJoinColumns annotation that can describe multiple join columns:

```
package javax.persistence;

@Target({TYPE, METHOD, FIELD})
public @interface PrimaryKeyJoinColumns {
   @PrimaryKeyJoinColumns[] value( );
}
```

Some persistence providers require a discriminator column for this mapping type. Most do not. Make sure to check your persistence provider implementation to see whether it is required.

Let's look at the XML mapping for this strategy type:

```
<entity-mappings>
   <entity class="com.titan.domain.Person">
      <inheritance strategy="JOINED"/>
      <attributes>
         <id>
            <generated-value/>
         </id>
      </attributes>
   </entity>
   <entity class="com.titan.domain.Customer"/>
   <entity class="com.titan.domain.Employee">
      <primary-key-join-column name="EMP_PK"/>
   </entity>
</entity-mappings>
```

The `<inheritance>` element is used to define that the `Person` class is part of an inheritance hierarchy mapped by the `JOINED` strategy. Then, for `Employee`, we need to define that its primary-key name is different from `Person`'s primary-key column.

Advantages

It is better to compare this mapping to other strategies to describe its advantages. Although it is not as fast as the `SINGLE_TABLE` strategy, you are able to define `NOT NULL` constraints on any column of any table and your model is normalized.

This mapping is better than the `TABLE_PER_CLASS` strategy for two reasons. One, the relational database model is completely normalized. Two, it performs better than the `TABLE_PER_CLASS` strategy if `SQL UNION`s are not supported.

Disadvantages

It does not perform as well as the `SINGLE_TABLE` strategy.

Mixing Strategies

The persistence specification currently makes mixing inheritance strategies optional. The rules for mixing strategies in an inheritance hierarchy may be defined in future versions of the spec.

Nonentity Base Classes

The inheritance mappings we described so far in this chapter concerned a class hierarchy of entity beans. Sometimes, however, you need to inherit from a nonentity superclass. This superclass may be an existing class in your domain model that you do not want to make an entity. The `@javax.persistence.MappedSuperclass` annotation allows you to define this kind of mapping. Let's modify our example class hierarchy and change `Person` into a mapped superclass:

```
@MappedSuperclass
public class Person {
   @Id @GeneratedValue
   public int getId( ) { return id; }
   public void setId(int id) { this.id = is; }

   public String getFirstName( ) { return firstName; }
   public void setFirstName(String first) { this.firstName = first; }

   public String getLastName( ) { return lastName; }
   public void setLastName(String last) { this.lastName = last; }
}

@Entity
@Table(name="CUSTOMER")
@Inheritance(strategy=InheritanceType.JOINED)
@AttributeOverride(name="lastname", column=@Column(name="SURNAME"))
public class Customer extends Person {
...
}

@Entity
@Table(name="EMPLOYEE")
@PrimaryKeyJoinColumn(name="EMP_PK")
public class Employee extends Customer {
...
}
```

Since it is not an entity, the mapped superclass does not have an associated table. Any subclass inherits the persistence properties of the base class. You can override any mapped property of the mapped class by using the `@javax.persistence.AttributeOverride` annotation (see Chapter 6). Here is how the database schema of the modified hierarchy would look:

```
create table CUSTOMER (
   id integer primary key not null,
   firstName varchar(255),
   SURNAME varchar(255),
   street varchar(255),
   city varchar(255),
   state varchar(255),
   zip varchar(255),
);

create table EMPLOYEE (
   EMP_PK integer primary key not null,
   employeeId integer
);
```

As you can see, the `Customer` entity class inherits the `id`, `firstName`, and `lastName` properties. Since an `@AttributeOverride` was specified, the column name for `lastName` will be `SURNAME`. This mapping strategy is useful for when you want to have a base class for an entity and you do not want to force it to be an entity itself.

You can have `@MappedSuperclass` annotated classes in between two `@Entity` annotated classes in a given hierarchy. Also, nonannotated classes (i.e., not annotated with `@Entity` nor `@MappedSuperclass`), are completely ignored by the persistence provider.

Let's look at the XML mapping:

```
<entity-mappings>
   <mapped-superclass class="com.titan.domain.Person">
      <attributes>
         <id>
            <generated-value/>
         </id>
      </attributes>
   </mapped-superclass>
   </entity>
   <entity class="com.titan.domain.Customer">
      <inheritance strategy="JOINED"/>
      <attribute-override name="lastName">
         <column name="SURNAME"/>
      </attribute-override>
   </entity>
   <entity class="com.titan.domain.Employee">
      <primary-key-join-column name="EMP_PK"/>
   </entity>
</entity-mappings>
```

The `<mapped-superclass>` element is a direct subelement of `<entity-mappings>` and declares all nonentity superclasses. The `<attribute-override>` element overrides any default column mappings that are declared in the superclass.

CHAPTER 9

Queries and EJB QL

Querying is a fundamental feature of all relational databases. It allows you to pull complex reports, calculations, and information about intricately related objects from persistence storage. Queries in Java Persistence are done using both the EJB QL query language and native Structured Query Language (SQL).

EJB QL is a declarative query language similar to the SQL used in relational databases, but it is tailored to work with Java objects rather than a relational schema. To execute queries, you reference the properties and relationships of your entity beans rather than the underlying tables and columns these objects are mapped to. When an EJQ QL query is executed, the entity manager uses the information you provided through the mapping metadata, discussed in the previous two chapters, and automatically translates it to one (or several) native SQL query. This generated native SQL is then executed through a JDBC driver directly on your database. Since EJB QL is a query language that represents Java objects, it is portable across vendor database implementations because the entity manager handles the conversion to raw SQL for you.

The EJB QL language is easy for developers to learn yet precise enough to be interpreted into native database code. This rich and flexible query language empowers developers while executing in fast native code at runtime. Plus, because EJB QL is object-oriented, queries are usually much more compact and readable than their SQL equivalent. EJB QL existed in the EJB 2.1 specification, and it is really the only feature that survived in the new release. Although it was well-formed, EJB QL in EJB 2. 1 was incomplete, forcing developers to escape to JDBC or write really inefficient code. EJB QL has been greatly improved and expanded to be more parallel to SQL and should now meet most of your needs. Things like projection, `GROUP BY`, and `HAVING` have been added, as well as bulk updates and deletes.

Sometimes, though, EJB QL is not enough. Because it is a portable query language, it cannot always take advantage of specific proprietary features of your database vendor. EJB QL does not allow you to execute stored procedures, for instance. The EJB 3.0 Expert Group foresaw the need for this and has provided an API to map native SQL calls to your entity beans.

EJB QL and native SQL queries are executed through the javax.persistence.Query interface. The Query interface is very analogous to the java.sql.PreparedStatement interface. This Query API gives you methods for paging your result set, as well as passing Java parameters to your query. Queries can be predeclared through annotations or XML, or created dynamically at runtime through EntityManager APIs.

Query API

A query in Java Persistence is a full-blown Java interface that you obtain at runtime from the entity manager:

```
package javax.persistence;

public interface Query {
   public List getResultList( );
   public Object getSingleResult( );
   public int executeUpdate( );
   public Query setMaxResults(int maxResult);
   public Query setFirstResult(int startPosition);
   public Query setHint(String hintName, Object value);
   public Query setParameter(String name, Object value);
   public Query setParameter(String name, Date value, TemporalType temporalType);
   public Query setParameter(String name, Calendar value, TemporalType temporalType);
   public Query setParameter(int position, Object value);
   public Query setParameter(int position, Date value, TemporalType temporalType);
   public Query setParameter(int position, Calendar value, TemporalType
temporalType);
   public Query setFlushMode(FlushModeType flushMode);
}
```

Queries are created using these EntityManager methods:

```
package javax.persistence;

public interface EntityManager {
    public Query createQuery(String ejbqlString);
    public Query createNamedQuery(String name);
    public Query createNativeQuery(String sqlString);
    public Query createNativeQuery(String sqlString, Class resultClass);
    public Query createNativeQuery(String sqlString, String resultSetMapping);
}
```

Let's first look at using EntityManager.createQuery( ) to create a query dynamically at runtime:

```
try {
   Query query = entityManager.creatQuery(
            "from Customer c where c.firstName='Bill' and c.lastName='Burke'");
   Customer cust = (Customer)query.getSingleResult( );
} catch (EntityNotFoundException notFound) {
} catch (NonUniqueResultException nonUnique) {
}
```

The previous query looks for a single, unique Customer entity named Bill Burke. The query is executed when the getSingleResult( ) method is called. This method expects that the call will return only one result. If no result is returned, then the method throws a javax.persistence.EntityNotFoundException runtime exception. If more than one result is found, then a javax.persistence.NonUniqueResultException runtime exception is thrown. Since both of these exceptions are RuntimeExceptions, the example code is not required to have a full *try/catch* block.

There is a good chance that the NonUniqueResultException would be thrown by this example. Believe it or not, there are a lot of Bill Burkes in the world (try Googling him), and this name seems to be as common as John Smith is in the U.S. You can change the query to use the getResultList( ) method to obtain a collection of results:

```
Query query = entityManager.creatQuery(
             "from Customer c where c.firstName='Bill' and c.lastName='Burke'");
java.util.List bills = query.getResultList( );
```

The getResultList( ) method does not throw an exception if there are no Bill Burkes. The returned list would just be empty.

Parameters

Much like a java.sql.PreparedStatement in JDBC, EJB QL allows you to specify parameters in query declarations so that you can reuse and execute the query multiple times on different sets of parameters. Two syntaxes are provided: named parameters and positional parameters. Let's modify our earlier Customer query to take both last name and first name as named parameters:

```
public List findByName(String first, String last) {
   Query query = entityManager.createQuery(
             "from Customer c where c.firstName=:first and c.lastName=:last");
   query.setParameter("first", first);
   query.setParameter("last", last);
   return query.getResultList( );
}
```

The : character followed by the parameter name is used in EJB QL statements to identify a named parameter. The setParameter( ) method in this example takes the name of the parameter first, and then the actual value. EJB QL also supports positional parameters. Let's modify the previous example to see this mode in action:

```
public List findByName(String first, String last) {
   Query query = entityManager.createQuery(
             "from Customer c where c.firstName=?1 and c.lastName=?2");
   query.setParameter(1, first);
   query.setParameter(2, last);
   return query.getResultList( );
}
```

Instead of a string named parameter, setParameter( ) also takes a numeric parameter position. The ? character is used instead of the : character that is used with named parameters.

Using named parameters over positional parameters is recommended as the EJB QL code becomes self-documenting. This is especially useful when working with predeclared queries.

Date Parameters

If you need to pass java.util.Date or java.util.Calendar parameters into a query, you need to use special setParameter methods:

```
package javax.persistence;

public enum TemporalType {
     DATE, //java.sql.Date
     TIME, //java.sql.Time
     TIMESTAMP //java.sql.Timestamp
}

public interface Query {
   Query setParameter(String name, java.util.Date value, TemporalType temporalType);
   Query setParameter(String name, Calendar value, TemporalType temporalType);

   Query setParameter(int position, Date value, TemporalType temporalType);
   Query setParameter(int position, Calendar value, TemporalType temporalType);
}
```

A Date or Calendar object can represent a real date, a time of day, or a numeric timestamp. Because these object types can represent different things at the same time, you need to tell your Query object how it should use these parameters. The javax.persistence.TemporalType passed in as a parameter to the setParameter( ) method tells the Query interface what database type to use when converting the java.util.Date or java.util.Calendar parameter to a native SQL type.

Paging Results

Sometimes an executed query returns too many results. For instance, maybe we're displaying a list of customers on a web page. The web page can display only so many customers, and maybe there are thousands or even millions of customers in the database. The Query API has two built-in functions to solve this type of scenario: setMaxResults( ) and setFirstResult( ):

```
public List getCustomers(int max, int index) {
   Query query = entityManager.createQuery("from Customer c");
   return query.setMaxResults(max).
                setFirstResult(index).
                getResultList( );
}
```

The getCustomers( ) method executes a query that obtains all customers from the database. We limit the number of customers it returns by using the setMaxResults( ) method, passing in the max method parameter. The method is also designed so that you can define an arbitrary set of results that you want returned by the execution of the query. The setFirstResult( ) method tells the query what position in the executed query's result set you want returned. So, if you had a max result of 3 and a first result of 5, customers 5, 6, and 7 would be returned. We set this value in the getCustomers( ) method with the index parameter. Let's take this method and write a code fragment that lists all customers in the database:

```
List results;
int first = 0;
int max = 10;

do {
   results = getCustomers(max, first);
   Iterator it = results.iterator( );
   while (it.hasNext( )) {
      Customer c = (Customer)it.next( );
      System.out.println(c.getFirstName() + " " + c.getLastName( ));
   }
   entityManager.clear( );
   first = first + results.getSize( );
} while (results.size( ) > 0);
```

In this example, we loop through all customers in the database and output their first and last names to the system output stream. If we had thousands or even millions of customers in the database, we could quickly run out of memory, as each execution of the getCustomers( ) method would return customers that were still managed by the entity manager. So, after we are finished outputting a block of customers, we call EntityManager.clear( ) to detach these customers and let them be garbage-collected by the Java VM. Use this pattern when you need to deal with a lot of entity objects within the same transaction.

Hints

Some Java Persistence vendors will provide additional add-on features that you can take advantage of when executing a query. For instance, the JBoss EJB 3.0 implementation allows you to define a timeout for the query. These types of add-on features can be specified as hints using the setHint( ) method on the query. Here's an example of defining a JBoss query timeout using hints:

```
Query query = manager.createQuery("from Customer c");
query.setHint("org.hibernate.timeout", 1000);
```

The setHint( ) method takes a string name and an arbitrary object parameter.

FlushMode

In Chapter 5, we talked about flushing and flush modes. Sometimes you would like a different flush mode to be enforced for the duration of a query. For instance, maybe a query wants to make sure that the entity manager does not flush before the query is executed (since the default value implies that the entity manager can). The `Query` interface provides a `setFlushMode()` method for this particular purpose:

```
Query query = manager.createQuery("from Customer c");
query.setFlushMode(FlushModeType.COMMIT);
```

In this example, we're telling the persistence provider that we do not want the query to do any automatic flushing before this particular query is executed. Using this commit mode can be dangerous if some correlated dirty entities are in the persistence context. You might return wrong entities from your query. Therefore, it is recommended that you use the `FlushModeType.AUTO`.

EJB QL

Now that you have a basic understanding of how to work with `Query` objects, you can learn what features are available to you for creating your own EJB QL queries. EJB QL is expressed in terms of the abstract persistence schema of an entity: its abstract schema name, basic properties, and relationship properties. EJB QL uses the abstract schema names to identify beans, the basic properties to specify values, and the relationship properties to navigate across relationships.

To discuss EJB QL, we will use the relationships among the Customer, Address, CreditCard, Cruise, Ship, Reservation, and Cabin entities defined in Chapter 7. Figure 9-1 is a class diagram that shows the direction and cardinality (multiplicity) of the relationships among these beans.

Abstract Schema Names

The abstract schema name can be defined by metadata or it can default to a specific value. It defaults to the unqualified name of the entity bean class if the `name()` attribute is not specified when declaring the `@Entity` annotation.

In the following example, the `@Entity.name()` attribute is not specified on the `Customer` bean class, so `Customer` is used to reference the entity within EJB QL calls:

```
package com.titan.domain;

@Entity
public class Customer {...}

entityManager.createQuery("SELECT c FROM Customer AS c");
```

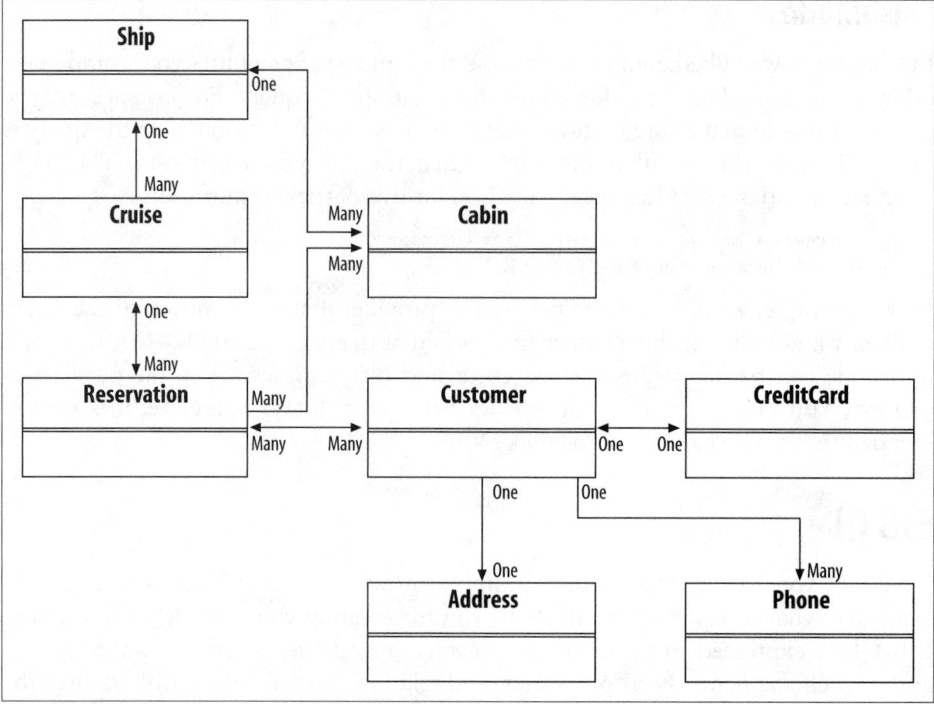

Figure 9-1. Titan Cruises class diagram

In the following example, since the `@Entity.name()` attribute is defined, you would reference Customer entities in EJB QL as `Cust`:

```
package com.titan.domain;

@Entity(name="Cust")
public class Customer {...}

entityManager.createQuery("SELECT c FROM Cust AS c");
```

Simple Queries

The simplest EJB QL statement has no `WHERE` clause and only one abstract schema type. For example, you could define a query method to select all Customer beans:

```
SELECT OBJECT( c ) FROM Customer AS c
```

The `FROM` clause determines which entity bean types will be included in the `SELECT` statement (i.e., it provides the *scope* of the select). In this case, the `FROM` clause declares the type to be `Customer`, which is the abstract schema name of the Customer entity. The `AS c` part of the clause assigns `c` as the identifier of the Customer entity. This is similar to SQL, which allows an identifier to be associated with a table. Identifiers can be any length and follow the same rules that are applied to field names in the Java programming language. However, identifiers cannot be the same as existing abstract schema name values. In addition, identification variable names are *not* case-sensitive, so an identifier of `customer` would be in conflict with an abstract schema name of `Customer`. For example, the following statement is illegal because `Customer` is the abstract schema name of the Customer EJB:

```
SELECT OBJECT( customer ) FROM Customer AS customer
```

The `AS` operator is optional, but it is used in this book to help make the EJB QL statements clearer. The following two statements are equivalent:

```
SELECT OBJECT(c) FROM Customer AS c

SELECT c FROM Customer c
```

The `SELECT` clause determines the type of any values that are returned. In this case, the statement returns the Customer entity bean, as indicated by the `c` identifier.

The `OBJECT( )` operator is optional and is a relic requirement of the EJB 2.1 spec. It is there for backward compatibility.

Identifiers cannot be EJB QL reserved words. In Java Persistence, the following words are reserved: `SELECT`, `FROM`, `WHERE`, `UPDATE`, `DELETE`, `JOIN`, `OUTER`, `INNER`, `GROUP`, `BY`, `HAVING`, `FETCH`, `DISTINCT`, `OBJECT`, `NULL`, `TRUE`, `FALSE`, `NOT`, `AND`, `OR`, `BETWEEN`, `LIKE`, `IN`, `AS`, `UNKNOWN`, `EMPTY`, `MEMBER`, `OF`, `IS`, `AVG`, `MAX`, `MIN`, `SUM`, `COUNT`, `ORDER ASC`, `DESC`, `MOD`, `UPPER`, `LOWER`, `TRIM`, `POSITION`, `CHARACTER_LENGTH`, `CHAR_LENGTH`, `BIT_LENGTH`, `CURRENT_TIME`, `CURRENT_DATE`, `CURRENT_TIMESTAMP`, and `NEW`. It's a good practice to avoid all SQL reserved words, because you never know which ones will be used by future versions of EJB QL. You can find more information in the appendix of *SQL in a Nutshell* (O'Reilly).

Selecting Entity and Relationship Properties

EJB QL allows `SELECT` clauses to return any number of basic or relationship properties. For example, we can define a simple `SELECT` statement to return the first and last names of all of Titan Cruises' customers:

```
SELECT c.firstName, c.lastName FROM Customer AS c
```

The `SELECT` clause uses a simple path to select the Customer entity's `firstName` and `lastName` properties as the return type. The persistence property names are identified by the access type of your entity bean class, regardless of whether you've applied your mapping annotations on a get or set method or on the member fields of the class.

If you use get or set methods to specify your persistent properties, then the property name is extracted from the method name. The get part of the method name is removed, and the first character of the remaining string is lowercase:

```
@Entity
public class Customer {
   private ind id;
```

```
    private String first;
    private String last;

    @Id
    public int getId( ) { return id; }
    public String getFirstName( ) { return first; }
    public String getLastName( ) { return first; }
```

In this example, we are using get and set methods to define our persistent properties. The SELECT clause would look like this:

```
SELECT c.firstName, c.lastName FROM Customer AS c
```

If you are mapping your entity directly on the member fields of your bean class, then the field name is used in the SELECT clause:

```
@Entity
public class Customer {
   @Id private int id;
   private String first;
   private String last;
}
```

Our example EJB QL statement would need to be rewritten with the changed property names first and last:

```
SELECT c.first, c.last FROM Customer AS c
```

When a query returns more than one item, you must use the Query.getResultList( ) method. If the SELECT clause queries more than one column or entity, the results are aggregated in an object array (Object[]) in the java.util.List returned by getResultList( ). The following code shows how to access the returned results:

```
Query query = manager.createQuery(
              "SELECT c.firstName, c.lastName FROM Customer AS c");
List results = query.getResultList( );
Iterator it = results.iterator( );
while (it.hasNext( )) {
   Object[] result = (Object[])it.next( );
   String first = (String)result[0];
   String last = (String)result[1];
}
```

You can also use single-valued relationship field types in simple select statements. The following EJB QL statement selects all CreditCards from their related Customer entities:

```
SELECT c.creditCard FROM Customer AS c
```

In this case, the EJB QL statement uses a path to navigate from the Customers to their creditCard relationship fields. The creditCard identifier is obtained by the same access type rules for basic properties.

Paths can be as long as required. It's common to use paths that navigate over one or more relationship fields to end at either a basic or a relationship property. For example, the following EJB QL statement selects all the `city` fields of all the Addresses in each Customer:

```
SELECT c.address.city  FROM Customer AS c
```

In this case, the path uses the abstract schema name of the Customer, the Customer's `address` relationship field, and the Address's `city` field.

To illustrate more complex paths, we'll need to expand the class diagram. Figure 9-2 shows that the CreditCard is related to a CreditCompany that has its own Address.

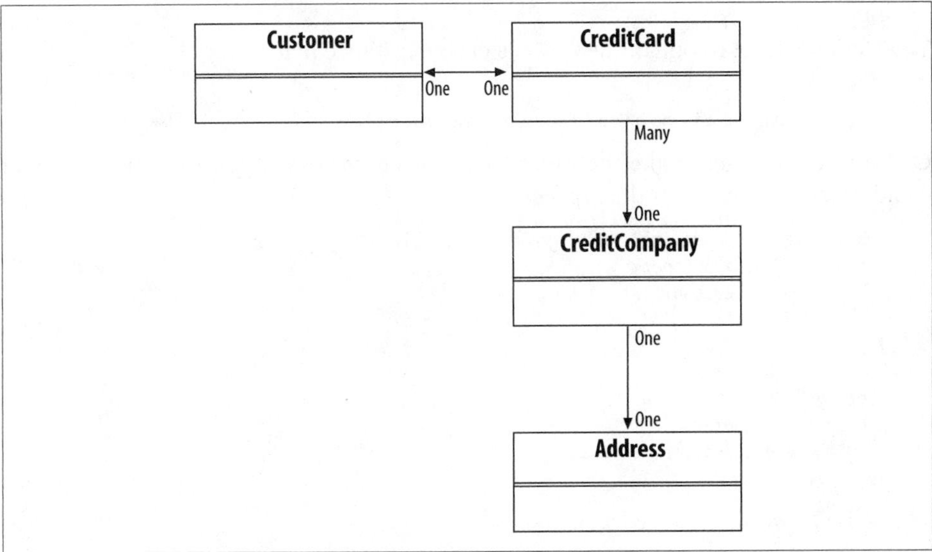

Figure 9-2. Expanded class diagram for CreditCard

Using these relationships, we can specify a more complex path that navigates from the Customer to the CreditCompany to the Address. Here's an EJB QL statement that selects the addresses of all the credit card companies used by Titan's customers:

```
SELECT c.creditCard.creditCompany.address FROM Customer AS c
```

The EJB QL statement could also navigate all the way to the Address bean's fields. The following statement selects all the cities in which the credit card companies that distribute credit cards used by Titan's customers are based:

```
SELECT c.creditCard.creditCompany.address.city FROM Customer AS c
```

Note that these EJB QL statements return `address` relationship properties or `city` properties only for those credit card companies responsible for cards owned by Titan's customers. The address information of any credit card companies whose cards are not currently used by Titan's customers won't be included in the results.

Paths cannot navigate beyond persistent properties. For example, imagine that the Address uses a ZipCode class as its zip property and this property is stored as a byte stream in the database:

```
public class ZipCode implements java.io.Serializable {
    public int mainCode;
    public int codeSuffix;
    ...
}

@Entity
public class Address {
   private ZipCode zip;
}
```

You can't navigate to one of the ZipCode class's instance fields:

```
// this is illegal
SELECT c.address.zip.mainCode FROM Customer AS c
```

Of course, you could make the ZipCode class @Embeddable. If you did this, then you could obtain properties of the ZipCode class:

```
public class ZipCode implements java.io.Serializable {
    public int mainCode;
    public int codeSuffix;
    ...
}

@Entity
public class Address {
   @Embedded private ZipCode zip;
}
```

This EJB QL would now be legal:

```
// @Embedded makes this legal now
SELECT c.address.zip.mainCode FROM Customer AS c
```

It's illegal to navigate across a collection-based relationship field. The following EJB QL statement is illegal, even though the path ends in a single-type relationship field:

```
// this is illegal
SELECT c.reservations.cruise FROM Customer AS c
```

If you think about it, this limitation makes sense. You can't use a navigation operator (.) in Java to access elements of a java.util.Collection object. For example, if getReservations( ) returns a java.util.Collection type, this statement is illegal:

```
// this is illegal in the Java programming language
customer.getReservations( ).getCruise( );
```

Referencing the elements of a collection-based relationship field is possible, but it requires the use of an IN or JOIN operator and an identification assignment in the FROM clause.

Constructor Expressions

One of the most powerful features of EJB QL is the ability to specify a constructor within the SELECT clause that can allocate plain Java objects (nonentities) and pass in columns you select into that constructor. For example, let's say we want to aggregate first and last names from our Customer entity into a plain Java object called Name:

```
public class Name {
   private String first;
   private String last;

   public Name(String first, String last) {
      this.first = first;
      this.last = last;
   }

   public String getFirst( ) { return this.first; }
   public String getLast( ) { return this.last; }
}
```

We can actually have our query return a list of Name classes instead of a plain list of strings. We do this by calling the constructor of Name directly within our query:

```
SELECT new com.titan.domain.Name(c.firstName, c.lastName) FROM Customer c
```

The Query object will automatically allocate an instance of Name for each row returned, passing in the firstName and lastName columns as arguments to the Name's constructor. This feature is incredibly useful for generating typed reports and can save you a lot of typing.

The IN Operator and INNER JOIN

Many relationships between entity beans are collection-based, and being able to access and select beans from these relationships is important. We've seen that it is illegal to select elements directly from a collection-based relationship. To overcome this limitation, EJB QL introduces the IN operator, which allows an identifier to represent individual elements in a collection-based relationship field.

The following query uses the IN operator to select the elements from a collection-based relationship. It returns all the reservations of all the customers:

```
SELECT r
FROM Customer AS c, IN( c.reservations ) r
```

The IN operator assigns the individual elements in the reservations property to the r identifier. Once we have an identifier to represent the individual elements of the collection, we can reference them directly and even select them in the EJB QL statement. We can also use the element identifier in path expressions. For example, the following statement selects every cruise for which Titan's customers have made reservations:

```
SELECT r.cruise
FROM Customer AS c, IN( c.reservations ) r
```

The identifiers assigned in the FROM clause are evaluated from left to right. Once you declare an identifier, you can use it in subsequent declarations in the FROM clause. The c identifier, which was declared first, was subsequently used in the IN operator to define the r identifier.

This query can also be expressed as an INNER JOIN:

```
SELECT r.cruise
FROM Customer c INNER JOIN c.reservations r
```

The INNER JOIN syntax parallels the SQL language much better and is more intuitive for developers coming from the relational world.

Identification chains can become very long. The following statement uses two IN operators to navigate two collection-based relationships and a single relationship. While not necessarily useful, this statement demonstrates how a query can use IN operators across many relationships.

```
SELECT cbn.ship
FROM Customer AS c, IN ( c.reservations ) r,
IN( r.cabins ) cbn
```

Alternatively, again, the INNER JOIN syntax could be used:

```
SELECT cbn.ship
FROM Customer c INNER JOIN c.reservations r
INNER JOIN r.cabins cbn
```

These queries select all ships for which customers have reservations. The INNER keyword is actually optional, so the previous query could be rewritten as:

```
SELECT cbn.ship
FROM Customer c JOIN c.reservations r
JOIN r.cabins cbn
```

LEFT JOIN

The LEFT JOIN syntax enables retrieval of a set of entities where matching values in the join statement may not exist. For values that do not exist, a null value is placed in the result set.

For example, let's say we want to generate a report with a customer's name and all the customer's phone numbers. Some customers may not have specified a phone number, but we still want to list their names. We would use a LEFT JOIN to acquire all of this information, including customers with no phone numbers:

```
SELECT c.firstName, c.lastName, p.number From Customer c
LEFT JOIN c.phoneNumbers p
```

If there were three customers in our system, and Bill Burke did not provide any phone numbers, the return values might look like this:

```
David Ortiz 617-555-0900
David Ortiz 617-555-9999
Trot Nixon 781-555-2323
Bill Burke null
```

The previous query can also be expressed as a `LEFT OUTER JOIN`. This is just syntax sugar to parallel SQL 92.

```
SELECT c.firstName, c.lastName, p.number From Customer c
LEFT OUTER JOIN c.phoneNumbers p
```

Fetch Joins

The `JOIN FETCH` syntax allows you to preload a returned entity's relationships even if the relationship property has a `FetchType` of `LAZY`. For example, let's say we have defined our customer's one-to-many relationship to Phone as follows:

```
@OneToMany(fetch=FetchType.LAZY)
public Collection<Phone> getPhones( ) { return phones; }
```

If we want to print out all customer information including their phone numbers, we would usually just query for all customers and then traverse the `getPhones( )` method inside a *for* loop:

```
1  Query query = manager.createQuery("SELECT c FROM Customer c");
2  List results = query.getResultList( );
3  Iterator it = results.iterator( );
4  while (it.hasNext( )) {
5     Customer c = (Customer)it.next( );
6     System.out.print(c.getFirstName( ) + " " + c.getLastName( ));
7     for (Phone p : c.getPhoneNumbers( )) {
8        System.out.print(p.getNumber( ) + " ");
9     }
10    System.out.println("");
11 }
```

There are performance problems with the preceding code. Because the Phone relationship is annotated as being lazily loaded in the `Customer` bean class, the `Phone` collection will not be initialized when we do the initial query at Line 1. When `getPhonesNumbers( )` is executed at Line 7, the persistence engine has to do an additional query to get the Phone entities associated with the customer. This is called the *N + 1 problem*, as we have to do *N* extra queries beyond our initial query. When tuning database applications, it is always important to reduce the number of round trips made to the database as much as possible. This is where the `JOIN FETCH` syntax comes into play. Let's modify our query to preload the Phone association:

```
SELECT c FROM Customer c LEFT JOIN FETCH c.phones
```

Using LEFT JOIN FETCH will additionally preload the Phone association. This can have a dramatic effect on performance because instead of $N + 1$ queries, only one query is made to the database.

Using DISTINCT

The DISTINCT keyword ensures that the query does not return duplicates. For example, the following query finds all customers with reservations. This query will return duplicates:

```
SELECT res FROM Reservation AS res, IN (res.customers) cust
```

If a customer has more than one reservation, there will be duplicate references to that customer in the result. Using the DISTINCT keyword ensures that each customer is represented only once in the result:

```
SELECT DISTINCT cust FROM Reservation AS res,
IN (res.customers) cust
```

The WHERE Clause and Literals

You can use literal values to narrow the scope of the elements selected. This is accomplished through the WHERE clause, which behaves in much the same way as the WHERE clause in SQL.

For example, you can define an EJB QL statement that selects all the Customer entities that use a specific brand of credit card. The literal in this case is a String literal. Literal strings are enclosed by single quotes. Literal values that include a single quote, like the restaurant name Wendy's, use two single quotes to escape the quote: Wendy''s. The following statement returns customers that use Capital One credit cards. (If you don't want to bother with such details, use a query parameter; the job will be done for you by the query API.)

```
SELECT c
FROM Customer AS c
WHERE c.creditCard.creditCompany.name = 'Capital One'
```

Path expressions in the WHERE clause are used in the same way as in the SELECT clause. When making comparisons with a literal, the path expression must evaluate to a basic property; you can't compare a relationship field with a literal.

In addition to literal strings, literals can be exact numeric values (long types) and approximate numeric values (double types). Exact numeric literal values are expressed using the Java integer literal syntax (321, -8932, +22). Approximate numeric literal values are expressed using Java floating-point literal syntax in scientific (5E3, -8.932E5) or decimal (5.234, 38282.2) notation. For example, the following EJB QL statement selects all the ships that weigh 100,000 metric tons:

```
SELECT s
FROM Ship AS s
WHERE s.tonnage = 100000.00
```

Boolean literal values use TRUE and FALSE. Here's an EJB QL statement that selects all the customers who have good credit:

```
SELECT c
FROM Customer AS c
WHERE c.hasGoodCredit = TRUE
```

The WHERE Clause and Operator Precedence

The WHERE clause is composed of conditional expressions that reduce the scope of the query and limit the number of items selected. Several conditional and logical operators can be used in expressions; they are listed here in order of precedence:

- Navigation operator (.)
- Arithmetic operators: +, - (unary); *, / (multiplication and division); +, - (addition and subtraction)
- Comparison operators: =, >, >=, <, <=, <> (not equal), LIKE, BETWEEN, IN, IS NULL, IS EMPTY, MEMBER OF
- Logical operators: NOT, AND, OR

The WHERE Clause and Arithmetic Operators

The arithmetic operators allow a query to perform arithmetic in the process of doing a comparison. Arithmetic operators can be used only in the WHERE clause, not in the SELECT clause.

The following EJB QL statement returns references to all the Reservation EJBs that will be charged a port tax of more than $300:

```
SELECT r
FROM Reservation AS r
WHERE (r.amountPaid * .01)  > 300.00
```

The rules applied to arithmetic operations are the same as those used in the Java programming language, where numbers are *widened*, or *promoted*, in the process of performing a calculation. For example, multiplying a double and an int value requires that the int first be promoted to a double value. (The result will always be that of the widest type used in the calculation, so multiplying an int and a double results in a double value.)

String, boolean, and entity object types cannot be used in arithmetic operations. For example, using the addition operator with two String values is considered an illegal operation. There is a special function for concatenating String values, covered later in this chapter in the section titled "Functional expressions in the WHERE clause."

The WHERE Clause and Logical Operators

Logical operators such as AND, OR, and NOT operate the same way in EJB QL as their corresponding logical operators in SQL.

Logical operators evaluate only Boolean expressions, so each operand (i.e., each side of the expression) must evaluate to true, false, or NULL. Logical operators have the lowest precedence so that all the expressions can be evaluated before they are applied.

The AND and OR operators don't behave like their Java language counterparts, && and ||. EJB QL does not specify whether the righthand operands are evaluated conditionally. For example, the && operator in Java evaluates its righthand operand *only* if the lefthand operand is true. Similarly, the || logical operator evaluates the righthand operand *only* if the lefthand operand is false. We can't make the same assumption for the AND and OR operators in EJB QL. Whether these operators evaluate righthand operands depends on the native query language into which the statements are translated. It's best to assume that both operands are evaluated on all logical operators.

NOT simply reverses the Boolean result of its operand; expressions that evaluate to the Boolean value of true become false, and vice versa

The WHERE Clause and Comparison Symbols

Comparison operators, which use the symbols =, >, >=, <, <=, and <>, should be familiar to you. The following statement selects all the Ship entities whose tonnage field is greater than or equal to 80,000 tons but less than or equal to 130,000 tons:

```
SELECT s
FROM Ship AS s
WHERE s.tonnage >= 80000.00 AND s.tonnage <= 130000.00
```

Only the = and <> (equals and not equals) operators may be used on boolean and entity object identifiers. The greater-than and less-than symbols (>, >=, <, <=) can be used on numeric values as well as strings. However, the semantics of these operations are not defined by the Java Persistence specification. Is character case (upper or lower) important? Does leading and trailing whitespace matter? Issues like these affect the ordering of string values. In order for EJB QL to maintain its status as an abstraction of native query languages, it cannot dictate String ordering, because native query languages may have very different ordering rules. In fact, even different relational database vendors vary on the question of String ordering, which makes it all but impossible to standardize ordering even for SQL "compliant" databases.

Of course, this is all academic if you plan on using the same database well into the future. In such a case, the best thing to do is to examine the documentation for the database you are using to find out how it orders strings in comparisons. This tells you exactly how your EJB QL comparisons will work.

The WHERE Clause and Equality Semantics

While it is legal to compare an exact numeric value (`short`, `int`, `long`) to an approximate numeric value (`double`, `float`), all other equality comparisons must compare the same types. You cannot, for example, compare a `String` value of `123` to the `Integer` literal `123`. However, you can compare two `String` types for equality.

You can compare numeric values for which the rules of numeric promotion apply. For example, a `short` may be compared to an `int`, an `int` to a `long`, etc. Java Persistence also states that primitives may be compared to primitive wrapper types—the rules of numeric promotion apply.

In older versions of the spec, `String` type comparisons had to match exactly, character for character. EJB 2.1 dropped this requirement, making the evaluation of equality between `String` types more ambiguous. This continued in Java Persistence. Again, this ambiguity arises from the differences between kinds of databases (relational versus object-oriented versus file), as well as differences between vendors of relational databases. Consult your vendor's documentation to determine exactly how `String` equality comparisons are evaluated.

You can also compare entity objects for equality, but these too must be of the same type. To be more specific, they must both be entity object references to beans from the same deployment. As an example, the following query finds all the Reservation entities made by a specific Customer. It takes a Customer entity as a parameter:

```
SELECT r
FROM Reservation r, IN ( r.customers ) AS cust
WHERE  cust = :specificCustomer
```

Once it's determined that the bean is the correct type, the actual comparison is performed on the beans' primary keys. If they have the same primary key, they are considered equal.

You may use `java.util.Date` objects in equality comparisons. See the earlier section titled "Date Parameters."

The WHERE Clause and BETWEEN

The `BETWEEN` clause is an inclusive operator specifying a range of values. In this example, we use it to select all ships weighing between 80,000 and 130,000 tons:

```
SELECT s
FROM Ship AS s
WHERE s.tonnage BETWEEN 80000.00 AND 130000.00
```

The `BETWEEN` clause may be used only on numeric primitives (`byte`, `short`, `int`, `long`, `double`, `float`) and their corresponding `java.lang.Number` types (`Byte`, `Short`, `Integer`, etc.). It cannot be used on `String`, `boolean`, or entity object references.

Using the NOT logical operator in conjunction with BETWEEN excludes the range specified. For example, the following EJB QL statement selects all the ships that weigh less than 80,000 tons or more than 130,000 tons but excludes everything in between:

```
SELECT s
FROM Ship AS s
WHERE s.tonnage NOT BETWEEN 80000.00 AND 130000.00
```

The net effect of this query is the same as if it had been executed with comparison symbols:

```
SELECT s
FROM Ship AS s
WHERE s.tonnage < 80000.00 OR s.tonnage > 130000.00
```

The WHERE Clause and IN

The IN conditional operator used in the WHERE clause is not the same as the IN operator used in the FROM clause (that's why the JOIN keyword in the FROM clause should be preferred over the IN keyword for collection navigation). In the WHERE clause, IN tests for membership in a list of literal values. For example, the following EJB QL statement uses the IN operator to select all the customers who reside in a specific set of states:

```
SELECT c
FROM Customer AS c
WHERE c.address.state  IN ('FL', 'TX', 'MI', 'WI', 'MN')
```

Applying the NOT operator to this expression reverses the selection, excluding all customers who reside in the list of states:

```
SELECT c
FROM Customer AS c
WHERE c.address.state NOT IN ('FL', 'TX', 'MI', 'WI', 'MN')
```

If the field tested is null, the value of the expression is "unknown," which means it cannot be predicted.

The IN operator can be used with operands that evaluate to either string or numeric values. For example, the following EJB QL statement uses the IN operator to select all cabins on deck levels 1, 3, 5, and 7:

```
SELECT cab
FROM Cabin AS cab
WHERE cab.deckLevel IN (1,3,5,7)
```

The IN operator can also be used with input parameters. For example, the following query selects all the customers who live in the designated states:

```
SELECT c
FROM Customer AS c
WHERE c.address.state IN ( ?1, ?2, ?3, 'WI', 'MN')
```

In this case, the input parameters (?1, ?2, and ?3) are combined with string literals ('WI' and 'MN') to show that mixing literal and input parameters is allowed, providing they are "like" types.

The WHERE Clause and IS NULL

The IS NULL comparison operator allows you to test whether a path expression is null. For example, the following EJB QL statement selects all the customers who do not have an address:

```
SELECT c
FROM Customer AS c
WHERE c.address IS NULL
```

Using the NOT logical operator, we can reverse the results of this query, selecting all the customers who do have an address:

```
SELECT c
FROM Customer AS c
WHERE c.address IS NOT NULL
```

Path expressions are composed using "inner join" semantics. If an entity has a null relationship field, any query that uses that field as part of a path expression eliminates that entity from consideration. For example, if the Customer entity representing "John Smith" has a null value for its address relationship field, then the "John Smith" Customer entity won't be included in the result set for the following query:

```
SELECT c FROM Customer AS c
WHERE c.address.state = 'TX'
AND c.lastName = 'Smith' AND c.firstName = 'John'
```

This seems obvious at first, but stating it explicitly helps eliminate much of the ambiguity associated with null relationship fields.

The NULL comparison operator can also be used to test input parameters. In this case, NULL is usually combined with the NOT operator to ensure that an input parameter is not a null value. For example, this query can be used to test for null input parameters. The EJB QL statement first checks that the city and state input parameters are not null and then uses them in comparison operations:

```
SELECT c FROM Customer AS c
WHERE :city IS NOT NULL AND :state IS NOT NULL
AND c.address.state = :state
AND c.address.city = :city
```

In this case, if either of the input parameters is a null value, the query returns an empty List, avoiding the possibility of UNKNOWN results from null input parameters. Your Java code should do these null checks up front to avoid an unnecessary database roundtrip.

If the results of a query include a null relationship or a basic field, the results must include null values. For example, the following query selects the addresses of customers whose last name is Smith:

```
SELECT c.address FROM Customer AS c
WHERE c.lastName = 'Smith'
```

If the Customer entity representing "John Smith" has a null value for its address relationship field, the previous query returns a List that includes a null value—the null represents the address relationship field of "John Smith"—in addition to a bunch of Address entity references. You can eliminate null values by including the NOT NULL operator in the query, as shown here:

```
SELECT c.address.city FROM Customer AS c
WHERE c.address.city NOT NULL AND c.address.state = 'FL'
```

The WHERE Clause and IS EMPTY

The IS EMPTY operator allows the query to test whether a collection-based relationship is empty. Remember from Chapter 7 that a collection-based relationship will never be null. If a collection-based relationship field has no elements, it returns an empty Collection or Set.

Testing whether a collection-based relationship is empty has the same purpose as testing whether a single relationship field or basic field is null: it can be used to limit the scope of the query and items selected. For example, the following query selects all the cruises that have not booked any reservations:

```
SELECT crs FROM Cruise AS crs
WHERE crs.reservations IS EMPTY
```

The NOT operator reverses the result of IS EMPTY. The following query selects all the cruises that have at least one reservation:

```
SELECT crs FROM Cruise AS crs
WHERE crs.reservations IS NOT EMPTY
```

It is illegal to use IS EMPTY against collection-based relationships that have been assigned an identifier in the FROM clause:

```
// illegal query
SELECT r
FROM Reservation AS r INNER JOIN r.customers AS c
WHERE
r.customers IS NOT EMPTY AND
c.address.city = 'Boston'
```

While this query appears to be good insurance against UNKNOWN results, it's not. It's illegal because the IS EMPTY operator cannot be used on a collection-based relationship identified within an INNER JOIN. Because the relationship is specified in the INNER

JOIN clause, only those Reservation entities that have a nonempty customers field will be included in the query; any Reservation entity that has an empty relationship field is already excluded because its customers elements cannot be assigned the c identifier.

The WHERE Clause and MEMBER OF

The MEMBER OF operator is a powerful tool for determining whether an entity is a member of a specific collection-based relationship. The following query determines whether a particular Customer entity (specified by the input parameter) is a member of any of the Reservation/Customer relationships:

```
SELECT crs
FROM Cruise AS crs, IN (crs.reservations) AS res, Customer AS cust
WHERE
cust = :myCustomer
  AND
cust MEMBER OF res.customers
```

Applying the NOT operator to MEMBER OF has the reverse effect, selecting all the cruises on which the specified customer does not have a reservation:

```
SELECT crs
FROM Cruise AS crs, IN (crs.reservations) AS res, Customer AS cust
WHERE
cust = :myCustomer
  AND
cust NOT MEMBER OF res.customers
```

Checking whether an entity is a member of an empty collection always returns false.

The WHERE Clause and LIKE

The LIKE comparison operator allows the query to select String type fields that match a specified pattern. For example, the following EJB QL statement selects all the customers with hyphenated names, like "Monson-Haefel" and "Berners-Lee":

```
SELECT OBJECT( c ) FROM Customer AS c
WHERE c.lastName LIKE '%-%'
```

You can use two special characters when establishing a comparison pattern: % (percent) stands for any sequence of characters and _ (underscore) stands for any single character. You can use these characters at any location within a string pattern. If a % or _ actually occurs in the string, you can escape it with the \ character. The NOT logical operator reverses the evaluation so that matching patterns are excluded. The following examples show how the LIKE clause evaluates String type fields:

phone.number LIKE '617%'

  True for "617-322-4151"

  False for "415-222-3523"

cabin.name LIKE 'Suite _100'
: True for "Suite A100"

  False for "Suite A233"

phone.number NOT LIKE '608%'
: True for "415-222-3523"

  False for "608-233-8484"

someField.underscored LIKE '_%'
: True for "_xyz"

  False for "abc"

someField.percentage LIKE '\%%'
: True for "% XYZ"

  False for "ABC"

The LIKE operator can also be used with input parameters:

```
SELECT c FROM Customer AS c
WHERE c.lastName LIKE :param
```

Functional Expressions

EJB QL has numerous functions that you can use to process strings and numeric values.

Functional expressions in the WHERE clause

EJB QL has seven functional expressions that allow for simple String manipulation and three functional expressions for basic numeric operations. The String functions are:

LOWER(String)
: Converts a string to lowercase.

UPPER(String)
: Converts a string to uppercase.

TRIM([[LEADING | TRAILING | BOTH] [trim_char] FROM] String)
: Allows you to trim a specified character from the beginning (LEADING), end (TRAILING), or both (BOTH). If you do not specify a trim character, the space character will be assumed.

CONCAT(String1, String2)
: Returns the String that results from concatenating String1 and String2.

LENGTH(String)
: Returns an int indicating the length of the string.

`LOCATE(String1, String2 [, start])`
: Returns an `int` indicating the position at which `String1` is found within `String2`. If it's present, `start` indicates the character position in `String2` at which the search should start. Support for the `start` parameter is optional; some containers will support it, and others will not. Don't use it if you want to ensure that the query is portable.

`SUBSTRING(String1, start, length)`
: Returns the `String` consisting of `length` characters taken from `String1`, starting at the position given by `start`.

The `start` and `length` parameters indicate positions in a `String` as integer values. You can use these expressions in the `WHERE` clause to refine the scope of the items selected. Here's how the `LOCATE` and `LENGTH` functions might be used:

```
SELECT c
FROM Customer AS c
WHERE
LENGTH(c.lastName) > 6
  AND
LOCATE( c.lastName, 'Monson') > -1
```

This statement selects all the customers with `Monson` somewhere in their last names but specifies that the names must be longer than six characters. Therefore, "Monson-Haefel" and "Monson-Ares" would evaluate to `true`, but "Monson" would return `false` because it has only six characters.

The arithmetic functions in EJB QL may be applied to primitive as well as corresponding primitive wrapper types:

`ABS(number)`
: Returns the absolute value of a number (`int`, `float`, or `double`)

`SQRT(double)`
: Returns the square root of a `double`

`MOD(int, int)`
: Returns the remainder for the first parameter divided by the second (i.e., MOD(7, 5) is equal to 2)

Functions returning dates and times

EJB QL has three functions that can return you the current date, time, and timestamp: `CURRENT_DATE`, `CURRENT_TIME`, and `CURRENT_TIMESTAMP`. Here's an example of searching for reservations made on the current date:

```
SELECT res FROM Reservation res WHERE res.date = CURRENT_DATE
```

Aggregate functions in the SELECT clause

Aggregate functions are used with queries that return a collection of values. They are fairly simple to understand and can be handy, especially the `COUNT( )` function.

COUNT (identifier or path expression). This function returns the number of items in the query's final result set. The return type is a `java.lang.Long`, depending on whether it is the return type of the query method. For example, the following query provides a count of all the customers who live in Wisconsin:

```
SELECT COUNT( c )
FROM Customers AS c
WHERE c.address.state = 'WI'
```

The `COUNT( )` function can be used with an identifier, in which case it always counts entities, or with path expressions, in which case it counts either CMR fields or CMP fields. For example, the following statement provides a count of all the Zip codes that start with the numbers 554:

```
SELECT  COUNT(c.address.zip)
FROM Customers AS c
WHERE c.address.zip LIKE '554%'
```

In some cases, queries that count a path expression have a corresponding query that can be used to count an identifier. For example, the result of the following query, which counts Customers instead of the `zip` field, is equivalent to the previous query:

```
SELECT COUNT( c )
FROM Customers AS c
WHERE c.address.zip LIKE '554%'
```

MAX(path expression), MIN(path expression). These functions can be used to find the largest or smallest value from a collection of any type of field. They cannot be used with identifiers or paths that terminate in a relationship field. The result type will be the type of field that is being evaluated. For example, the following query returns the highest price paid for a reservation:

```
SELECT MAX( r.amountPaid )
FROM Reservation AS r
```

The `MAX( )` and `MIN( )` functions can be applied to any valid value, including primitive types, strings, and even serializable objects. The result of applying the `MAX( )` and `MIN( )` functions to serializable objects is not specified, because there is no standard way to determine which serializable object is greater than or lesser than another one.

The result of applying the `MAX( )` and `MIN( )` functions to a `String` field depends on the underlying data store. This has to do with the inherent problems associated with `String` type comparisons.

AVG(numeric), SUM(numeric). The AVG( ) and SUM( ) functions can be applied only to path expressions that terminate in a numeric primitive field (byte, long, float, etc.) or in one of their corresponding numeric wrappers (Byte, Long, Float, etc.). The result of a query that uses the SUM( ) function has the same type as the numeric type it's evaluating. The result type of the AVG( ) function is a java.lang.Double, depending on whether it is used in the return type of the SELECT method.

For example, the following query uses the SUM( ) function to get the total amount paid by all customers for a specific cruise (specified by the input parameter):

```
SELECT SUM( r.amountPaid)
FROM Cruise c join c.reservations r
WHERE  c = :cr
```

DISTINCT, nulls, and empty arguments. The DISTINCT operator can be used with any of the aggregate functions to eliminate duplicate values. The following query uses the DISTINCT operator to count the number of *different* Zip codes that match the pattern specified:

```
SELECT DISTINCT COUNT(c.address.zip)
FROM Customers AS c
WHERE c.address.zip LIKE '554%'
```

The DISTINCT operator first eliminates duplicate Zip codes; if 100 customers live in the same area with the same Zip code their Zip code is counted only once. After the duplicates have been eliminated, the COUNT( ) function counts the number of items left.

Any field with a null value is automatically eliminated from the result set operated on by the aggregate functions. The COUNT( ) function also ignores values with null values. The aggregate functions AVG( ), SUM( ), MAX( ), and MIN( ) return null when evaluating an empty collection. For example, the following query attempts to obtain the average price paid by customers for a specific cruise:

```
SELECT AVG( r.amountPaid)
FROM Cruise As c JOIN c.reservations r
WHERE c = :myCruise
```

If the cruise specified by the input parameter has no reservations, the collection on which the AVG( ) function operates is empty (there are no reservations and therefore no amounts paid).

The COUNT( ) function returns 0 (zero) when the argument it evaluates is an empty collection. If the following query is evaluated on a cruise with no reservations, the result is 0 (zero) because the argument is an empty collection:

```
SELECT COUNT( r )
FROM Cruise AS c, IN( c.reservations ) AS r
WHERE c = ?1
```

The ORDER BY Clause

The ORDER BY clause allows you to specify the order of the entities in the collection returned by a query. The semantics of the ORDER BY clause are basically the same as in SQL. For example, we can construct a simple query that uses the ORDER BY clause to return an alphabetical list of all of Titan Cruises' customers:

```
SELECT c
FROM Customers AS c
ORDER BY c.lastName
```

This might return a Collection of Customer entities in the following order (assume that their last and first names are printed to output):

```
Aares, John
Astro, Linda
Brooks, Hank
.
.
Xerces, Karen
Zastro, William
```

You can use the ORDER BY clause with or without the WHERE clause. For example, we can refine the previous query by listing only those U.S. customers who reside in Boston:

```
SELECT c
FROM Customers AS c
WHERE c.address.city = 'Boston' AND c.address.state = 'MA'
ORDER BY c.lastName
```

The default order of an item listed in the ORDER BY clause is always ascending, which means that the lesser values are listed first and the greater values last. You can explicitly specify the order as *ascending* or *descending* by using the keywords ASC and DESC. The default is ASC. Null elements will be placed on top or at the bottom of the query result depending on the underlying database. Here's a statement that lists customers in reverse (descending) order:

```
SELECT c
FROM Customers AS c
ORDER BY c.lastName DESC
```

The results of this query are:

```
Zastro, William
Xerces, Karen
.
.
Brooks, Hank
Astro, Linda
Aares, John
```

You can specify multiple order-by items. For example, you can sort customers by lastName in ascending order and firstName in descending order:

```
SELECT c
FROM Customers AS c
ORDER BY c.lastName ASC, c.firstName DESC
```

If you have five Customer entities with the `lastName` equal to `Brooks`, this query sorts the results as follows:

```
Brooks, William
Brooks, Henry
Brooks, Hank
Brooks, Ben
Brooks, Andy
```

Although the fields used in the `ORDER BY` clause must be basic fields, the value selected can be an entity identifier, a relationship field, or a basic field. For example, the following query returns an ordered list of all Zip codes:

```
SELECT addr.zip
FROM Address AS addr
ORDER BY addr.zip
```

The following query returns all the Address entities for customers named Smith, ordered by their Zip code:

```
SELECT c.address
FOR Customer AS c
WHERE c.lastName = 'Smith'
ORDER BY c.address.zip
```

You must be careful which basic fields you use in the `ORDER BY` clause. If the query selects a collection of entities, then the `ORDER BY` clause can be used with only basic fields of the entity type that is selected. The following query is illegal, because the basic field used in the `ORDER BY` clause is not a field of the entity type selected:

```
// Illegal EJB QL
SELECT c
FROM Customer AS c
ORDER BY c.address.city
```

Because the `city` field is not a direct field of the Customer entity, you cannot use it in the `ORDER BY` clause.

A similar restriction applies to results. The field used in the `ORDER BY` clause must also be in the `SELECT` clause. The following query is illegal, because the field identified in the `SELECT` clause is not the same as the one used in the `ORDER BY` clause:

```
SELECT c.address.city
FROM Customer AS c
ORDER BY c.address.state
```

In the previous query, we wanted a list of all the cities ordered by their state. Unfortunately, this is illegal. You can't order by the `state` field if you are not selecting the `state` field.

GROUP BY and HAVING

The GROUP BY and HAVING clauses are commonly used to apply stricter organization to a query and to narrow the results for aggregate functions. The GROUP BY clause is usually used in combination with aggregate functions, because it allows you to cluster data by category.

Let's say you want to do a report to find out how many reservations each particular cruise had. You would want to use the COUNT function to count each reservation, but how would you group the calculation of the count on a per-cruise basis? This is what the GROUP BY syntax allows you to do. Here's a query that returns the cruise name and a count of each reservation per cruise:

```
SELECT cr.name, COUNT (res) FROM Cruise cr
LEFT JOIN cr.reservations res
GROUP BY cr.name
```

The GROUP BY clause must specify one of the columns that you are returning in the query. Because we are using a LEFT JOIN, cruises that do not have any reservations will be returned with a count of zero. If you wanted to exclude cruises from the report that did not have any reservations, you would use an INNER JOIN instead.

The GROUP BY syntax is even more interesting if we combine it with a constructor expression. Let's populate a list of ReservationSummary instances. ReservationSummary is a helper class comprised of the cruise name, the number of reservations, and how much money was collected:

```
public class ReservationSummary {
   public String cruise;
   public int numReservations;
   public double cashflow;

   public ReservationSummary(String c, int num, double cash) {
     this.cruise = c;
     this.numReservations = num;
     this.cashflow = cash;
   }
}
```

We will invoke the constructor directly within our query:

```
SELECT new ReservationSummary(cr.name, COUNT(res), SUM(res.amountPaid))
FROM Cruise cr
LEFT JOIN cr.reservations res
GROUP BY cr.name
```

The HAVING clause is used with a GROUP BY clause and acts as a filter, restricting the final output. The HAVING clause employs aggregate functional expressions using only the identifiers used in the SELECT clause. You can restrict the GROUP BY result by using the HAVING syntax. Let's restrict our report to show only those cruises with more than 10 reservations:

```
SELECT cr.name, COUNT (res) FROM Cruise cr
JOIN cr.reservations res
GROUP BY cr.name
HAVING count(res) > 10
```

The same rules that govern SELECT clauses govern HAVING clauses. Only grouped properties may appear outside of any function that you use, though.

Subqueries

Subqueries are SELECT statements embedded in another query. EJB QL supports subqueries in WHERE and HAVING clauses. Subqueries are very useful when normal mechanisms for narrowing your search cannot obtain the data you desire. Here's an example of finding the count of all reservations whose amount paid is greater than the average amount paid for all reservations:

```
SELECT COUNT(res)
FROM Reservation res
WHERE res.amountPaid > (SELECT avg(r.amountPaid) FROM Reservation r)
```

If you look carefully, you can see that this example can actually be broken up into two separate queries. You could execute one query that found the average amount paid and then pass this value into the second query to find all amounts paid that are greater than the average. For performance reasons, it is better to submit one query, as you can avoid the overhead of an extra network call to the database. It is also possible that the database could optimize this large query.

You can also reference identifiers in the FROM clause of the outer query of your subquery. For example, let's say we want to find all cruises that made more than $100,000. The query would look like this:

```
FROM Cruise cr
WHERE 100000 < (
   SELECT SUM(res.amountPaid) FROM cr.reservations res)
)
```

The subquery in this example references the reservation association of the cruise specified in the outer query's FROM clause.

ALL, ANY, SOME

When a subquery returns multiple rows, it is possible to quantify the results with the ALL, ANY, and SOME expressions.

The ALL operator returns true if all the things in the subquery match the conditional expression. For example, maybe we want to list the cruises for which every reservation has a down payment:

```
FROM Cruise cr
WHERE 0 < ALL (
   SELECT res.amountPaid from cr.reservations res
)
```

The ANY operator returns true if anything in the subquery matches the conditional expression. For example, maybe we want to find all cruises that have at least one reservation without a down payment:

```
FROM Cruise cr
WHERE 0 = ANY (SELECT res.amountPaid from cr.reservations res);
```

SOME is a synonym of ANY, and the two are syntactically equivalent. You can use a NOT expression to obtain the same query:

```
FROM Cruise cr
WHERE 0 < NOT ALL (SELECT res.amountPaid from cr.reservations res)
```

EXISTS

The EXISTS operator returns true if the subquery result consists of one or more values. If no values are returned by the subquery, then false is returned. We could rewrite our query to search for cruises for which some customers had not paid their balance due:

```
FROM Cruise cr
WHERE EXISTS (SELECT res FROM cr.reservations WHERE res.amountPaid = 0)
```

Bulk UPDATE and DELETE

Java Persistence has the ability to perform bulk UPDATE and DELETE operations. This can save you a lot of typing. For example, let's say we want to give a $10 credit across the board to any customer named Bill Burke. We can do the following bulk UPDATE:

```
UPDATE Reservation res SET res.amountPaid = (res.amountPaid + 10)
WHERE EXISTS (
   SELECT c FROM res.customers c
   WHERE c.firstName = 'Bill' AND c.lastName='Burke'
)
```

An example of DELETE could be that we want to remove all reservations made by Bill Burke:

```
DELETE FROM Reservation res
WHERE EXISTS (
   SELECT c FROM res.customers c
   WHERE c.firstName = 'Bill' AND c.lastName='Burke'
)
```

Be very careful how you use bulk UPDATE and DELETE. It is possible, depending on the vendor implementation, to create inconsistencies between the database and entities that are already being managed by the current persistence context. Vendor implementations are required only to execute the update or delete directly on the database. They do not have to modify the state of any currently managed entity. For this reason, it is recommended that you do these operations within their own transaction or at the beginning of a transaction (before any entities are accessed that might be affected by these bulk operations). Alternatively, executing `EntityManager.flush( )` and `EntityManager.clear( )` before executing a bulk operation will keep you safe.

Native Queries

EJB QL is a very rich syntax and should meet most of your querying needs. Sometimes, though, you want to take advantage of certain proprietary capabilities that are available only on a specific vendor's database.

The entity manager service provides a way to create native SQL queries and map them to your objects. Native queries can return entities, column values, or a combination of the two. The `EntityManager` interface has three methods for creating native queries: one for returning scalar values, one for returning one entity type, and one for defining a complex result set that can map to a mix of multiple entities and scalar values.

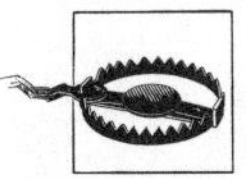

You can always get the underlying JDBC connection through a `javax.sql.DataSource` injected by the `@Resource` and execute any SQL statement you need. Be aware that your changes will not be reflected in the current persistence context.

Scalar Native Queries

```
Query createNativeQuery(String sql)
```

This creates a native query that returns scalar results. It takes one parameter: your native SQL. It executes as is and returns the result set in the same form as EJB QL returns scalar values.

Simple Entity Native Queries

```
Query createNativeQuery(String sql, Class entityClass)
```

A simple entity native query takes an SQL statement and implicitly maps it to one entity based on the mapping metadata you declared for that entity. It expects that the columns returned in the result set of the native query will match perfectly with the entity's O/R mapping. The entity the native SQL query maps to is determined by the `entityClass` parameter:

```
Query query = manager.createNativeQuery(
    "SELECT p.phone_PK, p.phone_number, p.type
        FROM PHONE AS p", Phone.class
);
```

All the properties of the entities must be pulled.

Complex Native Queries

```
Query createNativeQuery(String sql, String mappingName)
```

This entity manager method allows you to have complex mappings for your native SQL. You can return multiple entities and scalar column values at the same time. The `mappingName` parameter references a declared `@javax.persistence.SqlResultSetMapping`. This annotation is used to define how the native SQL results hook back into your O/R model. If your returned column names don't match the parallel annotated property mapping, you can provide a field-to-column mapping for them using `@javax.persistence.FieldResult`:

```
package javax.persistence;

public @interface SqlResultSetMapping {
   String name( );
   EntityResult[] entities( ) default {};
   ColumnResult[] columns( ) default {};
}

public @interface EntityResult {
   Class entityClass( );
   FieldResult[] fields( ) default {};
   String discriminatorColumn( ) default "";
}

public @interface FieldResult {
   String name( );
   String column( );
}

public @interface ColumnResult {
   String name( );
}
```

Let's do a series of examples to show how this would work.

Native queries with multiple entities

First, let's create a native query that returns multiple entity types: a Customer and its Credit Card:

```
@Entity
@SqlResultSetMapping(name="customerAndCreditCardMapping",
      entities={@EntityResult(entityClass=Customer.class),
                @EntityResult(entityClass=CreditCard.class,
                              fields={@FieldResult(name="id",
                                                   column="CC_ID"),
                                     @FieldResult(name="number",
                                                   column="number")}
                              )})
public class Customer {...}
```

```
// execution code
{
   Query query = manager.createNativeQuery(
       "SELECT c.id, c.firstName, cc.id As CC_ID, cc.number" +
              "FROM CUST_TABLE c, CREDIT_CARD_TABLE cc" +
              "WHERE c.credit_card_id = cc.id",
       "customerAndCreditCardMapping");
}
```

Because the result set returns multiple entity types, we must define an `@SqlResultSetMapping`. This annotation can be placed on an entity class or method. The `entities()` attribute is set to an array of `@EntityResult` annotations. Each `@EntityResult` annotation specifies the entities that will be returned by the native SQL query.

The `@javax.persistence.FieldResult` annotation is used to explicitly map columns in the query with properties of an entity. The `name()` attribute of `@FieldResult` identifies the entity bean's property, and the `column()` attribute identifies the result set column returned by the native query.

In this example, we do not need to specify any `@FieldResults` for Customer, as the native query pulls in each column for this entity. However, since we are only querying the ID and number columns of the CreditCard entity, an `@FieldResult` annotation should be specified. In the `@EntityResult` annotation for CreditCard, the `fields()` attribute defines what `CreditCard` properties each queried column maps to. Because the `Customer` and `CreditCard` primary-key columns have the same name, the SQL query needs to distinguish that they are different. The `cc.id As CC_ID` SQL fragment performs this identification.

We can express this in XML as well:

```
<entity-mappings>
   <sql-result-set-mapping name="customerAndCreditCardMapping">
      <entity-result entity-class="com.titan.domain.Customer"/>
      <entity-result entity-class="com.titan.domain.CreditCard"/>
         <field-result name="id" column="CC_ID"/>
         <field-result name="number" column="number"/>
      </entity-result>
   </sql-result-set-mapping>
</entity-mappings>
```

Mixed scalar and entity results

For our final example, let's show an entity and scalar value mix. We'll write a native SQL query that returns a list of cruises and how many reservations each cruise has.

```
@SqlResultSetMapping(name="reservationCount",
         entities=@EntityResult(name="com.titan.domain.Cruise",
                                fields=@FieldResult(name="id", column="id")),
         columns=@ColumnResult(name="resCount"))
@Entity
public class Cruise {...}
```

```
{
   Query query = manager.createNativeQuery(
      "SELECT c.id, count(Reservation.id) as resCount
       FROM Cruise c LEFT JOIN Reservation ON c.id = Reservation.CRUISE_ID
       GROUP BY c.id",
       "reservationCount");
}
```

The reservationCount mapping declares that the native SQL query represents a request for a Cruise entity and a count of all the reservations for that cruise. The @FieldResult annotation identifies the c.id column as being associated with a Cruise entity. The @ColumnResult annotation identifies the resCount column as a scalar value.

Here's the XML equivalent:

```
<entity-mappings>
   <sql-result-set-mapping name="reservationCount">
      <entity-result entity-class="com.titan.domain.Cruise">
         <field-result name="id" column="id"/>
      </entity-result>
      <column-result name="resCount"/>
   </sql-result-set-mapping>
</entity-mappings>
```

Named Queries

Java Persistence provides a mechanism so that you can predefine EJB QL or native SQL queries and reference them by name when creating a query. You would want to predeclare queries for the same reason you create String constant variables in Java: to reuse them in multiple different situations. If you predefine your queries in one place, you have an easy way to fine-tune or modify them as time goes on. The @javax.persistence.NamedQuery annotation is used for predefining EJB QL.

```
package javax.persistence;

public @interface NamedQuery {
   String name( );
   String query( );
   QueryHint[] hints( ) default {};
}

public @interface QueryHint {
   String name( );
   String value( );
}

public @interface NamedQueries {
   NamedQuery[] value( );
}
```

You use the @javax.persistence.NamedQueries annotation when you are declaring more than one query on a class or package. The @javax.persistence.QueryHint annotation declares vendor-specific hints. These hints work in the same way as the Query.setHint( ) method described earlier in this chapter. Here's an example:

```
package com.titan.domain;
import javax.persistence.*;

@NamedQueries({
   @NamedQuery(name="getAverageReservation",
               query=
                 "SELECT AVG( r.amountPaid)
                  FROM Cruise As c, JOIN c.reservations r
                  WHERE c = :cruise"),

   @NamedQuery(name="findFullyPaidCruises",
               query=
                 "FROM Cruise cr
                  WHERE 0 < ALL (
                     SELECT res.amountPaid from cr.reservations res
                  )")
})
@Entity
public class Cruise {...}
```

This example declares two EJB QL queries on the Cruise entity bean class. You can then reference these declarations in the EntityManager.createNamedQuery( ) method:

```
Query query = em.createNamedQuery("findFullyPaidCruises");
Query.setParameter("cruise", cruise);
```

There is, of course, an XML equivalent to @NamedQuery:

```
<entity-mappings>
   <named-query name="getAverageReservation">
      <query>
            SELECT AVG( r.amountPaid)
            FROM Cruise As c JOIN c.reservations r
            WHERE c = :cruise
      </query>
   </named-query>
</entity-mappings>
```

Named Native Queries

The @javax.persistence.NamedNativeQuery annotation is used for predefining native SQL queries:

```
package javax.persistence;

public @interface NamedNativeQuery {
   String name( );
   String query( );
   Class resultClass( ) default void.class;
   String resultSetMapping( ) default "";
}
```

```
public @interface NamedNativeQueries {
   NamedNativeQuery[] value( );
}
```

The `resultClass( )` attribute is for when you have a native query that returns only one entity type (see the "Native Queries" section earlier in this chapter). The `resultSetMapping( )` attribute must resolve to a predeclared `@SqlResultSetMapping`. Both attributes are optional, but you must declare at least one of them. Here is an example of predeclaring an `@NamedNativeQuery`:

```
@NamedNativeQuery(
   name="findCustAndCCNum",
   query="SELECT c.id, c.firstName, c.lastName, cc.number AS CC_NUM
           FROM CUST_TABLE c, CREDIT_CARD_TABLE cc
           WHERE c.credit_card_id = cc.id",
   resultSetMapping="customerAndCCNumMapping")
@SqlResultSetMapping(name="customerAndCCNumMapping",
     entities={@EntityResult(entityClass=Customer.class)},
     columns={@ColumnResult(name="CC_NUM")}
)
@Entity
public class Customer {...}
```

You can then reference this declaration in the `EntityManager.createNamedQuery( )` method:

```
Query query = em.createNamedQuery("findCustAndCCNum");
```

Here's the XML equivalent:

```
<entity-mappings>
   <named-native-query name="findCustAndCCNum"
                       result-set-mapping="customerAndCCNumMapping"/>
      <query>
            SELECT c.id, c.firstName, c.lastName,
            cc.number AS CC_NUM
            FROM CUST_TABLE c, CREDIT_CARD_TABLE cc
            WHERE c.credit_card_id = cc.id
      </query>
   </named-native-query>
</entity-mappings>
```

CHAPTER 10

Entity Callbacks and Listeners

When you execute EntityManager methods like persist( ), merge( ), remove( ), and find( ), or when you execute EJB QL queries, a predefined set of life cycle events are triggered. For instance, the persist( ) method triggers database inserts. Merging triggers updates to the database. The remove( ) method triggers database deletes. Querying entities triggers a load from the database. Sometimes it is very useful to have your entity bean class be notified as these events happen. For instance, maybe you want to create an audit log of every interaction done on each row in your database. The Java Persistence specification allows you to set up callback methods on your entity classes so that your entity instances are notified when these events occur. You can also register separate listener classes that can intercept these same events. These are called *entity listeners*. This chapter discusses how you register your entity bean classes for life cycle callbacks as well as how to write entity listeners that can intercept life cycle events on your entities.

Callback Events

A certain annotation represents each phase of an entity's life cycle:

```
@javax.persistence.PrePersist
@javax.persistence.PostPersist
@javax.persistence.PostLoad
@javax.persistence.PreUpdate
@javax.persistence.PostUpdate
@javax.persistence.PreRemove
@javax.persistence.PostRemove
```

The @PrePersist and @PostPersist events have to do with the insertion of an entity instance into the database. The @PrePersist event occurs immediately when the EntityManager.persist( ) call is invoked or whenever an entity instance is scheduled to be inserted into the database (as with a cascaded merge). The @PostPersist event is not triggered until the actual database insert.

The @PreUpdate event is triggered just before the state of the entity is synchronized with the database. The @PostUpdate event happens after. This synchronization could occur at transaction commit time, when EntityManager.flush( ) is executed, or whenever the persistence context deems it necessary to update the database.

The @PreRemove and @PostRemove events have to do with the removal of an entity bean from the database. @PreRemove is triggered whenever EntityManager.remove( ) is invoked on the entity bean, directly or because of a cascade. The @PostRemove event happens immediately after the actual database delete occurs.

The @PostLoad event is triggered after an entity instance has been loaded by a find( ) or getReference( ) method call on the EntityManager interface, or when an EJB QL query is executed. It is also called after the refresh( ) method is invoked.

Callbacks on Entity Classes

You can have an entity bean instance register for a callback on any of these life cycle events by annotating a public, private, protected, or package-protected method on the bean class. This method must return void, throw no checked exceptions, and have no arguments.

```
@Entity
public class Cabin {

   ...

   @PostPersist void afterInsert( ) {
    ...
   }

   @PostLoad void afterLoading( ) {
    ...
   }
}
```

When an event is triggered on a particular managed entity instance, the entity manager will invoke the appropriate annotated method on the entity bean class.

If you are annotation-averse, you can hook into these events by using the <pre-persist>, <post-persist>, <pre-update>, <post-update>, <pre-remove>, <post-remove>, and <post-load> subelements of <entity> in the ORM mapping deployment descriptor:

```
<entity class="com.titan.domain.Cabin">
   <post-persist name="afterInsert"/>
   <post-load name="afterLoading"/>
</entity>
```

These subelements have one attribute called name that takes the name of the method you want to invoke when the callback event happens.

Entity Listeners

Entity listeners are classes that can generically intercept entity callback events. They are not entity classes themselves, but they can be attached to an entity class through a binding annotation or XML. You can assign methods on an entity listener class to intercept a particular life cycle event. These methods return `void` and take one `Object` parameter that is the entity instance on which the event is being triggered. The method is annotated with the callback in which it is interested.

```
public class TitanAuditLogger {

   @PostPersist void postInsert(Object entity) {
      System.out.println("Inserted entity: " + entity.getClass().getName( ));
   }

   @PostLoad void postLoad(Object entity) {
      System.out.println("Loaded entity: " + entity.getClass().getName( ));
   }

}
```

The entity listener class must have a public no-arg constructor. It can be applied to an entity class by using the `@javax.persistence.EntityListeners` annotation:

```
package javax.persistence;

@Target(TYPE) @Retention(RUNTIME)
public @interface EntityListeners {
   Class[] value( );
}
```

You can specify one or more entity listeners that intercept the callback events of an entity class:

```
@Entity
@EntityListeners({TitanAuditLogger.class, EntityJmxNotifier.class})
public class Cabin {
...

   @PostPersist void afterInsert( ) {
    ...
   }

   @PostLoad void afterLoading( ) {
    ...
   }

}
```

By using the `@EntityListeners` annotation on the `Cabin` entity class, any callback methods within those entity listener classes will be invoked whenever `Cabin` entity instances interact with a persistence context. Entity listeners can also be applied using XML:

```
<entity class="com.titan.domain.Cabin">
   <entity-listeners>
      <entity-listener class="com.titan.listeners.TitanAuditLogger">
      </entity-listener>
      <entity-listener class="com.titan.listeners.EntityJmxNotifier">
         <pre-persist name="beforeInsert"/>
         <post-load name="afterLoading"/>
      </entity-listener>
   </entity-listeners>
</entity>
```

The `<entity-listeners>` element can be used within the declaration of an entity class. It lists the set of listeners that should be executed. Any entity listener class that doesn't use annotations to identify the callbacks can use the `<post-persist>` and other callback elements to specify these methods. Declaring `<entity-listeners>` also has the side effect of overriding any `@EntityListeners` annotation that might be applied to the entity class.

The execution order of entity listeners is the order they were declared in the `@EntityListeners` annotation or ORM XML mapping file. Any callbacks on the entity bean class itself are called last. Let's look at what would happen if we invoked the following operations:

```
1  EntityManager em = factory.createEntityManager( );
2  em.getTransaction().begin( );
3
4  Cabin cabin = new Cabin( );
5  em.persist(cabin);
6
7  Cabin anotherCabin = em.find(Cabin.class, 5);
8
9  em.getTransaction().commit( );
```

Pretend this code executes on the examples we have shown in this chapter. The `EntityJmxNotifier` class is interested in a `<pre-persist>` callback. The `EntityJmxNotifier.beforeInsert( )` method is executed when the `EntityManager.persist( )` method is invoked at Line 5.

At Line 7, the `TitanAuditLogger.postLoad( )`, `EntityJmxNotifier.afterLoading( )`, and `Cabin.afterLoading( )` methods are invoked, in that order, as the `@PostLoad` event is triggered by the `EntityManager.find( )` invocation. The `Cabin.afterLoading( )` method is invoked on the same instance returned by the `find( )` method.

Our persistence provider has decided to delay the database insert of the newly persisted cabin until the transaction commits. In Line 9, the `TitanAuditLogger.postPersist( )` and `Cabin.afterInsert( )` methods are called, in that order. The `Cabin.afterInsert( )` method is invoked on the same entity instance that we persisted in Line 5.

Default Entity Listeners

You can specify a set of default entity listeners that are applied to every entity class in the persistence unit by using the <entity-listeners> element under the top-level <entity-mappings> element in the ORM mapping file. For instance, if you wanted to apply the TitanAuditLogger to every entity class in a particular persistence unit, you would do the following:

```
<entity-mappings>
   <entity-listeners>
      <entity-listener class="com.titan.listeners.TitanAuditLogger">
         <post-persist name="afterInsert"/>
         <post-load name="afterLoading"/>
      </entity-listener>
      <entity-listener class="com.titan.listeners.EntityJmxNotifier"/>
   </entity-listeners>
</entity-mappings
```

If you want to turn off default entity listeners to a particular entity class, you can use the @javax.persistence.ExcludeDefaultListeners annotation:

```
@Entity
@ExcludeDefaultListeners
public class Cabin {
...
}
```

There is also an XML equivalent of this annotation:

```
<entity class="com.titan.domain.Cabin">
   <exclude-default-listeners/>
</entity
```

If either the @ExcludeDefaultListeners annotation or its XML equivalent are applied to the Cabin entity, the TitanAuditLogger is turned off for that entity.

Inheritance and Listeners

If you have an inheritance entity hierarchy in which the base class has entity listeners applied to it, any subclass will inherit these entity listeners. If the subclass also has entity listeners applied to it, then both the base and the subclass's listeners will be attached.

```
@Entity
@EntityListeners(TitanAuditLogger.class)
public class Person {

   @PostPersist void anotherCallback( ) {
    ...
   }
}
```

```
@Entity
@EntityListeners(EntityJmxNotifier.class)
public class Customer extends Person {
...
}
```

In this example, the TitanAuditLogger entity listener and EntityJmxNotifier will be attached to the Customer entity. If all of these listeners have an @PostPersist callback, the order of callback execution will be as follows:

- TitanAuditLogger's @PostPersist method
- EntityJmxNotifier's @PostPersist method
- Person's @PostPersist anotherCallback( ) method

Entity listeners applied to a base class happen before any listeners attached to a subclass. Callback methods defined directly in an entity class happen last.

You can turn off inherited entity listeners by using @javax.persistence.ExcludeSuperclassListeners:

```
@Entity
@EntityListeners(TitanAuditLogger.class)
public class Person {

}

@Entity
@EntityListeners(EntityJmxNotifier.class)
@ExcludeSuperclassListeners
public class Customer extends Person {
...
}
```

In this example, only the EntityJmxNotifier listener would be executed for Customer entity instances. @ExcludeSuperclassListeners has an XML equivalent in the <exclude-superclass-listeners/> element.

CHAPTER 11

Session Beans

Entity beans provide an object-oriented model that makes it easier for developers to create, modify, and delete data from the database. They allow developers to be more productive by encouraging reuse, thus reducing development costs. For example, once a bean has been defined to represent a concept like a ship, that bean can be reused throughout a business system without redefining, recoding, or retesting the business logic and data access.

However, entity beans are not the entire story. We have seen another kind of enterprise bean: the *session bean*. Session beans fill the gaps left by entity beans. They are useful for describing interactions between other beans (taskflow) and for implementing particular tasks. Unlike entity beans, session beans do not represent data in the database, but they can access data. This means that we can use session beans to read, update, and insert data in a business process. For example, we might use a session bean to provide lists of information, such as a list of all available cabins. Sometimes we might generate the list by interacting with entity beans, like the cabin list we developed in the TravelAgent EJB in Chapter 4.

When do you use an entity bean and when do you use a session bean? As a rule of thumb, an entity bean should provide a safe and consistent interface to a set of shared data that defines a concept. This data may be updated frequently. Session beans access data that spans concepts, is not shared, and is usually read-only. Session beans contain business logic and entity beans model persistent data.

In addition to accessing data directly, session beans can represent taskflow. Taskflow refers to all the steps required to accomplish a particular task, such as booking passage on a ship or renting a video. Session beans frequently manage the interactions among entity beans, describing how they work together to accomplish a specific task. The relationship between session beans and entity beans is like the relationship between a script for a play and the actors that perform the play. Actors are pointless without a script; they may represent something, but they can't tell a story. Similarly, entities represented in a database aren't meaningful unless you can create interactions between the entities. It makes no sense to have a database full of cabins, ships, customers, and such if we can't create interactions between them, such as booking a customer for a cruise.

Session beans are divided into two basic types: stateless and stateful. A *stateless* session bean is a collection of related services, each represented by a method; the bean maintains no state from one method invocation to the next. When you invoke a method on a stateless session bean, it executes the method and returns the result without knowing or caring what other requests have gone before or might follow. Think of a stateless session bean as a set of procedures or batch programs that execute a request based on some parameters and return a result.

A *stateful* session bean is an extension of the client application. It performs tasks on behalf of a client and maintains state related to that client. This state is called *conversational state* because it represents a continuing conversation between the stateful session bean and the client. Methods invoked on a stateful session bean can write and read data to and from this conversational state, which is shared among all methods in the bean. Stateful session beans tend to be specific to one scenario. They represent logic that might have been captured in the client application of a two-tier system.

Depending on the vendor, stateful session beans may have a timeout period. If the client fails to use the stateful bean before it times out, the bean instance is destroyed and the EJB object reference is invalidated. This prevents the stateful session bean from lingering long after a client has shut down or otherwise has finished using it. After all, clients can crash, and users can walk away from their desks and forget what they were doing; we don't want stateful session beans associated with dead clients or forgetful users cluttering up our server forever. A client can also explicitly remove a stateful session bean by calling one of its remove methods.

Stateless session beans have longer lives because they do not retain any conversational state and are not dedicated to one client. As soon as a stateless session bean has finished a method invocation, it can be reassigned to service a new client. Stateless session beans may also have a timeout period and can be removed by the client, but the impact of a bean timeout or removal is different than with a stateful session bean. A timeout or remove operation simply invalidates the EJB object reference for that client; the bean instance is not destroyed and is free to service other client requests.

Whether they are stateful or stateless, session beans are not persistent, like entity beans are. In other words, session beans don't represent persistent data and are not saved to the database.

The Stateless Session Bean

A stateless session bean is very efficient and relatively easy to develop. A session bean can be swapped freely between EJB objects because it isn't dedicated to one client and doesn't maintain any conversational state. As soon as it is finished servicing a method invocation it can be swapped to another EJB object. Because it does not maintain conversational state, a stateless session bean does not require passivation or activation, further reducing the overhead of swapping. In short, stateless session beans are lightweight and fast.

Saying that a stateless session bean doesn't maintain any conversational state means that every method invocation is independent of previous invocations and everything the method needs to know has to be passed via the method's parameters. Since stateless session beans can't remember anything from one method invocation to the next, they must take care of an entire task in one method invocation. The only exception to this rule is information obtainable from the `SessionContext` and the JNDI ENC, or environment references that are injected directly into the bean (we'll talk later about dependency injection). Stateless session beans are EJB's version of the traditional transaction-processing applications, which are executed using a procedure call. The procedure executes from beginning to end and then returns the result. Once the procedure finishes, nothing about the data that was manipulated or the details of the request is remembered.

These restrictions don't mean that a stateless session bean can't have instance variables or maintain any kind of internal state. Nothing prevents you from keeping a variable that tracks the number of times a bean has been called or that saves data for debugging. An instance variable can even hold a reference to a live resource, such as a URL connection for logging, verifying credit cards through a different EJB, or anything else that might be useful—the resource should be obtained from the JNDI ENC or be injected into fields directly using EJB's injection features. However, it is important to remember that this state can never be visible to a client. A client can't assume that the same bean instance will service all of its requests. Instance variables may have different values in different bean instances, so their values can appear to change randomly as stateless session beans are swapped from one client to another. Therefore, anything you reference in instance variables should be generic. For example, each bean instance might reasonably record debugging messages—that might be the only way to figure out what is happening on a large server with many bean instances. The client doesn't know or care where debugging output is going. However, it would clearly be inappropriate for a stateless bean to remember that it was in the process of making a reservation for Madame X—the next time it is called, it may be servicing another client entirely.

Stateless session beans can be used for report generation, batch processing, or some stateless services such as validating credit cards. Another good application might be a StockQuote EJB that returns a stock's current price. Any activity that can be accomplished in one method call is a good candidate for the high-performance stateless session bean.

The ProcessPayment EJB

Chapters 2 and 3 discussed the TravelAgent EJB, which has a business method called `bookPassage( )` that uses the ProcessPayment EJB. The next section develops a complete definition of the TravelAgent EJB, including the logic of the `bookPassage( )` method. At this point, however, we are primarily interested in the ProcessPayment EJB, which is a stateless bean the TravelAgent EJB uses to charge the customer for the price of the cruise. Charging customers is a common activity in Titan's business systems. Not only does the reservation system need to charge customers, so do Titan's gift shops, boutiques, and other related businesses. Because many different systems charge customers for services, we've encapsulated the logic for charging customers in its own bean.

Payments are recorded in a special database table called `PAYMENT`. The `PAYMENT` data is batch-processed for accounting purposes and is not normally used outside of accounting. In other words, the data is only inserted by Titan's system; it is not read, updated, or deleted. Because the process of making a charge can be completed in one method, and because the data is not updated frequently and is not shared, we will use a stateless session bean for processing payments. Several different forms of payment can be used: credit card, check, and cash. We will model these payment forms in our stateless ProcessPayment EJB.

The database table: PAYMENT

The ProcessPayment EJB accesses an existing table in Titan's system, called the `PAYMENT` table. In your database, create a table called `PAYMENT`, with this definition:

```
CREATE TABLE PAYMENT
(
    customer_id     INTEGER,
    amount          DECIMAL(8,2),
    type            CHAR(10),
    check_bar_code  CHAR(50),
    check_number    INTEGER,
    credit_number   CHAR(20),
    credit_exp_date DATE
)
```

The business interface: ProcessPayment

A stateless session bean has one or more business interfaces. The business interface for ProcessPayment obviously needs a `byCredit( )` method because the TravelAgent EJB uses it. We can also identify two other methods that we'll need: `byCash( )` for customers paying cash and `byCheck( )` for customers paying with a personal check.

A business interface can be a remote or local interface, but not both. Remote business interfaces are able to receive method invocations from networked clients. When a client invokes a method on a session bean's remote interface, the parameter values and return value are *copied*. This is true irregardless of whether the client is running in the same VM or on another machine in the network. This is known as *call-by-value* semantics.

Local interfaces are available only within the same JVM as the session bean. Invoking on a local interface does not copy the parameters or return value. Because of this, local interfaces are said to follow what is termed *call-by-reference* semantics.

Since the TravelAgent EJB will be in the same deployment, the ProcessPayment EJB should provide a local interface so that invocations on ProcessPayment are efficient. The ProcessPayment EJB also has remote clients, so we'll provide a remote business interface as well.

The local and remote interfaces will publish the same API. To make our design a little bit cleaner, we will have these interfaces extend a base interface called `com.titan.processpayment.ProcessPayment`:

```
package com.titan.processpayment;

import com.titan.domain.*;

public interface ProcessPayment {

    public boolean byCheck(Customer customer, CheckDO check, double amount)
        throws PaymentException;

    public boolean byCash(Customer customer, double amount)
        throws PaymentException;

    public boolean byCredit(Customer customer, CreditCardDO card,
        double amount) throws PaymentException;
}
```

The EJB specification allows you to define a common base class for your remote and local interfaces if they share the same methods. Three business methods have been defined: `byCheck( )`, `byCash( )`, and `byCredit( )`, which take information relevant to the form of payment used and return a `boolean` value that indicates whether the payment succeeded. These methods can throw application-specific exceptions, like `PaymentException`. `PaymentException` is thrown if any problems occur while processing the payment, such as a low check number or an expired credit card. Notice, however, that nothing about the `ProcessPayment` interface is specific to the reservation system. It could be used just about anywhere in Titan's system. In addition, each method defined in the base business interface is completely independent of the others. All the data that is required to process a payment is obtained through the method's arguments. Next, let's specify both the remote and local interfaces:

```
package com.titan.processpayment;

import javax.ejb.Remote;
```

```
@Remote
public interface ProcessPaymentRemote extends ProcessPayment {
}

package com.titan.processpayment;

import javax.ejb.Local;

@Local
public interface ProcessPaymentLocal extends ProcessPayment{
}
```

The `ProcessPaymentRemote` and `ProcessPaymentLocal` interfaces extend the base `ProcessPayment` interface so that they do not have to duplicate the method definitions. `ProcessPaymentRemote` is identified as a remote interface by the `@javax.ejb.Remote` annotation and `ProcessPaymentLocal` by the `@javax.ejb.Local` annotation.

Entities as parameters

Each method of the ProcessPayment EJB's business interface takes a Customer entity bean as a parameter. Because entity beans are plain Java objects, they can be serialized across the network as plain Java objects as long as they implement `java.io.Serializable` or `Externalizable`. This is important because the ProcessPayment EJB accesses the internal state of the Customer entity. If every call to the Customer's get methods went over a remote interface (as is required in the EJB 2.1 specification), the ProcessPayment EJB would be very inefficient, because network calls are expensive. This is yet another example of the simplicity of the EJB 3.0 specification. In EJB 2.1, because entities were first-class components, one had to write parallel value object classes if one wanted to pass around the state of an entity instead of accessing it through the old remote interface model.

Domain objects: the CreditCardDO and CheckDO classes

The ProcessPayment EJB's business interface uses two classes that are particularly interesting, `CreditCardDO` and `CheckDO`:

```
/* CreditCardDO.java */
package com.titan.processpayment;

import java.util.Date;

public class CreditCardDO implements java.io.Serializable {
    final static public String MASTER_CARD = "MASTER_CARD";
    final static public String VISA = "VISA";
    final static public String AMERICAN_EXPRESS = "AMERICAN_EXPRESS";
    final static public String DISCOVER = "DISCOVER";
    final static public String DINERS_CARD = "DINERS_CLUB_CARD";

    public String number;
    public Date expiration;
    public String type;
```

```
    public CreditCardDO(String nmbr, Date exp, String typ) {
        number = nmbr;
        expiration = exp;
        type = typ;
    }
}

/* CheckDO.java */
package com.titan.processpayment;

public class CheckDO implements java.io.Serializable {
    public String checkBarCode;
    public int checkNumber;

    public CheckDO(String barCode, int number) {
        checkBarCode = barCode;
        checkNumber = number;
    }
}
```

`CreditCardDO` and `CheckDO` are *domain objects*. They are simply serializable Java classes, not enterprise beans; they provide a convenient mechanism for transporting related data. `CreditCardDO`, for example, collects all the credit card data together in one class, making it easier to pass the information across the network as well as making our interfaces a little cleaner.

An application exception: PaymentException

Any remote or local interface can throw application exceptions. Application exceptions should describe a business logic problem—in this case, a problem making a payment. Application exceptions should be meaningful to the client, providing a brief and relevant identification of the error.

It is important to understand what exceptions you should use, and when you should use them. Exceptions such as `javax.naming.NamingException` and `java.sql.SQLException` are thrown by other Java subsystems and have nothing to do with the business process an EJB is supposed to be modeling. These types of Java subsystem exceptions expose the implementation of your session bean. Another thing (which you will learn in Chapter 16) is that checked exceptions (non-`RuntimeException`s), by default, do not cause a transaction rollback. Instead of throwing these types of exceptions directly, you should catch them in a *try/catch* block and throw a more appropriate exception. A common practice is to wrap these checked exceptions in a `javax.ejb.EJBException`, as these types of subsystem errors are unrecoverable.

An `EJBException` indicates that the container ran into problems processing a business interface invocation. `EJBException` is unchecked (it extends `java.lang.RuntimeException`), so you won't get a compile error if you don't catch it. However, under certain circumstances, it is a good idea to catch `EJBException`, and in other circumstances, it should be propagated.

A PaymentException describes a specific business problem that is possibly recoverable. This makes it an application exception. The EJB container treats any exception that does not extend RuntimeException as an application exception. Here is the definition of PaymentException:

```
package com.titan.processpayment;

public class PaymentException extends java.lang.Exception {
    public PaymentException( ) {
        super( );
    }
    public PaymentException(String msg) {
        super(msg);
    }
}
```

An application exception is propagated to the calling client as is. Any instance variables you include in these exceptions should be serializable. Nonapplication exceptions are always wrapped in an EJBException. This means that any exception you throw that is or extends RuntimeException will be caught by the EJB container and wrapped in an EJBException. This is especially important for session beans that interact with entity beans. All exceptions thrown by Java Persistence interfaces are RuntimeExceptions. Your client code must be aware of this if it needs to take action on specific persistence exceptions. Exception behavior can be declared explicitly using the @javax.ejb.ApplicationException and the <application-exception> XML deployment descriptor metadata. These constructs are discussed in detail in Chapter 16, as they have a huge impact on transactional behavior.

The bean class: ProcessPaymentBean

The ProcessPayment EJB models a specific business process, so it is an excellent candidate for a stateless session bean. This bean really represents a set of independent operations—another indication that it is a good candidate for a stateless session bean. Here is the definition of the ProcessPaymentBean class:

```
package com.titan.processpayment;
import com.titan.domain.*;

import java.sql.*;
import javax.ejb.*;
import javax.annotation.Resource;

import javax.sql.DataSource;
import javax.ejb.EJBException;

@Stateless
public class ProcessPaymentBean
        implements ProcessPaymentRemote, ProcessPaymentLocal {
```

```
final public static String CASH = "CASH";
final public static String CREDIT = "CREDIT";
final public static String CHECK = "CHECK";

@Resource(mappedName="titanDB") DataSource dataSource;

@Resource(name="min") int minCheckNumber;

public boolean byCash(Customer customer, double amount)
    throws PaymentException {
    return process(customer.getId( ), amount, CASH, null, -1, null, null);
}

public boolean byCheck(Customer customer, CheckDO check, double amount)
    throws PaymentException {
    if (check.checkNumber > minCheckNumber) {
        return process(customer.getId( ), amount, CHECK,
            check.checkBarCode, check.checkNumber, null, null);
    }
    else {
        throw new PaymentException("Check number is too low.
            Must be at least "+minCheckNumber);
    }
}
public boolean byCredit(Customer customer, CreditCardDO card,
    double amount) throws PaymentException {
    if (card.expiration.before(new java.util.Date( ))) {
        throw new PaymentException("Expiration date has passed");
    }
    else {
        return process(customer.getId( ), amount, CREDIT, null,
        -1, card.number, new java.sql.Date(card.expiration.getTime( )));
    }
}
private boolean process(int customerID, double amount, String type,
    String checkBarCode, int checkNumber, String creditNumber,
    java.sql.Date creditExpDate) throws PaymentException {

    Connection con = null;

    PreparedStatement ps = null;

    try {
        con = dataSource.getConnection( );
        ps = con.prepareStatement
            ("INSERT INTO payment (customer_id, amount, type,"+
            "check_bar_code,check_number,credit_number,"+
            "credit_exp_date) VALUES (?,?,?,?,?,?,?)");
        ps.setInt(1,customerID);
        ps.setDouble(2,amount);
        ps.setString(3,type);
        ps.setString(4,checkBarCode);
        ps.setInt(5,checkNumber);
```

```
                ps.setString(6,creditNumber);
                ps.setDate(7,creditExpDate);
                int retVal = ps.executeUpdate( );
                if (retVal!=1) {
                    throw new EJBException("Payment insert failed");
                }
                return true;
            } catch(SQLException sql) {
                throw new EJBException(sql);
            } finally {
                try {
                    if (ps != null) ps.close( );
                    if (con!= null) con.close( );
                } catch(SQLException se) {
                    se.printStackTrace( );
                }
            }
        }
    }
```

The bean class is annotated with the `@javax.ejb.Stateless` annotation to identify that it is a stateless session bean:

```
Package javax.ejb;

@Target(TYPE) @Retention(RUNTIME)
public @interface Stateless {
   String name( ) default "";
}
```

The `name( )` attribute identifies the EJB name of the session bean. The EJB name defaults to the unqualified name of the bean class if you initialize this attribute. For ProcessPayment EJBs, the EJB name would default to `ProcessPaymentBean`. In most cases, you don't have to be aware of the concept of an EJB name. It is useful when you want to override or augment metadata with an XML deployment descriptor.

The bean class identifies its remote and local interfaces by implementing the `ProcessPaymentRemote` and `ProcessPaymentLocal` interfaces. When an EJB is deployed, the container looks at the interfaces of the bean class to see if they are annotated with `@javax.ejb.Local` or `@javax.ejb.Remote`. This introspection determines the remote and local interfaces of the bean class. Alternatively, the bean class does not have to implement any interfaces, and the `@Local` and `@Remote` annotations can be applied directly on the bean class.

```
@Stateless
@Local(ProcessPaymentLocal.class)
@Remote(ProcessPaymentRemote.class)
public class ProcessPaymentBean {

    final public static String CASH = "CASH";
    final public static String CREDIT = "CREDIT";
    final public static String CHECK = "CHECK";
```

When used on the bean class, the @Local and @Remote annotations take an array of interface classes. It is not recommended that you use this approach unless you have to, as implementing your business interfaces directly enforces the contract between the bean class and these interfaces.

The three payment methods use the private helper method process( ), which does the work of adding the payment to the database. This strategy reduces the possibility of programmer error and makes the bean easier to maintain. The process( ) method does not use entity beans but simply inserts the payment information directly into the PAYMENT table using JDBC. The JDBC connection is obtained from the datasource field of the bean class.

The byCheck( ) and byCredit( ) methods contain some logic to validate the data before processing it. byCredit( ) verifies that the credit card's expiration date does not precede the current date. If it does, a PaymentException is thrown. byCheck( ) verifies that the serial number of the check is higher than a certain minimum. This is determined by the minCheckNumber field. If the check number is lower than this value, a PaymentException is thrown.

Accessing environment properties (injection)

The datasource and minCheckNumber fields are examples of session bean fields that are initialized by the EJB's environment. Each EJB container has its own internal registry where it stores configuration values and references to external resources and services. This registry is called the Enterprise Naming Context (ENC). If you look at the declaration of these member variables, you will see that they are annotated with @javax.annotation.Resource. This tells the EJB container that when an instance of the bean class is instantiated, those fields must be initialized with values in the container's ENC.

When the EJB container is deployed, the ENC is populated with metadata embedded in annotations like @Resource, and with information stored in any EJB XML deployment descriptor. For example, the @Resource annotation that tags the datasource field contains a mappedName( ) attribute which identifies the external JDBC data source that should be mapped into the ENC. For minCheckNumber, the @Resource annotation identifies a named value within the ENC that may be used to initialize the field externally. This named value can be configured using the EJB's XML deployment descriptor:

```
<ejb-jar
      xmlns="http://java.sun.com/xml/ns/javaee"
      xmlns:xsi="http://www.w3.org/2001/XMLSchema-instance"
      xsi:schemaLocation="http://java.sun.com/xml/ns/javaee
                          http://java.sun.com/xml/ns/javaee/ejb-jar_3_0.xsd"
      version="3.0">
   <enterprise-beans>
     <session>
```

```
        <ejb-name>ProcessPaymentBean</ejb-name>
        <env-entry>
            <env-entry-name>min</env-entry-name>
            <env-entry-type>java.lang.Integer</env-entry-type>
            <env-entry-value>250</env-entry-value>
        </env-entry>
    </session>
  </enterprise-beans>
</ejb-jar>
```

The XML populates the EJB's ENC under the name `min` with a value of `250`. It is a good idea to capture thresholds and other limits in the bean's environment properties instead of hardcoding them: it gives you greater flexibility. If, for example, Titan decided to raise the minimum check number, you would need to change only the bean's XML deployment descriptor, not the class definition. The exact semantics of the `<env-entry>` and `@Resource` annotation are discussed in detail in Chapter 14.

The XML Deployment Descriptor

EJB has an optional XML deployment descriptor defined in the *META-INF/ejb-jar.xml* file of the EJB's JAR file. You can use this descriptor as an alternative to annotations, to augment metadata that is not declared as an annotation, or to override an annotation. The choice is up to you. Here is a deployment descriptor that provides a complete annotation-alternative definition of the ProcessPayment EJB:

```
<?xml version="1.0"?>
<ejb-jar
       xmlns="http://java.sun.com/xml/ns/javaee"
       xmlns:xsi="http://www.w3.org/2001/XMLSchema-instance"
       xsi:schemaLocation="http://java.sun.com/xml/ns/javaee
                           http://java.sun.com/xml/ns/javaee/ejb-jar_3_0.xsd"
       version="3.0">
   <enterprise-beans>
      <session>
         <ejb-name>ProcessPaymentBean</ejb-name>
         <remote>com.titan.processpayment.ProcessPaymentRemote</remote>
         <local>com.titan.processpayment.ProcessPaymentLocal</local>
         <ejb-class>com.titan.processpayment.ProcessPaymentBean</ejb-class>
         <session-type>Stateless</session-type>
         <resource-ref>
             <res-ref-name>theDatasource</res-ref-name>
             <res-type>javax.sql.DataSource</res-type>
             <res-auth>Container</res-auth>
             <mapped-name>titandb</mapped-name>
             <injection-target>
                <injection-target-class>
                   com.titan.processpayment.ProcessPaymentBean
                </injection-target-class>
                <injection-target-name>dataSource</injection-target-name>
             </injection-target>
         </resource-ref>
```

```
            <env-entry>
               <env-entry-name>min</env-entry-name>
               <env-entry-type>java.lang.Integer</env-entry-type>
               <env-entry-value>250</env-entry-value>
               <injection-target>
                  <injection-target-class>
                     com.titan.processpayment.ProcessPaymentBean
                  </injection-target-class>
                  <injection-target-name>minCheckNumber</injection-target-name>
               </injection-target>
            </env-entry>
         </session>
      </enterprise-beans>
   </ejb-jar>
```

What's interesting about an XML-only deployment is that if you used RuntimeException rather than EJBException within your bean class, your Java code would have no references to any EJB-specific APIs. If you looked at the Java code, you wouldn't even know that it was an EJB.

The <enterprise-beans> element contained in <ejb-jar> defines the set of EJBs you are deploying. The <session> element denotes that you are deploying a session bean. <ejb-name> gives the session bean an identity that you can reference. The <remote> and <local> elements identify the business interfaces of the bean, and <ejb-class> declares the bean class. The <session-type> element identifies the session bean as a stateless session bean. <resource-ref> and <env-entry> initialize the datasource and minCheckNumber fields of the bean class (details are provided in Chapter 14).

The XML deployment descriptor schema also supports partial XML definitions. For example, if you just wanted to configure the minCheckNumber field in XML, you wouldn't have to declare every piece of metadata about the EJB:

```
<ejb-jar>
   <session>
      <ejb-name>ProcessPaymentBean</ejb-name>
      <env-entry>
         <env-entry-name>min</env-entry-name>
         <env-entry-type>java.lang.Integer</env-entry-type>
         <env-entry-value>250</env-entry-value>
      </env-entry>
   </session>
</ejb-jar>
```

SessionContext

The javax.ejb.SessionContext interface provides a view into the EJB container's environment. The SessionContext object can be used as the bean instance's interface to the EJB container to obtain information about the context of the method invocation call and to provide quick access to various EJB services. A session bean can obtain a reference to its SessionContext by using the @Resource annotation:

```
@Stateless
public class ProcessPaymentBean implements ProcessPaymentLocal {

   @Resource SessionContext ctx;
...
}
```

SessionContext allows you to obtain information such as the current user that is invoking on the EJB or to look up entries within the EJB's ENC. Let's look at the javax.ejb.SessionContext interface:

```
public interface javax.ejb.SessionContext extends javax.ejb.EJBContext {
    EJBLocalObject getEJBLocalObject( ) throws IllegalStateException
    EJBObject getEJBObject( ) throws IllegalStateException;
    MessageContext getMessageContext( ) throws IllegalStateException;

    <T> getBusinessObject(Class<T> businessInterface) throws IllegalStateException;
    Class getInvokedBusinessInterface( );
}
```

The getEJBObject( ) and getEJBLocalObject( ) methods are obsolete and will throw an exception if invoked on. They are objects that are specific to the EJB 2.1 style of defining EJBs.

The SessionContext.getBusinessObject( ) method returns a reference to the current EJB that can be invoked on by other clients. This reference is the EJB equivalent to Java's this pointer. The businessInterface parameter must be one of the EJB's remote or local interfaces so that the container knows whether to create a remote or local reference to the current EJB. The getBusinessObject( ) method allows the bean instance to get its own EJB object reference, which it can then pass to other beans. Here is an example:

```
@Stateless
public class A_Bean implements A_BeanRemote {
    @Resource private SessionContext context;
    public void someMethod( ) {
        B_BeanRemote  b = ... // Get a remote reference to B_Bean.
        A_BeanRemote mySelf =  getBusinessObject(A_BeanRemote.class);
        b.aMethod( mySelf );
    }
    ...
         }
```

It is illegal for a bean instance to pass a this reference to another bean; instead, it passes its remote or local EJB object reference, which the bean instance gets from its SessionContext.

The SessionContext.getInvokedBusinessInterface( ) method allows you to determine whether your EJB was invoked on through its remote, local, or web service interface. It returns the invoked business interface as a class.

EJBContext

SessionContext extends the javax.ejb.EJBContext class. EJBContext defines several methods that provide useful information to a bean at runtime.

Here is the definition of the EJBContext interface:

```
package javax.ejb;
public interface EJBContext {

    public Object lookup(String name);

    // EJB 2.1 only: TimerService
    public TimerService getTimerService( )
       throws java.lang.IllegalStateException;

    // security methods
    public java.security.Principal getCallerPrincipal( );
    public boolean isCallerInRole(java.lang.String roleName);

    // transaction methods
    public javax.transaction.UserTransaction getUserTransaction( )
        throws java.lang.IllegalStateException;
    public boolean getRollbackOnly( )
        throws java.lang.IllegalStateException;
    public void setRollbackOnly( )
        throws java.lang.IllegalStateException;

    // deprecated and obsolete methods
    public java.security.Identity getCallerIdentity( );
    public boolean isCallerInRole(java.security.Identity role);
    public java.util.Properties getEnvironment( );

    public EJBHome getEJBHome( )
       java.lang.IllegalStateException;
    public EJBLocalHome getEJBLocalHome( )
       java.lang.IllegalStateException;

}
```

EJBContext.lookup( ) is a convenience method that allows you to look up entries in the EJB's ENC.

The EJBContext.getTimerService( ) method returns a reference to the container's Timer Service, which allows the stateless bean to set up notifications of timed events for itself. In other words, a session bean can set alarms so that the container will call it when a specific date arrives or some interval of time has passed. The Timer Service can also be injected using the @Resource annotation. The Timer Service is covered in detail in Chapter 13.

The EJBContext.getCallerPrincipal( ) method is used to obtain the java.security.Principal object representing the client that is currently accessing the bean. The Principal object can, for example, be used by an EJB to track the identities of clients making updates:

```
@Stateless
public class BankBean implements Bank {
    @Resource SessionContext context;
    ...
    public void withdraw(int acctid, double amount) throws AccessDeniedException {
        String modifiedBy = principal.getName( );
        ...
    }
    ...
}
```

The EJBContext.isCallerInRole( ) method tells you whether the client accessing the bean is a member of a specific role, identified by a role name. This method is useful when more access control is needed than simple method-based access control can provide. In a banking system, for example, you might allow the Teller role to make most withdrawals but only the Manager role to make withdrawals of more than $10,000. This kind of fine-grained access control cannot be addressed through EJB's security attributes, because it involves a business logic problem. Therefore, we can use the isCallerInRole( ) method to augment the automatic access control provided by EJB. First, let's assume that all managers are also tellers. The business logic in the withdraw( ) method uses isCallerInRole( ) to make sure that only the Manager role can withdraw sums of more than $10,000:

```
@Stateless
public class BankBean implements Bank {
    @Resource SessionContext context;

    public void withdraw(int acctid, double amount) throws AccessDeniedException {

        if (amount > 10000) {
            boolean isManager = context.isCallerInRole("Manager");
            if (!isManager) {
                // Only Managers can withdraw more than 10k.
                throw new AccessDeniedException( );
            }
        }

    }
    ...
}
```

The transactional methods—getUserTransaction( ), setRollbackOnly( ), and getRollbackOnly( )—are described in detail in Chapter 16.

EJBContext contains some methods that were used in older EJB specifications but have been abandoned in EJB 3.0. The security methods that interact with Identity classes, as well as the getEnvironment( ), EJBContext.getEJBHome( ), and EJBContext.getEJBLocalHome( ) methods, are now obsolete. A RuntimeException is thrown if these methods are executed.

The material on EJBContext covered in this section applies equally well to message-driven beans. There are some exceptions, however, and these differences are covered in Chapter 12.

The Life Cycle of a Stateless Session Bean

The life cycle of a stateless session bean is very simple. It has only two states: *Does Not Exist* and *Method-Ready Pool*. The Method-Ready Pool is an instance pool of stateless session bean objects that are not in use. Because of all the injection and such that can happen, it can be more efficient to save stateless bean instances when they are not in use. This is an important difference between stateless and stateful session beans; stateless beans define instance pooling in their life cycles and stateful beans do not.* Figure 11-1 illustrates the states and transitions a stateless session bean instance goes through in its lifetime.

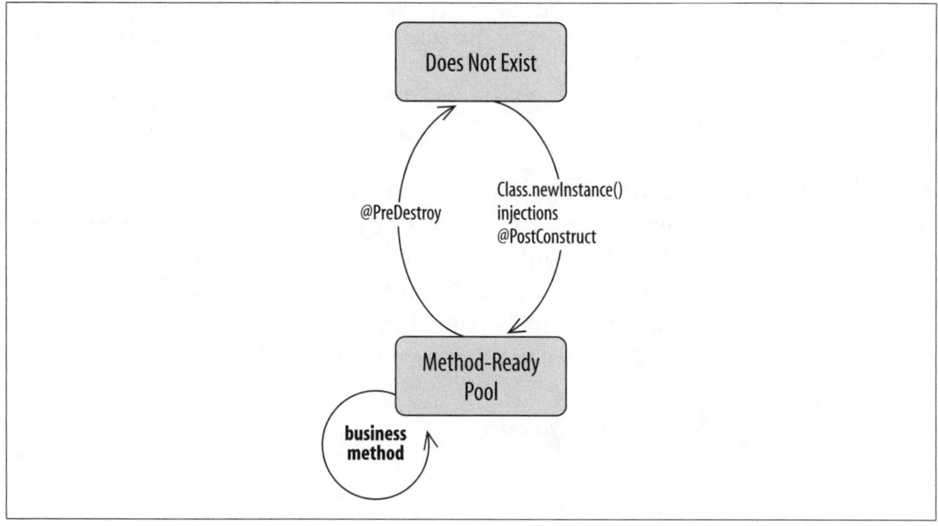

Figure 11-1. Stateless session bean life cycle

* Some vendors may *not* pool stateless instances but may instead create and destroy instances with each method invocation. This is an implementation-specific decision that shouldn't affect the specified life cycle of the stateless bean instance.

The Does Not Exist State

When a bean is in the Does Not Exist state, it is not an instance in the memory of the system. In other words, it has not been instantiated yet.

The Method-Ready Pool

Stateless bean instances enter the Method-Ready Pool as the container needs them. When the EJB server is first started, it may create a number of stateless bean instances and enter them into the Method-Ready Pool. (The actual behavior of the server depends on the implementation.) When the number of stateless instances servicing client requests is insufficient, more can be created and added to the pool.

Transitioning to the Method-Ready Pool

When an instance transitions from the Does Not Exist state to the Method-Ready Pool, three operations are performed on it. First, the bean instance is instantiated by invoking the `Class.newInstance()` method on the stateless bean class. Second, the container injects any resources that the bean's metadata has requested via an injection annotation or XML deployment descriptor.

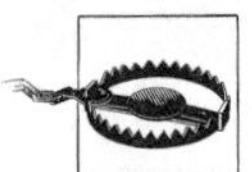

You must always provide a *default constructor*. A default constructor is a public constructor with no parameters. The container instantiates instances of the bean class using `Class.newInstance()`, which requires a no-arg constructor. If no constructors are defined, the no-arg constructor is implicit.

Finally, the EJB container will post a post-construction event. The bean class can register for this event by annotating a method with `@javax.annotation.PostConstruct`. This annotated method is called by the container after the bean is instantiated. The callback method can be of any name, but it must return `void`, have no parameters, and throw no checked exceptions. The bean class may define only one `@PostConstruct` method (but it is not required to do so).

```
@Stateless
public class MyBean implements MyLocal {

   @PostConstruct
   public void myInit() {}
```

Alternatively, you can declare your `@PostConstruct` method in the EJB's XML deployment descriptor:

```
<ejb-jar>
   <enterprise-beans>
      <session>
         <ejb-name>MyBean</ejb-name>
         <post-construct>
```

```
            <lifecycle-callback-method>myInit</lifecycle-callback-method>
        </post-construct>
    </session>
  </enterprise-beans>
</ejb-jar>
```

Stateless session beans are not subject to activation, so they can maintain open connections to resources for their entire life cycles.* The @PreDestroy method should close any open resources before the stateless session bean is evicted from memory at the end of its life cycle. You'll read more about @PreDestroy later in this section.

Life in the Method-Ready Pool

Once an instance is in the Method-Ready Pool, it is ready to service client requests. When a client invokes a business method on an EJB object, the method call is delegated to any available instance in the Method-Ready Pool. While the instance is executing the request, it is unavailable for use by other EJB objects. Once the instance has finished, it is immediately available to any EJB object that needs it. Stateless session instances are dedicated to an EJB object only for the duration of a single method call.

When an instance is swapped in, its SessionContext changes to reflect the context of the EJB object and the client invoking the method. The bean instance may be included in the transactional scope of the client's request and it may access SessionContext information specific to the client request: for example, the security and transactional methods. Once the instance has finished servicing the client, it is disassociated from the EJB object and returned to the Method-Ready Pool.

Clients that need a remote or local reference to a stateless session bean begin by having the reference injected (servlet support injection, for example), or by looking up the stateless bean in JNDI. The reference returned does not cause a session bean instance to be created or pulled from the pool until a method is invoked on it.

PostConstruct is invoked only once in the life cycle of an instance: when it is transitioning from the Does Not Exist state to the Method-Ready Pool. It is not reinvoked every time a client requests a remote reference to the bean.

Transitioning out of the Method-Ready Pool: the death of a stateless bean instance

Bean instances leave the Method-Ready Pool for the Does Not Exist state when the server no longer needs them—that is, when the server decides to reduce the total size of the Method-Ready Pool by evicting one or more instances from memory. The

* The duration of a stateless bean instance's life is assumed to be very long. However, some EJB servers may actually destroy and create instances with every method invocation, making this strategy less attractive. Consult your vendor's documentation for details on how your EJB server handles stateless instances.

process begins when a PreDestroy event on the bean is triggered. The bean class can register for this event by annotating a method with @javax.annotation.PreDestroy. The container calls this annotated method when the PreDestroy event is fired. This callback method can be of any name, but it must return void, have no parameters, and throw no checked exceptions. The bean class may define only one @PreDestroy method (but it is not required to do so). An @PreDestroy callback method can perform any cleanup operations, such as closing open resources.

```
@Stateless
public class MyBean implements MyLocal {

   @PreDestroy
   public void cleanup( ) {
      ...
   }
```

Alternatively, you can declare your @PreDestroy method in the EJB's XML deployment descriptor:

```
<ejb-jar>
   <enterprise-beans>
      <session>
          <ejb-name>MyBean</ejb-name>
          <pre-destroy>
             <lifecycle-callback-method>cleanup</lifecycle-callback-method>
          </pre-destroy>
      </session>
   </enterprise-beans>
</ejb-jar>
```

As with @PostConstruct, @PreDestroy is invoked only once: when the bean is about to transition to the Does Not Exist state. During this callback method, the SessionContext and access to the JNDI ENC are still available to the bean instance. Following the execution of the @PreDestroy method, the bean is dereferenced and eventually garbage-collected.

The Stateful Session Bean

Each stateful session bean is dedicated to one client for the life of the bean instance; it acts on behalf of that client as its agent. Stateful session beans are not swapped among EJB objects nor are they kept in an instance pool, like stateless session bean instances are. Once a stateful session bean is instantiated and assigned to an EJB object, it is dedicated to that EJB object for its entire life cycle.*

* This is a conceptual model. Some EJB containers may actually use instance swapping with stateful session beans but make it appear as if the same instance is servicing all requests. Conceptually, however, the same stateful session bean instance services all requests.

Stateful session beans maintain conversational state, which means that the instance variables of the bean class can maintain data specific to the client between method invocations. This makes it possible for methods to be interdependent so that changes made to the bean's state in one method call can affect the results of subsequent method invocations. Therefore, every method call from a client must be serviced by the same instance (at least conceptually), so the bean instance's state can be predicted from one method invocation to the next. In contrast, stateless session beans don't maintain client-specific data from one method call to the next, so any instance can be used to service any method call from any client.

Although stateful session beans maintain conversational state, they are not themselves persistent, like entity beans are. Entity beans represent data in the database; their persistence fields are written directly to the database. Stateful session beans can access the database but do not represent data in the database.

Stateful session beans are often considered extensions of the client. This makes sense if you think of a client as being made up of operations and state. Each task may rely on some information gathered or changed by a previous operation. A GUI client is a perfect example: when you fill in the fields on a GUI client you are creating conversational state. Pressing a button executes an operation that might fill in more fields, based on the information you entered previously. The information in the fields is conversational state.

Stateful session beans allow you to encapsulate some of the business logic and conversational state of a client and move it to the server. Moving this logic to the server thins the client application and makes the system as a whole easier to manage. The stateful session bean acts as an agent for the client, managing processes or taskflow to accomplish a set of tasks; it manages the interactions of other beans in addition to direct data access over several operations to accomplish a complex set of tasks. By encapsulating and managing taskflow on behalf of the client, stateful beans present a simplified interface that hides the details of many interdependent operations on the database and other beans from the client.

Getting Set Up for the TravelAgent EJB

The TravelAgent EJB will use the Cabin, Cruise, Reservation, and Customer entity beans developed in Chapters 6 and 7. It will coordinate the interaction of these entity beans to book a passenger on a cruise. We'll modify the Reservation entity that was used in Chapter 7 so that it can be created with all of its relationships identified right away. In other words, we will define another constructor in addition to a default constructor:

```
public class Reservation {

    public Reservation( ) {}
```

```
    public Reservation(Customer customer, Cruise cruise,
        Cabin cabin, double price, Date dateBooked) {

        setAmountPaid(price);
        setDate(dateBooked);
        setCruise(cruise);

        Set cabins = new HashSet( );
        cabins.add(cabin);
        this.setCabins(cabins);
        Set customers = new HashSet( );
        customers.add(customer);
        this.setCustomers(customers);
    }
```

Creating this constructor will allow us to avoid calling all of those *setter* methods within our TravelAgent EJB code and will make it less cluttered.

The TravelAgent EJB

The TravelAgent EJB, which we have already seen, is a stateful session bean that encapsulates the process of making a reservation on a cruise. We will develop this bean further to demonstrate how stateful session beans can be used as taskflow objects. We won't develop a local interface for the TravelAgent EJB, partly because it is designed to be used by remote clients (and therefore doesn't require local component interfaces), and partly because the rules for developing local interfaces for stateful session beans are the same as those for stateless session beans.

The remote interface: TravelAgent

As a stateful session bean that models taskflow, the TravelAgent EJB manages the interactions among several other beans while maintaining conversational state. Here's the modified `TravelAgentRemote` interface:

```
package com.titan.travelagent;

import com.titan.processpayment.CreditCardDO;
import javax.ejb.Remote;
import com.titan.domain.Customer;

@Remote
public interface TravelAgentRemote {

    public Customer findOrCreateCustomer(String first, String last);

    public void updateAddress(Address addr);

    public void setCruiseID(int cruise);

    public void setCabinID(int cabin);
```

```
        public TicketDO bookPassage(CreditCardDO card, double price)
            throws IncompleteConversationalState;
    }
```

The purpose of the TravelAgent EJB is to make cruise reservations. To accomplish this task, the bean needs to know which cruise, cabin, and customer make up the reservation. Therefore, the client using the TravelAgent EJB needs to gather this kind of information before booking the reservation. The `TravelAgentRemote` interface provides methods for setting the IDs of the cruise and cabin that the customer wants to book. We can assume that the cabin ID comes from a list and that the cruise ID comes from some other source. The client will pass in the customer's name to the `findOrCreateCustomer( )` method. If the customer exists in the database, the TravelAgent EJB will use that customer; otherwise, one will be created.

Once the customer, cruise, and cabin are chosen, the TravelAgent EJB is ready to process the reservation. This operation is performed by the `bookPassage( )` method, which needs the customer's credit card information and the price of the cruise. `bookPassage( )` is responsible for charging the customer's account, reserving the chosen cabin in the right ship on the right cruise, and generating a ticket for the customer. How this is accomplished is not important to us at this point; when we are developing the remote interface, we are concerned only with the business definition of the bean. We will discuss the implementation when we talk about the bean class.

Note that the `bookPassage()` method throws an application-specific exception, `IncompleteConversationalState`. This exception is used to communicate business problems encountered while booking a customer on a cruise. The `IncompleteConversationalState` exception indicates that the TravelAgent EJB did not have enough information to process the booking. Here's the `IncompleteConversationalState` class:

```
package com.titan.travelagent;

public class IncompleteConversationalState extends java.lang.Exception {
    public IncompleteConversationalState( ){super( );}
    public IncompleteConversationalState(String msg){super(msg);}
}
```

Domain objects: the TicketDO class

Like the `CreditCardDO` and `CheckDO` classes used in the ProcessPayment EJB, the `TicketDO` class is defined as a pass-by-value object. One could argue that a ticket should be the Reservation entity bean, since it is a plain Java object and could be serialized back to the client. However, determining how a business object is used can also dictate whether it should be a bean or simply a class. Because the Reservation entity bean references a lot of interrelated entities, the number of objects serialized back to the client could become quite large, and thus very inefficient. With the `TicketDO` object, you can pull together the exact information you want to send back to the client.

The constructor for TicketDO uses the entities from which it pulls the data:

```
package com.titan.travelagent;

import com.titan.domain.Cruise;
import com.titan.domain.Cabin;
import com.titan.domain.Customer;

public class TicketDO implements java.io.Serializable {
    public int customerID;
    public int cruiseID;
    public int cabinID;
    public double price;
    public String description;

    public TicketDO(Customer customer, Cruise cruise,
        Cabin cabin, double price) {
            description = customer.getFirstName( )+
                " " + customer.getLastName( ) +
                " has been booked for the "
                + cruise.getName( ) +
                " cruise on ship " +
                  cruise.getShip( ).getName( ) + ".\n" +
                " Your accommodations include " +
                  cabin.getName( ) +
                " a " + cabin.getBedCount( ) +
                " bed cabin on deck level " + cabin.getDeckLevel( ) +
                ".\n Total charge = " + price;
            customerID = customer.getId( );
            cruiseID = cruise.getId( );
            cabinID = cabin.getId( );
            this.price = price;
        }

    public String toString( ) {
        return description;
    }
}
```

Taking a peek at the client view

Before settling on definitions for your component interfaces, it is a good idea to figure out how clients will use the bean. Imagine that the TravelAgent EJB is used by a Java application with GUI fields. These fields capture the customer's preference for the type of cruise and cabin. We start by examining the code used at the beginning of the reservation process:

```
Context jndi = getInitialContext( );
Object ref = jndi.lookup("TravelAgentBean/remote");
TravelAgentRemote agent = (TravelAgentRemote)
    PortableRemoteObject.narrow(ref, TravelAgentRemote.class);
```

This code simply looks up the TravelAgent EJB in JNDI. The act of doing this creates a session that is dedicated to the client and is represented by the agent variable.

Every time you look up a stateful session bean in JNDI, a new session is created.

```
Customer cust = agent.findOrCreateCustomer(textField_firstName.getText( ),
                                   textField_lastName.getText( ));
```

This code locates an existing customer or creates a new customer based on information the travel agent gathered over the phone. The act of calling `findOrCreateCustomer( )` will store the customer being referenced in the TravelAgent EJB's internal state. The real-life travel agent also gathers any address changes to the client and makes those changes on the server.

```
Address updatedAddress = new Address(textField_street.getText( ), ...);
agent.updateAddress(updatedAddress);
```

Next, we gather the cruise and cabin choices from another part of the client application:

```
Integer cruise_id = new Integer(textField_cruiseNumber.getText( ));

Integer cabin_id = new Integer( textField_cabinNumber.getText( ));

agent.setCruiseID(cruise_id);
agent.setCabinID(cabin_id);
```

The travel agent chooses the cruise and cabin the customer wishes to reserve. These IDs are set in the TravelAgent EJB, which maintains the conversational state for the whole process.

At the end of the process, the travel agent completes the reservation by processing the booking and generating a ticket. Because the TravelAgent EJB has maintained the conversational state, caching the customer, cabin, and cruise information, only the credit card and price are needed to complete the transaction:

```
String cardNumber = textField_cardNumber.getText( );
Date date = dateFormatter.parse(textField_cardExpiration.getText( ));
String cardBrand = textField_cardBrand.getText( );
CreditCardDO card = new CreditCardDO(cardNumber,date,cardBrand);
double price = double.valueOf(textField_cruisePrice.getText( )).doubleValue( );
TicketDO ticket = agent.bookPassage(card,price);
PrintingService.print(ticket);
```

This summary of how the client will use the TravelAgent EJB confirms that our remote interface is workable. We can now move ahead with development.

The bean class: TravelAgentBean

We can now implement all of the behavior expressed in the new remote interface for the TravelAgent EJB. Here is a partial definition of the new TravelAgentBean class:

```
package com.titan.travelagent;

import com.titan.processpayment.*;
import com.titan.domain.*;
import javax.ejb.*;
import javax.persistence.*;
import javax.annotation.EJB;
import java.util.Date;

@Stateful
public class TravelAgentBean implements TravelAgentRemote {

    @PersistenceContext(unitName="titan")
    private EntityManager entityManager;

    @EJB private ProcessPaymentLocal processPayment;

    private Customer customer;
    private Cruise cruise;
    private Cabin cabin;

    public Customer findOrCreateCustomer(String first, String last) {
        try {
           Query q = entityManager.createQuery("from Customer c where c.firstName = :
first and c.lastName = :last");
           q.setParameter("first", first);
           q.setParameter("last", last);
           this.customer = (Customer)q.getSingleResult( );
        } catch (NoResultException notFound) {
           this.customer = new Customer( );
           this.customer.setFirstName(first);
           this.customer.setLastName(last);
           entityManager.persist(this.customer);
        }
        return this.customer;
    }

    public void updateAddress(Address addr) {
        this.customer.setAddress(addr);
        this.customer = entityManager.merge(customer);
    }

    public void setCabinID(int cabinID) {
        this.cabin = entityManager.find(Cabin.class, cabinID);
        if (cabin == null) throw new NoResultException("Cabin not found");
    }

    public void setCruiseID(int cruiseID) {
        this.cruise = entityManager.find(Cruise.class, cruiseID);
```

```
        if (cruise == null) throw new NoResultException("Cruise not found");
    }

    @Remove
    public TicketDO bookPassage(CreditCardDO card, double price)
        throws IncompleteConversationalState {

        if (customer == null || cruise == null || cabin == null)
        {
            throw new IncompleteConversationalState( );
        }
        try {
            Reservation reservation = new Reservation(
                               customer, cruise, cabin, price, new Date( ));
            entityManager.persist(reservation);

            processPayment.byCredit(customer, card, price);

            TicketDO ticket = new TicketDO(customer, cruise, cabin, price);
            return ticket;
        } catch(Exception e) {
            throw new EJBException(e);
        }
    }
}
```

This is a lot of code to digest, so we will approach it in small pieces.

```
@Stateful
public class TravelAgentBean implements TravelAgentRemote {

    @PersistenceContext(unitName="titan")
    private EntityManager entityManager;

    @EJB private ProcessPaymentLocal processPayment;
```

The TravelAgent EJB needs a reference to Titan's entity manager service so that it can find, update, and create the entity beans that are needed. The `@javax.persistence.PersistenceContext` annotation causes the EJB container to initialize the `entityManager` field for this purpose. The ProcessPayment EJB is also needed to be able to set up a credit card payment. The `@javax.ejb.EJB` annotation is used to pull in a reference to this stateless session bean in much the same way as the `@Resource` annotation was used to initialize its `datasource` field in the ProcessPayment EJB's bean class. Chapter 14 discusses the semantics of these annotations in detail.

Next, let's examine the `findOrCreateCustomer( )` method:

```
    public Customer findOrCreateCustomer(String first, String last) {
        try {
           Query q = entityManager.createQuery("select c " +
                 + "from Customer c "
                 + "where c.firstName = :first and c.lastName = :last");
           q.setParameter("first", first);
           q.setParameter("last", last);
```

```
            this.customer = (Customer)q.getSingleResult( );
        } catch (NoResultException notFound) {
            this.customer = new Customer( );
            this.customer.setFirstName(first);
            this.customer.setLastName(last);
            entityManager.persist(this.customer);
        }
        return this.customer;
    }
```

The findOrCreateCustomer( ) method dynamically creates a query to search for an existing customer based on the first- and last-name parameters passed in. The Query.getSingleResult( ) method throws a javax.persistence.NoResultException. If thrown, this exception tells us that a brand-new Customer entity must be created.

```
    public void updateAddress(Address addr) {
        this.customer.setAddress(addr);
        this.customer = entityManager.merge(customer);
    }
```

The updateAddress( ) method simply synchronizes the address changes made on the client into the database. The customer field is no longer managed by the persistence context, as it was initialized separately in the findOrCreateCustomer( ) method and detached when that method finished. Since the Customer instance is detached, the EntityManager.merge( ) method is used to update changes made to the customer's address.

The TravelAgent EJB has methods for setting the desired cruise and cabin. These methods take int IDs as arguments and retrieve references to the appropriate Cruise or Cabin entity from the injected EntityManager. These references are also part of the TravelAgent EJB's conversational state. Here's how setCabinID( ) and getCabinID( ) are defined:

```
    public void setCabinID(int cabinID) {
        this.cabin = entityManager.find(Cabin.class, cabinID);
        if (cabin == null) throw new NoResultException("Cabin not found");
    }

    public void setCruiseID(int cruiseID) {
        this.cruise = entityManager.find(Cruise.class, cruiseID);
        if (cruise == null) throw new NoResultException("Cruise not found");
    }
```

We look up the Cabin and Cruise entities via the EntityManager.find( ) method. If this method returns null, we throw a NoResultException back to the client so that it is notified that the Cabin or Cruise entity is no longer valid.

It may seem strange that we set these values using int IDs, but we keep them in the conversational state as entity bean references. Using int IDs is simpler for the client, which does not work with their entity bean references. In the client code, we get the cabin and cruise IDs from text fields. Why make the client obtain a bean reference to the Cruise and Cabin entities when an ID is simpler? Also, we could have waited until the bookPassage( ) method was invoked before reconstructing the remote references, but this strategy keeps the bookPassage( ) method simple.

The bookPassage( ) method

The last point of interest in our bean definition is the bookPassage( ) method. This method uses the conversational state accumulated by the findOrCreateCustomer( ), setCabinID( ), and setCruiseID( ) methods to process a reservation for a customer. Here's how the bookPassage( ) method is defined:

```
@Remove
public TicketDO bookPassage(CreditCardDO card, double price)
    throws IncompleteConversationalState {

    if (customer == null || cruise == null || cabin == null)
    {
        throw new IncompleteConversationalState( );
    }
    try {
        Reservation reservation = new Reservation(
                               customer, cruise, cabin, price, new Date( ));
        entityManager.persist(reservation);

        process.byCredit(customer, card, price);

        TicketDO ticket = new TicketDO(customer, cruise, cabin, price);
        return ticket;
    } catch(Exception e) {
        throw new EJBException(e);
    }
}
```

This method demonstrates the taskflow concept. It uses several beans, including the ProcessPayment EJB and the Reservation, Customer, Cabin, and Cruise entities, to accomplish one task: booking a customer on a cruise. Deceptively simple, this method encapsulates several interactions that ordinarily might have been performed on the client. For the price of one bookPassage( ) call from the client, the TravelAgent EJB performs the following operations, in this order:

1. Creates a new Reservation object
2. Persists the new Reservation object with the entity manager service
3. Charges the customer's credit card using the ProcessPayment EJB
4. Generates a new TicketDO with all the pertinent information describing the customer's purchase

Notice that the bookPassage( ) method is annotated with the @javax.ejb.Remove annotation. The @Remove annotation tells the EJB container that when the method completes, the client no longer needs the session. After the `bookPassage()` method completes, the EJB container removes the session from the EJB container.

The TravelAgent EJB is now complete. We've learned that from a design standpoint, encapsulating the taskflow in a stateful session bean means a less complex interface for the client and more flexibility for implementing changes. We could easily change `bookPassage()` to check for overlapped bookings (when a customer books passage on two cruises with overlapping dates). This type of enhancement does not change the remote interface, so the client application does not need modification. Encapsulating taskflow in stateful session beans allows the system to evolve without impacting clients.

In addition, the type of clients used can change. One of the biggest problems with two-tier architectures—besides scalability and transactional control—is that the business logic is intertwined with the client logic. As a result, it is difficult to reuse the business logic in a different kind of client. With stateful session beans, this is not a problem, because stateful session beans are an extension of the client but are not bound to the client's presentation. Let's say that our first implementation of the reservation system used a Java applet with GUI widgets. The TravelAgent EJB would manage conversational state and perform all the business logic while the applet focused on the GUI presentation. If, at a later date, we decide to go to a thin client (HTML generated by a Java servlet, for example), we would simply reuse the TravelAgent EJB in the servlet. Because all the business logic is in the stateful session bean, the presentation (Java applet or servlet or something else) can change easily.

The TravelAgent EJB also provides transactional integrity for processing the customer's reservation. If any of the operations within the body of the `bookPassage()` method fails, all the operations are rolled back so that none of the changes is accepted. If the credit card cannot be charged by the ProcessPayment EJB, the newly created Reservation EJB and its associated record are not created. The transactional aspects of the TravelAgent EJB are explained in detail in Chapter 16.

The remote and local EJB references can be used within the same taskflow. For example, the `bookPassage()` method uses a local reference when accessing the ProcessPayment EJB. This usage is totally appropriate. The EJB container ensures that the transaction is atomic—i.e., that failures in either the remote or the local EJB reference will affect the entire transaction.

The XML Deployment Descriptor

Here is a deployment descriptor that provides a complete annotation-alternative definition of the TravelAgent EJB:

```
<?xml version="1.0"?>
<ejb-jar
       xmlns="http://java.sun.com/xml/ns/javaee"
       xmlns:xsi="http://www.w3.org/2001/XMLSchema-instance"
       xsi:schemaLocation="http://java.sun.com/xml/ns/javaee
                           http://java.sun.com/xml/ns/javaee/ejb-jar_3_0.xsd"
```

```
            version="3.0">
   <enterprise-beans>
      <session>
         <ejb-name>TravelAgentBean</ejb-name>
         <remote>com.titan.travelagent.TravelAgentRemote</remote>
         <ejb-class>com.titan.travelagent.TravelAgentBean</ejb-class>
         <session-type>Stateful</session-type>
         <ejb-local-ref>
             <ejb-ref-name>ejb/PaymentProcessor</ejb-ref-name>
             <ejb-ref-type>Session</ejb-ref-type>
             <local>com.titan.processpayment.ProcessPaymentLocal</local>
             <injection-target>
                <injection-target-class>
                   com.titan.travelagent.TravelAgentBean
                </injection-target-class>
                <injection-target-name>processPayment</injection-target-name>
             </injection-target>
          </ejb-local-ref>
          <persistence-context-ref>
             <persistence-context-ref-name>
                persistence/titan
             </persistence-context-ref-name>
             <persistence-unit-name>titan</persistence-unit-name>
             <injection-target>
                 <injection-target-class>
                    com.titan.travelagent.TravelAgentBean
                 </injection-target-class>
                 <injection-target-name>entityManager</injection-target-name>
             </injection-target>
          </persistence-context-ref>
      </session>
   </enterprise-beans>
</ejb-jar>
```

There is one minor difference between the stateful session bean syntax and that for stateless beans. The `<session-type>` element is set to `Stateful` rather than `Stateless`. You also see that we are using `<ejb-local-ref>` and `<persistence-context-ref>` to initialize the `processPayment` and `entityManager` fields of the bean class. These elements are explained in more detail in Chapter 14.

The Life Cycle of a Stateful Session Bean

The biggest difference between the stateful session bean and the other bean types is that stateful session beans do not use instance pooling. Stateful session beans are dedicated to one client for their entire lives, so swapping or pooling of instances isn't possible.* When they are idle, stateful session bean instances are simply evicted from

* Some vendors use pooling with stateful session beans, but that is a proprietary implementation and should not affect the specified life cycle of the stateful session bean.

memory. The EJB object remains connected to the client, but the bean instance is dereferenced and garbage-collected during inactive periods. This means that each stateful bean must be passivated before it is evicted in order to preserve the conversational state of the instance, and it must be activated to restore its state when the EJB object becomes active again.

The bean's perception of its life cycle depends on whether it implements a special interface called `javax.ejb.SessionSynchronization`. This interface defines an additional set of callback methods that notify the bean of its participation in transactions. A bean that implements `SessionSynchronization` can cache database data across several method calls before making an update. We have not discussed transactions in detail yet; we will consider this part of the bean's life cycle in Chapter 16. This section describes the life cycle of stateful session beans that do not implement the `SessionSynchronization` interface.

The life cycle of a stateful session bean has three states: Does Not Exist, Method-Ready, and Passivated. This sounds a lot like a stateless session bean, but the Method-Ready state is significantly different from the Method-Ready Pool of stateless beans. Figure 11-2 shows the state diagram for stateful session beans.

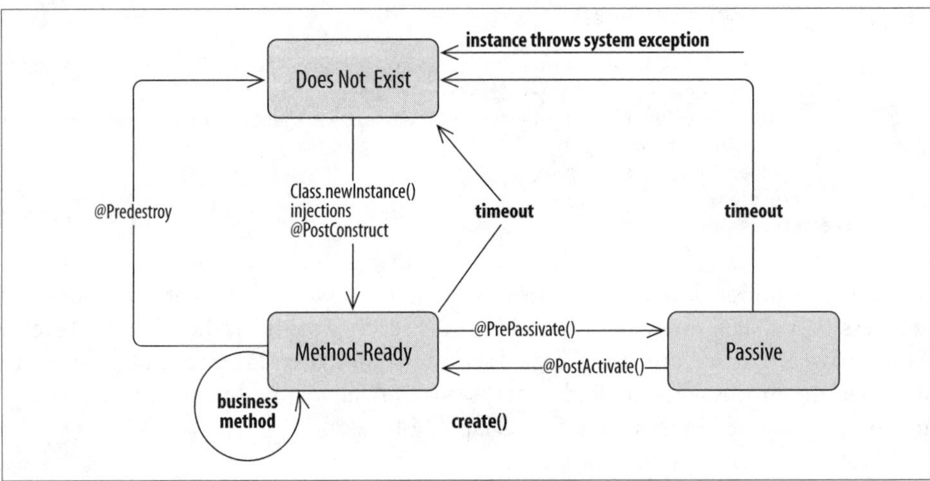

Figure 11-2. Stateful session bean life cycle

The Does Not Exist State

A stateful bean instance in the Does Not Exist state has not been instantiated yet. It doesn't exist in the system's memory.

The Method-Ready State

The Method-Ready state is the state in which the bean instance can service requests from its clients. This section explores the instance's transition into and out of the Method-Ready state.

Transitioning into the Method-Ready state

When a client invokes the first method on the stateful session bean reference, the bean's life cycle begins. The container invokes `newInstance( )` on the bean class, creating a new instance of the bean. Next, the container injects any dependencies into the bean instance. At this point, the bean instance is assigned to the client referencing it. Finally, just like stateless session beans, the container invokes any `@PostConstruct` callbacks if there is a method in the bean class that has this annotation applied. Once `@PostConstruct` has completed, the container continues with the actual method call.

Life in the Method-Ready state

While in the Method-Ready state, the bean instance is free to receive method invocations from the client, which may involve controlling the taskflow of other beans or accessing the database directly. During this time, the bean can maintain conversational state and open resources in its instance variables.

Transitioning out of the Method-Ready state

Bean instances leave the Method-Ready state to enter either the Passivated state or the Does Not Exist state. Depending on how the client uses the stateful bean, the EJB container's load, and the passivation algorithm used by the vendor, a bean instance may be passivated (and activated) several times in its life, or not at all. If the bean is removed, it enters the Does Not Exist state. A client application can remove a bean by invoking a business interface method annotated as `@Remove`.

The container can also move the bean instance from the Method-Ready state to the Does Not Exist state if the bean times out. Timeouts are declared at deployment time in a vendor-specific manner. When a timeout occurs in the Method-Ready state, the container may, but is not required to, call any `@PreDestroy` callback methods. A stateful bean cannot time out while a transaction is in progress.

The Passivated State

During the lifetime of a stateful session bean, there may be periods of inactivity when the bean instance is not servicing methods from the client. To conserve resources, the container can passivate the bean instance by preserving its conversational state and evicting the bean instance from memory. A bean's conversational state may consist of primitive values, objects that are serializable, and the following special types:

- `javax.ejb.SessionContext`
- `javax.jta.UserTransaction` (bean transaction interface)
- `javax.naming.Context` (only when it references the JNDI ENC)
- `javax.persistence.EntityManager`
- `javax.persistence.EntityManagerFactory`
- References to managed resource factories (e.g., `javax.sql.DataSource`)
- References to other EJBs

The types in this list (and their subtypes) are handled specially by the passivation mechanism. They do not need to be serializable; they will be maintained through passivation and restored automatically when the bean instance is activated.

When a bean is about to be passivated, a method on the bean class may be annotated with `@PrePassivate` to receive a callback for this event. This can be used to alert the bean instance that it is about to enter the Passivated state. At this time, the bean instance should close any open resources and set all nontransient, nonserializable fields to `null`. This prevents problems from occurring when the bean is serialized. Transient fields are simply ignored.

How does the container store the bean's conversational state? It's largely up to the container. Containers can use standard Java serialization to preserve the bean instance, or some other mechanism that achieves the same result. Some vendors, for example, simply read the values of the fields and store them in a cache. The container is required to preserve remote references to other beans with the conversational state. When the bean is activated, the container must restore any bean references automatically. The container must also restore any references to the special types listed earlier.

When the client makes a request on an EJB object whose bean is passivated, the container activates the instance. This involves deserializing the bean instance and reconstructing the `SessionContext` reference, bean references, and managed resource factories held by the instance before it was passivated. When a bean's conversational state has been successfully restored, an `@PostActivate` callback method is invoked on the bean instance if one is declared on the bean class. The bean instance should open any resources that cannot be passivated and initialize the values of any transient fields within the `@PostActivate` method. Once `@PostActivate` is complete, the bean is back in the Method-Ready state and is available to service client requests delegated by the EJB object.

The activation of a bean instance follows the rules of Java serialization, regardless of how the bean's state was actually stored. The exception to this is transient fields. In Java serialization, transient fields are set to their default values when an object is deserialized; primitive numbers become zero, Boolean fields `false`, and object references `null`. In EJB, transient fields can contain arbitrary values when the bean is activated. The values held by transient fields following activation are unpredictable across vendor implementations, so do not depend on them to be initialized. Instead, use an `@PostActivate` callback method to reset their values.

The container can also move the bean instance from the Passivated state to the Does Not Exist state if the bean times out. When a timeout occurs in the Passivated state, any `@PreDestroy` callback methods are not invoked.

System exceptions

Whenever a system exception is thrown by a bean method, the container invalidates the EJB object and destroys the bean instance. The bean instance moves directly to the Does Not Exist state, and any `@PreDestroy` call methods are *not* invoked.*

A system exception is any unchecked exception not annotated as an `@ApplicationException`, including `EJBException`. Application and system exceptions are explained in more detail in Chapter 16.

Stateful Session Beans and Extended Persistence Contexts

In Chapter 5, we discussed the differences between a transaction-scoped persistence context and an extended one. The `EntityManager` injected into the `TravelAgentBean` class with the `@PersistenceContext` annotation is a transaction-scoped persistence context. In Chapter 16, we will see that every method within `TravelAgentBean` has a transaction started and ended within the scope of that method. This means that any entity bean instance you persist or fetch is detached from the persistence context at the end of the method call. Any local caching the `EntityManager` instance had done is lost. This is why we have to call `EntityManager.merge( )` and reset the customer member variable in the `TravelAgentBean.updateAddress( )` method. The `Customer` instance we fetched in `findOrCreateCustomer( )` became unmanaged at the end of the method call, and the `EntityManager` no longer tracked the instance for state changes.

Wouldn't it be nice if all loaded entities could remain managed after any `TravelAgentBean` method call? This is exactly what an `EXTENDED` persistence context is used for. Stateful session beans are the only EJB component type that is allowed to inject an `EXTENDED` persistence context through the `@PersistenceContext` annotation. The extended persistence context is created and attached to the stateful bean instance before `@PostConstruct`. When the stateful bean instance is removed, the extended persistence context is also cleaned up. Because a stateful bean represents a

* Yes, this is a hole in the specification.

conversation with a client, it makes sense to cache and manage entity instances across method invocations. Stateless and message-driven beans are pooled, and managed entity instances would easily become stale and unusable. Let's look at how the `TravelAgentBean` class would change to use an extended persistence context:

```
import static javax.persistence.PersistenceContextType.EXTENDED;

@Stateful
public class TravelAgentBean implements TravelAgentRemote {

    @PersistenceContext(unitName="titan", type=EXTENDED)
    private EntityManager entityManager;

    public void updateAddress(Address addr) {
       customer.setAddress(addr);
    }
...
}
```

When the persistence context type is marked as `EXTENDED`, queried entities will remain managed and attached to the stateful session bean's `EntityManager`. With this setting, the `updateAddress( )` method can get a little simpler, as the `EntityManager.merge( )` method is no longer needed. Any extended persistence context that a stateful bean has will automatically be registered with a transaction when any transactional method is invoked. When the `updateAddress( )` method completes, the EJB container will automatically commit the state changes made to `customer` without having to manually call the `merge( )` or `flush( )` method.

Nested Stateful Session Beans

Stateful session beans behave in interesting ways when you inject other stateful session beans within them. When you inject a stateful session bean into an EJB with the `@EJB` annotation, a session is created for that injected instance:

```
@Stateful
public class ShoppingCartBean implements ShoppingCart{

   @EJB AnotherStatefulLocal another;

   @Remove void checkout {}
}
```

When a stateful bean reference is injected into another stateful session bean, the containing bean owns the injected session. This means that when the containing bean is created, a unique session is created for the injected reference. When the containing bean is removed, the contained stateful bean is also removed. In the `ShoppingCartBean` example, an `AnotherStatefulLocal` session is created for the another member variable when an instance of it is created. When the `checkout( )`

method is called, another's stateful session is also removed. This feature of the specification allows you to cleanly aggregate conversational business processes without having to worry about managing the life cycle of the contained stateful sessions.

Nested stateful session beans also have an interesting effect when they inject an EXTENDED persistence context that also exists in the containing stateful bean. When this scenario happens, the containing and contained stateful session beans share the same EXTENDED persistence context:

```
@Stateful
public class ShoppingCartBean implements ShoppingCart{

   @EJB AnotherStatefulLocal another;

   @PersistenceContext(unitName="titan", type=EXTENDED)
   private EntityManager entityManager;

   @Remove void checkout {}
}

@Stateful
public class AnotherStatefulBean implements AnotherStatefulLocal
{
   @PersistenceContext(unitName="titan", type=EXTENDED)
   private EntityManager entityManager;

}
```

The AnotherStatefulBean.entityManager and ShoppingCartBean.entityManager fields actually reference the same persistence context. This means that they also share the same managed entity instances. It is important to note that this persistence context nesting works only when a reference to a local stateful session interface is injected. If a remote interface were nested instead, then the beans would not share the same EXTENDED persistence context.

CHAPTER 12
Message-Driven Beans

The message-driven bean was introduced in EJB 2.0 to support the processing of asynchronous messages from a JMS provider. EJB 2.1 expanded the definition of the message-driven bean so that it can support any messaging system, not just JMS through the JCA. EJB 3.0 does not really expand on the feature set of earlier specification versions, but it does simplify configuration with the use of annotations. This chapter examines both JMS-based message-driven beans as well as the expanded message-driven bean model available to EJB 3.0 developers.

JMS and Message-Driven Beans

All EJB 3.0 vendors must support a JMS provider. Most vendors have a JMS provider built in and must support other JMS providers through the JCA. However, regardless of whether your vendor has its own JMS provider or allows you to integrate some other provider, a JMS provider is an absolute necessity for supporting message-driven beans. By forcing the adoption of JMS, Sun has guaranteed that EJB developers can expect to have a working JMS provider on which messages can be both sent and received.

JMS as a Resource

JMS is a vendor-neutral API that can be used to access enterprise messaging systems. Enterprise messaging systems (a.k.a. message-oriented middleware) facilitate the exchange of messages between software applications over a network. The role of JMS isn't unlike the role of JDBC: just as JDBC provides a common API for accessing many different relational databases, JMS provides vendor-independent access to enterprise messaging systems. Although messaging products aren't as familiar as database products, there's no shortage of messaging systems that support JMS, including JBossMQ, IBM's MQSeries, BEA's WebLogic JMS service, Sun Microsystems' Sun ONE Message Queue, and Sonic's SonicMQ. Software applications that use the JMS API for sending or receiving messages are portable from one JMS vendor to another.

Applications that use JMS are called *JMS clients*, and the messaging system that handles routing and delivery of messages is called the *JMS provider*. A *JMS application* is a business system composed of many JMS clients and, generally, one JMS provider. A JMS client that sends a message is called a *producer*, and a JMS client that receives a message is called a *consumer*. A single JMS client can be both a producer and a consumer.

In EJB, enterprise beans of all types can use JMS to send messages. The messages are consumed by other Java applications or by message-driven beans. JMS facilitates sending messages from enterprise beans using a *messaging service*, sometimes called a *message broker* or *router*. Message brokers have been around for a couple of decades—the oldest and most established is IBM's MQSeries—but JMS is fairly new, and it is specifically designed to deliver a variety of message types from one Java application to another.

Reimplementing the TravelAgent EJB with JMS

We can modify the TravelAgent EJB developed in Chapter 11 so that it uses JMS to alert some other Java application that a reservation has been made. The following code shows how to modify the bookPassage( ) method so that the TravelAgent EJB sends a simple text message based on a description obtained from the TicketDO object:

```
@Resource(mappedName="ConnectionFactoryNameGoesHere")
private ConnectionFactory connectionFactory;

@Resource(mappedName="TicketTopic")
private Topic topic;

@Remove
public TicketDO bookPassage(CreditCardDO card, double price)
    throws IncompleteConversationalState {

    if (customer == null || cruise == null || cabin == null) {
        throw new IncompleteConversationalState( );
    }
    try {
        Reservation reservation = new Reservation(
                              customer, cruise, cabin, price, new Date( ));
        entityManager.persist(reservation);

        process.byCredit(customer, card, price);

        TicketDO ticket = new TicketDO(customer, cruise, cabin, price);

        Connection connect = factory.createConnection( );
        Session session = connect.createSession(true,0);
        MessageProducer producer = session.createProducer(topic);
        TextMessage textMsg = session.createTextMessage( );
        textMsg.setText(ticketDescription);
```

```
            producer.send(textMsg);
            connect.close( );

            return ticket;
        } catch(Exception e) {
            throw new EJBException(e);
        }
    }
```

While all the code we added might look a little overwhelming, the basics of JMS are not all that complicated.

ConnectionFactory and Topic

In order to send a JMS message, we need a connection to the JMS provider and a destination address for the message. A JMS connection factory makes the connection to the provider possible; the destination address is identified by a `Topic` object. Both the connection factory and the `Topic` object are obtained by using `@javax.annotation.Resource` to inject these objects directly into the fields of the TravelAgent EJB:

```
@Resource(mappedName="ConnectionFactoryNameGoesHere")
private ConnectionFactory connectionFactory;

@Resource(mappedName="TicketTopic")
private Topic topic;
```

The `ConnectionFactory` is similar to a `DataSource` in JDBC. Just as the `DataSource` provides a JDBC connection to a database, the `ConnectionFactory` provides a JMS connection to a message router.*

The `Topic` object itself represents a network-independent destination to which the message will be addressed. In JMS, messages aren't sent directly to applications; they're sent to topics or queues. A *topic* is analogous to an email list or newsgroup; any application with the proper credentials can receive messages from and send messages to a topic. When a JMS client receives messages from a topic, the client is said to *subscribe* to that topic. JMS decouples applications by allowing them to send messages to each other through a destination, which serves as a virtual channel. A *queue* is another type of destination that we'll discuss in detail later.

Connection and Session

The `ConnectionFactory` is used to create a `Connection`, which is an actual connection to the JMS provider:

```
Connection connect = connectionFactory.createConnection( );
Session session = connect.createSession(true,0);
```

* This analogy is not perfect. One might also say that the `Session` is analogous to the `DataSource`, since both represent transaction-resource connections.

Once you have a Connection, you can use it to create a Session. A Session allows you to group the actions of sending and receiving messages. In this case, you need only a single Session. Using multiple Sessions is helpful if you wish to produce and consume messages in different threads. Session objects use a single-threaded model, which prohibits concurrent access to a single Session from multiple threads. The thread that creates a Session is usually the thread that uses that Session's producers and consumers (i.e., MessageProducer and MessageConsumer objects). If you wish to produce and consume messages using multithreading, you must create a different Session object for each thread.

The createSession( ) method has two parameters:

```
createSession(boolean transacted, int acknowledgeMode)
```

According to the EJB specifications, these arguments are ignored at runtime because the EJB container manages the transaction and acknowledgment mode of any JMS resource obtained from the JNDI ENC. The specification recommends that developers use the arguments true for transacted and 0 for acknowledgeMode, but since they are supposed to be ignored, it should not matter what you use. Unfortunately, not all vendors adhere to this part of the specification. Some vendors ignore these parameters; others do not.

It's good programming practice to close a Connection after it has been used:

```
Connection connect = factory.createConnection( );
...
connect.close( );
```

MessageProducer

The Session is used to create a MessageProducer, which sends messages from the TravelAgent EJB to the destination specified by the Topic object. Any JMS clients that subscribe to that topic will receive a copy of the message:

```
MessageProducer producer = session.createProducer(topic);

TextMessage textMsg = session.createTextMessage( );
textMsg.setText(ticketDescription);
producer.send(textMsg);
```

Message types

In JMS, a message is a Java object with two parts: a *header* and a *message body*. The header is composed of delivery information and metadata, and the message body carries the application data, which can take several forms: text, serializable objects, byte streams, etc. The JMS API defines several message types (TextMessage, MapMessage, ObjectMessage, and others) and provides methods for delivering messages to and receiving messages from other applications.

For example, we can change the TravelAgent EJB so that it sends a MapMessage rather than a TextMessage:

```
TicketDO ticket = new TicketDO(customer,cruise,cabin,price);
...
MessageProducer producer = session.createProducer(topic);

MapMessage mapMsg = session.createMapMessage( );
mapMsg.setInt("CustomerID", ticket.customerID.intValue( ));
mapMsg.setInt("CruiseID", ticket.cruiseID.intValue( ));
mapMsg.setInt("CabinID", ticket.cabinID.intValue( ));
mapMsg.setDouble("Price", ticket.price);

producer.send(mapMsg);
```

The attributes of MapMessage (CustomerID, CruiseID, CabinID, and Price) can be accessed by name from those JMS clients that receive it. As an alternative, the TravelAgent EJB could be modified to use the ObjectMessage type, which would allow us to send the entire TicketDO object as the message using Java serialization:

```
TicketDO ticket = new TicketDO(customer,cruise,cabin,price);
...
MessageProducer producer = session.createProducer(topic);

ObjectMessage objectMsg = session.createObjectMessage( );
ObjectMsg.setObject(ticket);

producer.send(mapMsg);
```

In addition to TextMessage, MapMessage, and ObjectMessage, JMS provides two other message types: StreamMessage and BytesMessage. StreamMessage can take the contents of an I/O stream as its payload. BytesMessage can take any array of bytes, which it treats as opaque data.

JMS Application Client

To get a better idea of how JMS is used, we can create a Java application whose sole purpose is receiving and processing reservation messages. This application is a simple JMS client that prints a description of each ticket as it receives the messages. We'll assume that the TravelAgent EJB is using TextMessage to send a description of the ticket to the JMS clients. Here's how the JMS application client might look:

```
import javax.jms.Message;
import javax.jms.TextMessage;
import javax.jms.ConnectionFactory;
import javax.jms.Connection;
import javax.jms.Session;
import javax.jms.Topic;
import javax.jms.JMSException;
import javax.naming.InitialContext;
```

```
public class JmsClient_1 implements javax.jms.MessageListener {

    public static void main(String [] args) throws Exception {

        if(args.length != 2)
            throw new Exception("Wrong number of arguments");
        new JmsClient_1(args[0], args[1]);
        while(true){Thread.sleep(10000);}
    }

    public JmsClient_1(String factoryName, String topicName) throws Exception {

        InitialContext jndiContext = getInitialContext( );

        ConnectionFactory factory = (ConnectionFactory)
            jndiContext.lookup("ConnectionFactoryNameGoesHere");
        Topic topic = (Topic)jndiContext.lookup("TopicNameGoesHere");
        Connection connect = factory.createConnection( );
        Session session =
            connect.createSession(false,Session.AUTO_ACKNOWLEDGE);
        MessageConsumer consumer = session.createConsumer(topic);
        consumer.setMessageListener(this);

        connect.start( );
    }

    public void onMessage(Message message) {
        try {

            TextMessage textMsg = (TextMessage)message;
            String text = textMsg.getText( );
            System.out.println("\n RESERVATION RECEIVED:\n"+text);

        } catch(JMSException jmsE) {
            jmsE.printStackTrace( );
        }
    }

    public static InitialContext getInitialContext( ) {
        // create vendor-specific JNDI context here
    }
}
```

The constructor of `JmsClient_1` obtains the `ConnectionFactory` and `Topic` from the JNDI `InitialContext`. This context is created with vendor-specific properties so that the client can connect to the same JMS provider as the one used by the TravelAgent EJB. For example, here's how the `getInitialContext( )` method for the JBoss application server would be coded:*

* JNDI also allows the properties to be set in a *jndi.properties* file that contains the property values for the `InitialContext` and that can be discovered dynamically at runtime. In this book, I chose to set the properties explicitly.

```
public static InitialContext getInitialContext( ) {
    Properties env = new Properties( );
    env.put(Context.SECURITY_PRINCIPAL, "guest");
    env.put(Context.SECURITY_CREDENTIALS, "guest");
    env.put(Context.INITIAL_CONTEXT_FACTORY,
       " org.jboss.security.jndi.JndiLoginInitialContextFactory");
    env.put(Context.PROVIDER_URL, " jnp://hostname:1099");
    return new InitialContext(env);
}
```

Once the client has the `ConnectionFactory` and `Topic`, it creates a `Connection` and a `Session` in the same way as the TravelAgent EJB does. The main difference is that the `Session` object is used to create a `MessageConsumer` rather than a `MessageProducer`. The `MessageConsumer` is designed to process incoming messages that are published to its `Topic`:

```
Session session =
    connect.createSession(false,Session.AUTO_ACKNOWLEDGE);
MessageConsumer consumer = session.createConsumer(topic);
consumer.setMessageListener(this);
connect.start( );
```

The `MessageConsumer` can receive messages directly or delegate message processing to a `javax.jms.MessageListener`. We chose to have `JmsClient_1` implement the `MessageListener` interface so that it can process the messages itself. `MessageListener` objects implement a single method, `onMessage( )`, which is invoked every time a new message is sent to the subscriber's topic. In this case, every time the TravelAgent EJB sends a reservation message to the topic, the JMS client's `onMessage( )` method is invoked to receive and process a copy of the message:

```
public void onMessage(Message message) {
    try {
        TextMessage textMsg = (TextMessage)message;
        String text = textMsg.getText( );
        System.out.println("\n RESERVATION RECEIVED:\n"+text);
    } catch(JMSException jmsE) {
        jmsE.printStackTrace( );
    }
}
```

JMS Is Asynchronous

One of the principal advantages of JMS messaging is that it's *asynchronous*. In other words, a JMS client can send a message without having to wait for a reply. Contrast this flexibility with the synchronous messaging of Java RMI or JAX-RPC. Each time a client invokes a bean's method, it blocks the current thread until the method completes execution. This lock-step processing makes the client dependent on the availability of the EJB server, resulting in a tight coupling between the client and the enterprise bean. JMS clients send messages asynchronously to a destination (topic or queue) from which other JMS clients can also receive messages. When a JMS client sends a message, it doesn't wait for a reply; it sends the message to a router, which is responsible for forwarding the message to other clients. There's no effect on the client if one or more recipients are unavailable; it just goes ahead with its work. It's the router's responsibility to make sure that the message eventually reaches its destination. Clients sending messages are decoupled from the clients receiving them; senders are not dependent on the availability of receivers.

The limitations of RMI make JMS an attractive alternative for communicating with other applications. Using the standard JNDI environment-naming context, an enterprise bean can obtain a JMS connection to a JMS provider and use it to deliver asynchronous messages to other Java applications. For example, a TravelAgent session bean can use JMS to notify other applications that a reservation has been processed, as shown in Figure 12-1.

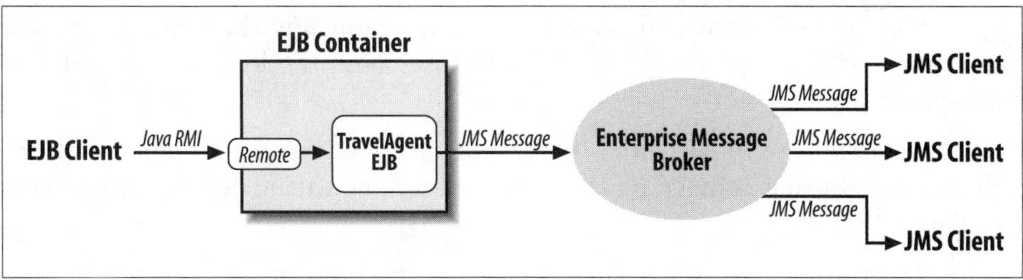

Figure 12-1. Using JMS with the TravelAgent EJB

In this case, the applications receiving JMS messages from the TravelAgent EJB may be message-driven beans, other Java applications in the enterprise, or applications in other organizations that benefit from being notified that a reservation has been processed. Examples might include business partners who share customer information or an internal marketing application that adds customers to a catalog mailing list.

Because messaging is inherently decoupled and asynchronous, the transactions and security contexts of the sender are not propagated to the receiver. For example, when the TravelAgent EJB sends the ticket message, the JMS provider may authenticate it, but the message's security context won't be propagated to the JMS client that received the message. When a JMS client receives the message from the TravelAgent EJB, the client has no idea about the security context under which the message was sent. This is how it should be, because the sender and receiver often operate in environments with different security domains.

Similarly, transactions are never propagated from the sender to the receiver. For one thing, the sender has no idea who the receivers of the message will be. If the message is sent to a topic, there could be one receiver or thousands; managing a distributed transaction under such ambiguous circumstances is not tenable. In addition, the clients receiving the message may not get it for a long time after it is sent; there may be a network problem, the client may be down, or there may be some other problem.

Transactions are designed to be executed quickly because they lock up resources, and applications can't tolerate the possibility of a long transaction with an unpredictable end.

A JMS client can, however, have a distributed transaction with the JMS provider so that it manages the send or receive operation in the context of a transaction. For example, if the TravelAgent EJB's transaction fails for any reason, the JMS provider discards the ticket message sent by the TravelAgent EJB. Transactions and JMS are covered in more detail in Chapter 16.

JMS Messaging Models

JMS provides two types of messaging models: *publish-and-subscribe* and *point-to-point*. The JMS specification refers to these as *messaging domains*. In JMS terminology, publish-and-subscribe and point-to-point are frequently shortened to *pub/sub* and *p2p* (or *PTP*), respectively. This chapter uses both the long and short forms throughout.

In the simplest sense, publish-and-subscribe is intended for a one-to-many broadcast of messages, and point-to-point is intended for one-to-one delivery of messages (see Figure 12-2).

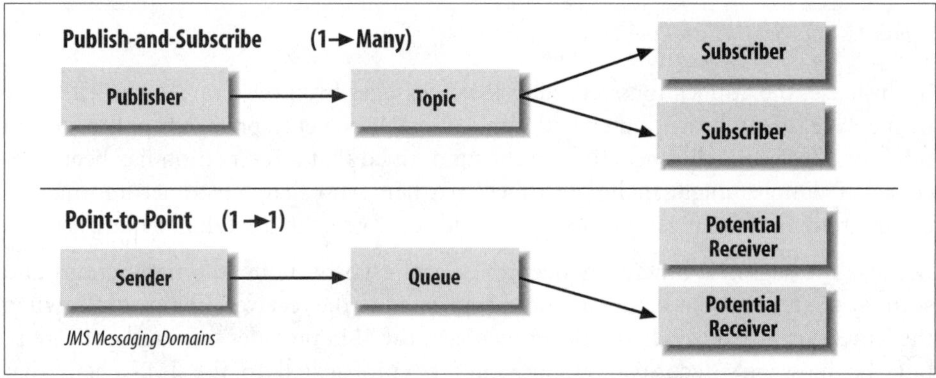

Figure 12-2. JMS messaging domains

Each messaging domain (i.e., pub/sub and p2p) has its own set of interfaces and classes for sending and receiving messages. This results in two different APIs, which share some common types. JMS 1.1 introduced a Unified API that allows developers to use a single set of interfaces and classes for both messaging domains. Only the Unified API is used in this chapter.

Publish-and-subscribe

In publish-and-subscribe messaging, one producer can send a message to many consumers through a virtual channel called a *topic*. Consumers can choose to subscribe to a topic. Any messages addressed to a topic are delivered to all the topic's consumers. The pub/sub messaging model is largely a *push-based model*, in which messages are automatically broadcast to consumers without the consumers having to request or poll the topic for new messages.

In the pub/sub messaging model, the producer sending the message is not dependent on the consumers receiving the message. JMS clients that use pub/sub can establish durable subscriptions that allow consumers to disconnect and later reconnect and collect messages that were published while they were disconnected. The TravelAgent EJB in this chapter uses the pub/sub programming model with a `Topic` object as a destination.

Point-to-point

The point-to-point messaging model allows JMS clients to send and receive messages both synchronously and asynchronously via virtual channels known as *queues*. The p2p messaging model has traditionally been a *pull-* or *polling-based model*, in which messages are requested from the queue instead of being pushed to the client automatically.* A queue may have multiple receivers, but only one receiver may receive each message. As shown earlier in Figure 12-2, the JMS provider takes care of doling out the messages among JMS clients, ensuring that each message is consumed by only one JMS client. The JMS specification does not dictate the rules for distributing messages among multiple receivers.

Which messaging model should you use?

The rationale behind the two models lies in the origin of the JMS specification. JMS started out as a way of providing a common API for accessing existing messaging systems. At the time of its conception, some messaging vendors had a p2p model and some had a pub/sub model. Hence, JMS needed to provide an API for both models to gain wide industry support.

Almost anything that can be done with the pub/sub model can be done with point-to-point, and vice versa. An analogy can be drawn to developers' programming language preferences. In theory, any application that can be written with Pascal can also be written with C. Anything that can be written in C++ can also be written in Java. In some cases, it comes down to a matter of preference, or which model you are already familiar with.

In most cases, the decision about which model to use depends on which model is a better fit for the application. With pub/sub, any number of subscribers can be listening on a topic, and all of them will receive copies of the same message. The publisher

* The JMS specification does not specifically state how the p2p and pub/sub models must be implemented. Either model can use push or pull—but conceptually, pub/sub is push and p2p is pull.

may not care if everybody is listening, or even if nobody is listening. For example, consider a publisher that broadcasts stock quotes. If any particular subscriber is not currently connected and misses out on a great quote, the publisher is not concerned. In contrast, a point-to-point session is likely to be intended for a one-on-one conversation with a specific application at the other end. In this scenario, every message really matters. The range and variety of the data the messages represent can be a factor as well. Using pub/sub, messages are dispatched to the consumers based on filtering that is provided through the use of specific topics. Even when messaging is being used to establish a one-on-one conversation with another known application, it can be advantageous to use pub/sub with multiple topics to segregate different kinds of messages. Each kind of message can be dealt with separately through its own unique consumer and `onMessage( )` listener.

Point-to-point is more convenient when you want a particular receiver to process a given message once. This is perhaps the most critical difference between the two models: p2p guarantees that only one consumer processes each message. This ability is extremely important when messages need to be processed separately but in tandem.

Session Beans Should Not Receive Messages

`JmsClient_1` was designed to consume messages produced by the TravelAgent EJB. Can another session bean receive those messages also? The answer is yes, but it's a really bad idea.

Session beans respond to calls from EJB clients and they cannot be programmed to respond to JMS messages, as can message-driven beans. It's impossible to write a session or entity bean that is driven by incoming messages. It is possible to develop a session bean that can consume a JMS message from a business method, but an EJB client must call the method first. For example, when the business method on the Hypothetical EJB is called, it sets up a JMS session and then attempts to read a message from a queue:

```
@Stateless
public class HypotheticalBean implements HypotheticalRemote {
    @Resource(mappedName="ConnectionFactory");
    private ConnectionFactory factory;

    @Resource(mappedName="MyQueue")
    private Queue queue;

    public String businessMethod( ) {

        try{
            Connection connect = factory.createConnection( );
            Session session = connect.createSession(true,0);
            MessageConsumer receiver = session.createConsumer(queue);
            TextMessage textMsg = (TextMessage)receiver.receive( );
```

```
            connect.close( );

            return textMsg.getText( );
        } catch(Exception e) {
            throws new EJBException(e);
        }

    }
    ...
}
```

The message consumer is used to proactively fetch a message from the queue. While this operation has been programmed correctly, it is dangerous because a call to the `MessageConsumer.receive( )` method blocks the thread until a message becomes available. If a message is never delivered, the thread is blocked indefinitely! If no one ever sends a message to the queue, the `MessageConsumer` just sits there waiting, forever.

To be fair, there are other `receive( )` methods that are less dangerous. For example, `receive(long timeout)` allows you to specify a time after which the `MessageConsumer` should stop blocking the thread and give up waiting for a message. There is also `receiveNoWait( )`, which checks for a message and returns `null` if none is waiting, thus avoiding a prolonged thread block. However, this operation is still dangerous. There is no guarantee that the less risky `receive( )` methods will perform as expected, and the risk of programmer error (e.g., using the wrong `receive( )` method) is too great.

The moral of the story is simple: don't write convoluted code trying to force session beans to receive messages. If you need to receive messages, use a message-driven bean; MDBs are specially designed to consume JMS messages.

Learning More About JMS

JMS (and enterprise messaging in general) represents a powerful paradigm in distributed computing. While this chapter has provided a brief overview of JMS, it has presented only enough material to prepare you for the discussion of message-driven beans in the next section. To understand JMS and how it is used, you will need to study it independently.* Taking the time to learn JMS is well worth the effort.

JMS-Based Message-Driven Beans

Message-driven beans (MDBs) are stateless, server-side, transaction-aware components for processing asynchronous messages delivered via JMS. While a message-driven bean is responsible for processing messages, its container manages the component's environment, including transactions, security, resources, concurrency, and

* For a detailed treatment of JMS, see *Java Message Service* (O'Reilly).

message acknowledgment. It's particularly important to note that the container manages concurrency. The thread safety provided by the container gives MDBs a significant advantage over traditional JMS clients, which must be custom built to manage resources, transactions, and security in a multithreaded environment. An MDB can process hundreds of JMS messages concurrently because numerous instances of the MDB can execute concurrently in the container.

A message-driven bean is a complete enterprise bean, just like a session or entity bean, but there are some important differences. While a message-driven bean has a bean class, it does not have a remote or local business interface. These interfaces are absent because the message-driven bean responds only to asynchronous messages.

The ReservationProcessor EJB

The ReservationProcessor EJB is a message-driven bean that receives JMS messages notifying it of new reservations. The ReservationProcessor EJB is an automated version of the TravelAgent EJB that processes reservations sent via JMS. These messages might come from another application in the enterprise or from an application in some other organization—perhaps another travel agent. When the ReservationProcessor EJB receives a message, it creates a new Reservation EJB (adding it to the database), processes the payment using the ProcessPayment EJB, and sends out a ticket. This process is illustrated in Figure 12-3.

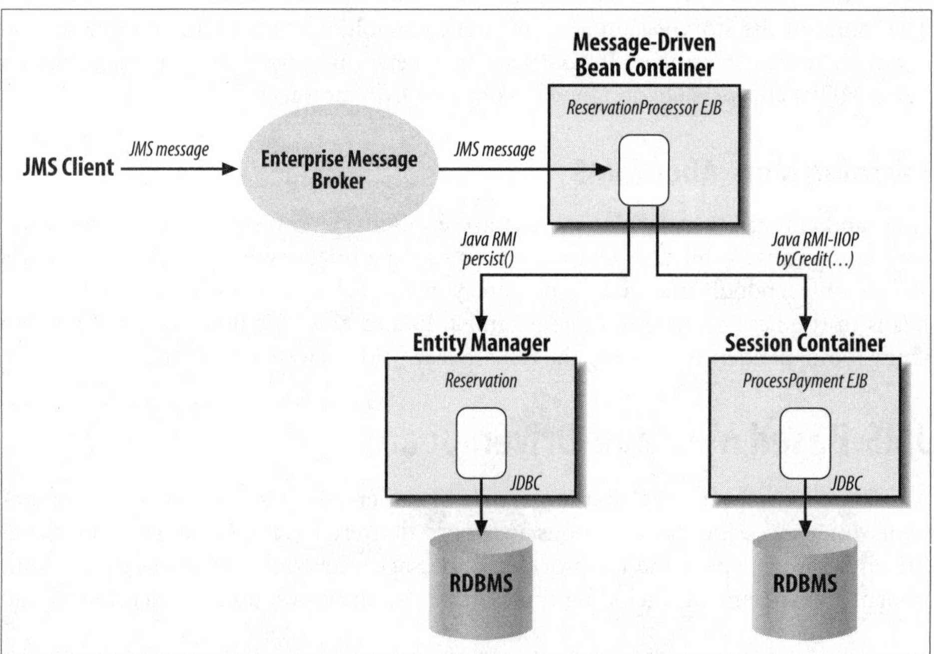

Figure 12-3. The ReservationProcessor EJB processing reservations

The ReservationProcessorBean Class

Here is a partial definition of the ReservationProcessorBean class. Some methods are left empty; they will be filled in later. Notice that the onMessage( ) method contains the business logic; it is similar to the business logic developed in the bookPassage( ) method of the TravelAgent EJB in Chapter 11. Here's the code:

```
package com.titan.reservationprocessor;

import javax.jms.*;
import com.titan.domain.*;
import com.titan.processpayment.*;
import com.titan.travelagent.*;
import java.util.Date;
import javax.ejb.*;
import javax.annotation.*;
import javax.persistence.*;

@MessageDriven(activationConfig={
                @ActivationConfigProperty(
                     propertyName="destinationType",
                     propertyValue="javax.jms.Queue"),
                @ActivationConfigProperty(
                     propertyName="messageSelector",
                     propertyValue="MessageFormat = 'Version 3.4'"),
                @ActivationConfigProperty(
                     propertyName="acknowledgeMode",
                     propertyValue="Auto-acknowledge")})
public class ReservationProcessorBean implements javax.jms.MessageListener {
    @PersistenceContext(unitName="titanDB")
    private EntityManager em;

    @EJB
    private ProcessPaymentLocal process;

    @Resource(mappedName="ConnectionFactory")
    private ConnectionFactory connectionFactory;

    public void onMessage(Message message) {
        try {
            MapMessage reservationMsg = (MapMessage)message;

            int customerPk = reservationMsg.getInt("CustomerID");
            int cruisePk = reservationMsg.getInt("CruiseID");
            int cabinPk = reservationMsg.getInt("CabinID");

            double price = reservationMsg.getDouble("Price");

            // get the credit card
            Date expirationDate =
                new Date(reservationMsg.getLong("CreditCardExpDate"));
            String cardNumber = reservationMsg.getString("CreditCardNum");
            String cardType = reservationMsg.getString("CreditCardType");
```

```
            CreditCardDO card = new CreditCardDO(cardNumber,
                expirationDate, cardType);

            Customer customer = em.find(Customer.class, customerPk);
            Cruise cruise = em.find(Cruise.class, cruisePk);
            Cabin cabin = em.find(Cabin.class, cabinPk);

            Reservation reservation = new Reservation(
                         customer, cruise, cabin, price, new Date( ));
            em.persist(reservation);

            process.byCredit(customer, card, price);

            TicketDO ticket = new TicketDO(customer,cruise,cabin,price);

            deliverTicket(reservationMsg, ticket);
        } catch(Exception e) {
            throw new EJBException(e);
        }
    }

    public void deliverTicket(MapMessage reservationMsg, TicketDO ticket) {

        // send it to the proper destination
    }

}
```

MessageDrivenContext

Message-driven beans also have a context object that is similar in functionality to that of the javax.ejb.SessionContext described in Chapter 11. This object may be injected using the @javax.annotation.Resource annotation:

```
@Resource MessageDrivenContext context;
```

The MessageDrivenContext simply extends the EJBContext; it does not add any new methods. The EJBContext is defined as follows:

```
package javax.ejb;
public interface EJBContext {

    // transaction methods
    public javax.transaction.UserTransaction getUserTransaction( )
        throws java.lang.IllegalStateException;
    public boolean getRollbackOnly( ) throws java.lang.IllegalStateException;
    public void setRollbackOnly( ) throws java.lang.IllegalStateException;

    // EJB home methods
    public EJBHome getEJBHome( );
    public EJBLocalHome getEJBLocalHome( );

    // security methods
    public java.security.Principal getCallerPrincipal( );
    public boolean isCallerInRole(java.lang.String roleName);
```

```
        // deprecated methods
        public java.security.Identity getCallerIdentity( );
        public boolean isCallerInRole(java.security.Identity role);
        public java.util.Properties getEnvironment( );

    }
```

Only the transactional methods that `MessageDrivenContext` inherits from `EJBContext` are available to message-driven beans. The home methods—`getEJBHome( )` and `getEJBLocalHome( )`—throw a `RuntimeException` if invoked, because MDBs do not have home interfaces or EJB home objects. The security methods—`getCallerPrincipal( )` and `isCallerInRole( )`—also throw a `RuntimeException` if invoked on a `MessageDrivenContext`. When an MDB services a JMS message, there is no "caller," so there is no security context to be obtained from the caller. Remember that JMS is asynchronous and doesn't propagate the sender's security context to the receiver—that wouldn't make sense, since senders and receivers tend to operate in different environments.

MDBs usually execute in a container-initiated or bean-initiated transaction, so the transaction methods allow the MDB to manage its context. The transaction context is not propagated from the JMS sender; it is either initiated by the container or initiated by the bean explicitly using `javax.jta.UserTransaction`. The transaction methods in `EJBContext` are explained in more detail in Chapter 16.

Message-driven beans also have access to their own JNDI ENCs, which provide the MDB instances access to environment entries, other enterprise beans, and resources. For example, the ReservationProcessor EJB takes advantage of the ENC to obtain references to the Titan `EntityManager`, the ProcessPayment EJB, and a JMS `ConnectionFactory` and `Queue` for sending out tickets.

MessageListener interface

MDBs usually implement the `javax.jms.MessageListener` interface, which defines the `onMessage( )` method. This method processes the JMS messages received by a bean.

```
package javax.jms;
public interface MessageListener {
    public void onMessage(Message message);
}
```

Although MDBs usually implement this interface, we will see later in this chapter that MDBs can integrate with other messaging systems that define a different interface contract.

Taskflow and integration for B2B: onMessage( )

The `onMessage( )` method is where all the business logic goes. As messages arrive, the container passes them to the MDB via the `onMessage( )` method. When the method returns, the MDB is ready to process a new message. In the ReservationProcessor

EJB, the onMessage( ) method extracts information about a reservation from a MapMessage and uses that information to create a reservation in the system:

```
public void onMessage(Message message) {
    try {
        MapMessage reservationMsg = (MapMessage)message;

        int customerPk = reservationMsg.getInt("CustomerID");
        int cruisePk = reservationMsg.getInt("CruiseID");
        int cabinPk = reservationMsg.getInt("CabinID");

        double price = reservationMsg.getDouble("Price");

        // get the credit card

        Date expirationDate =
            new Date(reservationMsg.getLong("CreditCardExpDate"));
        String cardNumber = reservationMsg.getString("CreditCardNum");
        String cardType = reservationMsg.setString("CreditCardType");
        CreditCardDO card = new CreditCardDO(cardNumber,
            expirationDate, cardType);
```

JMS is frequently used as an integration point for business-to-business (B2B) applications, so it's easy to imagine the reservation message coming from one of Titan's business partners (perhaps a third-party processor or branch travel agency).

The ReservationProcessor EJB needs to access the Customer, Cruise, and Cabin entities in order to process the reservation. The MapMessage contains the primary keys for these entities; the ReservationProcessor EJB uses the injected EntityManager to look up the entity beans:

```
public void onMessage(Message message) {
    ...
    Customer customer = em.find(Customer.class, customerPk);
    Cruise cruise = em.find(Cruise.class, cruisePk);
    Cabin cabin = em.find(Cabin.class, cabinPk);
    ...
}
```

Once the information is extracted from the MapMessage, it is used to create a reservation and process the payment. This is basically the same taskflow that was used by the TravelAgent EJB in Chapter 11. A Reservation entity is created that represents the reservation itself, and a ProcessPayment EJB is created to process the credit card payment:

```
Reservation reservation = new Reservation(
               customer, cruise, cabin, price, new Date( ));
em.persist(reservation);

process.byCredit(customer, card, price);

TicketDO ticket = new TicketDO(customer,cruise,cabin,price);

deliverTicket(reservationMsg, ticket);
```

Like a session bean, the MDB can access any other session bean and use that bean to complete a task. An MDB can manage a process and interact with other beans as well as resources. For example, it is commonplace for an MDB to use JDBC to access a database based on the contents of the message it is processing.

Sending messages from a message-driven bean

An MDB can also send messages using JMS. The `deliverTicket( )` method sends the ticket information to a destination defined by the sending JMS client:

```
public void deliverTicket(MapMessage reservationMsg, TicketDO ticket)
    throws JMSException{

    Queue queue = (Queue)reservationMsg.getJMSReplyTo( );
    Connection connect = connectionFactory.createConnection( );
    Session session = connect.createSession(true,0);
    MessageProducer sender = session.createProducer(queue);
    ObjectMessage message = session.createObjectMessage( );
    message.setObject(ticket);
    sender.send(message);

    connect.close( );
}
```

Every message type has two parts: a message header and a message body (a.k.a. the *payload*). The message header contains routing information and may also have properties for message filtering and other attributes. One of these attributes may be `JMSReplyTo`. The message's sender may set the `JMSReplyTo` attribute to any destination accessible to its JMS provider. In the case of the reservation message, the sender set the `JMSReplyTo` attribute to the queue to which the resulting ticket should be sent. Another application can access this queue to read tickets and distribute them to customers or store the information in the sender's database.

You can also use the `JMSReplyTo` address to report business errors. For example, if the cabin is already reserved, the ReservationProcessor EJB might send an error message to the `JMSReplyTo` queue explaining that the reservation could not be processed. Including this type of error handling is left as an exercise for the reader.

@MessageDriven

MDBs are identified using the `@javax.ejb.MessageDriven` annotation or, alternatively, are described in an EJB deployment descriptor. An MDB can be deployed alone, but it's more often deployed with the other enterprise beans that it references. For example, the ReservationProcessor EJB uses the ProcessPayment EJB as well as the Titan `EntityManager`, so it is feasible to deploy all of these beans within the same Java EE deployment.

@ActivationConfigProperty

We'll see later that because MDBs can receive messages from arbitrary messaging providers, the configuration must be very flexible to be able to describe the proprietary properties that different providers will have. JCA-based MDBs don't necessarily use JMS as the message service, so this requirement is very important. To facilitate this, the `@MessageDriven.activationConfig( )` attribute takes an array of `@ActivationConfigProperty` annotations. These annotations are simply a set of name/value pairs that describe the configuration of your MDB.

```
@MessageDriven(activationConfig={
                @ActivationConfigProperty(
                     propertyName="destinationType",
                     propertyValue="javax.jms.Queue"),
                @ActivationConfigProperty(
                     propertyName="messageSelector",
                     propertyValue="MessageFormat = 'Version 3.4'"),
                @ActivationConfigProperty(
                     propertyName="acknowledgeMode",
                     propertyValue="Auto-acknowledge")})
public class ReservationProcessorBean implements javax.jms.MessageListener {
   ...
}
```

The property names and values used in the `activationConfig( )` attribute to describe the messaging service vary depending on the type of message service used, but EJB 3.0 defines a set of fixed properties for JMS-based message-driven beans. These properties are `acknowledgeMode`, `messageSelector`, `destinationType`, and `subscriptionDurability`.

Message selector

An MDB can declare a *message selector*. Message selectors allow an MDB to be more selective about the messages it receives from a particular topic or queue. Message selectors use `Message` properties as criteria in conditional expressions.* These conditional expressions use Boolean logic to declare which messages should be delivered. A message selector is declared using the standard property name, `messageSelector`, in an activation configuration element:

```
@ActivationConfigProperty(
               propertyName="messageSelector",
               propertyValue="MessageFormat = 'Version 3.4'"),
```

Message selectors are based on message properties. Message properties are additional headers that can be assigned to a message; they allow vendors and developers to attach information to a message that isn't part of the message's body. The `Message` interface provides several methods for reading and writing properties. Properties can have a `String` value or one of several primitive values (`boolean`, `byte`, `short`, `int`, `long`,

* Message selectors are also based on message headers, which are outside the scope of this chapter.

float, double). The naming of properties, together with their values and conversion rules, is strictly defined by JMS.

The ReservationProcessor EJB uses a message selector filter to select messages of a specific format. In this case, the format is "Version 3.4"; this is a string that Titan uses to identify messages of type MapMessage that contain the name values CustomerID, CruiseID, CabinID, CreditCard, and Price. In other words, adding a MessageFormat to each reservation message allows us to write MDBs that are designed to process different kinds of reservation messages. If a new business partner needs to use a different type of Message object, Titan would use a new message version and an MDB to process it.

Here's how a JMS producer would go about setting a MessageFormat property on a Message:

```
Message message = session.createMapMessage( );
message.setStringProperty("MessageFormat","Version 3.4");

// set the reservation named values

sender.send(message);
```

The message selectors are based on a subset of the SQL-92 conditional expression syntax that is used in the WHERE clauses of SQL statements. They can become fairly complex, including the use of literal values, Boolean expressions, unary operators, and so on.

Acknowledge mode

A JMS *acknowledgment* means that the JMS client notifies the JMS provider (message router) when a message is received. In EJB, it's the MDB container's responsibility to send an acknowledgment when it receives a message. Acknowledging a message tells the JMS provider that an MDB container has received and processed the message. Without an acknowledgment, the JMS provider does not know whether the MDB container has received the message, and unwanted redeliveries can cause problems. For example, once we have processed a reservation message using the ReservationProcessor EJB, we don't want to receive the same message again.

The acknowledgment mode is set using the standard acknowledgeMode activation configuration property, as shown in the following code snippet:

```
@ActivationConfigProperty(
          propertyName="acknowledgeMode",
          propertyValue="Auto-acknowledge")
```

Two values can be specified for acknowledgment mode: Auto-acknowledge and Dups-ok-acknowledge. Auto-acknowledge tells the container that it should send an acknowledgment to the JMS provider soon after the message is given to an MDB instance to process. Dups-ok-acknowledge tells the container that it doesn't have to send the acknowledgment immediately; anytime after the message is given to the MDB instance will be fine. With `Dups-ok-acknowledge`, it's possible for the MDB container to delay acknowledgment for so long that the JMS provider assumes the message was not received and sends a "duplicate" message. Obviously, with `Dups-ok-acknowledge`, your MDBs must be able to handle duplicate messages correctly.

`Auto-acknowledge` avoids duplicate messages because the acknowledgment is sent immediately. Therefore, the JMS provider won't send a duplicate. Most MDBs use `Auto-acknowledge` to avoid processing the same message twice. `Dups-ok-acknowledge` exists because it can allow a JMS provider to optimize its use of the network. In practice, though, the overhead of an acknowledgment is so small, and the frequency of communication between the MDB container and the JMS provider is so high, that `Dups-ok-acknowledge` doesn't have a big impact on performance.

Having said all of this, the acknowledgment mode is ignored most of the time—in fact, it is ignored unless the MDB executes with bean-managed transactions, or with the container-managed transaction attribute `NotSupported` (see Chapter 16). In all other cases, transactions are managed by the container, and acknowledgment takes place within the context of the transaction. If the transaction succeeds, the message is acknowledged. If the transaction fails, the message is not acknowledged. When using container-managed transactions with a `Required` transaction attribute, the acknowledgment mode is usually not specified; however, it is included in the deployment descriptor for the sake of discussion.

Subscription durability

When a JMS-based MDB uses a `javax.jms.Topic`, the deployment descriptor must declare whether the subscription is `Durable` or `NonDurable`. A `Durable` subscription outlasts an MDB container's connection to the JMS provider, so if the EJB server suffers a partial failure, shuts down, or otherwise disconnects from the JMS provider, the messages that it would have received are not lost. The provider stores any messages that are delivered while the container is disconnected; the messages are delivered to the container (and from there to the MDB) when the container reconnects. This behavior is commonly referred to as *store-and-forward messaging*. `Durable` MDBs are tolerant of disconnections, whether intentional or the result of a partial failure.

If the subscription is `NonDurable`, any messages the bean would have received while it was disconnected are lost. Developers use `NonDurable` subscriptions when it is not critical for all messages to be processed. Using a `NonDurable` subscription improves the performance of the JMS provider but significantly reduces the reliability of the MDBs.

```
@ActivateConfigProperty(
      propertyName="subscriptionDurability",
      propertyValue="Durable")
```

When the destination type is javax.jms.Queue, as is the case in the ReservationProcessor EJB, durability is not a factor because of the nature of queue-based messaging systems. With a queue, messages may be consumed only once and they remain in the queue until they are distributed to one of the queue's listeners.

The XML Deployment Descriptor

Here is a deployment descriptor that provides a complete annotation-alternative definition of the ReservationProcessor EJB:

```
<?xml version="1.0"?>
<ejb-jar
       xmlns="http://java.sun.com/xml/ns/javaee"
       xmlns:xsi="http://www.w3.org/2001/XMLSchema-instance"
       xsi:schemaLocation="http://java.sun.com/xml/ns/javaee
                          http://java.sun.com/xml/ns/javaee/ejb-jar_3_0.xsd"
       version="3.0">
   <enterprise-beans>
      <message-driven>
         <ejb-name>ReservationProcessorBean</ejb-name>
         <ejb-class>
             com.titan.reservationprocessor.ReservationProcessorBean
         </ejb-class>
         <messaging-type>javax.jms.MessageListener</messaging-type>
         <transaction-type>Container</transaction-type>
         <message-destination-type>
             javax.jms.Queue
         </message-destination-type>
         <activation-config>
             <activation-property>
                 <activation-config-property-name>destinationType
                 </activation-config-property-name>
                 <activation-config-property-value>javax.jms.Queue
                 </activation-config-property-value>
             <activation-property>
             <activation-property>
                 <activation-config-property-name>messageSelector
                 </activation-config-property-name>
                 <activation-config-property-value>MessageFormat = 'Version 3.4'
                 </activation-config-property-value>
             <activation-property>
             <activation-property>
                 <activation-config-property-name>acknowledgeMode
                 </activation-config-property-name>
                 <activation-config-property-value>Auto-acknowledge
                 </activation-config-property-value>
             <activation-property>
         </activation-config>
         <ejb-local-ref>
             <ejb-ref-name>ejb/PaymentProcessor</ejb-ref-name>
             <ejb-ref-type>Session</ejb-ref-type>
             <local>com.titan.processpayment.ProcessPaymentLocal</local>
```

```
            <injection-target>
               <injection-target-class>
                  com.titan.reservationprocessor.ReservationProcessorBean
               </injection-target-class>
               <injection-target-name>process</injection-target-name>
            </injection-target>
         </resource-ref>
         <persistence-context-ref>
            <persistence-context-ref-name>
persistence/titan
</persistence-context-ref-name>
            <persistence-unit-name>titan</persistence-unit-name>
                <injection-target-class>
                   com.titan.reservationprocessor.ReservationProcessorBean
                </injection-target-class>
                <injection-target-name>em</injection-target-name>
            </injection-target>
         </env-entry>
        <resource-ref>
            <resource-ref-name>jms/ConnectionFactory</resource-ref-name>
            <resource-type>javax.jms.ConnectionFactory</res-type>
            <res-auth>Container</res-auth>
            <mapped-name>ConnectionFactory</mapped-name>
            <injection-target>
               <injection-target-class>
                  com.titan. reservationprocessor. ReservationProcessorBean
               </injection-target-class>
               <injection-target-name>datasource</injection-target-name>
            </injection-target>
         </resource-ref>
      </message-driven>
   </enterprise-beans>
</ejb-jar>
```

In addition to the `<activation-config>` element that describes the messaging properties, there are the `<messaging-type>` and `<message-destination-type>` elements. An MDB is declared in a `<message-driven>` element within the `<enterprise-beans>` element, alongside `<session>` beans. Similar to `<session>` bean types, it defines an `<ejb-name>` and a `<transaction-type>` but does not define component interfaces (local or remote). MDBs do not have remote or local interfaces, so these definitions aren't needed.

The ReservationProcessor Clients

In order to test the ReservationProcessor EJB, we need to develop two new client applications: one to send reservation messages and the other to consume ticket messages produced by the ReservationProcessor EJB.

The reservation message producer

The JmsClient_ReservationProducer sends 100 reservation requests very quickly. The speed with which it sends these messages forces many containers to use multiple MDB instances to process them. The code for JmsClient_ReservationProducer looks like this:

```
import javax.jms.Message;
import javax.jms.MapMessage;
import javax.jms.ConnectionFactory;
import javax.jms.Connection;
import javax.jms.Session;
import javax.jms.Queue;
import javax.jms.MessageProducer;
import javax.jms.JMSException;
import javax.naming.InitialContext;
import java.util.Date;

import com.titan.processpayment.CreditCardDO;

public class JmsClient_ReservationProducer {

    public static void main(String [] args) throws Exception {

        InitialContext jndiContext = getInitialContext( );

        ConnectionFactory factory = (ConnectionFactory)
            jndiContext.lookup("ConnectionFactoryNameGoesHere");

        Queue reservationQueue = (Queue)
            jndiContext.lookup("QueueNameGoesHere");

        Connection connect = factory.createConnection( );

        Session session =
            connect.createSession(false,Session.AUTO_ACKNOWLEDGE);

        MessageProducer sender = session.createProducer(reservationQueue);

        for(int i = 0; i < 100; i++){
            MapMessage message = session.createMapMessage( );
            message.setStringProperty("MessageFormat","Version 3.4");

            message.setInt("CruiseID",1);
            message.setInt("CustomerID",i%10);
            message.setInt("CabinID",i);
            message.setDouble("Price", (double)1000+i);

            // the card expires in about 30 days
            Date expirationDate = new Date(System.currentTimeMillis( )+43200000);
            message.setString("CreditCardNum", "923830283029");
            message.setLong("CreditCardExpDate", expirationDate.getTime( ));
            message.setString("CreditCardType", CreditCardDO.MASTER_CARD);
```

```
            sender.send(message);
        }
        connect.close( );
    }

    public static InitialContext getInitialContext( )
        throws JMSException {
        // create vendor-specific JNDI context here
    }
}
```

This code is very similar to the code we extended our TravelAgent EJB with earlier. It obtains a ConnectionFactory from JNDI and sets up the relevant JMS objects that will be used to send messages. It then creates 100 reservations and sends them to the JMS queue to be processed asynchronously.

The ticket message consumer

The JmsClient_TicketConsumer is designed to consume all the ticket messages delivered by ReservationProcessor EJB instances to the queue. It consumes the messages and prints out the descriptions:

```
import javax.jms.Message;
import javax.jms.ObjectMessage;
import javax.jms.ConnectionFactory;
import javax.jms.Connection;
import javax.jms.Session;
import javax.jms.Queue;
import javax.jms.MessageConsumer;
import javax.jms.JMSException;
import javax.naming.InitialContext;

import com.titan.travelagent.TicketDO;

public class JmsClient_TicketConsumer
    implements javax.jms.MessageListener {

    public static void main(String [] args) throws Exception {

        new JmsClient_TicketConsumer( );

        while(true){Thread.sleep(10000);}

    }

    public JmsClient_TicketConsumer( ) throws Exception {

        InitialContext jndiContext = getInitialContext( );

        ConnectionFactory factory = (ConnectionFactory)
            jndiContext.lookup("QueueFactoryNameGoesHere");
        Queue ticketQueue = (Queue)jndiContext.lookup("QueueNameGoesHere");
        Connection connect = factory.createConnection( );
```

```
            Session session =
                connect.createSession(false,Session.AUTO_ACKNOWLEDGE);
            MessageConsumer receiver = session.createConsumer(ticketQueue);

            receiver.setMessageListener(this);

            connect.start( );
        }

        public void onMessage(Message message) {
            try {
                ObjectMessage objMsg = (ObjectMessage)message;
                TicketDO ticket = (TicketDO)objMsg.getObject( );
                System.out.println("********************************");
                System.out.println(ticket);
                System.out.println("********************************");

            } catch(JMSException jmsE) {
                jmsE.printStackTrace( );
            }
        }
        public static InitialContext getInitialContext( ) throws JMSException {
            // create vendor-specific JNDI context here
        }
    }
```

To make the ReservationProcessor EJB work with the two client applications, `JmsClient_ReservationProducer` and `JmsClient_TicketConsumer`, you must configure your EJB container's JMS provider so that it has two queues: one for reservation messages and another for ticket messages.

The Life Cycle of a Message-Driven Bean

Just as session beans have well-defined life cycles, so does the MDB bean. The MDB instance's life cycle has two states: *Does Not Exist* and *Method-Ready Pool*. The Method-Ready Pool is similar to the instance pool used for stateless session beans.* Figure 12-4 illustrates the states and transitions that an MDB instance goes through in its lifetime.

The Does Not Exist State

When an MDB instance is in the Does Not Exist state, it is not an instance in the memory of the system. In other words, it has not been instantiated yet.

* Some vendors may *not* pool MDB instances but may instead create and destroy instances with each new message. This is an implementation-specific decision that should not affect the specified life cycle of the stateless bean instance.

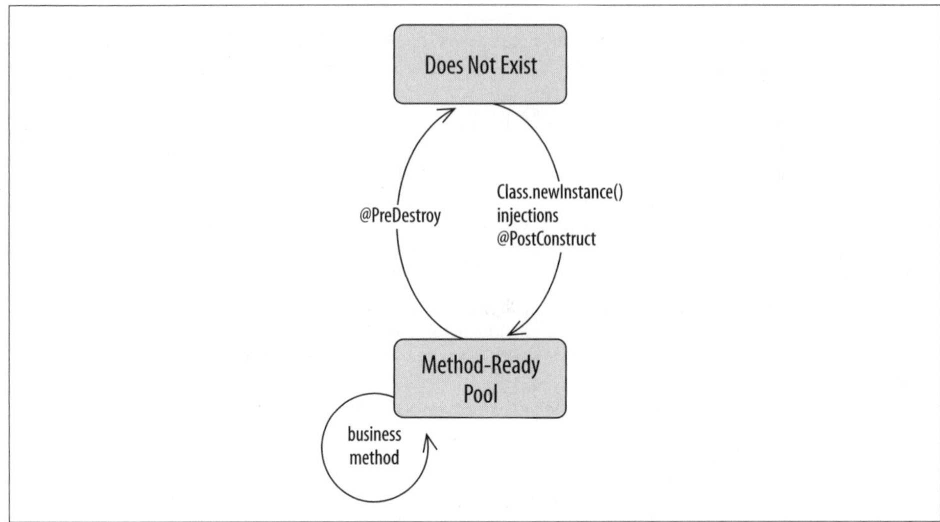

Figure 12-4. MDB life cycle

The Method-Ready Pool

MDB instances enter the Method-Ready Pool as the container needs them. When the EJB server is first started, it may create a number of MDB instances and enter them into the Method-Ready Pool. (The actual behavior of the server depends on the implementation.) When the number of MDB instances handling incoming messages is insufficient, more can be created and added to the pool.

Transitioning to the Method-Ready Pool

When an instance transitions from the Does Not Exist state to the Method-Ready Pool, three operations are performed on it. First, the bean instance is instantiated by invoking the `Class.newInstance( )` method on the stateless bean class. Second, the container injects any resources that the bean's metadata has requested via an injection annotation or XML deployment descriptor.

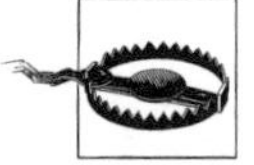

You must always provide a default constructor. A default constructor is a constructor with no parameters. The container instantiates instances of the bean class using `Class.newInstance( )`, which requires a no-arg constructor. If no constructors are defined, the no-arg constructor is implicit.

Finally, the EJB container will invoke the `PostConstruct` callback if there is one. The bean class may or may not have a method that is annotated with `@javax.ejb.PostConstruct`. If it is present, this annotated method will be called by the container after the bean is instantiated. This `@PostConstruct` annotated method can be of any name, but it must return void, have no parameters, and throw no checked exceptions. The bean class may define only one @PostConstruct method (but it is not required to do so).

```
@MessageDriven
public class MyBean implements MessageListener {

   @PostConstruct
   public void myInit( ) {}
```

MDBs are not subject to activation, so they can maintain open connections to resources for their entire life cycles.* The @PreDestroy method should close any open resources before the stateless session bean is evicted from memory at the end of its life cycle. You'll read more about @PreDestroy later in this section.

Life in the Method-Ready Pool

When a message is delivered to an MDB, it is delegated to any available instance in the Method-Ready Pool. While the instance is executing the request, it is unavailable to process other messages. The MDB can handle many messages simultaneously, delegating the responsibility of handling each message to a different MDB instance. When a message is delegated to an instance by the container, the MDB instance's MessageDrivenContext changes to reflect the new transaction context. Once the instance has finished, it is immediately available to handle a new message.

Transitioning out of the Method-Ready Pool: the death of an MDB instance

Bean instances leave the Method-Ready Pool for the Does Not Exist state when the server no longer needs them—that is, when the server decides to reduce the total size of the Method-Ready Pool by evicting one or more instances from memory. The process begins by invoking an @PreDestroy callback method on the bean instance. Again, as with @PostConstruct, this callback method is optional to implement and its signature must return a void type, have zero parameters, and throw no checked exceptions. An @PreDestroy callback method can perform any cleanup operation, such as closing open resources.

```
@MessageDriven
public class MyBean implements MessageListener {

   @PreDestroy
   public void cleanup( ) {
      ...
   }
```

* The duration of a stateless bean instance's life is assumed to be very long. However, some EJB servers may actually destroy and create instances with every method invocation, making this strategy less attractive. Consult your vendor's documentation for details on how your EJB server handles stateless instances.

As with @PostConstruct, @PreDestroy is invoked only once: when the bean is about to transition to the Does Not Exist state. During this callback method, the MessageDrivenContext and access to the JNDI ENC are still available to the bean instance. Following the execution of the @PreDestroy method, the bean is dereferenced and eventually garbage-collected.

Connector-Based Message-Driven Beans

Although the JMS-based MDB has proven very useful, it has limitations. Perhaps the most glaring limitation is that EJB vendors are able to support only a small number of JMS providers (usually only one). In pre-EJB 2.1 days, most vendors supported only their own JMS provider, and no others. Obviously, this limits your choices: if your company or a partner company uses a JMS provider that is not supported by your EJB vendor, you will not be able to process messages from that JMS provider.*

The root of the problem is complex and requires a fairly deep understanding of transaction management. In a nutshell, the delivery of the message by the JMS provider to the MDB, and all the work performed by the MDB (e.g., using JDBC, invoking methods on other beans, etc.), must be part of the same transaction, which is initiated by the EJB container. This requires that the EJB container have prior knowledge that message delivery is imminent so that it can initiate a transaction before the message is actually delivered. Unfortunately, the JMS API doesn't support this kind of functionality. So in the early days of EJB, JMS providers had to perform custom integration with each and every EJB vendor. Custom integration was expensive (businesswise), so old EJB 2.0 vendors generally choose to integrate with very few JMS providers.

Another limitation with JMS-based MDBs is that you are tied to the JMS programming model; no other messaging systems are supported. While JMS is very useful, it's not the only messaging system available. SOAP, email, CORBA messaging, proprietary messaging systems used in ERP systems (SAP, PeopleSoft, etc.), and legacy messaging systems are examples of other non-JMS messaging systems.

EJB 3.0 (and 2.1) supports an expanded, more open definition of message-driven beans that allows them to service any kind of messaging system from any vendor. The only requirement is that new types of message-driven beans adhere to the message-driven bean life cycle. EJB vendors can build custom code to support a new messaging system (something other than JMS), but they must also support any message-driven bean type that's based on JCA 1.5.

* A workaround is to use a JMS gateway, which routes messages from one JMS provider to another, but this is a custom solution outside the EJB specification.

The JCA provides a standard Service Provider Interface (SPI) that allows any EIS to plug into any Java EE container system. Version 1.0 of the connector architecture applies only to request/reply resources in which the Java EE component (EJB or servlet/JSP) initiates the request. The current version of the connector architecture (1.5), which is required by J2EE 1.4 and higher, is much more general and can work with any asynchronous messaging systems. In such systems, the Java EE component waits for messages to arrive, instead of initiating an interaction with an EIS; the EIS initiates the interaction by delivering a message.

JCA 1.5 defines a messaging contract specifically tailored to message-driven beans. It defines the contracts between an EJB container and an asynchronous Connector so that message-driven beans automatically process incoming messages from the EIS. MDBs based on an asynchronous Connector can implement a specific messaging interface defined by the Connector itself. Instead of implementing the `javax.jms.MessageListener` interface, the MDB implements some other type of interface that is specific to the EIS.

For example, Chapter 3 introduced a hypothetical Email Connector that allows MDBs to process email—similar to how JMS-based MDBs process JMS messages. The Email Connector is purchased from Vendor X and is delivered in a JAR file called a Resource ARchive (RAR). The RAR contains all the Connector code and deployment descriptors necessary to plug into the EJB container system. It also defines a messaging interface that the developer uses to create an email MDB. Here is the hypothetical email messaging interface that must be implemented by an email MDB:

```
package com.vendorx.email;

public interface EmailListener {
    public void onMessage(javax.mail.Message message);
}
```

The bean class that implements this interface is responsible for processing email messages delivered by the Email Connector. The following code shows an MDB that implements the `EmailListener` interface and processes email:

```
package com.titan.email;

@MessageDriven(activationConfig={
                @ActivationConfigProperty(
                     propertyName="mailServer",
                     propertyValue="mail.ispx.com"),
                @ActivationConfigProperty(
                     propertyName="serverType",
                     propertyValue="POP3 "),
                @ActivationConfigProperty(
                     propertyName="messageFilter",
                     propertyValue="to='submit@titan.com'")})
public class EmailBean implements com.vendorx.email.EmailListener {
```

```
        public void onMessage(javax.mail.Message message){
            javax.mail.internet.MimeMessage msg =
                (javax.mail.internet.MimeMessage) message;
            Address [] addresses = msg.getFrom( );
            //  continue processing Email message
        }
    }
```

In this example, the container calls onMessage( ) to deliver a JavaMail Message object, which represents an email message including MIME attachments. However, the messaging interfaces used by a Connector-based MDB don't have to use onMessage( ). The method name and method signature can be whatever is appropriate to the EIS; it can even have a return type. For example, a Connector might be developed to handle request/reply-style messaging for SOAP. This connector might use the ReqRespListener defined by the Java API for XML Messaging (JAXM), which is a SOAP messaging API defined by Sun Microsystems that is not part of the Java EE platform:

```
package javax.xml.messaging;
import javax.xml.soap.SOAPMessage;

public interface ReqRespListener {
    public SOAPMessage onMessage(SOAPMessage message);
}
```

In this interface, onMessage( ) has a return type of SOAPMessage. This means the EJB container and Connector are responsible for coordinating the reply message back to the sender (or to some destination defined in the deployment descriptor). In addition to supporting different method signatures, the messaging interface may have several methods for processing different kinds of messages using the same MDB.

There's no limit to the new kinds of message-driven beans that EJB container systems can support. The real beauty of all of this is that Connector-based MDBs are completely portable across EJB vendors—because all vendors must support them. If you use a Connector-based MDB with EJB Vendor A and later change to EJB Vendor B, you can continue to use the same Connector-based MDB with no portability problems.

The activation configuration properties used with non-JMS-based MDBs depend on the type of Connector and its requirements. Let's see an example of this:

```
@MessageDriven(activationConfig={
                @ActivationConfigProperty(
                     propertyName="mailServer",
                     propertyValue="mail.ispx.com"),
                @ActivationConfigProperty(
                     propertyName="serverType",
                     propertyValue="POP3"),
                @ActivationConfigProperty(
                     propertyName="messageFilter",
                     propertyValue="to='submit@titan.com'")})
```

We talked about @ActivationConfigProperty annotations before. As you can see from the preceding example, any name/value pair is supported within this annotation, so it can easily support the email-specific configuration for this Connector type.

Message Linking

Message linking is a feature that allows the messages being sent by any enterprise bean to be routed to a specific message-driven bean in the same deployment. By using message linking, you can orchestrate a flow of messages between components in the same application. For example, in the beginning of this chapter, the Travel-Agent EJB from Chapter 11 was reimplemented so that it sent a JMS message with the ticket information to a Topic destination. Here's a different implementation of the TravelAgent EJB's bookPassage( ) method, this time using an ObjectMessage type:

```
@Resource(mappedName="ConnectionFactory")
private ConnectionFactory connectionFactory;

@Resource(mappedName="TicketTopic")
private Topic topic;

@Remove
public TicketDO bookPassage(CreditCardDO card, double price)
    throws IncompleteConversationalState {

    if (customer == null || cruise == null || cabin == null) {
        throw new IncompleteConversationalState( );
    }
    try {
        Reservation reservation = new Reservation(
                              customer, cruise, cabin, price, new Date( ));
        entityManager.persist(reservation);

        process.byCredit(customer, card, price);

        TicketDO ticket = new TicketDO(customer, cruise, cabin, price);



        Connection connect = topicFactory.createConnection( );
        Session session = connect.createSession(true,0);
        MessageProducer publisher = session.createProducer(topic);

        ObjectMessage objectMsg = session.createObjectMessage( );
        objectMsg.setObject(ticket);
        publisher.send(objectMsg);
        connect.close( );

        return ticket;
    } catch(Exception e) {
        throw new EJBException(e);
    }
}
```

When we discussed this method earlier in the chapter, we never really mentioned where the ticket message was being sent. It could go to the reservation agent or to some other department of Titan Cruises. However, message linking makes sure that the message goes directly to a message-driven bean that we deploy.

For example, we might deploy a message-driven bean, the TicketDistributor EJB, which is responsible for distributing ticket information to several different targets such as legacy databases, partner organizations, marketing, etc. Figure 12-5 shows how the TicketDistributor EJB (an MDB) works with the TravelAgent EJB to distribute ticket information to several different targets.

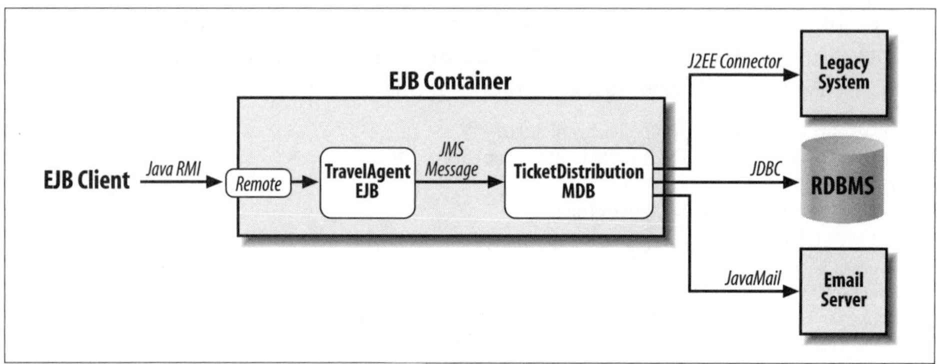

Figure 12-5. Message flow with message linking

The TicketDistributor distributes the ticket information to a variety of disparate targets, including a separate relational database using JDBC, a legacy system (e.g., IMS, CICS, etc.) using a Java EE Connector, and email using JavaMail. The TravelAgent EJB could have handled this type of distribution directly, but defining a separate MDB to do distribution provides more flexibility and better performance.

The TicketDistributor MDB is more flexible because the routing for the message can be changed without modifying the TravelAgent EJB. The TravelAgent EJB always sends messages to the same JMS topic; it's the TicketDistributor's responsibility to distribute the ticket information to other sources. The TicketDistributor also improves performance, because the TicketAgent doesn't have to wait on the various targets (a separate database, legacy system, and email) to accept and process the message before finishing the reservation. The TicketAgent just sends the ticket information and forgets about it. It's the TicketDistribution MDB's responsibility to distribute the ticket information to the appropriate parties. In addition, the TravelAgent EJB doesn't have to coordinate a distributed transaction across different resources, which can create significant bottlenecks and affect throughput.

The EJB specification does not have an annotation to wire message linking, so we'll have to create a partial XML deployment descriptor to enable this feature. In order to link the outgoing messages sent by the TravelAgent EJB with the incoming messages consumed and processed by the TicketDistribution MDB, we need to define

<message-destination-link> elements in the deployment descriptor. The <message-destination-link> element is defined by the <message-destination-ref> element of the TravelAgent EJB. The TicketDistributor EJB also declares the <message-destination-link> element. Both elements reference the same logical destination declared in the assembly descriptor:

```
<ejb-jar>
  <enterprise-beans>
    <session>
        <ejb-name>com.titan.travelagent.TravelAgentBean</ejb-name>
        <message-destination-ref>
            <message-destination-ref-name>
                   jms/TicketTopic
            </message-destination-ref-name>
            <message-destination-type>javax.jms.Topic</message-destination-type>
            <message-destination-usage>Produces</message-destination-usage>
            <message-destination-link>
                 Distributor
            </message-destination-link>
            <injection-target>
                 <injection-target-class>javax.jms.Topic</injection-target-class>
                 <injection-target-name>topic</injection-target-name>
            </injection-target>
        </message-destination-ref>
    </session>
    <message-driven>
        <ejb-name>TicketDistributorEJB</ejb-name>
        <message-destination-link>
            Distributor
        </message-destination-link>
    </message-driven>
  </enterprise-beans>
  <assembly-descriptor>
    <message-destination>
       <message-destination-name>Distributor</message-destination-name>
    </message-destination>
  </assembly-descriptor>
</ejb-jar>
```

A <message-destination-ref> element declares the destination to which an enterprise bean sends or receives messages. When the <message-destination-ref> includes a <message-destination-link> element, it means that message senders and receivers will be sharing a logical destination described in the assembly descriptor. In the preceding example, the TravelAgent EJB's <message-destination-ref> declares a <message-destination-link>, which points to the <message-destination> element in the <assembly-descriptor> that has the name Distributor. The <message-destination-link> defined by the TicketDistributor MDB points to the same <message-destination> element. This means the messages sent by the TravelAgent EJB to the Distributor message destination will go to the TicketDistributor MDB.

The <injection-target> is a common XML fragment that allows you to inject the reference into a field or *setter* method of the bean class. Here, the descriptor says it will inject the Topic destination of the topic field of the TravelAgent EJB's bean class. We'll go over this in more detail in Chapter 14.

Message-driven beans always consume messages from the destination defined by the <message-destination-link> element defined directly under the <message-bean> element. However, they can also produce messages that are sent to a logical message destination if they use the message API described by their own <message-destination-ref> element. The following listing shows that the TicketDistributor consumes messages from the Distributor destination, but it also uses the JMS to send messages to a completely different destination, called Partner:

```
<ejb-jar>
  <enterprise-beans>
    <message-driven>
      <ejb-name>TicketDistributorEJB</ejb-name>
      <message-destination-link>
         Distributor
      </message-destination-link>
      <message-destination-ref>
          <message-destination-ref-name>
                jms/PartnerCompany
          </message-destination-ref-name>
          <message-destination-type>javax.jms.Topic</message-destination-type>
          <message-destination-usage>Produces</message-destination-usage>
          <message-destination-link>
             Partner
           </message-destination-link>
        </message-destination-ref>
    </message-driven>
  </enterprise-beans>
  <assembly-descriptor>
    <message-destination>
       <message-destination-name>Distributor</message-destination-name>
    </message-destination>
    <message-destination>
       <message-destination-name>Partner</message-destination-name>
    </message-destination>
  </assembly-descriptor>
</ejb-jar>
```

At deployment time, each <message-destination> element is mapped to a real messaging destination in the target environment. In most cases, this will be a JMS topic or queue, but it could be a destination of some other type of messaging system.

The Java EE application server doesn't have to route the messages through an actual destination. It can asynchronously send them from the sender to the receiver; in this case, from the TravelAgent EJB to the TicketDistributor MDB. However, if the application server handles message delivery itself, instead of going through a messaging provider, it must follow the semantics of the messaging system. For JMS, transactions, persistence, durability, security, and acknowledgments should be handled correctly whether the message is sent directly from one component to another, or via a JMS provider.

CHAPTER 13

Timer Service

Business systems frequently use scheduling systems to run programs at specified times. Scheduling systems typically run applications that generate reports, reformat data, or do audit work at night. In other cases, scheduling systems provide callback APIs that can alert subsystems of events such as due dates, deadlines, etc. Scheduling systems often run *batch jobs* (a.k.a. *scheduled jobs*), which perform routine work automatically at a prescribed time. Users in the Unix world frequently run scheduled jobs using *cron*, a simple but useful scheduling system that runs programs listed in a configuration file. Other job-scheduling systems include the OMG's COS Timer Event Service, which is a CORBA API for timed events, as well as commercial products.

Regardless of the software, scheduling systems are used in many different scenarios:

- In a credit card processing system, credit card charges are processed in batches so that all the charges made for an entire day are settled together rather than separately. This work is scheduled to be done in the evening to reduce the impact of processing on the system.
- In a hospital or clinical system, Electronic Data Interface (EDI) software is used to send medical claims to various HMOs. Each HMO has its own processing requirements, but all of them are routine, so jobs are scheduled to gather claim data, put it in the proper format, and transfer it to the HMO.
- In just about any company, managers need specific reports run on a regular basis. A scheduling system can be configured to run those reports automatically and deliver them via email to managers.

Scheduling systems are also common in *workflow applications*, which are systems that manage document processing that typically spans days or months and involves many systems and lots of human intervention. In workflow applications, scheduling is employed for auditing tasks that periodically take inventory of the state of an application, invoice, sales order, etc., in order to ensure everything is proceeding as scheduled. The scheduling system maintains timers and delivers events to alert applications and components when a specified date and time are reached, or when some period has expired. Here are some examples of workflow scheduling:

- In a mortgage system, a lot of tasks have to be completed (i.e., appraisal, rate lock-in, closing appointment, etc.) before the mortgage can be closed. Timers can be set on mortgage applications to perform periodic audits that ensure everything is proceeding on schedule.
- In a healthcare claims-processing system, claims must be processed within 90 days according to terms negotiated by in-network physicians and clinics. Each claim could have a timer set to go off seven days before the deadline.
- In a stockbroker system, buy-at-limit orders can be created for a specific number of shares, but only at a specified price or lower. These buy-at-limit orders typically have a time limit. If the stock price falls below the specified price before the time limit, the buy-at-limit order is carried out. If the stock price does not fall below the specified price before the time limit, the timer expires and the buy-at-limit order is canceled.

In the EJB world, there has been a general interest in scheduling systems that can work directly with enterprise beans. However, prior to EJB 2.1, there has been no standard Java EE scheduling system. Enterprise JavaBeans 2.1 introduced a standardized but limited scheduling system called the Timer Service that hasn't been expanded at all in EJB 3.0.

The Java Standard Edition includes the `java.util.Timer` class, which allows threads to schedule tasks for future execution in a background thread. This facility is useful for a variety of applications, but it's too limited to be used in enterprise computing. Note, however, that the scheduling semantics of `java.util.Timer` are similar to those of the EJB Timer Service.

The Timer Service is a facility of the EJB container system that provides a timed-event API, which can be used to schedule timers for specified dates, periods, and intervals. A timer is associated with the enterprise bean that set it, and it calls that bean's `ejbTimeout( )` method or a method annotated with `@javax.ejb.Timeout` when it goes off. The rest of this chapter describes the EJB Timer Service API and its use with stateless session and message-driven beans, as well as providing some criticism of and suggested improvements for the Timer Service.

Titan's Maintenance Timer

Titan Cruises has a policy of performing regular maintenance on its ships. For example, the engines require extensive and varied maintenance activities throughout the year, as do navigation equipment, communications, sewer and water systems, etc. In fact, there are literally thousands of maintenance functions to be performed on a ship throughout the year. To manage all of these items, Titan uses the EJB Timer Service to alert the proper maintenance crews when an item needs to be serviced. In this chapter, we modify the Ship Maintenance EJB to manage its own maintenance schedule. Titan's Health and Safety Department can use business methods on the Ship Maintenance EJB to schedule and cancel maintenance items, and the Ship Maintenance EJB will take care of alerting the correct maintenance crew when an item needs to be serviced.

Timer Service API

The Timer Service enables an enterprise bean to be notified when a specific date has arrived, when some period of time has elapsed, or at recurring intervals. To use the Timer Service, an enterprise bean must implement the `javax.ejb.TimedObject` interface, which defines a single callback method, `ejbTimeout( )`:

```
package javax.ejb;

public interface TimedObject {
    public void ejbTimeout(Timer timer) ;
}
```

In EJB 3.0, the `@javax.ejb.Timeout` annotation can be applied to a method whose signature returns `void` and has one `javax.ejb.Timer` parameter. We'll show examples of both.

When the scheduled time is reached or the specified interval has elapsed, the container system invokes the enterprise bean's timeout callback method. The enterprise bean can then perform any processing it needs to respond to the timeout, such as run reports, audit records, modify the states of other beans, etc. For example, the Ship Maintenance EJB can be modified to implement the `TimedObject` interface, as shown:

```
@Stateless
public class ShipMaintenanceBean implements ShipMaintenanceRemote
      implements javax.ejb.TimedObject {

    public void ejbTimeout(javax.ejb.Timer timer) {
       // business logic for timer goes here
    }
}
```

Alternatively, the `@javax.ejb.Timeout` annotation can be used:

```
@Stateless
public class ShipMaintenanceBean implement ShipMaintenanceRemote {

    @Timeout
    public void maintenance(javax.ejb.Timer timer) {
       // business logic for timer goes here
    }
}
```

An enterprise bean schedules itself for a timed notification using a reference to the TimerService, which can be obtained from the EJBContext or injected directly into your bean using the @javax.annotation.Resource annotation. The TimerService allows a bean to register itself for notification on a specific date, after some period of time, or at recurring intervals. The following code shows how a bean would register for notification exactly 30 days from now:

```
// Create a Calendar object that represents the time 30 days from now.
Calendar time = Calendar.getInstance( );  // the current time.
time.add(Calendar.DATE, 30); // add 30 days to the current time.
Date date = time.getTime( );

// Create a timer that will go off 30 days from now.
TimerService timerService = // from EJBContext or injected
timerService.createTimer( date,  null);
```

This example creates a Calendar object that represents the current time and then increments this object by 30 days so that it represents the time 30 days from now. The code obtains a reference to the container's TimerService and calls the TimerService.createTimer( ) method, passing it the java.util.Date value of the Calendar object, thus creating a timer that will go off after 30 days.

We can add a method, scheduleMaintenance( ), to the Ship Maintenance EJB that allows a client to schedule a maintenance item for a particular ship. When the method is called, the client passes in the name of the ship on which maintenance will be performed, a description of the maintenance item, and the date on which it is to be performed. For example, a client could schedule a maintenance item for the cruise ship *Valhalla* on April 2, 2006, as shown in the following code snippet:

```
InitialContext jndiCntxt = new InitialContext( );
ShipMaintenanceRemote maintenance =
  (ShipMaintenanceRemote) jndiCntxt.lookup("ShipMaintenanceRemote ");
ShipMaintenanceRemote Calendar april2nd = Calendar.getInstance( );
april2nd.set(2006, Calendar.APRIL, 2);
String description = "Stress Test: Test Drive Shafts A & B ...";
maintenance.scheduleMaintenance("Valhalla", description, april2nd.getTime( ));
```

The ShipMaintenanceBean implements the scheduleMaintenance( ) method and takes care of scheduling the event using the Timer Service, as shown here:

```
@Stateless
public class ShipMaintenanceBean implements ShipMaintenanceRemote {

    @Resource javax.ejb.TimerService timerService;
    @PersistenceContext(unitName="titanDB") entityManager;

    public void scheduleMaintenance(String ship, String description,
                                    Date dateOfTest) {
        String item = ship + " is scheduling maintenance of " + description;
        timerService.createTimer(dateOf, msg);
    }
```

```
        @Timeout
        public void maintenance(javax.ejb.Timer timer) {
           // business logic for timer goes here
        }
        ...
    }
```

As you can see, the Ship Maintenance EJB is responsible for obtaining a reference to the Timer Service and scheduling its own events. When April 2, 2006 rolls around, the Timer Service calls the annotated `maintenance( )` method on the Ship Maintenance EJB representing the *Valhalla*. When this callback method is invoked, the Ship Maintenance EJB sends a JMS message containing the description of the test to the Health and Safety Department at Titan Cruises, alerting it that a stress test is required. Here's how the implementation of maintenance looks:

```
@Stateless
public class ShipMaintenanceBean implements ShipMaintenanceRemote {

    @Resource javax.ejb.TimerService timerService;

    public void scheduleMaintenance(String ship, String description,
                                    Date dateOfTest) {
        String item = ship + " is scheduling maintenance of " + description;
        timerService.createTimer(dateOf, item);
    }

    @Resource(mappedName="ConnectionFactory") ConnectionFactory factory;
    @Resource(mappedName="MaintenanceTopic") topic;

    @Timeout
    public void maintenance(javax.ejb.Timer timer) {
      try{
        String item = (String)timer.getInfo( );

        Connection connect = factory.createConnection( );
        Session session = connect.createSession(true,0);
        MessageProducer publisher = session.createProducer(topic);

        TextMessage msg = session.createTextMessage( );
        msg.setText(item);
        publisher.send(msg);
        connect.close( );
      }catch(Exception e){
        throw new EJBException(e);
      }
    }
}
```

The TimerService Interface

The `TimerService` interface provides an enterprise bean with access to the EJB container's Timer Service so that new timers can be created and existing timers can be listed. The TimerService interface is part of the javax.ejb package in EJB 3.0 and has the following definition:

```
package javax.ejb;
import java.util.Date;
import java.io.Serializable;
public interface TimerService {

   // Create a single-action timer that expires on a specified date.
   public Timer createTimer(Date expiration, Serializable info)
      throws IllegalArgumentException,IllegalStateException,EJBException;
   // Create a single-action timer that expires after a specified duration.
   public Timer createTimer(long duration, Serializable info)
      throws IllegalArgumentException,IllegalStateException,EJBException;
   // Create an interval timer that starts on a specified date.
   public Timer createTimer(
      Date initialExpiration, long intervalDuration, Serializable info)
      throws IllegalArgumentException,IllegalStateException,EJBException;
   // Create an interval timer that starts after a specified duration.
   public Timer createTimer(
      long initialDuration, long intervalDuration, Serializable info)
      throws IllegalArgumentException,IllegalStateException,EJBException;
   // Get all the active timers associated with this bean
   public java.util.Collection getTimers( )
      throws IllegalStateException,EJBException;
}
```

Each of the four TimerService.createTimer( ) methods establishes a timer with a different type of configuration. There are essentially two types of timers: *single-action* and *interval*. A single-action timer expires once, and an interval timer expires many times, at specified intervals. When a timer expires, the Timer Service calls the bean's ejbTimeout( ) method or a callback method with @javax.ejb.Timeout.

Here's how each of the four createTimer( ) methods works. At this point, we are discussing only the expiration and duration parameters and their uses. The Serializable info parameter is discussed later in this chapter.

createTimer(Date expiration, Serializable info)
: Creates a single-action timer that expires once. The timer expires on the date set for the expiration parameter. Here's how to set a timer that expires on July 4, 2006:

```
Calendar july4th = Calendar.getInstance( );
july4th.set(2006, Calendar.JULY, 4);
timerService.createTimer(july4th.getTime( ), null);
```

createTimer(long duration, Serializable info)
: Creates a single-action timer that expires only once. The timer expires after duration time (measured in milliseconds) has elapsed. Here's how to set a timer that expires in 90 days:

```
long ninetyDays = 1000 * 60 * 60 * 24 * 90; // 90 days
timerService.createTimer(ninetyDays, null);
```

`createTimer(Date initialExpiration, long intervalDuration, Serializable info)`
: Creates an interval timer that expires many times. The timer first expires on the date set for the `initialExpiration` parameter. After the first expiration, subsequent expirations occur at intervals equal to the `intervalDuration` parameter (in milliseconds). Here's how to set a timer that expires on July 4, 2006 and continues to expire every three days after that date:

```
Calendar july4th = Calendar.getInstance( );
july4th.set(2006, Calendar.JULY, 4);
long threeDaysInMillis = 1000 * 60 * 60 * 24 * 3; // 3 days
timerService.createTimer(july4th.getTime( ), threeDaysInMillis, null);
```

`createTimer(long initialDuration, long intervalDuration, Serializable info)`
: Creates an interval timer that expires many times. The timer first expires after the period given by `initialDuration` has elapsed. After the first expiration, subsequent expirations occur at intervals given by the `intervalDuration` parameter. Both `initialDuration` and `intervalDuration` are in milliseconds. Here's how to set a timer that expires in 10 minutes and continues to expire every hour thereafter:

```
long tenMinutes = 1000 * 60 * 10;  // 10 minutes
long oneHour = 1000 * 60 * 60; // 1 hour
timerService.createTimer(tenMinutes, oneHour, null);
```

When a timer is created, the Timer Service makes it persistent in some type of secondary storage, so it will survive system failures. If the server goes down, the timers are still active when the server comes back up. While the specification isn't clear, it's assumed that any timers that expire while the system is down will go off when it comes back up again. If an interval timer expires many times while the server is down, it may go off multiple times when the system comes up again. Consult your vendor's documentation to learn how they handle expired timers following a system failure.

The `TimerService.getTimers( )` method returns all the timers that have been set for a particular enterprise bean. For example, if this method is called on the EJB representing the cruise ship *Valhalla*, it returns only the timers that are set for the *Valhalla*, not timers set for other ships. The `getTimers( )` method returns a `java.util.Collection`, an unordered collection of zero or more `javax.ejb.Timer` objects. Each `Timer` object represents a different timed event that has been scheduled for the bean using the Timer Service.

The `getTimers( )` method is often used to manage existing timers. A bean can look through the `Collection` of `Timer` objects and cancel any timers that are no longer valid or need to be rescheduled. For example, the Ship Maintenance EJB defines the `clearSchedule( )` method, which allows a client to cancel all scheduled maintenance. Here's the implementation of `clearSchedule( )`:

```
@Stateless
public class ShipMaintenanceBean implements ShipMaintenanceRemote {

    @Resource javax.ejb.TimerService timerService;
```

```
        public void clearSchedule( ) {
            for (Object obj : timerService.getTimers( )) {
                javax.ejb.Timer timer = (javax.ejb.Timer)obj;
                timer.cancel( );
            }
        }

        public void scheduleMaintenance(String name, String desc, Date date) {
           // business logic goes here

        public void ejbTimeout(javax.ejb.Timer timer) {
           // business logic for timer goes here
        }
        ...
    }
```

The logic here is simple. After getting a reference to the `TimerService`, we get a `Collection` that contains all of the `Timers`. Then we loop through the `Collection`, canceling each timer whose `MaintenanceItem` is the desired ship. The `Timer` objects implement a `cancel( )` method, which removes the timed event from the Timer Service so that it never expires.

Exceptions

The `TimerService.getTimers( )` method can throw an `IllegalStateException` or an `EJBException`. All of the `createTimer( )` methods declare these two exceptions, plus a third exception, the `IllegalArgumentException`. Here are the reasons why the `TimerService` methods would throw these exceptions:

`java.lang.IllegalArgumentException`
: The duration and expiration parameters must have valid values. This exception is thrown if a negative number is used for one of the duration parameters or a null value is used for the expiration parameter, which is of type `java.util.Date`.

`java.lang.IllegalStateException`
: This exception is thrown if the enterprise bean attempts to invoke one of the `TimerService` methods from a method where it's not allowed. Each enterprise bean type (i.e., entity, stateless session, and message driven) defines its own set of allowed operations. However, in general, the `TimerService` methods can be invoked from anywhere except the `EJBContext` methods (i.e., `setEntityContext( )`, `setSessionContext( )`, and `setMessageDrivenContext( )`).

`javax.ejb.EJBException`
: This exception is thrown when some type of system-level exception occurs in the Timer Service.

The Timer

A `Timer` is an object that implements the `javax.ejb.Timer` interface. It represents a timed event that has been scheduled for an enterprise bean using the Timer Service.

Timer objects are returned by the TimerService.createTimer( ) and TimerService.getTimers( ) methods, and a Timer is the only parameter of the TimedObject.ejbTimeout( ) method or annotated @javax.ejb.Timeout callback. The Timer interface is:

```
package javax.ejb;

public interface Timer {

    // Cause the timer and all its associated expiration
    // notifications to be canceled
    public void cancel( )
         throws IllegalStateException,NoSuchObjectLocalException,EJBException;

    // Get the information associated with the timer at the time of creation.
    public java.io.Serializable getInfo( )
         throws IllegalStateException,NoSuchObjectLocalException,EJBException;

    // Get the point in time at which the next timer
    // expiration is scheduled to occur.
    public java.util.Date getNextTimeout( )
         throws IllegalStateException,NoSuchObjectLocalException,EJBException;

    // Get the number of milliseconds that will elapse
    // before the next scheduled timer expiration
    public long getTimeRemaining( )
         throws IllegalStateException,NoSuchObjectLocalException,EJBException;

    //Get a serializable handle to the timer
    public TimerHandle getHandle( )
         throws IllegalStateException,NoSuchObjectLocalException,EJBException;
}
```

A Timer instance represents exactly one timed event and can be used to cancel the timer, obtain a serializable handle, obtain the application data associated with the timer, and find out when the timer's next scheduled expiration will occur.

Canceling timers

The previous section used the Timer.cancel( ) method. It's used to cancel a specific timer from the Timer Service so that it never expires. It is useful if a particular timer needs to be removed completely or simply rescheduled. To reschedule a timed event, cancel the timer and create a new one. For example, when one of the ship's components fails and is replaced, that component must have its maintenance rescheduled: it doesn't make sense to perform a yearly overhaul on an engine in June if it was replaced in May. The scheduleMaintenance( ) method can be modified so that it can add a new maintenance item or replace an existing one by canceling it and adding the new one:

```
package com.titan.maintenance;

import javax.ejb.*;
import java.util.Date;
import javax.annotation.Resource;
```

```
@Stateless
public class ShipMaintenanceBean implements ShipMaintenanceRemote {

    @Resource javax.ejb.TimerService timerService;

    public void scheduleMaintenance(String ship, String description,
                                    Date dateOf) {
        String item = ship + " is scheduling maintenance of " + description;

        for (Object obj : timerService.getTimers( )) {
            javax.ejb.Timer timer = (javax.ejb.Timer)obj;
            String scheduled = (String)timer.getInfo( );
            if (scheduled.equals(item)) {
                timer.cancel( );
            }
        }

        timerService.createTimer(dateOf, item);
    }

    @Timeout
    public void maintenance(javax.ejb.Timer timer) {
       // business logic for timer goes here
    }
}
```

The `scheduleMaintenance( )` method first obtains a `Collection` of all timers defined for the ship. It then compares the description of each timer to the description passed into the method. If there is a match, it means a timer for that maintenance item was already scheduled and should be canceled. After the *for* loop, the new `Timer` is added to the Timer Service.

Identifying timers

Of course, comparing descriptions is a fairly unreliable way of identifying timers, since descriptions tend to vary over time. What is really needed is a far more robust information object that can contain both a description and a precise identifier.

All of the `TimeService.createTimer( )` methods declare an `info` object as their last parameter. The `info` object is application data that is stored by the Timer Service and delivered to the enterprise bean when its timeout callback is invoked. The serializable object used as the `info` parameter can be anything, as long as it implements the `java.io.Serializable` interface and follows the rules of serialization.* The `info` object can be put to many uses, but one obvious use is to associate the timer with some sort of identifier.

* In the most basic cases, all an object needs to do to be serializable is implement the `java.io.Serializable` interface and make sure any nonserializable fields (e.g., JDBC connection handles) are marked as `transient`.

To get the info object from a timer, you call the timer's getInfo( ) method. This method returns a serializable object, which you'll have to cast to an appropriate type. So far, we've been using strings as info objects, but there are much more elaborate (and reliable) possibilities. For example, instead of comparing maintenance descriptions to find duplicate timers, Titan decided to use unique Maintenance Item Numbers (MINs). MINs and maintenance descriptions can be combined into a new MaintenanceItem object:

```
public class MaintenanceItem implements java.io.Serializable {
    private long maintenanceItemNumber;
    private String shipName;
    private String description;
    public MaintenanceItem(long min, String ship, String desc) {
        maintenanceItemNumber = min;
        shipName = ship;
        description = desc;
    }
    public long getMIN( ) {
        return maintenanceItemNumber;
    }
    public String getShipName( ) {
        return shipName;
    }
    public String getDescription( ) {
        return description;
    }
}
```

Using the MaintenanceItem type, we can modify the scheduleMaintenance( ) method to be more precise, as shown here (changes are in bold):

```
@Stateless
public class ShipMaintenanceBean implements ShipMaintenanceRemote {

    @Resource javax.ejb.TimerService timerService;

    public void scheduleMaintenance(
              MaintenanceItem maintenanceItem, Date dateOfTest) {
        for (Object obj : timerService.getTimers( )) {
            MaintenanceItem scheduled = (MaintenanceItem)timer.getInfo( );
            if (scheduled.getMIN() == maintenanceItem.getMIN( )) {
                Timer.cancel( );
            }
        }
    }

    @Timeout
    public void maintenance(javax.ejb.Timer timer) {
        // business logic for timer goes here
    }

}
```

The MaintenanceInfo class contains information about the maintenance work that is to be done and is sent to the maintenance system using JMS. When one of the timers expires, the Timer Service calls the maintenance( ) method on the Ship Maintenance EJB. When the maintenance( ) method is called, the info object is obtained from the Timer object and used to determine which timer logic should be executed.

Retrieving other information from timers

The Timer.getNextTimeout( ) method simply returns the date—represented by a java.util.Date instance—on which the timer will expire next. If the timer is a single-action timer, the Date returned is the time at which the timer will expire. If, however, the timer is an interval timer, the Date returned is the time remaining until the next expiration. Oddly, there is no way to determine subsequent expirations or the interval at which an interval timer is configured. The best way to handle this is to put that information into your info object.

The Timer.getTimeRemaining( ) method returns the number of milliseconds before the timer will next expire. Like the getNextTimeout( ) method, this method only provides information about the next expiration.

The TimerHandle object

The Timer.getHandle( ) method returns a TimerHandle object. The TimerHandle object is similar to the javax.ejb.Handle and javax.ejb.HomeHandle discussed in Chapter 5. It's a reference that can be saved to a file or some other resource and then used later to regain access to the Timer. The TimerHandle interface is simple:

```
package javax.ejb;
public interface TimerHandle extends java.io.Serializable {
    public Timer getTimer( ) throws NoSuchObjectLocalException, EJBException;
}
```

The TimerHandle is only valid as long as the timer has not expired (if it's a single-action timer) or been canceled. If the timer no longer exists, calling the TimerHandle.getTimer( ) method throws a javax.ejb.NoSuchObjectException.

TimerHandle objects are local, which means they cannot be used outside the container system that generated them. Passing the TimerHandle as an argument to a remote or endpoint interface method is illegal. However, a TimerHandle can be passed between local enterprise beans using their local interface, because local enterprise beans must be co-located in the same container system.

Exceptions

All the methods defined in the Timer interface declare two exceptions:

`javax.ejb.NoSuchObjectLocalException`
: This exception is thrown if you invoke any method on an expired single-action timer or a canceled timer.

`javax.ejb.EJBException`
: This exception is thrown when some type of system-level exception occurs in the Timer Service.

Transactions

When a bean calls `createTimer( )`, the operation is performed in the scope of the current transaction. If the transaction rolls back, the timer is undone: it's not created (or, more precisely, it's uncreated). For example, if the Ship Maintenance EJB's `scheduleMaintenance( )` method has a transaction attribute of `RequiresNew`, a new transaction will be created when the method is called. If an exception is thrown by the method, the transaction rolls back and the new timer event is not created.

In most cases, the timeout callback method on beans should have a transaction attribute of `RequiresNew`. This ensures that the work performed by the callback method is in the scope of container-initiated transactions. Transactions are covered in more detail in Chapter 16.

Stateless Session Bean Timers

Our Ship Maintenance EJB example was an example of a stateless session bean's usage of the Timer Service. Stateless session bean timers can be used for *auditing* or *batch processing*. As an auditing agent, a stateless session timer can monitor the state of the system to ensure that tasks are being completed and that data is consistent. This type of work spans entities and possibly data sources. Such EJBs can also perform batch-processing work such as database cleanup, transfer of records, etc. Stateless session bean timers can also be deployed as agents that perform some type of intelligent work on behalf of the organization they serve. An agent can be thought of as an extension of an audit: it monitors the system but it also fixes problems automatically.

Stateless session bean timers are associated with only a specific type of session bean. When a timer for a stateless session bean goes off, the container selects an instance of that stateless bean type from the instance pool and calls its timeout callback method. This makes sense, because all stateless session beans in the instance pool are logically equivalent. Any instance can serve any client, including the container itself.

Stateless session timers are often used to manage taskflow; they're also used when the timed event applies to a collection of entities instead of just one. For example, stateless session timers might be used to audit all maintenance records to ensure that they meet state and federal guidelines: at specific intervals, a timer notifies the bean to look up the maintenance records from all the ships and generate a report. A stateless session timer can also be used to do something like send notifications to all the passengers for a particular cruise, thus avoiding the timer attack problem.

The stateless session bean can access an injected `TimerService` from the `SessionContext` in the `@PostConstruct`, `@PreDestroy`, or any business method, but it cannot access the Timer Service from any *setter* injection method. This means a client must call some method on a stateless session bean (either `create` or a business method) in order for a timer to be set. This is the only way to guarantee that the timer is set.

Setting a timer on the `@PostConstruct` method is problematic. First, there is no guarantee that an `@PostConstruct` callback will ever be called. An `@PostConstruct` callback method's stateless session bean is called sometime after the bean is instantiated, before it enters the Method-Ready Pool. However, a container might not create a pool of instances until the first client accesses that bean, so if a client (remote or otherwise) never attempts to access the bean, the `@PostConstruct` callback may never be called and the timer will never be set. Another problem with using`@PostConstruct` is that it's called on every instance before it enters the pool; you have to prevent subsequent instances (instances created after the first instance) from setting the timer—the first instance created would have already done this. It's tempting to use a static variable to avoid re-creating timers, as in the following code, but this can cause problems:

```
public class StatelessTimerBean javax.ejb.TimedObject {

    static boolean isTimerSet = false;

    @Resource TimerService timerService;
    @Resource SessionContext ctx;

    @PostConstruct
    public void init(){
        if( isTimerSet == false) {
            long expirationDate = (Long)ctx.lookup("expirationDate");
            timerService.createTimer(expirationDate, null );
            isTimerSet = true;
        }
    }
```

While this may seem like a good solution, it works only when your application is deployed within a single server with one VM and one classloader. If you are using a clustered system, a single server with multiple VMs, or multiple classloaders (very common), it won't work because bean instances that are not instantiated in the same VM with the same classloader will not have access to the same static variable. In this scenario, it's easy to end up with multiple timers doing the same thing. An alternative is to have `@PostCreate` access and remove all preexisting timers to see if the timer is already established, but this can affect performance because it's likely that new instances will be created and added to the pool many times, resulting in many calls to @PostCreate and, therefore, many calls to TimerService.getTimers( ). Also, there is no requirement that the Timer Service work across a cluster, so timers set on one node in a cluster may not be visible to timers set on some other node in the cluster.

With stateless session beans, you should never use the @PreDestroy callback method to cancel or create timers. The @PreDestroy callback is called on individual instances before they are evicted from memory. It is not called in response to client calls to the remote or local remove method. Also, the @PreDestroy callback doesn't correspond to an undeployment of a bean; it's specific to only a single instance. As a result, you cannot determine anything meaningful about the EJB as a whole from a call to the ejbRemove( ) method and you should not use it to create or cancel timers.

When a stateless session bean implements the javax.ejb.TimedObject interface, or contains an @javax.ejb.Timeout callback method, its life cycle changes to include the servicing of timed events. The Timer Service pulls an instance of the bean from the instance pool when a timer expires; if there are no instances in the pool, the container creates one. Figure 13-1 shows the life cycle of a stateless session bean that implements the TimedOut interface.

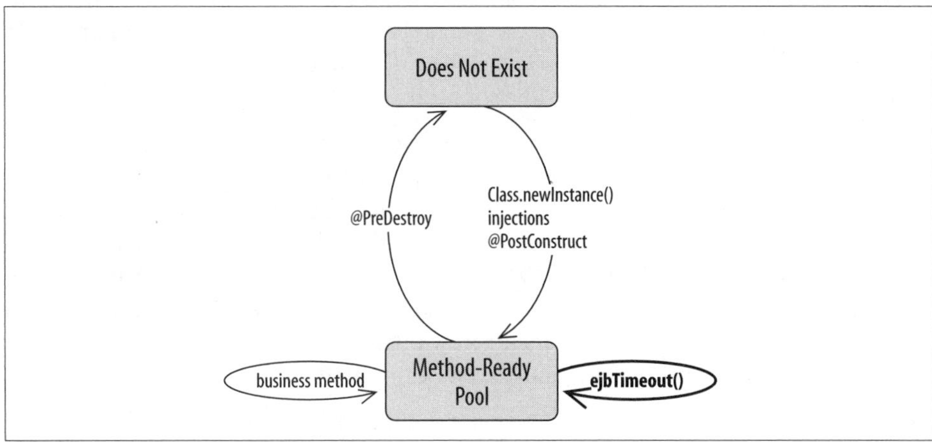

Figure 13-1. Stateless session bean life cycle with TimedObject

Message-Driven Bean Timers

Message-driven bean timers are similar to stateless session bean timers in several ways. Timers are associated only with the type of bean. When a timer expires, a message-driven bean instance is selected from a pool to execute the timeout callback method. In addition, message-driven beans can be used for performing audits or other types of batch jobs. The primary difference between a message-driven bean timer and a stateless session bean timer is the way in which they're initiated: timers are created in response to an incoming message or, if the container supports it, from a configuration file.

In order to initialize a message-driven bean timer from an incoming message, you simply put the call to the TimerService.createTimer( ) method in the message-handling method. For a JMS-based message-driven bean, the method call goes in the onMessage( ) method:

```
@MessageDriven
public class JmsTimerBean implements MessageListener {
    @Resource TimerService timerService

    public void onMessage(Message message){
        MapMessage mapMessage = (MapMessage)message;
        long expirationDate = mapMessage.getLong("expirationDate");

        timerService.createTimer(expirationDate, null );
    }

    @Timeout
    public void timeout( ){
        // put timeout logic here
    }
```

The incoming JMS message should contain information about the timer: the beginning (start) date, duration, or even the Serializable info object. Combining JMS with the Timer Service can offer some powerful design options for implementing audits, batch processing, and agent-like solutions.

Although it's not standardized, it is possible that vendors will allow message-driven bean timers to be configured at deployment time. This would require a proprietary solution, since standard configuration options for message-driven bean timers do not exist. The advantage of configured timers is that they do not require a client to initiate some action to start the timer. When the bean is deployed, its timer is set automatically. This capability makes message-driven bean timers more like Unix cron jobs, which are preconfigured and then run. Consult your vendor to see if it offers a proprietary configuration for message-driven bean timers.

As was the case for stateless session beans, the TimedObject interface or the presence of an @Timeout method changes the life cycle of the message-driven bean slightly (see Figure 13-2). When a timed event occurs, the container must pull a message-driven bean instance from the pool. If there are no instances in the pool, then an instance must be moved from the Does Not Exist state to the Method-Ready Pool before it can receive the timed event.

Problems with the Timer Service

The Timer Service is an excellent addition to the EJB platform, but it's limited. A lot can be learned from cron, the Unix scheduling utility that's been around for years. Here are some proposals for improving the service. If you are interested only in

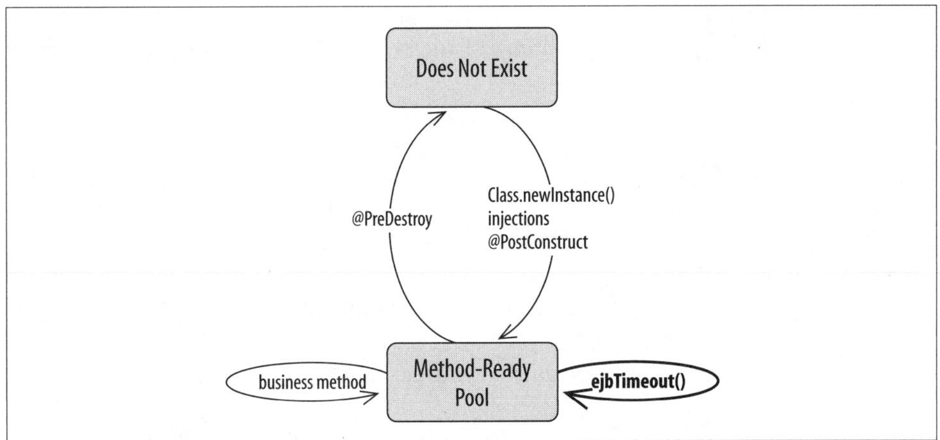

Figure 13-2. Message-driven bean life cycle with TimedObject

learning how timers work now, as opposed to how they may be improved, feel free to skip the rest of this chapter—it's not required reading. With that said, understanding how timers can be improved helps you understand their limitations. If you have some time and want to expand your understanding of timers, keep reading.

A very little bit about cron

Cron is a Unix program that allows you to schedule scripts (similar to batch files in DOS), commands, and other programs to run at specified dates and times. Unlike the EJB Timer Service, cron allows for flexible, calendar-based scheduling. Cron jobs (anything cron runs is called a *job*) can be scheduled to run at intervals, including a specific minute of the hour, hour of the day, day of the week, day of the month, and month of the year.

For example, you can schedule a cron job to run every Friday at 12:15 p.m., or every hour, or the first day of every month. While this level of refinement may sound complicated, it is actually very easy to specify. Cron uses a simple text format of five fields of integer values, separated by spaces or tabs, to describe the intervals at which scripts should be run. Figure 13-3 shows the field positions and their meanings.

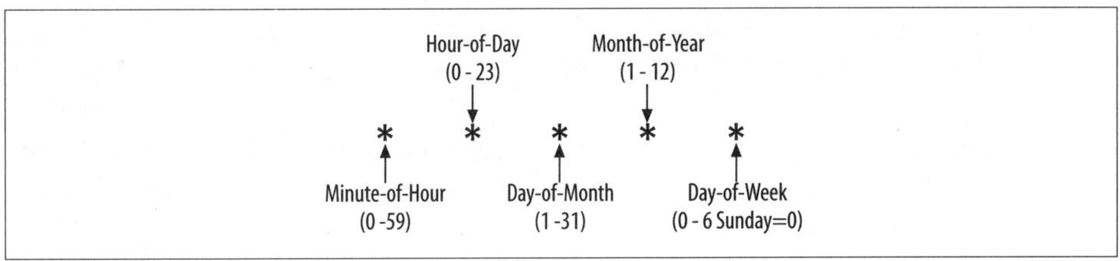

Figure 13-3. Cron date/time format

The order of the fields is significant, since each specifies a different calendar designator: minute, hour, day, month, and day of the week. The following examples show how to schedule cron jobs:

```
20   *   *   *   *   --->   20 minutes after every hour. (00:20, 01:20, etc.)
 5  22   *   *   *   --->   Every day at 10:05 p.m.
 0   8   1   *   *   --->   The first day of every month at 8:00 a.m.
 0   8   4   7   *   --->   The fourth of July at 8:00 a.m.
15  12   *   *   5   --->   Every Friday at 12:15 p.m.
```

An asterisk indicates that all values are valid. For example, if you use an asterisk for the minute field, you're scheduling cron to execute the job every minute of the hour. You can define more complex intervals by specifying multiple values, separated by commas, for a single field. In addition, you can specify ranges of time using the hyphen:

```
0  8  *  *  1,3,5  --->  Every Monday, Wednesday, and Friday at 8:00 a.m.
0  8  1,15  *  *   --->  The first and 15th of every month at 8:00 a.m.
0  8-17  *  *  1-5 --->  Every hour from 8:00 a.m. through 5:00 p.m., Mon-Fri.
```

Cron jobs are scheduled using *crontab* files, which are simply text files in which you configure the date/time fields and a command—usually a command to run a script.

Improving the Timer Service

The cron date/time format provides a lot more flexibility than is currently offered by the EJB Timer Service. The Timer Service requires you to designate intervals in exact milliseconds, which is a bit awkward to work with (you have to convert days, hours, and minutes to milliseconds), but more importantly, it's not flexible enough for many real-world scheduling needs. For example, there is no way to schedule a timer to expire on the first and 15th of every month, or every hour between 8:00 a.m. and 5:00 p.m., Monday through Friday. You can derive some of the more complex intervals but only at the cost of adding logic to your bean code to calculate them, and in more complicated scenarios, you'll need multiple timers for the same task.

Cron is not perfect either. Scheduling jobs is like setting a timer on a VCR: everything is scheduled according to the clock and calendar. You can specify that cron run a job at specific times of the day on specific days of the year, but you can't have it run a job at relative intervals from an arbitrary starting point. For example, cron's date/time format doesn't let you schedule a job to run every 10 minutes, starting now. You have to schedule it to run at specific minutes of the hour (e.g., 0, 10, 20, 30, 40, 50). Cron is also limited to scheduling recurring jobs; you can't set up a single-action timer, and you can't set a start date. A problem with both cron and the EJB Timer Service is that you can't program a stop date—a date when the timer will automatically cancel itself.

You also may have noticed that cron granularity is to the minute rather than to the millisecond. At first glance, this looks like a weakness, but in practice, it's perfectly acceptable. For calendar-driven scheduling, more precision simply isn't very useful.

The Timer Service interface would be improved if it could handle a cron-like date/time format, with a start date and end date. Instead of discarding the current createTimer( ) calls (which are useful, especially for single-action timers and arbitrary millisecond intervals), it would be preferable simply to add a new method with cron-like semantics. Instead of using 0–6 to designate the day of the week, it would be better to use the values Sun, Mon, Tue, Wed, Thu, Fri, and Sat (as in the Linux version of cron). For example, code to schedule a timer that would run every weekday at 11:00 p.m. starting October 1, 2006 and ending May 31, 2007 would look like this:

```
TimerService timerService = ejbContext.getTimerService( );
Calendar start = Calendar.getInstance( ).set(2006, Calendar.OCTOBER, 1);
Calendar end = Calendar.getInstance( ).set(2007, Calendar.MAY, 31);

String dateTimeString = "23   *   *   *    Mon-Fri";
timerService.createTimer(dateTimeString, start, end, null);
```

This proposed change to the Timer Service retains the millisecond-based createTimer( ) methods because they are very useful. While cron-like configuration is powerful, it's not a silver bullet. If you need to schedule a timer to go off every 30 seconds starting now (or at any arbitrary point in time), you need to use one of the existing createTimer( ) methods. True millisecond accuracy is difficult; first, normal processing and thread contention tend to delay response time, and second, a server clock must be properly synchronized with the correct time (i.e., UTC)* to the millisecond, and most are not.

Message-driven beans: standard configuration properties

Although the previous suggestions would improve usability a bit, they are not crucial for the use of an EJB timer. There is enormous potential for using message-driven beans as cron-like jobs that are configured at deployment and run automatically. Unfortunately, there is no standard way to configure a message-driven bean timer at deployment time. Some vendors may support this, but others do not. Preconfigured message-driven bean timers are going to be in high demand by developers who want to schedule message-driven beans to perform work at specific dates and times. Without support for deployment-time configuration, the only reliable way to program an enterprise bean timer is to have a client call a method or send a JMS message. This is not an acceptable solution. Developers need deployment-time configuration, and it should be added to the next version of the specification.

Building on the cron-like semantics proposed in the previous subsection, it would be easy to devise standard activation properties for configuring message-driven bean

* Coordinated Universal Time (UTC) is the international standard reference time. Servers can be coordinated with UTC using the Network Time Protocol (NTP) and public time servers. Coordinated Universal Time is abbreviated UTC as a compromise among standardizing nations. A full explanation is provided by the National Institute of Standards and Technology's FAQ on UTC at *http://www.boulder.nist.gov/timefreq/general/misc.htm#Anchor-14550*.

timers at deployment time. For example, the following code configures a message-driven bean, the Audit EJB, to run at 11:00 p.m., Monday through Friday, starting October 1, 2006 and ending May 31, 2007 (start and end dates are not required):

```
<activation-config>
  <description>Run Monday through Friday at 11:00 p.m.
             Starting on Oct 1st,2003 until May 31st, 2004</description>
  <activation-config-property>
    <activation-config-property-name>dateTimeFields
    </activation-config-property-name>
    <activation-config-property-value> 23   *   *   *   Mon-Fri
    </activation-config-property-value>
  </activation-config-property>
  <activation-config-property>
    <activation-config-property-name>startDate</activation-config-property-name>
    <activation-config-property-value>October 1, 2003
    </activation-config-property-value>
  </activation-config-property>
  <activation-config-property>
    <activation-config-property-name>endDate</activation-config-property-name>
    <activation-config-property-value>May 31, 2004
    </activation-config-property-value>
  </activation-config-property>
</activation-config>
```

This type of configuration would be fairly easy for providers to implement if they supported enhanced cron-like semantics. In addition, you could configure message-driven beans to use the millisecond-based timers EJB 2.1 already supports.

Other problems with the Timer API

The semantics of the `Timer` object convey little information about the object itself. There is no way to determine whether a timer is a single-action timer or an interval timer. If it's an interval timer, there is no way to determine the configured interval or whether the timer has executed its first expiration. To solve these problems, additional methods should be added to the `Timer` interface to provide this information. As a stopgap, it's a good idea to place this information in the `info` object so that it can be accessed by applications that need it.

Final Words

Whether the changes outlined in this chapter are adopted is a matter for the EJB Expert Group, which should be responsive to the EJB developer community. It's likely that others will find ways to improve on these proposed changes. Regardless of the outcome, the limited semantics of the Timer Service and the lack of support for configurable message-driven bean timers are problems. As you develop timers, you will quickly discover the need for a much richer way of describing expirations, and some way to configure timers at deployment time, instead of having to use a client application to initiate a scheduled event.

CHAPTER 14

The JNDI ENC and Injection

Every EJB container that is deployed in an application server has its own personal internal registry called the Enterprise Naming Context (ENC). This ENC is implemented by JNDI and is a sandbox where the EJB container can hold specific references to its environment. Think of it as the EJB container's personal address book, where it writes down addresses to various Java EE services that it wants to look up and use within its business logic.

In Chapter 11, we started to talk a little bit about the ENC, showing how you can use annotations like `@javax.annotation.EJB` and `@javax.annotation.Resource` to inject references to Java EE services directly into the fields of your bean. This injection process is driven by the EJB container's ENC. In this chapter, we'll show you how you can populate the ENC and use it as your own JNDI registry, and we'll show you how you can use it to inject environment references into your bean fields.

The JNDI ENC

The ENC has been around in the EJB specification since the early 1.0 days. It began as a local JNDI namespace that was specific to an EJB container. Developers could define aliases to resources, EJBs, and environment entries in the JNDI ENC through EJB XML deployment descriptors. These aliases could then be looked up directly in JNDI within business logic. In EJB 3.0, this mechanism was enhanced so that JNDI ENC references could be injected directly into the fields of a bean class. Annotations are the primary mechanism for doing this, but XML deployment descriptor support is available for those who wish to use that abstraction.

What Can Be Registered in the JNDI ENC?

Many different items can be bound to the ENC: references to any EJB interface, a JMS queue or topic destination, JMS connection factories, data sources, any JCA resource, and even primitive values. Java EE services such as `javax.transaction.`

UserTransaction, javax.ejb.TimerService, and org.omg.CORBA.ORB are also available in the ENC.

How Is the JNDI ENC Populated?

The ENC's JNDI namespace is populated in two separate ways: via XML or via annotations. Any reference that you declare in XML to a service or resource automatically populates the JNDI ENC with the reference's name. Any environment annotation that you use in your bean class also causes the ENC to be populated. Once an item is bound to the JNDI ENC of the EJB container, it can be referenced by a JNDI lookup.

XML Population

To illustrate how XML population works, let's define a reference to the stateless session bean we wrote in Chapter 11. Here we define a local interface reference to the ProcessPayment EJB for the TravelAgent EJB:

```
<ejb-jar>
   <enterprise-beans>
      <session>
         <ejb-name>TravelAgentBean</ejb-name>
         <ejb-local-ref>
            <ejb-ref-name>ejb/ProcessPayment</ejb-ref-name>
            <ejb-ref-type>Session</ejb-ref-type>
            <local>com.titan.processpayment.ProcessPaymentLocal</local>
            <ejb-link>ProcessPaymentBean</ejb-link>
         </ejb-local-ref>
   </enterprise-beans>
</ejb-jar>
```

The <ejb-local-ref> element tells the EJB container that the TravelAgentBean wants a reference to the ProcessPayment EJB. A reference to this bean is registered in the TravelAgentBean's JNDI ENC under the name ejb/ProcessPayment. This is defined by the <ejb-ref-name> element. Other referenceable things, like resources and JMS destinations, have similar XML elements such as <ejb-local-ref> to specify how and where the reference will be bound into their JNDI ENCs. Each service type in Java EE has its own reference syntax. We'll see examples of all of them in this chapter.

Annotation Population

Each referenceable type also has a corresponding annotation that can be used as an alternative to XML. If you specify these annotations on the bean class, they will cause the JNDI ENC to be populated with the information defined in the annotation:

```
import javax.annotation.EJB;

@Stateful
@EJB(name="ejb/ProcessPayment",
```

```
        beanInterface=ProcessPaymentLocal.class,
        beanName="ProcessPaymentBean")
public class TravelAgentBean implements TravelAgentRemote {
...
}
```

In this example, we are registering a reference to the ProcessPayment EJB under the `ejb/ProcessPayment` name. Business logic running inside the `TravelAgentBean` is able to do JNDI lookups to find this reference. Each environment annotation, such as `@javax.annotation.EJB`, has a `name()` attribute that specifies the JNDI ENC name to which you want the service reference to be bound. The second half of this chapter describes all the details of each of these different environment annotations.

How Are Things Referenced from the ENC?

Anything registered in the JNDI ENC can be looked up by name under the `java:comp/env` context. The `comp` part of this name corresponds to *component*. The JNDI name resolves to a different context depending on where you invoke the lookup. For example, if you invoke `jndi.lookup("java:comp/env")` within the `TravelAgentBean`, you will get that EJB container's ENC. If you do the same within `ProcessPaymentBean`, you will get a different ENC registry specific to that bean. The application server knows what ENC is active when you perform the lookup.

```
@Stateful
@EJB(name="ejb/ProcessPayment",
        beanInterface=ProcessPaymentLocal.class,
        beanName="ProcessPaymentBean")
public class TravelAgentBean implements TravelAgentRemote {

    public TicketDO bookPassage(CreditCardDO card, double amount) {
        ProcessPaymentLocal payment = null;
        try {
            javax.naming.InitialContext ctx = new InitialContext( );
            payment = (ProcessPaymentLocal)
                    ctx.lookup("java:comp/env/ejb/ProcessPayment");
        } catch (javax.naming.NamingException ne) {
            throw new EJBException(ne);
        }
        payment.process(card, customer, amount);
...
}
```

In this example, the `bookPassage( )` method from our TravelAgent EJB needs a reference to the ProcessPayment EJB so that it can bill the customer for the reservation. A reference to the ProcessPayment EJB was created in the TravelAgent's ENC by annotating the bean class with the `@EJB` annotation. The preceding code does a JNDI lookup to find this reference. While the `ProcessPayment.process( )` method is invoked, the `java:comp/env/ejb/ProcessPayment` reference is no longer available because the ProcessPayment's ENC is active instead of the TravelAgent's ENC.

Using EJBContext

In Chapters 11 and 12, we talked a little bit about the `javax.ejb.SessionContext` and `javax.ejb.MessageDrivenContext` interfaces. Both extend the `javax.ejb.EJBContext` and they can be used to look up ENC entries. The `EJBContext` interface has a convenience ENC lookup method. This method is a bit simpler than a direct JNDI lookup because it does not throw a checked exception and it takes a relative name into the ENC instead of the full `java:comp/env` string we saw before. `SessionContext` or `MessageDrivenContext` can be injected into your session or message-driven beans by using the `@javax.annotation.Resource` annotation.

```
@Stateful
@EJB(name="ejb/ProcessPayment",
     beanInterface=ProcessPaymentLocal.class,
     beanName="ProcessPaymentBean")
public class TravelAgentBean implements TravelAgentRemote {

   @Resource private javax.ejb.SessionContext ejbContext;

   public TicketDO bookPassage(CreditCardDO card, double amount) {
      ProcessPaymentLocal payment = (ProcessPaymentLocal)
           ejbContext.lookup("ejb/ProcessPayment");
      payment.process(card, customer, amount);
...
}
```

This example uses the `EJBContext.lookup( )` method to look up the `TravelAgentBean`'s reference to ProcessPayment. This context object is injected into the `ejbContext` field using the `@Resource` annotation. You do not append the `java:comp/env` string to the name when performing the lookup but instead use the relative name defined in the annotation or XML reference.

Annotation injection

Instead of an ENC lookup, the ProcessPayment EJB reference can be injected directly into a member variable of the TravelAgent EJB. This injection can be done through environment annotations or an XML deployment descriptor fragment:

```
@Stateful
public class TravelAgentBean implements TravelAgentRemote {
   @EJB private ProcessPaymentLocal payment;

...
}
```

By using the `@javax.ejb.EJB` annotation on the `payment` field of the `TravelAgentBean` class, the EJB container will automatically inject a reference to the ProcessPayment EJB directly into the `payment` field when the `TravelAgent` bean instance is created. Alternatively, if you do not like this form of injection, the specification also supports injecting via a bean *setter* method:

```
@Stateful
public class TravelAgentBean implements TravelAgentRemote {
   private ProcessPaymentLocal payment;

   @EJB public void setProcessPayment(ProcessPaymentLocal payment) {
   this.payment = payment;
}
```

Unlike the previous example, when the TravelAgentBean instance is allocated, the EJB container will instead invoke the setProcessPayment( ) method, passing in the EJB reference as a parameter. This pattern works for all other injection annotations discussed in this chapter. *Setter* method injection is more verbose than direct field injection, but its advantage is that it can be mocked more easily in unit tests.

A number of different environment annotations such as @EJB are described in detail in the second half of this chapter. All of them function similarly and follow the same usage patterns as@EJB.

Default ENC name

Annotating a field or a *setter* method of a bean class also creates an entry in the JNDI ENC for the injected element. This is true for all environment annotations, not just @EJB. If the name( ) attribute of the injection annotation is specified, then the reference is stored in the ENC under that name. If no name is specified, then the ENC name is extracted from the name of the annotated field or *setter* method. In this case, a default ENC name is derived from the fully qualified class name of the field or method, as well as the base name of the field or method. So, for the payment field of the previous example, the ENC name would be com.titan.travelagent.TravelAgentBean/payment. For the setProcessPayment( ) method, the default ENC name would be com.titan.travelagent.TravelAgentBean/processPayment. These injected EJB references can then be looked up in JNDI under java:comp/env/com.titan.travelagent.TravelAgentBean/payment and java:comp/env/com.titan.travelagent.TravelAgentBean/processPayment, respectively. The ENC name becomes very important when you want to override an injection annotation within XML.

XML injection

If you prefer not to use annotations to initialize the fields of your bean class, then the <injection-target> element is available to you in your ejb-jar.xml deployment descriptor:

```
<ejb-jar>
   <enterprise-beans>
      <session>
         <ejb-name>TravelAgentBean</ejb-name>
         <ejb-local-ref>
            <ejb-ref-name>ProcessPayment</ejb-ref-name>
            <ejb-ref-type>Session</ejb-ref-type>
            <local>com.titan.processpayment.ProcessPaymentLocal</local>
```

```
            <ejb-link>ProcessPaymentBean</ejb-link>
            <injection-target>
               <injection-target-class>
                  com.titan.travelagent.TravelAgentBean
               </injection-target-class>
               <injection-target-name>payment</injection-target-name>
            </injection-target>
         </ejb-ref>
      </enterprise-beans>
   </ejb-jar>
```

Each XML environment element such as <ejb-local-ref> can use <injection-target> to populate a field or call a *setter* method with the referenced item. The <injection-target-class> element is the class where your field or method is declared. This may seem unnecessarily verbose, but this becomes important when there are inheritance hierarchies. The <injection-target-name> specifies the target field or method name into which you want the reference injected. In this case, we're injecting into the payment field. If you wanted to inject into a *setter* method instead, it would be processPayment.

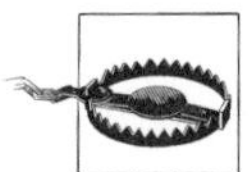

You cannot inject into a field and method with the same base name. For instance, if you had a setProcessPayment( ) method as well as a processPayment field, you could not define injections into both of those items, as they will represent the same ENC name and will not be distinguishable by the EJB container.

XML overrides

Using injection annotations is sometimes considered hardcoding configuration into the code of your bean class. Although there is an element of hardcoding here, the EJB specification allows you to override injection annotations via the XML deployment descriptor. Let's re-examine our use of the @EJB annotation:

```
@Stateful
public class TravelAgentBean implements TravelAgentRemote {
   @EJB private ProcessPaymentLocal payment;

...
}
```

In the original deployment of the TravelAgent EJB, the EJB container could figure out what EJB reference to inject based on the type of the annotated payment field. ProcessPaymentLocal was unique across the application. What if in a new deployment, multiple process payment engines were deployed into the same application? You might want to configure, per deployment of your application, which process payment engine the TravelAgentBean used. You can override this annotation within XML:

```
<ejb-jar>
   <enterprise-beans>
```

```
      <session>
         <ejb-name>TravelAgentBean</ejb-name>
         <ejb-local-ref>
            <ejb-ref-name>
               come.titan.travelagent.TravelAgentBean/payment
            </ejb-ref-name>
            <ejb-ref-type>Session</ejb-ref-type>
            <local>com.titan.processpayment.ProcessPaymentLocal</local>
            <ejb-link>MasterCardProcessPaymentBean</ejb-link>
         </ejb-local-ref>
   </enterprise-beans>
</ejb-jar>
```

In this example, we are providing a more exact mapping for the @EJB annotation within XML. The <ejb-ref-name> must match the default ENC name of the injected field; this is how the EJB container knows you are overriding an annotated field. The <ejb-link> element provides a more specific reference to the process payment engine that the TravelAgent EJB will use. If the name( ) attribute was used with the @EJB annotation, then <ejb-ref-name> would have to match that value:

```
@Stateful
public class TravelAgentBean implements TravelAgentRemote {
   @EJB(name="ejb/ProcessPayment") private ProcessPaymentLocal payment;

...
}
```

The @EJB annotation tells the EJB container that it wants to inject an EJB with the ProcessPaymentLocal interface into the payment field. This EJB reference is registered in the ENC under the ejb/ProcessPayment entry. The XML must use this ENC name to override what is injected:

```
<ejb-jar>
   <enterprise-beans>
      <session>
         <ejb-name>TravelAgentBean</ejb-name>
         <ejb-local-ref>
            <ejb-ref-name>ejb/ProcessPayment</ejb-ref-name>
            <ejb-ref-type>Session</ejb-ref-type>
            <local>com.titan.processpayment.ProcessPaymentLocal</local>
            <ejb-link>MasterCardProcessPaymentBean</ejb-link>
         </ejb-local-ref>
   </enterprise-beans>
</ejb-jar>
```

The same ejb/ProcessPayment name is referenced using the <ejb-ref-name> element.

XML always takes precedence over annotation metadata. XML provides the means to reconfigure hardcoded annotation configuration.

Injection and inheritance

It is possible for a bean class to be part of a class hierarchy. If any fields or methods have injection annotations on them, they will still be populated, but certain injection rules are followed:

```
public class BaseClass {

   @Resource DataSource data;

   @EJB(beanName="ProcessPaymentBean ")
   public void setProcessPayment(ProcessPaymentLocal pp) {
   ...
   }
}

@Stateless
public class MySessionBean extends BaseClass implements MySessionRemote {
...
}
```

In this example, we have a stateless session bean class that inherits from a base class. All instances of MySessionBean would have the appropriate resource injected into the base class's data field as well as the setProcessPayment( ) method. It is possible to change what is injected into the setProcessPayment( ) method by reimplementing and overriding it in the subclass:

```
@Stateless
public class MySessionBean extends BaseClass implements MySessionRemote {
   @EJB(beanName="AcmeProcessPayment")
   public void setProcessPayment(ProcessPaymentLocal pp) {
      ...
   }
...
}
```

The ProcessPaymentBean would no longer be injected into the setProcessPayment( ) method. Instead, the new overridden reference, AcmeProcessPayment, would be injected. There is one exception to this rule. If the setProcessPayment( ) method in the BaseClass was a private method rather than a protected or public method, then the base class would still be injected with the old reference:

```
Public class BaseClass {

   @Resource DataSource data;

   @EJB(beanName="ProcessPaymentBean")
   private void setProcessPayment(ProcessPaymentLocal pp) {
   ...
   }
}
@Stateless
public class MySessionBean extends BaseClass implements MySessionRemote {
```

```
        @EJB(beanName="AcmeProcessPayment")
        public void setProcessPayment(ProcessPaymentLocal pp) {
           ...
        }
     ...
     }
```

So, in the previous example, both setProcessPayment( ) methods would be invoked and set with a different ProcessPaymentLocal reference. The BaseClass's setProcessPayment( ) method would get a reference to the ProcessPaymentBean, and the setProcessPayment( ) method of MySessionBean would get AcmeProcessPayment.

Reference and Injection Types

The first half of this chapter focused on the semantics of the JNDI ENC and how to reference things within it. You learned the base semantics of both annotation and XML injection. This section dives into the various services and configurations you can reference from your ENC. Other chapters within this book have touched briefly on most of these injectable and referenceable types, but this chapter groups all of it into one place and discusses the intricacies and dirty details.

EJB References

As you saw in Chapter 11 and early in this chapter, your EJB bean classes can reference and aggregate other EJBs either through JNDI ENC lookups or by directly injecting these references into member fields.

@javax.ejb.EJB

The @javax.ejb.EJB annotation can be used on your bean class's *setter* methods, on member fields, or directly on the class itself:

```
package javax.ejb;

@Target({TYPE, METHOD, FIELD}) @Retention(RUNTIME)
public @interface EJB {
   String name( ) default "";
   Class beanInterface( ) default Object.class;
   String beanName( ) default "";
   String mappedName( ) default "";
}
```

The name( ) attribute refers to what the JNDI ENC name will be for the referenced EJB. This name is relative to the java:comp/env context.

The beanInterface( ) attribute is the interface you are interested in and usually is used by the container to distinguish whether you want a remote or local reference to the EJB. If your EJB needs to be integrated with EJB 2.1 beans, `beanInterface()` can also be a reference to a home interface.

The `beanName()` is the EJB name of the EJB referenced. It is equal to either the value you specify in the `@Stateless.name()` or `@Stateful.name()` annotation, or the value you put in the `<ejb-name>` field in the XML deployment descriptor.

The `mappedName()` attribute is a placeholder for a vendor-specific identifier. This identifier may be a key into the vendor's global registry. Many vendors store references to EJBs within the global JNDI tree so that clients can reference them, and `mappedName()` may reference that global JNDI name.

When placed on the bean class, the `@EJB` annotation will register a reference into the JNDI ENC of the bean:

```
@Stateful
@EJB(name="ejb/ProcessPayment",
     beanInterface=ProcessPaymentLocal.class)
public class TravelAgentBean implements TravelAgentRemote {
...
}
```

In this example, code within the `TravelAgentBean` can look up the ProcessPayment EJB under the `java:comp/env/ejb/ProcessPayment` JNDI ENC name. Here's how a client bean would use this context to look up a reference to the ProcessPayment EJB:

```
InitialContext jndiContext = new InitialContext();
Object ref = jndiContext.lookup("java:comp/env/ejb/ProcessPayment");
ProcessPaymentLocal local = (ProcessPaymentLocal)ref;
```

When the `@EJB` annotation is used on the bean class, the `name()` and `beanInterface()` attributes are required. Most of the time, only the bean's interface is needed to distinguish which EJB you are referring to. Sometimes, though, you may be reusing the same business interface for multiple deployed EJBs. In that case, the `beanName()` or `mappedName()` attribute must be used to provide a unique identifier for the EJB you want to reference.

The `@EJB` annotation can be used only once on your bean class. When you need to reference multiple EJBs, the `@javax.ejb.EJBs` annotation is available:

```
package javax.ejb;

@Target({TYPE}) @Retention(RUNTIME)
public @interface EJBs {
   EJB[] value();
}
```

This kind of annotation is required because only one annotation of a given type can be applied to any given artifact in the Java language. This plural name pattern is duplicated for the other reference annotations described in this chapter:

```
@Stateful
@EJBs({
```

```
    @EJB(name="ProcessPayment",
         beanInterface=ProcessPaymentLocal.class),
    @EJB(name="CustomerReferralEngine",
         beanInterface=CustomerReferralLocal.class)
})
public class TravelAgentBean implements TravelAgentRemote {
...
}
```

In this example, the TravelAgentBean creates an ENC reference to both the ProcessPayment and CustomerReferralEngine local interfaces.

The @EJB annotation can also be placed on a *setter* method or member field so that the EJB referenced will be injected directly into the bean class instance:

```
@Stateful
public class TravelAgentBean implements TravelAgentRemote {
   @EJB private ProcessPaymentLocal payment;

...
}
```

When used on a *setter* method or member field, no annotation attribute like beanName( ) is required, as long as the business interface can be determined by the type of the field or method.

XML-based remote EJB references

The <ejb-ref> element defines a reference to remote EJBs. It contains the subelements <description> (optional), <ejb-ref-name> (required), <ejb-ref-type> (required), <remote> (required), <home> (optional), <ejb-link> (optional), and <mapped-name> (optional), as well as the element <injection-target> (optional) described in the first part of this chapter. Here is a remote reference to the ProcessPayment EJB:

```
<ejb-jar>
   <enterprise-beans>
      <session>
         <ejb-name>TravelAgentBean</ejb-name>
         <ejb-ref>
            <ejb-ref-name>ejb/ProcessPaymentRemote </ejb-ref-name>
            <ejb-ref-type>Session</ejb-ref-type>
            <remote>com.titan.processpayment.ProcessPaymentRemote</remote>
         </ejb-ref>
   </enterprise-beans>
</ejb-jar>
```

The <ejb-ref-name> element is equivalent to the name( ) attribute of the @EJB annotation in that it represents the ENC name to which the reference will be bound. This name is relative to the java:comp/env context. Here's how a client bean would use this ENC context to look up a reference to the ProcessPayment EJB:

```
InitialContext jndiContext = new InitialContext( );
Object ref = jndiContext.lookup("java:comp/env/ejb/ProcessPaymentRemote");
```

```
ProcessPaymentRemote remote = (ProcessPaymentRemote)
   javax.rmi.PortableRemoteObject.narrow(ref, ProcessPaymentRemote.class);
```

The `<ejb-ref-type>` element can have one of two values, `Session` or `Entity`, according to whether it is a session bean or an EJB 2.1 entity bean home interface.

The `<remote>` element specifies the fully qualified class name of the bean's remote interface. If you are referencing an old EJB 2.1 bean, then the `<home>` element must be provided with the fully qualified name of the bean's home interface.

The `<ejb-ref>` element can be linked directly to a specific EJB container by using the `<ejb-link>` element. This element is equivalent in description to the `beanName()` attribute of the `@EJB` annotation. It references the `EJB-name` of the referenced EJB. The EJB linked can be in the same JAR deployment as the referencing EJB, or in another deployment within an Enterprise ARchive (*.ear*) (EARs are explained in Chapter 20).

```
<ejb-jar>
   <enterprise-beans>
      <session>
         <ejb-name>TravelAgentBean</ejb-name>
         <ejb-ref>
            <ejb-ref-name>ejb/ProcessPaymentRemote </ejb-ref-name>
            <ejb-ref-type>Session</ejb-ref-type>
            <remote>com.titan.processpayment.ProcessPaymentRemote</remote>
            <ejb-link>processPaymentEJB</ejb-link>
         </ejb-ref>
      </session>

      <session>
         <ejb-name>ProcessPaymentEJB</ejb-name>
         <remote>com.titan.processpayment.ProcessPaymentRemote</remote>
         ...
      </session>
   </enterprise-beans>
</ejb-jar>
```

The `<mapped-name>` element is equivalent to the `mappedName()` attribute of the `@EJB` annotation in that it is a vendor-specific, optional unique identifier.

The `<injection-target>` element is used if you want to inject the EJB reference into a field or *setter* method of your bean class. Here is an example of using `<injection-target>` with `<ejb-ref>`:

```
<ejb-jar>
   <enterprise-beans>
      <session>
         <ejb-name>TravelAgentBean</ejb-name>
         <ejb-ref>
            <ejb-ref-name>ejb/ProcessPaymentRemote </ejb-ref-name>
            <ejb-ref-type>Session</ejb-ref-type>
            <remote>com.titan.processpayment.ProcessPaymentRemote</remote>
            <injection-target>
               <injection-target-class>
```

```
                com.titan.travelagent.TravelAgentBean
            </injection-target-class>
            <injection-target-name>payment</injection-target-name>
         </injection-target>
      </ejb-ref>
   </enterprise-beans>
</ejb-jar>
```

In this example, the remote reference to the ProcessPayment EJB is injected into a member field named payment or passed as a parameter to a *setter* method named setPayment( ) in the TravelAgentBean class

XML-based local EJB references

The <ejb-local-ref> element defines a reference to remote EJBs. It contains the subelements <description> (optional), <ejb-ref-name> (required), <ejb-ref-type> (required), <local> (required), <local-home> (optional), <ejb-link> (optional), and <mapped-name> (optional), as well as the element <injection-target> (optional) described in the first part of this chapter. Here is a local reference to the ProcessPayment EJB:

```
<ejb-jar>
   <enterprise-beans>
      <session>
         <ejb-name>TravelAgentBean</ejb-name>
         <ejb-local-ref>
            <ejb-ref-name>ejb/ProcessPaymentRemote </ejb-ref-name>
            <ejb-ref-type>Session</ejb-ref-type>
            <local>com.titan.processpayment.ProcessPaymentLocal</local>
         </ejb-local-ref>
   </enterprise-beans>
</ejb-jar>
```

The <ejb-ref-name> element is equivalent to the name( ) attribute of the @EJB annotation in that it represents the ENC name to which the reference will be bound. This name is relative to the java:comp/env context.

The <ejb-ref-type> element can have one of two values, Session or Entity, according to whether it is a session bean or an EJB 2.1 entity bean home interface.

The <local> element specifies the fully qualified class name of the bean's local interface. If you are referencing an old EJB 2.1 bean, then the <local-home> element must be provided with the fully qualified name of the bean's home interface.

The <ejb-ref> element can be linked directly to a specific EJB container by using the <ejb-link> element. This element is equivalent in description to the beanName( ) attribute of the @EJB annotation. It references the EJB-name of the referenced EJB. The EJB linked can be in the same JAR deployment as the referencing EJB, or in another deployment within an Enterprise ARchive (*.ear*), which is discussed in Chapter 20.

```
<ejb-jar>
   <enterprise-beans>
```

```
      <session>
         <ejb-name>TravelAgentBean</ejb-name>
         <ejb-local-ref>
            <ejb-ref-name>ejb/ProcessPaymentLocal</ejb-ref-name>
            <ejb-ref-type>Session</ejb-ref-type>
            <local>com.titan.processpayment.ProcessPaymentLocal</local>
            <ejb-link>processPaymentEJB</ejb-link>
         </ejb-local-ref>
      </session>

      <session>
         <ejb-name>ProcessPaymentEJB</ejb-name>
         <local>com.titan.processpayment.ProcessPaymentLocal</local>
         ...
      </session>
   </enterprise-beans>
</ejb-jar>
```

The <mapped-name> element is equivalent to the mappedName( ) attribute of the @EJB annotation in that it is a vendor-specific, optional unique identifier.

Enterprise beans declared in the <ejb-local-ref> elements are local enterprise beans, so they do not require use of the javax.rmi.PortableRemoteObject.narrow( ) method to narrow the reference to the appropriate type. Instead, you can use a simple native cast operation:

```
InitialContext jndiContext = new InitialContext( );
ProcessPaymentLocal local = (ProcessPaymentRemote)
   jndiContext.lookup("java:comp/env/ejb/ProcessPaymentLocal");
```

The <injection-target> element is used if you want to inject your reference into your EJB instead of doing a lookup in the JNDI ENC. The exact semantics of <injection-target> were described earlier in this chapter, but here is an example of using it:

```
<ejb-jar>
   <enterprise-beans>
      <session>
         <ejb-name>TravelAgentBean</ejb-name>
         <ejb-local-ref>
            <ejb-ref-name>ejb/ProcessPaymentLocal</ejb-ref-name>
            <ejb-ref-type>Session</ejb-ref-type>
            <local>com.titan.processpayment.ProcessPaymentLocal</local>
            <injection-target>
               <injection-target-class>
                  com.titan.travelagent.TravelAgentBean
               </injection-target-class>
               <injection-target-name>payment</injection-target-name>
            </injection-target>
         </ejb-local-ref>
   </enterprise-beans>
</ejb-jar>
```

In this example, the local reference to the ProcessPayment EJB would be injected into a member field named `payment` or passed as a parameter to a *setter* method named `setPayment( )` in the `TravelAgentBean` class.

Ambiguous and overloaded EJB names

The `<ejb-name>` element and any `@Stateless.name( )` or `@Stateful.name( )` attributes must be unique within a given EJB JAR deployment. Unfortunately, this is not the case for all EJB JARs deployed in an Enterprise ARchive (*.ear* files are described in Chapter 20). In an *.ear* file, EJB names can be duplicated in different EJB-JAR deployments. To differentiate references with duplicate EJB names, the EJB specification has an extended syntax for `<ejb-link>` and the `beanName( )` attribute of the `@EJB` annotation. This extended syntax has a relative path to the JAR file in which the EJB is located, followed by the # character, followed by the EJB name of the referenced bean:

```
@EJB(beanName="inventory-ejb.jar#InventoryEJB") InventoryLocal inventory;
```

In this example, the *inventory-ejb.jar* file is in the root directory of the EAR file along with the JAR the referencing EJB is deployed in. The `@EJB` annotation references the `InventoryEJB` within that *inventory.jar* deployment.

Resolving EJB references

The simplest example of using the `@javax.ejb.EJB` annotation is using it with no other annotation attributes:

```
@EJB ProcessPaymentLocal processPayment;
```

The specification isn't very detailed in terms of exactly how the EJB container should resolve this reference. To give you a feel for how this process works, let's see how the JBoss application server resolves this reference:

1. The only possible identifier for this EJB reference is the business interface type. The application server first looks for a unique EJB in the referencing EJB's EJB-JAR deployment that uses `ProcessPaymentLocal` as its local or remote interface. If more than one EJB uses the same business interface, it throws a deployment exception.
2. If the EJB-JAR is deployed as part of an Enterprise ARchive (*.ear*), it looks in other EJB-JARs for a unique EJB that uses the `ProcessPaymentLocal` interface. Again, if more than one EJB uses the same business interface, it throws a deployment exception.
3. If the EJB reference is not found in the *.ear* file, it looks for it in other global EJB-JAR deployments.

If the `beanName( )` attribute is specified, then JBoss uses the same search process, but it uses the `beanName( )`'s value as an additional identifier.

If the mappedName() attribute is specified, then no search process is performed. The application server expects that a specific EJB is bound into the global JNDI under the mappedName()'s value.

EntityManagerFactory References

A javax.persistence.EntityManagerFactory can be registered in the JNDI ENC of an EJB and then injected. It is sometimes useful to obtain a reference to an EntityManagerFactory directly so that you can have full control over the EntityManager instance and persistence context you want to work with. Although you can obtain an EntityManagerFactory through the javax.persistence.Persistence API, it is always better to use the facilities of Java EE so that the life cycle of the EntityManagerFactory can be controlled by the application server. When you let the application server populate your ENC or inject your EntityManagerFactory, the Java EE runtime will handle the cleanup of this instance and you do not have to call EntityManagerFactory.close(). Like all other services and resources, an EntityManagerFactory can be bound to the JNDI ENC or injected into your bean class by using either annotations or XML.

@javax.persistence.PersistenceUnit

The @javax.persistence.PersistenceUnit annotation can be used on your bean class's *setter* methods or member fields, or directly on the class itself:

```
package javax.persistence;

@Target({TYPE, METHOD, FIELD}) @Retention(RUNTIME)
public @interface PersistenceUnit {
   String name() default "";
   String unitName() default "";
}
```

The name() attribute refers to what the JNDI ENC name will be for the referenced EntityManagerFactory. This name is relative to the java:comp/env context.

The unitName() attribute identifies which EntityManagerFactory you are interested in referencing and refers to the name you have given your persistence unit that you declared in a *persistence.xml* file. If left unspecified, a deployment error is raised unless the EJB-JAR has only one persistence unit deployed within it. In that case, it defaults to this sole persistence unit.

When placed on the bean class, the @PersistenceUnit annotation will register a reference to the EntityManagerFactory in the JNDI ENC of the EJB bean class:

```
@Stateful
@PersistenceUnit(name="persistence/TitanDB",
     unitName="TitanDB")
public class TravelAgentBean implements TravelAgentRemote {
...
}
```

In this example, code that is within the TravelAgentBean can look up an EntityManagerFactory that manages a TitanDB persistence unit under the java:comp/env/persistence/TitanDB JNDI ENC name. Here's how a client bean would use this context to look up the reference to this EntityManagerFactory:

```
InitialContext jndiContext = new InitialContext( );
EntityManagerFactory titan = (EntityManagerFactory)
       jndiContext.lookup("java:comp/env/persistence/TitanDB");
```

When the @PersistenceUnit annotation is used on the bean class, the name( ) attribute is always required so that the EJB container knows where in the JNDI ENC to bind the EntityManagerFactory.

The @PersistenceUnit annotation can be used only once on your bean class. When you need to reference multiple persistence units, the @javax.persistence.PersistenceUnits annotation is available:

```
package javax.persistence;

@Target({TYPE}) @Retention(RUNTIME)
public @interface PersistenceUnits {
   PersistenceUnit[] value( );
}
```

This kind of annotation is required because only one annotation of a given type can be applied to any given artifact in the Java language:

```
@Stateful
@PersistenceUnits({
   @PersistenceUnit(name="persistence/TitanDB",
        unitName="TitanDB"),
   @PersistenceUnit(name="Customers",
        unitName="crmDB")
})
public class TravelAgentBean implements TravelAgentRemote {
...
}
```

In this example, the TravelAgentBean creates an ENC reference to both the TitanDB and crmDB persistence units.

The @PersistenceUnit annotation can also be placed on a *setter* method or member field so that the EntityManagerFactory that is referenced is injected directly into the bean class instance:

```
@Stateful
public class TravelAgentBean implements TravelAgentRemote {
   @PersistenceUnit(unitName="crmDB") private EntityManagerFactory crm;

...
}
```

When used on a *setter* method or member field, no annotation attribute is required, because both the name( ) and the unitName( ) attributes have valid defaults, as described earlier in this chapter.

XML-based EntityManagerFactory references

The <persistence-unit-ref> element defines a reference to a given EntityManagerFactory. It contains the subelements <description> (optional), <persistence-unit-ref-name> (required), and <persistence-unit-name> (required), as well as the element <injection-target> (optional) described in the first section of this chapter. Here is an example of a reference to the TitanDB persistence unit:

```
<ejb-jar>
   <enterprise-beans>
      <session>
         <ejb-name>TravelAgentBean</ejb-name>
         <persistence-unit-ref>
            <persistence-unit-ref-name>persistence/TitanDB</persistence-unit-ref-
name>
            <persistence-unit-name>TitanDB</persistence-unit-name>
         </persistence-unit-ref>
   </enterprise-beans>
</ejb-jar>
```

The <persistence-unit-ref-name> element is equivalent to the name( ) attribute of the @PersistenceUnit annotation in that it represents the ENC name to which the reference will be bound. Here's how a client bean would use this ENC context to look up a reference to this EntityManagerFactory:

```
InitialContext jndiContext = new InitialContext( );
EntityManagerFactory titan = (EntityManagerFactory)
       jndiContext.lookup("java:comp/env/persistence/TitanDB");
```

The <persistence-unit-name> element is equivalent to the unitName( ) attribute of the @PersistenceUnit annotation. It represents the same name you have declared in your persistence.xml deployment descriptor.

The <injection-target> element is used if you want to inject your EntityManagerFactory into your EJB's bean class. Here is an example of using <injection-target>:

```
<ejb-jar>
   <enterprise-beans>
      <session>
         <ejb-name>TravelAgentBean</ejb-name>
         <persistence-unit-ref>
            <persistence-unit-ref-name>persistence/TitanDB</persistence-unit-ref-
name>
            <persistence-unit-name>TitanDB</persistence-unit-name>
            <injection-target>
               <injection-target-class>com.titan.travelagent.TravelAgentBean</
injection-target-class>
```

```
                <injection-target-name>ships</injection-target-name>
            </injection-target>
        </persistence-unit-ref>
    </enterprise-beans>
</ejb-jar>
```

In this example, the EntityManagerFactory would be injected into field named ships or passed as a parameter to a *setter* method named setShips( ) in the TravelAgentBean class.

Scoped and overloaded unit names

A persistence unit can be declared in many different places. It can be defined in an EJB-JAR, an EAR/lib JAR, or even a WAR file (see Chapter 20 for more details on these file types). Persistence units are scoped when defined in a WAR or EJB-JAR file and they cannot be referenced by components deployed outside of that archive. Persistence units deployed in a JAR in the *.ear*'s *lib/* directory are available to all other components in that enterprise archive. Sometimes you may have the same persistence unit name defined in your EJB or WAR file as the name you declared in a persistence JAR in the *EAR/lib* directory. To differentiate references with duplicate persistence unit names, the specification has an extended syntax for <persistence-unit-name> and the unitName( ) attribute of the @PersistenceUnit annotation. This extended syntax has a relative path to a JAR file that contains the persistence unit, followed by the # character, followed by the persistence unit name:

```
@PersistenceUnit(unitName="inventory.jar#InventoryDB")
EntityManagerFactory inventory;
```

In this example, the *inventory.jar* is in the same directory of the EAR file as the persistence unit's JAR file. The @PersistenceUnit annotation references the InventoryDB persistence unit within that *inventory.jar* deployment.

EntityManager References

An EntityManager can be registered in the JNDI ENC of an EJB. When you are registering an EntityManager into the JNDI ENC or injecting it into your EJB, the EJB container has full control over the life cycle of the underlying persistence context of the EntityManager. The EntityManager object reference itself is really just a proxy around an actual persistence context that may not even exist yet, depending on the type of persistence context you are injecting. When you let the application server populate your ENC or inject your EntityManager, the EJB container handles the cleanup of this instance and you do not have to call EntityManager.close( ). In fact, it is illegal to call close( ) on an injected EntityManager instance, and an exception will be thrown if you do. Like all other services and resources, an EntityManager can be bound to the JNDI ENC or injected into your bean class by using either annotations or XML.

@javax.persistence.PersistenceContext

The @javax.persistence.PersistenceContext annotation can be used on your bean class's *setter* methods or member fields, or directly on the class itself:

```
package javax.persistence;

public enum PersistenceContextType {
   TRANSACTION,
   EXTENDED
}

@Target({}) @Retention(RUNTIME)
public @interface PersistenceProperty {
   String name( );
   String value( );
}

@Target({TYPE, METHOD, FIELD}) @Retention(RUNTIME)
public @interface PersistenceContext {
   String name( ) default "";
   String unitName( ) default "";
   PersistenceContextType type( ) default TRANSACTION;
   PersistenceProperty[] properties( ) default {};
}
```

The name( ) attribute refers to the JNDI ENC name under which the EntityManager is referenced. This name is relative to the java:comp/env context.

The unitName( ) attribute identifies which persistence unit you are interested in referencing. This identifier is the same as what you have declared in your *persistence.xml* file. If left unspecified, a deployment error is raised unless the EJB-JAR has only one persistence unit deployed within it. In that case, it defaults to this sole persistence unit.

The type( ) attribute specifies the type of persistence context you want. PersistenceContextType.TRANSACTION specifies that you want a transaction-scoped persistence context. This is the default. PersistenceContextType.EXTENDED gives you an extended persistence context. The EXTENDED type can be used only on stateful session beans. You will receive a deployment error if you use it with any other bean type. Review Chapter 5 for more information on the differences between EXTENDED- and TRANSACTION-based persistence contexts.

The properties( ) attribute allows you to pass in additional vendor-specific properties for the created EntityManager instance. You set this attribute with an array of @javax.persistence.PersistenceProperty annotation declarations.

When placed on the bean class, the @PersistenceContext annotation will register a reference to the EntityManager into the JNDI ENC of the EJB bean class:

```
@Stateful
@PersistenceContext(name="persistence/TitanDB",
```

```
        unitName="TitanDB"
        type=PersistenceContextType.EXTENDED)
public class TravelAgentBean implements TravelAgentRemote {
...
}
```

In this example, code within the TravelAgentBean can look up an EntityManager that manages a TitanDB persistence unit under the java:comp/env/persistence/TitanDB JNDI ENC name. Here's how a client bean would use this context to look up the reference to this EntityManager:

```
InitialContext jndiContext = new InitialContext( );
EntityManager titan = (EntityManagerFactory)
        jndiContext.lookup("java:comp/env/persistence/TitanDB");
```

When the @PersistenceContext annotation is used on the bean class, the name( ) attribute is required so that the EJB container knows where in the JNDI ENC to bind the EntityManager. The type( ) and unitName( ) attributes have valid defaults.

The @PersistenceContext annotation can be used only once on your bean class. When you need to reference multiple persistence contexts, the @javax.persistence.PersistenceContexts annotation is available:

```
package javax.persistence;

@Target({TYPE, METHOD, FIELD}) @Retention(RUNTIME)
public @interface PersistenceContexts {
   PersistenceContext[] value( );
}
```

This kind of annotation is required because only one annotation of a given type can be applied to any given artifact in the Java language:

```
@Stateful
@PersistenceContexts({
   @PersistenceContext(name="persistence/TitanDB",
        unitName="TitanDB",
        type=PersistenceContextType.EXTENDED),
   @PersistenceContext(name="Customers",
        unitName="crmDB")
})
public class TravelAgentBean implements TravelAgentRemote {
...
}
```

In this example, the TravelAgentBean creates an ENC reference to both the TitanDB and crmDB persistence units.

The @PersistenceContext annotation can also be placed on a *setter* method or member field so that the EntityManager referenced is injected directly into the bean class instance:

```
@Stateful
public class TravelAgentBean implements TravelAgentRemote {
```

```
    @PersistenceContext(unitName="crmDB") private EntityManager crm;

   ...
   }
```

When used on a *setter* method or member field, no annotation attribute is required, as the name( ), unitName( ), and type( ) attributes have valid defaults.

XML-based EntityManager references

The <persistence-context-ref> element defines a reference to a given EntityManager. It contains the subelements <description> (optional), <persistence-context-ref-name> (required), <persistence-unit-name> (required), <persistence-context-type> (optional), and one or more <persistence-property> (optional) elements as well as the element <injection-target> (optional) described in the first section of this chapter. Here is an example of a reference to the TitanDB persistence unit:

```
<ejb-jar>
   <enterprise-beans>
      <session>
         <ejb-name>TravelAgentBean</ejb-name>
         <persistence-context-ref>
            <persistence-context-ref-name>
               persistence/TitanDB
            </persistence-context-ref-name>
            <persistence-unit-name>TitanDB</persistence-unit-name>
            <persistence-context-type>EXTENDED</persistence-context-ref>
            <persistence-property>
               <name>hibernate.show_sql</name>
               <value>true</value>
            </persistence-property>
   </enterprise-beans>
</ejb-jar>
```

The <persistence-context-ref-name> element is equivalent to the name( ) attribute of the @PersistenceContext annotation in that it represents the ENC name to which the reference is bound. Here's how a client bean would use this ENC context to look up a reference to this EntityManager:

```
InitialContext jndiContext = new InitialContext( );
EntityManager titan = (EntityManager)
       jndiContext.lookup("java:comp/env/persistence/TitanDB");
```

The <persistence-unit-name> element is equivalent to the unitName( ) attribute of the @PersistenceContext annotation in that it represents the same name you have declared in your persistence.xml deployment descriptor.

The <persistence-property> element is equivalent to the properties( ) attribute of the @PersistenceContext annotation. This element is optional and you may specify more than one.

The <injection-target> element is used if you want to inject an EntityManager into an EJB. Here is an example of using <injection-target>:

```
<ejb-jar>
   <enterprise-beans>
      <session>
         <ejb-name>TravelAgentBean</ejb-name>
         <persistence-context-ref>
            <persistence-context-ref-name>
               persistence/TitanDB
            </persistence-context-ref-name>
            <persistence-unit-name>TitanDB</persistence-unit-name>
            <injection-target>
               <injection-target-class>
                  com.titan.travelagent.TravelAgentBean
               </injection-target-class>
               <injection-target-name>ships</injection-target-name>
            </injection-target>
         </persistence-context-ref>
   </enterprise-beans>
</ejb-jar>
```

In this example, the EntityManager would be injected into the field named ships or passed as a parameter to a *setter* method named setShips( ) in the TravelAgentBean class.

Scoped and overloaded unit names

The referencing of the persistence unit of a referenced EntityManager has the same possible ambiguities that were discussed in the "XML-based EntityManagerFactory references" section earlier in this chapter. To differentiate references with duplicate persistence unit names, the specification has an extended syntax for <persistence-unit-name> and the unitName( ) attribute of the @PersistenceContext annotation. This extended syntax has a relative path to a JAR file that contains the persistence unit, followed by the # character, followed by the persistence unit name:

```
@PersistenceContext(unitName="inventory.jar#InventoryDB")
EntityManager inventory;
```

In this example, the *inventory.jar* file is in the same directory of the EAR file as the persistence unit's hard file. The @PersistenceContext annotation references the InventoryDB persistence unit within that *inventory.jar* deployment.

Resource References

In Chapter 11, we saw how the ProcessPayment EJB needed a reference to a JDBC data source to perform its business logic. Enterprise beans use the JNDI ENC to look up external resources, such as database connections, that they need to access. The mechanism for doing this is similar to the mechanism used for referencing other EJB and environment entries: the external resources are mapped into a name within the

JNDI ENC namespace and are optionally injected into member fields or *setter* methods of bean instances. This is accomplished using annotations or an XML deployment descriptor fragment.

External resources can be of the type javax.sql.DataSource, javax.jms.ConnectionFactory, javax.jms.QueueConnectionFactory, javax.jms.TopicConnectionFactory, javax.mail.Session, java.net.URL, or javax.resource.cci.ConnectionFactory, or any other type defined by a JCA resource adapter. In this section, we'll focus on javax.sql.DataSource as an example.

@javax.annotation.Resource

The @javax.annotation.Resource annotation is used to reference an external resource. It can be applied to your bean class's *setter* methods or member fields, or directly on the class itself. This annotation is highly overloaded and overused in the Java EE specification in that in addition to external resources, it is also used to reference JMS message destinations, environment entries, EJBContexts, and Java EE core services. For now, we'll focus solely on using this annotation to access external resources:

```
package javax.annotation;

@Target({TYPE, METHOD, FIELD}) @Retention(RUNTIME)
public @interface Resource {

   public enum AuthenticationType {
      CONTAINER,
      APPLICATION
   }

   String name( ) default "";
   Class type( ) default Object.class;
   AuthenticationType authenticationType( ) default AuthenticationType.CONTAINER;
   boolean shareable( ) default true;
   String description( ) default "";
   String mappedName( ) default "";
}
```

The name( ) attribute refers to what the JNDI ENC name is for the referenced external resource. This name is relative to the java:comp/env context.

The type( ) attribute declares the fully qualified class name of the resource's Java type. When the @Resource annotation is applied to the bean class, this attribute may be important to the EJB container to truly identify the resource in which you are interested. Usually, this attribute is unneeded and the default value is good enough.

The mappedName( ) attribute is a vendor-specific identifier for the external resource. Since Java EE has no specified mechanism or global registry for finding global resources, many vendors require this attribute so that they can locate and bind the resource. Many times, this mappedName( ) attribute will be equivalent to a global JNDI name.

When placed on the bean class, the @Resource annotation registers a reference to the external resource into the JNDI ENC of the EJB bean class:

```
@Stateful
@Resource(name="jdbc/OracleDB",
          type=javax.sql.DataSource,
          mappedName="java:/DefaultDS")
public class TravelAgentBean implements TravelAgentRemote {
...
}
```

In this example, the @Resource annotation is binding a javax.sql.DataSource into the jdbc/OracleDB ENC name. The mappedName( ) attribute provides a global, vendor-specific identifier so that the application server can locate the desired resource. Code within the TravelAgentBean can locate this data source under the java:comp/env/jdbc/OracleDB JNDI ENC name. Here's how a client bean would use this context to look up the reference:

```
InitialContext jndiContext = new InitialContext( );
DataSource oracle = (DataSource)
       jndiContext.lookup("java:comp/env/jdbc/OracleDB");
```

When the @Resource annotation is used on the bean class, the name( ) and type( ) attributes are required. As stated earlier, mappedName( ) or additional vendor-specific annotation metadata may be required by the vendor to truly identify the resource.

The authenticationType( ) attribute tells the server who is responsible for authentication when the resource is accessed. It can have one of two values: CONTAINER or APPLICATION. If CONTAINER is specified, the container will automatically perform authentication (sign on or log in) to use the resource, as specified at deployment time. If APPLICATION is specified, the bean itself must perform the authentication before using the resource. Here's how a bean might sign on to a connection factory when APPLICATION is specified:

```
@Stateful
@Resource(name="jdbc/OracleDB",
          type=javax.sql.DataSource,
          authenticationType=AuthenticationType.APPLICATION,
          mappedName="java:/DefaultDS")
public class TravelAgentBean implements TravelAgentRemote {
   @Resource SessionContext ejbContext;

   private java.sql.Connection getConnection( ) {
      DataSource source = (DataSource)
         ejbContext.lookup("jdbc/OracleDB");
      String loginName = ejbContext.getCallerPrincipal().getName( );
      String password = ...;  // get password from somewhere
```

```
        // use login name and password to obtain a database connection
        java.sql.Connection con = source.getConnection(loginName, password);
}
```

In this case, the connection will be authenticated programmatically. In the CONTAINER option, the caller principal could be extracted internally by the resource itself, or configured statically by the application deployment.

The @Resource annotation can be used only once on your bean class. When you need to reference multiple persistence units, the @javax.annotation.Resources annotation is available:

```
package javax.annotation;

@Target({TYPE }) @Retention(RUNTIME)
public @interface Resources {
   Resource[] value();
}
```

This kind of annotation is required because only one annotation of a given type can be applied to any given artifact in the Java language:

```
@Stateful
@Resources({
   @Resource(name="jdbc/OracleDB",
             type=javax.sql.DataSource.class,
             mappedName="java:/DefaultDS"),
   @Resource(name="jdbc/SybaseDB",
             type=javax.sql.DataSource.class,
             mappedName="java:/OtherDS")
})
public class TravelAgentBean implements TravelAgentRemote {
...
}
```

In this example, the TravelAgentBean creates an ENC reference to both the OracleDB and SybaseDB data sources.

The @Resource annotation can also be placed on a *setter* method or member field so that the resources referenced will be injected directly into the bean class instance:

```
@Stateful
public class TravelAgentBean implements TravelAgentRemote {
   @Resource(mappedName="java:/DefaultDS") private javax.sql.DataSource oracle;

...
}
```

When used on a *setter* method or member field, only the mappedName( ) attribute may be required to identify the resource, as the type and ENC name can be determined from the type and name of the method or field.

Shareable resources

When several enterprise beans in a transaction use the same resource, you will want to configure your EJB server to share that resource. Sharing a resource means that each EJB will use the same connection to access the resource (e.g., database or JMS provider), a strategy that is more efficient than using separate resource connections.

In terms of a database, EJBs that are referencing the same database will probably want to use the same database connection during a transaction so that all CRUD operations return consistent results. EJB containers share resources by default, but resource sharing can be turned on or off explicitly with the `shareable( )` attribute of the `@Resource` annotation.

Occasionally, advanced developers may run into situations where resource sharing is not desirable, and having the option to turn off resource sharing is beneficial. Unless you have a good reason for turning off resource sharing, we recommend that you set the `shareable( )` attribute to `true`.

XML-based resource references

The `<resource-ref>` element defines a reference to a given resource. It contains the subelements `<description>` (optional), `<res-ref-name>` (required), `<res-type>` (required), `<res-auth>` (required), `<res-sharing-scope>` (optional), and `<mapped-name>` (optional), as well as the element `<injection-target>` (optional) described in the first section of this chapter. Here is an example of a reference to a data source of `TitanDB`:

```
<ejb-jar>
   <enterprise-beans>
      <session>
         <ejb-name>TravelAgentBean</ejb-name>
         <resource-ref>
            <res-ref-name>jdbc/OracleDB</res-ref-name>
            <res-type>javax.sql.DataSource</res-type>
            <res-auth>Container</res-auth>
            <mapped-name>java:/DefaultDS</mapped-name>
         </resource-ref>
   </enterprise-beans>
</ejb-jar>
```

The `<res-ref-name>` element is equivalent to the `name( )` attribute of the `@Resource` annotation. `<res-type>` is equivalent to the `type( )` attribute. `<res-auth>` is the same as the `authenticationType( )` attribute and can have one of two values: `Container` or `Application`. The `<mapped-name>` element is equivalent to the `mappedName( )` attribute of the `@Resource` annotation.

The `<injection-target>` element is used if you want to inject the resource into your EJB, as described earlier in this chapter. Here is an example of using `<injection-target>`:

```
<ejb-jar>
   <enterprise-beans>
```

```
<session>
   <ejb-name>TravelAgentBean</ejb-name>
   <resource-ref>
      <res-ref-name>jdbc/OracleDB</res-ref-name>
      <res-type>javax.sql.DataSource</res-type>
      <res-auth>Container</res-auth>
      <mapped-name>java:/DefaultDS</mapped-name>
      <injection-target>
         <injection-target-class>com.titan.travelagent.TravelAgentBean</
injection-target-class>
         <injection-target-name>oracle</injection-target-name>
      </injection-target>
   </resource-ref>
</enterprise-beans>
</ejb-jar>
```

In this example, the data source would be injected into a field named `oracle` or passed as a parameter to a *setter* method named `setOracle()` in the `TravelAgentBean` class.

Resource Environment and Administered Objects

Resource environment entries are objects that do not fall into the resource reference category. Some resources may have other, additional administered objects that need to be obtained from the JNDI ENC or injected into your bean class. An administered object is a resource that is configured at deployment time and is managed by the EJB container at runtime. They are usually defined and deployed by a JCA resource adapter.

Besides administered objects, resource environment entries are also used to reference services such as `javax.transaction.UserTransaction` and `javax.transaction.TransactionSynchronizationRegistry`.

To obtain a reference to one of these services, the `@Resource` annotation can be used. When using this annotation, the `authenticationType()` and `shareable()` attributes are meaningless and are illegal even to specify:

```
@Stateful
public class TravelAgentBean implements TravelAgentRemote {
   @Resource private javax.transaction.UserTransaction utx;

...
}
```

If you are using XML, you must use a separate `<resource-env-ref>` element. It contains the subelements `<resource-env-ref-name>` (required), `<resource-env-ref-type>` (required), and `<mapped-name>` (optional), as well as the element `<injection-target>` (optional).

The <resource-env-ref-name> element corresponds to the JNDI ENC name. <resource-env-ref-type> is the type of the reference, and <mapped-name> and <injection-target> are used in the same way as they are used in <resource-ref>:

```
<ejb-jar>
   <enterprise-beans>
      <session>
         <ejb-name>TravelAgentBean</ejb-name>
         <resource-env-ref>
            <resource-env-ref-name>UserTransaction</res-ref-name>
            <resource-env-ref-type>javax.transaction.UserTransaction</res-type>
            <injection-target>
               <injection-target-class>
                 com.titan.travelagent.TravelAgentBean
               </injection-target-class>
               <injection-target-name>utx</injection-target-name>
            </injection-target>
         </resource-env-ref>
   </enterprise-beans>
</ejb-jar>
```

This XML grabs a reference to a javax.transaction.UserTransaction object and injects it into the utx field of the TravelAgentBean class.

Environment Entries

In Chapter 11, the ProcessPayment EJB had a configurable property for minimum check number. These types of configurable properties are called *environment entries*. The bean can use environment entries to customize its behavior.

Although they can be defined using annotations, environment entries are almost always configured via XML, as they really are configuration values and not metadata. The <env-entry> element is used to define them. This element contains the subelements <description> (optional), <env-entry-name> (required), <env-entry-type> (required), and <env-entry-value> (optional), as well as the element <injection-target> (optional). Here is a typical <env-entry> declaration:

```
<ejb-jar>
   <enterprise-beans>
      <session>
         <ejb-name>ProcessPaymentBean</ejb-name>
         <env-entry>
            <env-entry-name>minCheckNumber</env-entry-name>
            <env-entry-type>java.lang.Integer</env-entry-type>
            <env-entry-value>2000</env-entry-value>
         </env-entry>
   </enterprise-beans>
</ejb-jar>
```

The <env-entry-name> element is relative to the java:comp/env context. For example, the minCheckNumber entry can be accessed using the path java:comp/env/minCheckNumber in a JNDI ENC lookup:

```
InitialContext jndiContext = new InitialContext( );
int minValue = (Integer)
        jndiContext.lookup("java:comp/env/minCheckNumber");
```

Alternatively, it can be looked up with the `EJBContext.lookup( )` method using the `minCheckNumber` name.

`<env-entry-type>` can be of type `String` or one of the several primitive wrapper types, including `Integer`, `Long`, `Double`, `Float`, `Byte`, `Boolean`, and `Short`.

`<env-entry-value>` is optional. The value can be specified by the bean developer or deferred to the application assembler or deployer.

The `<injection-target>` element can be used to initialize a field or *setter* method with the environment entry's value:

```
<ejb-jar>
   <enterprise-beans>
      <session>
         <ejb-name>ProcessPaymentBean</ejb-name>
         <env-entry>
            <env-entry-name>minCheckNumber</env-entry-name>
            <env-entry-type>java.lang.Integer</env-entry-type>
            <env-entry-value>2000</env-entry-value>
            <injection-target>
               <injection-target-class>
                  com.titan.processpayment.ProcessPaymentBean
               </injection-target-class>
               <injection-target-name>minCheckNumber</injection-target>
            </injection-target>
         </env-entry>
   </enterprise-beans>
</ejb-jar>
```

The preceding XML will inject the value `2000` into the field named `minCheckNumber` or invoke a *setter* method named `setMinCheckNumber( )` in the bean class.

The `@javax.annotation.Resource` annotation can be used to pull in the environment entry instead of the `<injection-target>` element:

```
@Resource(name="minCheckNumber") private int minCheckNumber = 100;
```

In this example, the value of `2000` will be pulled from the environment entry described in XML and injected into the `minCheckNumber` field. If no XML is used to configure this value, the default will be `100`, but no entry is created in the ENC. A common pattern is to annotate your field with `@Resource` and provide a default value for the field that can optionally be overridden in XML. Using the `@Resource` annotation with a `String` or primitive value type identifies it as an environment entry to the EJB container. When `@Resource` designates an environment entry, only the `name( )` attribute is allowed to be specified. Also, it doesn't make much sense to use `@Resource` for environment entries at the class level, as there is no way to initialize the value in the annotation.

Message Destination References

Message destination references populate the JNDI ENC with a pointer to a JMS topic or queue. You need these references if you are sending messages within your EJB. Chapter 12 gave a more complete description of this type of reference, so only an overview will be provided here, with additional instructions on how to inject using an annotation instead.

XML-based resource references

The `<message-destination-ref>` element defines a reference to a JMS message destination. It contains the subelements `<description>` (optional), `<message-destination-ref-name>` (required), `<message-destination-type>` (required), `<message-destination-usage>` (required), `<message-destination-link>` (optional), and `<mapped-name>` (optional), as well as the element `<injection-target>` (optional) described in the first section of this chapter. Here is an example of a reference to a topic:

```
<ejb-jar>
   <enterprise-beans>
      <session>
         <ejb-name>TravelAgentBean</ejb-name>
         <message-destination-ref>
            <message-destination-ref-name>
               jms/TicketTopic
            </message-destination-ref-name>
            <message-destination-type>javax.jms.Topic</message-destination-type>
            <message-destination-usage>Produces</message-destination-usage>
            <message-destination-link>Distributor</message-destination-link>
            <mapped-name>topic/TicketTopic</mapped-name>
            <injection-target>
               <injection-target-class>com.titan.travelagent.TravelAgentBean</
injection-target-class>
               <injection-target-name>ticketTopic</injection-target-name>
            </injection-target>
         </message-destination-ref>
   </enterprise-beans>
</ejb-jar>
```

The `<message-destination-ref-name>` element is the JNDI ENC name the topic will be bound to and is relative to the path `java:comp/env`.

The `<message-destination-type>` element is either a `javax.jms.Topic` or a `javax.jms.Queue` and is required.

The `<message-destination-usage>` element specifies whether the EJB produces or consumes messages to or from this destination.

The `<message-destination-link>` element creates a message flow, as described in Chapter 12.

Sometimes a vendor-specific identify is required, and `<mapped-name>` optionally fulfills this role.

As with all other resource reference types, the `<injection-target>` element can be used to inject the destination into a field or *setter* method.

Using @Resource

The `@javax.annotation.Resource` annotation is overloaded to support referencing JMS destinations. Unfortunately, the specification does not provide annotation metadata to set up a message destination link, so you'll have to rely on XML to do this sort of thing.

When placed on the bean class, the `@Resource` annotation registers a reference to the JMS queue or topic destination into the JNDI ENC of the EJB bean class:

```
@Stateful
@Resource(name="jms/TicketTopic",
          type=javax.jms.Topic,
          mappedName="topic/TicketTopic")
public class TravelAgentBean implements TravelAgentRemote {
...
}
```

In this example, the `@Resource` annotation is binding a `javax.jms.Topic` into the `jms/TicketTopic` ENC name. The `mappedName()` attribute provides a global, vendor-specific identifier so that the application server can locate the desired destination.

When the `@Resource` annotation is used on the bean class, the `name()` and `type()` attributes are required. As stated earlier, `mappedName()` or additional vendor-specific annotation metadata may be required by the vendor to truly identify the resource. Only these three attributes can be set by application code. All others are illegal and they will create a deployment error.

The `@Resource` annotation can also be placed on a *setter* method or member field so that the destination referenced will be injected directly into the bean class instance:

```
@Stateful
public class TravelAgentBean implements TravelAgentRemote {
   @Resource(mappedName="topic/TicketTopic")
   private javax.jms.Topic ticketTopic;

...
}
```

When used on a *setter* method or member field, only the `mappedName()` attribute may be required to identify the resource, as the type and ENC name can be determined from the field type and name.

Web Service References

Web service references populate the JNDI ENC with a pointer to either the service interface or the service endpoint interface. Chapter 19 gives a more complete description of this type of reference, so only an overview will be provided here, with additional instructions on how to inject using an annotation instead.

XML-based resource references

The `<service-ref>` element defines a reference to a JAX-WS service interface. From this reference, a stub that implements the service endpoint interface can be obtained and invoked upon. This element contains the subelements `<description>` (optional), `<service-ref-name>` (required), `<service-interface>` (required), `<wsdl-file>` (required), `<jaxrpc-mapping-file>` (required), `<service-qname>` (required), and `<mapped-name>` (optional), as well as the element `<injection-target>` (optional) described in the first section of this chapter. Here is what a `<service-ref>` might look like:

```
<ejb-jar>
  <enterprise-beans>
     <session>
        <ejb-name>TravelAgentBean</ejb-name>
        <service-ref>
           <service-ref-name>service/ChargeItProcessorService</service-ref-name>
           <service-interface>com.charge_it.ProcdessorService</service-interface>
           <wsdl-file>META-INF/wsdl/ChargeItProcessor.wsdl</wsdl-file>
           <jaxrpc-mapping-file>META-INF/mapping.xml</jaxrpc-mapping-file>
           <service-qname>chargeIt:ProcessorService</service-qname>
           <mapped-name>webservice/ChargeItProcessorService</mapped-name>
           <injection-target>
              <injection-target-class>
                 com.titan.travelagent.TravelAgentBean
              </injection-target-class>
              <injection-target-name>chargeService</injection-target-name>
           </injection-target>
        </service-ref>
  </enterprise-beans>
</ejb-jar>
```

The `<service-ref-name>` element declares the JNDI ENC lookup name of the JAX-RPC service: it is always relative to the `java:comp/env` context. For more details about various web service deployment descriptors, see Chapter 19.

Using @javax.xml.ws.WebServiceRef

The `@javax.xml.ws.WebServiceRef` annotation can be used to vastly simplify the referencing of web services. It can be used to reference or inject a service interface or a service endpoint interface:

```
package javax.xml.ws;

@Target({TYPE, METHOD, FIELD}) @Retention(RUNTIME)
public @interface WebServiceRef {

   String name( ) default "";
   String wsdlLocation( ) default "";
   Class type( ) default Object.class;
   Class value( ) default Object.class;
   String mappedName( ) default "";
}
```

The `name( )` attribute is used to map the JNDI ENC name. The `wsdlLocation( )` attribute is used to define the location of the WSDL file. You can usually leave this empty, and the deployer will generate or locate it for you automatically. When referencing a service endpoint directly, the `value( )` attribute can be filled with the class of the service interface from which to obtain the endpoint. The `mappedName( )` attribute may be used to specify a vendor-specific reference. Here is an example of obtaining both a service interface and a service endpoint interface:

```
@Stateful
public class TravelAgentBean implements TravelAgentRemote {
   @WebServiceRef ProcessorService service;

   @WebServiceRef(ProcessorService.class) Processor endpoint;
...
}
```

More information on this annotation is available in Chapter 19.

CHAPTER 15

Interceptors

Interceptors are objects that are able to interpose themselves on method calls or the life cycle events of session and message-driven beans. They allow you to encapsulate common behavior that cuts across large parts of your application. This behavior is usually common code that you don't want to pollute your business logic. Where most of the changes to the EJB 3.0 specification were designed to make EJB easier to use for application developers, interceptors are an advanced feature that provide you another way to modularize your application or even extend your EJB container. This chapter teaches you how to write an interceptor as well as shows you various real-world examples of where interceptors can be used.

Intercepting Methods

To understand when to use interceptors, we'll look at some modified code of our TravelAgent EJB's `bookPassage( )` method. The application developer of this code has added some profiling logic to time how long the `bookPassage( )` method takes to be invoked. It is as simple as polling the current time at the start of the method and printing out the time it took at the end of it within a *finally* block:

```
@Remove
public TicketDO bookPassage(CreditCardDO card, double price)
    throws IncompleteConversationalState {

   long startTime = System.currentTimeMillis( );
   try {
      if (customer == null || cruise == null || cabin == null) {
            throw new IncompleteConversationalState( );
      }
      try {
         Reservation reservation = new Reservation(
                           customer, cruise, cabin, price, new Date( ));
         entityManager.persist(reservation);

         process.byCredit(customer, card, price);
```

```
            TicketDO ticket = new TicketDO(customer, cruise, cabin, price);
            return ticket;
         } catch(Exception e) {
            throw new EJBException(e);
         }
      } finally {
        long endTime = System.currentTimeMillis( ) - startTime;
        System.out.println("bookPassage( ) took: " + endTime + " (ms)");
      }
   }
```

Although this code will compile and run fine, it has a lot of design flaws:

- The bookPassage( ) method is polluted with code that has nothing to do with the business logic of the method. Not only has the developer added six lines of code to the method, but he has also made the code a bit harder to read.
- It is difficult to turn profiling off and on since you have to comment out the code and recompile the bean class.
- This profiling logic is obviously a template that could be reused across many methods of your application. If this profiling code is littered throughout your EJB methods, you would need to potentially modify a lot of different classes to expand the functionality of your profiling logic.

Interceptors provide a mechanism to encapsulate this profiling logic and an easy way to apply it to your methods without making the code harder to read. Interceptors provide a structure for this type of behavior so that it can easily be extended and expanded in one class. Finally, they provide a simple, configurable mechanism for applying their behavior wherever you like.

Interceptor Class

Encapsulating this profile logic into an interceptor is as simple as creating a plain Java class that has a method with the @javax.interceptor.AroundInvoke annotation and the following signature:

```
@AroundInvoke
Object <any-method-name>(javax.interceptor.InvocationContext invocation)
    throws Exception;
```

The @AroundInvoke method in an interceptor class does just what it implies. It wraps around the call to your business method and is actually invoked in the same Java call stack and in the same transaction and security context as the bean method it is intercepting. The javax.interceptor.InvocationContext parameter is a generic representation of the business method the client is invoking. You can obtain information such as the target bean instance on which you are invoking, access to its parameters expressed as an array of objects, and a reference to a java.lang.reflect.Method object that is the generic representation of the actual invoked method. InvocationContext is also used to drive the invocation. Let's convert our profiling logic into an @AroundInvoke method:

```
1  import javax.ejb.*;
2
3  public class Profiler {
4     @AroundInvoke
5     public Object profile(InvocationContext invocation) throws Exception {
6        long startTime = System.currentTimeMillis( );
7        try {
8           return invocation.proceed( );
9        } finally {
10          long endTime = System.currentTimeMillis( ) - startTime;
11          System.out.println("Method " + invocation.getMethod( )
12                            + " took " + endTime + " (ms)");
13       }
14    }
15 }
```

The @AroundInvoke method of our interceptor class is the profile( ) method. It looks pretty much the same as the code in our bookPassage( ) method, except that the business logic is gone and all that is left is our generic profiling logic. In Line 8, the InvocationContext.proceed( ) method is called. If another interceptor must be invoked as part of the method call, then proceed( ) calls the @AroundInvoke method of that other interceptor. If no other interceptors need executing, then the EJB container calls the bean method on which the client is invoking. Because the profile( ) method is invoked in the same Java call stack as the business method on which you are invoking, proceed( ) must be called by the interceptor code or the actual EJB method is not called at all.

In Lines 10 and 11, the profile( ) method calculates the execution time and prints out the time the method took to execute. The InvocationContext.getMethod( ) operation gives the profile( ) code access to the java.lang.reflect.Method object that represents the actual bean method being invoked. It is used in Line 11 to print out the name of the method being called. Besides getMethod( ), the InvocationContext interface has some other interesting methods:

```
package javax.interceptor;

public interface InvocationContext {
   public Object getTarget( );
   public Method getMethod( );
   public Object[] getParameters( );
   public void setParameters(Object[] newArgs);
   public java.util.Map<String, Object> getContextData( );
   public Object proceed( ) throws Exception;
}
```

The getTarget( ) method returns a reference to the target bean instance. We could change our profile( ) method to also print out the parameters of the invoked bean method by using the getParameters( ) method. The setParameters( ) method allows you to actually modify the parameters of the method that is being invoked. Use this with care. The getContextData( ) method returns a Map object that is active for the entire method invocation. Interceptors can use this map to pass contextual data between each other within the same method invocation.

Applying Interceptors

Now that the interceptor class has been written, it is time to apply it to an EJB. One or more interceptors can be applied to all EJBs within a deployment (default interceptors), to all methods of one EJB, or to a single method of an EJB. Interceptors can be applied via an annotation or by using an XML deployment descriptor. We'll discuss all options in this section.

Annotated methods and classes

The `@javax.interceptor.Interceptors` annotation can be used to apply interceptors to individual methods or to every method in the EJB's bean class:

```
package javax.interceptor;

import java.lang.annotation.*;

@Retention(RetentionType.RUNTIME)
@Target({ElementType.CLASS, ElementType.METHOD})
public @interface Interceptors {
   Class[] value( );
}
```

Profiling the `bookPassage( )` method of our TravelAgent EJB is as easy as applying the `@Interceptors` annotation:

```
@Remove
@Interceptors(Profiler.class)
public TicketDO bookPassage(CreditCardDO card, double price)
    throws IncompleteConversationalState {
      if (customer == null || cruise == null || cabin == null) {
            throw new IncompleteConversationalState( );
      }
      try {
         Reservation reservation = new Reservation(
                              customer, cruise, cabin, price, new Date( ));
         entityManager.persist(reservation);

         process.byCredit(customer, card, price);

         TicketDO ticket = new TicketDO(customer, cruise, cabin, price);
         return ticket;
      } catch(Exception e) {
         throw new EJBException(e);
     }
}
```

When the `@Interceptors` annotation is applied to an individual method, that interceptor is executed only when that particular method is invoked. If you use the

@Interceptors annotation on the bean class, all interceptor classes listed will interpose on every method invocation of every business method of the EJB:

```
@Stateful
@Interceptors(Profiler.class)
public class TravelAgentBean implement TravelAgentRemote {

   @Remove
   public TicketDO bookPassage(CreditCardDO card, double price)
      throws IncompleteConversationalState {
      ...
   }
...
}
```

Whether you want to apply the @Interceptors annotation on the class or the method is really determined by the interceptor you are using.

Applying interceptors through XML

Although the @Interceptors annotation allows you to apply the profiling interceptor easily, it does force you to modify and recompile your class every time you want to remove profiling from or add it to a particular method or EJB. Unless an interceptor is part of your business logic, it may not be the best idea to annotate your code; using XML bindings instead might be a better approach. Because the EJB 3.0 specification supports partial XML deployment descriptors, it is quite painless and easy to apply an interceptor through XML:

```
<ejb-jar
       xmlns="http://java.sun.com/xml/ns/javaee"
       xmlns:xsi="http://www.w3.org/2001/XMLSchema-instance"
       xsi:schemaLocation="http://java.sun.com/xml/ns/javaee
                          http://java.sun.com/xml/ns/javaee/ejb-jar_3_0.xsd"
       version="3.0">
   <assembly-descriptor>
      <interceptor-binding>
         <ejb-name>TravelAgentBean</ejb-name>
         <interceptor-class>com.titan.Profiler</interceptor-class>
         <method-name>bookPassage</method-name>
         <method-params>
            <method-param>com.titan.CreditCardDO</method-param>
            <method-param>double</method-param>
         </method-params>
      </interceptor-binding>
   </assembly-descriptor>
</ejb-jar>
```

The preceding XML is a complete deployment descriptor. The <interceptor-binding> element specifies that we want the Profiler interceptor to be executed whenever the bookPassage( ) method of the TravelAgent EJB is invoked. Because the bookPassage( ) method is not overloaded in the bean class, the <method-params> element isn't really required.

If you want to apply an interceptor to every business method of a particular EJB, then leave out the <method-name> and <method-params> elements:

```
<ejb-jar
       xmlns="http://java.sun.com/xml/ns/javaee"
       xmlns:xsi="http://www.w3.org/2001/XMLSchema-instance"
       xsi:schemaLocation="http://java.sun.com/xml/ns/javaee
                           http://java.sun.com/xml/ns/javaee/ejb-jar_3_0.xsd"
       version="3.0">
   <assembly-descriptor>
      <interceptor-binding>
         <ejb-name>TravelAgentBean</ejb-name>
         <interceptor-class>com.titan.Profiler</interceptor-class>
      </interceptor-binding>
   </assembly-descriptor>
</ejb-jar>
```

As you can see, you can use an XML deployment descriptor only when you need it and leave the rest of the EJB metadata expressed as annotations. In this particular interceptor use case, it makes more sense to use XML than an annotation because profiling is probably something you'd want to do in development, not in a production application.

Default interceptors

XML has some other advantages as well. For instance, the <ejb-name> element in an <interceptor-binding> can take a wildcard. In this case, you are applying one or more interceptors that you declare in the interceptor-binding to every EJB in that particular JAR file deployment:

```
<ejb-jar
       xmlns="http://java.sun.com/xml/ns/javaee"
       xmlns:xsi="http://www.w3.org/2001/XMLSchema-instance"
       xsi:schemaLocation="http://java.sun.com/xml/ns/javaee
                           http://java.sun.com/xml/ns/javaee/ejb-jar_3_0.xsd"
       version="3.0">
   <assembly-descriptor>
      <interceptor-binding>
         <ejb-name>*</ejb-name>
         <interceptor-class>com.titan.Profiler</interceptor-class>
      </interceptor-binding>
   </assembly-descriptor>
</ejb-jar>
```

Disabling interceptors

If you are using default interceptors or class-level interceptors, there may be times when you want to disable them for a particular EJB or for a particular method of an EJB. You can do this via an annotation or through XML. Let's look at disabling default interceptors first:

```
<ejb-jar
       xmlns="http://java.sun.com/xml/ns/javaee"
       xmlns:xsi="http://www.w3.org/2001/XMLSchema-instance"
       xsi:schemaLocation="http://java.sun.com/xml/ns/javaee
                           http://java.sun.com/xml/ns/javaee/ejb-jar_3_0.xsd"
       version="3.0">
   <assembly-descriptor>
      <interceptor-binding>
         <ejb-name>*</ejb-name>
         <interceptor-class>com.titan.Profiler</interceptor-class>
      </interceptor-binding>
   </assembly-descriptor>
</ejb-jar>
```

In the preceding XML, we have enabled the `Profiler` interceptor for every EJB deployed in the particular JAR file in which the XML is placed. Let's say we do not want the `Profiler` to be executed for our TravelAgent EJB. We can turn off all default interceptors by using the `@javax.interceptor.ExcludeDefaultInterceptors` annotation:

```
@Stateful
@ExcludeDefaultInterceptors
@Interceptors(com.titan.SomeOtherInterceptor.class)
public class TravelAgentBean implements TravelAgentRemote {
...
}
```

In the preceding example, the `Profiler` will not be executed. Just because the `@ExcludeDefaultInterceptors` annotation has been used, it does not mean we cannot specify an `@Interceptors` annotation that triggers other interceptor classes. This exclusion can be done within XML as well:

```
<ejb-jar
       xmlns="http://java.sun.com/xml/ns/javaee"
       xmlns:xsi="http://www.w3.org/2001/XMLSchema-instance"
       xsi:schemaLocation="http://java.sun.com/xml/ns/javaee
                           http://java.sun.com/xml/ns/javaee/ejb-jar_3_0.xsd"
       version="3.0"
   >
      <interceptor-binding>
         <ejb-name>*</ejb-name>
         <interceptor-class>com.titan.Profiler</interceptor-class>
      </interceptor-binding>
      <interceptor-binding>
         <ejb-name>TravelAgentBean</ejb-name>
         <exclude-default-interceptors/>
         <interceptor-class>com.titan.SomeOtherInterceptor</interceptor-class>
      </interceptor-binding>
   </assembly-descriptor>
</ejb-jar>
```

What we're really doing in the preceding examples is giving the TravelAgent EJB a brand-new interceptor stack that overrides and supercedes any default interceptors.

The same overriding and disabling of interceptors can be done at the method level as well. You can turn off interceptors entirely for a particular method by using the `@javax.interceptor.ExcludeDefaultInterceptors` and `@javax.interceptor.ExcludeClassInterceptors` annotations:

```
@Stateful
@Interceptors(com.titan.SomeOtherInterceptor.class)
public class TravelAgentBean implements TravelAgentRemote {
...
   @Remove
   @ExcludeClassInterceptors
   @ExcludeDefaultInterceptors
   public TicketDO bookPassage(CreditCardDO cc, double amount) {
      ...
   }
...
}
```

The `@ExcludeClassInterceptors` annotation turns off any applied class-level interceptors, and the `@ExcludeDefaultInterceptors` annotation turns off any default interceptors defined in XML. You could also specify an `@Interceptors` annotation on the `bookPassage( )` method to define a different interceptor stack compared to the rest of the methods in the bean class. This is also available in XML format:

```
<ejb-jar
       xmlns="http://java.sun.com/xml/ns/javaee"
       xmlns:xsi="http://www.w3.org/2001/XMLSchema-instance"
       xsi:schemaLocation="http://java.sun.com/xml/ns/javaee
                           http://java.sun.com/xml/ns/javaee/ejb-jar_3_0.xsd"
       version="3.0">
   <assembly-descriptor>
      <interceptor-binding>
         <ejb-name>*</ejb-name>
         <interceptor-class>com.titan.Profiler</interceptor-class>
      </interceptor-binding>
      <interceptor-binding>
         <ejb-name>TravelAgentBean</ejb-name>
         <interceptor-class>com.titan.SomeOtherInterceptor</interceptor-class>
      </interceptor-binding>
      <interceptor-binding>
         <ejb-name>TravelAgentBean</ejb-name>
         <exclude-default-interceptors/>
         <exclude-class-interceptors/>
         <interceptor-class>com.titan.MyMethodInterceptor</interceptor-class>
         <method-name>bookPassage</method-name>
         <method-params>
            <method-param>com.titan.CreditCardDO</method-param>
            <method-param>double</method-param>
         </method-params>
      </interceptor-binding>
   </assembly-descriptor>
</ejb-jar>
```

Usually, you will not be concerned with disabling interceptors, but it is good to know you have the tools to do so if you need to.

Interceptors and Injection

Interceptors belong to the same ENC as the EJBs they intercept. Like the EJBs they intercept, interceptor classes have full support for all the injection annotations, as well as injection through XML. So, you can use annotations like `@Resource`, `@EJB`, and `@PersistenceContext` within your interceptor class if you so desire. Let's illustrate this in an auditing interceptor:

```
package com.titan.interceptors;

import javax.ejb.*;
import javax.persistence.*;
import javax.annotation.Resource;
import javax.interceptor.*;

public class AuditInterceptor {
   @Resource EJBContext ctx;
   @PersistenceContext(unitName="auditdb") EntityManager manager;

   @AroundInvoke
   public Object audit(InvocationContext invocation) throws Exception {
      Audit audit = new Audit( ) ;
      audit.setMethod(invocation.getMethod().toString( ));
      audit.setUser(ctx.getCallerPrincipal().toString( ));
      audit.setTime(new Date( ));

      try {
         Object returnValue = invocation.proceed( );
      } catch (Exception ex) {
         audit.setFailure(ex.getMessage( ));
         throw ex;
      } finally {
         manager.persist(audit);
      }
   }
}
```

The purpose of this interceptor is to log in a database every method invocation done on a particular bean so that an audit trail is created. From this audit trail, system administrators can research security breaches or replay the actions of a particular user. The interceptor obtains the calling user by invoking `getCallerPrincipal( )` on the `javax.ejb.EJBContext` injected into the `ctx` member variable. It allocates an Audit entity bean and sets properties like the method being invoked, the calling principal, and the current time. If the method throws an exception, this is also stored in the Audit entity. At the end of the `@AroundInvoke` method, the Audit entity is persisted to the database by the `EntityManager` injected into the `manager` member variable.

As with bean classes, interceptor injection annotations create additional entries in the ENC of the EJB to which the interceptor class is bound. This means that the persistence context referenced by the manager field is also available in JNDI with the string java:comp/env/com.titan.interceptors.AuditInterceptor/manager.

XML Injection

If you do not want to use annotations to inject dependencies into your interceptor classes, the XML alternative is to define an <interceptor> element within your ejb-jar.xml deployment descriptor:

```
<ejb-jar
       xmlns="http://java.sun.com/xml/ns/javaee"
       xmlns:xsi="http://www.w3.org/2001/XMLSchema-instance"
       xsi:schemaLocation="http://java.sun.com/xml/ns/javaee
                           http://java.sun.com/xml/ns/javaee/ejb-jar_3_0.xsd"
       version="3.0">
   <interceptors>
      <interceptor>
         <interceptor-class>
             com.titan.interceptors.AuditInterceptor
         </interceptor-class>
         <around-invoke>
            <method-name>audit</method-name>
         </around-invoke>
         <persistence-context-ref>
            <persistence-context-name>
               com.titan.interceptors.AuditInterceptor/manager
            </persistence-context-name>
            <persistence-context-unit-name>auditdb</persistence-context-unit-name>
            <injection-target>
               <injection-target-class>
                  com.titan.interceptors.AuditInterceptor
               </injection-target-class>
               <injection-target-name>manager</injection-target-name>
            </injection-target>
         </persistence-context-ref>
      </interceptor>
   </interceptors>
</ejb-jar>
```

The <interceptors> element is a new, top-level element in <ejb-jar>. The <interceptor> subelement accepts any environment entries that are available within an EJB description. Also, if you elect not to use annotations in your class definitions, you can specify metadata like @AroundInvoke using the <around-invoke> element.

There may be times when you want to override injections specified on the interceptor class on a per-EJB basis. This can be done through annotations or via XML. For instance, say you want to use a different persistence unit for the interceptor bound to your TravelAgent EJB other than the auditdb unit that is currently being injected into your AuditInterceptor class. You can do this by overriding the environment name of the injected property in your EJB definition:

```
@Stateful
@PersistenceContext(name="com.titan.interceptors.AuditInterceptor/manager",
                    unitName="EnterpriseWideAuditDB")
public class TravelAgentBean implements TravelAgentRemote {
 ...
}
```

Since all injections are based on the ENC name, the preceding code uses the @PersistenceContext annotation on the EJB bean class to override the interceptor's persistence context reference. This can be done in XML as well:

```
<ejb-jar
       xmlns="http://java.sun.com/xml/ns/javaee"
       xmlns:xsi="http://www.w3.org/2001/XMLSchema-instance"
       xsi:schemaLocation="http://java.sun.com/xml/ns/javaee
                           http://java.sun.com/xml/ns/javaee/ejb-jar_3_0.xsd"
       version="3.0">
   <enterprise-beans>
      <session>
         <ejb-name>TravelAgentBean</ejb-name>
          <persistence-context-ref>
             <persistence-context-name>
                com.titan.interceptors.AuditInterceptor/manager
             </persistence-context-name>
             <persistence-context-unit-name>auditdb</persistence-context-unit-name>
          </persistence-context-ref>
      </session>
   </enterprise-beans>
</ejb-jar>
```

The <persistence-context-unit-name> element references the default ENC name of the manager field in the AuditInterceptor class.

Intercepting Life Cycle Events

Not only can you intercept EJB method invocations, but you can also intercept EJB life cycle events. These callbacks can be used to initialize the state of your EJB bean classes, as well as the interceptor class itself. Life cycle interception looks very similar to the @AroundInvoke style:

```
@<callback-annotation> void <method-name>(InvocationContext ctx);
```

To intercept an EJB callback, define a method within your interceptor class that is annotated with the callback in which you are interested. The return value of the method must be void because EJB callbacks have no return value. The method name can be anything and must not throw any checked exceptions (no throws clause). InvocationContext is the only parameter to this method. As with @AroundInvoke methods, callback interception is invoked in one big Java call stack. This means you must call InvocationContext.proceed( ) to complete the life cycle event. When calling proceed( ) the next interceptor class that has the same callback is invoked. If there are no other interceptors, then the callback method of the EJB's bean class is invoked, if one exists. If the EJB has no callback method, then proceed( ) is a no-op. Because there may be no callback method, InvocationContext.getMethod( ) always returns null.

Custom Injection Annotations

Why would you want to intercept an EJB callback? One concrete example is when you want to create and define your own injection annotations. The EJB specification has a bunch of annotations for injecting Java EE resources, services, and EJB references into your bean classes. Some application servers or applications like to use JNDI as a global registry for configuration or for non-Java EE services. Unfortunately, the specification defines no way to inject something directly from global JNDI into your beans. What we can do is define our own annotation for providing this functionality and implement it as an interceptor.

The first thing we must do is to define the annotation we will use to inject from JNDI:

```
package com.titan.annotations;

import java.lang.annotation.*;

@Target({ElementType.METHOD, ElementType.FIELD})
@Retention(RetentionPolicy.RUNTIME)
public @interface JndiInjected {
   String value( );
}
```

The value( ) attribute of the @com.titan.annotations.JndiInjected annotation is the global JNDI name of the object we want injected into our field or *setter* method. Here is an example of how we might use this custom annotation:

```
@Stateless
public class MySessionBean implements MySession {
   @JndiInject("java:/TransactionManager")
   private javax.transaction.TransactionManager tm;

...
}
```

Some applications might be interested in obtaining a reference to the Java EE JTA Transaction Manager service. Many application servers store a reference to this service in global JNDI. In this instance, we use the @JndiInjected annotation to pull a reference to the Transaction Manager directly into the field of our session bean. Now that we have defined our custom injection annotation and we've defined how it might be used, we need to code the interceptor class that implements this behavior:

```
package com.titan.interceptors;

import java.lang.reflect.*;
import com.titan.annotations.JndiInjected;
import javax.ejb.*;
import javax.naming.*;
import javax.interceptor.*;
import javax.annotation.*;

public class JndiInjector {

   @PostConstruct
   public void jndiInject(InvocationContext invocation) {
      Object target = invocation.getTarget( );
      Field[] fields = target.getClass().getDeclaredFields( );
      Method[] methods = target.getClass().getDeclaredMethods( );

      // find all @JndiInjected fields/methods and set them
      try {
         InitialContext ctx = new InitialContext( );
         for (Method method : methods) {
            JndiInjected inject = method.getAnnotation(JndiInjected.class);
            if (inject != null) {
               Object obj = ctx.lookup(inject.value( ));
               method.setAccessible(true);
               method.invoke(target, obj);
            }
         }
         for (Field field : fields) {
            JndiInjected inject = field.getAnnotation(JndiInjected.class);
            if (inject != null) {
               Object obj = ctx.lookup(inject.value( ));
               field.setAccessible(true);
               field.set(target, obj);
            }
         }
         invocation.proceed( );
      } catch (Exception ex) {
         throw new EJBException("Failed to execute @JndiInjected", ex);
      }
   }
}
```

The `jndiInject( )` method is annotated with `@javax.annotation.PostConstruct` to tell the EJB container that the `JndiInjector` interceptor is interested in intercepting that particular EJB callback. The method begins by obtaining a reference to the bean instance it is intercepting. It then reflects on the object to find all methods and fields that are annotated with `@JndiInjected`, looks up the referenced JNDI name, and initializes the field or method of the target bean instance. Notice that this is done in a *try/catch* block. When intercepting a callback method, you can never throw a checked exception; therefore, all checked exceptions must be caught and wrapped in an `EJBException`.

Now that the interceptor class has been implemented, we can apply this interceptor to our EJBs:

```
<ejb-jar>
   <assembly-descriptor>
      <interceptor-binding>
         <ejb-name>*</ejb-name>
         <interceptor-class>com.titan.interceptors.JndiInjector</interceptor-class>
      </interceptor-binding>
   </assembly-descriptor>
</ejb-jar>
```

One particularly interesting thing about this example is that it shows that you can use EJB interceptors as a framework for writing custom annotations that add your own customer behavior to your EJBs. Default interceptors, through XML, give you a clean, simple way of applying the interceptors that implement the behavior of your annotations. Finally, this custom behavior is portable and can be used in any vendor implementation. Not only is EJB 3.0 easy to use, but it is now finally easy to extend as well.

Exception Handling

Exception handling with interceptors is simple yet powerful. Since interceptors sit directly in the Java call stack of the bean method or callback that is being invoked, you can put a *try/catch/finally* block around the `InvocationContext.proceed( )` method. You can abort an invocation before it reaches the actual bean method by throwing an exception within the `@AroundInvoke` or callback method. You are also allowed to catch a bean-method-thrown exception and throw a different exception, or suppress the exception. With `@AroundInvoke` interception, you are even allowed to retry the bean method call after catching an exception from the bean method. Let's look at some examples.

Aborting a Method Invocation

Parameter validation is business logic that checks to see that the parameters of a business method are valid values before proceeding with the logic of the method. The ProcessPayment EJB method, `byCheck( )`, uses validation to determine whether the `CheckDO` parameter has a minimum check number. Maybe we are selling our Titan Cruise reservation software as an ERP system to various cruise companies throughout the world. We may want to turn off check validation for one deployment of our ProcessPayment EJB. For another deployment, we might want to add more complex validation, such as checking the name and account number of the check against a fraud database. Interceptors give us the ability to encapsulate our validation logic in an interceptor class and to configure and apply it as needed to different deployments of our ProcessPayment EJB. Because interceptors allow you to abort the EJB method invocation in the interceptor class itself before even reaching the actual bean method, it is possible to modularize validation logic in this way:

```
package com.titan.interceptors;

import javax.ejb.*;
import javax.annotation.*;
import javax.interceptor.*;

public class CheckValidation {
   @Resource int minimumCheckNumber;

   @AroundInvoke
   public Object validateCheck(InvocationContext ctx) throws Exception {
      CheckDO check = ctx.getParameters( )[1];
      if (check.checkNumber < minimumCheckNumber) {
         throw new PaymentException("Check number is too low");
      }
      return ctx.proceed( );
   }
}
```

This `CheckValidation` class has encapsulated the validation logic of the `ProcessPaymentBean.byCheck( )` method. It uses the `InvocationContext.getParameters( )` method to obtain the `CheckDO` parameter. The minimum check number is injected into the `minimumCheckNumber` variable of the interceptor class from an `<env-entry>`. The `validateCheck( )` method verifies that the check number in the `CheckDO` parameter is greater than the minimum check number. It aborts the invocation with a `PaymentException` if the validation fails.

Validation is just one example of where you might want to abort an EJB invocation within an `@AroundInvoke` method. Another example is the case where you are implementing your own custom security framework. EJB security is pretty basic and sometimes you have larger security requirements. For instance, you may want to integrate your EJB with a rules engine that analyzes the user as well as the method and parameters to determine whether the user is allowed to invoke the method. This can also be done from within an interceptor.

Catch and Rethrow Exceptions

Besides aborting a given method invocation, you can also catch exceptions thrown by the bean method within the interceptor's `@AroundInvoke` method. For example, you can use interceptor classes as an abstraction mechanism to create exception-handling frameworks. Consider JDBC and the `java.sql.SQLException`. When an `SQLException` is thrown, your code, programmatically, does not know the cause of the exception without looking at the error number or the message of the exception. Unfortunately, error codes and messages differ per database vendor and thus, if you wanted to handle certain exceptions in certain ways, your code would be nonportable between database vendors.

Let's take two common SQLExceptions: deadlocking and cursor not available. First, we will create concrete exceptions that extend SQLException:

```
@ApplicationException(rollback=true)
public class DatabaseDeadlockException extends java.sql.SQLException {
   public DatabaseDeadlockException(Exception cause) {
      Super(cause);
   }
}
@ApplicationException(rollback=true)
public class DatabaseCursorNotAvailable extends java.sql.SQLException {
   public DatabaseCursorNotAvailable(Exception cause) {
      super(cause);
   }
}
```

With these exceptions, we have abstracted away the dependency on the error number to determine the actual database error that occurred. Our client code can use these exceptions in a portable way and not be concerned with the underlying database vendor. But before we can use these exceptions, we need to write the interceptor class that does the exception handling:

```
public class MySQLExceptionHandler {
   @AroundInvoke
   public Object handleException(InvocationContext ctx) Exception {
      try {
         return ctx.proceed( );
   } catch (SQLException sql) {
       int ernum = sql.getErrorCode( );
       switch(ernum) {
       case 32343:
          throw new DatabaseDeadlockException(sql);
       case 22211:
          throw new DatabaseCursorNotAvailable(sql);
       ...
       default:
          throw new RollbackAlwaysOnException(sql);
       }
   }
}
```

The @AroundInvoke method simply catches any SQLException thrown by the bean method and converts it to an appropriate exception type that you can catch in your client code. Of course, there would be one exception-handler interceptor class per database vendor. Here's how your application code could then take advantage of this interceptor behavior:

```
// application client code
{
   try {
      ejbref.invokeSomeDatabaseOperation( );
   } catch (DatabaseDeadlockException deadlock) {
      // handle this specific error case in a special way
```

```
    }
}
```

So, combining the exception handler interceptor with EJB invocations allows you to have specific code that handles specific database errors like deadlock, without having to worry that your code is not portable between vendors.

Interceptor Life Cycle

Interceptor classes have the same life cycles as the EJBs they intercept. Consider an interceptor class as an extension of the EJB's bean instance. They are created along with bean instances. They are destroyed, passivated, and activated along with their bean instances as well. Also, it is important to note that interceptor classes have the same restrictions as the beans to which they are attached. For instance, you cannot inject an extended persistence context into an interceptor class if that interceptor does not intercept a stateful session bean.

Because interceptors have life cycles and hook into life cycle events, they can also hold internal state. This might be extremely useful when you want the interceptor class to obtain an open connection to a remote system and then close that connection at destroy time. You may also be interested in maintaining state that is particular to the bean instance on which the interceptor class is intercepted. Maybe you have a custom injection annotation that you have built and it needs special cleanup after the bean instance is destroyed. You can hold internal state within the interceptor class and do the cleanup when the interceptor and bean instance are destroyed.

Bean Class @AroundInvoke Methods

This chapter has mostly discussed interceptor classes. `@AroundInvoke` methods can also exist inside EJB bean classes. When used inside a bean class, the `@AroundInvoke` method will be the last "interceptor" to be invoked before the actual bean method:

```
@Stateless
public class MySessionBean implements MySessionRemote {

   public void businessMethod( ) {
      ...
   }

   @AroundInvoke
   public Object beanClassInterceptor(InvocationContext ctx) {
      try {
         System.out.println("entering: " + ctx.getMethod( ));
         return ctx.proceed( );
      } finally {
         System.out.println("leaving: " + ctx.getMethod( ));
      }
   }
}
```

This is a simple example of a bean class @AroundInvoke method. For what sorts of things would you want to use it? You may want to have a dynamic implementation of your bean class, or you may have an interceptor whose logic is specific to the bean.

Future Interceptor Improvements

The EJB 3.0 Expert Group mulled over a few other interceptor features while the specification was being written, but they didn't make the cut when the final draft was made public. Let's go over one of them so that you can decide for yourself whether it is a good idea.

Annotations with Behavior

Let's go back to the auditing example described earlier in this chapter. To apply this auditing behavior, you had to either annotate the bean method with @Interceptors or specify some XML in ejb-jar.xml. There are a couple of problems with this approach. If you use the @Interceptors annotation, then your bean class is tied to the auditing implementation. If you use XML, well, you're stuck writing a verbose XML file and adding it to your deployment. Wouldn't it be nice if you could just express this auditing functionality with its own annotation?

```
@Interceptors(com.titan.interceptors.AuditInterceptor)
public @interface Audit {
}
```

The idea is that you annotate your custom annotation with the interceptor functionality you want to apply to the bean. When writing the custom annotation, you apply the @Interceptors annotation to the definition of that annotation. This will automatically cause the interceptor to be applied wherever the @Audit annotation is applied:

```
@Stateful
public class TravelAgentBean implements TravelAgentRemote {

   @Audit
   public TicketDO bookPassage(CreditCardDO cc, double amount) {
    ...
   }
}
```

The preceding example uses the new @Audit annotation. Applying @Audit to bookPassage( ) will trigger the addition of the AuditInterceptor to the invocation of the method. It is much clearer what is happening here and the @Audit annotation gives you, as an interceptor developer, another level of indirection.

Feedback Welcome

The EJB 3.0 Expert Group always welcomes feedback. If you like this feature or want a different one, feel free to email the group at *ejb3-feedback@sun.com*.

CHAPTER 16
Transactions

ACID Transactions

To understand how transactions work, we will revisit the TravelAgent EJB, the stateful session bean developed in Chapter 11 that encapsulates the process of making a cruise reservation for a customer. The TravelAgent EJB's bookPassage( ) method looks like this:

```
public TicketDO bookPassage(CreditCardDO card, double price)
    throws IncompleteConversationalState {

    if (customer == null || cruise == null || cabin == null) {
        throw new IncompleteConversationalState( );
    }
    try {
        Reservation reservation = new Reservation(
            customer, cruise, cabin, price);
        entityManager.persist(reservation);

        this.processPayment.byCredit(customer, card, price);

        TicketDO ticket = new TicketDO(customer,cruise,cabin,price);

        return ticket;
    } catch(Exception e) {
        throw new EJBException(e);
    }
}
```

The TravelAgent EJB is a fairly simple session bean, and its use of other EJBs is typical of business-object design and taskflow. Unfortunately, good business-object design is not enough to make these EJBs useful in an industrial-strength application. The problem is not with the definition of the EJBs or the taskflow; the problem is that a good design does not, in and of itself, guarantee that the TravelAgent EJB's bookPassage( ) method represents a good *transaction*. To understand why, we will take a closer look at what a transaction is and what criteria a transaction must meet to be considered reliable.

In business, a transaction usually involves an exchange between two parties. When you purchase an ice cream cone, you exchange money for food; when you work for a company, you exchange skill and time for money (which you use to buy more ice cream). When you are involved in these exchanges, you monitor the outcome to ensure that you aren't "ripped off." If you give the ice cream vendor a $20 bill, you don't want him to drive off without giving you your change; likewise, you want to make sure that your paycheck reflects all the hours that you worked. By monitoring these commercial exchanges, you are attempting to ensure the reliability of the transactions; you are making sure that each transaction meets everyone's expectations.

In business software, a transaction embodies the concept of a commercial exchange. A business system transaction (transaction for short) is the execution of a unit-of-work that accesses one or more shared resources, usually databases. A *unit-of-work* is a set of activities that relate to each other and must be completed together. The reservation process is a unit-of-work made up of several activities: recording a reservation, debiting a credit card, and generating a ticket.

The object of a transaction is to execute a unit-of-work that results in a reliable exchange. Here are some types of business systems that employ transactions:

ATM
: The ATM (automatic teller machine) you use to deposit, withdraw, and transfer funds executes these units-of-work as transactions. In an ATM withdrawal, for example, the ATM checks to make sure you don't overdraw; then it debits your account and spits out some money.

Online book order
: You've probably purchased many of your Java books—maybe even this book—from an online bookseller. This type of purchase is also a unit-of-work that takes place as a transaction. In an online book purchase, you submit your credit card number, it is validated, and a charge is made for the price of the book. Then an order to ship the book is sent to the bookseller's warehouse.

Medical system
: In a medical system, important data—some of it critical—is recorded about patients every day, including information about clinical visits, medical procedures, prescriptions, and drug allergies. The doctor prescribes the drug, then the system checks for allergies, contraindications, and appropriate dosages. If all tests pass, the drug can be administered. These tasks make up a unit-of-work. A unit-of-work in a medical system may not be financial, but it's just as important. Failure to identify a drug allergy in a patient could be fatal.

As you can see, transactions are often complex and usually involve the manipulation of a lot of data. Mistakes in data can cost money, or even lives. Transactions must therefore preserve data integrity, which means that the transaction must work perfectly every time or not be executed at all. This is a pretty tall order. As difficult as this requirement is, however, when it comes to commerce, there is no room for error. Units-of-work involving money or anything of value always require the utmost reliability because errors affect the revenues and the well-being of the parties involved.

To give you an idea of the accuracy required by transactions, think about what would happen if a transactional system suffered from seemingly infrequent errors. ATMs provide customers with convenient access to their bank accounts and represent a significant percentage of the total transactions in personal banking. The transactions handled by ATMs are simple but numerous, providing us with a great example of why transactions must be error-proof. Let's say that a bank has 100 ATMs in a metropolitan area, and each ATM processes 300 transactions (deposits, withdrawals, and transfers) a day, for a total of 30,000 transactions per day. If each transaction involves the deposit, withdrawal, or transfer of an average of $100, then about $3 million will move through the ATM system per day. In the course of a year, that's a little more than $1 billion:

365 days × 100 ATMs × 300 transactions × $100 = $1,095,000,000

How well do the ATMs have to perform to be considered reliable? For the sake of argument, let's say that ATMs execute transactions correctly 99.99% of the time. This seems to be more than adequate: after all, only one out of every 10,000 transactions executes incorrectly. But if you do the math, that could result in more than $100,000 in errors over the course of a year!

$1,095,000,000 × .01% = $109,500

Obviously, this example is an oversimplification of the problem, but it illustrates that even a small percentage of errors is unacceptable in high-volume or mission-critical systems. For this reason, experts have identified four characteristics of a transaction that must be met for a system to be considered safe. Transactions must be *atomic*, *consistent*, *isolated*, and *durable* (ACID)—the four horsemen of transaction services:

Atomic
: An atomic transaction must execute completely or not at all. This means that every task within a unit-of-work must execute without error. If any of the tasks fail, the entire unit-of-work or transaction is aborted, meaning that any changes to the data are undone. If all the tasks execute successfully, the transaction is committed, which means that the changes to the data are made permanent or durable.

Consistent
: Consistency refers to the integrity of the underlying data store. It must be enforced by both the transactional system and the application developer. The transactional system fulfills this obligation by ensuring that a transaction is atomic, isolated, and durable. The application developer must ensure that the

database has appropriate constraints (primary keys, referential integrity, and so forth) and that the unit-of-work—the business logic—doesn't result in inconsistent data (i.e., data that is not in harmony with the real world it represents). In an account transfer, for example, the debit to one account must equal the credit to another account.

Isolated
: Isolation means that a transaction must be allowed to execute without interference from other processes or transactions. In other words, the data that a transaction accesses cannot be affected by any other part of the system until the transaction or unit-of-work is completed.

Durable
: Durability means that all the data changes made during the course of a transaction must be written to some type of physical storage before the transaction is successfully completed. This ensures that the changes are not lost if the system crashes.

To get a better idea of what these principles mean, we will examine the TravelAgent EJB in terms of the four ACID properties.

Is the TravelAgent EJB Atomic?

Our first measure of the TravelAgent EJB's reliability is its atomicity: does it ensure that the transaction executes completely or not at all? What we are really concerned with are the critical tasks that change or create information. In the `bookPassage( )` method, a Reservation entity is created, the ProcessPayment EJB debits a credit card, and a `TicketDO` object is created. All of these tasks must be successful for the entire transaction to be successful.

To understand the importance of the atomic characteristic, imagine what would happen if even one of the subtasks failed to execute. If, for example, the creation of a Reservation entity failed but all other tasks succeeded, your customer would probably end up getting bumped from the cruise or sharing the cabin with a stranger. As far as the travel agent is concerned, the `bookPassage( )` method executed successfully because a `TicketDO` object was generated. If a ticket is generated without the creation of a reservation, the state of the business system becomes inconsistent with reality because the customer paid for a ticket, but the reservation was not recorded. Likewise, if the ProcessPayment EJB fails to charge the customer's credit card, the customer gets a free cruise. He may be happy, but management won't be. Finally, if the `TicketDO` object is never created, the customer will have no record of the transaction and probably will not be allowed onto the ship.

So the only way `bookPassage( )` can be completed is if all the critical tasks execute successfully. If something goes wrong, the entire process must be aborted. Aborting a transaction requires more than simply not finishing the tasks; in addition, all the tasks that did execute within the transaction must be undone. If, for example, the creation of the Reservation entity and `ProcessPayment.byCredit( )` method succeeded, but the creation of the `TicketDO` object failed (throwing an exception from the constructor) the reservation and payment records must not be added to the database.

Is the TravelAgent EJB Consistent?

In order for a transaction to be consistent, the business system must make sense after the transaction has completed. In other words, the *state* of the business system must be consistent with the reality of the business. This requires the transaction to enforce the atomic, isolated, and durable characteristics, and it also requires diligent enforcement of integrity constraints by the application developer. If, for example, the application developer fails to include the credit card charge operation in the `bookPassage( )` method, the customer will be issued a ticket but will never be charged. The data will be inconsistent with the expectation of the business—a customer should be charged for passage.

In addition, the database must be set up to enforce integrity constraints. For example, it should not be possible for a record to be added to the `RESERVATION` table unless the `CABIN_ID`, `CRUISE_ID`, and `CUSTOMER_ID` foreign keys map to corresponding records in the `CABIN`, `CRUISE`, and `CUSTOMER` tables, respectively. If a `CUSTOMER_ID` that does not map to a `CUSTOMER` record is used, referential integrity should cause the database to throw an error message.

Is the TravelAgent EJB Isolated?

If you are familiar with the concept of thread synchronization in Java or row-locking schemes in relational databases, isolation will be a familiar concept. To be isolated, a transaction must protect the data it is accessing from other transactions. This is necessary to prevent other transactions from interacting with data that is in transition. In the TravelAgent EJB, the transaction is isolated to prevent other transactions from modifying the entities and tables that are being updated. Imagine the problems that would arise if separate transactions were allowed to change any entity bean at any time—transactions would walk all over each other. Several customers could easily book the same cabin because their travel agents happened to make their reservations at the same time.

The isolation of data accessed by EJBs does not mean that the entire application shuts down during a transaction. Only those entity beans and data directly affected by the transaction are isolated. In the TravelAgent EJB, for example, the transaction isolates only the Reservation EJB created. Many Reservation entities can exist; there's no reason these other EJBs can't be accessed by other transactions.

Is the TravelAgent EJB Durable?

To be durable, the `bookPassage()` method must write all changes and new data to a permanent data store before it can be considered successful. While this may seem like a no-brainer, often it is not what happens in real life. In the name of efficiency, changes are often maintained in memory for long periods of time before being saved on a disk drive. The idea is to reduce disk accesses—which slow systems down—and only periodically write the cumulative effect of data changes. While this approach is great for performance, it is also dangerous because data can be lost when the system goes down and memory is wiped out. Durability requires the system to save all updates made within a transaction as the transaction successfully completes, thus protecting the integrity of the data.

In the TravelAgent EJB, this means that the new `RESERVATION` and `PAYMENT` records inserted are made persistent before the transaction can complete successfully. Only when the data is made durable are those specific records accessible through their respective entities from other transactions. Hence, durability also plays a role in isolation. A transaction is not finished until the data is successfully recorded.

Ensuring that transactions adhere to the ACID principles requires careful design. The system has to monitor the progress of a transaction to ensure that it does all of its work, that the data is changed correctly, that transactions do not interfere with each other, and that the changes can survive a system crash. Engineering all of this functionality into a system is a lot of work, and not something you would want to reinvent for every business system on which you work. Fortunately, EJB is designed to support transactions automatically, making the development of transactional systems easier. The rest of this chapter examines how EJB supports transactions implicitly (through declarative transaction attributes) and explicitly (through the Java Transaction API, or JTA).

Declarative Transaction Management

One of the primary advantages of Enterprise JavaBeans is that it allows for *declarative transaction management*. Without this feature, transactions must be controlled using explicit transaction demarcation, which involves the use of fairly complex APIs like the OMG's Object Transaction Service (OTS) or its Java implementation, the Java Transaction Service (JTS). At best, explicit demarcation is difficult if you use the aforementioned APIs, particularly if you are new to transactional systems. In addition, it requires that the transactional code be written within the business logic, which reduces the clarity of the code. We talk more about explicit transaction management and EJB later in this chapter.

With declarative transaction management, the transactional behavior of EJBs can be controlled using the `@javax.ejb.TransactionAttribute` annotation or the EJB *deployment descriptor*, both of which can set transaction attributes for individual enterprise bean methods. This means that the transactional behavior of an EJB can be changed without changing the EJB's business logic by simply annotating the method in a different way or modifying XML. Declarative transaction management reduces the complexity of transactions for EJB developers and application developers and makes it easier to create robust transactional applications.

Transaction Scope

Transaction scope is a crucial concept for understanding transactions. In this context, transaction scope refers to those EJBs—both session and entity—that are participating in a particular transaction. In the `bookPassage()` method of the TravelAgent EJB, all the EJBs involved are part of the same transaction scope. The scope of the transaction starts when a client invokes the TravelAgent EJB's `bookPassage()` method. Once the transaction scope has started, it is propagated to both the entity manager service that is responsible for creating reservations and the ProcessPayment EJB.

As you know, a transaction is a unit-of-work made up of one or more tasks. In a transaction, all the tasks that make up the unit-of-work must succeed for the entire transaction to succeed; in other words, the transaction must be atomic. If any task fails, the updates made by all the other tasks in the transaction will be rolled back or undone. In EJB, tasks are expressed as enterprise bean methods, and a unit-of-work consists of every enterprise bean method invoked in a transaction. The scope of a transaction includes every EJB that participates in the unit-of-work.

It is easy to trace the scope of a transaction by following the thread of execution. If the invocation of the `bookPassage()` method begins a transaction, then logically, the transaction ends when the method completes. The scope of the `bookPassage()` transaction would include the TravelAgent EJB, the `EntityManager` service, and the ProcessPayment EJB—every EJB or transactional-aware service touched by the `bookPassage()` method. A transaction is propagated to an EJB when that EJB's method is invoked and included in the scope of that transaction. The transaction is also propagated to the persistence context of an `EntityManager`. The persistence context keeps track of changes made to persistent managed objects and commits them if the transaction succeeds.

A transaction can end if an exception is thrown while the `bookPassage()` method is executing. The exception can be thrown from one of the other EJBs or from the `bookPassage()` method itself. An exception may or may not cause a rollback, depending on its type. We'll discuss exceptions and transactions in more detail later.

The thread of execution is not the only factor that determines whether an EJB is included in the scope of a transaction; the EJB's transaction attributes also play a role. Determining whether an EJB participates in the transaction scope of any unit-of-work is accomplished implicitly, using the EJB's transaction attributes, or explicitly, using the JTA.

Transaction Attributes

As an application developer, you don't normally need to control transactions explicitly when using an EJB server. EJB servers can manage transactions implicitly, based on the transaction attributes established at deployment time. When an EJB is deployed, you can set its runtime transaction attribute in the `@javax.ejb.TransactionAttribute` annotation or deployment descriptor to one of several values:

```
NotSupported
Supports
Required
RequiresNew
Mandatory
Never
```

You can set a transaction attribute for the entire EJB (in which case it applies to all methods) or you can set different transaction attributes for individual methods. The former method is much simpler and less error-prone, but setting attributes at the method level offers more flexibility. The code in the following sections shows how to set the default transaction attribute of an EJB in the EJB's deployment descriptor.

Using the @TransactionAttribute annotation

The `@javax.ejb.TransactionAttribute` annotation can be used to apply transaction attributes to your EJB's bean class. The attribute is defined using the `javax.ejb.TransactionAttributeType` Java enum:

```
public enum TransactionAttributeType {
   MANDATORY,
   REQUIRED,
   REQUIRES_NEW,
   SUPPORTS,
   NOT_SUPPORTED,
   NEVER
}

@Target({METHOD, TYPE})
public @interface TransactionAttribute {
   TransactionAttributeType value( ) default TransactionAttributeType.REQUIRED;
}
```

The `@TransactionAttribute` can be applied per method, or you can use it on the bean class to define the default transaction attribute for the entire bean class:

```
import static TransactionAttributeType.*;

@Stateless
@TransactionAttribute(NOT_SUPPORTED)
public class TravelAgentBean implements TravelAgentRemote {
```

```
    public void setCustomer(Customer cust) {...}

    @TransactionAttribute(REQUIRED)
    public TicketDO bookPassage(CreditCardDO card, double price) {
        ...
    }
}
```

In this example, the default transaction attribute will be NOT_SUPPORTED for every method of the class because we have applied the @TransactionAttribute annotation to the bean class. This default can be overridden by applying @TransactionAttribute individually to the bookPassage( ) method so that it has a REQUIRED transaction attribute.

If you do not specify any @TransactionAttribute and there is no XML deployment descriptor, the default transaction attribute will be REQUIRED. One of the ideas behind EJB 3.0 is to provide common defaults so that you do not have to be explicit about transaction demarcation. In the majority of cases, EJB methods will be transactional, especially if they are interacting with an entity manager.

Setting a transaction attribute within XML

In the XML deployment descriptor, a <container-transaction> element specifies the transaction attributes for the EJBs described in the deployment descriptor:

```
<ejb-jar xmlns="http://java.sun.com/xml/ns/javaee"
         xmlns:xsi="http://www.w3.org/2001/XMLSchema-instance"
         xsi:schemaLocation="http://java.sun.com/xml/ns/javaee
                             http://java.sun.com/xml/ns/javaee/ejb-jar_3_0.xsd"
         version=3.0>
    <assembly-descriptor>
        <container-transaction>
            <method>
                <ejb-name>TravelAgentEJB</ejb-name>
                <method-name> * </method-name>
            </method>
            <trans-attribute>NotSupported</trans-attribute>
        </container-transaction>
        <container-transaction>
            <method>
                <ejb-name>TravelAgentEJB</ejb-name>
                <method-name>bookPassage</method-name>
            </method>
            <trans-attribute>Required</trans-attribute>
        </container-transaction>
    </assembly-descriptor>
</ejb-jar>
```

This deployment descriptor specifies the transaction attributes for the TravelAgent EJB. Each <container-transaction> element specifies a method and that method's transaction attribute. The first <container-transaction> element specifies that all methods have a transaction attribute of NotSupported by default; the * is a wildcard that indicates all the methods of the TravelAgent EJB. The second <container-transaction> element overrides the default setting to specify that the bookPassage() method has a Required transaction attribute. Note that we have to specify which EJB we are referring to with the <ejb-name> element; an XML deployment descriptor can cover many EJBs.

Transaction attributes defined

Here are the definitions of the transaction attributes listed earlier. In a few of the definitions, the client transaction is described as *suspended*. This means the transaction is not propagated to the enterprise bean method being invoked; propagation of the transaction is temporarily halted until the enterprise bean method returns. To make things easier, we will talk about attribute types as if they were bean types: for example, we'll say "a Required EJB" as shorthand for "an enterprise bean with the Required transaction attribute." The attributes are:

`NotSupported`

Invoking a method on an EJB with this transaction attribute suspends the transaction until the method is completed. This means that the transaction scope is not propagated to the NotSupported EJB or to any of the EJBs it calls. Once the method on the NotSupported EJB is done, the original transaction resumes its execution.

Figure 16-1 shows that a NotSupported EJB does not propagate the client transaction when one of its methods is invoked.

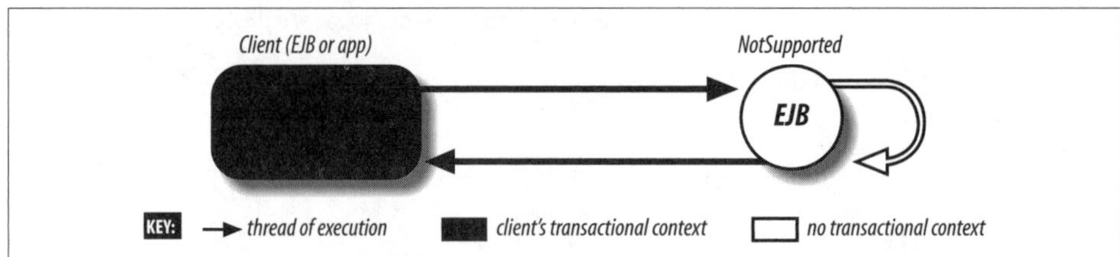

Figure 16-1. The NotSupported attribute

`Supports`

This attribute means that the enterprise bean method will be included in the transaction scope if it is invoked within a transaction. In other words, if the EJB or client that invokes the Supports EJB is part of a transaction scope, the Supports EJB and all EJBs accessed by it become part of the original transaction. However, the Supports EJB doesn't have to be part of a transaction and can interact with clients and other EJBs that are not included in a transaction scope.

Figure 16-2a shows the `Supports` EJB being invoked by a transactional client and propagating the transaction. Figure 16-2b shows the `Supports` EJB being invoked by a nontransactional client.

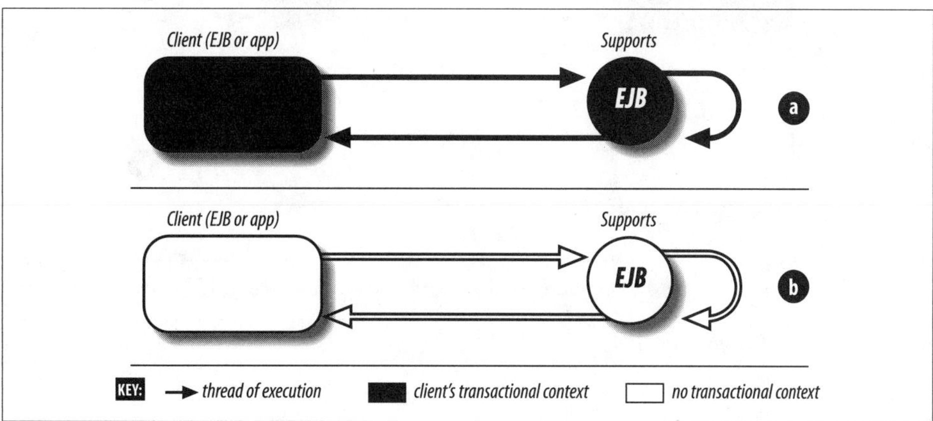

Figure 16-2. The Supports attribute

`Required`

This attribute means that the enterprise bean method must be invoked within the scope of a transaction. If the calling client or EJB is part of a transaction, the `Required` EJB is automatically included in its transaction scope. If, however, the calling client or EJB is not involved in a transaction, the `Required` EJB starts its own new transaction. The new transaction's scope covers only the `Required` EJB and all other EJBs accessed by it. Once the method invoked on the `Required` EJB is done, the new transaction's scope ends.

Figure 16-3a shows the `Required` EJB being invoked by a transactional client and propagating the transaction. Figure 16-3b shows the `Required` EJB being invoked by a nontransactional client, which causes it to start its own transaction.

`RequiresNew`

This attribute means that a new transaction is always started. Regardless of whether the calling client or EJB is part of a transaction, a method with the `RequiresNew` attribute begins a new transaction when invoked. If the calling client is already involved in a transaction, that transaction is suspended until the `RequiresNew` EJB's method call returns. The new transaction's scope covers only the `RequiresNew` EJB and all the EJBs accessed by it. Once the method invoked on the `RequiresNew` EJB is done, the new transaction's scope ends and the original transaction resumes.

Figure 16-4a shows the `RequiresNew` EJB being invoked by a transactional client. The client's transaction is suspended while the EJB executes under its own transaction. Figure 16-4b shows the `RequiresNew` EJB being invoked by a nontransactional client; the `RequiresNew` EJB executes under its own transaction.

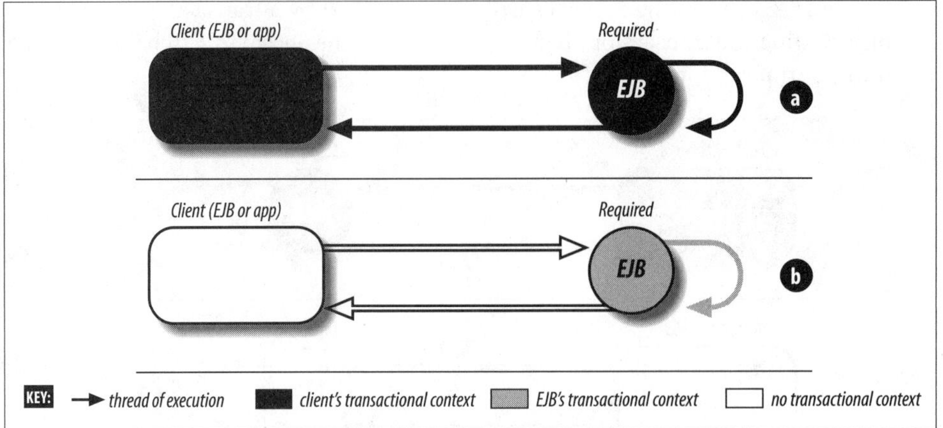

Figure 16-3. The Required attribute

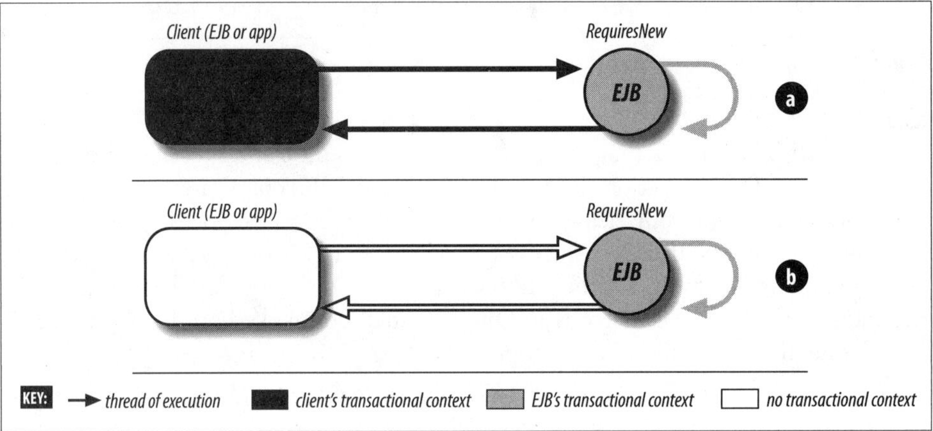

Figure 16-4. The RequiresNew attribute

`Mandatory`

This attribute means that the enterprise bean method must always be made part of the transaction scope of the calling client. The EJB may not start its own transaction; the transaction must be propagated from the client. If the calling client is not part of a transaction, the invocation will fail, throwing a `javax.ejb.EJBTransactionRequiredException`.

Figure 16-5a shows the `Mandatory` EJB invoked by a transactional client and propagating the transaction. Figure 16-5b shows the `Mandatory` EJB invoked by a nontransactional client; the method throws an `EJBTransactionRequiredException` because there is no transaction scope.

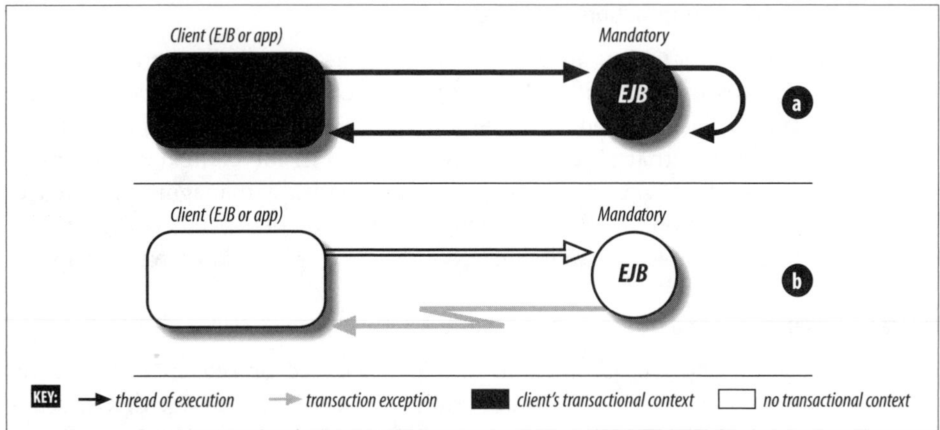

Figure 16-5. The Mandatory attribute

`Never`

This attribute means that the enterprise bean method must not be invoked within the scope of a transaction. If the calling client or EJB is part of a transaction, the `Never` EJB will throw an `EJBException`. However, if the calling client or EJB is not involved in a transaction, the `Never` EJB will execute normally without a transaction.

Figure 16-6a shows the `Never` EJB being invoked by a nontransactional client. Figure 16-6b shows the `Never` EJB being invoked by a transactional client; the method throws an `EJBException` to EJB clients because a client or EJB that is included in a transaction can never invoke the method.

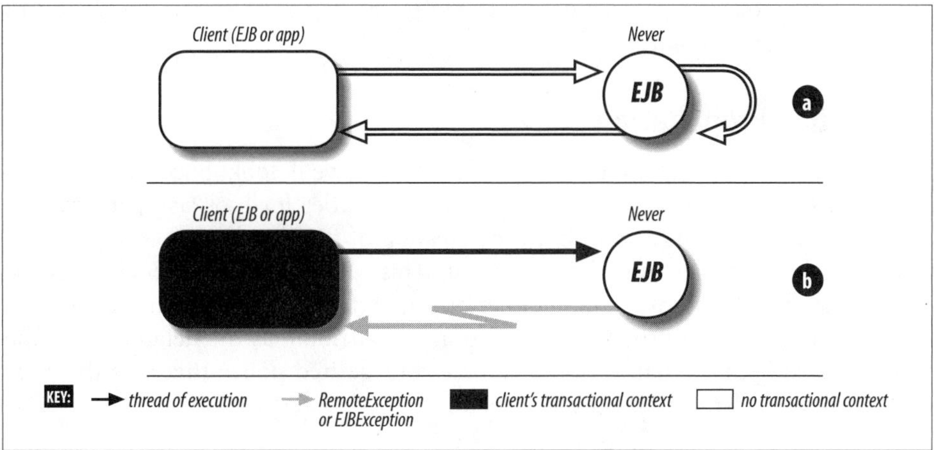

Figure 16-6. The Never attribute

EJB 3.0 persistence and transaction attributes

The EJB specification strongly advises that EntityManagers be accessed within the scope of a JTA transaction. So, if you are wrapping access to your persistent entities with EJBs, use only the Required, RequiresNew, and Mandatory transaction attributes. This restriction ensures that all database access occurs in the context of a transaction, which is important when the container is automatically managing persistence. There are valid exceptions to this rule when using extended persistence contexts with stateful session beans, but we'll talk about these exceptions later in the chapter.

Message-driven beans and transaction attributes

Message-driven beans may declare only the NotSupported or Required transaction attribute. The other transaction attributes don't make sense in message-driven beans because they apply to client-initiated transactions. The Supports, RequiresNew, Mandatory, and Never attributes are all relative to the transaction context of the client. For example, the Mandatory attribute requires the client to have a transaction in progress before calling the enterprise bean. This is meaningless for a message-driven bean, which is decoupled from the client.

The NotSupported transaction attribute indicates that the message will be processed without a transaction. The Required transaction attribute indicates that the message will be processed with a container-initiated transaction.

EJB endpoints and transaction attributes

The Mandatory transaction attribute cannot be used with EJB endpoints because an EJB endpoint does not propagate a client transaction. This may change when web service transactions become standardized, but for now, using Mandatory with an EJB endpoint method is prohibited.

Transaction Propagation

To illustrate the impact of transaction attributes, we'll look once again at the bookPassage( ) method of the TravelAgent EJB. In order for bookPassage( ) to execute as a successful transaction, both the creation of the Reservation entity and the charge to the customer must be successful. This means both operations must be included in the same transaction. If either operation fails, the entire transaction fails. We could have specified the Required transaction attribute as the default for all the EJBs involved because that attribute enforces our desired policy that all EJBs must execute within a transaction and thus ensures data consistency.

As a transaction monitor, an EJB server watches each method call in the transaction. If any of the updates fail, all the updates to all the EJBs and entities will be reversed or *rolled back*. A rollback is like an undo command. If you have worked with relational databases, the concept of a rollback should be familiar to you. Once an update is executed, you can either *commit* the update or roll it back. A commit makes the changes requested by the update permanent; a rollback aborts the update and leaves the database in its original state. Making EJBs transactional provides the same kind of rollback/commit control. For example, if the Reservation entity cannot be created by the `EntityManager`, the charge made by the ProcessPayment EJB is rolled back. Transactions make updates an all-or-nothing proposition. This ensures that the unit-of-work, like the `bookPassage( )` method, executes as intended, and it prevents inconsistent data from being written to databases.

In cases in which the container implicitly manages the transaction, the commit and rollback decisions are handled automatically. When transactions are managed explicitly within an enterprise bean or by the client, the responsibility falls on the enterprise bean or application developer to commit or roll back a transaction. Programmatic demarcation of transactions is covered in detail later in this chapter.

Let's assume that the TravelAgent EJB is created and used on a client as follows:

```
TravelAgent agent = (TravelAgent)jndi.lookup("TravelAgent");
agent.setCabinID(cabin_id);
agent.setCruiseID(cruise_id);
try {
    agent.bookPassage(card,price);
} catch(Exception e) {
    System.out.println("Transaction failed!");
}
```

Furthermore, let's assume that the `bookPassage( )` method has been given the transaction attribute `RequiresNew`. In this case, the client that invokes the `bookPassage( )` method is not itself part of a transaction. When `bookPassage( )` is invoked on the TravelAgent EJB, a new transaction is created, as dictated by the `RequiresNew` attribute. This means the TravelAgent EJB registers itself with the EJB server's transaction manager, which will manage the transaction automatically. The transaction manager coordinates transactions, propagating the transaction scope from one EJB to the next to ensure that all EJBs touched by a transaction are included in the transaction's unit-of-work. That way, the transaction manager can monitor the updates made by each enterprise bean and decide, based on the success of those updates, whether to commit all changes made by all enterprise beans to the database, or roll them all back. If a *system exception* or a *rollback application exception* is thrown by the `bookPassage( )` method, the transaction is automatically rolled back. We talk more about exceptions later in this chapter.

When the `byCredit( )` method is invoked within the `bookPassage( )` method, the ProcessPayment EJB registers with the transaction manager under the transactional context that was created for the TravelAgent EJB; the transactional context is propagated to the ProcessPayment EJB. When the new Reservation entity is persisted by the entity manager, the entity manager's persistent context is also registered with the transaction manager under the same transaction. When all the EJBs and persistence contexts are registered and their updates are made, the transaction manager checks to ensure that their updates will work. If all the updates will work, the transaction manager allows the changes to become permanent. If one of the EJBs or entity managers reports an error or fails, any changes made in either the ProcessPayment or TravelAgent EJB are rolled back by the transaction manager. Figure 16-7 illustrates the propagation and management of the TravelAgent EJB's transactional context.

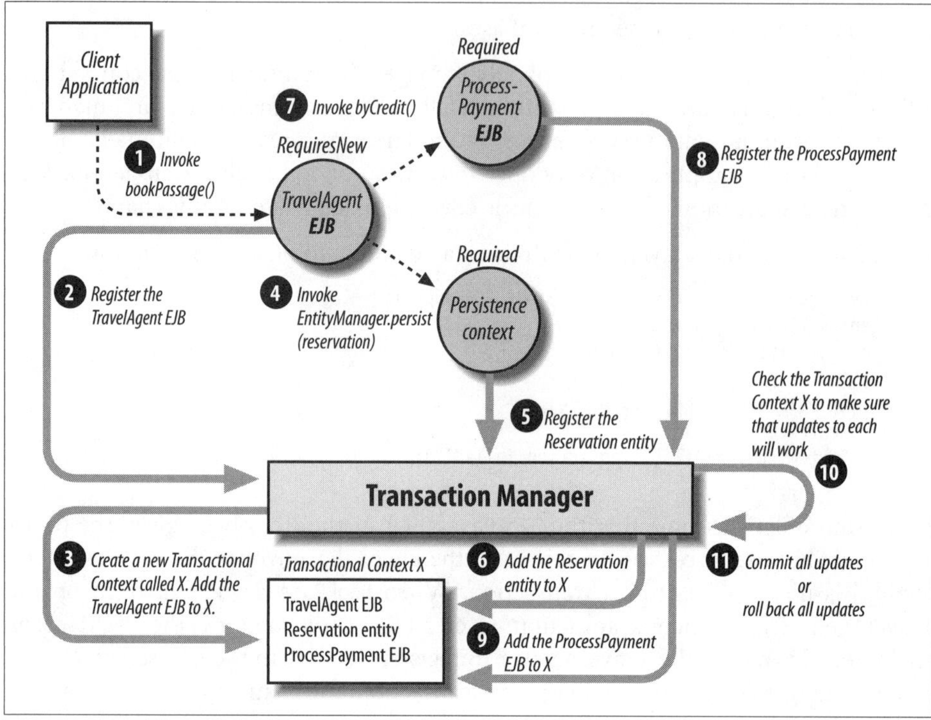

Figure 16-7. Managing the TravelAgent EJB's transactional context

In addition to managing transactions in its own environment, an EJB server can coordinate with other transactional systems. If, for example, the ProcessPayment EJB actually came from a different application server than the TravelAgent EJB, the two application servers would cooperate to manage the transaction as one unit-of-work. This is called a *distributed transaction*.* A distributed transaction requires what is called a *two-phase commit* (2-PC or TPC). A 2-PC allows transactions to be managed across different servers and resources (e.g., databases and JMS providers). The details of a 2-PC are beyond the scope of this book, but a system that supports it will not require any extra operations by an EJB or application developer. If distributed transactions are supported, the protocol for propagating transactions, as discussed

* Not all EJB servers support distributed transactions.

earlier, will be supported. In other words, as an application or EJB developer, you should not notice a difference between local and distributed transactions.

A number of books on transaction processing and 2-PC are available. Perhaps the best books on the subject are *Principles of Transaction Processing* (Morgan Kaufmann) and *Transaction Processing: Concepts and Techniques* (Morgan Kaufmann). A much lighter resource is the series of "XA Exposed" articles (I, II, and III) by Mike Spille, which you can find at *http://jroller.com/page/pyrasun/?anchor=xa_exposed*.

Transactions and persistence context propagation

There are some transaction propagation rules to consider when invoking on multiple different EJBs within the same transaction that use entity managers. For instance, if our ProcessPayment EJB was reimplemented to use Java Persistence rather than JDBC to log payments, its entity manager would share the same persistence context as the `TravelAgentBean`'s `bookPassage( )` method. This is because the `bookPassage( )` method invokes the `ProcessPaymentBean` within the same transaction. Here is a more detailed list of persistence context-propagation rules:

- When a transaction-scoped entity manager is invoked outside the scope of a transaction, it creates a persistence context for the duration of that method call. After the method call completes, any managed objects produced by the call are immediately detached. Chapter 5 gives a detailed list of methods that are allowed to be invoked outside of a transaction.
- If a transaction-scoped entity manager is invoked from within a transaction, a new persistence context is created if there isn't one already and associated with that transaction.
- If an entity manager is invoked upon and a persistence context is already associated with the transaction, use that persistence context. The persistence context is propagated between EJB invocations in the same transaction. This means that if an EJB interacts with an injected entity manager within a transaction and then invokes on another EJB within that same transaction, that EJB call will use the same enlisted persistence context.
- If an EJB with a transaction-scoped persistence context invokes on a stateful session bean that uses an extended persistence context, an error is thrown.
- If a stateful session bean with an extended persistence context calls another EJB that has injected a transaction-scoped persistence context, the extended persistence context is propagated.
- If an EJB calls another EJB with a different transaction scope, the persistence context, whether it is extended or not, is not propagated.
- If a stateful session bean with an extended persistence context calls another non-injected stateful session bean with an extended persistence context, an error is

thrown. We saw in Chapter 11 that if you inject a stateful session bean into another stateful session bean, those beans share the same extended persistence context. However, if you manually create a stateful session, there is no sharing of persistence contexts.

Isolation and Database Locking

Transaction isolation (the "I" in ACID) is a critical part of any transactional system. This section explains isolation conditions, database locking, and transaction isolation levels. These concepts are important when deploying any transactional system.

Dirty, Repeatable, and Phantom Reads

Transaction isolation is defined in terms of isolation conditions called *dirty reads*, *repeatable reads*, and *phantom reads*. These conditions describe what can happen when two or more transactions operate on the same data.* To illustrate these conditions, let's think about two separate client applications using their own instances of the TravelAgent EJB to access the same data—specifically, a cabin record with a primary key of 99. These examples revolve around the `RESERVATION` table, which is accessed by both the `bookPassage( )` method (through the Reservation entity) discussed at the beginning of this chapter and in Chapter 11, and a new `listAvailableCabins( )` method that uses EJB QL to query cabin lists:

```
public List listAvailableCabins(int bedCount)
    throws IncompleteConversationalState {
    if (cruise == null)
        throw new IncompleteConversationalState( );

    Query query = entityManager.createQuery("SELECT name FROM Cabin c
            WHERE c.ship = :ship AND c.bedCount = :beds AND
            NOT ANY (SELECT cabin from Reservation res
            WHERE res.cruise = :cruise");
    query.setParameter("ship", cruise.getShip( ));
    query.setParameter("beds", bedCount);
    query.setParameter("cruise", cruise);

    return query.getResultList( );
}
```

When two users execute these methods concurrently, different problems can surface or be avoided entirely, depending on the isolation level used by the database. For this example, assume that both methods have a transaction attribute of `Required`.

* Isolation conditions are covered in detail by the ANSI SQL-92 Specification, Document Number: ANSI X3. 135-1992 (R1998).

Dirty reads

A *dirty read* occurs when a transaction reads uncommitted changes made by a previous transaction. If the first transaction is rolled back, the data read by the second transaction becomes invalid because the rollback undoes the changes. The second transaction will not be aware that the data it has read has become invalid. Here's a scenario showing how a dirty read can occur (illustrated in Figure 16-8):

1. Time 10:00:00: Client 1 executes the `TravelAgent.bookPassage()` method. Along with the Customer and Cruise entities, Client 1 had previously chosen Cabin 99 to be included in the reservation.
2. Time 10:00:01: Client 1's TravelAgent EJB creates a Reservation entity within the `bookPassage()` method. The `EntityManager` inserts a record into the `RESERVATION` table, which reserves Cabin 99.
3. Time 10:00:02: Client 2 executes `TravelAgent.listAvailableCabins()`. Client 1 has reserved Cabin 99, so it is not in the list of available cabins that is returned from this method.
4. Time 10:00:03: Client 1's TravelAgent EJB executes the `ProcessPayment.byCredit()` method within the `bookPassage()` method. The `byCredit()` method throws an exception because the expiration date on the credit card has passed.
5. Time 10:00:04: the exception thrown by the ProcessPayment EJB causes the entire `bookPassage()` transaction to be rolled back. As a result, the record inserted into the `RESERVATION` table when the Reservation EJB was created is not made durable (i.e., it is removed). Cabin 99 is now available.

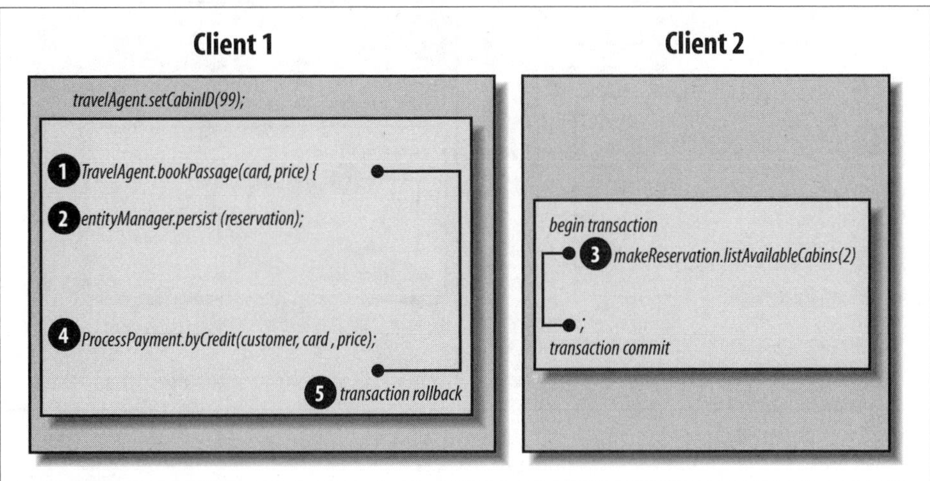

Figure 16-8. A dirty read

Client 2 is now using an invalid list of available cabins because Cabin 99 is available but not included in the list. This omission would be serious if Cabin 99 was the last available cabin, because Client 2 would inaccurately report that the cruise was booked. The customer would presumably try to book a cruise on a competing cruise line.

Repeatable reads

A *repeatable read* occurs when the data read is guaranteed to look the same if read again during the same transaction. Repeatable reads are guaranteed in one of two ways: either the data read is locked against changes, or it is a snapshot that doesn't reflect changes. If the data is locked, it cannot be changed by any other transaction until the current transaction ends. If the data is a snapshot, other transactions can change the data, but these changes will not be seen by this transaction if the read is repeated. Here's an example of a repeatable read (illustrated in Figure 16-9):

1. Time 10:00:00: Client 1 begins an explicit `javax.transaction.UserTransaction`.
2. Time 10:00:01: Client 1 executes `TravelAgent.listAvailableCabins(2)`, asking for a list of available cabins that have two beds. Cabin 99 is in the list of available cabins.
3. Time 10:00:02: Client 2 is working with an interface that manages cabins. Client 2 attempts to change the bed count on Cabin 99 from 2 to 3.
4. Time 10:00:03: Client 1 re-executes `TravelAgent.listAvailableCabins(2)`. Cabin 99 is still in the list of available cabins.

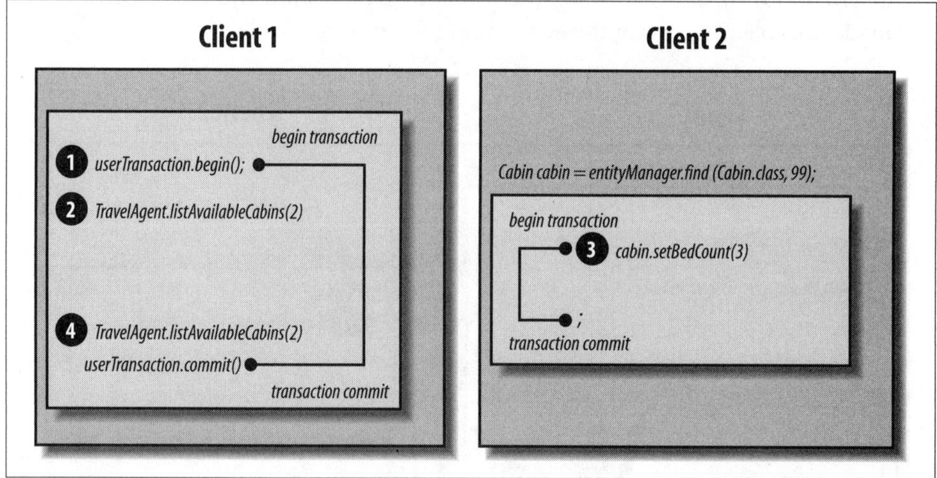

Figure 16-9. A repeatable read

This example is somewhat unusual because it uses `javax.transaction.UserTransaction`, which is covered in more detail later in this chapter. Essentially, what it does is allow a client application to control the scope of a transaction explicitly. In this case, Client 1 places transaction boundaries around both calls to listAvailableCabins() so that they are a part of the same transaction. If Client 1 didn't do this, the two listAvailableCabins() methods would have executed as separate transactions and our repeatable read condition would not have occurred.

Although Client 2 attempted to change the bed count for Cabin 99 to 3, Cabin 99 still shows up in the Client 1 call to listAvailableCabins() when a bed count of 2 is requested. Either Client 2 was prevented from making the change (because of a lock) or Client 2 was able to make the change, but Client 1 is working with a snapshot of the data that doesn't reflect that change.

A *nonrepeatable read* occurs when the data retrieved in a subsequent read within the same transaction can return different results. In other words, the subsequent read can see the changes made by other transactions.

Phantom reads

A *phantom read* occurs when new records added to the database are detectable by transactions that started prior to the insert. Queries will include records added by other transactions after their transaction has started. Here's a scenario that includes a phantom read (illustrated in Figure 16-10):

1. Time 10:00:00: Client 1 begins an explicit javax.transaction.UserTransaction.
2. Time 10:00:01: Client 1 executes TravelAgent.listAvailableCabins(2), asking for a list of available cabins that have two beds. Cabin 99 is in the list of available cabins.
3. Time 10:00:02: Client 2 executes bookPassage() and creates a reservation. The reservation inserts a new record into the RESERVATION table, reserving Cabin 99.
4. Time 10:00:03: Client 1 reexecutes TravelAgent.listAvailableCabins(2). Cabin 99 is no longer in the list of available cabins.

Client 1 places transaction boundaries around both calls to listAvailableCabins() so that they are part of the same transaction. In this case, the reservation was made between the listAvailableCabins() queries in the same transaction. Therefore, the record inserted in the RESERVATION table did not exist when the first listAvailableCabins() method was invoked, but it did exist and was visible when the second listAvailableCabins() method was invoked. The inserted record is called a *phantom record*.

Database Locks

Databases, especially relational databases, normally use several different locking techniques. The most common are *read locks*, *write locks*, and *exclusive write locks*. (I've taken the liberty of adding *"snapshots"* to this list of techniques, although this isn't a formal term.) These locking mechanisms control how transactions access data concurrently. Locking mechanisms impact the read conditions described in the

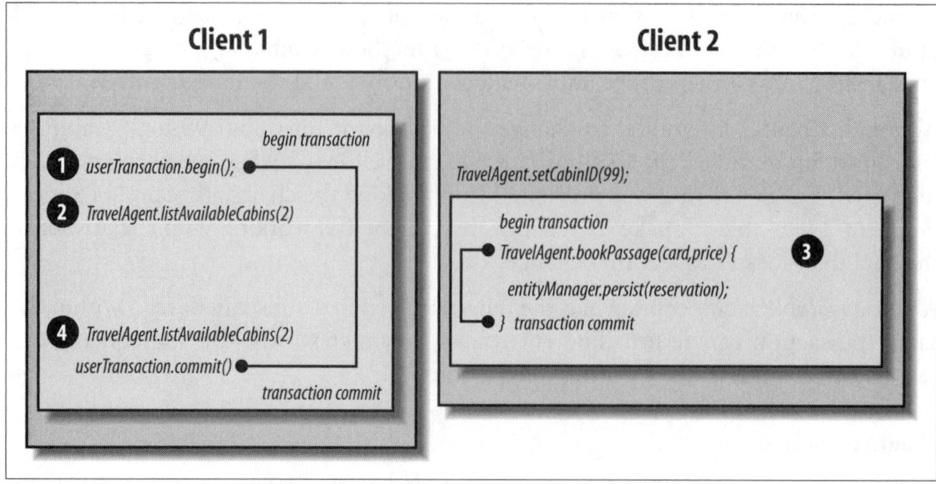

Figure 16-10. A phantom read

previous section. These types of locks are simple concepts that are addressed to a degree by the Java Persistence specification, but we'll discuss this later. Database vendors implement these locks differently, so you should understand how your database addresses these locking mechanisms to best predict how the isolation levels described in this section will work.

The four types of locks are:

Read locks
: Read locks prevent other transactions from changing data read during a transaction until the transaction ends, thus preventing nonrepeatable reads. Other transactions can read the data but not write to it. The current transaction is also prohibited from making changes. Whether a read lock locks only the records read, a block of records, or a whole table depends on the database being used.

Write locks
: Write locks are used for updates. A write lock prevents other transactions from changing the data until the current transaction is complete but allows dirty reads by other transactions and by the current transaction itself. In other words, the transaction can read its own uncommitted changes.

Exclusive write locks
: Exclusive write locks are used for updates. An exclusive write lock prevents other transactions from reading or changing the data until the current transaction is complete. It also prevents dirty reads by other transactions. Some databases do not allow transactions to read their own data while it is exclusively locked.

Snapshots

A snapshot is a frozen view of the data that is taken when a transaction begins. Some databases get around locking by providing every transaction with its own snapshot. Snapshots can prevent dirty reads, nonrepeatable reads, and phantom reads. They can be problematic because the data is not real-time data; it is old the instant the snapshot is taken.

Transaction Isolation Levels

Transaction isolation is defined in terms of the isolation conditions (dirty reads, repeatable reads, and phantom reads). Isolation levels are commonly used in database systems to describe how locking is applied to data within a transaction.* The following terms are used to discuss isolation levels:

Read Uncommitted

The transaction can read uncommitted data (i.e., data changed by a different transaction that is still in progress). Dirty reads, nonrepeatable reads, and phantom reads can occur. Bean methods with this isolation level can read uncommitted changes.

Read Committed

The transaction cannot read uncommitted data; data that is being changed by a different transaction cannot be read. Dirty reads are prevented; nonrepeatable reads and phantom reads can occur. Bean methods with this isolation level cannot read uncommitted data.

Repeatable Read

The transaction cannot change data that is being read by a different transaction. Dirty reads and nonrepeatable reads are prevented; phantom reads can occur. Bean methods with this isolation level have the same restrictions as those in the Read Committed level and can execute only repeatable reads.

Serializable

The transaction has exclusive read and update privileges; different transactions can neither read nor write to the same data. Dirty reads, nonrepeatable reads, and phantom reads are prevented. This isolation level is the most restrictive.

These isolation levels are the same as those defined for JDBC. Specifically, they map to the static final variables in the `java.sql.Connection` class. The behavior modeled by the isolation levels in the connection class is the same as the behavior described here.

* Isolation conditions are covered in detail by ANSI SQL-92 Specification, Document Number: ANSI X3.135-1992 (R1998).

The exact behavior of these isolation levels depends largely on the locking mechanism used by the underlying database or resource. How the isolation levels work depends in large part on how your database supports them.

In EJB, the deployer sets transaction isolation levels in a vendor-specific way if the container manages the transaction. The EJB developer sets the transaction isolation level if the enterprise bean manages its own transactions. Up to this point, we have discussed only container-managed transactions; we will discuss bean-managed transactions later in this chapter.

Balancing Performance Against Consistency

Generally speaking, as the isolation levels become more restrictive, the performance of the system decreases because transactions are prevented from accessing the same data. If isolation levels are very restrictive—in other words, if they are at the Serializable level—then all transactions, even simple reads, must wait in line to execute. This can result in a system that is very slow. EJB systems that process a large number of concurrent transactions and need to be very fast will therefore avoid the Serializable isolation level where it is not necessary.

Isolation levels, however, also enforce consistency of data. More restrictive isolation levels help to ensure that invalid data is not used for performing updates. The old adage, "garbage in, garbage out," applies. The Serializable isolation level ensures that data is never accessed concurrently by transactions, thus ensuring that the data is always consistent.

Choosing the correct isolation level requires some research about the database you are using and how it handles locking. You must also carefully analyze how each piece of data in your application is being used. For instance, almost every entity in the Titan Cruises reservation system has data that will seldom, if ever, change. A ship's name never changes. The number of cabins in a ship rarely changes. Cruise names and dates never change because customers have to make vacation plans based on this information. Even if these types of data do change, they would rarely affect the integrity of the system. Therefore, a low isolation level can be specified when a piece of business logic is only viewing this type of data. Reservations, on the other hand, can greatly affect the integrity of our Titan reservation system. If you look at the `bookPassage( )` method carefully, you may see that it is quite possible for the system to double-book a cabin of a particular cruise. If two customers are making a reservation concurrently for the same cabin and cruise, then a double booking would happen because there are no checks in `bookPassage( )` to prevent it. Let's fix this problem:

```
public TicketDO bookPassage(CreditCardDO card, double price)
    throws IncompleteConversationalState {

    if (customer == null || cruise == null || cabin == null) {
        throw new IncompleteConversationalState( );
    }
```

```
    try {
        Query isReserved = entityManager.createQuery(
           "select count(res) from Reservation res" +
            "where res.cabin = :cabin AND res.cruise = :cruise");
        isReserved.setParameter("cabin", cabin);
        isReserved.setParameter("cruise", cruise);
        int count = (Integer) isReserved.getSingleResult( );
        if (count > 0) throw new EJBException("Cabin already reserved");

        Reservation reservation = new Reservation(
            customer, cruise, cabin, price);
        entityManager.persist(reservation);

        this.process.byCredit(customer, card, price);

        TicketDO ticket = new TicketDO(customer,cruise,cabin,price);

        return ticket;
    } catch(Exception e) {
        throw new EJBException(e);
    }
}
```

What we've done is added an isReserved query to bookPassage( ) that will check to see if a cabin has already been reserved for a particular cruise. If that query returns any number of cabins, then the reservation cannot be made. If the bookPassage( ) method interacts with the EntityManager and data source using a Serializable isolation level database connection, then executing the isReserved query will obtain the necessary locks in the database to ensure that the value returned by this query will be valid for the duration of the transaction. No isolation level can be used other than Serializable because the other levels do not adequately isolate the query from changes made by other transactions.

Controlling isolation levels

Different EJB servers allow different levels of granularity for isolation levels; some servers defer this responsibility to the database. Most EJB servers and EntityManager implementations control the isolation level through the resource access API (e.g., JDBC and JMS) and may allow different resources to have different isolation levels. However, they will generally require a consistent isolation level for access to the same resource within a single transaction. Consult your vendor's documentation to find out the level of control your server offers.

Bean-managed transactions in session beans and message-driven beans, however, allow you to specify the transaction isolation level using the database's API. The JDBC API, for instance, provides a mechanism for specifying the isolation level of the database connection. For example:

```
DataSource source = (javax.sql.DataSource)
    jndiCntxt.lookup("java:comp/env/jdbc/titanDB");
```

```
Connection con = source.getConnection( );
con.setTransactionIsolation(Connection.TRANSACTION_SERIALIZABLE);
```

You can have different isolation levels for different resources within the same transaction, but all enterprise beans using the same resource in a transaction should use the same isolation level.

Optimistic Locking

The `isReserved` query we used earlier in combination with the `Serializable` isolation level allowed the `bookPassage( )` method to prevent double bookings. With this query in place, there will be far fewer angry customers. This solution for double bookings has a serious performance drawback, though. In order for the `isReserved` query to work, no other reservation referencing the cabin the customer is trying to book, or the query may be invalid. In most databases, an exclusive lock would need to be obtained on the entire `RESERVATION` table to make this work. This means that any `bookPassage( )` or `listAvailableCabin( )` invocations could happen only one at a time. This is a huge scalability problem. As Titan's business grows and adds more ships, cruises, and customers, our system will not be able to handle the new processing load, no matter how many machines we buy or CPUs we upgrade. This is because there will be a high contention on a shared resource (i.e., on the `RESERVATION` table).

So, how can we solve this concurrency problem? One solution is to use the *optimistic locking* design pattern. Optimistic locking isn't locking in the traditional sense. The way it works is that in our `bookPassage( )` method, we assume that no other customer is trying to book the same cabin at the same time. Then, at transaction commit time, we let the database resolve whether the cabin has been reserved. If it has been reserved, we throw an exception and roll back the transaction. In other words, we are being optimistic that no other customer is reserving the same cabin. How does this work? How does this avoid table-level locks? Well, to use optimistic locking we have to redesign our Titan reservation system a little and use a special feature of Java Persistence.

The first thing we need to do is create a new entity class that holds information about a particular cabin for a particular cruise. Let's call this new entity class `CruiseCabin`. A `CruiseCabin` entity class will be created for each cabin for each cruise:

```
package com.titan.domain;

import javax.persistence.*;

@Entity
public class CruiseCabin {
   private int id;
   private Cabin cabin;
   private Cruise cruise;
   private boolean isReserved;
   private long version;
```

```
    @Id @GeneratedValue
    public int getId( ) {
       return id;
    }
    public void setId(int id) {
       this.id = id;
    }

    @OneToOne
    public Cabin getCabin( ) {
       return cabin;
    }
    public void setCabin(Cabin cabin) {
       this.cabin = cabin;
    }

    @OneToOne
    public Cruise getCruise( ) {
       return cruise;
    }

    public void setCruise(Cruise cruise) {
       this.cruise = cruise;
    }

    public boolean getIsReserved( ) {
       return isReserved;
    }
    public void setIsReserved(boolean is) {
      isReserved = is;
    }

    @Version
    protected long getVersion( ) {
       return version;
    }
    protected void setVersion(long version) {
       this.version = version;
    }
}
```

The CruiseCabin entity class references the cabin and cruise to which it belongs. The isReserved property lets us know whether somebody has reserved the cabin for that cruise. The new and interesting property is the version property, which is annotated with @javax.persistence.Version. An @Version property is a column in the CruiseCabin table that will hold a version ID of a particular CruiseCabin row. Whenever the CruiseCabin entity class is updated, the version column is incremented. When a transaction beginning the commit process and business logic has updated the CruiseCabin, the entity manager first checks to see if the version property of the in-memory CruiseCabin instance matches the version column currently stored in the database. If the versions match, then the version property is incremented. If they don't match, then the entity manager throws an exception and the whole transaction rolls back. Let's change bookPassage( ) to use this new feature:

```
public TicketDO bookPassage(CreditCardDO card, double price)
    throws IncompleteConversationalState {

    if (customer == null || cruise == null || cabin == null) {
        throw new IncompleteConversationalState( );
    }
    try {
        Query getCruiseCabin = entityManager.createQuery(
           "SELECT cc FROM CruiseCabin cc WHERE" +
           "cc.cabin = :cabin AND cc.cruise = :cruise");
        getCruiseCabin.setParameter("cabin", cabin);
        getCruiseCabin.setParameter("cruise", cruise);
        CruiseCabin cc = (CruiseCabin)getCruiseCabin.getSingleResult( );

        if (cc.getIsReserved( ))
           throw new EJBException("Cabin is already reserved for cruise");
        cc.setIsReserved(true);

        Reservation reservation = new Reservation(
            customer, cruise, cabin, price);
        entityManager.persist(reservation);

        this.process.byCredit(customer, card, price);

        TicketDO ticket = new TicketDO(customer,cruise,cabin,price);

        return ticket;
    } catch(Exception e) {
        throw new EJBException(e);
    }
}
```

The bookPassage( ) method conducts a query for the relevant CruiseCabin entity class. If it is reserved, it aborts the transaction. If not, then it sets the isReserved property and continues with the rest of the method. At transaction commit time, the entity manager invokes an SQL query that both verifies and increments the version column of the entity. Let's assume that the queried CruiseCabin has an ID of 1 and the current version is 101:

```
update CRUISE_CABIN set isReserved=true, version=version + 1
where id = 1 AND version = 101;
```

If this update returns zero modified rows, then the entity manager knows that the CruiseCabin has been updated by another transaction and a concurrency error has occurred. In this error condition, it throws the javax.persistence.OptimisticLock-Exception and rolls back the transaction. Otherwise, the transaction completes successfully, and the queried CruiseCabin is updated as reserved and its version property is incremented. This optimistic locking solution creates a quick *write-lock* on one row in our database instead of the vastly unscalable table lock in the Serializable solution that was presented earlier in this chapter.

It should be noted that the optimistic locking design pattern does not work all the time. If you have a row in your database that has a high concurrent write contention, then it is probably less efficient to use the optimistic locking pattern because it will create a lot of rollbacks, which create a lot of overhead in your system. In that scenario, the Serializable solution is possibly more scalable. A redesign of your data model is probably more appropriate in this situation, however. If you have high concurrent access to one particular row in your database, then your system probably won't scale much anyway.

Programmatic Locking

The EntityManager interface has a specific lock( ) method for performing entity locks. To use it, you pass in the entity object you want to lock and indicate whether you want a read or write lock:

```
package javax.persistence;

public enum LockModeType{
   READ,
   WRITE
}

public interface EntityManager {
   void lock(Object entity, LockModeType type);
}
```

LockModeType.READ ensures that no dirty and nonrepeatable reads can occur on the locked entity. LockModeType.WRITE has the same semantics as READ, but it also forces an increment of the entity's @Version property. To implement these semantics, a database row lock is usually performed (i.e., SELECT ... FOR UPDATE).

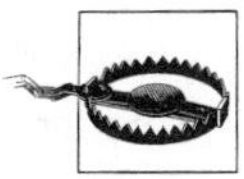

Vendor implementations are not required to support locking on entities that do not have an @Version property.

Programmatic locking becomes important when you want to ensure nonrepeatable reads on entity beans that may be read within the transaction but not updated.

Nontransactional EJBs

Beans outside of a transaction's scope normally provide some kind of stateless service that does not manipulate data in a data store. While these types of enterprise beans may be necessary as utilities during a transaction, they do not need to meet the ACID requirements. Consider a nontransactional stateless session bean, the Quote

EJB, which provides live stock quotes. This EJB may respond to a request from an EJB involved in a stock purchase transaction. The success or failure of the stock purchase as a transaction will not impact the state or operations of the Quote EJB, so it does not need to be part of the transaction. Beans that are involved in transactions are subjected to the isolated ACID property, which means that their services *cannot* be shared during the life of the transaction. Making an enterprise bean transactional can be expensive at runtime. Declaring an EJB to be nontransactional (i.e., `NotSupported`) leaves it out of the transaction scope, which may improve the performance and availability of that service.

Explicit Transaction Management

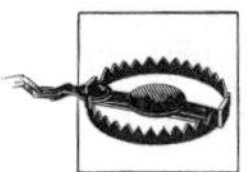

Although this section covers JTA, it is strongly recommended that you do not attempt to manage transactions explicitly. Through transaction attributes, Enterprise JavaBeans provides a comprehensive and simple mechanism for delimiting transactions at the method level and propagating transactions automatically. Only developers with a thorough understanding of transactional systems should attempt to use JTA with EJB.

EJB provides implicit transaction management on the method level: we can define transactions that are delimited by the scope of the method being executed. This is one of the primary advantages of EJB over cruder distributed object implementations; it reduces complexity, and therefore, programmer error. In addition, declarative transaction demarcation, as used in EJB, separates the transactional behavior from the business logic; a change to transactional behavior does not require changes to the business logic. In rare situations, however, it may be necessary to take control of transactions explicitly.

Explicit management of transactions is normally accomplished using the OMG's Object Transaction Service (OTS) or the Java implementation of OTS, the Java Transaction Service (JTS). OTS and JTS provide APIs that allow developers to work with transaction managers and resources (e.g., databases and JMS providers) directly. While the JTS implementation of OTS is robust and complete, it is not the easiest API to work with; it requires clean and intentional control over the bounds of enrollment in transactions.

Enterprise JavaBeans supports a much simpler API, the Java Transaction API (JTA), for working with transactions. This API is implemented by the `javax.transaction` package. JTA actually consists of two components: a high-level transactional client interface and a low-level X/Open XA interface. We are concerned with the high-level client interface, since it is accessible to enterprise beans and is recommended for client applications. The low-level XA interface is used by the EJB server and container to coordinate transactions with resources such as databases.

Your use of explicit transaction management will probably focus on one simple interface: javax.transaction.UserTransaction. UserTransaction allows you to manage the scope of a transaction explicitly. Here's how explicit demarcation might be used in an EJB or client application:

```
TravelAgent tr1 = (TravelAgent)getInitialContext( ).lookup("TravelAgentRemote");
tr1.setCruiseID(cruiseID);
tr1.setCabinID(cabin_1);
tr1.setCustomer(customer0;
TravelAgent tr2 = (TravelAgent)getInitialContext( ).lookup("TravelAgentRemote");;
tr2.setCruiseID(cruiseID);
tr2.setCabinID(cabin_2);
tr2.setCustomer(customer);

javax.transaction.UserTransaction tran = ...; // Get the UserTransaction.
tran.begin( );
tr1.bookPassage(visaCard,price);
tr2.bookPassage(visaCard,price);
tran.commit( );
```

The client application needs to book two cabins for the same customer. In this case, the customer is purchasing a cabin for himself and his children. The customer does not want to book either cabin unless he can get both, so the client application is designed to include both bookings in the same transaction. This is accomplished by explicitly marking the transaction's boundaries through use of the javax.transaction.UserTransaction object. Each enterprise bean method invoked by the current thread between the UserTransaction.begin( ) and UserTransaction.commit( ) methods is included in the same transaction scope, according to the transaction attributes of the enterprise bean methods invoked.

Obviously, this example is contrived, but the point it makes is clear. Transactions can be controlled directly, instead of depending on method scope to delimit them. The advantage of using explicit transaction demarcation is that it gives the client control over the bounds of a transaction. The client, in this example, may be a client application or another enterprise bean.* In either case, the same javax.transaction.UserTransaction is used, but it is obtained from different sources depending on whether it is needed on the client or in an enterprise bean.

Java Enterprise Edition (Java EE) specifies how a client application can obtain a UserTransaction object using JNDI. Here's how a client obtains a UserTransaction object if the EJB container is part of a Java EE system (Java EE and its relationship with EJB are covered in more detail in Chapter 18):

```
Context jndiCntx = new InitialContext( );
UserTransaction tran = (UserTransaction)
    jndiCntx.lookup("java:comp/UserTransaction");
```

* Only beans declared as managing their own transactions (bean-managed transaction beans) can use the UserTransaction interface.

```
utx.begin( );
...
utx.commit( );
```

Enterprise beans can also manage transactions explicitly. Only session beans and message-driven beans that define a `javax.ejb.TransactionManagementType` of `Bean` using the `@javax.ejb.TransactionManager` annotation can manage their own transactions. Enterprise beans that manage their own transactions are frequently referred to as bean-managed transaction (BMT) beans. Entity beans can never be BMT beans. BMT beans do not declare transaction attributes for their methods. Here's how a session bean declares that it will manage transactions explicitly:

```
import javax.ejb.* ;
import javax.annotation.* ;
import javax.transaction.UserTransaction;

@Stateless
@TransactionManagement(TransactionManagerType.BEAN)
public class HypotheticalBean implements HypotheticalLocal {
...
}
```

To manage its own transaction, an enterprise bean needs to obtain a `UserTransaction` object. An enterprise bean obtains a reference to the `UserTransaction` from the `EJBContext` or from `@Resource` injection:

```
import javax.ejb.* ;
import javax.annotation.* ;
import javax.transaction.UserTransaction;

@Stateless
@TransactionManagement(TransactionManagerType.BEAN)
public class HypotheticalBean implements HypotheticalLocal {
    @Resource SessionContext ejbContext;

    public void someMethod( ) {
        try {
            UserTransaction ut = ejbContext.getUserTransaction( );
            ut.begin( );

            // Do some work.

            ut.commit( );
    } catch(IllegalStateException ise) {...}
        catch(SystemException se) {...}
        catch(TransactionRolledbackException tre) {...}
        catch(HeuristicRollbackException hre) {...}
        catch(HeuristicMixedException hme) {...}
```

Alternatively, the `UserTransaction` can be injected directly into the bean:

```
import javax.ejb.* ;
import javax.annotation.* ;
import javax.transaction.UserTransaction;
```

```
@Stateless
@TransactionManagement(TransactionManagerType.BEAN)
public class HypotheticalBean implements HypotheticalLocal {
    @Resource UserTransaction ut;
...
}
```

Finally, an enterprise bean can also access the UserTransaction from the JNDI ENC. The enterprise bean performs the lookup using the java:comp/env/UserTransaction context:

```
InitialContext jndiCntx = new InitialContext( );
UserTransaction tran = (UserTransaction)
    jndiCntx.lookup("java:comp/env/UserTransaction");
```

Transaction Propagation in Bean-Managed Transactions

With stateless session beans, transactions that are managed using UserTransaction must be started and completed within the same method. In other words, UserTransaction transactions cannot be started in one method and ended in another. This makes sense because stateless session bean instances are shared across many clients; while one stateless instance may service a client's first request, a completely different instance may service a subsequent request by the same client. With stateful session beans, however, a transaction can begin in one method and be committed in another because a stateful session bean is used by only one client. Therefore, a stateful session bean can associate itself with a transaction across several different client-invoked methods. As an example, imagine the TravelAgent EJB as a BMT bean. In the following code, the transaction is started in the setCruiseID( ) method and completed in the bookPassage( ) method. This allows the TravelAgent EJB's methods to be associated with the same transaction. The definition of the TravelAgentBean class looks like this:

```
import com.titan.reservation.*;

import javax.ejb.EJBException;

@Stateful
@TransactionManagement(TransactionManagerType.BEAN)
public class TravelAgentBean implements TravelAgentRemote {
    ...
    public void setCruiseID(Integer cruiseID) {
        try {
            ejbContext.getUserTransaction().begin( );
            cruise = entityManager.getReference(Cruise.class, cruiseID);
        } catch(Exception re) {
            throw new EJBException(re);
        }

    }
    public TicketDO bookPassage(CreditCardDO card, double price)
        throws IncompleteConversationalState {
```

```
            try {
                if (ejbContext.getUserTransaction().getStatus( ) !=
                    javax.transaction.Status.STATUS_ACTIVE) {

                    throw new EJBException("Transaction is not active");
                }

            } catch(javax.transaction.SystemException se) {
                 throw new EJBException(se);
            }

            if (customer == null || cruise == null || cabin == null)
            {
                throw new IncompleteConversationalState( );
            }
            try {
                Reservation reservation =
                    new Reservation(customer, cruise, cabin, price);

                process.byCredit(customer, card, price);

                TicketDO ticket = new TicketDO(customer,cruise,cabin,price);

                ejbContext.getUserTransaction().commit( );

                return ticket;
            } catch(Exception e) {
                throw new EJBException(e);
            }
        }
        ...
    }
```

Repeated calls to the `EJBContext.getUserTransaction( )` method return a reference to the same `UserTransaction` object. The container is required to retain the association between the transaction and the stateful bean instance across multiple client calls, until the transaction terminates.

In the `bookPassage( )` method, we can check the status of the transaction to ensure that it is still active. If the transaction is no longer active, we throw an exception. The use of `getStatus( )` is covered in more detail later in this chapter.

When a client that is already involved in a transaction invokes a bean-managed transaction method, the client's transaction is suspended until the method returns. This suspension occurs regardless of whether the BMT bean explicitly started its own transaction within the method or the transaction was started in a previous method invocation. The client transaction is always suspended until the BMT method returns.

Transaction control across methods is strongly discouraged because it can result in improperly managed transactions and long-lived transactions that lock up or even leak resources.

Message-driven beans and bean-managed transactions

Message-driven beans also have the option of managing their own transactions. In the case of MDBs, the scope of the transaction must begin and end within the onMessage( ) method—it is not possible for a bean-managed transaction to span onMessage( ) calls.

You can transform the ReservationProcessor EJB you created in Chapter 12 into a BMT bean simply by changing its javax.ejb.TransactionManagementType value to Bean:

```
@MessageDriven
@TransactionManagement(BEAN)
public class ReservationProcessorBean implements MessageListener {
...
}
```

In this case, the ReservationProcessorBean class would be modified to use javax.transaction.UserTransaction to mark the beginning and end of the transaction:

```
@MessageDriven
@TransactionManagement(BEAN)
public class ReservationProcessorBean implements javax.jms.MessageListener {
    @PersistenceContext(unitName="titanDB")
    private EntityManager em;

    @EJB
    private ProcessPaymentLocal process;

    @Resource(name="ConnectionFactory")
    private ConnectionFactory connectionFactory;

    @Resource UserTransaction ut;

    public void onMessage(Message message) {
        try {
            ut.begin( );

            MapMessage reservationMsg = (MapMessage)message;

            int customerPk = reservationMsg.getInt("CustomerID");
            int cruisePk = reservationMsg.getInt("CruiseID");
            int cabinPk = reservationMsg.getInt("CabinID");

            double price = reservationMsg.getDouble("Price");

            // get the credit card
            Date expirationDate =
                new Date(reservationMsg.getLong("CreditCardExpDate"));
            String cardNumber = reservationMsg.getString("CreditCardNum");
            String cardType = reservationMsg.getString("CreditCardType");
            CreditCardDO card = new CreditCardDO(cardNumber,
                expirationDate, cardType);
```

```
            Customer customer = em.getReference(Customer.class, customerPk);
            Cruise cruise = em.getReference(Cruise.class, cruisePk);
            Cabin cabin = em.getReference(Cabin.class, cabinPk);

            Reservation reservation = new Reservation(
                          customer, cruise, cabin, price, new Date( ));
            em.persist(reservation);

            process.byCredit(customer, card, price);

            TicketDO ticket = new TicketDO(customer,cruise,cabin,price);

            deliverTicket(reservationMsg, ticket);

            ut.commit( );

        } catch(Exception e) {
            throw new EJBException(e);
        }
    }

    ...
```

It is important to understand that in a BMT, the message consumed by the MDB is not part of the transaction. When an MDB uses container-managed transactions, the message it is handling is a part of the transaction, so if the transaction is rolled back, the consumption of the message is also rolled back, forcing the JMS provider to redeliver the message. But with bean-managed transactions, the message is not part of the transaction, so if the BMT is rolled back, the JMS provider will not be aware of the transaction's failure. However, all is not lost, because the JMS provider can still rely on message acknowledgment to determine if the message was successfully delivered.

The EJB container will acknowledge the message if the `onMessage( )` method returns successfully. If, however, a `RuntimeException` is thrown by the `onMessage( )` method, the container will not acknowledge the message and the JMS provider will suspect a problem and probably attempt to redeliver the message. If redelivery of a message is important when a transaction fails, your best course of action is to ensure that the `onMessage( )` method throws an `EJBException` so that the container will *not* acknowledge the message received from the JMS provider.

Vendors use proprietary (declarative) mechanisms to specify the number of attempts to redeliver messages to BMT/`NotSupported` MDBs that "fail" to acknowledge receipt. The JMS-MDB provider may provide a "dead message" area into which such messages will be placed if they cannot be successfully processed according to the retry count. Administrators can monitor the dead message area so that delivered messages can be detected and handled manually.

Other than the message, everything between the `UserTransaction.begin()` and `UserTransaction.commit()` methods is part of the same transaction. This includes creating a new Reservation EJB and processing the credit card using the ProcessPayment EJB. If a transaction failure occurs, these operations will be rolled back. The transaction also includes the use of the JMS API in the `deliverTicket()` method to send the ticket message. If a transaction failure occurs, the ticket message will not be sent.

Heuristic Decisions

Transactions are normally controlled by a *transaction manager* (often the EJB server), which manages the ACID characteristics across several enterprise beans, databases, and servers. The transaction manager uses a two-phase commit (2-PC) to manage transactions. 2-PC is a protocol for managing transactions that commits updates in two stages. 2-PC is complex, but basically it requires that servers and databases cooperate through an intermediary—the transaction manager—in order to ensure that all of the data is made durable together. Some EJB servers support 2-PC and others do not, and the value of this transaction mechanism is a source of some debate. The important point to remember is that a transaction manager controls the transaction; based on the results of a poll against the resources (databases, JMS providers, and other resources), it decides whether all the updates should be committed or rolled back. A *heuristic decision* takes place when one of the resources makes a unilateral decision to commit or roll back without permission from the transaction manager. When a heuristic decision has been made, the atomicity of the transaction is lost and data-integrity errors can occur.

`UserTransaction` throws a few different exceptions related to heuristic decisions; these are discussed in the following section.

UserTransaction

EJB servers are required to support `UserTransaction` but are not required to support the rest of JTA, nor are they required to use JTS for their transaction service. `UserTransaction` is defined as follows:

```
public interface javax.transaction.UserTransaction {

    public abstract void begin( ) throws IllegalStateException, SystemException;
    public abstract void commit( ) throws IllegalStateException, SystemException,
        TransactionRolledbackException, HeuristicRollbackException,
        HeuristicMixedException;
    public abstract int getStatus( );
    public abstract void rollback( ) throws IllegalStateException, SecurityException,
        SystemException;
    public abstract void setRollbackOnly( ) throws IllegalStateException,
        SystemException;
    public abstract void setTransactionTimeout(int seconds)
        throws SystemException;

}
```

Here's what the methods defined in this interface do:

`begin()`
: Invoking the `begin()` method creates a new transaction. The thread that executes the `begin()` method is immediately associated with the new transaction, which is then propagated to any EJB that supports existing transactions. The `begin()` method can throw one of two checked exceptions. An `IllegalStateException` is thrown when `begin()` is called by a thread that is already associated with a transaction. You must complete any transactions associated with that thread before beginning a new transaction. A `SystemException` is thrown if the transaction manager (i.e., the EJB server) encounters an unexpected error condition.

`commit()`
: The `commit()` method completes the transaction that is associated with the current thread. When `commit()` is executed, the current thread is no longer associated with a transaction. This method can throw several checked exceptions. An `IllegalStateException` is thrown if the current thread is not associated with a transaction. A `SystemException` is thrown if the transaction manager (the EJB server) encounters an unexpected error condition. A `TransactionRolledbackException` is thrown when the entire transaction is rolled back rather than committed; this can happen if one of the resources was unable to perform an update or if the `UserTransaction.rollBackOnly()` method was called. A `HeuristicRollbackException` indicates that one or more resources made a heuristic decision to roll back the transaction. A `HeuristicMixedException` indicates resources made heuristic decisions to both roll back and commit the transaction; that is, some resources decided to roll back and others decided to commit.

`rollback()`
: The `rollback()` method is invoked to roll back the transaction and undo updates. The `rollback()` method can throw one of three different checked exceptions. A `SecurityException` is thrown if the thread using the `UserTransaction` object is not allowed to roll back the transaction. An `IllegalStateException` is thrown if the current thread is not associated with a transaction. A `SystemException` is thrown if the transaction manager (the EJB server) encounters an unexpected error condition.

`setRollbackOnly()`
: The `setRollbackOnly()` method is invoked to mark the transaction for rollback. This means that, regardless of whether the updates executed within the transaction succeed, the transaction must be rolled back when completed. This method can be invoked by any BMT EJB participating in the transaction, or by the client application. The `setRollBackOnly()` method can throw one of two checked exceptions. An `IllegalStateException` is thrown if the current thread is not associated with a transaction; a `SystemException` is thrown if the transaction manager (the EJB server) encounters an unexpected error condition.

`setTransactionTimeout(int seconds)`
: The `setTransactionTimeout(int seconds)` method sets the lifespan of a transaction, i.e., how long it will live before timing out. The transaction must complete before the transaction timeout is reached. If this method is not called, the transaction manager (EJB server) automatically sets the timeout. If this method is invoked with a value of `0` seconds, the default timeout of the transaction manager will be used. This method must be invoked after the `begin( )` method. A `SystemException` is thrown if the transaction manager (EJB server) encounters an unexpected error condition.

`getStatus( )`
: The `getStatus( )` method returns an integer that can be compared to constants defined in the `javax.transaction.Status` interface. A sophisticated programmer can use this method to determine the status of a transaction associated with a `UserTransaction` object. A `SystemException` is thrown if the transaction manager (EJB server) encounters an unexpected error condition.

Status

`Status` is a simple interface that contains constants but no methods. Its sole purpose is to provide a set of constants that describe the status of a transactional object—in this case, `UserTransaction`:

```
interface javax.transaction.Status
{
    public final static int STATUS_ACTIVE;
    public final static int STATUS_COMMITTED;
    public final static int STATUS_COMMITTING;
    public final static int STATUS_MARKED_ROLLBACK;
    public final static int STATUS_NO_TRANSACTION;
    public final static int STATUS_PREPARED;
    public final static int STATUS_PREPARING;
    public final static int STATUS_ROLLEDBACK;
    public final static int STATUS_ROLLING_BACK;
    public final static int STATUS_UNKNOWN;
}
```

The value returned by `getStatus( )` tells the client using the `UserTransaction` the status of a transaction. Here's what the constants mean:

`STATUS_ACTIVE`
: An active transaction is associated with the `UserTransaction` object. This status is returned after a transaction has been started and prior to a transaction manager beginning a two-phase commit. (Transactions that have been suspended are still considered active.)

`STATUS_COMMITTED`
: A transaction is associated with the `UserTransaction` object; the transaction has been committed. It is likely that heuristic decisions have been made; otherwise,

the transaction would have been destroyed and the STATUS_NO_TRANSACTION constant would have been returned instead.

STATUS_COMMITTING
: A transaction is associated with the UserTransaction object; the transaction is in the process of committing. The UserTransaction object returns this status if the transaction manager has decided to commit but has not yet completed the process.

STATUS_MARKED_ROLLBACK
: A transaction is associated with the UserTransaction object; the transaction has been marked for rollback, perhaps as a result of a UserTransaction.setRollbackOnly( ) operation invoked somewhere else in the application.

STATUS_NO_TRANSACTION
: No transaction is currently associated with the UserTransaction object. This occurs after a transaction has completed or if no transaction has been created. This value is returned instead of throwing an IllegalStateException.

STATUS_PREPARED
: A transaction is associated with the UserTransaction object. The transaction has been prepared, which means that the first phase of the two-phase commit process has completed.

STATUS_PREPARING
: A transaction is associated with the UserTransaction object; the transaction is in the process of preparing, which means that the transaction manager is in the middle of executing the first phase of the two-phase commit.

STATUS_ROLLEDBACK
: A transaction is associated with the UserTransaction object; the outcome of the transaction has been identified as a rollback. It is likely that heuristic decisions have been made; otherwise, the transaction would have been destroyed and the STATUS_NO_TRANSACTION constant would have been returned.

STATUS_ROLLING_BACK
: A transaction is associated with the UserTransaction object; the transaction is in the process of rolling back.

STATUS_UNKNOWN
: A transaction is associated with the UserTransaction object; its current status cannot be determined. This is a transient condition and subsequent invocations will ultimately return a different status.

EJBContext Rollback Methods

Only BMT beans can access UserTransaction from EJBContext and the JNDI ENC. Container-managed transaction (CMT) beans cannot use UserTransaction. CMT beans use the setRollbackOnly( ) and getRollbackOnly( ) methods of EJBContext to interact with the current transaction instead. Later in this chapter, we'll see that exceptions can be used to roll back the transaction.

The setRollbackOnly( ) method gives an enterprise bean the power to veto a transaction, which can be used if the enterprise bean detects a condition that would cause inconsistent data to be committed when the transaction completes. Once an enterprise bean invokes the setRollbackOnly( ) method, the current transaction is marked for rollback and cannot be committed by any other participant in the transaction, including the container.

The getRollbackOnly( ) method returns true if the current transaction has been marked for rollback. This information can be used to avoid executing work that would not be committed anyway. For example, if an exception is thrown and captured within an enterprise bean method, getRollbackOnly( ) can be used to determine whether the exception caused the current transaction to be rolled back. If it did, there is no sense in continuing the processing. If it did not, the EJB has an opportunity to correct the problem and retry the task that failed. Only expert EJB developers should attempt to retry tasks within a transaction. Alternatively, if the exception did not cause a rollback (i.e., getRollbackOnly( ) returns false), a rollback can be forced using the setRollbackOnly( ) method.

BMT beans must *not* use the setRollbackOnly( ) and getRollbackOnly( ) methods of the EJBContext. BMT beans should use the getStatus( ) and rollback( ) methods on the UserTransaction object to check for rollback and force a rollback, respectively.

Exceptions and Transactions

Exceptions have a large impact on the outcome of transactions.

Application Exceptions Versus System Exceptions

System exceptions represent unknown internal errors. The EJB container throws system exceptions when it encounters an internal application server failure. Business logic can throw system exceptions when it wants to abort the business process. Application exceptions are exceptions that are part of your business logic. They denote a strongly typed definition of a specific business problem or failure but do not necessarily abort or roll back the business process.

System exceptions

System exceptions include java.lang.RuntimeException and its subclasses. EJBException is a subclass of RuntimeException, so it is considered a system exception. System exceptions also include java.rmi.RemoteException and its subclasses. The RuntimeException and RemoteException subclasses differ in that they can be turned into application exceptions using the @javax.ejb.ApplicationException annotation. This annotation is discussed later in this chapter.

System exceptions always cause a transaction to roll back when they are thrown from an enterprise bean method. Any `RuntimeException` not annotated with `@ApplicationException` that is thrown within the `bookPassage( )` method (for instance, `EJBException`, `NullPointerException`, `IndexOutOfBoundsException`, and so on) is handled by the container automatically and results in a transaction rollback. In Java, `RuntimeException` types do not need to be declared in the `throws` clause of the method signature or handled using *try/catch* blocks; they are automatically thrown from the method.

The container handles system exceptions automatically and it will always do the following:

- Roll back the transaction.
- Log the exception to alert the system administrator.
- Discard the EJB instance.

When a system exception is thrown from any callback method (`@PostConstruct`, `@PostActivate`, and so on), it is treated the same way as exceptions thrown from any business method.

Although EJB requires system exceptions to be logged, it does not specify how they should be logged or the format of the logfile. The exact mechanism for recording exceptions and reporting them to the system administrator is left to the vendor.

When a system exception occurs, the EJB instance is discarded, which means that it is dereferenced and garbage collected. The container assumes that the EJB instance may have corrupt variables or otherwise be unstable and is therefore unsafe to use.

The impact of discarding an EJB instance depends on the enterprise bean's type. In the case of stateless session beans, the client does not notice that the instance has been discarded. These instance types are not dedicated to a particular client; they are swapped in and out of an instance pool, so any instance can service a new request. With stateful session beans, however, the impact on the client is severe. Stateful session beans are dedicated to a single client and maintain conversational state. Discarding a stateful bean instance destroys the instance's conversational state and invalidates the client's reference to the EJB. When stateful session instances are discarded, subsequent invocations of the EJB's methods by the client result in a `NoSuchEJBException`, which is a subclass of `RuntimeException`.*

With message-driven beans, a system exception thrown by the `onMessage( )` method or one of the callback methods (`@PostConstruct` or `@PreDestroy`) will cause the bean instance to be discarded. If the MDB was a BMT bean, the message it was handling may or may not be redelivered, depending on when the EJB container acknowledges

* Although the instance is always discarded with a `RuntimeException`, the impact on the remote reference may vary depending on the vendor.

delivery. In the case of container-managed transactions, the container will roll back the transaction, so the message will not be acknowledged and may be redelivered.

In session beans, when a system exception occurs and the instance is discarded, a `RuntimeException` is always thrown whether the client is a remote or a local invocation. If the client started the transaction, which was then propagated to the EJB, a system exception (thrown by the enterprise bean method) will be caught by the container and rethrown as a `javax.ejb.EJBTransactionRolledbackException`. `EJBTransactionRolledbackException` is a subtype of `RuntimeException` and gives a more explicit indication to the client that a rollback occurred. If the client did not propagate a transaction to the EJB, the system exception will be caught and rethrown as an `EJBException`.

An `EJBException` should generally be thrown when a nonbusiness subsystem throws an exception, such as JDBC throwing an `SQLException` or JMS throwing a `JMSException`. In some cases, however, the bean developer may attempt to handle the exception and retry an operation instead of throwing an `EJBException`. This should be done only when the exceptions thrown by the subsystem and their repercussions on the transaction are well understood. As a rule of thumb, rethrow nonbusiness subsystem exceptions as `EJBExceptions` (or `@ApplicationExceptions` that cause a rollback) and allow the EJB container to roll back the transaction and discard the bean instance automatically.

Application exceptions

An *application exception* is normally thrown in response to a business-logic error, as opposed to a system error. Application exceptions are always delivered directly to the client without being repackaged as an `EJBException` type. By default, they do not cause a transaction to roll back. In this case, the client has an opportunity to recover after an application exception is thrown. For example, the `bookPassage()` method throws an application exception called `IncompleteConversationalState`; this is an application exception because it does not extend `RuntimeException` or `RemoteException`. The `IncompleteConversationalState` exception is thrown if one of the arguments passed into the `bookPassage()` method is `null`. (Application errors are frequently used to report validation errors in this manner.) In this case, the exception is thrown before tasks are started and is clearly not the result of a subsystem failure (e.g., JDBC, JMS, Java RMI, and JNDI).

Because it is an application exception, an `IncompleteConversationalState` exception does not result in a transaction rollback by default. The exception is thrown before any work is done, avoiding unnecessary processing by the `bookPassage()` method and providing the client (the enterprise bean or application that invoked the `bookPassage()` method) with an opportunity to recover and possibly retry the method call with valid arguments. The @javax.ejb.ApplicationException annotation may be used to force an application exception to roll back the transaction automatically:

```
package javax.ejb;

@Target(TYPE) @Retention(RUNTIME)
public @interface ApplicationException {
   boolean rollback( ) default false;
}
```

For instance, the PaymentException used in the ProcessPayment EJB in Chapter 11 is a good candidate for an application exception that causes an automatic rollback:

```
@ApplicationException(rollback=true)
public class PaymentException extends java.lang.Exception {
    public PaymentException( ) {
        super( );
    }
    public PaymentException(String msg) {
        super(msg);
    }
}
```

We want the transaction to be rolled back automatically, but business logic may be able to catch PaymentExceptions and retry the transaction automatically (as it would if another credit card were on file, for example).

The @ApplicationException annotation can also be used on subclasses of java.lang.RuntimeException and java.rmi.RemoteException. This is useful because you may not want a thrown RuntimeException to be wrapped in an EJBException, or you may not want a particular subclass of RemoteException to roll back the exception.

Application exceptions are declarable in XML, as well, with the <application-exception> element:

```
<ejb-jar>
   <assembly-descriptor>
      <application-exception>
         <exception-class>java.sql.SQLException</exception-class>
         <rollback>true</rollback>
      </application-exception>
   </assembly-descriptor>
</ejb-jar>
```

The <application-exception> element is a subelement of <assembly-descriptor>. XML gives you the added capability of declaring a third-party exception as an application exception. In this example, we made java.sql.SQLException an application exception that causes a rollback. We could then let the ProcessPayment EJB throw SQLExceptions directly instead of wrapping them in an EJBException.

Table 16-1 summarizes the interactions among different types of exceptions and transactions in session and entity beans.

Table 16-1. Exception summary for session and entity beans

Transaction scope	Transaction type attributes	Exception thrown	Container's action	Client's view
Client-initiated transaction. The transaction is started by the client (application or EJB) and propagated to the enterprise bean method.	`transaction-type = Container` `transaction-attribute = Required | Mandatory |Supports`	Application exception	If the EJB invoked `setRollbackOnly()` or the application exception is annotated with `@ApplicationException(rollback=true)`, mark the client's transaction for rollback. ethrow the application exception.	Receives the application exception. The client's transaction may or may not have been marked for rollback.
		System exception	Mark the client's transaction for rollback. Log the error. Discard the instance. Rethrow the `javax.ejb.EJBTransactionRolledbackException`.	Clients receive the JTA `javax.ejb.EJBTransactionRolledbackException`. The client's transaction has been rolled back.
Container-managed transaction. The transaction started when the EJB's method was invoked and will end when the method completes.	`transaction-type = Container` `transaction-attribute = Required | RequiresNew`	Application exception	If the EJB invoked `setRollbackOnly()` or the application exception is annotated with `@ApplicationException(rollback=true)`, roll back the transaction and rethrow the application exception. If the EJB did not explicitly roll back the transaction, attempt to commit the transaction and rethrow the application exception.	Receives the application exception. The EJB's transaction may or may not have been rolled back. The client's transaction is not affected.

Table 16-1. Exception summary for session and entity beans (continued)

Transaction scope	Transaction type attributes	Exception thrown	Container's action	Client's view
		System exception	Roll back the transaction. Log the error. Discard the instance. Rethrow the `RemoteException` or `EJBException`.	Remote clients receive the `RemoteException` or `EJBException`. The EJB's transaction was rolled back. The client's transaction may be marked for rollback, depending on the vendor.
The bean is not part of a transaction. The EJB was invoked but doesn't propagate the client's transaction and doesn't start its own transaction.	`transaction-type = Container` `transaction-attribute = Never | NotSupported | Supports |`	Application exception	Rethrow the application exception.	Receives the application exception. The client's transaction is not affected.
		System exception	Log the error. Discard the instance. Rethrow the `RemoteException` or `EJBException`.	Remote clients receive the `RemoteException` or `EJBException`. The client's transaction may or may not be marked for rollback, depending on the vendor.
Bean-managed transaction. The stateful or stateless session EJB uses the `EJBContext` to explicitly manage its own transaction.	`transaction-type = Bean` `transaction-attribute = Bean-managed transaction` EJBs do not use transaction attributes.	Application exception	Rethrow the application exception.	Receives the application exception. The client's transaction is not affected.
		System exception	Roll back the transaction. Log the error. Discard the instance. Rethrow the `RemoteException` or `EJBException`.	Remote clients receive the `RemoteException` or `EJBException`. The client's transaction is not affected.

Table 16-2 summarizes the interactions among different types of exceptions and transactions in message-driven beans.

Table 16-2. Exception summary for message-driven beans

Transaction scope	Transaction type attributes	Exception thrown	Container's action
Container-initiated transaction. The transaction started before the `onMessage()` method was invoked and will end when the method completes.	`transaction-type =Container` `transaction-attribute = Required`	System exception	Roll back the transaction. Log the error. Discard the instance.
		Application exception	If the instance called `setRollbackOnly()` or the exception is annotated with `@ApplicationException(rollback=true)`, roll back the transaction and rethrow to the resource adapter.
Container-initiated transaction. No transaction was started.	`transaction-type =Container` `transaction-attribute = NotSupported`	System exception	Log the error. Discard the instance.
		Application exception	Rethrow the exception to the resource adapter.
Bean-managed transaction. The message-driven bean uses `EJBContext` to manage its own transaction explicitly.	`transaction-type = Bean` `transaction-attribute` = Bean-managed transaction EJBs do not use transaction attributes.	System exception	Roll back the transaction. Log the error. Discard the instance.
		Application exception	Rethrow the exception to the resource adapter.

Transactional Stateful Session Beans

Session beans can interact directly with the database as easily as they can manage the taskflow of other enterprise beans. The ProcessPayment EJB, for example, makes inserts into the `PAYMENT` table when the `byCredit()` method is invoked, and the TravelAgent EJB queries the database directly when the `listAvailableCabins()` method is invoked. Stateless session beans—such as the ProcessPayment EJB—have no conversational state, so each method invocation must make changes to the database immediately. With stateful session beans, however, we may not want to make changes to the database until the transaction is complete. Remember, a stateful session bean can be one of many participants in a transaction, so it may be advisable to postpone database updates until the entire transaction is committed or to avoid updates if it is rolled back.

There are several different scenarios in which a stateful session bean might cache changes before applying them to the database. For example, think of a shopping cart implemented by a stateful session bean that accumulates several items for purchase. If the stateful bean implements `SessionSynchronization`, it can cache the items and write them to the database only when the transaction is complete.

The `javax.ejb.SessionSynchronization` interface allows a session bean to receive additional notification of the session's involvement in transactions. The addition of these transaction callback methods by the `SessionSynchronization` interface expands the EJB's awareness of its life cycle to include a new state, the *Transactional Method-Ready state*. This third state, although not discussed in Chapter 11, is always a part of the life cycle of a transactional stateful session bean. Implementing the `SessionSynchronization` interface simply makes it visible to the EJB. Figure 16-11 shows the stateful session bean with the additional state.

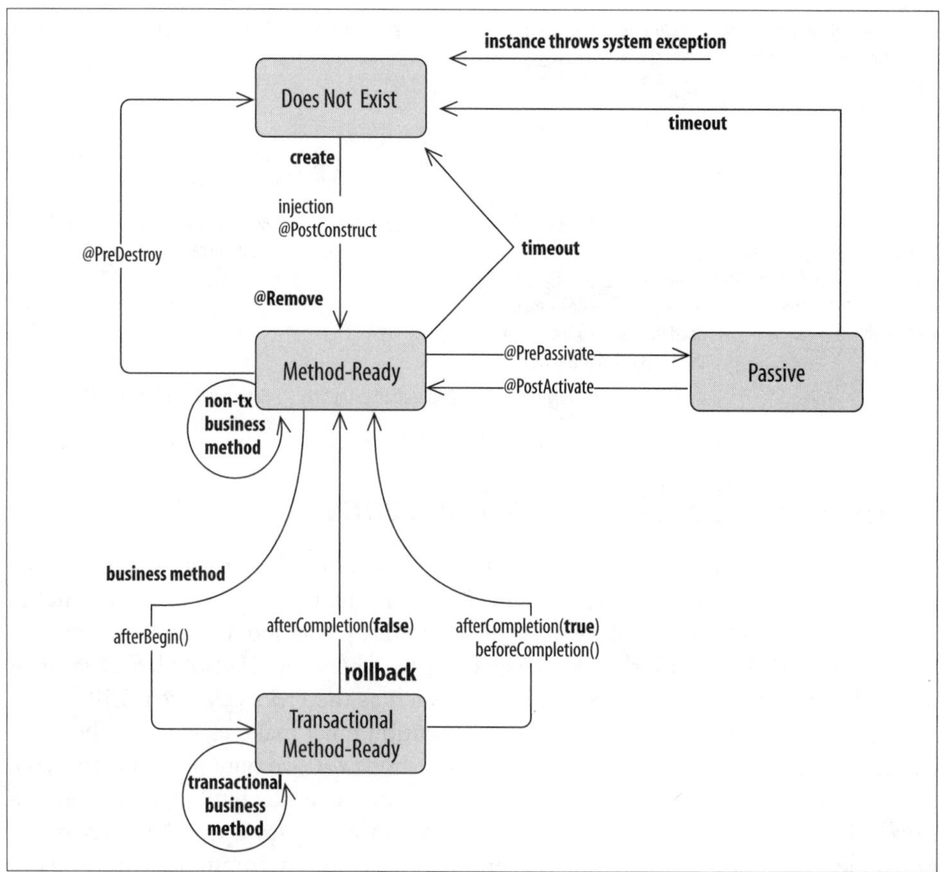

Figure 16-11. Life cycle of a stateful session bean

The SessionSynchronization interface is defined as follows:

```
package javax.ejb;

public interface javax.ejb.SessionSynchronization {
    public abstract void afterBegin( ) throws RemoteException;
    public abstract void beforeCompletion( ) throws RemoteException;
    public abstract void afterCompletion(boolean committed)
        throws RemoteException;
}
```

When a method of the SessionSynchronization bean is invoked outside of a transaction scope, the method executes in the Method-Ready state, as discussed in Chapter 11. However, when a method is invoked within a transaction scope (or creates a new transaction), the EJB moves into the Transactional Method-Ready state.

The Transactional Method-Ready State

The SessionSynchronization methods are called in the Transactional Method-Ready state.

Transitioning into the Transactional Method-Ready state

When a transactional method is invoked on a SessionSynchronization bean, the stateful bean becomes part of the transaction, causing the afterBegin( ) callback method defined in the SessionSynchronization interface to be invoked. This method should take care of reading any data from the database and storing the data in the bean's instance fields. The afterBegin( ) method is called before the EJB object delegates the business-method invocation to the EJB instance.

Life in the Transactional Method-Ready state

When the afterBegin( ) callback method completes, the business method originally invoked by the client is executed on the EJB instance. Any subsequent business methods invoked within the same transaction will be delegated directly to the EJB instance.

Once a stateful session bean is a part of a transaction—whether it implements SessionSynchronization or not—it cannot be accessed by any other transactional context. This is true regardless of whether the client tries to access the EJB with a different context or the EJB's own method creates a new context. If, for example, a method with a transaction attribute of RequiresNew is invoked, the new transactional context causes an error to be thrown. Since the NotSupported and Never attributes specify a different transactional context (no context), invoking a method with these attributes also causes an error. A stateful session bean cannot be removed while it is involved in a transaction. This means that invoking an @Remove annotated method while the SessionSynchronization bean is in the middle of a transaction will cause an error to be thrown.

At some point, the transaction in which the SessionSynchronization bean has been enrolled will come to an end. If the transaction is committed, the SessionSynchronization bean will be notified through its beforeCompletion( ) method. At this time, the EJB should write its cached data to the database. If the transaction is rolled back, the beforeCompletion( ) method will not be invoked, avoiding the pointless effort of writing changes that won't be committed to the database.

The afterCompletion( ) method is always invoked, whether the transaction ended successfully with a commit or unsuccessfully with a rollback. If the transaction was a success—which means that beforeCompletion( ) was invoked—the committed parameter of the afterCompletion( ) method will be true. If the transaction was unsuccessful, then the committed parameter will be false.

It may be desirable to reset the stateful session bean's instance variables to some initial state if the afterCompletion( ) method indicates that the transaction was rolled back.

Conversational Persistence Contexts

Entity managers participate in transactions just like any other resource. We've seen examples of this throughout this book. Extended persistence contexts have some interesting transactional behavior that you can exploit. You are allowed to invoke EntityManager operations such as persist( ), merge( ), and remove( ) outside of a transaction when you interact with an extended persistence context. These inserts, updates, and deletes are queued until the extended persistence context is enlisted in an active transaction and is committed. In other words, the database is not touched until the persistence context becomes involved with a transaction. Also, any executed queries do not hold their database connection after they complete. Let's look at an example of this:

```
1  EntityManager manager = entityManagerFactory.createEntityManager(EXTENDED);
2  manager.persist(newCabin);
3  manager.merge(someCustomer);
4  manager.remove(someReservation);
5
6  userTransaction.begin( );
7  manager.flush( );
8  userTransaction.commit( );
```

Line 1 creates an extended persistence context. Lines 2–4 create, update, and delete some entity beans. These actions are queued until the persistence context becomes enlisted in a transaction in Line 6. The act of calling an EntityManager method enlists the persistence context in the transaction. The batched actions are then committed in Line 7.

You can really exploit this behavior by using it with stateful session beans. Earlier, we showed the example of creating two reservations through the TravelAgentBean:

```
TravelAgent tr1 = (TravelAgent)getInitialContext( ).lookup("TravelAgentRemote");
tr1.setCruiseID(cruiseID);
tr1.setCabinID(cabin_1);
tr1.setCustomer(customer0);
TravelAgent tr2 = (TravelAgent)getInitialContext( ).lookup("TravelAgentRemote");;
tr2.setCruiseID(cruiseID);
tr2.setCabinID(cabin_2);
tr2.setCustomer(customer);

javax.transaction.UserTransaction tran = ...; // Get the UserTransaction.
tran.begin( );
tr1.bookPassage(visaCard,price);
tr2.bookPassage(visaCard,price);
tran.commit( );
```

The idea was that we had one customer that wanted to create multiple reservations for his family. These multiple reservations would participate in one transaction initiated by the client. This is actually very poor system design because you have a transaction that spans multiple remote invocations. Remote clients, in general, are very unreliable entities, especially those clients that are driven by human interaction. Database update locks are held in between the remote `bookPassage( )` invocations and the database connections remain open. If the human travel agent decided to go to lunch in the middle of a transaction, these resources and connections would be held until the transaction timed out. To solve this problem, we can use the queuing behavior of nontransactional entity manager operations. Let's modify `TravelAgentBean` using the optimistic locking example as a base:

```
import javax.ejb.*;
import javax.persistence.*;
import static javax.persistence.PersistenceContextType.*;
import static javax.ejb.TransactionAttributeType.*;

@Stateful
@TransactionAttribute(NOT_SUPPORTED)
public class TravelAgentBean implements TravelAgentRemote {

   @PersistenceContext(unitName="titan", type=EXTENDED)
   private EntityManager entityManager;

   @EJB ProcessPaymentLocal processPayment;

   private Customer customer;
   private Cruise cruise;
   private Cabin cabin;

   public Customer findOrCreateCustomer(String first, String last) {
     ...
   }

   public void setCabinID(int id) {
     ...
   }
```

```
    public void setCruiseID(int id) {
      ...
    }

    public TicketDO bookPassage(CreditCardDO card, double price)
       throws IncompleteConversationalState {

       if (customer == null || cruise == null || cabin == null) {
         throw new IncompleteConversationalState( );
       }
       try {
           Query getCruiseCabin = entityManager.createQuery(
                 "SELECT cc FROM CruiseCabin cc WHERE" +
                 "cc.cabin = :cabin AND cc.cruise = :cruise");
           getCruiseCabin.setParameter("cabin", cabin);
           getCruiseCabin.setParameter("cruise", cruise);
           CruiseCabin cc = (CruiseCabin)getCruiseCabin.getSingleResult( );

           if (cc.getIsReserved( ))
               throw new EJBException ("Cabin is already reserved");
           cc.setIsReserved(true);

           Reservation reservation = new Reservation(
               customer, cruise, cabin, price);
           entityManager.persist(reservation);

           this.process.byCredit(customer, card, price);

           TicketDO ticket = new TicketDO(customer,cruise,cabin,price);

           return ticket;
       } catch(Exception e) {
           throw new EJBException(e);
       }
    }

    @TransactionAttribute(REQUIRED)
    @Remove
    public void checkout( ) {
       entityManager.flush( ); // really not necessary
    }
}
```

We changed a few things from the previous example. The first thing we did was to make every business method nontransactional by annotating the bean class with @TransactionAttribute(NOT_SUPPORTED). Next, an extended persistence context was injected into the entityManager field so that we can interact with it outside of a transaction. The @Remove annotation was moved from bookPassage( ) to a new checkout( ) method so that multiple bookPassage( ) method calls could be invoked on the same TravelAgent session. Since bookPassage( ) is now nontransactional, any reservation created by this method is now queued and no database resources are held in between invocations. The reservations are committed to the database when the extended persistence context is enlisted in a transaction within the checkout( ) method.

The EntityManager.flush( ) operation within the checkout( ) method wasn't really necessary: extended persistence contexts are automatically enlisted in a transaction when the method begins. It is good practice, though, to call flush( ) anyway because it reminds developers reading the code of what is actually happening.

The last thing that needs to be modified is the ProcessPayment EJB. Since ProcessPaymentBean uses raw JDBC to log payments, these payments are not queued like the entity manager operations are. To facilitate this, we need to write another entity bean to represent a payment and change the ProcessPayment EJB to use an entity manager, rather than JDBC:

```
@Entity
public class Payment implements java.io.Serializable
{
   private int id;
   private Customer customer;
   private double amount;
   private String type;
   private String checkBarCode;
   private int checkNumber;
   private String creditCard;
   private Date creditCardExpiration;

   @Id @GeneratedValue
   public int getId( ) { return id; }
   public void setId(int id) { this.id = id; }

   @ManyToOne
   public Customer getCustomer( ) { return customer; }
   public void setCustomer(Customer cust) { this.customer = cust; }

   public double getAmount( ) { return amount; }
   public void setAmount(double amount) { this.amount = amount; }

   public String getType( ) { return type; }
   public void setType(String type) { this.type = type; }

   public String getCheckBarCode( ) { return checkBarCode; }
   public void setCheckBarCode(String checkBarCode) { this.checkBarCode =
checkBarCode; }

   public int getCheckNumber( ) { return checkNumber; }
   public void setCheckNumber(int checkNumber) { this.checkNumber = checkNumber; }

   public String getCreditCard( ) { return creditCard; }
   public void setCreditCard(String creditCard) { this.creditCard = creditCard; }

   public Date getCreditCardExpiration( ) { return creditCardExpiration; }
   public void setCreditCardExpiration(Date creditCardExpiration) {
       this.creditCardExpiration = creditCardExpiration; }

}
```

This entity represents the PAYMENT table we used in previous ProcessPayment EJB examples. Next, let's modify ProcessPaymentBean to use this new entity:

```
package com.titan.processpayment;

import com.titan.domain.*;

import javax.ejb.*;
import javax.annotation.Resource;
import javax.persistence.*;
import static javax.ejb.TransactionAttributeType.*;
import static javax.persistence.PersistenceContextType.*;

@Stateful
@TransactionAttribute(SUPPORTS)
public class ProcessPaymentBean implements ProcessPaymentLocal
{

   final public static String CASH = "CASH";
   final public static String CREDIT = "CREDIT";
   final public static String CHECK = "CHECK";

   @PersistenceContext(unitName="titan", type=EXTENDED)
   private EntityManager entityManager;

   @Resource(name="min") int minCheckNumber = 100;

   public boolean byCash(Customer customer, double amount)
      throws PaymentException
   {
      return process(customer, amount, CASH, null, -1, null, null);
   }

   public boolean byCheck(Customer customer, CheckDO check, double amount)
      throws PaymentException
   {
      if (check.checkNumber > minCheckNumber)
      {
         return process(customer, amount, CHECK,
                     check.checkBarCode, check.checkNumber, null, null);
      }
      else
      {
         throw new PaymentException("Check number is too low. Must be at least
"+minCheckNumber);
      }
   }
   public boolean byCredit(Customer customer, CreditCardDO card,
                           double amount) throws PaymentException
   {
      if (card.expiration.before(new java.util.Date( )))
      {
         throw new PaymentException("Expiration date has passed");
      }
```

```
        else
        {
           return process(customer, amount, CREDIT, null,
                          -1, card.number, new java.sql.Date(card.expiration.getTime(
)));
        }
     }
     private boolean process(Customer cust, double amount, String type,
                             String checkBarCode, int checkNumber, String creditNumber,
                             java.sql.Date creditExpDate) throws PaymentException
     {
        Payment payment = new Payment( );
        payment.setCustomer(cust);
        payment.setAmount(amount);
        payment.setType(type);
        payment.setCheckBarCode(checkBarCode);
        payment.setCheckNumber(checkNumber);
        payment.setCreditCard(creditNumber);
        payment.setCreditCardExpiration(creditExpDate);
        entityManager.persist(payment);
        return true;
     }
}
```

The ProcessPaymentBean class is annotated with @TransactionAttribute(SUPPORTS) because it may or may not be executed within a transaction. The changes to the process( ) method were quite easy and actually removed a lot of the verbose JDBC syntax from the original version. We did have to do a few other contrived, ugly things in the ProcessPayment EJB to force this example to work. The Java Persistence specification does not allow you to propagate an extended persistence context to a stateless session bean when there is no transaction. Therefore, ProcessPayment was turned into a stateful session bean that has an extended persistence context injected into it. Because ProcessPayment is an EJB that is nested inside TravelAgentBean, they share the same extended persistence context (see Chapter 11 for more details). We can use this loophole to circumvent the propagation problem.

Given the ugly changes we had to make to ProcessPayment to get this example to work, I don't recommend using the queuing features of extended persistence contexts if you need to interact with other EJBs. It is unfortunate that the EJB 3.0 Expert Group could not fix the obvious usability problems exposed in this section. Since the group couldn't agree on a solution because of one or two stubborn members, a couple of vendors have decided to fix these problems in their own implementations.

With the TravelAgentBean and ProcessPaymentBean changes complete, we can now focus on reimplementing the client:

```
TravelAgent tr1 = (TravelAgent)getInitialContext( ).lookup("TravelAgentRemote");
tr1.setCruiseID(cruiseID);
tr1.setCabinID(cabin_1);
tr1.setCustomer(customer0);
tr1.bookPassage(visaCard,price);
```

```
tr1.setCruiseID(cruiseID);
tr1.setCabinID(cabin_2);
tr1.setCustomer(customer);
tr1.bookPassage(visaCard,price);

tr1.checkout( );
```

Compared to the client code from the original example, this code has been greatly simplified. As you can see, we managed to refactor the TravelAgentBean with very little code changes and simplify the client logic. We solved our original use case of allowing multiple calls to bookPassage( ). At the same time, we managed to use our database resources more efficiently and still represent one unit-of-work.

The combination of stateful session beans, extended persistence contexts, and specific transaction demarcation gives you a lot of power to optimize and control your conversational state. Without these integrated features, you would have the painstaking task of managing all of these state changes within the stateful session bean itself. Now you can let the entity manager do most of the work for you.

CHAPTER 17

Security

Most Java EE applications need to provide identity to users who access them and security for that access. Applications may want to prevent hostile users from logging into their systems. They might also want to restrict the actions of the individuals using their systems. The Java EE and EJB specifications provide a core set of security services that application developers can integrate declaratively and programmatically. These include:

Authentication
: Authentication is the process of validating the identity of a user who is trying to access a secured system. When authenticating, the application server verifies that the user actually exists in the system and has provided the correct credentials, such as a password.

Authorization
: Once a user is authenticated in a system, he will want to interact with the application. Authorization involves determining whether a user is allowed to execute a certain action. Authorization can police a user's access to subsystems, data, and business objects, or it can monitor more general behavior. Certain users, for example, may be allowed to update information, while others are allowed only to view the data. For web applications, maybe only certain users are permitted to access certain URLs. For EJB applications, the user can be authorized on a per-method basis.

Confidentiality and integrity protection
: When a user is interacting with an application over a network through a browser or through remote EJB invocations, it is possible for rogue individuals to intercept network packets and interpret the data if the connection is not secured. Data transfer should be protected and attackers should not be able to read or modify this data in transit. Data transfer can be secured through cryptographic services such as SSL. Encryption is vendor-specific and is not covered in this chapter.

Although a small programmatic API is available for interacting with Java EE security services, users rarely have to write any code to secure their applications because setting up security is usually a static declarative process. Only session beans can be secured in EJB land. Java Persistence does not yet have a mechanism to secure access, but it is possible—depending on the RDBMS system you are using—to assign privileges at the database level. This chapter focuses on how to set up authentication and authorization for your session beans.

Authentication and Identity

In a secure EJB application, authentication involves verifying that a user is who she says she is. When a remote client logs on to the EJB system, it is associated with a security identity for the duration of that session. Once a remote client application has been associated with a security identity, it is ready to use beans to accomplish some task. When a client invokes a method on a bean, the EJB server implicitly passes the client's identity with the method invocation. When the EJB object receives the method invocation, it checks the identity to ensure that the client is valid and is allowed to invoke that method.

Unfortunately (or fortunately, depending on your perspective), the EJB specification does not specify how authentication happens. Although it defines how security information is propagated from a client to the server (through CORBA/IIOP), it does not specify how the client is supposed to obtain and associate identity and credentials with an EJB invocation. It also does not define how the application server stores and retrieves authentication information. The vendor must decide how to package and provide these services on the client and server.

When invoking on a remote EJB, many application servers accomplish authentication by using the JNDI API. For example, a client using JNDI can provide authenticating information using the JNDI API to access a server or resource in the server. This information is frequently passed when the client attempts to initiate a JNDI connection on the EJB server. The following code shows how a client's password and username can be added to the connection properties for obtaining a JNDI connection to the EJB server:

```
properties.put(Context.SECURITY_PRINCIPAL, userName);
properties.put(Context.SECURITY_CREDENTIALS, userPassword);

InitialContext ctx = new InitialContext(properties);
Object ref = jndiContext.lookup("TravelAgent");
TravelAgentRemote remote = (TravelAgentRemote)
    PortableRemoteObject.narrow(ref, TravelAgentRemote.class);
```

In this example, the user is authenticated with the connection to the JNDI `InitialContext`. The username and password are associated with the client thread and propagated to the server internally when calls are made to remote EJBs.

Although JNDI is a common way for most application servers to perform authentication, sometimes users need a better abstraction for obtaining security information. For instance, what if the credentials were a thumbprint instead of a password? Many application servers provide a mechanism other than JNDI with which to authenticate. For instance, the JBoss application server uses the JAAS specification, which provides a rich API for performing authentication.

Authorization

Once a user is authenticated by a vendor-specific mechanism, he must be checked to see if he is allowed to invoke a particular EJB method. Authorization is performed in Java EE and EJB by associating one or more roles with a given user and then assigning method permissions based on that role. While an example of a user might be "Scott" or "Gavin," roles are used to identify a group of users—for instance, "administrator," "manager," or "employee." In EJB, you assign access control on a per-method basis. You do not assign these permissions on a per-user basis, but rather, on a per-role basis.

The roles used to describe authorization are considered logical roles because they do not directly reflect users, groups, or any other security identities in a specific operational environment. EJB security roles are mapped to real-world user groups and users when the bean is deployed. This mapping allows a bean to be portable; every time the bean is deployed in a new system, the roles can be mapped to the users and groups specific to that operational environment.

Unlike authentication, authorization is something that the EJB specification clearly defines. You begin by declaring the roles that are accessed programmatically in your code base. Then you assign permissions for each method in your class. This is done declaratively through Java annotations or through the `ejb-jar.xml` deployment descriptor. To illustrate, let's secure access to the ProcessPayment EJB defined in Chapter 11.

Assigning Method Permissions

Titan Cruises must be very careful when determining to whom it will grant access to the ProcessPayment EJB. This bean allows users to charge money against a customer's credit card, so it is in Titan's best interest to make sure its customers feel safe giving out their credit card numbers. Only users who are authorized travel agents will be allowed to process payments at Titan Cruises. Furthermore, only authorized agents with an automatic check fraud-detection system for their bank accounts will be allowed to make check payments. However, any valid user will be allowed to make cash payments.

To assign method permissions to an EJB's methods, use the @javax.annotation.security.RolesAllowed annotation:

```
package javax.annotation.security;

@Target({TYPE, METHOD}) @Retention(RUNTIME)
public @interface RolesAllowed {
   String[] value();
}
```

This annotation defines one or more logical roles that are allowed to access the method. When placed on the bean class, the @RolesAllowed annotation specifies the default set of roles that are permitted to access bean methods. Each EJB method can override this behavior by using the same annotation.

The @javax.annotation.security.PermitAll annotation specifies that any authenticated user is permitted to invoke the method. As with @RolesAllowed, you can use this annotation on the bean class to define the default for the entire bean class, or you can use it on a per-method basis. @PermitAll is also the default value if no default or explicit security metadata is provided for a method. This means that if you do not use any security annotations on your bean class, every user is granted unlimited access.

Let's apply these annotations to ProcessPaymentBean using the permissions we discussed earlier:

```
package com.titan.processpayment;

import com.titan.domain.*;

import javax.ejb.*;
import javax.annotation.Resource;
import javax.annotation.security.*;

@Stateless
@RolesAllowed("AUTHORIZED_TRAVEL_AGENT")
public class ProcessPaymentBean implements ProcessPaymentRemote,
                                           ProcessPaymentLocal
{
...
   @PermitAll
   public boolean byCash(Customer customer, double amount)
      throws PaymentException
   {
      ...
   }

   @RolesAllowed("CHECK_FRAUD_ENABLED")
   public boolean byCheck(Customer customer, CheckDO check, double amount)
      throws PaymentException
   {
      ...
   }
```

```
    public boolean byCredit(Customer customer, CreditCardDO card,
                            double amount) throws PaymentException
    {
       ...
    }
    private boolean process(int customerID, double amount, String type,
                            String checkBarCode, int checkNumber, String creditNumber,
                            java.sql.Date creditExpDate) throws PaymentException
    {
       ...
    }
}
```

The AUTHORIZED_MERCHANT role identifies Titan users who are authorized to make payments on the system. The bean class is annotated with @RolesAllowed to specify that all methods in ProcessPaymentBean, by default, can be executed only by AUTHORIZED_MERCHANT users. The byCredit( ) method inherits this default setting. Titan Cruises will accept cash payments from anybody, so the byCash( ) method is annotated with @PermitAll to allow payments from any user. For the byCheck( ) method, we have an additional requirement that only merchants that have CHECK_FRAUD_ENABLED are allowed to process check payments. For this method, an additional @RolesAllowed annotation is used to override the default one applied on the bean class. When a client invokes on an EJB method for which it doesn't have the appropriate permissions, the EJB container throws a javax.ejb.EJBAccessException.

Let's apply this security metadata with XML instead:

```
<ejb-jar version="3.0">
   <assembly-descriptor>
      <security-role>
         <description>This role represents an authorized merchant</description>
         <role-name>AUTHORIZED_MERCHANT</role-name>
      </security-role>
      <security-role>
         <description>
          This role represents a merchant that has check fraud enabled
         </descripton>
         <role-name>CHECK_FRAUD_ENABLED</role-name>
      </security-role>
      <method-permission>
         <role-name>AUTHORIZED_MERCHANT</role-name>
         <method>
            <ejb-name>ProcessPaymentBean</ejb-name>
            <method-name>byCredit</method-name>
         </method>
      </method-permission>
      <method-permission>
          <role-name>CHECK_FRAUD_ENABLED</role-name>
          <method>
             <ejb-name>ProcessPaymentBean</ejb-name>
             <method-name>byCheck</method-name>
          </method>
```

```
        </method-permission>
        <method-permission>
            <unchecked/>
            <method>
                <ejb-name>ProcessPaymentBean</ejb-name>
                <method-name>byCheck</method-name>
            </method>
        </method-permission>
    </assembly-descriptor>
</ejb-jar>
```

Method permission declarations are defined within the `<assembly-descriptor>` element. Each role that is used to map method permissions must be identified first within `<security-role>` elements. These elements have an optional `<description>` element that describes the role's use. The `<role-name>` element declares the role that will be used in the deployment. It is unclear to me why the `<security-role>` element is required by the specification because the referenced roles could be determined by looking at all the `<method-permission>` elements. It seems like complete syntactic sugar to me.

The method permissions themselves are declared with multiple `<method-permission>` elements. Each `<method-permission>` element defines one or more `<role-name>` elements that declare the roles allowed to access a particular `<method>`. The `<unchecked>` element is equivalent to the `@PermitAll` annotation. The `<method>` element declares the method you want to secure. The `<method-name>` element is allowed to take a * wildcard. If a `<method-permission>` declaration can be applied to one or more bean methods, then the union is taken.

Identifying Specific Methods in XML

The `<method>` element is used by the `<method-permission>` element to identify a specific group of methods in a particular bean. The `<method>` element always contains an `<ejb-name>` element that specifies the bean's name and a `<method-name>` element that specifies the method. It may also include a `<description>` element, `<method-params>` elements specifying which method parameters will be used to resolve overloaded methods, and a `<method-intf>` element that specifies whether the method belongs to the bean's remote or local interface. This last element resolves the possibility that the same method name might be used in more than one interface.

Wildcard declarations

The method name in a `<method>` element can be a simple wildcard (*). A wildcard applies to all methods of the bean's home and remote interfaces. For example:

```
<method>
    <ejb-name>ProcessPaymentBean</ejb-name>
    <method-name>*</method-name>
</method>
```

Although it's tempting to combine the wildcard with other characters, don't do this. The value get*, for example, is illegal. The asterisk character can only be used by itself.

Named method declarations

Named declarations apply to all methods defined in the bean's remote and local interfaces that have the specified name. For example:

```
<method>
    <ejb-name>ProcessPaymentBean</ejb-name>
    <method-name>byCheck</method-name>
</method>
```

This declaration applies to all methods with the given name in any business interface. It does not distinguish between overloaded methods. For example, if the local interface for the ProcessPayment EJB is modified so that it has three overloaded byCheck( ) methods, the previous <method> declaration would apply to all methods, as illustrated here:

```
@Local
public interface ProcessPaymentLocal {
   boolean byCheck(Customer cust, CheckDO check, double amount);

   boolean byCheck(double[] amounts);

   boolean byCheck( );
}
```

Specific method declarations

Specific method declarations use the <method-params> element to pinpoint a method by listing its parameters, which allows you to differentiate between overloaded methods. The <method-params> element contains zero or more <method-param> elements that correspond, in order, to each parameter type (including multidimensional arrays) declared in the method. To specify a method with no arguments, use a <method-params> element with no <method-param> elements nested within it.

For example, let's look again at our ProcessPayment EJB, to which we have added some overloaded byCheck( ) methods. Here are three <method> elements, each of which unambiguously specifies one of the methods by listing its parameters:

```
<method>
    <ejb-name>ProcessPaymentBean</ejb-name>
    <method-name>byCheck</method-name>
    <method-params>
            <method-param>com.titan.domain.Customer</method-param>
            <method-param>com.titan.processpayment.CheckDO</method-param>
            <method-param>double</method-param>
    </method-params>
</method>
```

```
<method>
    <ejb-name>ProcessPaymentBean</ejb-name>
    <method-name>byCheck</method-name>
    <method-params></method-params>
</method>
<method>
    <ejb-name>ProcessPaymentBean</ejb-name>
    <method-name>byCheck</method-name>
    <method-params>double[]</method-params>
</method>
```

Remote/home/local differentiation

There's one problem left. The same method name can be used in the remote interface and the local interface. To resolve this ambiguity, add the `<method-intf>` element to a method declaration as a modifier. Five values are allowed for a `<method-intf>` element: `Remote`, `Home`, `LocalHome`, `Local`, and `ServiceEndpoint`.

All of these styles of method declarations can be used in any combination and within any element that uses the `<method>` element. The `<method-permission>` elements are combined to form a union of role-to-method permissions. For example, in the following code, the first `<method-permission>` element declares that only administrators have access to the remote methods of the ProcessPayment EJB:

```
<method-permission>
    <role-name>administrator</role-name>
    <method>
        <ejb-name>ProcessPaymentBean</ejb-name>
        <method-name>*</method-name>
        <method-intf>Remote</method_intf>
    </method>
</method-permission>
```

Excluded Methods

EJB security metadata has a rarely used feature that allows you to forbid access to one or more methods. Excluded methods are identified with the `@javax.annotation.security.DenyAll` annotation or with the `<exclude-list>` element. Denying access to a particular method with an annotation isn't a very useful proposition. Why would you write a bean class method, add it to the business interface, and then annotate it so that it couldn't be used? Using this feature in XML, though, does have some uses. What if the ProcessPayment EJB was part of a third-party vendor library? The `<exclude-list>` element could be used to turn off various features of the API per deployment. Let's look at an example:

```
<ejb-jar>
    <assembly-descriptor>
        <exclude-list>
            <method>
                <ejb-name>ProcessPaymentBean</ejb-name>
```

```
                <method-name>byCash</method-name>
            </method>
        </exclude-list>
    </assembly-descriptor>
</ejb-jar>
```

This example disallows all access to the ProcessPaymentBean.byCash( ) method. The <exclude-list> element can take one or more method signatures.

The RunAs Security Identity

In addition to specifying the roles that have access to an enterprise bean's methods, the deployer can also specify the *runAs* role for the entire enterprise bean. While the @RolesAllowed annotation and <method-permission> elements specify which roles have access to the bean's methods, runAs specifies the role under which the method will run. In other words, the runAs role is used as the enterprise bean's identity when it tries to invoke methods on other beans—and this identity isn't necessarily the same as the identity that's currently accessing the bean. The @javax.annotation.security.RunAs annotation is used to specify this special role. Although they are not allowed to use method permissions, message-driven beans can use the @RunsAs feature:

```
package javax.annotation.security;

public @interface RunAs {
   String value( );
}
```

@RunAs could be used to simplify our role mapping for the ProcessPayment EJB. We could mark our TravelAgentBean to run as an AUTHORIZED_MERCHANT so that we would not have to map any of the TravelAgentBean's roles to the ProcessPayment EJB's roles. This could be especially important if a third-party vendor bought the ProcessPayment EJB from Titan Cruises. Let's look at how TravelAgentBean would use the @RunAs annotation:

```
package com.titan.travelagent;

import javax.ejb.*;
import javax.annotation.security.*;

@Stateful
@RunAs("AUTHORIZED_MERCHANT")
public class TravelAgentBean implements TravelAgentRemote
{
...
}
```

This can also be expressed in ejb-jar.xml:

```
<ejb-jar version="3.0">
  <enterprise-beans>
```

```
    <session>
        <ejb-name>TravelAgentBean</ejb-name>
        <security-identity>
            <run-as>
                <role-name>AUTHORIZED_MERCHANT</role-name>
            </run-as>
        </security-identity>
    </session>
  </enterprise-beans>
</ejb-jar>
```

The <security-identity> element is a subelement of the session bean or message-driven bean for which you are declaring a <run-as> element. The <run-as> element defines the role you want to be assigned to the EJB after the caller has been successfully authenticated and authorized.

To specify that an enterprise bean will execute under the caller's identity rather than a propagated run-as identity, the <security-identity> role contains a single empty element, <use-caller-identity/>. The following declarations specify that the EmployeeService EJB should always execute under the caller's identity:

```
<enterprise-beans>
    <entity>
        <ejb-name>EmployeeService</ejb-name>
        <security-identity>
            <user-caller-identity/>
        </security-identity>
    </entity>
</enterprise-beans>
```

The use of <security-identity> applies to session beans. Message-driven beans have only a `runAs` identity; they never execute under the caller identity because there is no "caller." The messages that a message-driven bean processes are not considered calls, and the clients that send them are not associated with the messages. With no caller identity to propagate, message-driven beans must always specify a `runAs` security identity if they interact with other secured session beans.

Programmatic Security

Most of the security features in this chapter have focused solely on declarative security metadata, or metadata that is statically defined before an application even runs. EJB also has a small programmatic API for gathering information about a secured session. Specifically, the `javax.ejb.EJBContext` interface has a method for determining the concrete user that is invoking on the EJB. It also has a method that allows you to check whether the current user belongs to a certain role:

```
package javax.ejb;

public interface EJBContext {
   javax.security.Principal getCallerPrincipal( );
```

```
    boolean isCallerInRole(String roleName);
}
```

The getCallerPrincipal( ) method returns a standard Java SE javax.security.Principal security interface. A Principal object represents the individual user that is currently invoking on the EJB. We can expand our ProcessPayment EJB to store the travel agent that logged the payment for a customer as well. This addition allows us to audit the payment if there are any problems with the transaction.

```
package com.titan.processpayment;

import javax.security.Principal;
import javax.ejb.*;
import javax.annotation.*;

@Stateless
public class ProcessPaymentBean implements ProcessPaymentLocal {

   @Resource SessionContext ctx;
...
   private boolean process(int customerID, double amount, String type,
                           String checkBarCode, int checkNumber,
                           String creditNumber, java.sql.Date creditExpDate)
             throws PaymentException
   {
      Principal caller = ctx.getCallerPrincipal( );
      String travelAgent = caller.getName( );
      // add travelAgent to payment record
      ...
   }
}
```

The EJBContext.isCallerInRole( ) method allows you to determine whether the current calling user belongs to a certain role. For instance, we might want to forbid large payment transactions above a certain dollar amount for junior travel agents.

If you want to use isCallerInRole, you must provide a little bit of syntactic sugar. Because EJB roles are logical, the application server needs to be aware of all roles with which the EJB interacts so that it can map them to real-world corporate environments. The EJB container can easily determine method permission roles by introspecting the annotation and XML metadata defined for the EJB. A harder job is determining whether programmatic security is referencing a certain role that is not defined in metadata. To make the EJB container's job easier, you must declare all programmatic role access using the @javax.annotation.security.DeclareRoles annotation:

```
package javax.annotation.security;

@Target(TYPE) @Retention(RUNTIME)
public @interface DeclareRoles {
   String[] value( );
}
```

Let's use isCallerInRole( ) with the ProcessBean EJB:

```
package com.titan.processpayment;

import javax.security.Principal;
import javax.ejb.*;
import javax.annotation.*;
import javax.annotation.security.*;

@Stateless
@DeclareRoles("JUNIOR_TRAVEL_AGENT")
public class ProcessPaymentBean implements ProcessPaymentLocal {

   @Resource SessionContext ctx;

   @Resource double maximumJuniorTrade = 10000.0;
...
   private boolean process(int customerID, double amount, String type,
                           String checkBarCode, int checkNumber,
                           String creditNumber, java.sql.Date creditExpDate)
             throws PaymentException
   {
      if (amount > maximumJuniorTrade &&
          ctx.isCallerInRole("JUNIOR_TRAVEL_AGENT"))
           throw new PaymentException("Travel agent is not authorized to make such
                                      a large purchase.
                                     Manager approval is required.");
      ...
   }
}
```

In this example, we expand the private process( ) method to check if the payment is greater than a certain amount and whether the user of the system is a junior travel agent. If he is, then he needs a manager to approve the sale and a PaymentException is thrown. Because we are using the EJBContext.isCallerInRole( ) method to implement this behavior, we must annotate the bean class with the @DeclareRoles annotation, specifying that we are referencing the JUNIOR_TRAVEL_AGENT role. If you do not use the @DeclareRoles annotation, then you must use the <security-role-ref> element within the session bean's declaration:

```
<ejb-jar version="3.0">
   <enterprise-beans>
      <session>
         <ejb-name>ProcessPaymentBean</ejb-name>
         <security-role-ref>
            <role-name>JUNIOR_TRAVEL_AGENT</role-name>
         </security-role-ref>
      </session>
   </enterprise-beans>
</ejb-jar>
```

The <security-role-ref> element is defined within a <session> or <message-driven> element. It has one subelement, <role-name>, which names the role that is being referenced.

CHAPTER 18

EJB 3.0: Web Services Standards

Web services have taken the enterprise computing industry by storm in the past couple of years, and for good reason. They present the opportunity for real interoperability across hardware, operating systems, programming languages, and applications. Based on the XML, SOAP, and WSDL standards, web services have enjoyed widespread adoption by nearly all of the major enterprise players, including Microsoft, IBM, BEA, JBoss, Oracle, Hewlett-Packard, and others. Sun Microsystems has integrated web services into the Java EE platform; specifically, Sun and the Java Community Process have introduced several web services APIs, including the Java API for XML Web Services (JAX-WS), the Java API for XML-based RPC (JAX-RPC), the SOAP with Attachments API for Java (SAAJ), and the Java API for XML Registries (JAXR). These web services APIs were integrated into J2EE 1.4 and have been expanded upon in Java EE 5 and EJB 3.0.

This chapter provides an overview of the technologies that are the foundation of web services: XML Schema and XML Namespaces, SOAP, and WSDL. Chapter 19 provides an overview of JAX-WS and JAX-RPC, the most important web services APIs.

Web Services Overview

The term *web services* means different things to different people, but thankfully, the definition is straightforward for EJB developers because the Java EE platform has adopted a rather narrow view of them. Specifically, a web service is a remote application described using the Web Service Description Language (WSDL) and accessed using the Simple Object Access Protocol (SOAP) according to the rules defined by the WS-I Basic Profile 1.1. The WS-I (Web Services Integration Organization) is a group of vendors (Microsoft, IBM, BEA, Sun Microsystems, Oracle, HP, and others) that have banded together to ensure web services are interoperable across all platforms. To do this, they have created a recommendation called the Basic Profile 1.1, which defines a set of rules for using XML, SOAP, and WSDL together to create interoperable web services.

In order to understand SOAP and WSDL, you must understand XML Schema and XML Namespaces. The rest of this chapter conducts a whirlwind tour of XML, SOAP, and WSDL. Although it's not the purpose of this book to cover these subjects in depth, you should be able to understand the basics. For more in-depth coverage, you can turn to *J2EE Web Services* (Addison-Wesley) or *Java Web Services* (O'Reilly).

XML Schema and XML Namespaces

We'll start with the basics of XML Schema and XML Namespaces. It's assumed that you already understand how to use basic XML elements and attributes. If you don't, you should probably read a primer on XML before proceeding. I recommend the book *Learning XML* (O'Reilly). If you already understand how XML Schema and XML Namespaces work, skip ahead to the section on SOAP.

XML Schema

An *XML Schema* is similar in purpose to a *Document Type Definition* (DTD), which validates the structure of an XML document. To illustrate some of the basic concepts of XML Schema, let's start with an XML document with address information:

```
<?xml version='1.0' encoding='UTF-8' standalone='yes'?>
<address>
  <street>3243 West 1st Ave.</street>
  <city>Madison</city>
  <state>WI</state>
  <zip>53591</zip>
</address>
```

In order to ensure that the XML document contains the proper type of elements and data, the address information must be evaluated for *correctness*. You measure the correctness of an XML document by determining two criteria: whether the document is *well formed* and whether it is *valid*. To be well formed, an XML document must obey the syntactic rules of the XML markup language: it must use proper attribute declarations, the correct characters to denote the start and end of elements, and so on. Most XML parsers based on standards like SAX and DOM detect documents that aren't well formed automatically.

In addition to being well formed, the document must use the right types of elements and attributes in the correct order and structure. A document that meets these criteria is called *valid*. However, the criteria for validity have nothing to do with XML itself; they have more to do with the application in which the document is used. For example, the Address document would not be valid if it didn't include the Zip Code or state elements. In order to validate an XML document, you need a way to represent these application-specific constraints.

The XML Schema for the Address XML document looks like this:

```
<?xml version='1.0' encoding='UTF-8' ?>
<schema xmlns="http://www.w3.org/2001/XMLSchema"
    xmlns:titan="http://www.titan.com/Reservation"
    targetNamespace="http://www.titan.com/Reservation">

  <element name="address" type="titan:AddressType"/>

  <complexType name="AddressType">
    <sequence>
      <element name="street" type="string"/>
      <element name="city" type="string"/>
      <element name="state" type="string"/>
      <element name="zip" type="string"/>
    </sequence>
  </complexType>

</schema>
```

The first thing to focus on in this XML Schema is the `<complexType>` element, which declares a type of element in much the same way that a Java class declares a type of object. The `<complexType>` element explicitly declares the names, types, and order of elements that an `AddressType` element may contain. In this case, it may contain four elements of type `string`, in the following order: `street`, `city`, `state`, and `zip`. Validation is pretty strict, so any XML document that claims conformity to this XML Schema must contain exactly the right elements with the right data types, in the correct order.

XML Schema automatically supports about two dozen simple data types, called *built-in types*. Built-in types are a part of the XML Schema language and are automatically supported by any XML Schema-compliant parser. Table 18-1 provides a short list of some of the built-in types. It also includes Java types that correspond to each built-in type. (Table 18-1 presents only a subset of all the XML Schema [XSD] built-in types, but it's more than enough for this book.)

Table 18-1. XML Schema built-in types and their corresponding Java types

XML Schema built-in type	Java type
byte	Byte, byte
boolean	Boolean, boolean
short	Short, short
int	Integer, int
long	Long, long
float	Float, float
double	Double, double
string	java.lang.String
dateTime	java.util.Calendar

Table 18-1. XML Schema built-in types and their corresponding Java types (continued)

XML Schema built-in type	Java type
integer	java.math.BigInteger
decimal	java.math.BigDecimal

By default, each element declared by a `<complexType>` must occur once in an XML document, but you can specify that an element is optional or that it must occur more than once by using the occurrence attributes. For example, we can say that the `street` element *must* occur once but *may* occur twice:

```
<complexType name="AddressType">
  <sequence>
    <element name="street" type="string" maxOccurs="2" minOccurs="1" />
    <element name="city" type="string"/>
    <element name="state" type="string"/>
    <element name="zip" type="string"/>
  </sequence>
</complexType>
```

By default, the `maxOccurs` and `minOccurs` attributes are always `1`, indicating that the element must occur exactly once. Setting `maxOccurs` to `2` allows an XML document to have either two `street` elements or just one. You can also set `maxOccurs` to `unbounded`, which means the element may occur as many times as needed. Setting `minOccurs` to `0` means the element is optional and can be omitted.

The `<element>` declarations are nested under a `<sequence>` element, which indicates that the elements must occur in the order they are declared. You can also nest the elements under an `<all>` declaration, which allows the elements to appear in any order. The following shows the `AddressType` declared with an `<all>` element rather than a `<sequence>` element:

```
<complexType name="AddressType">
   <all>
     <element name="street" type="string" maxOccurs="2" minOccurs="1" />
     <element name="city" type="string"/>
     <element name="state" type="string"/>
     <element name="zip" type="string"/>
   </all>
</complexType>
```

In addition to declaring elements of XSD built-in types, you can declare elements based on complex types. This is similar to how Java class types declare fields that are other Java class types. For example, we can define a `CustomerType` that uses the `AddressType`:

```
<?xml version='1.0' encoding='UTF-8' ?>
<schema xmlns="http://www.w3.org/2001/XMLSchema"
    xmlns:titan="http://www.titan.com/Reservation"
    targetNamespace="http://www.titan.com/Reservation">
```

```
  <element name="customer" type="titan:CustomerType"/>

<complexType name="CustomerType">
    <sequence>
      <element name="last-name" type="string"/>
      <element name="first-name" type="string"/>
      <element name="address" type="titan:AddressType"/>
    </sequence>
  </complexType>
<complexType name="AddressType">
    <sequence>
      <element name="street" type="string" />
      <element name="city" type="string"/>
      <element name="state" type="string"/>
      <element name="zip" type="string"/>
    </sequence>
 </complexType>

</schema>
```

This XSD tells us that an element of CustomerType must contain a <last-name> and <first-name> element of the built-in type string, and an element of type AddressType. This is straightforward, except for the titan: prefix on AddressType. That prefix identifies the XML Namespace of the AddressType; we'll discuss namespaces later in the chapter. For now, just think of it as declaring that the AddressType is a custom type defined by Titan Cruises. It's not a standard XSD built-in type. An XML document that conforms to the Customer XSD would look like this:

```
<?xml version='1.0' encoding='UTF-8' ?>
<customer>
  <last-name>Jones</last-name>
  <first-name>Sara</first-name>
  <address>
    <street>3243 West 1st Ave.</street>
    <city>Madison</city>
    <state>WI</state>
    <zip>53591</zip>
  </address>
</customer>
```

Building on what you've learned so far, we can create a Reservation schema using the CustomerType, the AddressType, and a new CreditCardType:

```
<?xml version='1.0' encoding='UTF-8' ?>
<schema xmlns="http://www.w3.org/2001/XMLSchema"
    xmlns:titan="http://www.titan.com/Reservation"
    targetNamespace="http://www.titan.com/Reservation">

  <element name="reservation" type="titan:ReservationType"/>

  <complexType name="ReservationType">
    <sequence>
      <element name="customer" type="titan:CustomerType"/>
```

```
        <element name="cruise-id" type="int"/>
        <element name="cabin-id" type="int"/>
        <element name="price-paid" type="double"/>
      </sequence>
    </complexType>
    <complexType name="CustomerType">
      <sequence>
        <element name="last-name" type="string"/>
        <element name="first-name" type="string"/>
        <element name="address" type="titan:AddressType"/>
        <element name="credit-card" type="titan:CreditCardType"/>
      </sequence>
    </complexType>
    <complexType name="CreditCardType">
      <sequence>
        <element name="exp-date" type="dateTime"/>
        <element name="number" type="string"/>
        <element name="name" type="string"/>
        <element name="organization" type="string"/>
      </sequence>
    </complexType>
    <complexType name="AddressType">
      <sequence>
        <element name="street" type="string"/>
        <element name="city" type="string"/>
        <element name="state" type="string"/>
        <element name="zip" type="string"/>
      </sequence>
    </complexType>
  </schema>
```

An XML document that conforms to the Reservation XSD would include information describing the customer (name and address), credit card information, and the identity of the cruise and cabin that are being reserved. This document might be sent to Titan Cruises from a travel agency that cannot access the TravelAgent EJB to make reservations. Here's an XML document that conforms to the Reservation XSD:

```
<?xml version='1.0' encoding='UTF-8' ?>
<reservation>
  <customer>
    <last-name>Jones</last-name>
    <first-name>Sara</first-name>
    <address>
      <street>3243 West 1st Ave.</street>
      <city>Madison</city>
      <state>WI</state>
      <zip>53591</zip>
    </address>
    <credit-card>
      <exp-date>09-2007/exp-date>
      <number>0394029302894028930</number>
      <name>Sara Jones</name>
      <organization>VISA</organization>
```

```
      </credit-card>
    </customer>
    <cruise-id>123</cruise-id>
    <cabin-id>333</cabin-id>
    <price-paid>6234.55</price-paid>
</reservation>
```

At runtime, the XML parser compares the document to its schema, ensuring that the document conforms to the schema's rules. If the document doesn't adhere to the schema, it is considered invalid, and the parser produces error messages. An XML Schema checks that XML documents received by your system are properly structured, so you won't encounter errors while parsing the documents and extracting the data. For example, if someone sent your application a Reservation document that omitted the credit card element, the XML parser could reject the document as invalid before your code even sees it; you don't have to worry about errors in your code caused by missing information in the document.

This brief overview represents only the tip of the iceberg. XML Schema is a very rich XML typing system and can be given sufficient attention only in a text dedicated to the subject. For in-depth and insightful coverage of XML Schema, read *XML Schema: The W3C's Object-Oriented Descriptions for XML* (O'Reilly), or read the XML Schema specification, starting with the primer at the World Wide Web Consortium (W3C) web site (*http://www.w3.org/TR/xmlschema-0*).

XML Namespaces

The Reservation schema defines an XML markup language that describes the structure of a specific kind of XML document. Just as a class is a type of Java object, an *XML markup language* is a type of XML document defined by an XML Schema. In some cases, it's convenient to combine two or more XML markup languages into a single document so that the elements from each markup language can be validated separately using different XML Schema. This is especially useful when you want to reuse a markup language in many different contexts. For example, the `AddressType` defined in the previous section is useful in a variety of contexts, not just the Reservation XSD, so it could be defined as a separate markup language in its own XML Schema:

```
<?xml version='1.0' encoding='UTF-8' ?>
<schema xmlns="http://www.w3.org/2001/XMLSchema"
    targetNamespace="http://www.titan.com/Address">

  <complexType name="AddressType">
    <sequence>
      <element name="street" type="string"/>
      <element name="city" type="string"/>
      <element name="state" type="string"/>
      <element name="zip" type="string"/>
    </sequence>
  </complexType>
</schema>
```

To use different markup languages in the same XML document, you must clearly identify the markup language to which each element belongs. The following example is an XML document for a reservation, but this time we are using XML Namespaces to separate the address information from the reservation information:

```
<?xml version='1.0' encoding='UTF-8' ?>
<res:reservation xmlns:res="http://www.titan.com/Reservation">
  <res:customer>
    <res:last-name>Jones</res:last-name>
    <res:first-name>Sara</res:first-name>

    <addr:address xmlns:addr="http://www.titan.com/Address">
      <addr:street>3243 West 1st Ave.</addr:street>
      <addr:city>Madison</addr:city>
      <addr:state>WI</addr:state>
      <addr:zip>53591</addr:zip>
    </addr:address>

    <res:credit-card>
      <res:exp-date>09-2007</res:exp-date>
      <res:number>0394029302894028930</res:number>
      <res:name>Sara Jones</res:name>
      <res:organization>VISA</res:organization>
    </res:credit-card>
  </res:customer>
  <res:cruise-id>123</res:cruise-id>
  <res:cabin-id>333</res:cabin-id>
  <res:price-paid>6234.55</res:price-paid>
</res:reservation>
```

All of the elements for the address information are prefixed with the characters `addr:` and all the reservation elements are prefixed with `res:`. These prefixes allow parsers to identify and separate the elements that belong to the Address markup from those that belong to the Reservation markup. As a result, the address elements can be validated against the Address XSD and the reservation elements can be validated against the Reservation XSD. The prefixes are assigned using XML Namespace declarations, which are shown in bold in the previous listing. An XML Namespace declaration follows this format:

```
xmlns:prefix="URI"
```

The prefix can be anything you like, as long as it does not include blank spaces or any special characters. We use prefixes that are abbreviations for the name of the markup language: `res` stands for Reservation XSD and `addr` stands for Address XSD. Most XML documents follow this convention, but it's not a requirement; you could use a prefix like `foo` or `bar` or anything else you fancy.

While the prefix can be any arbitrary token, the Universal Resource Identifier (URI) must be very specific. A *URI* is an identifier that is a superset of the Universal Resource Locator (URL), which you use every day to look up web pages. In most cases, people use the stricter URL format for XML Namespaces because URLs are familiar and easy to understand. The URI used in the XML Namespace declaration identifies the exact markup language that is employed. It doesn't have to point at a web page or an XML document; it only needs to be unique to that markup language. For example, the XML Namespace used by the Address markup is different from the URL used for the Reservation markup:

```
xmlns:addr="http://www.titan.com/Address"
xmlns:res="http://www.titan.com/Reservation"
```

The URI in the XML Namespace declaration should match the target namespace declared by the XML Schema. The following example shows the Address XSD with the target namespace declaration in bold. The URL value of the `targetNamespace` attribute is identical to the URL assigned to the `add:` prefix in the Reservation document shown earlier:

```
<?xml version='1.0' encoding='UTF-8' ?>
<schema xmlns="http://www.w3.org/2001/XMLSchema"
    targetNamespace="http://www.titan.com/Address">

  <complexType name="AddressType">
    <sequence>
      <element name="street" type="string"/>
      <element name="city" type="string"/>
      <element name="state" type="string"/>
      <element name="zip" type="string"/>
    </sequence>
  </complexType>
</schema>
```

The `targetNamespace` attribute identifies the unique URI of the markup language; it is the permanent identifier for that XML Schema. Whenever elements from the Address XSD are used in some other document, the document must use an XML Namespace declaration to identify those elements as belonging to the Address markup language.

Prefixing every element in an XML document with its namespace identifier is a bit tedious, so the XML Namespace allows you to declare a default namespace that applies to all nonprefixed elements. The default namespace is simply an XML Namespace declaration that has no prefix (`xmlns="`*`URL`*`"`). For example, we can use a default name in the Reservation document for all reservation elements:

```
<?xml version='1.0' encoding='UTF-8' ?>
<reservation xmlns="http://www.titan.com/Reservation">
  <customer>
    <last-name>Jones</last-name>
    <first-name>Sara</first-name>

    <addr:address xmlns:addr="http://www.titan.com/Address">
      <addr:street>3243 West 1st Ave.</addr:street>
      <addr:city>Madison</addr:city>
      <addr:state>WI</addr:state>
      <addr:zip>53591</addr:zip>
    </addr:address>
```

```
    <credit-card>
      <exp-date>09-2007</exp-date>
      <number>0394029302894028930</number>
      <name>Sara Jones</name>
      <organization>VISA</organization>
    </credit-card>
  </customer>
  <cruise-id>123</cruise-id>
  <cabin-id>333</cabin-id>
  <price-paid>6234.55</price-paid>
</reservation>
```

None of the reservation element names are prefixed. Any nonprefixed element belongs to the default namespace. The address elements do not belong to the *http://www.titan.com/Reservation* namespace, so they are prefixed to indicate to which namespace they belong. The default namespace declaration has *scope*; in other words, it applies to the element in which it is declared (if that element has no namespace prefix), and to all nonprefixed elements nested under that element. We can apply the scoping rules of namespace to simplify the Reservation document further by allowing the address elements to override the default namespace with their own default namespace:

```
<?xml version='1.0' encoding='UTF-8' ?>
<reservation xmlns="http://www.titan.com/Reservation">
  <customer>
    <last-name>Jones</last-name>
    <first-name>Sara</first-name>

    <address xmlns="http://www.titan.com/Address">
      <street>3243 West 1st Ave.</street>
      <city>Madison</city>
      <state>WI</state>
      <zip>53591</zip>
    </address>

    <credit-card>
      <exp-date>09-2007</exp-date>
      <number>0394029302894028930</number>
      <name>Sara Jones</name>
      <organization>VISA</organization>
    </credit-card>
  </customer>
  <cruise-id>123</cruise-id>
  <cabin-id>333</cabin-id>
  <price-paid>6234.55</price-paid>
</reservation>
```

The `Reservation` default namespace applies to the `<reservation>` element and all of its children, except for the address elements. The `<address>` element and its children have defined their own default namespace, which overrides the default namespace of the `<reservation>` element.

Default namespaces do not apply to attributes. As a result, any attributes used in an XML document should be prefixed with a namespace identifier. The only exceptions to this rule are attributes defined by the XML language itself, such as the xmlns attribute, which establishes an XML Namespace declaration. This attribute doesn't need to be prefixed because it is part of the XML language.

XML Namespaces are URIs that uniquely identify a namespace but do not actually point at a resource. In other words, you don't normally use the URI of an XML Namespace to look something up. It's usually only an identifier. However, you might want to indicate the location of the XML Schema associated with an XML Namespace so that a parser can upload it and use it in validation. This is accomplished using the schemaLocation attribute:

```
<?xml version='1.0' encoding='UTF-8' ?>
<reservation xmlns="http://www.titan.com/Reservation"
             xmlns:xsi="http://www.w3.org/2001/XMLSchema-Instance"
             xsi:schemaLocation="http://www.titan.com/Reservation
                                 http://www.titan.com/schemas/reservation.xsd">
  <customer>
    <last-name>Jones</last-name>
    <first-name>Sara</first-name>

    <address xmlns="http://www.titan.com/Address"
                 xsi:schemaLocation="http://www.titan.com/Address
                                 http://www.titan.com/schemas/address.xsd">
      <street>3243 West 1st Ave.</street>
      <city>Madison</city>
      <state>WI</state>
      <zip>53591</zip>
    </address>

    <credit-card>
      <exp-date>09-2007</exp-date>
      <number>0394029302894028930</number>
      <name>Sara Jones</name>
      <organization>VISA</organization>
    </credit-card>
  </customer>
  <cruise-id>123</cruise-id>
  <cabin-id>333</cabin-id>
  <price-paid>6234.55</price-paid>
</reservation>
```

The schemaLocation attribute provides a list of values as Namespace-Location value pairs. The first value is the URI of the XML Namespace; the second is the physical location (URL) of the XML Schema. The following schemaLocation attribute states that all elements belonging to the Reservation namespace (http://www.titan.com/Reservation) can be validated against an XML Schema located at the URL *http://www.titan.com/schemas/reservation.xsd*:

```
xsi:schemaLocation="http://www.titan.com/Reservation
                    http://www.titan.com/schemas/reservation.xsd">
```

The schemaLocation attribute is not a part of the XML language, so we'll actually need to prefix it with the appropriate namespace in order to use it. The XML Schema specification defines a special namespace that can be used for schemaLocation (as well as other attributes). That namespace is http://www.w3.org/2001/XMLSchema-Instance. To declare the schemaLocation attribute properly, you must declare its XML Namespace and prefix it with the identifier for that namespace, as shown in the following snippet:

```
<?xml version='1.0' encoding='UTF-8' ?>
<reservation xmlns="http://www.titan.com/Reservation"
                      xmlns:xsi="http://www.w3.org/2001/XMLSchema-Instance"
                      xsi:schemaLocation="http://www.titan.com/Reservation
                                       http://www.titan.com/schemas/reservation.xsd">
```

A namespace declaration needs to be defined only once; it applies to all elements nested under the element in which it's declared. The convention is to use the prefix xsi for the XML Schema Instance namespace (http://www.w3.org/2001/XMLSchema-Instance).

XML Schema also uses XML Namespaces. Let's look at XML Schema for the Address markup language with a new focus on the use of XML Namespaces:

```
<?xml version='1.0' encoding='UTF-8' ?>
<schema
    xmlns="http://www.w3.org/2001/XMLSchema"
    targetNamespace="http://www.titan.com/Address"
    xmlns:addr="http://www.titan.com/Address">

  <element name="address" type="addr:AddressType"/>

  <complexType name="AddressType">
    <sequence>
      <element name="street" type="string"/>
      <element name="city" type="string"/>
      <element name="state" type="string"/>
      <element name="zip" type="string"/>
    </sequence>
  </complexType>
```

In this file, namespaces are used in three separate declarations. The first declaration states that the default namespace is http://www.w3.org/2001/XMLSchema, which is the namespace of the XML Schema specification. This declaration makes it easier to read the XSD because most of the elements do not need to be prefixed. The second declaration states that the target namespace of the XML Schema is the namespace of the Address markup. This tells us that all the types and elements defined in this XSD belong to that namespace. Finally, the third namespace declaration assigns the prefix addr to the target namespace so that types can be referenced exactly. For example, the top-level <element> definition uses the name addr:AddressType to state that the element is of type AddressType, belonging to the namespace http://www.titan.com/Address.

Why do you have to declare a prefix for the target namespace? The reason is clearer when you examine the Reservation XSD:

```
<?xml version='1.0' encoding='UTF-8' ?>
<schema
    xmlns="http://www.w3.org/2001/XMLSchema"
    xmlns:xsi="http://www.w3.org/2001/XMLSchema-Instance"
    xmlns:addr="http://www.titan.com/Address"
    xmlns:res="http://www.titan.com/Reservation"
    targetNamespace="http://www.titan.com/Reservation">

  <import namespace="http://www.titan.com/Address"
               xsi:schemaLocation="http://www.titan.com/Address.xsd" />

  <element name="reservation" type="res:ReservationType"/>

  <complexType name="ReservationType">
    <sequence>
      <element name="customer" type="res:CustomerType"/>
      <element name="cruise-id" type="int"/>
      <element name="cabin-id" type="int"/>
      <element name="price-paid" type="double"/>
    </sequence>
  </complexType>
  <complexType name="CustomerType">
    <sequence>
      <element name="last-name" type="string"/>
      <element name="first-name" type="string"/>
      <element name="address" type="addr:AddressType"/>
      <element name="credit-card" type="res:CreditCardType"/>
    </sequence>
  </complexType>
  <complexType name="CreditCardType">
    <sequence>
      <element name="exp-date" type="dateTime"/>
      <element name="number" type="string"/>
      <element name="name" type="string"/>
      <element name="organization" type="string"/>
    </sequence>
  </complexType>
</schema>
```

The Reservation XSD imports the Address XSD so that the `AddressType` can be used to define the `CustomerType`. You can see the use of namespaces in the definition of `CustomerType`, which references types from both the Address and Reservation namespaces (prefixed by addr and res, respectively):

```
<?xml version='1.0' encoding='UTF-8' ?>
<schema
    xmlns="http://www.w3.org/2001/XMLSchema"
    xmlns:xsi="http://www.w3.org/2001/XMLSchema-Instance"
    xmlns:addr="http://www.titan.com/Address"
    xmlns:res="http://www.titan.com/Reservation"
    targetNamespace="http://www.titan.com/Reservation">
```

```
...
<complexType name="CustomerType">
   <sequence>
     <element name="last-name" type="string"/>
     <element name="first-name" type="string"/>
     <element name="address" type="addr:AddressType"/>
     <element name="credit-card" type="res:CreditCardType"/>
   </sequence>
 </complexType>
```

Assigning a prefix to the `Reservation` namespace allows us to distinguish between elements that are defined as Reservation types (e.g., `credit-card`) and elements that are defined as Address types (e.g., `address`). All the `type` attributes that reference the built-in `string` and `int` types also belong to the XML Schema namespace, so we don't need to prefix them. We could, though, for clarity. That is, we'd replace `string` and `int` with `xsd:string` and `xsd:int`. The prefix `xsd` references the `XML Schema` namespace; it allows us to identify built-in types defined as XML Schema more clearly. It's not a problem that the default namespace is the same as the namespace prefixed by `xsd`. By convention, the `xsd` prefix is the one used in most XML Schema.

SOAP 1.1

SOAP 1.1 is simply a distributed object protocol such as DCOM, CORBA's IIOP, and JRMP (the primary transport used by RMI). The most significant difference between SOAP 1.1 and other distributed object protocols is that SOAP 1.1 is based on XML.

SOAP is defined by its own XML Schema and relies heavily on the use of XML Namespaces. Every SOAP message that is sent across the wire is an XML document consisting of standard SOAP elements and application data. The use of namespaces differentiates the standard SOAP elements from the application data. Here's a SOAP request message that might be sent from a client to a server:

```
<?xml version='1.0' encoding='UTF-8' ?>
<env:Envelope xmlns:env="http://schemas.xmlsoap.org/soap/envelope/">
   <env:Header />
   <env:Body>
       <reservation xmlns="http://www.titan.com/Reservation">
             <customer>
                      <!-- customer info goes here -->
             </customer>
             <cruise-id>123</cruise-id>
             <cabin-id>333</cabin-id>
             <price-paid>6234.55</price-paid>
       </reservation>
   </env:Body>
</env:Envelope>
```

The standard SOAP elements are shown in bold and the application data, or the Reservation XML document fragment, is shown in regular text. SOAP's primary purpose is to establish a standard XML framework for packaging application data that is exchanged between different software platforms, such as Java and Perl, or Java and .NET. To do this, SOAP defines a set of elements, each designed to carry different data. The `<Envelope>` element is the root of the SOAP message; all other elements are contained by it. Within the `<Envelope>` element are two direct children: the `<Header>` element and the `<Body>` element.

The `<Header>` element is generally used for carrying infrastructure data such as security tokens, transaction IDs, routing information, and so on. In the previous example, the `<Header>` element is empty, which is not unusual for basic web services. In many cases, we are only interested in exchanging information and not in more advanced issues, such as those relating to security and transactions. Although the `<Body>` element is required, the `<Header>` element is not. From this point forward, the `<Header>` element will be omitted from examples.

The `<Body>` element carries the application information that is being exchanged. In the previous example, the `<Body>` element contains a `<reservation>` element, which is the application data. It's an XML document fragment based on the Reservation XSD developed earlier in this chapter. It's called a "fragment" because it's embedded inside a SOAP message, instead of standing alone.

Web Services Styles

The SOAP message in the previous example is a *Document/Literal message*, which means that the message body is a single XML Schema instance document, and thus the full message can be validated. For this reason, Document/Literal is becoming the preferred message style of the web services community.

The `schemaLocation` attribute could have been included; it's omitted because we assume that the receiver is already familiar with the schema used for that type of SOAP message.

The other style allowed by the WS-I Basic Profile 1.1 and supported by EJB 3.0 is *RPC/Literal*. RPC/Literal represents SOAP messages as RPC calls with parameters and return values, each with its own schema type. The following Java interface defines a single method called `makeReservation( )`:

```
public interface TravelAgent {
    public void makeReservation(int cruiseID, int cabinID,
                                int customerId, double price);
}
```

The `makeReservation( )` method can be modeled as a SOAP message using the RPC/Literal messaging style:

```
<env:Envelope
    xmlns:env="http://schemas.xmlsoap.org/soap/envelope/"
    xmlns:titan="http://www.titan.com/TravelAgent"/>
   <env:Body>
```

```
        <titan:makeReservation>
              <cruiseId>23</cruiseId>
              <cabinId>144</cabinId>
              <customerId>9393</customerId>
              <price>5677.88</price>
        </titan:makeReservation>
    </env:Body>
</env:Envelope
```

The first element within the <Body> identifies the web services operation being invoked. In this case, it's the makeReservation operation. Directly under the <titan:makeReservation> element are the parameters of the RPC call, each represented by an element with a value.

EJB 3.0, but not the WS-I Basic Profile 1.1, supports the *RPC/Encoded* mode of SOAP messaging. Most SOAP applications used RPC/Encoded when web services were first created. However, the web services industry has moved toward Document/Literal and RPC/Literal, primarily because interoperability between platforms using RPC/Encoded proved to be less than perfect and sometimes downright difficult. While RPC/Encoded SOAP messages rely on SOAP-defined types for arrays, enumeration, unions, lists, and the like, RPC/Literal and Document/Literal depend only on XML Schema for their data types, which seems to provide a better system for interoperability across programming languages. Although EJB 3.0 supports RPC/Encoded messaging, it's not a very good option to use in web services. RPC/Encoded messaging will not be addressed in this book.

Exchanging SOAP Messages with HTTP

SOAP messages are *network-protocol agnostic*, which means that a SOAP message is not aware of or dependent on the type of network or protocol used to carry it. With that said, SOAP is primarily exchanged using HTTP. The reason for using HTTP is simple. Most Internet products, including web servers, application servers, and wireless devices, are designed to handle the HTTP protocol. This widespread support provides an instant infrastructure for SOAP messaging. The fact that SOAP can leverage the ubiquity of HTTP is one of the reasons it has become so popular so quickly.

Another advantage of using HTTP is that SOAP messages can slip through firewalls without any hassles. If you have ever tried to support internal or external customers who are separated from you by a firewall (yours or theirs), you know the headaches it can create. Unless you have direct control over the firewall, your chances of communicating with arbitrary clients using anything but HTTP or SMTP (email) are slim to none. However, because SOAP can be transmitted with HTTP, it slips through the firewall unnoticed. This ability makes life a lot simpler for the application developer, but it's a point of contention with the security folks. Understandably, they're a bit irked by the idea of application developers circumventing their defenses. Using HTTP to carry an application protocol such as SOAP is commonly called *HTTP tunneling*. In the past, support for tunneling by vendors of other distributed object protocols (CORBA IIOP, DCOM, and so on) was sporadic and proprietary, making interoperability extremely difficult. However, tunneling over HTTP is built into the SOAP 1.1 specification, which means interoperability is no longer a problem. Because almost every application server vendor rapidly adopts SOAP, SOAP-HTTP tunneling is becoming ubiquitous.

You can use SOAP 1.2 with other protocols, such as SMTP, FTP, and even raw TCP/IP, but HTTP is the only protocol for which a binding is currently specified. As a result, EJB 3.0 and Java EE 5 require support for SOAP 1.1 over HTTP 1.1 but not other protocols.

Now You See It, Now You Don't

All this talk about SOAP is intended to give you a better idea of what is going on under the hood, but in practice, you are unlikely to interact with the protocol directly. As with most protocols, SOAP is designed to be produced and consumed by software and is usually encapsulated by a developer API. In EJB 3.0, the API you use to exchange SOAP messages is the Java API for XML-based Web Services (JAX-WS), which hides the details of SOAP messaging so that you can focus on developing and invoking web services. While using JAX-WS, you will rarely have to deal with the SOAP protocol, which is nice because it makes you a lot more productive. JAX-WS is covered in Chapter 19.

WSDL 1.1

The Web Service Description Language (WSDL) is an XML document used to describe a web service. WSDL is programming-language, platform, and protocol agnostic. The fact that WSDL is protocol agnostic means that it can describe web services that use protocols other than SOAP and HTTP. This ability makes WSDL very flexible, but it has the unfortunate side effect of also making WSDL abstract and difficult to understand. Fortunately, the WS-I Basic Profile 1.1 endorses only SOAP 1.1 or 1.2 over HTTP, so we'll discuss WSDL as if that's the only combination of protocols supported.

Imagine that you want to develop a web services component that implements the following interface:

```
public interface TravelAgent {
    public String makeReservation(int cruiseID, int cabinID,
                                  int customerId, double price);
}
```

Any application should be able to invoke this method using SOAP, regardless of the language in which it was written or the platform on which it is running. Because other programming languages don't understand Java, we have to describe the web service in a language they do understand: XML. Using XML, and specifically the WSDL markup language, we can describe the type of SOAP messages that must be sent to invoke the `makeReservation( )` method. A WSDL document that describes the `makeReservation( )` method might look like this:

```
<?xml version="1.0"?>
<definitions name="TravelAgent"
   xmlns="http://schemas.xmlsoap.org/wsdl/"
   xmlns:soap="http://schemas.xmlsoap.org/wsdl/soap/"
   xmlns:xsd="http://www.w3.org/2001/XMLSchema"
   xmlns:titan="http://www.titan.com/TravelAgent"
   targetNamespace="http://www.titan.com/TravelAgent">

<!-- message elements describe the parameters and return values -->
<message name="RequestMessage">
   <part name="cruiseId"   type="xsd:int" />
   <part name="cabinId"    type="xsd:int" />
   <part name="customerId" type="xsd:int" />
   <part name="price"      type="xsd:double" />
</message>
<message name="ResponseMessage">
   <part name="reservationId" type="xsd:string" />
</message>

<!-- portType element describes the abstract interface of a web service -->
<portType name="TravelAgent">
  <operation name="makeReservation">
     <input message="titan:RequestMessage"/>
     <output message="titan:ResponseMessage"/>
  </operation>
</portType>

<!-- binding element tells us which protocols and encoding styles are used  -->
<binding name="TravelAgentBinding" type="titan:TravelAgent">
   <soap:binding style="rpc"
              transport="http://schemas.xmlsoap.org/soap/http"/>
   <operation name="makeReservation">
      <soap:operation soapAction="" />
      <input>
        <soap:body use="literal"
              namespace="http://www.titan.com/TravelAgent"/>
      </input>
      <output>
        <soap:body use="literal"
              namespace="http://www.titan.com/TravelAgent"/>
      </output>
   </operation>
</binding>

<!-- service element tells us the Internet address of a web service -->
<service name="TravelAgentService">
  <port name="TravelAgentPort" binding="titan:TravelAgentBinding">
     <soap:address location="http://www.titan.com/webservices/TravelAgent" />
```

```
    </port>
  </service>

  </definitions>
```

If you find the previous WSDL listing indecipherable, don't despair. Most people can't understand a WSDL document the first time they see one. Like many things that are complicated, the best approach to understanding WSDL is to study it in pieces. And fortunately, modern web services platforms, like JBoss, provide tools to generate the WSDL for you. WSDL should be something you need to look at only when things break. At this point, things still break often, so it's helpful to be familiar with WSDL: it will show you what the server expects when a method is called. But don't think that you'll be called on to write a WSDL document by yourself.

The <definitions> Element

The root element of a WSDL document is the `<definitions>` element. Usually, a WSDL document declares all the XML Namespaces used in the root element. In the previous example, the `<definitions>` element makes four XML Namespace declarations:

```
<?xml version="1.0"?>
<definitions name="TravelAgent"
   xmlns="http://schemas.xmlsoap.org/wsdl/"
   xmlns:soap="http://schemas.xmlsoap.org/wsdl/soap/"
   xmlns:xsd="http://www.w3.org/2001/XMLSchema"
   xmlns:titan="http://www.titan.com/TravelAgent"
   targetNamespace="http://www.titan.com/TravelAgent">
```

The default namespace (`xmlns="http://schemas.xmlsoap.org/wsdl/"`) is the WSDL namespace. The `xsd` prefix is assigned to the `XML Schema` namespace. It is used primarily to identify simple data types such as `xsd:string`, `xsd:int`, and `xsd:dateTime` in `<message>` elements:

```
<message name="RequestMessage">
   <part name="cruiseId"   type="xsd:int" />
   <part name="cabinId"    type="xsd:int" />
   <part name="customerId" type="xsd:int" />
   <part name="price"      type="xsd:double" />
</message>
<message name="ResponseMessage">
   <part name="reservationId" type="xsd:string" />
</message>
```

The `titan` prefix is assigned to a Titan Cruises URL, which indicates that it's an XML Namespace belonging to Titan Cruises. This namespace is also the value of the `targetNamespace` attribute. This attribute is similar to the one used in XML Schema. For example, the `<portType>` element references `<message>` elements and the `<binding>` element references a `<portType>` element using the target namespace:

```
<!-- message elements describe the parameters and return values -->
<message name="RequestMessage">
   <part name="cruiseId"   type="xsd:int" />
   <part name="cabinId"    type="xsd:int" />
   <part name="customerId" type="xsd:int" />
   <part name="price"      type="xsd:double" />
</message>
<message name="ResponseMessage">
   <part name="reservationId" type="xsd:string" />
</message>

<!-- portType element describes the abstract interface of a web service -->
<portType name="TravelAgent">
  <operation name="makeReservation">
     <input message="titan:RequestMessage"/>
     <output message="titan:ResponseMessage"/>
  </operation>
</portType>

<!-- binding element tells us which protocols and encoding styles are used  -->
<binding name="TravelAgentBinding" type="titan:TravelAgent">
   ...
</binding>
```

As you can see, the different WSDL types reference each other by name, and a named WSDL type automatically takes on the namespace declared by the `targetNamespace` attribute.

The <portType> and <message> Elements

The `<portType>` and `<message>` elements are the immediate children of the `<definitions>` element. Here's what they look like:

```
<!-- message elements describe the parameters and return values -->
<message name="RequestMessage">
   <part name="cruiseId"   type="xsd:int" />
   <part name="cabinId"    type="xsd:int" />
   <part name="customerId" type="xsd:int" />
   <part name="price"      type="xsd:double" />
</message>
<message name="ResponseMessage">
   <part name="reservationId" type="xsd:string" />
</message>

<!-- portType element describes the abstract interface of a web service -->
<portType name="TravelAgent">
  <operation name="makeReservation">
     <input message="titan:RequestMessage"/>
     <output message="titan:ResponseMessage"/>
  </operation>
</portType>
```

The <portType> element describes the web services operations (Java methods) that are available. An operation can have input, output, and fault messages. An *input message* describes the type of SOAP message a client should send to the web service. An *output message* describes the type of SOAP message a client should expect to get back. A *fault message* (not shown in the example) describes any SOAP error messages that the web service might send back to the client. A fault message is similar to a Java exception.

JAX-WS, and therefore EJB 3.0, supports two styles of web services messaging: *request-response* and *one-way*. You know you are dealing with request-response if the <operation> element contains a single <input> element, followed by a single <output> element, and optionally, zero or more <fault> elements. The TravelAgent <portType> is an example of the request-response messaging style:

```
<!-- portType element describes the abstract interface of a web service -->
<portType name="TravelAgent">
  <operation name="makeReservation">
     <input message="titan:RequestMessage"/>
     <output message="titan:ResponseMessage"/>
  </operation>
</portType>
```

The one-way message style, on the other hand, is implied by the presence of a single <input> element but no <output> or <fault> element. Here is a web service that supports one-way messaging:

```
<!-- portType element describes the abstract interface of a web service -->
<portType name="ReservationProcessor">
  <operation name="submitReservation">
     <input message="titan:ReservationMessage"/>
  </operation>
</portType>
```

The request-response style of messaging is the kind you expect in RPC programming; you send a message and get a response. The one-way style tends to be used for asynchronous messaging; you send a message but do not expect a response. In addition, one-way messaging is frequently used to deliver XML documents, such as the Reservation document, rather than parameters and return values. However, both request-response and one-way messaging styles can be used with either RPC or document-style messaging.

WSDL also supports two other messaging styles: *notification* (a single <output> and no <input>) and *solicitation* (a single <output> followed by a single <input>). While WSDL makes these messaging styles available, they are not supported by WS-I Basic Profile 1.1 or JAX-RPC.

The <types> Element

If your service needs any custom types, they are defined in the <types> element, which is the first child of the <definitions> element. The complete WSDL document shown earlier did not include a <types> element because it didn't define any new types (it used XML Schema built-in types). The <types> element allows us to declare more complex XML types. For example, instead of declaring each parameter of the makeReservation operation as an individual part, you can combine them into a single structure that serves as the parameter of the operation:

```
<?xml version="1.0"?>
<definitions name="TravelAgent"
   xmlns="http://schemas.xmlsoap.org/wsdl/"
   xmlns:soap="http://schemas.xmlsoap.org/wsdl/soap/"
   xmlns:xsd="http://www.w3.org/2001/XMLSchema"
   xmlns:titan="http://www.titan.com/TravelAgent"
   targetNamespace="http://www.titan.com/TravelAgent">

<!-- types element describes complex XML data types -->
<types>
  <xsd:schema
    targetNamespace="http://www.titan.com/TravelAgent">

    <xsd:complexType name="ReservationType">
      <xsd:sequence>
        <xsd:element name="cruiseId" type="xsd:int"/>
        <xsd:element name="cabinId" type="xsd:int"/>
        <xsd:element name="customerId" type="xsd:int"/>
        <xsd:element name="price-paid" type="xsd:double"/>
      </xsd:sequence>
    </xsd:complexType>
  </xsd:schema>
</types>

<!-- message elements describe the parameters and return values -->
<message name="RequestMessage">
   <part name="reservation" type="titan:ReservationType" />
</message>
<message name="ResponseMessage">
   <part name="reservationId" type="xsd:string" />
</message>
```

The <types> element is frequently used with document-oriented messaging. For example, the following WSDL binding defines an XML Schema for the Reservation markup so that Reservation documents can be submitted to Titan as one-way messages. The schema is embedded within the WSDL document as the content of the <types> element:

```
<?xml version="1.0"?>
<definitions name="Reservation"
   xmlns="http://schemas.xmlsoap.org/wsdl/"
   xmlns:soap="http://schemas.xmlsoap.org/wsdl/soap/"
```

```
   xmlns:xsd="http://www.w3.org/2001/XMLSchema"
   xmlns:titan="http://www.titan.com/Reservation"
   targetNamespace="http://www.titan.com/Reservation">

<!-- types element describes complex XML data types -->
<types>
  <xsd:schema
    targetNamespace="http://www.titan.com/Reservation">

  <xsd:element name="reservation" type="titan:ReservationType"/>

  <xsd:complexType name="ReservationType">
    <xsd:sequence>
      <xsd:element name="customer" type="titan:CustomerType"/>
      <xsd:element name="cruise-id" type="xsd:int"/>
      <xsd:element name="cabin-id" type="xsd:int"/>
      <xsd:element name="price-paid" type="xsd:double"/>
    </xsd:sequence>
  </xsd:complexType>
  <xsd:complexType name="CustomerType">
    <xsd:sequence>
      <xsd:element name="last-name" type="xsd:string"/>
      <xsd:element name="first-name" type="xsd:string"/>
      <xsd:element name="address" type="titan:AddressType"/>
      <xsd:element name="credit-card" type="titan:CreditCardType"/>
    </xsd:sequence>
  </xsd:complexType>
  <xsd:complexType name="CreditCardType">
    <xsd:sequence>
      <xsd:element name="exp-date" type="xsd:dateTime"/>
      <xsd:element name="number" type="xsd:string"/>
      <xsd:element name="name" type="xsd:string"/>
      <xsd:element name="organization" type="xsd:string"/>
    </xsd:sequence>
  </xsd:complexType>
  <xsd:complexType name="AddressType">
    <xsd:sequence>
      <xsd:element name="street" type="xsd:string"/>
      <xsd:element name="city" type="xsd:string"/>
      <xsd:element name="state" type="xsd:string"/>
      <xsd:element name="zip" type="xsd:string"/>
    </xsd:sequence>
  </xsd:complexType>
 </xsd:schema>
</types>

<!-- message elements describe the parameters and return values -->
<message name="ReservationMessage">
   <part name="inmessage" element="titan:reservation"/>
</message>
<!-- portType element describes the abstract interface of a web service -->
<portType name="ReservationProcessor">
  <operation name="submitReservation">
     <input message="titan:ReservationMessage"/>
```

```
    </operation>
  </portType>
  <!-- binding tells us which protocols and encoding styles are used  -->
  <binding name="ReservationProcessorBinding" type="titan:ReservationProcessor">
     <soap:binding style="document"
                   transport="http://schemas.xmlsoap.org/soap/http"/>
     <operation name="submitReservation">
        <soap:operation soapAction="" />
        <input>
          <soap:body use="literal"/>
        </input>
     </operation>
  </binding>
  <!-- service tells us the Internet address of a web service -->
  <service name="ReservationProcessorService">
    <port name="ReservationProcessorPort" binding="titan:ReservationProcessorBinding">
       <soap:address location="http://www.titan.com/webservices/Reservation" />
    </port>
  </service>

  </definitions>
```

The <binding> and <service> Elements

In addition to the `<portType>` and `<message>` elements, a WSDL document also defines `<binding>` and `<service>` elements. JAX-WS specifies these elements to generate marshaling and network communication code that is used to send and receive messages.

The `<binding>` element describes the type of encoding used to send and receive messages as well as the protocol on which the SOAP messages are carried. The `<binding>` definition for the `TravelAgent` port type looks like this:

```
  <!-- binding element tells us which protocols and encoding styles are used  -->
  <binding name="TravelAgentBinding" type="titan:TravelAgent">
     <soap:binding style="rpc"
                   transport="http://schemas.xmlsoap.org/soap/http"/>
     <operation name="makeReservation">
        <soap:operation soapAction="" />
        <input>
          <soap:body use="literal"
                namespace="http://www.titan.com/TravelAgent"/>
        </input>
        <output>
          <soap:body use="literal"
                namespace="http://www.titan.com/TravelAgent"/>
        </output>
     </operation>
  </binding>
```

A binding element is always interlaced with protocol-specific elements—usually, the elements describe the SOAP protocol binding. (In fact, this is the only binding that is allowed by the WS-I Basic Profile 1.1.) Because Java EE web services must support SOAP with attachments, the MIME binding is also supported when attachments (images, documents, and so on) are sent with SOAP messages. However, that subject is a bit involved and is outside the scope of this book.

Similar to the <portType> element, the <binding> element contains <operation>, <input>, <output>, and <fault> elements. In fact, a binding is specific to a particular <portType>: its <operation>, <input>, and <output> elements describe the implementation details of the corresponding <portType>. The previous example used the HTTP protocol with RPC/Literal-style messaging. The WSDL binding for Document/Literal-style messaging is different:

```
<!-- binding element tells us which protocols and encoding styles are used  -->
<binding name="TravelAgentBinding" type="titan:TravelAgent">
   <soap:binding style="document"
                 transport="http://schemas.xmlsoap.org/soap/http"/>
   <operation name="submitReservation">
      <soap:operation soapAction=""/>
      <input>
        <soap:body use="literal"/>
      </input>
   </operation>
</binding>
```

The <binding> element describes a one-way web service that accepts an XML document fragment. The <portType> associated with this <binding> also defines a single input message (consistent with one-way messaging) within an operation called submitReservation:

```
<!-- portType element describes the abstract interface of a web service -->
<portType name="ReservationProcessor">
  <operation name="submitReservation">
     <input message="titan:ReservationMessage"/>
  </operation>
</portType>
```

UDDI 2.0

Universal Description, Discovery, and Integration (UDDI) is a specification that describes a standard for publishing and discovering web services on the Internet. It's essentially a repository with a rigid data structure describing companies and the web services they provide. UDDI is not as fundamental to web services as XML, SOAP, and WSDL, but it is considered a basic constituent of web services in Java EE.

The analogy normally used to describe UDDI is that it provides electronic White, Yellow, and Green pages for companies and their web services. You can look up companies by name or identifier (White pages) or by business or product category (Yellow pages). You can also discover information about web services hosted by a company by examining the technical entities of a UDDI registry (Green pages). In other words, UDDI is an electronic directory that allows organizations to advertise their business and web services and to locate other organizations and web services.

Not only does a UDDI registry provide information about web services and their hosts, a UDDI repository is itself a web service. You can search, access, add, update, and delete information in a UDDI registry using a set of standard SOAP messages. All UDDI registry products must support the standard UDDI data structures and SOAP messages, which means that you can access any UDDI-compliant registry using the same standard set of SOAP messages.

Although organizations can set up private UDDI registries, there is a free UDDI registry that anyone can use, called the Universal Business Registry (UBR). This registry is accessed at one of four sites hosted by Microsoft, IBM, SAP, and NTT. If you publish information about your company in any one of these sites, the data will be replicated to each of the other three. You can find out more about the UBR and the sites that host it at *http://www.uddi.org*.

From Standards to Implementation

Understanding the fundamental web services standards (XML, SOAP, and WSDL) is essential to becoming a competent web services developer. However, you'll also need to understand how to implement web services in software. Numerous web services platforms allow you to build production systems based on the web services standards, including .NET, Perl, and Java EE. The focus of this book is obviously the Java EE platform, and specifically, support for web services in EJB. The next chapter explains how JAX-WS and its precursor (JAX-RPC) are used to support web services in Enterprise JavaBeans.

CHAPTER 19

EJB 3.0 and Web Services

Support for web services in EJB 3.0 is based on the Java API for XML-based Web Services (JAX-WS) 2.0 specification, as well its predecessor, the Java API for XML-based RPC (JAX-RPC) 1.1. The name was changed primarily to avoid the common misconception that web services are only about RPC. Other specifications included in EJB 3.0 are the SOAP with Attachments API for Java (SAAJ) and the Java API for XML Registries (JAXR). JAX-WS and JAX-RPC are similar to RMI and CORBA, except they use the SOAP protocol; SAAJ is an API for manipulating the structure of a SOAP message; and JAXR allows you to access web services registries, usually UDDI.

Although this chapter and Chapter 18 provide you with a launching pad for learning about web services in Java EE (specifically EJB), the subject is too huge to cover in a book about EJB. In order to cover Java EE web services comprehensively, we would need another 500 pages. Since you'll need to lift this book to read it, we wrote a lighter approach to the subject. This chapter provides you with an introduction to both JAX-WS and JAX-RPC, but you should not consider it a comprehensive guide to the APIs.

If you are interested in learning more about the standard web services technologies (XML, SOAP, WSDL, and UDDI) and Java EE APIs (JAX-RPC, SAAJ, and JAXR), you might want to read *J2EE Web Services* (Addison-Wesley), which provides complete and thorough coverage of these topics.

The main purpose of a web services API is to bridge Java components with the standard web services protocols. Unlike other distributed technologies, web services were designed to be very flexible and very extendable. Although this makes the technology more open and more adaptable, it also makes transparency harder to achieve. A good web services API will go to great lengths to achieve transparency. The process of invoking and defining a web service in Java should be as close as possible to invoking and defining a normal object in Java. Both JAX-RPC and JAX-WS attempt to achieve this goal, although we think you will see that JAX-WS does a much better job. We will start with JAX-RPC and then move into the newer JAX-WS API.

Accessing Web Services with JAX-RPC

JAX-RPC provides a client-side programming model that allows you to access web services on other platforms from your EJBs. In other words, by using JAX-RPC, EJBs can access web services across the network hosted on both Java and non-Java platforms (Perl, .NET, C++, and so on). There are three APIs for accessing web services: generated stubs, dynamic proxies, and the Dynamic Invocation Interface (DII). When JAX-RPC is accessed from a Java EE/EJB 3.0 environment, the decision to use a dynamic proxy or a stub is up to the specific container on which you are running. In this case, however, a dynamic proxy will most likely be used because a stub is not portable between Java EE platforms.

A *dynamic proxy* is very much like the classic Java RMI or CORBA programming model, where the client accesses a remote service via a remote interface implemented by a network stub. The stub translates calls made on the remote interface into network messages that are sent to the remote service. It's similar to using an EJB remote reference; however, the protocol is SOAP over HTTP rather than CORBA IIOP. Figure 19-1 illustrates the remote execution loop executed with a JAX-RPC dynamic proxy.

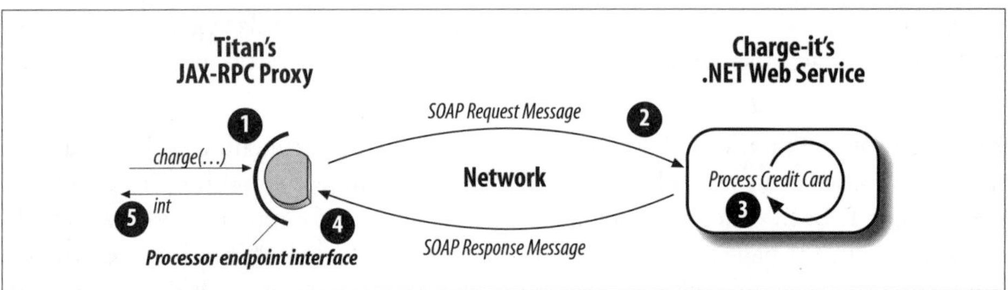

Figure 19-1. The JAX-RPC RMI loop

The execution loop in JAX-RPC is the same as any other RMI loop. In Step 1, the client invokes a method on the JAX-RPC proxy that implements the service endpoint interface. The method invocation is transformed into a SOAP message that is sent to the server in Step 2. In Step 3, the web service processes the request and sends the results back as a SOAP response message in Step 4. In Step 5, the SOAP response message is transformed into either a return value or an exception (if it was a SOAP fault) and is then returned to the client.

Generating JAX-RPC Artifacts from WSDL

The primary interface that describes a JAX-RPC web service is called a *service endpoint interface*. A JAX-RPC-compliant compiler generates the endpoint interface from a WSDL `<portType>` definition. This interface, when combined with WSDL `<binding>` and `<port>` definitions, is used to create the dynamic proxy at deploy time. The organization that hosts the web service provides the WSDL document.

Imagine that Titan Cruises subcontracts a company, Charge-It Inc., to process payments made by customers using credit cards. Charge-It runs a system based on .NET and exposes its credit card processing application to clients via a web service. A WSDL document describes the web service. The WSDL document for Charge-It's web service looks like this:

```
<?xml version="1.0" encoding="UTF-8"?>
<definitions xmlns="http://schemas.xmlsoap.org/wsdl/"
    xmlns:wsdl="http://schemas.xmlsoap.org/wsdl/"
    xmlns:xsd="http://www.w3.org/2001/XMLSchema"
    xmlns:soap="http://schemas.xmlsoap.org/wsdl/soap/"
    xmlns:tns="http://charge-it.com/Processor"
    targetNamespace="http://charge-it.com/Processor">

<message name="chargeRequest">
  <part name="name" type="xsd:string"/>
  <part name="number" type="xsd:string"/>
  <part name="exp-date" type="xsd:dateTime"/>
  <part name="card-type" type="xsd:string"/>
  <part name="amount" type="xsd:float"/>
</message>
<message name="chargeResponse">
  <part name="return" type="xsd:int"/>
</message>
<portType name="Processor">
  <operation name="charge">
    <input message="tns:chargeRequest"/>
    <output message="tns:chargeResponse"/>
  </operation>
</portType>
<binding name="ProcessorSoapBinding" type="tns:Processor">
  <soap:binding style="rpc"
      transport="http://schemas.xmlsoap.org/soap/http"/>
  <operation name="charge">
    <soap:operation soapAction="" style="rpc"/>
    <input>
      <soap:body use="literal"
          namespace="http://charge-it.com/Processor"/>
    </input>
    <output>
      <soap:body use="literal"
          namespace="http://charge-it.com/Processor"/>
    </output>
  </operation>
</binding>
<service name="ProcessorService">
   <port name="ProcessorPort" binding="tns:ProcessorSoapBinding">
      <soap:address
       location="http://www.charge-it.com/ProcessorService"/>
   </port>
</service>
</definitions>
```

The endpoint interface is based on the WSDL <portType> and its corresponding <message> definitions. Based on these definitions, a JAX-RPC compiler would generate the following interface:

```
package com.charge_it;

public interface Processor extends java.rmi.Remote {
    public int charge(String name, String number, java.util.Calendar expDate,
                      String cardType, float amount)
                      throws java.rmi.RemoteException;
}
```

An endpoint interface is a plain Java interface that extends the `java.rmi.Remote` interface. All methods on the service endpoint interface must throw RemoteException, although the bean implementation class is not required to. Application exceptions can be thrown from any business method. The interface name, method names, parameters, and exceptions are derived from the WSDL document. Figure 19-2 shows the mapping between the <portType> and <message> definitions and the endpoint interface.

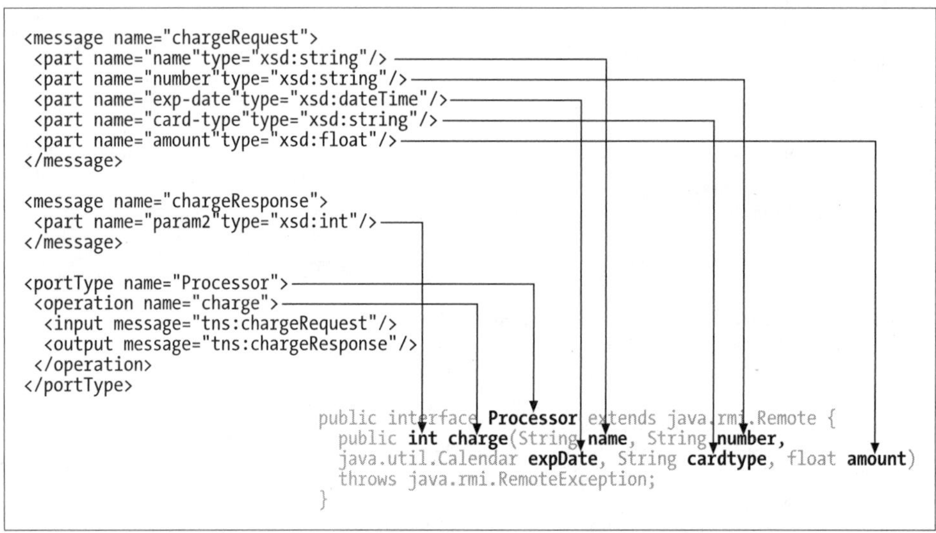

Figure 19-2. Mapping a WSDL <portType> to a JAX-RPC endpoint interface

The name of the endpoint interface comes from the name of the <portType>, which is `Processor`. The methods defined by the endpoint interface are derived from the <operation> elements declared by the WSDL <portType>. In this case, there is one <operation> element, which maps a single method: `charge( )`. The parameters of the `charge( )` method are derived from the <operation> element's input message. For each <part> element of the input message, there will be a corresponding parameter in the `charge( )` method. The output message, in this case, declares a single <part> element, which maps to the return type of the `charge( )` method.

The JAX-RPC specification defines an exact mapping between many of the XML Schema built-in types and Java. This is how the XML Schema types declared by the WSDL <part> elements are mapped to the parameters and the return type of an endpoint method. Table 19-1 shows the mapping between XML Schema built-in types and Java primitives and classes.

Table 19-1. XML Schema built-in types and their corresponding Java types

XML Schema built-in type	Java type
xsd:byte	Byte
xsd:Boolean	Boolean
xsd:short	Short
xsd:int	Int
xsd:long	Long
xsd:float	float
xsd:double	Double
xsd:string	java.lang.String
xsd:dateTime	java.util.Calendar
xsd:integer	java.math.BigInteger
xsd:decimal	java.math.BigDecimal
xsd:QName	java.xml.namespace.QName
xsd:base64Binary	byte []
xsd:hexBinary	byte []

JAX-RPC also maps *nillable* types (types that can be null), based on XML Schema built-in types, to Java primitive wrappers. For example, a nillable `xsd:int` type would map to a `java.lang.Integer` type and a nillable `xsd:double` would map to a `java.lang.Double` type.

In addition, JAX-RPC defines a mapping between complex types defined in the WSDL <types> element and Java bean classes.

When a service is deployed, the proxy, which implements the endpoint interface, is generated from the <binding> and <port> definitions. The JAX-RPC proxy translates the messaging style specified by the <binding> definition into a marshaling algorithm for converting method calls made on the endpoint stub into SOAP request and reply messages. Charge-It's WSDL document defines the following <binding> element:

```
<binding name="ProcessorSoapBinding" type="tns:Processor">
  <soap:binding style="rpc"
      transport="http://schemas.xmlsoap.org/soap/http"/>
  <operation name="charge">
    <soap:operation soapAction="" style="rpc"/>
    <input>
      <soap:body use="literal"
          namespace="http://charge-it.com/Processor"/>
    </input>
```

```
    <output>
      <soap:body use="literal"
          namespace="http://charge-it.com/Processor"/>
    </output>
  </operation>
</binding>
```

According to the <binding> element, the web service employs RPC/Literal SOAP 1.1 messages with a request-response-style operation. The proxy is responsible for converting method calls made on the endpoint interface into SOAP messages that are sent to the web service. It's also responsible for converting SOAP response messages sent back to the stub into a return value—or, if it's a SOAP fault message, into an exception thrown by the endpoint method.

The proxy also takes into consideration the <port> definition, which declares the Internet address where the web service is located. The Charge-It WSDL document defines the following <port> element:

```
<service name="ProcessorService">
   <port name="ProcessorPort" binding="tns:ProcessorSoapBinding">
      <soap:address
       location="http://www.charge-it.com/ProcessorService"/>
   </port>
</service>
```

The address attribute (*http://www.charge-it.com/ProcessorService*) specifies the URL with which the proxy will exchange SOAP messages. Figure 19-1, shown earlier, illustrates how the processor endpoint interface and stub are used to access the Charge-It credit card processing web service.

In addition to the service endpoint interface, the JAX-RPC compiler also creates a service interface, which is used to get an instance of the proxy at runtime. The service interface is based on the <service> element of the WSDL document. Here's the definition of the ProcessorService interface generated from Charge-It's WSDL document:

```
package com.charge_it;

public interface ProcessorService extends javax.xml.rpc.Service {
   public com.charge_it.Processor getProcessorPort( )
      throws javax.xml.rpc.ServiceException;
   public java.lang.String getProcessorPortAddress( );
   public com.charge_it.Processor getProcessorPort(java.net.URL portAddress)
      throws javax.xml.rpc.ServiceException;
}
```

The getProcessorPort( ) method returns a proxy that is ready to invoke methods on the web service. The getProcessPortAddress( ) method returns the URL that the proxy accesses by default. The getProcessorPort(URL) method allows you to create an endpoint stub that accesses a different URL than the default defined in the WSDL document.

Calling a Service from an EJB

As with other resources (JDBC, JMS, and so on), the generated JAX-RPC service can be injected directly into a field or *setter* method of the bean class. It can also be bound to a specific namespace in the JNDI ENC at deployment time. The service can then obtain the proxy, as described in the previous section.

To illustrate how EJBs use a service, we will modify the bookPassage( ) method of the TravelAgentBean defined in Chapter 11. Instead of using the ProcessPayment EJB to process credit cards, the TravelAgent EJB will use Charge-It's Processor web service. We could look up the service directly using JNDI, but injection will save us the extra step. The following code shows the changes to the TravelAgentBean class:

```
package com.titan.travelagent;
import com.charge_it.Processor;
import com.charge_it.ProcessorService;
...

@Stateful
public class TravelAgentBean implements TravelAgentRemote {
    @PersistenceContext(unitName="titanDB")
    private EntityManager em;

    @PersistenceContext EntityManager em;

    Customer customer;
    Cruise cruise;
    private Cabin cabin;

    private ProcessorService processorService;
    ...
    public TicketDO bookPassage(CreditCardDO card, double price)
        throws IncompleteConversationalState {

        if (customer == null || cruise == null || cabin == null)
        {
            throw new IncompleteConversationalState( );
        }
        try {
            Reservation reservation = new Reservation(
                customer, cruise, cabin, price, new Date( ));

            em.persist(reservation);

            String customerName = customer.getFirstName( )+" "+
                                  customer.getLastName( );
            java.util.Calendar expDate = new Calendar(card.date);
            Processor processor = processorService.getProcessorPort( );
            processor.charge(customerName, card.number,
                             expDate, card.type, price);
```

```
                TicketDO ticket = new TicketDO(customer, cruise, cabin, price);
                return ticket;
            } catch(Exception e) {
                throw new EJBException(e);
            }
        }
        ...
    }
```

ProcessorService is injected directly into the processorService field on the bean class. From this field, we can obtain the proxy object that implements the service endpoint interface. You will see in the next section how to configure an XML deployment descriptor to populate the field.

Invoking this proxy within a transactional business process such as bookPassage() presents a few problems of which you should be aware. If the proxy encounters a networking problem or SOAP processing error, it throws a RemoteException, which is caught and rethrown as an EJBException, causing the entire transaction to roll back. However, if an error occurs after the web service has executed but before the EJB method successfully returns, a partial rollback occurs; the reservation is rolled back, but the charge made using the Charge-It web service is not. *Invocations on web services do not participate in the caller's transaction context!*

The <service-ref> Deployment Element

We still need to specify where and how this web service reference is defined. To do this we need a <service-ref> element in our EJB deployment descriptor. This XML element binds a JAX-RPC service to the JNDI ENC and injects it into the processorService field of our bean class. EJB XML is allowed to be a partial deployment descriptor. This means that we do not have to define every single piece of metadata in XML just because we want to inject a web service into our bean class. The partial XML deployment descriptor of the TravelAgent EJB declares a <service-ref> element that looks like this:

```
<?xml version='1.0' encoding='UTF-8' ?>
<ejb-jar
 xmlns="http://java.sun.com/xml/ns/j2ee"
 xmlns:xsi="http://www.w3.org/2001/XMLSchema-instance"
 xmlns:chargeIt="http://charge-it.com/Processor"
 xsi:schemaLocation="http://java.sun.com/xml/ns/j2ee
                     http://java.sun.com/xml/ns/j2ee/ejb-jar_3_0.xsd"
 version="2.1">
   <enterprise-beans>
     <session>
       <ejb-name>TravelAgentEJB</ejb-name>
       <service-ref>
         <service-ref-name>service/ChargeItProcessorService</service-ref-name>
         <service-interface>com.charge_it.ProcessorService</service-interface>
         <wsdl-file>META-INF/wsdl/ChargeItProcessor.wsdl</wsdl-file>
         <jaxrpc-mapping-file>META-INF/mapping.xml</jaxrpc-mapping-file>
```

```
            <service-qname>chargeIt:ProcessorService</service-qname>
            <mapped-name>webservices/ProcessorService</mapped-name>
            <injection-target>
               <injection-target-class>
                    com.titan.travelagent.TravelAgentBean
               </injection-target-class>
               <injection-target-name>processorService</injection-target-name>
            </injection-target>
         </service-ref>
      </session>
   </enterprise-beans>
</ejb-jar>
```

The `<service-ref-name>` element declares the name of the JAX-RPC service in the JNDI ENC—it's always relative to the `java:comp/env` context. The `<service-interface>` element identifies the JAX-RPC service interface, which is implemented by a JAX-RPC service object. The `<wsdl-file>` identifies the location of the WSDL document that describes the Charge-It web service. The WSDL document must be packaged in the same EJB-JAR file as the EJB that is making the web service call, whether you are using a `<service-ref>` element or an annotation to inject your web service. The path is always relative to the root of the EJB-JAR file. In this case, a copy of the Charge-It WSDL document, `ChargeItProcessor.wsdl`, is stored in the *META-INF* directory of the EJB-JAR file. The `<jaxrpc-mapping-file>` element identifies the location of the JAX-RPC mapping file relative to the root of the EJB-JAR file. In this case, it's also located in the *META-INF* directory. (The *JAX-RPC mapping file* is an additional deployment file that helps the EJB container to understand the mapping between the WSDL document and the service endpoint interfaces.) The `<service-qname>` element identifies the fully qualified XML name of the WSDL `<service>` definition to which this reference pertains. The qualified service name is relative to the WSDL document identified by the `<wsdl-file>` element. The `<mapped-named>` element is a vendor-specific identifier that can map to a global registry of the application server (usually the global JNDI). The `<injection-target>` element is used to tell the EJB container to inject an instance of `ProcessorService` into the `processorService` field of the `TravelAgentBean` class. You can find more information about using `<injection-target>` in Chapter 14.

The JAX-RPC Mapping File

A JAX-RPC service or client in a Java EE environment must have a JAX-RPC mapping file. The mapping file format is defined in the "Implementing Enterprise Web Services" (JSR-109) specification. There are many possible ways to map or bind Java to WSDL, and WSDL to Java. This can cause portability problems between different JAX-RPC implementations, since they may bind Java and WSDL in different ways. The JAX-RPC mapping file addresses this problem by configuring the specific details for how binding is supposed to occur. This allows for a service and a client to be portable across different Java EE implementations. The mapping file for the *ChargeItProcessor.wsdl* document follows:

```
<?xml version='1.0' encoding='UTF-8' ?>
<java-wsdl-mapping
  xmlns="http://java.sun.com/xml/ns/j2ee"
  xmlns:chargeIt="http://charge-it.com/Processor"
  xmlns:xsi="http://www.w3.org/2001/XMLSchema-instance"
  xmlns:xsd="http://www.w3.org/2001/XMLSchema"
  xsi:schemaLocation="http://java.sun.com/xml/ns/j2ee
          http://www.ibm.com/webservices/xsd/j2ee_jaxrpc_mapping_1_1.xsd"
  version="1.1">

  <package-mapping>
   <package-type>com.charge_it</package-type>
   <namespaceURI>http://charge-it.com/Processor</namespaceURI>
  </package-mapping>
  <service-interface-mapping>
    <service-interface>com.charge_it.ProcessorService</service-interface>
    <wsdl-service-name>chargeIt:ProcessorService</wsdl-service-name>
    <port-mapping>
      <port-name>chargeIt:ProcessorPort</port-name>
      <java-port-name>ProcessorPort</java-port-name>
    </port-mapping>
  </service-interface-mapping>
  <service-endpoint-interface-mapping>
    <service-endpoint-interface>com.charge_it.Processor
    </service-endpoint-interface>
    <wsdl-port-type>chargeIt:Processor</wsdl-port-type>
    <wsdl-binding>chargeIt:ProcessorSoapBinding</wsdl-binding>
    <service-endpoint-method-mapping>
      <java-method-name>charge</java-method-name>
      <wsdl-operation>chargeIt:charge</wsdl-operation>
      <method-param-parts-mapping>
        <param-position>0</param-position>
        <param-type>java.lang.String</param-type>
        <wsdl-message-mapping>
          <wsdl-message>chargeIt:chargeRequest</wsdl-message>
          <wsdl-message-part-name>name</wsdl-message-part-name>
          <parameter-mode>IN</parameter-mode>
        </wsdl-message-mapping>
      </method-param-parts-mapping>
      <method-param-parts-mapping>
        <param-position>1</param-position>
        <param-type>java.lang.String</param-type>
        <wsdl-message-mapping>
          <wsdl-message>chargeIt:chargeRequest</wsdl-message>
          <wsdl-message-part-name>number</wsdl-message-part-name>
          <parameter-mode>IN</parameter-mode>
        </wsdl-message-mapping>
      </method-param-parts-mapping>
      <method-param-parts-mapping>
        <param-position>2</param-position>
        <param-type>java.util.Calendar</param-type>
```

```
      <wsdl-message-mapping>
        <wsdl-message>chargeIt:chargeRequest</wsdl-message>
        <wsdl-message-part-name>exp-date</wsdl-message-part-name>
        <parameter-mode>IN</parameter-mode>
      </wsdl-message-mapping>
    </method-param-parts-mapping>
    <method-param-parts-mapping>
      <param-position>3</param-position>
      <param-type>java.lang.String</param-type>
      <wsdl-message-mapping>
        <wsdl-message>chargeIt:chargeRequest</wsdl-message>
        <wsdl-message-part-name>card-type</wsdl-message-part-name>
        <parameter-mode>IN</parameter-mode>
      </wsdl-message-mapping>
    </method-param-parts-mapping>
    <method-param-parts-mapping>
      <param-position>4</param-position>
      <param-type>float</param-type>
      <wsdl-message-mapping>
        <wsdl-message>chargeIt:chargeRequest</wsdl-message>
        <wsdl-message-part-name>amount</wsdl-message-part-name>
        <parameter-mode>IN</parameter-mode>
      </wsdl-message-mapping>
    </method-param-parts-mapping>
    <wsdl-return-value-mapping>
      <method-return-value>int</method-return-value>
      <wsdl-message>chargeIt:chargeResponse</wsdl-message>
      <wsdl-message-part-name>return</wsdl-message-part-name>
    </wsdl-return-value-mapping>
  </service-endpoint-method-mapping>
 </service-endpoint-interface-mapping>
</java-wsdl-mapping>
```

As you can see, the service interface is mapped to a WSDL `<service>` element, the endpoint interface is mapped to a WSDL `<portType>`, each method is mapped to a WSDL `<operation>`, and every parameter and return value is mapped to a specific WSDL `<part>` of a specific WSDL `<message>` definition.

The complete JAX-RPC mapping file is too complicated to discuss in detail. Don't worry, though, you normally don't write these by hand. A Java EE implementation will provide tools to generate these files for you. Also, the JAX-RPC mapping file is no longer used in JAX-WS. We will discuss how it handles binding in the section "Using JAX-WS," later in this chapter.

Defining a Web Service with JAX-RPC

Java EE provides two different programming models for defining a JAX-RPC web service: the web container model (or servlet model) and the EJB container model. Given that this book is about EJB 3.0, we assume you are more interested in the EJB model.

The core component in the EJB model is called an *EJB endpoint*. An EJB endpoint is a stateless session bean that is exposed as a web service. In addition to the remote and local component interfaces, there is another component interface, called the *service endpoint interface*. The service endpoint interface defines the abstract web services contract that the EJB endpoint provides to a web services client.

Because an EJB endpoint is simply a SOAP-accessible stateless session bean, it has the same advantages as other EJBs. An EJB endpoint runs in the same EJB container that automatically manages transactions and security and provides access to other EJBs and resources via injection or the JNDI ENC.

To illustrate how an EJB endpoint is developed, we'll create a new version of the TravelAgent EJB. The revised TravelAgent EJB will use the same logic as the TravelAgent EJB developed in Chapter 11 and the ReservationProcessor EJB developed in Chapter 12, but it will be deployed as a stateless session bean with an endpoint interface. The TravelAgent endpoint is based on the WSDL document shown earlier in this chapter.

The WSDL Document

Every EJB endpoint must have a WSDL document that describes the web service. You can create this document by hand, or you can use the tools provided by your Java EE vendor to generate it. The `<portType>` declared by the WSDL document must be aligned with the endpoint interface of the web service. In other words, the mapping between the WSDL `<portType>` and the endpoint interface must be correct according to the JAX-RPC specification. One way to ensure this is to create the WSDL document first, and then use it to generate the service endpoint interface:

```
<?xml version="1.0"?>
<definitions name="TravelAgent"
   xmlns="http://schemas.xmlsoap.org/wsdl/"
   xmlns:soap="http://schemas.xmlsoap.org/wsdl/soap/"
   xmlns:xsd="http://www.w3.org/2001/XMLSchema"
   xmlns:titan="http://www.titan.com/TravelAgent"
   targetNamespace="http://www.titan.com/TravelAgent">

<!-- message elements describe the parameters and return values -->
<message name="RequestMessage">
   <part name="cruiseId"   type="xsd:int" />
   <part name="cabinId"    type="xsd:int" />
   <part name="customerId" type="xsd:int" />
   <part name="price"      type="xsd:double" />
</message>
<message name="ResponseMessage">
   <part name="reservationId" type="xsd:string" />
</message>

<!-- portType element describes the abstract interface of a web service -->
<portType name="TravelAgentEndpoint">
```

```
  <operation name="makeReservation">
     <input message="titan:RequestMessage"/>
     <output message="titan:ResponseMessage"/>
  </operation>
</portType>

<!-- binding element tells us which protocols and encoding styles are used  -->
<binding name="TravelAgentBinding" type="titan:TravelAgentEndpoint">
   <soap:binding style="rpc"
                transport="http://schemas.xmlsoap.org/soap/http"/>
   <operation name="makeReservation">
      <soap:operation soapAction="" />
      <input>
        <soap:body use="literal"
              namespace="http://www.titan.com/TravelAgent"/>
      </input>
      <output>
        <soap:body use="literal"
              namespace="http://www.titan.com/TravelAgent"/>
      </output>
   </operation>
</binding>

<!-- service element tells us the Internet address of a web service -->
<service name="TravelAgentService">
  <port name="TravelAgentPort" binding="titan:TravelAgentBinding">
     <soap:address location="http://www.titan.com/webservices/TravelAgent" />
  </port>
</service>

</definitions>
```

The Service Endpoint Interface

The process for generating a service endpoint interface for an EJB endpoint is identical to the process we used to generate a JAX-RPC client. The JAX-RPC compiler generates it from the <portType> and <message> definitions (and <types>, if present). The resulting interface looks like the following:

```
package com.titan.webservice;

public interface TravelAgentEndpoint extends java.rmi.Remote {
    public java.lang.String makeReservation(int cruiseId, int cabinId,
                                             int customerId, double price)
                            throws java.rmi.RemoteException;
}
```

Alternatively, you can start from Java by writing the service endpoint interface by hand. You can then generate the WSDL and the JAX-RPC mapping file from this interface. Refer to Table 19-1, earlier in the chapter, to determine the schema types that will be mapped from the Java parameters in each method.

The Stateless Bean Class

The bean class defined for the TravelAgent endpoint must implement the methods defined by the endpoint interface. As with remote and local interfaces, a stateless bean class can implement the service endpoint interface directly. Here's the new definition for the TravelAgentBean class:

```
package com.titan.webservice;
import com.titan.domain.*;
import com.titan.cabin.*;
import com.titan.processpayment.*;
import javax.ejb.EJBException;
import java.util.Date;
import java.util.Calendar;
import javax.persistence.*;

@Stateless
public class TravelAgentBean implements TravelAgentEndpoint {
    @PersistenceContext EntityManager em;

    @EJB ProcessPaymentLocal process;

    public String makeReservation(int cruiseId, int cabinId,
                                  int customerId, double price){
      try {
            Cruise cruise = em.find(Cruise.class, cruiseId);
            Cabin cabin = em.find(Cabin.class, cabinId);
            Customer customer = em.find(Customer.class, customerId);
            CreditCardDO card = this.getCreditCard(customer);

            Reservation reservation = new Reservation(
                        customer, cruise, cabin, price, new Date( ));
            process.byCredit(customer, card, price);

            return reservation.getId( );

        } catch(Exception e) {
            throw new EJBException(e);
        }
    }

    public CreditCardDO getCreditCard(Customer cust) throws Exception{
        CreditCard card = customer.getCreditCard( );
        return new CreditCardDO(card.getNumber(),card.getExpirationDate( ),
                                card.getCreditOrganization( ));
    }
}
```

The TravelAgentBean class is not that different from the TravelAgent EJB developed earlier in this chapter (the version that uses the Charge-It credit card processing web service). The primary differences are that it responds to web service calls rather than remote or local calls, and it is a stateless session bean rather than a stateful session bean.

The Deployment Files

The TravelAgent endpoint requires three deployment files: a WSDL file, a JAX-RPC mapping file, and a *webservices.xml* file. In this section, we will create these files manually, although you would typically use the tools provided by your Java EE implementation to assist in this process.

The WSDL file

The WSDL file used to represent the endpoint interface must be packaged with the EJB endpoint. Normally, the WSDL document is placed in the *META-INF* directory of the JAR file, but it can go anywhere as long as it's in the same JAR file as the EJB endpoint.

The JAX-RPC mapping file

EJB endpoints, like JAX-RPC service references, require you to define a JAX-RPC mapping file. The mapping file can have any name, but it should be descriptive, and the file type should be XML. It's common to name this file *jaxrpc-mapping.xml* or *travelagent_mapping.xml*, or something along those lines. We covered the JAX-RPC mapping file earlier in this chapter in the section titled "The JAX-RPC Mapping File."

The webservices.xml file

The *webservices.xml* file is the baling wire that ties the separate deployment files together. It defines the relationships between the stateless session bean, the WSDL file, and the JAX-RPC mapping file:

```
<?xml version='1.0' encoding='UTF-8' ?>
<webservices
   xmlns="http://java.sun.com/xml/ns/j2ee"
   xmlns:xsi="http://www.w3.org/2001/XMLSchema-instance"
   xmlns:titan="http://www.titan.com/TravelAgent"
   xsi:schemaLocation="http://java.sun.com/xml/ns/j2ee
              http://www.ibm.com/webservices/xsd/j2ee_web_services_1_1.xsd"
   version="1.1">

      <webservice-description>
         <webservice-description-name>TravelAgentService
         </webservice-description-name>
         <wsdl-file>META-INF/travelagent.wsdl</wsdl-file>
         <jaxrpc-mapping-file>/META-INF/travelagent_mapping.xml
         </jaxrpc-mapping-file>
         <port-component>
            <port-component-name>TravelAgentEndpoint</port-component-name>
            <wsdl-port>titan:TravelAgentPort</wsdl-port>
            <service-endpoint-interface>
               com.titan.webservice.TravelAgentEndpoint
            </service-endpoint-interface>
            <service-impl-bean>
```

```
                <ejb-link>TravelAgentBean</ejb-link>
            </service-impl-bean>
        </port-component>
    </webservice-description>
</webservices>
```

The `<webservice-description>` element describes an EJB endpoint; there may be one or more of these elements in a single *webservices.xml* file.* `<webservice-description-name>` is a unique name assigned to the web services description. It can be anything you like. The `<wsdl-file>` element points to the WSDL document of the EJB endpoint. Each EJB endpoint has exactly one WSDL document, which is usually located in the *META-INF* directory of the EJB-JAR file. When the EJB endpoint is deployed, your deployment tool will probably provide you with the option of copying the WSDL document to some type of public URL or registry so that others can discover the web service. The `<jaxrpc-mapping-file>` element indicates the location of the JAX-RPC mapping file that is associated with the EJB endpoint and the WSDL document. It, too, is usually located in the *META-INF* directory of the EJB-JAR file.

The `<port-component>` element maps a stateless session bean declared in the *ejb-jar.xml* file to a specific `<port>` in the WSDL document. `<port-component-name>` is the logical name you assign the EJB endpoint. It can be anything. The `<wsdl-port>` element maps the EJB endpoint deployment information to a specific WSDL `<port>` element in the WSDL document. `<service-endpoint-interface>` is the fully qualified name of the endpoint interface—it must be the same interface declared by the `<service-endpoint>` element for the EJB in the *ejb-jar.xml* file. `<service-impl-bean>` and its `<ejb-link>` element link the `<port-component>` to a specific EJB. The value of `<ejb-link>` must match the value of the EJB name, which is `TravelAgentBean` in this example.

Using JAX-WS

The WSDL, JAX-RPC mapping, and *webservices.xml* files sure are a lot of things to define just to expose your stateless EJB as a web service. It should be easier to publish an EJB as a web service, and it is. One of the goals of the JAX-WS specification was to make the JAX-RPC API and deployment model easier to use. To this end, the specification provides an extensive set of annotations, most of which are based on JSR-181 ("Web Services Metadata for the Java Platform"). These annotations make it much simpler to define a web service. Keeping with the spirit of EJB 3.0, all JAX-WS annotations have reasonable defaults. In the following example, it takes nothing more than adding two annotations to transform a stateless EJB into a web service:

* The `<webservice-description>` element can also describe a JAX-RPC service endpoint, which is a servlet-based web service that is outside the scope of this book.

```
package com.titan.webservice;

import javax.ejb.Stateless;
import javax.jws.WebService;
import javax.jws.WebMethod;

@Stateless
@WebService
public class TravelAgentBean
{
   @WebMethod
   public String makeReservation(int cruiseId, int cabinId,
                                 int customerId, double price) {
   ...
   }
}
```

The @WebService Annotation

The main annotation for defining a web service is `@javax.jws.WebService`. This annotation must be placed on the stateless session bean implementation class in order to expose it as a web service:

```
package javax.jws;

@Target({TYPE}) @Retention(value=RetentionPolicy.RUNTIME)
public @interface WebService {
   String name( ) default "";
   String targetNamespace( ) default "";
   String serviceName( ) default "";
   String wsdlLocation( ) default "";
   String portName( ) default "";
   String endpointInterface( ) default "";
}
```

The `name( )` attribute is the name of the web service and it is used as the name of the `portType` when mapped to WSDL. This defaults to the short name of the Java class or Java interface to which you are applying it. The `targetNamespace( )` attribute specifies the XML namespace used for the WSDL and XML elements that are generated from this annotation. The default value is generated from the package name of the annotated type. The `wsdlLocation( )` attribute defines the URL of the WSDL document that represents this web service. You need this attribute only if you are mapping your service to a preexisting WSDL document. The `endpointInterface( )` attribute is used to externalize the contract of the web service by specifying that contract in the form of a Java interface. We'll talk more about this option later. The `portName( )` attribute specifies which WSDL port you will use. In most cases, you can use the default values for each of these attributes.

The @WebMethod Annotation

If a stateless session bean is annotated with `@java.jws.WebService`, and it contains no methods that are annotated with `@javax.jws.WebMethod`, then all methods are made available to the web service. Otherwise, only those methods that are annotated with `@javax.jws.WebMethod` will be made available. This is an important feature because web services tend to be coarser-grained than a standard EJB. Also, it is generally considered good design practice to reduce dependencies between modules. The `@javax.jws.WebMethod` annotation also offers attributes for customizing the generated WSDL:

```
package javax.jws;

@Target({ElementType.METHOD}) @Retention(value = RetentionPolicy.RUNTIME)
public @interface WebMethod
{
   String operationName( ) default "";
   String action( ) default "";
}
```

The `operationName( )` attribute is used to define the WSDL operation that the annotated method implements. If it is not specified, the literal Java method name is used. The `action( )` attribute is used to set the `SOAPAction` hint that corresponds with this operation. This hint allows a service endpoint to determine the destination by simply looking at the `SOAPAction` HTTP header instead of analyzing the contents of the SOAP message body. This has the potential for a slight performance increase, although it depends on the Java EE implementation you are using. The following example demonstrates setting the operation name for a Java method:

```
package com.titan.webservice;

import javax.ejb.Stateless;
import javax.jws.WebService;
import javax.jws.WebMethod;

@Stateless
@WebService(name = "TravelAgent")
public class TravelAgentBean
{
   @WebMethod(operationName = "Reserve")
   public String makeReservation(int cruiseId, int cabinId,
                                 int customerId, double price) {
   ...
   }
}
```

This will result in the following WSDL portType definition:

```
<portType name="TravelAgent">
   <operation name="Reserve">
    ...
   </operation>
</portType>
```

The @SOAPBinding Annotation

In Chapter 18, we discussed the web services styles supported in EJB 3.0. You can customize the web services style that the EJB endpoint uses with the `@javax.jws.soap.SOAPBinding` annotation:

```
@Target(value = {ElementType.TYPE}) @Retention(value = RetentionPolicy.RUNTIME)
public @interface SOAPBinding {
   public enum Style {DOCUMENT, RPC};
   public enum Use {LITERAL, ENCODED};
   public enum ParameterStyle {BARE, WRAPPED}

   Style style( ) default Style.DOCUMENT;
   Use use( ) default Use.LITERAL;
   ParameterStyle parameterStyle( ) default ParameterStyle.WRAPPED;
}
```

Table 19-2 describes the supported attribute value combinations. It is important to note that the `use( )` attribute must always be set to `LITERAL`. `ENCODED` refers to SOAP encoding, which has been disallowed by the WS-I Basic Profile 1.1. Furthermore, an EJB implementation is not required to support it. If this annotation is not specified, the default style is Document/Literal Wrapped.

Table 19-2. @SOAPBinding behavior

Style	Use	Parameter style	Description
RPC	LITERAL	N/A	Each parameter is mapped to a `wsdl:part`, which is mapped to a schema type definition.
DOCUMENT	LITERAL	BARE	Only one parameter is allowed, and that parameter is mapped to a root schema element that fully defines the content of the message.
DOCUMENT	LITERAL	WRAPPED	All parameters are wrapped in a root schema element with the same name as the operation to which they belong .

The @WebParam Annotation

The `@javax.jws.WebParam` annotation allows you to control the WSDL that is generated for a Java method annotated with `@javax.jws.WebMethod`:

```
package javax.jws;

@Target({PARAMETER})@Retention(value=RetentionPolicy.RUNTIME)
public @interface WebParam {
   public enum Mode {IN, OUT, INOUT};
   String name( ) default "";
   String targetNamespace( ) default "";
   Mode mode( ) default Mode.IN;
   boolean header( ) default false;
}
```

If the style is RPC/Literal, the name( ) attribute sets the wsdl:part name. Otherwise, it sets the XML local name of the element within the schema document that corresponds to the annotated parameter. If it is not specified, the default value is computed in the form of arg*N*, where *N* is the 0-based position of the parameter in the method signature.* The targetNamespace( ) attribute, used only if the style is Document/Literal, sets the targetNamespace of the schema definition that contains the element.† The header( ) attribute is used to indicate that the parameter should be put in a SOAP header rather than in the SOAP body. The mode( ) attribute is used to indicate whether the parameter is to be used for input, output, or both. Due to Java semantics, if a parameter is used for output, it must be wrapped using a special holder type. The following example shows the use of a JAX-WS holder on an RPC-style service:

```
@WebMethod(operationName = "CheckStatus")
public int checkStatus(
   @WebParam(name = "ReservationID")
   String reservationId,
   @WebParam(name = "CustomerID", mode = WebParam.Mode.OUT)
   javax.xml.ws.Holder<Integer> customerId
){
   ...
   // return customer id and status
   customerId.value = getCustomerId(reservationId);
   return status;
}
```

This produces the following WSDL:

```
<message name="CheckStatus">
   <part name="ReservationID" type="xsd:string"/>
</message>
<message name="CheckStatusResponse">
   <part name="return" type="xsd:int"/>
   <part name="CustomerID" type="xsd:int"/>
</message>
<portType name="TravelAgent">
   <operation name="CheckStatus" parameterOrder="ReservationID CustomerID">
      <input message="tns:CheckStatus"/>
      <output message="tns:CheckStatusResponse"/>
   </operation>
</portType>
```

* At the time of this writing, this convention was still in draft.

† The behavior of targetNamespace( ) on Document/Literal wrapped was not fully explained in the original JSR-181 release. The maintenance release is expected to disallow it.

The @WebResult Annotation

This `@javax.jws.WebResult` annotation provides the same, although somewhat reduced, functionality for return values that `@javax.jws.WebParam` provides for method parameters:

```
@Target(value = {ElementType.METHOD}) @Retention(value = RetentionPolicy.RUNTIME)
public @interface WebResult
{
   String name( ) default "";
   String targetNamespace( ) default "";
}
```

The attributes behave the same as they do in `@javax.jws.WebParam`, with the exception of the default value for `name( )`. If the `name( )` attribute is not specified, and the style is Document/Literal bare, then its value will be the WSDL operation name concatenated with `"Response"`. For all other styles, the default is `"return"`. The following example demonstrates the use of this annotation:

```
package com.titan.webservice;

import javax.ejb.Stateless;
import javax.jws.WebService;
import javax.jws.WebMethod;
import javax.jws.WebResult;


@Stateless
@WebService(name = "TravelAgent")
public class TravelAgentBean
{
   @WebMethod(operationName = "Reserve")
   @WebResult(name = "ReservationID")
   public String makeReservation(int cruiseId, int cabinId,
                                 int customerId, double price) {
   ...
   }
}
```

This produces the following relevant WSDL sections:

```
<xs:element name="ReserveResponse" type="ReserveResponse"/>
<xs:complexType name="ReserveResponse">
  <xs:sequence>
     <xs:element name="ReservationID" type="xs:string" nillable="true"/>
  </xs:sequence>
</xs:complexType>
...
<message name="ReserveResponse">
    <part name="parameters" element="tns:ReserveResponse"/>
</message>
...
<portType name="TravelAgent">
   <operation name="Reserve">
```

```
        <input message="tns:Reserve"/>
        <output message="tns:ReserveResponse"/>
    </operation>
</portType>
```

The @OneWay Annotation

The `@javax.jws.OneWay` annotation is used to declare that the corresponding web services operation will return an empty message. This allows the server and the client to optimize the operation by performing the method invocation asynchronously. Whether the method is actually executed asynchronously is determined by the Java EE implementation. The resulting WSDL for a one-way operation will not have an `<output>` tag.

Separating the Web Services Contract

Up to this point, we have been defining everything within the EJB implementation class. An alternative approach is to use the `endpointInterface()` attribute of the `@javax.jws.WebService` annotation. The web services contract can then be maintained in an external Java interface. With this methodology, the *only required annotation* on the endpoint interface is `@javax.jws.WebService`. All other annotations are optional. Unlike the previous approach of keeping everything within the EJB implementation, *all methods in the interface are exposed* in the web service. Technically, the EJB implementation does not have to implement this interface, although there is no reason not to. We can modify the `TravelAgentBean` example to utilize this approach by first extracting the desired web methods:

```
package com.titan.webservice;

import javax.jws.WebService;

@WebService
public interface TravelAgentEndpoint {
    public java.lang.String makeReservation(int cruiseId, int cabinId,
                                             int customerId, double price);
}
```

The implementation bean then references the endpoint interface from the `@javax.jws.WebService` annotation:

```
package com.titan.webservice;

import javax.jws.WebService;

@WebService(endpointInterface = "com.titan.webservice.TravelAgentEndpoint")
public class TravelAgentBean implements TravelAgentEndpoint {
...
}
```

The Service Class

Similar to the JAX-RPC client methodology we discussed earlier, JAX-WS contains a service class that the JAX-WS client uses to communicate with a web service. The service class must extend `javax.xml.ws.Service` and provide a method to retrieve the service endpoint interface. It should also use the `@javax.xml.ws.WebServiceClient` annotation to define the name, namespace, and WSDL location of the service. The `@javax.xml.ws.WebEndpoint` annotation is necessary to resolve for which WSDL `<port>` to return a proxy. The following is an example `Service` class that communicates with the Charge-It web service:

```
package com.charge_it;

import javax.xml.ws.WebServiceClient;
import javax.xml.ws.WebEndpoint;

@WebServiceClient(name="ProcessorService",
                  targetNamespace="http://charge-it.com/Processor"
                  wsdlLocation="http://charge-it.com/Processor?wsdl")
public class ProcessorService extends javax.xml.ws.Service {
   public ProcessorService( ) {
      super(new URL("http://charge-it.com/Processor?wsdl"),
            new QName("http://charge-it.com/Processor", "ProcessorService"));
   }

   public ProcessorService(String wsdlLocation, QName serviceName) {
      super(wsdlLocation, serviceName);
   }

   @WebEndpoint(name = "ProcessorPort")
   public Processor getProcessorPort( ) {
      return (Processor)
         super.getPort(
            new QName("http://charge-it.com/Processor", "ProcessorPort"),
            Processor.class);
   }
}
```

The Service Endpoint Interface

We discussed a JAX-WS service endpoint interface in the earlier section "Separating the Web Services Contract." Our client can use the same interface. This means that the client uses all of the annotations we defined for the server side. However, remember that you are not limited to just talking to JAX-WS web services. A web service can be running on *any platform* in *any language*. So, in those scenarios, you will not reuse the service endpoint interface but will instead use a tool to generate one for you. However, we will go ahead and do this by hand:

```
package com.charge_it;

import javax.jws.WebService;
import javax.jws.soap.SOAPBinding;

@WebService
@SOAPBinding(style = SOAPBinding.Style.RPC)
public interface Processor{
    public int charge(String name, String number, java.util.Calendar expDate,
                      String cardType, float amount);
}
```

The @WebServiceRef Annotation

In addition to the <service-ref> XML tag in ejb-jar.xml, a JAX-WS client can use the @javax.xml.ws.WebServiceRef annotation to reference either a service interface or a service endpoint interface directly:

```
package javax.xml.ws;

@Target({TYPE, METHOD, FIELD}) @Retention(RUNTIME)
public @interface WebServiceRef {
     String name( ) default "";
     String wsdlLocation( ) default "";
     Class type default Object.class;
     Class value default Object.class;
     String mappedName( ) default "";
};
```

The name( ) attribute defines how the web service will be bound into the JNDI ENC. The wsdlLocation( ) attribute specifies the URL where the WSDL file lives in the EJB-JAR. HTTP URLs are allowed. If not specified, the value for this attribute will be pulled from the service class, provided it is annotated with the @javax.xml.ws.WebServiceClient annotation.

The mappedName( ) attribute is a vendor-specific global identifier for the web service. You need to consult your vendor documentation to determine whether you need this attribute.

The type( ) and value( ) attributes are used to determine whether to inject a service class or service endpoint interface into a field or property. In order to inject a service endpoint interface, value( ) must be set to the service interface. The type( ) attribute can then refer to the service endpoint interface that will be injected. This does not have to be specified if the container can infer that information from the field type:

```
// Injected SEI, inferred from type
@WebServiceRef(ProcessorService.class)
private Processor endpoint;
```

In order to inject a service interface, both the value( ) and type( ) attributes can be set to the service interface class; otherwise, it can be inferred from the type:

```
// Inject Service, inferred from type
@WebServiceRef
private ProcessorService service;
```

Let's modify our TravelAgent EJB bean class to use this annotation:

```
package com.titan.travelagent;
import com.charge_it.ProcessorService;
import com.charge_it.Processor;
...

@Stateful
public class TravelAgentBean implements TravelAgentRemote {
    @PersistenceContext(unitName="titanDB")
    private EntityManager em;

    @PersistenceContext EntityManager em;

    Customer customer;
    Cruise cruise;
    private Cabin cabin;

    @WebServiceRef(ProcessorService.class)
    Processor processor;
    ...
    public TicketDO bookPassage(CreditCardDO card, double price)
        throws IncompleteConversationalState {

        if (customer == null || cruise == null || cabin == null)
        {
            throw new IncompleteConversationalState( );
        }
        try {
            Reservation reservation = new Reservation(
                customer, cruise, cabin, price, new Date( ));

            em.persist(reservation);

            String customerName = customer.getFirstName( )+" "+
                                  customer.getLastName( );
            java.util.Calendar expDate = new Calendar(card.date);

            processor.charge(customerName, card.number,
                             expDate, card.type, price);

            TicketDO ticket = new TicketDO(customer, cruise, cabin, price);
            return ticket;
        } catch(Exception e) {
            throw new EJBException(e);
        }
    }
    ...
}
```

In this example, the annotation will cause a dynamic proxy that implements the Processor interface to be injected into the processor field. Because we are injecting a service endpoint interface directly into the field, the `value()` attribute must be employed to specify which JAX-WS service class will be used to create the endpoint.

You can also override attributes of this annotation with the `<service-ref>` tag we covered earlier.

Other Annotations and APIs

Another big change in JAX-WS is the delegation of all binding concerns to the Java API for XML Binding (JAXB) 2.0. So, under the hood, JAX-WS actually passes the SOAP body to a JAXB `Unmarshaller`, which constructs the resulting Java object graph. This means that you can further customize the binding process by putting highly detailed JAXB annotations on the JavaBeans that your service implementation uses. JAX-WS also provides a few more annotations for advanced customization, as well as some additional client APIs for invoking services dynamically. However, this book does not expand on those topic because they would detract from our focus. For more information on them, please see the relevant specifications.

CHAPTER 20
Java EE

The specification for Java Enterprise Edition 5 (Java EE 5) defines a platform for developing web-enabled applications that includes Enterprise JavaBeans, servlets, and JavaServer Pages (JSP). Java EE products are application servers that provide a complete implementation of the EJB, servlet, and JSP technologies. In addition, Java EE outlines how these technologies work together to provide a complete solution for developing applications. To help you understand Java EE, we must introduce servlets and JSP and explain the synergy between these technologies and Enterprise JavaBeans.

At the risk of spoiling the story, Java EE provides three kinds of "glue" to make it easier for components to interact. First, the JNDI *Enterprise Naming Context* (ENC) is used to standardize the way components look up and inject resources they need. We discussed the ENC in the context of enterprise beans; in this chapter, we will look briefly at how servlets, JSPs, and even some clients can use injection and the ENC to reference and find resources. Second, the use of *deployment descriptors* and *annotations* is extended to servlets and JSP. Java servlets and JSP pages can mix and match the use of annotations or XML deployment descriptors to define their relationship to their environment. Third, Java EE provides additional packaging formats, beyond the basic EJB JAR, so that entire applications can be bundled in reusable, deployable units.

Servlets

The servlet specification defines a server-side component model that can be implemented by web server vendors. *Servlets* provide a simple but powerful API for generating web pages dynamically. (Although servlets can be used for many different request-response protocols, they are predominantly used to process HTTP requests for web pages.)

Servlets are developed in the same fashion as enterprise beans; they are Java classes that extend a base component class and have a deployment descriptor. Once a servlet is developed and packaged in a JAR file, it can be deployed in a web server. When a servlet is deployed, it is assigned to handle requests for a specific web page or to assist other servlets in handling page requests. The following servlet, for example, might be assigned to handle any request for the *helloworld.html* page on a web server:

```
import javax.servlet.*;
import javax.servlet.http.*;

public class HelloWorld extends HttpServlet {

    protected void doGet(HttpServletRequest req, HttpServletResponse response)
        throws ServletException,java.io.IOException {

    try {
        ServletOutputStream writer = response.getWriter( );
        writer.println("<HTML><BODY>");
        writer.println("<h1>Hello World!!</h1>");
        writer.println("</BODY></HTML>");
    } catch(Exception e) {
        // handle exception
    }
    ...
}
```

When a browser sends a request for the page to the web server, the server delegates the request to the appropriate servlet instance by invoking the servlet's `doGet()` method.* The servlet is provided with information about the request in the `HttpServletRequest` object and can use the `HttpServletResponse` object to reply to the request. This simple servlet sends a short HTML document (including the text "Hello World!!") back to the browser, which displays it. Figure 20-1 illustrates how a request is sent by a browser and serviced by a servlet running in a web server.

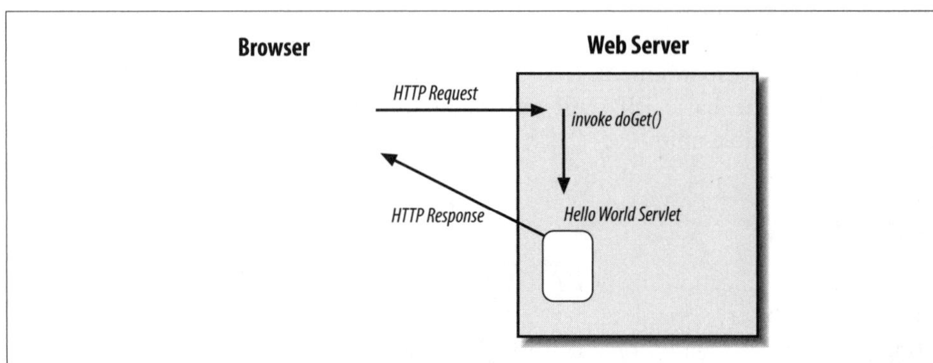

Figure 20-1. Servlet servicing an HTTP request

* `HttpServlets` also have a `doPost( )` method that handles requests for forms.

Servlets are similar to session beans because both perform a service and can directly access backend resources (e.g., databases) through JDBC, but they do not represent persistent data. Unlike session beans, however, servlets do not have support for container-managed transactions and are not composed of business methods. Servlets deal with very specific (usually HTTP) requests and respond by writing to an output stream.

The servlet specification is extensive and robust but also simple and elegant. To learn more about servlets, read *Java Servlet Programming* (O'Reilly).

JavaServer Pages

JavaServer Pages is an extension of the servlet component model that simplifies the process of generating HTML dynamically. JSP essentially allows you to incorporate Java directly into an HTML page as a scripting language. In Java EE, the Java code in a JSP page can access the JNDI ENC, just like the code in a servlet, and can even use all the injection annotations discussed in Chapter 14. In fact, JSP pages (text documents) are translated and compiled into Java servlets, which are then run in a web server just like any other servlet—some servers do the compilation automatically at runtime. You can also use JSP to generate XML documents dynamically. If you want to learn more about JSP, take a look at *JavaServer Pages* (O'Reilly).

Web Components and EJB

Together, servlets and JSP provide a powerful platform for generating web pages dynamically. Servlets and JSP, which are collectively called *web components*, can access resources such as JDBC and enterprise beans. Because web components can access databases using JDBC, they allow an enterprise to expose its business systems to the Web through an HTML interface. HTML interfaces have several advantages over more conventional client interfaces. The most important advantages have to do with distribution and firewalls. Conventional clients need to be installed and distributed on client machines; they require additional work for deployment and maintenance. Applets, which are downloaded dynamically, can eliminate the headache of installation but have their own limitations—such as sandbox restrictions and lengthy downloads. In contrast, HTML is extremely lightweight, does not require prior installation, and does not suffer from security restrictions. In addition, HTML interfaces can be modified and enhanced at their source without having to update the clients.

Firewalls present another significant problem in e-commerce. HTTP, the protocol over which web pages are requested and delivered, can pass through most firewalls without a problem, but protocols such as IIOP or JRMP cannot. This limitation is extremely important. It means that a client usually cannot access a server using IIOP or JRMP without modifications to the firewall, which is often not under the control of the groups who need the application to run. HTTP does not suffer from this limitation because almost all firewalls allow HTTP to pass unhindered.

The problems with distribution and firewalls have prompted most of the EJB industry to adopt an architecture based on web components (servlets/JSP) and Enterprise JavaBeans. Web components provide the presentation logic for generating web pages; EJB supplies a middle tier for business logic. Web components access enterprise beans using the same API as application clients. Each technology is doing what it does best: servlets and JSP are excellent components for generating dynamic HTML, and EJB is an excellent platform for business logic. Figure 20-2 illustrates how the architecture works.

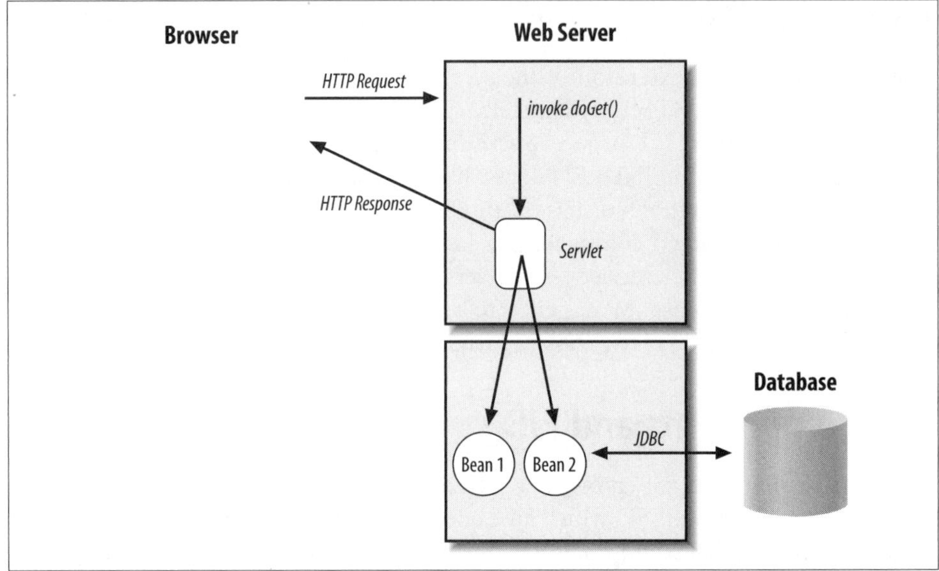

Figure 20-2. Using servlets/JSP and EJB together

This web component/EJB architecture is so widely accepted that it begs the question, "Should there be a united platform?" The Java EE specification answers this question. Java EE defines a single application server platform that focuses on the interaction among servlets, JSP, and EJB. Java EE is important because it provides a specification for the interaction of web components with enterprise beans, making solutions more portable across vendors that support both component models.

Filling in the Gaps

The Java EE specification attempts to fill in the gaps between the web components and Enterprise JavaBeans by defining how these technologies come together to form a complete platform. One of the ways in which Java EE adds value is by creating a consistent programming model across web components and enterprise beans through use of annotations, injection, JNDI ENC, and XML deployment descriptors. A servlet in Java EE can access JDBC `DataSource` objects, environment entries, and references to enterprise beans through injection annotations or the JNDI ENC in exactly the same way that enterprise beans use them. If you do not want to use injection annotations such as `@EJB`, `@Resource`, and `@PersistenceContext` directly within your servlet and JSP code, web components have their own XML deployment descriptors that allow you to declare the same elements that are available in EJB (`<ejb-ref>`, `<resource-ref>`, `<env-entry>`, and `<persistence-context-ref>`), as well as security roles and other elements specific to web components. In Java EE, web components are packaged along with any XML deployment descriptors and are deployed in JAR files with the extension *.war*, which stands for *web archive*. A *.war* file can contain several servlets and JSP documents that share an XML deployment descriptor. The use of injection annotations, the JNDI ENC, deployment descriptors, and JAR files in web components makes them consistent with the EJB programming model and unifies the entire Java EE platform.

Using the JNDI ENC makes it much simpler for web components to access Enterprise JavaBeans. The web component developer does not need to be concerned with the network location of enterprise beans; the server will map any `@EJB` or `<ejb-ref>` elements listed in the deployment descriptor to the enterprise beans at deployment time.

Optionally, Java EE vendors can allow web components to access the EJB local component interfaces of enterprise beans. This strategy makes a lot of sense if the web component and the bean are located in the same Java Virtual Machine, because the Java RMI-IIOP semantics can hurt performance if the communicating components are in the same virtual machine. Most Java EE vendors are expected to support this option.

Besides injecting resources, persistence contexts, and EJBs, you also have access to a `javax.jta.UserTransaction` object, as is the case in EJB. The `UserTransaction` object allows the web component to manage transactions explicitly. The transaction context must be propagated to any enterprise beans accessed within the scope of the transaction (according to the transaction attribute of the enterprise bean method).

Java EE also defines a *.ear* file (*enterprise archive file*), which is a JAR file for packaging EJB JAR files and web component JAR files (*.war* files) together into one complete deployment, called a *Java EE application*. A Java EE application may have its own optional XML deployment descriptor that points to the EJB and web component JAR files (called *modules*) as well as other elements such as icons, descriptions, and the like. This *.ear* deployment descriptor is not required. When a Java EE application is created, interdependencies such as `@EJB` and `@PersistenceContext` annotations can be resolved and security roles can be edited to provide a unified view of the entire web application. Figure 20-3 illustrates the file structure of a Java EE archive file.

Persistence Unit Scope

In previous chapters, we discussed a little bit about the scope of a persistence unit within a *.ear* file. There are a few rules governing the visibility of a persistence unit,

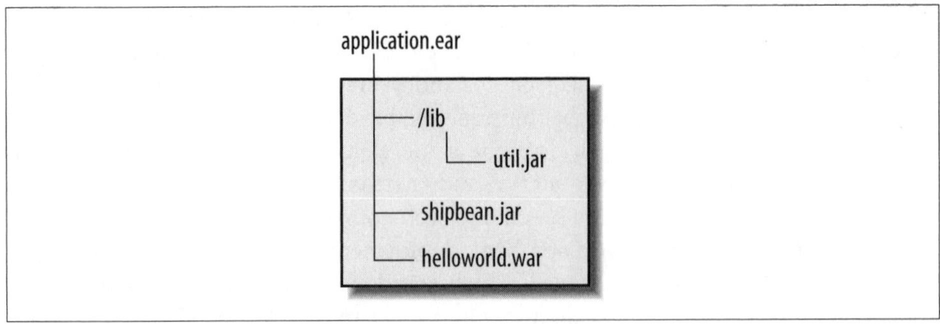

Figure 20-3. Contents of a Java EE .ear file

depending on how it is packaged. A persistence unit can be packaged within an EJB-JAR file, within a WAR's *WEB-INF/lib* directory, or within an EAR's *lib/* directory. A persistence unit packaged within an EAR's *lib/* directory is visible to every component deployed in the *.ear*. Any EJB, servlet, or JSP can reference the persistence unit by name with the `@PersistenceContext` and `@PersistenceUnit` annotations, or with the `<persistence-context-ref>` and `<persistence-unit-ref>` XML deployment descriptor elements. This isn't the case for persistence units that are defined within an EJB-JAR or a WAR file. Only EJBs or servlets defined within the scope of that archive are allowed to reference a scoped persistence unit.

If only one persistence unit is defined in a scoped archive, then that persistence unit may be referenced with an empty string, "", for the persistence unit name. If an EJB or WAR archive has a persistence unit with the same name as one defined in an EAR's *lib/* directory, then the # syntax discussed in Chapter 14 can be used to distinguish the name:

```
@PersistenceUnit(unitName="../lib/titan.jar#MyPU")
```

These types of name clashes are very rare and should be avoided if possible so that the structure of your deployment is not reflected in code or configuration.

Java EE Application Client Components

In addition to integrating web and enterprise bean components, Java EE introduces a new component model: the application client component. An *application client component* is a Java application that resides on a client machine and accesses enterprise bean components on the Java EE server. Client components also have access to a JNDI ENC that operates the same way as the JNDI ENC for web and enterprise bean components. The client component includes an XML deployment descriptor that declares the `<env-entry>`, `<ejb-ref>`, and `<resource-ref>` elements of the JNDI ENC in addition to a `<description>`, `<display-name>`, and `<icon>` that can be used to represent the component in a deployment tool. As with all other Java EE components, the injection annotations (`@PersistenceContext`, `@EJB`, `@Resource`) are also supported.

A client component is simply a Java program that uses the JNDI ENC to access environment properties, enterprise beans, and resources (JDBC, JavaMail, and so on) made available by the Java EE server. Client components reside on the client machine, not on the Java EE server. Here is an extremely simple component:

```
public class MyJavaEEClient {
    private static @EJB ProcessPaymentRemote processPayment;

    public static void main(String [] args) {

        InitialContext jndiCntx = new InitialContext( );

        Object ref = jndiCntx.lookup("java:comp/env/ejb/TravelAgent");
        TravelAgentRemote bean = (TravelAgentRemote)
            PortableRemoteObject.narrow(ref,TravelAgentRemote.class);

        Customer cust = new Customer( );
        cust.setName("Bill");
        bean.setCustomer(cust);
        TicketDO ticket = bean.bookPassage(...);

    }
}
```

`MyJavaEEClient` illustrates how a client component is written. Notice that the client component did not need to use a network-specific JNDI `InitialContext`. In other words, we did not have to specify the service provider in order to connect to the Java EE server. This is the real power of the Java EE application client component: *location transparency*. The client component does not need to know the exact location of the Ship EJB or choose a specific JNDI service provider; the JNDI ENC takes care of locating the enterprise bean.

When application components are developed, an XML deployment descriptor is created that specifies the JNDI ENC entries. At deployment time, a vendor-specific Java EE tool generates the class files needed to deploy the component on client machines. A client component is packaged into a JAR file with its XML deployment descriptor and can be included in a Java EE application. Once a client component is included in the Java EE application deployment descriptor, it can be packaged in the *.ear* file with the other components, as Figure 20-4 illustrates.

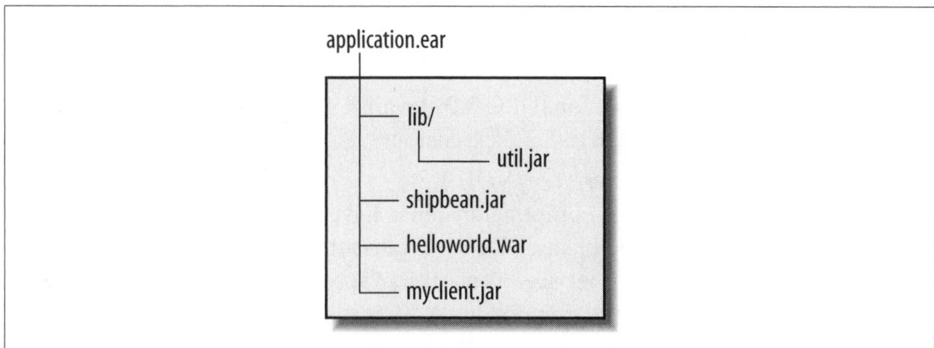

Figure 20-4. Contents of a Java EE .ear file with application components

Guaranteed Services

The Java EE specifications require application servers to support a specific set of protocols and Java enterprise extensions, ensuring a consistent platform for deploying Java EE applications. Java EE application servers must provide the following "standard" services:

Java Virtual Machine
: Java EE 5 products must support Java JDK 5.

Enterprise JavaBeans
: Java EE 5 products must support EJB 2.1 as well as EJB 3.0.

Servlets
: Java EE 5 products must support Servlets 2.5.

JavaServer Pages
: Java EE 5 products must support JSP 2.1.

HTTP and HTTPS
: Web components in a Java EE server service both HTTP and HTTPS requests. The Java EE product must be capable of advertising HTTP 1.0 and HTTPS (HTTP 1.0 over SSL 3.0) on ports 80 and 443, respectively. Components must have full access to HTTP/HTTPS client APIs.

JavaServer Faces 1.2
: This framework simplifies the building and assembly of reusable user interface components for the Web and for Swing applications.

Java RMI-IIOP
: Support for Java RMI-IIOP is required. However, the vendor may also use other protocols, as long as they are compatible with Java RMI-IIOP semantics.

Java RMI-JRMP
: Java EE components can be native Java RMI (JRMP) clients.

Java IDL
: Web components and enterprise beans must be able to access CORBA services that are hosted outside the Java EE environment using JavaIDL, a standard part of the Java 2 platform.

JDBC
: Java EE 5 requires support for JDBC 3.0. Java EE 1.3 requires support for JDBC 2.0 and some parts of the JDBC 2.0 extension.

Java Naming and Directory Interface (JNDI) 1.2
: Web and enterprise bean components must have access to the JNDI ENC to access things such as `EJB` objects, JTA `UserTransaction` objects, JDBC `DataSource` objects, Java Message Service `ConnectionFactory` objects, and JAX-RPC `ConnectionFactory` objects.

JavaMail and JAF
: Java EE 5 products must support JavaMail 1.3, including access to a message store. The platform must also support the Java Activation Framework (JAF) 1.0, which is needed to support different MIME types and required for JavaMail.

Java Message Service (JMS)
: Java EE 5 products must support JMS 1.1 and provide support for point-to-point (p2p) and publish-and-subscribe (pub/sub) messaging models, as well as the unified messaging model.

Java API for XML Parsing (JAXP)
: Java EE 5 products must support JAXP 1.2, which includes XML Schema validation, and Java EE 1.3 products must support JAXP 1.1.

Java EE Connector Architecture (JCA)
: Java EE 5 products must support JCA 1.5, which includes asynchronous messaging.

Java Authentication and Authorization Service (JAAS)
: Java EE 5 products must support the use of JAAS 1.0, as described in the JCA specifications.

Java Transaction API 1.0.1
: Java EE 5 and 1.3 products must support JTA 1.0.1 and must have access to the `UserTransaction` objects via the JNDI ENC.

Web Services for Java EE (WS-Java EE)
: Java EE 5 must support web services for Java EE 1.1. The specification includes JAX-RPC 1.1, JAXR 1.0, and SAAJ 1.2.

Web Services Metadata for Java EE
: This specification defines annotations that can be used to describe web services.

Java Logging API
: Java EE 5 products must support the logging of events using the `java.util.logging` package, which is part of the J2SDK 5 core.

Java EE Management API
: Java EE 5 products must support the Java EE Management API 1.0, including support for some features of JMX 1.2.

Java EE Deployment API
: Java EE 5 products must support the Java EE Deployment API 1.1. Vendors must support the plug-in component for tool vendors.

Java Authorization Service Provider Contract (JACC)
: Java EE 5 must support JACC 1.0, which defines a contract between a Java EE application server and an authorization policy provider.

Fitting the Pieces Together

To illustrate how a Java EE platform might function, imagine using a Java EE server in Titan's reservation system. To build this system, we would use the TravelAgent, ProcessPayment, and other EJBs, as well as the Cabin, Customer, and other entity beans we defined in this book, along with web components that would provide an HTML interface. The web components would access the enterprise beans in the same way that any Java client would, using the enterprise beans' remote and local interfaces. The web components would generate HTML to represent the reservation system.

Figure 20-5 shows a web page generated by a servlet or JSP page for the Titan reservation system. This web page was generated by web components on the Java EE server. When this page appears, the user has been guided through a login page, a customer selection page, and a cruise selection page, and is about to choose an available cabin for a reservation.

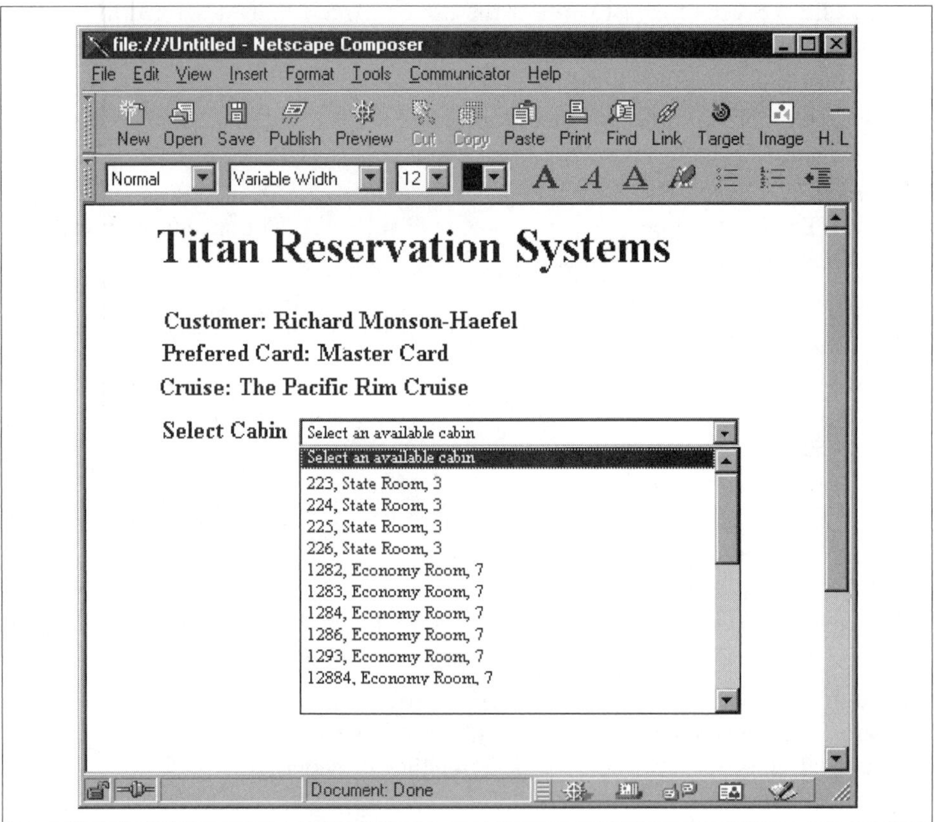

Figure 20-5. HTML interface to the Titan reservation system

The list of available cabins is obtained from the TravelAgent EJB, whose `listAvailableCabins( )` method is invoked by the servlet that generated the web page. The list of cabins creates an HTML listbox in a web page that is loaded into the user's browser. When the user chooses a cabin and submits the selection, an HTTP request is sent to the Java EE server. The Java EE server receives the request and delegates it to the `ReservationServlet`, which invokes the `TravelAgent.bookPassage( )` method to book the actual reservation. The ticket information returned by the `bookPassage( )` method is then used to create another web page, which is sent back to the user's browser. Figure 20-6 shows how the different components work together to process the request.

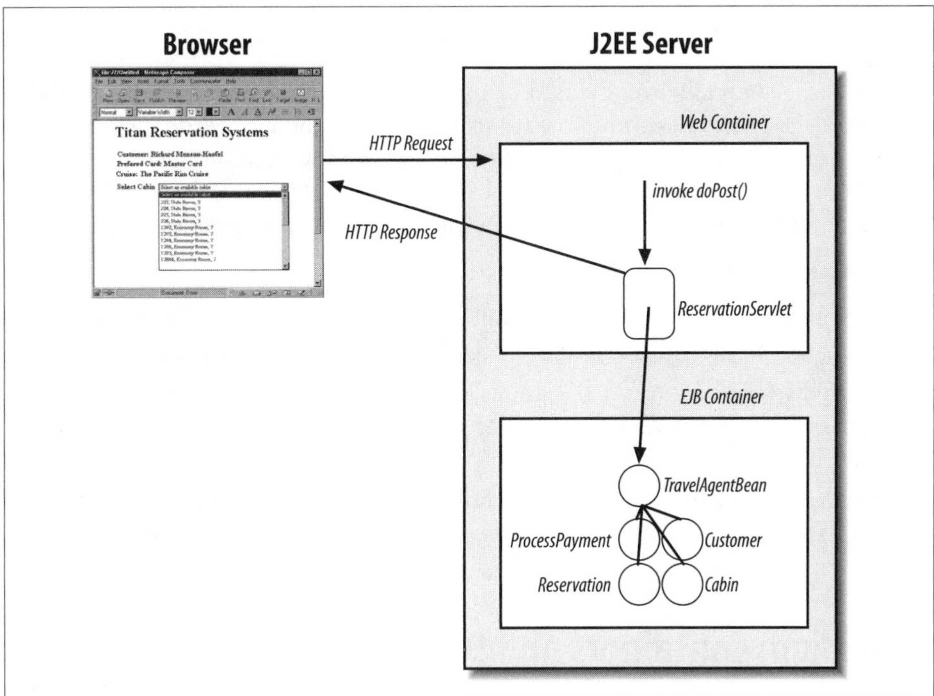

Figure 20-6. Java EE Titan reservation system

CHAPTER 21

EJB Design in the Real World

EJB has changed rapidly over the past couple of years with the introduction of EJB 3.0 and Java Persistence. Best practices for using EJBs "in the real world" are just now being documented, and already entire books have been written on how to use them. We cannot hope to cover everything in a single chapter. However, we can hit on the important topics regarding designing EJBs for use in real-world business applications.

This chapter covers:

- The questions you need to ask about your EJB container, persistence provider, and database selections *before* you begin designing your EJBs and entity beans.
- A step-by-step how-to for designing EJBs and entities from functional requirements to completed design, including the identification of potential base classes and EJB-helper classes.
- Alternatives to EJB. In some places, Enterprise JavaBeans are not the best choice. The last section in this chapter helps you identify those places and introduces some alternatives.

Predesign: Containers and Databases

Before you begin designing your application, it is essential that you consider the execution environment in which your code is run. The execution environment includes the following specifics regarding your system:

Hardware platform
Operating system
Java Virtual Machine (JVM) implementation
Application server (EJB container and persistence provider)
Database server

Each of these elements has a direct effect on your application design's success. We won't talk about hardware and operating systems (about which you may have little choice anyway), and we'll stay away from arguments about who has a better JVM.

Instead, we'll focus on the last two issues; they have the greatest effect on EJB application architecture.

Container Capabilities

Which EJB container you choose has a significant effect on your application's implementation and design. Regardless of your application's functional requirements, spend some time familiarizing yourself with how your application server works. Ideally, you'd develop that familiarity *before* choosing your application server.

When learning your container's capabilities, you are trying to find out how the application server's vendor has implemented its key features. Here are the primary areas on which to focus:

What vendor-specific functionality or extensions does it implement?
: Almost all EJB containers introduce some vendor-specific features. If you choose to use them, your application will be tied to that vendor's container. Switching to another vendor later may be costly. While this is often unavoidable (several popular development tools, for example, tie you closely to a vendor's implementation), there are tools out there that help to alleviate some of the risk.

How does the container's design or implementation affect performance?
: Because every vendor's implementation of the EJB spec is unique, containers from different vendors will perform differently. If possible, research the performance of your various container options for the specific functionality you need before choosing.

Can the container scale in a clustered environment?
: As your business ramps up, you may find that you need to add additional hardware to meet the load and demands of your new business. Does your vendor work well in a clustered environment of networked computers? Does it provide load balancing, failover, and replication of critical data? Ask your vendor these questions before you make your decision.

How much is this going to cost me?
: Open source application servers are starting to commoditize and dominate the application server market. They compete head-to-head in functionality, stability, and scalability with their commercial counterparts. Why pay for empty software licenses when you can get the same features for free? The JBoss* workbook at the end of this book is one example of an open source solution, but you should check out Glassfish, JOnAS, and Apache Geronimo as well.

Most vendors do a good job of implementing the specification, and it's relatively easy to move from one vendor to another. But don't walk into the EJB arena with your

* The author works for JBoss, so this is a little tongue-and-cheek. Hope you don't mind!

eyes closed. Ask the same kinds of questions that you would ask before making any other major software purchase, and you'll be OK.

Database Capabilities

While we place a lot of emphasis on the EJB container and persistence provider, the database server is just as influential on the overall system. Although the EJB container and Java Persistence isolate you from the database, the database is still there, and every data-related function depends on it.

The most critical function of a database is to ensure that data is available and consistent. Availability and consistency are qualities that depend on how your application uses transactions and how the database implements transactions.* When investigating how your database implements transactions, your primary concern should be the database's locking, isolation levels, and other resource management issues. Here are some questions to ask:

What transaction isolation levels does the database support?
: Although most databases support the four isolation levels discussed in Chapter 16 (Read Uncommitted, Read Committed, Repeatable Read, and Serializable), some do not. For example, PostgreSQL 7.3.x† offers only Read Committed and Serializable.

What are the lock types and lock scopes? What factors influence them?
: *Lock scope* is the number of rows that are protected when a lock is enacted. Depending on the vendor, the database may lock only the rows used by the transaction, blocks of rows (pages) that contain the rows used, or the entire table. The more rows are protected, the more likely it is that another process won't be able to access the data it needs. If such contention occurs, the other process will either fail or wait until the lock is released.

: As for what factors influence lock types and lock scopes, the database may "promote" locks under certain situations, such as when a query cannot use an index. This could mean that a nonexclusive write lock becomes an exclusive write lock or that a row-specific lock becomes a table-wide lock, should an index on that table not be usable in the write.

How are database resources handled within a transaction?
: During a transaction, especially a multistep transaction, the database has certain resources that it must manage. A good example is the number of open cursors involved in executing the transaction. Depending on how the database handles reclaiming those open cursors, a series of database operations that work fine outside of a transaction may not work at all when included in one because needed

* Transactions are discussed in Chapter 16.

† The most recent version of PostgreSQL at the time this was written.

cursors are left committed until after the last operation. In this case, large, multi-step, iterative processes ("batch" processes) can hit the maximum number of open cursors and fail. Knowing how your database manages resources such as open cursors can help you plan your transaction structure to ensure success.

Obviously, more is involved in the selection of a database server for your application/system than we've described here. However, all of these issues have direct ramifications on your EJB application.

Design

In this section, we go through the process of designing several EJBs. Although the design process of an EJB application is 95% identical to the design process of a non-EJB application (maybe even 99% identical), some steps in this process require special attention.

To discuss design, we need to change our thinking a bit. Throughout this book, we have focused on the details of EJBs and entity beans, and on how their individual components work. In this section, we consider the Titan EJB application as a system meeting a business need and not simply as a collection of fine-grained components. We will look at the design of such a system from the ground up, taking the application as a whole instead of continuing to view only the EJB components themselves (though we'll obviously pay special attention to those components, since this is a book on EJBs). Let's start by looking at its requirements.

At a high level, the application will be used by:

- Travel agents to sell reservations
- The general public to view cruise details
- Cruise administrators to manage the application's ship and cruise data

The application will be accessed via three mechanisms. The first two mechanisms are for "person" users (as opposed to "system" users, described shortly):

- Web interface (general public, travel agents, and cruise administrators)
- Standalone Java application (travel agents)

The third access mechanism is for systems that need direct access to the business layer. For our application, this includes access by:

- External travel agency systems (which includes both travel agents not working for Titan and reservation distribution services acting as clearinghouses for cruise line availability)
- Ship provisioning companies that need to know physical specifications for Titan's ships in order to provide auto-ordering of provisions (ship capacity, fuel type, and so on)

All three communications mechanisms (web client, standalone application, and business-to-business) must allow only secure actions to be executed by users. Connectivity to the external travel agencies and to the ship provisioning vendors is not guaranteed, so the communications mechanism will need to handle disconnects. Finally, we want to generate reservation confirmations and other forms in PDF format. Figure 21-1 is a system diagram of our requirements so far.

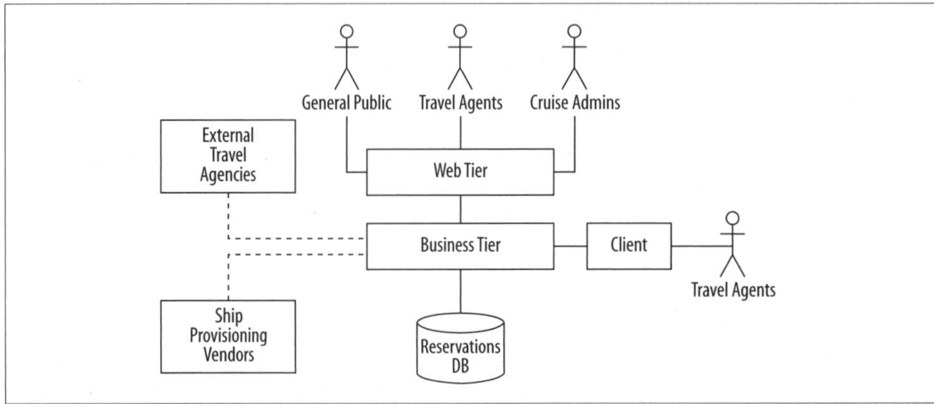

Figure 21-1. Application system diagram

Business Entity Identification

Now that we know our application's requirements, at least at a high level, we can identify the key business entities that the application needs to represent. This is generally a lengthy process, and we will go over only some of the results here. Although in our example, this is presented as a systematic, one-time process, it is really iterative. You will probably take a first stab at identifying business entities and then go through the process repeatedly before having a final list.

Here are some of the business entities for the Titan application:

Reservation
: Reservations are created by Travel Agents and belong to a Customer. They are associated with a Cruise and zero or more Cabins. A Reservation has a financial subtotal.

Travel Agent
: Travel Agents create and update Reservations and view Cruise information. Travel Agents are a kind of Person.

Customer
: A Customer is also a kind of Person. Customers have zero or more Reservations.

Ship
: A Ship has zero or more Cabins and belongs to zero or more Cruises.

Cruise

A Cruise has a Ship and a date period and is associated with zero or more Reservations.

Cabin

A Cabin belongs to a Ship and is associated with zero or more Reservations. All associated Reservations must have a Cruise with a Ship matching the Ship for the Cabin on the Reservation.

There's more structure to this list than is immediately apparent. It follows a number of guidelines that help reveal the important aspects of each entity:

Capitalization

Business entities are capitalized, and simpler pieces of information (date period, subtotal) are not.

Kind of, belongs, has, and is associated with

These phrases indicate fundamental connections between two entities. We have guessed at specific connection types for now, though the reality may change as we proceed. *Kind of* may indicate inheritance. *Has* and *have* may indicate that an entity is the parent in a parent/child relationship, and *belongs* may indicate that the entity is a child of another entity. *Is associated with* is a relationship too, but with a weaker sense of ownership (i.e., not parent-child).

Concrete verbs

There are three concrete verbs (*create*, *update*, and *view*) all in the description of the Travel Agent business entity. These verbs indicate processes or significant responsibilities handled by the entity.

Because we focus on the components that will end up being EJBs, our functional analysis is complete—selecting business entities is the most important part of the EJB design process for us.*

The next step is to look at the technical architecture and its implications for our entities. We'll get to that in just a moment. First, let's take a minute to diagram our business entities using UML so that we have a clear understanding of their relationships. While the textual descriptions help define the business relationships, a UML diagram depicts them more exactly. Figure 21-2 is a UML diagram of our business entities and their relationships.

The UML diagram introduces a Person entity from which we will derive both the TravelAgent and Customer entities. We've also introduced a mapping entity for

* Business entity identification is part of a complete functional analysis. A great deal more is involved in functional analysis for an application. User interface comps, lists of fields or attributes for each entity, and nonfunctional requirements (the number of users, usage patterns, and so on) are examples of additional items you may need to include in a functional analysis in order to design the complete application.

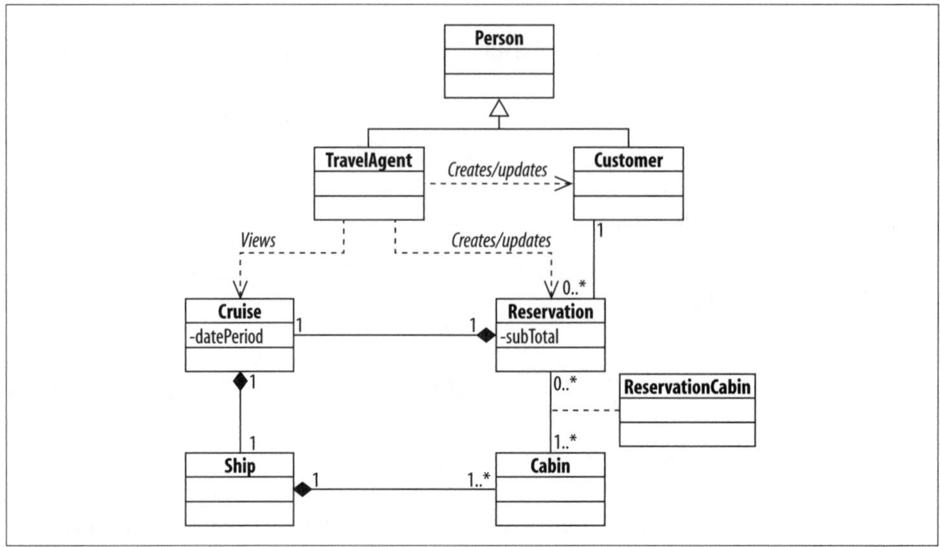

Figure 21-2. UML diagram of the application's business entities

mapping Reservation entities to Cabin entities. Otherwise, the UML diagram states exactly what we described earlier in the text.

The next step is to consider which objects to implement as EJBs and entity beans, and what types of EJBs to use. But first, it will help to understand the technical architecture of the system because aspects of it will have direct implications on our entity implementation choices.

Technical Architecture

Earlier, we depicted our system in a high-level diagram (Figure 21-1). This diagram depicts relationships between various entities and our system, but not much more. What else do we know about the various interactions of these entities and our Titan application?

- We know that connectivity between the external travel agencies and our system is not guaranteed. Because we are working with a Java implementation of this system, we may want to consider JMS as the communications mechanism between our system and theirs.
- Furthermore, we know that communication between our application and external travel agencies will be two-way (our application must be able to accept reservation requests), but communication between our application and the shop provision entities need only be one-way (we will tell them how many people are attending a cruise, for example).

- From our initial description, we can infer that making reservations is transactional and involves the following steps:
    a. Reserve a Cabin for use by a Customer.
    b. Reduce the total number of Cabins by one.
    c. Increase the total number of Customers for whom the provisioning vendor must provide food.
- These steps could involve up to three different database tables. At a minimum, this might involve the following database objects and systems:
    - One to store Reservations
    - One to store Cabin availability
    - One to store Customer information for provisioning

  While the complexity of these operations is not clearly defined, we can assume that reservation systems and the management of cruise and ship data are probably of moderate to high complexity. When combined with the need for transactional enforcement and the fact that only certain users will be able to execute certain actions (implied), using EJBs to represent the entities is appropriate.
- We know that customers and travel agents will be able to access the Titan application over the Web. This indicates that part of our system will involve controlling a user interface. EJBs are not well suited to user-interface work, so we'll include the use of servlets and JSPs in our system view.
- We also know that travel agents will be able to further access the system via a standalone Java application, indicating that some of the communications with the business tier of our application might not come via the Web.

Using this information, our technical system diagram can be amended as shown in Figure 21-3.

Although it may not look like it at first, we've gotten much closer to identifying our EJBs and entity benas. Between the new architecture diagram and our business entity UML diagram, we have all we need to move forward.

EJB and Entity Bean Identification

Not all of our business entities will turn out to be EJBs or entity beans, so the next step in our design process is to identify which of them *should*. Our understanding of the application's technical architecture helps. This is not a simple or well-defined process, like completing a jigsaw puzzle or building a bridge. For all but the simplest of applications, the process of identifying EJBs and entities in the application's technical architecture presents ambiguity and conflicting requirements. It's not easy to make the right choices. Fortunately, several rules of thumb will help guide the process.

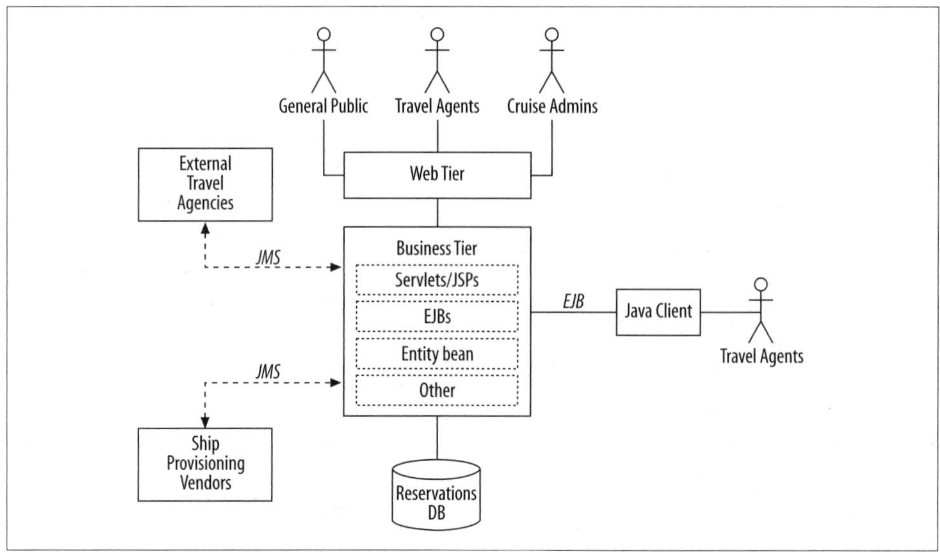

Figure 21-3. Amended system diagram

Let's quickly review the component types:

Entity beans
: Represent records persisted in a database. Entity beans can often be used to represent the nouns or *things* from our functional description. If a business entity has a real-world counterpart, it is probably an entity bean.

Session beans
: Manage processes or tasks, often calling other EJBs and non-EJB business objects as well as interacting with persistence units. Session beans represent *task-flows*. They are invoked locally or via RMI, both of which are synchronous mechanisms.

Message-driven beans
: Manage processes or tasks, like session beans, but are invoked *asynchronously* via JMS or possibly another messaging system. A message is received by the system and some function of the MDB is executed.

Identifying entity beans

With these characteristics in mind, let's start out by identifying entity beans in our application:

Guideline #1
: The description of entity beans gives us our first guideline: entity beans represent the entities (significant nouns) from the functional requirements. They are rows in a database table.

Our class diagram was created from the list of business entities in our functional analysis, which are essentially the *things* in our functional requirements. We know right away that all of the components in the diagram are candidates for implementation as entity beans. Although it is tempting to use straight JDBC for pieces of data that are read-only, it is strongly suggested that you don't. Since you would probably be populating a Java object anyway from the result set of any JDBC invocation, why not let Java Persistence do the work for you? More importantly, though, most persistence providers supply nice caching layers so that frequently accessed data remains in memory and you can avoid making expensive network calls to your database.

Identifying session beans

While entity beans are the *things* in our application, session beans implement *taskflow*. They are the processors and workhorses; they *do* stuff. We will identify them by considering the work that our application must do. A good starting place is reviewing the responsibilities depicted in the class diagram.

Looking over the class diagram, we see that `TravelAgent` has the following responsibilities:

- Views Cruises
- Creates and updates Reservations
- Creates and updates Customers

In any application, functionality seems to collect around one or more entities. Such a grouping of responsibilities often indicates that a session bean is needed, which brings us to the next guideline:

Guideline #2

Each session bean encapsulates access to data spanning concepts that are identified in the functional requirements analysis and initial technical architecture. So, when we see the grouping, as we do with `TravelAgent` in our class diagram, we know that a new session bean needs to be added to the design. However, the business entity, or actor (`TravelAgent`, in this case), will not become the session bean. Instead it indicates where a session bean is needed. The session bean represents the *action* the entity takes, not the entity itself. Think of the entity—implemented as an entity bean—as the subject of a sentence and the session bean as the sentence's verb.*

As for the name for the session bean, a good tactic is to create a name that reflects a combination of the target of the action and the action itself. For example, the

* To extend the metaphor, the direct objects of the sentence will be the other entity beans (or possibly even session beans) that will be used by the session bean when it executes. This approach is the starting point from which we evolve the Session Façade design pattern, in which session beans encapsulate a taskflow that uses one or more components.

TravelAgent creates and updates or "manages" Reservations, so a good name for our session bean might be ReservationManager. The primary objective of the name is to communicate what the session bean does. As the session bean encapsulates the responsibilities, each responsibility corresponds to a method in the EJB. So, our ReservationManager session bean will initially have three methods: `bookReservation( )`, `updateReservation( )`, and `cancelReservation( )`. These methods are also named intuitively to suggest what they do.

If we follow this line of reasoning, we may think we need to have a separate session bean called CruiseManager. However, the only interaction the TravelAgent has with a Cruise is to list it. Furthermore, it could be argued that in the overwhelming majority of cases, the TravelAgent will list Cruises only when making a Reservation. For these reasons, it might make more sense to combine the Cruise functionality and simply add a new `listCruises( )` method to the ReservationManager.

The `listCruises( )` method stands apart from the other methods a bit, both in effect (it reads data, while the other methods write data) and in direct object (it returns a collection of cruises, while the other methods manipulate a single reservation). This suggests Guideline #3:

Guideline #3

If a given session bean has a method that's *almost always* called in the context of another session bean's function(s), combine the session beans or move the method.

We have now accounted for all the responsibilities depicted in the class diagram, but we haven't accounted for all the functionality specified in the functional requirements. Creating the initial class diagram from the business entities initially misses functionality that has no "source" entity. For example, we've focused only on the reservations and the actions and entities around them. However, a reservation involves a Cruise that has certain characteristics. Some part of our application must be available to administer these Cruises. Cruises are made up of Cabins and Ships. Our administration functionality should focus on the management of all three entities: `Cruise`, `Ship`, and `Cabin`.

Our application revolves around travel agency functionality, but without the configuration of the cruises themselves, that functionality (creation of reservations, and so on) would be meaningless. Let's add a general session bean around this and other (to be determined) configuration chores. Although we may need to break this into multiple session beans later, we can start with one called `ConfigurationManager`.

Here too, we want to give it methods based on the functionality it encapsulates. Because no taskflows are detailed at this point, we will assume that all three items need to be created, updated, and deactivated. Thus, these actions (for the three entities) become nine initial methods:

```
addCruise
updateCruise
cancelCruise
addShip
updateShip
inactivateShip
addCabin
updateCabin
inactivateCabin*
```

We can now expand our entity diagram into the class diagram shown in Figure 21-4.

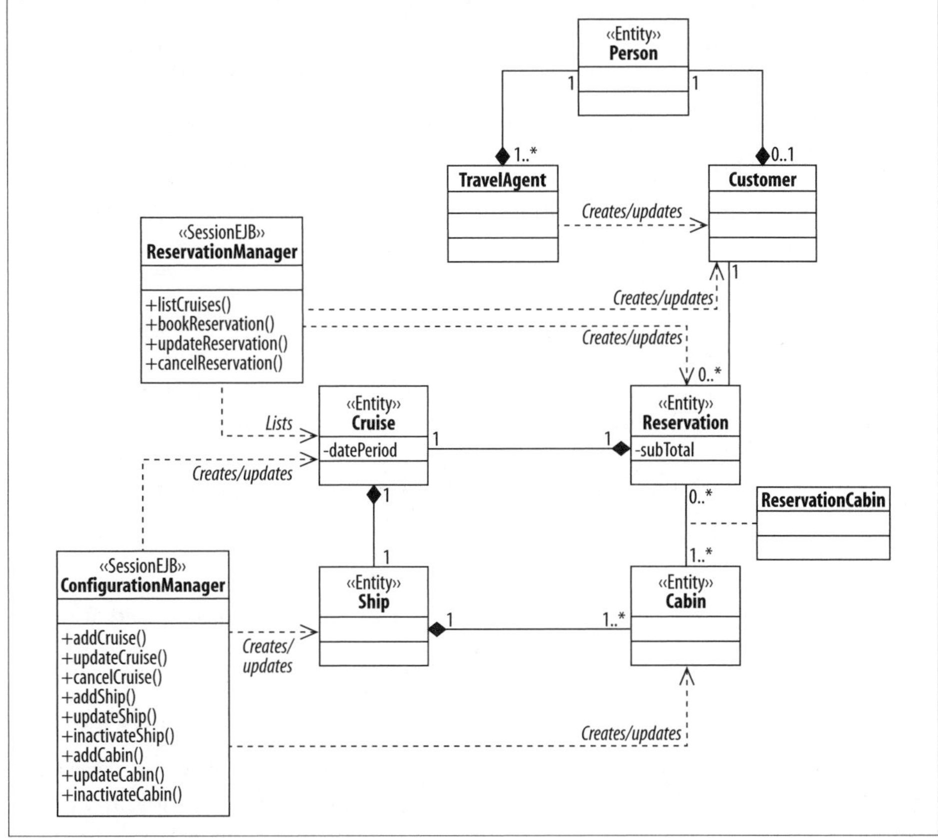

Figure 21-4. Expanded into a class diagram

* Most developers would expect to see "deleted" rather than "inactivated," but we have found that it is more prudent not to let the business tier delete configuration data (and possibly all application data). Instead, data should be deactivated by the business tier and deleted only during archival or export to a data warehouse, according to an agreed-upon process.

Identifying message-driven beans

Now we need to look for the message-driven beans in the application. As our review of the EJB types reminds us, message-driven beans (MDBs) implement *taskflows* like session beans, but they can be invoked *asynchronously*. Roughly put, they are transactional message handlers.* This suggests Guideline #4:

Guideline #4
: Each message-driven bean encapsulates related functionality that must be invoked in a transactional manner when an asynchronous message is received. So, as with session beans, in order to tell where we might want to use message-driven beans, we look for groups of functionality. However, for MDBs, the functionality is usually initiated with the reception of an asynchronous message.

Here's where our system architecture diagram helps us. Messaging takes place between our system and another (ostensibly external) system in two places:

- Between external travel agencies and the Titan application
- Between ship provisioning vendors and the Titan application

As you can see from our functional requirements and the technical architecture diagram, our system *receives* messages only from external travel agencies, so we'll focus on the travel agent functionality.

Since we've not been told anything to the contrary, we assume that external travel agent systems function like ours. Thus, ours should include all the functionality incorporated into `ReservationManager`. Additionally, the external travel agencies need some way to retrieve a list of ships and their cabins. This listing ability is included because the external travel agency systems can communicate only via messaging. This suggests that one or more MDBs could be used to implement this functionality.

For the Titan application, we will have two MDBs:

ReservationListener
: The ReservationListener creates, updates, or cancels one or more reservations in response to a reservation function message.

QueryListener
: The QueryListener retrieves cruise and ship data in response to a query message.

Compare the responsibilities of ReservationListener with those of ReservationManager. The cruise-listing behavior and the reservation-specific behavior are implemented in separate MDBs. Why? Guideline #4 tells us that if we are only going to execute a given piece of functionality in the context of a given process, we should combine that function with the others. This guideline is appropriate for session

* EJB qualities such as object distribution and role-based security enforcement are irrelevant in this context, because the MDB has no connection to the message sender.

The Naming of MDBs

MDB names, like session bean names, should suggest what the component does. A rule of thumb is to combine a description of the kinds of messages that the MDB receives with the word *Listener*. *Processor* is a common alternative to *Listener*, but it is less definitive and thus easier to confuse.

beans. Adding another method to a session bean does not introduce any complexity to the bean; it's just another method. However, in JMS-based MDBs, you have only one `onMessage( )` function. While you can certainly have many different types of messages coming into the queue on which the MDB is listening, each one must be processed separately. Each message type adds another significant condition to the MDB's processing logic. Furthermore, the functionality represented by the various messages for the ReservationListener will be largely the same, but messages representing queries for cruise information might be different.

While we're covering JMS-based MDBs, it makes sense to discuss the importance of message design. When a message listener is invoked, the only information it has is the message that it has been passed. In many cases, the message listener needs specific business information to do its work, and that information is packaged in the message.

Exactly how it is packaged depends on which message type you choose: `javax.jms.Message` or its subinterfaces (`BytesMessage`, `MapMessage`, `ObjectMessage`, `StreamMessage`, and `TextMessage`). A general rule of thumb is to use `ObjectMessage` for messaging between systems that are guaranteed to be Java-based and to use `TextMessage` for messaging between potentially non-Java systems. Because `ObjectMessage` carries a full Java object, its data is already structured for easy access by the MDB, whereas all but the simplest data in a `TextMessage` (and the other types, to varying extents) will generally have to be processed before it can be used (by a `StringTokenizer`, an XML parser, `Integer.parseInt`, or something similar).

On the upside, `TextMessage` (and maybe `BytesMessage`) is the universal message type—every messaging system knows how to send and receive simple text (and binary data). With that said, you should investigate message types and their tradeoffs before making final decisions.

Because we need to accept messages from the greatest variety of external travel agency systems, we will use `TextMessage` messages carrying XML payloads. Although it requires a heavy XML parser when processing messages, `TextMessage` provides interoperability benefits that fit our needs.

We've now identified all of the EJBs and entity beans in our sample application. Figure 21-5 shows an updated class diagram.

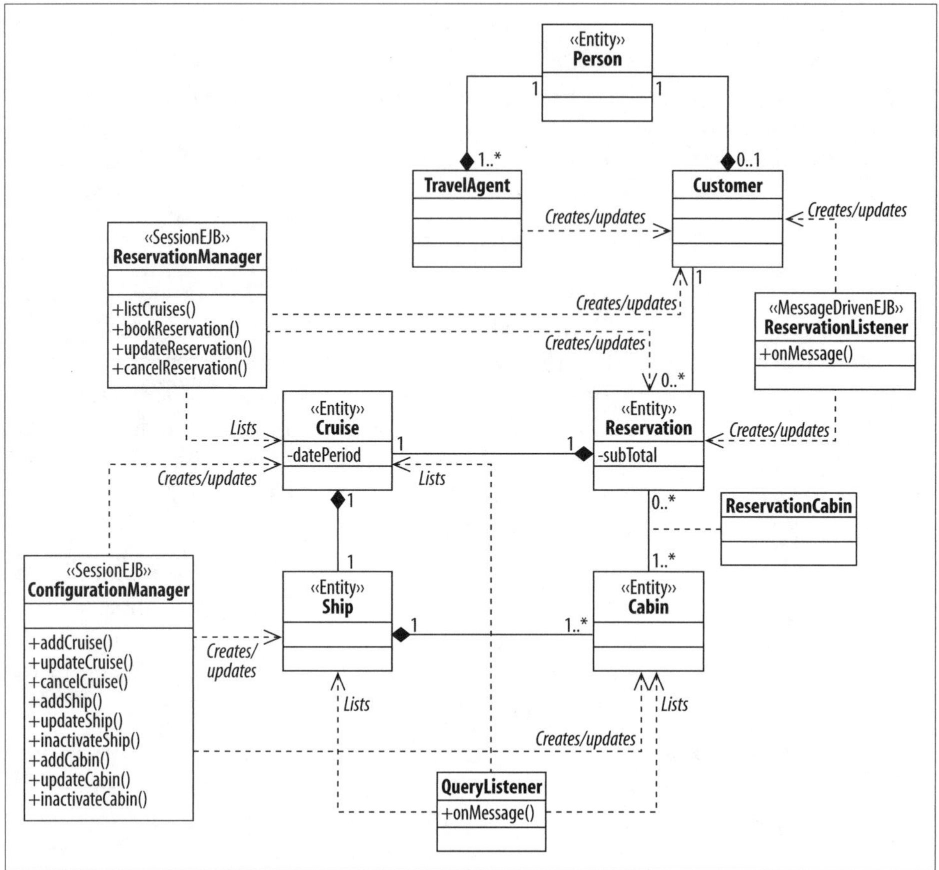

Figure 21-5. Updated class diagram

EJB Details

Now that we have identified the EJBs in our application along with some of their methods, we have completed about two-thirds of our design. So far, much of the design has flowed almost naturally from our business and technical requirements. The remaining one-third of the design is more difficult and requires some hard decisions.

Stateless versus stateful session beans

As their names indicate, the difference between the two subtypes of session beans is the maintenance of state. A common source of confusion is that we use similar words when we talk about web session state, servlets, and other aspects of web-based applications. Session bean state is taskflow related and should have little or no relation to the Web or to presentation tiers of your application. Session bean state is a way of sharing information among multiple methods of the same session bean. For example, the stateful version of `ReservationManager` contains the current `Customer` so that it is not passed into the `bookReservation( )`, `updateReservation( )`, and `cancelReservation( )` methods (see Figure 21-6).

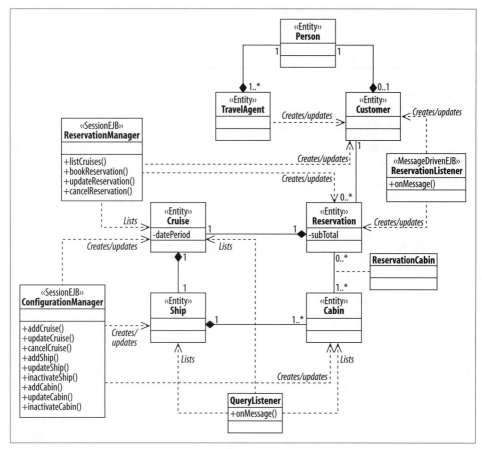

Figure 21-6. Stateful version of ReservationManager

Contrast that with the stateless version of `ReservationManager`, in which the current `Customer` is a parameter for those methods (see Figure 21-7).

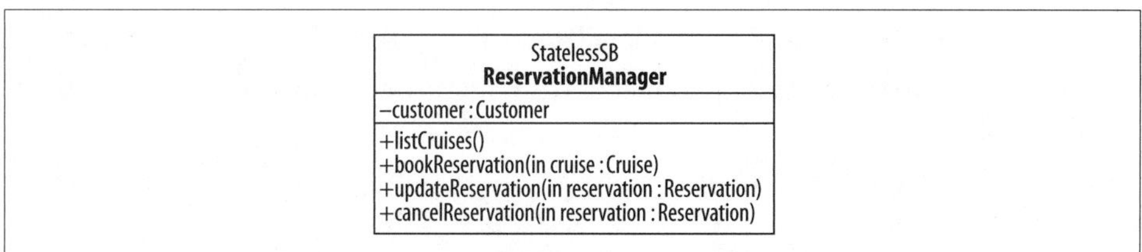

Figure 21-7. Stateless version of ReservationManager

The stateful session bean is more elegant when we need to call `bookReservation`, `updateReservation`, or `cancelReservation` multiple times, especially if you are using some of the extended persistence context queuing and batching features we discussed in Chapter 16.

However, there are certain performance considerations to think about. A stateful session bean must be created for each client that needs one. This stateful bean instance stays in memory until it is removed by its client or is passivated by the EJB container. This is probably not an issue in most applications, but if you have tens of thousands of stateful bean clients, it may become an issue. The side effects of using a stateful bean in this scenario can be minimized by making sure clients release their stateful bean references when they don't need them anymore, and by tuning the passivation timeout of your EJB container.

There are also performance considerations when you are clustering your stateful session beans. Clustered stateful session beans must have their state replicated to other nodes in the cluster so that client requests can successfully failover if a machine goes down. This can create a lot of network traffic and CPU cycles. In general, distributed systems should be designed to be as stateless as possible. However, if a client needs to have a stateful conversation with your application, then you're going to have to pay the cost of state replication somewhere in your application, whether it is in the web tier or in your EJB tier.

Local versus remote interfaces

Don't use remote interfaces unless you really have to—we can't emphasize this enough. Distributing your EJBs adds a whole layer of complication that is often unnecessary. There are the basic, only somewhat irritating issues, such as handling `RemoteExceptions` in your client code, and there are the complex, intractable issues, such as loss of performance and reliability when your components must operate across a network. One big complication is that remote interfaces (and the implementation they present) are often difficult to change because they will be used by other systems or applications that may be resistant to change.

Our application clearly needs to be distributed; it must support the standalone Java client that our internal travel agents will use. In your application, take a long, hard look at any requirements that push you in the direction of distributed components. Approach such requirements with common sense:

- Understand the requirements in detail and validate them.
- Determine whether the requirements truly merit being implemented as distributed EJBs.
- Document the detailed requirements before initiating development in order to ensure agreement and to prevent scope creep.

If, after this process, you determine that you need distributed functionality, your next task is to identify which EJBs should be implemented with remote interfaces and which should stay as local interfaces. In our application, travel agents will use the standalone client to access the full range of application functionality. We already know that session beans are the workhorses of our application, which is why we have exposed the session beans via remote interfaces.

How do we pass entity data, such as cruise information, across the remote interface? Good answers to this question are provided in the upcoming section "Returning entity data from EJBs." Because entity beans are plain Java objects, they can be serialized to remote clients. Entity beans can be a part of the interface of an EJB component.

It is a good idea to implement both remote and local interfaces for our session beans. While this results in slightly more code to build and maintain, it is a good idea to use the local interfaces in the code that runs inside the application server, such as servlets or JSPs. The small duplication is worth avoiding the remote interface.

Thus, our interface recommendations are:

- Use remote interfaces only if you must.
- Implement local interfaces for session beans if code will be calling them from inside your application server.

Entity Details

We may have finished identifying our entity beans and the relationships between them, but we still need to make a few design decisions regarding the persistence layer. One thing that needs consideration is how you transfer entity data from your session beans to your client code. Another thing that requires careful planning is how you interact with your data model. Database access usually has the most impact on the performance and scalability of your system. We'll discuss both of these issues in this section.

Returning entity data from EJBs

If you have remote clients that access your EJBs, you need to figure out how you will transfer entity information to and from the server. Because entity beans are plain Java objects, this job can be as simple as having your entity classes implement the `java.io.Serializable` or `Externalizable` interface and passing them as parameters in the remote interface of your EJBs:

```
@Entity
public Customer implements java.io.Serializable {
  ...
}

@Remote
public interface TravelAgentRemote {
```

```
    Ticket makeReservation(Reservation reservation);

    Reservation findReservation(Customer cust, Cruise cruise);

    void updateReservation(Reservation res);
}
```

For example, let's say you have a Swing GUI application that interacts with remote EJBs. It could create `Reservation` objects locally and send them to the server to be processed. The session bean could take the `Reservation` object as is and only call `EntityManager.persist()`. Later, the Swing GUI might want to update this reservation. It would call the `findReservation()` method mentioned earlier, and it would display the `Reservation` on the GUI locally. Edits could be made directly to the `Reservation` instance on the client, sent back to the server, and merged with the `EntityManager.merge()` operation.

There is one pitfall to this kind of design, though. An entity bean may have many nested relationships that create a complex object graph. You don't want to serialize entire object graphs over the wire to your remote clients because they may be too large. Therefore, it is good practice to set the `javax.persistence.FetchType` of all your relationships to `LAZY` so that they are lazily loaded on demand on the server. In your server logic that obtains and returns references to these complex entities, you can choose which information you want to be loaded—based on the business process you are performing—by using features such as `JOIN FETCH` queries.

Minimizing database access

The biggest bottleneck in EJB applications is usually the database. It is usually a highly contended resource that requires the most optimizations. Why is this so? First, the database is quite likely in another process on the same machine as the application server or, more likely, on another machine in the network. We mentioned earlier (in the local versus remote interface debate) that network invocations are expensive. This is also true of database calls. Second, the databases have to synchronize to disk any updates that you perform. A disk can go only so fast and is a resource that can be highly contended. Hard drives have a maximum throughput, and once you reach this limit, you can't go much further to increase the performance of your system. Therefore, you want to minimize database interaction as much as possible in your application design, which means limiting the number of round trips to the database and even combining multiple updates and/or queries into single operations. There are a couple of portable ways to tune your database access that we'll discuss in this section: caching and minimizing database invocations.

Caching

Caching will probably have the biggest impact on performance for your system. *Caching* is the act of leaving data in memory so that when a business process needs access to a certain entity bean, the persistence provider does not have to communicate to the database to obtain this information. Although caching is not discussed in the Java Persistence specification, all vendors will at least have some sort of single VM global cache that can hold data in memory until it is needed. Most vendors will additionally have distributed caching available so that you can retain this performance benefit when you run your application in a cluster of networked computers. Caching usually works with only the `find()` and `getReference()` `EntityManager` methods because the cache usually comprises only simple maps, with the primary key as the identifier. EJB QL queries are usually never cached, but some vendors do provide some ability in this area as well. It is a good idea to check your vendor's caching capabilities before making any purchasing decisions.

One thing to remember about caching is that one size does not fit all of the entity beans in your system. Although you can have a very large heap size with 64-bit systems nowadays, memory is still a finite resource. Some entities in your system may be accessed very rarely, and they may be using space that is needed by frequently accessed entities. In our Titan Reservation system, Ships, Cruises, and Cabins are f entities, and Customers and Reservations are rarely accessed after the initial order is placed in the system. In this case, it might make sense to eliminate or reduce the cache size for Customers and Reservations so that other entities that need caching can take up more room in memory. Another type of entity that you may not want to cache is one that is updated frequently. In this case, the cache is continuously being updated. While this isn't so important on applications that run on a single server, it can have performance penalties in a cluster because the updating server must send network messages to other nodes in the system to ensure that these remote caches are up-to-date.

So, some good common-sense rules for caching are:

- Create large cache sizes for frequently accessed entities.
- Create smaller caches or have no cache at all for infrequently accessed entities.
- Consider not caching frequently updated entities.

Which entities you should cache and how large your cache should be are factors that depend on the size of your database and the amount of memory you have available on your servers. It is best to create real-world simulations of the traffic your system will receive to fine-tune your cache settings. Don't make caching decisions blindly.

Combining queries

Even if you have optimal cache settings, you can still do a lot to minimize the number of times you hit the database. One thing you can do is to combine queries. In the earlier section titled "Returning entity data from EJBs," we discussed how it is good practice to set the `FetchType` of your related entities to be `LAZY` so that you don't pull entire object graphs. A lazy fetch mode may have the side effect of forcing the underlying persistence provider to make multiple extra queries to traverse a relationship, when this relationship could have been fetched along with the root entity. For example, let's look at the @OneToMany Cruise-Reservation relationship:

```
1  Cruise cruise = entityManager.find(Cruise.class, 1) ;
2  ... // do some work on base cruise
3  Collection<Reservation> reservations = cruise.getReservations( );
4  for (Reservation res : reservations ) "
5  {
6     res.setDate(newDate);
7  }
```

If our @OneToMany Cruise-Reservation were set to LAZY fetching, then the preceding business process would result in two separate database queries. Line 1 would load the base cruise object. Line 3 would execute a separate query to pull in the reservations associated with the cruise. It is more optimal to pull in the reservations by doing a join when the cruise is first loaded to eliminate the extra queries. Your first reaction might be to change the FetchType to EAGER for this relationship. This is not a good choice because different business processes might not be interested in the reservations relationship. A better solution is to use the JOIN FETCH feature of EJB QL:

```
Query query = entityManager.createQuery("FROM Cruise c LEFT FETCH JOIN c.reservations
   WHERE c.id = 1");
Cruise cruise = (Cruise)query.getSingleResult( );
... // do some work on base cruise
Collection<Reservation> reservations = cruise.getReservations( );
for (Reservation res : reservations )
{
   res.setDate(newDate);
}
```

In this code, even though the Reservation side of the relationship is marked as LAZY, the LEFT FETCH JOIN causes the relationship to be loaded when the cruise is queried.

Minimizing updates

Certain circumstances in your code can pop up, causing additional, unneeded database updates within a transaction. Because improving performance is mostly about reducing database access, you should be aware of these circumstances. Consider the following transaction:

```
Reservation res = entityManager.find(Reservation.class, 1);
res.setAmountPaid(amount);

Query query = entityManager.createQuery("FROM Reservation res WHERE res.dateReserved
   > 'APR-06-2005'");
List list = query.getResultList( );
for (Object obj : list) {
   Reservation reservation = (Reservation)obj;
   Reservation.setDateReserved(today);
}
```

The default FlushModeType for an EntityManager and for a Query is AUTO. This means that Line 4 may cause a database update of the Reservation updated in Line 2. The persistence provider may not be able to figure out whether the update in Line 2 affects the executed query. Because Lines 6–9 update reservations again, the same reservation might be updated in the database twice. A solution to this problem is to set FlushModeType to COMMIT. This defers any database updates, inserts, and deletes until the transaction commits.

```
entityManager.setFlushMode(FlushModeType.COMMIT);

Reservation res = entityManager.find(Reservation.class, 1);
res.setAmountPaid(amount);

Query query = entityManager.createQuery("FROM Reservation res WHERE res.dateReserved
> 'APR-05-2006'");
List list = query.getResultList( );
for (Object obj : list) {
   Reservation reservation = (Reservation)obj;
   Reservation.setDateReserved(today);
}
```

In many cases, the persistence provider can do batch queries when COMMIT is used and send all these changes in one network call. Another solution might be to always perform your queries upfront before any updates are made to the queried entities.

Fleshing Out the Design

Now that you've determined the major aspects of your EJBs, all that remains is to complete the design down to the class and method levels. This is the same task you would perform for any application, so we will not cover it here. However, this stage can undo or compromise good EJB design if it is executed poorly. This section discusses the two most critical lessons we have learned to keep an EJB design in good shape.

Don't confuse EJB types

This may seem like a no-brainer, but don't try to make one EJB type behave like another. If you've been paying attention throughout this book (you have, haven't you?), the differences between EJB types should be pretty clear in your head. Session and message-driven beans manage processes (synchronously and asynchronously, respectively), entity beans persist data, and everyone is happy. That's great! There are two possible wrinkles, however:

- Not everyone will have read this book; some people will have different understandings of how to design EJBs.
- Your application will evolve, and the changes may alter your EJB design.

As a consequence, you may find some of the following in your application:

- A custom JMS listener that calls a session bean
- Session beans presenting *getters/setters* for individual data items
- Entity beans containing complex business logic*

These are all *bad things*.† If you see these or any similar misconceptions about what each kind of EJB does, do everything you can to fix them ASAP. Depending on the exact circumstances, the consequences may be minor—an additional class or two requiring creation and maintenance—or they may make the EJB nonfunctional or impossible to maintain.

Minimize transaction scope

As you flesh out your EJBs, especially session beans, make sure that your transactions have the smallest scope possible. By *scope*, we mean the number of operations executed and the number of components used. Operations executed inside a transactional context require more container management than nontransactional operations, and this management generally results in limitations and performance costs. The limitations depend on the container, database, and other transactional components of your application. Exceeding these limitations can create problems that depend greatly on the execution environment and the exact processing being done.

This variability often makes diagnosis and troubleshooting of transactional problems difficult, so the best approach is to minimize transactional scope during design or early in coding. Here is how to identify possible transaction resource problems:

1. Understand the transactional capabilities and constraints of your EJB container, your database, and other subsystems. You should be concerned with what resources are limited during a transaction. Remember to check both the vendor documentation and any specification documentation.
2. Identify the complex taskflows in your application. Focus on functionality that iterates through EJBs, aggregates through data, or chains EJBs (where one EJB calls another, which calls another, and so on) inside a single transaction.‡
3. Estimate the amount of processing that the taskflows will perform. Consider the data entities used in the taskflows, and determine the maximum number of each

* We once saw a BMP entity bean designed to retrieve and manage a hierarchical collection—a tree—of key-value pairs. The entity bean contained data elements from the key table and the value table, all held in multiple instances of the same kind of entity bean. The entity bean contained the necessary logic to populate, traverse, and persist the entire tree of data.

† Can you identify the kinds of EJBs the examples should represent? Hint: a message-driven bean, an entity bean, and a session bean.

‡ Remember that the transaction scope is propagated to all EJBs touched by the thread of execution, except for those EJB methods that have `NotSupported` or `RequiresNew` specified for their transaction attributes in the deployment descriptor.

entity that your application will support.* This knowledge can help you determine how many EJBs will be used. Also, consider non-EJB resources, such as database cursors. Combine this data with the steps and dependencies of each taskflow to produce a list of resources used.

4. Compare the list of resources used by each taskflow to the relevant setting or constraint. For example, the total number of EJB instances is limited by the `max-beans-in-pool` deployment descriptor setting. Where the resources used could exceed the available resources, you will need to minimize the transactional scope.

Repeat this evaluation if you make significant changes to your EJBs, especially after revisions that affect your session beans.

Exceptions

Exceptions are fundamental to error notification and management in Java. Understanding exceptions and how to handle them is even more important in EJB because exceptions have a significant effect on transaction control. Be sure to review the section on exceptions and transactions in Chapter 16.

Exception design for EJBs is essentially the same as general exception design. With EJBs, though, you need to be aware of what types of exceptions roll back a transaction. Any exception annotated with `@ApplicationException(rollback=true)` causes a transaction rollback. Any exception annotated with `@ApplicationException(rollback=false)` does not roll back the transaction. If the `<application-exception>` element is used within the EJB XML deployment descriptor, the same rules apply. If there is no `@ApplicationException` annotation, or no EJB XML deployment descriptor metadata that defines the transaction rollback behavior, any `java.lang.RuntimeException` or `java.rmi.RemoteException` class, or any exception class that extends them, automatically causes a rollback.

Although the EJB specification allows you to manually roll back a transaction with the `EJBContext.setRollbackOnly( )` method, it is usually a best practice to let thrown exceptions determine the transaction's viability. This will shrink the number of *try/catch* blocks in your code base and will generally simplify exception handling. You must be thorough with your application of `@ApplicationException`, `<application-exception>`, and runtime or remote exceptions, however, to make sure that the behavior of your system remains consistent.

Here are the fundamental steps in exception design:

1. Identify business exceptions.
2. Design an exception hierarchy for business exceptions.

* This kind of information is also necessary for accurate database sizing.

3. Decide the rollback behavior for each business exception and use `@ApplicationException` and `<application-exception>` appropriately.
4. Decide whether each business exception should be an unchecked or a checked exception.
5. Declare or wrap subsystem or third-party exceptions that cause rollbacks.

Identifying business exceptions

The first step is to determine the business exceptions. Business exceptions encapsulate business errors that prevent the completion of a taskflow. The user should be notified, or the application should attempt to recover from the error, or both. The essential criterion is that the error needs to be propagated several layers (at least) up the application call stack. For example, the Titan application would throw a business exception if a reservation could not be completed because the desired cruise was sold out, and this exception would cause the user interface to display an error message. Avoid scenarios where business exceptions are used as costly `if-then` statements or other forms of flow control. Exceptions are *exceptional*.*

Business exceptions can often be identified almost straight from your business requirements, so if the requirements are fully defined, much of the work in this step is already done. The trick is to make sure your exceptions focus on error conditions. Some developers have used exceptions for user interface control, which is bad. For example, if a query for cabin information from the Titan application produced no results, it is better to return an empty `Collection` than to throw an exception. Exceptions should be reserved for errors, and other mechanisms should be employed for controlling user interaction.

Designing the exception hierarchy

Examine your object model and object interaction diagrams to pinpoint all business exceptions that need to be thrown. After you have determined what business exceptions you need, incorporate them into a class hierarchy. A hierarchy provides at least two benefits:

- Common functionality can be implemented in superclasses.
- You can use a package-specific superclass in *throws* clauses instead of listing multiple subclasses. For example, the signature can show `InventoryException` rather than `CabinSoldOutException`, `DeckSoldOutException`, and `CruiseSoldOutException`.

* Because throwing exceptions is costly, your application should take reasonable steps to avoid predictable exceptions. In other words, be sure to check the preconditions at the beginning of all taskflows and methods. This also avoids performing part of a taskflow only to have to roll it back, which is a waste of time and resources. For example, check if the cruise is sold out before attempting to create a reservation. While the cruise might sell out in the split second between the check and the creation, it's unlikely 99% of the time.

Here are some specific steps to assist in creating the hierarchy:

1. Always have a base class, probably abstract, to contain general exception functionality. This can be called `AbstractException`.
2. `AbstractException` should also contain code and attributes for passing at least two error codes: one for user notification and another for developer notification. The codes should correspond to entries in a resource bundle or other text localization mechanism. Short, mnemonic textual codes (`AVAILABLE_INVENTORY_EXCEEDED`) rather than numeric or otherwise cryptic codes (`I-01765`) are preferable.
3. Create a subclass of `AbstractException` for each major package—e.g., `InventoryException`, `GuestException`.
4. Package-specific exceptions can be subclassed as necessary to indicate particular error conditions. As mentioned earlier, `CabinSoldOutException`, `DeckSoldOutException`, and `CruiseSoldOutException` are possible subclasses of `InventoryException`. Use as many subclasses as you need.
5. When designing the EJB interfaces, start out by listing all exceptions that each method can throw. A rule of thumb is that if three or more exceptions thrown by a method are subclasses of the same package-level exception, replace them with the package-level exception.

Deciding on rollback exceptions

Now that you have your exception hierarchy, walk through it to determine whether each exception will cause an automatic transaction rollback. Even if you are annotation averse, this is the time to swallow your pride and use `@ApplicationException` to identify this behavior. This is good practice because the application code may want to determine generically whether a rollback happened.

```
try {
   ejb.doOperation( );
} catch (com.titan.exceptions.AbstractException ex) {
   ApplicationException ae = ex.getAnnotation(ApplicationException.class);
   if (ae.rollback( ) == true) System.out.println("unrecoverable error");
   else // try and recover
}
```

If you are thorough and use `@ApplicationException` everywhere in your exception hierarchy, you can examine this annotation metadata at runtime, without knowing the concrete type of the exception, to determine whether the transaction was rolled back.

Don't forget to annotate `Runtime` or `RemoteExceptions` that do not roll back the transaction automatically with `@ApplicationException`!

Checked versus unchecked exceptions

In most cases, you will want to use unchecked exceptions for your exception hierarchy. With checked exceptions, a lot of unnecessary *try/catch* blocks turn up all over the place. Usually, when an exception is thrown, nothing can be done and the thread of execution needs to be aborted anyway. Use checked exceptions only when you want to force the calling code to handle the exception. Even though you will primarily use unchecked exceptions, it is a good idea to put the unchecked exception in the *throws* clause of your methods. Most IDEs have automatic *try/catch* block generation around invoked methods. If the calling code wants to catch a particular unchecked exception, the IDE automatically creates the correct *catch* block if the exception is in the *throws* clause of the called method.

There is an informal category of checked exceptions that deserves special treatment. We call them *subsystem exceptions*. As the name indicates, subsystem exceptions are checked exceptions thrown by a subsystem of the JVM or a resource, such as JDBC or JMS. For example, `IOException` is thrown by the I/O subsystem; `JMSException` is thrown by JMS; `SQLException` is thrown by JDBC, and so on. These exceptions usually mean that the transaction needs to be rolled back, so you must take appropriate measures to handle them.

Wrap subsystem exceptions

Whether or not subsystem exceptions should appear in your EJB method signatures is circumstantial. If the client can recover or retry the business operation based on information available from the subsystem exception, then it might be a good idea to put it within the *throws* clause. For instance, if you are doing straight JDBC, you may run into deadlock exceptions when doing the JDBC operation. In this case, you will want the exception to be rolled back, but the client may want to retry the operation because the deadlock conditions may have been cleared up with the rollback. In this case, you can add `SQLException` to your method signature, but you must also declare it as an `<application-exception>` in your XML deployment descriptor:

```
<ejb-jar>
   <assembly-descriptor>
      <application-exception>
         <exception-class>java.sql.SQLException</exception-class>
         <rollback>true</rollback>
      </application-exception>
   </assembly-descriptor>
</ejb-jar>
```

If the subsystem exception is not recoverable or retryable, then don't put it in the *throws* clause of your methods. In this case, you should catch and wrap the exception in an `EJBException` or an appropriate business exception:

```
try {
   ...
} catch ( SQLException se ) {
```

```
        throw new EJBException("SQLException caught during processing: " +
                               se.getMessage( ), se);
    } catch ( RemoteException re ) {
        throw new EJBException("RemoteException caught during processing: "
                               + re.getMessage( ), re);
    }
```

Utility Classes

As you design your EJBs, you will begin to spot areas of common functionality. For example, since several classes and functions deal with reservations in the Titan application, several of the implementations may require the use of `startDate` and `endDate` parameters. They may even be of a similar type (i.e., `java.util.Date`). As another example, suppose the DBA for your application's database decides that there will be a timestamp column named `L*_MODIFIED` in all database tables. Every single entity bean in your application will support this field. Furthermore, the implementation of this field will have to remain consistent across all implementations of all entity beans in order to be of use.

You'll start to notice that a bunch of regular Java objects will begin to pop up in your design. These are called *utility classes*. Utility classes are hard to define precisely because they include generalized data-holding classes, such as a `DateRange` class that encapsulates a start date and an end date, and nondata classes that contain infrastructure-related, library-like, and convenience methods. Examples of nondata classes include a `StringUtils` class containing `String` manipulation functionality, an `ObjectUtils` class containing various equality and comparison convenience methods, and a `DatabaseUtils` class containing primary key generation and database connection functionality. Data-holding classes can be more ambiguous. Determining whether they are utility classes or domain-specific types will depend on your particular application and design. For example, a `Money` class that combines an amount and a currency could be considered a generalized, cross-package class or a finance-specific class.

The primary benefit of utility classes is reducing code duplication, which makes it easier to fix or improve your application without risking shotgun surgery.* Utility classes can also increase code readability.

You will discover candidate utility classes as you implement your design. The biggest sign that you might need a utility class is code duplication. If your code performs the same or very similar logic multiple times, or if two or more classes always accompany each other in methods or method signatures, you have a possible utility

* *Shotgun surgery* takes place "...when every time you make a kind of change, you have to make a lot of little changes to a lot of different classes." (From *Refactoring: Improving the Design of Existing Code*, published by Addison-Wesley.)

class (more correctly, a possible utility method or a possible utility class). Here's a method that might belong in a utility class:

```
public static boolean isEmpty(String str) {
   return ((str == null) || (str.trim( ).equals("")));
}
```

The `isEmpty` method is very simple, but implementing it in a utility class is worthwhile if you check for null or empty strings often enough—for instance, when validating method arguments. I would put this method in a `StringUtils` class.

Here's an example of a data-holding utility class; suppose you have a series of classes with method signatures that require both a currency and an amount parameter every time:

```
public Ticket bookPassage(CreditCard card, double price, Integer currency)
```

If you created a `Money` class, the modified method from the `TravelAgent` session bean would look like this:

```
public Ticket bookPassage(CreditCard card, Money amount)
```

A `DateRange` utility class is a common requirement in handling reservations. For example, imagine that we had added `startDate` and `endDate` virtual persistence fields to the `Cruise` EJB:

```
public Date getStartDate( );
public void setStartDate(Date start);

public Date getEndDate( );
public void setEndDate(Date end);
```

Because travel agents will want to search for cruises by these fields, we have added a `listMatchingCruises` method to the `TravelAgent` EJB:

```
public Collection listMatchingCruises(Date start, Date end)
   throws RemoteException;
```

After a `DateRange` class is created, this method changes to:

```
public Collection listMatchingCruises(DateRange range) throws RemoteException;
```

An additional benefit of reduced duplication is that it makes the interface more coherent; it's easier to understand a method signature with a date range than one with separate parameters for the start and end dates. Likewise, it's easier to understand a `Money` parameter than separate price and currency parameters. Everyone who touches the revised `bookPassage` and `listMatchingCruises` methods—their developers, the developers of any client code, or some college intern tasked with maintaining the code a year or two down the line—will have a more intuitive grasp of what those methods expect.

Unfortunately, knowing when to implement this type of refactoring comes with experience. Fortunately, there is an excellent book on refactoring: Martin Fowler's *Refactoring: Improving the Design of Existing Code* (Addison-Wesley). Take a look for other ways to identify candidates for utility classes (and for other ways to refactor your code).

Should You Use EJBs?

This book assumes that you've already decided to use EJBs. However, in several instances, EJBs are not the best solution to a problem. It makes sense, therefore, to review where EJBs are strong and then discuss situations in which EJBs don't make as much sense. In several situations—even some enterprise database-centric applications—EJBs are simply not the best choice. At the end of this section, we'll look at some of the alternative approaches and where they might fit.

When to Use EJBs

Here's a list of situations where EJBs are strong; we haven't distinguished between different types of EJBs:

Single and multisystem business transactions
: The ability to maintain transactional integrity for complex business entities is one of an EJB's key strengths. EJBs aren't alone in providing straightforward transactional control over a single data repository. However, EJBs shine where multiple resources (relational databases, messaging systems, etc.) are involved because they allow transactions to spread across as many different resources as you like, so long as the resources support distributed transactions.

Distributed functionality
: Business services often live on a remote server. For example, a business enterprise will have many different systems, ranging in degrees of inflexibility and entrenchment. One of these systems may need to access another. EJBs, which are inherently distributed, are often the simplest way to distribute remote services. EJB also allows you to provide business services to remote clients more easily than some alternatives. Remote access through components is easier to maintain than direct database access because the component code can shield the client from database schema changes.

Portable components (not classes)
: Until recently, if you wanted to share your business services with another application developer, you were forced to share classes or at least packages. Java did not allow for the easy creation of *enterprise components*, or reusable software building blocks that can be assembled with other components to form an application. EJBs allow you to package your business logic into a tidy, distributable unit that can be shared in a loosely coupled fashion. The user of your component need only tweak a descriptor file for her environment.

Applications relying on asynchronous messaging
EJBs (specifically MDBs) provide a strong technology for handling asynchronous communication such as JMS-based messaging or web services.

Security roles
If your application's business operations can be mapped to specific business roles in your enterprise, then EJBs may be a good choice. So much is made of the transaction management capability of EJBs that their deployment-descriptor-based security management features are overlooked. This capability is very powerful; if your application's users fit into distinct roles and the rules for those roles dictate which users can write what data, EJBs are a good choice.

Persistence context management
Managing the life cycle of an `EntityManager` created by an `EntityManagerFactory` can become cumbersome. If you make any nested object method calls, you'll need to pass around the `EntityManager` instance as a parameter. Even if your application is simple, EJBs provide nice persistence context management that will shrink and simplify your code.

When Not to Use EJBs

In several situations when building a software application—even an "enterprise" software application—using EJBs may actually be a barrier to meeting your business goals. The following list represents places where you might not want to use EJBs:

Applications requiring thread control
If your application design requires extensive use of threads, then the EJB spec actually prevents you from using EJBs (although some EJB container vendors may provide nonportable ways around this restriction). Container systems manage resources, transactions, security, and other qualities of service using threads; threads you create are outside of the container's control and can potentially cause system failures. Also, EJB containers may distribute EJBs across multiple JVMs, preventing the synchronization of threads.

Performance
Because EJBs do so much more than plain Java classes, they are slower than plain Java classes. The EJB container has to do a lot: maintain transactional integrity, manage bean instances and the bean pools, enforce security roles, manage resources and resource pools, coordinate distributed operations, synchronize shared services (if the vendor offers clustering capabilities), and so on. In most applications, this overhead is extremely marginal, but if you're doing a lot of CPU-intensive operations, using EJBs may not be appropriate.

Database babysitting
Applications that just babysit a database may not need the nice persistence context control that EJBs provide because they are only doing monotonous database upgrades or batch processing. In this case, EJBs may be overkill.

Alternatives to EJBs

A few frameworks out there try to duplicate the functionality that EJBs provide. Here is the most popular:

Spring (http://www.springframework.org)
: Spring pioneered many of the dependency injection concepts you see in the EJB 3.0 specification. However, it is a bit richer in functionality in this area in that entire object graphs can be represented in XML and injected into Spring-configured beans. The framework has much of the capabilities that EJB has to offer, such as integrated transaction demarcation and declarative security. It also provides a lot of integration helper classes that wrap some of the most popular open source frameworks out there. Spring also provides an integrated web framework similar to Struts and JSF. Spring is open source and available as a free download. The downside to Spring is that even though it is open source, it is controlled solely by one vendor. It is also entirely proprietary and not standards-based, as EJB is. Finally, although it has some annotation support, you'll find it very verbose in the XML department, so you'll need to really like XML deployment descriptors if you want to use Spring as your framework.

Alternatives to Java Persistence

There are a few alternatives to Java Persistence; some of them are growing in popularity and maturity. Java Persistence and the old EJB CMP specification still rank as the de facto standards for enterprise transactional needs.

JDBC

The first (and likely most common) alternative to using Java Persistence is to write straight JDBC functions. Although JDBC was a viable alternative to EJB 2.1 CMP, Java Persistence and vendor-provided tooling actually make it much more worthwhile and productive to go with Java Persistence. Java Persistence has much of the power that straight SQL does, but it can provide all the caching layers and object population that are difficult to write by hand with JDBC. Given that Java Persistence can also be used outside of the application server, it even makes sense now for database applications that are one-off plain Java programs.

The situations in which straight JDBC is preferable to Java Persistence are not concrete. You should use straight JDBC when the need for speed outweighs the need for transactional support or security provided by Java Persistence. Here's a simple example that uses JDBC:

```
import java.sql.*;

public class JDBCExample {
```

```
    public static void main(java.lang.String[] args) {
      try {
        // Load driver
        Class.forName("sun.jdbc.odbc.JdbcOdbcDriver");
      }
      catch (ClassNotFoundException e) {
        System.out.println("Cannot load driver.");
        return;
      }

      try {
        // Connect to database.
        Connection con = DriverManager.getConnection("jdbc:odbc:contactdb",
                "", "");

        // Create SQL Statement and execute.
        Statement stmt = con.createStatement( );
        ResultSet rs = stmt.executeQuery("SELECT name FROM contacts");

        // Display the SQL Results.
        while(rs.next( )) {
          System.out.println(rs.getString("name"));
        }

        // Release database resources.
        rs.close( );
        stmt.close( );
        con.close( );

        }
        catch (SQLException se) {
          // Display error message upon exception.
          System.out.println("SQL Exception: " + se.getMessage( ));
          se.printStackTrace(System.out);
         }
      }
  }
```

JDBC is very straightforward; it allows you to access your data repository directly. However, you must understand a fair amount of the underlying mechanics (SQL, database connection properties, and so on) in order to use it. Now, in a "real" application using JDBC, you centralize most of this code into a few classes, but you still must write all the SQL yourself.

Others

There are, of course, alternatives to Java Persistence other than straight JDBC. Here are a few worth reviewing for suitability, should you determine that your application does not require Java Persistence or that certain requirements demand an alternative approach:

Hibernate (http://www.hibernate.org)

Hibernate is another Java class-to-database table mapping project. Although Hibernate is itself a Java Persistence open source project, it existed as a separate, well-established, and popular API long before Java Persistence existed. It is a superset of the Java Persistence specification and it has a richer API and toolset than the standard version. The founder of Hibernate, Gavin King, was one of the EJB 3.0 Expert Group members and brought the Hibernate project into the JCP process. You may have more complex mappings than EJB 3.0 persistence can handle, or you just may find the proprietary interfaces with which Hibernate works a bit more usable. If your company is not married to standards, using straight Hibernate APIs may be the way to go.

iBatis (http://ibatis.apache.org)

iBatis is another open source framework that allows you to map straight native SQL calls to Java classes. It is a bit different from Java Persistence in that instead of being a full O/R mapping with an object-specific query language, it maps SQL result sets directly into an object graph through an XML deployment descriptor. The advantages of this approach are that you can use it against stored procedures and complex vendor-specific SQL, and you can wrap it around legacy systems that are using JDBC to simplify and refactor the code. The downside of iBatis is that you lose a lot of the advantages that a full O/R tool gives you, such as automatic optimizations, caching, and an object query language. However, if you want to remain close to SQL but you have a cleaner abstraction to JDBC, iBatis is a fine solution.

JDO (http://java.sun.com/products/jdo)

JDO stands for Java Data Objects and is a JCP standard. Although it used to be a viable alternative to EJB 2.1 CMP, it is now a dead specification. A lot of the brains behind JDO, in conjunction with the minds behind JBoss's Hibernate and Oracle's Toplink products, were part of the Java Persistence specification efforts. Now that Java Persistence has been incorporated as part of the Java EE, JDO will probably be retired and a migration path to Java Persistence specified.

As you can see, there are a few alternatives to EJB and Java Persistence. If your application doesn't need the complexity or some of their features, take a look around. Data persistence, security, and distributed object components with Java have been around for some time, and a wide assortment of approaches exist.

Wrapping Up

The main purpose of this book is to teach you how to use the Enterprise JavaBeans components and Java Persistence APIs, as opposed to how to design and architect enterprise systems. Although this chapter focuses on design considerations and alternatives to EJB and Java Persistence, it is not a comprehensive or complete treatment of architecture or design—that requires an entire book dedicated to that subject.

We feel that a number of books complement this chapter and will extend your understanding of design and architecture of EJB and Java EE systems. Chief among them is *Core J2EE Patterns: Best Practices and Design Strategies*, Second Edition (Addison-Wesley), *Patterns of Enterprise Application Architecture* (Addison-Wesley), and *Hibernate in Action* (Manning Publications). These books are excellent resources for a more in-depth understanding of design and architecture issues. With that said, they provide only shallow, if any, discussion of the EJB APIs, life cycles, deployment, and components. To master those topics, which are critical during development, you'll need this book.

PART II

The JBoss Workbook

Introduction

This workbook is designed to be a companion to O'Reilly's *Enterprise JavaBeans 3.0*, Fifth Edition, for users of JBoss™, an open source Java EE™ application server. Its goal is to provide step-by-step instructions for installing, configuring, and using JBoss, and for deploying and running the examples from *Enterprise JavaBeans*.

This workbook is based on the production release of JBoss 4.0.4 and many of the EJB 3.0 examples from *Enterprise JavaBeans 3.0*, Fifth Edition. All of the examples will work properly with JBoss 4.0.4 and above, but not with earlier versions of JBoss.

Contents of the JBoss Workbook

The workbook is divided into three sections:

JBoss Installation and Configuration
: Walks you through downloading, installing, and configuring JBoss. It also provides a brief overview of the structure of the JBoss installation.

Exercises
: Contains step-by-step instructions for downloading, building, and running the example programs in *Enterprise JavaBeans 3.0*, Fifth Edition (for brevity, the workbook refers to this book as "the EJB book"). The text also walks through the various deployment descriptors and source code to point out JBoss features and concerns.

Appendix
: Provides useful information that did not fit neatly in the other sections, including a collection of XML snippets for configuring a few popular JDBC drivers from various database vendors.

The length of each exercise in the workbook depends on the level of configuration required, but generally, each exercise also includes instructions on:

- Compiling and building the example code
- Deploying the EJB components to the application server

- Running the example programs and evaluating the results

Each exercise also provides basic information about JBoss relating to the example.

The exercises were designed to be built and executed in order. Every effort was made to remove any dependencies between exercises by including all necessary components in the directory for that exercise, but some dependencies still exist. The workbook text will guide you through these where they arise.

Also note that this workbook is not intended to be a course on database configuration or design. The exercises have been designed to work out-of-the-box with the open source database Hypersonic SQL, which is shipped with JBoss, and the application server creates all database tables automatically at runtime.

Online Resources

This workbook is designed for use with the EJB book and with downloadable example code, both available from our web site:

http://examples.oreilly.com/entjbeans5

We will post any errata here, and any updates required to support changes in specifications or products. This site also contains links to many popular EJB-related sites on the Internet.

We hope you find this workbook useful in your study of Enterprise JavaBeans and the JBoss open source J2EE implementation. Comments, suggestions, and error reports on the text of this workbook or the downloaded example files are welcome and appreciated. Please post on the JBoss Forum:

http://www.jboss.com/index.html?module=bb&op=viewforum&f=241

To obtain more information about JBoss or the JBoss project, visit the project's web site:

http://www.jboss.com

There, you will find links to detailed JBoss documentation, online forums, and events in the JBoss community. You can also obtain detailed information on JBoss training, support, and consulting services.

WORKBOOK 1

JBoss Installation and Configuration

This chapter guides you through the steps required to install a fully working JBoss server. Along the way, you will learn about JBoss 4.0's microkernel architecture, and the last section will show you how to install the code for the forthcoming exercises. If you need more detailed information about JBoss configuration, visit the JBoss web site, *http://www.jboss.com*, where you will find comprehensive online documentation.

About JBoss

JBoss is a collaborative effort of a worldwide group of developers to create an open source application server based on the Java 2 Platform, Enterprise Edition (J2EE). With more than six million downloads in the last four years, JBoss is the leading J2EE application server.

JBoss implements the full J2EE stack of services:

- Enterprise JavaBeans (EJB)
- Java Persistence
- Java Message Service (JMS)
- Java Transaction Service/Java Transaction API (JTS/JTA)
- Servlets and JavaServer Pages (JSP)
- Java Naming and Directory Interface (JNDI)

It also provides advanced features such as clustering, JMX, web services, and Internet Inter-ORB Protocol (IIOP) integration.

Because JBoss code is licensed under the GNU Lesser General Public License (LGPL; see *http://www.gnu.org/copyleft/lesser.txt*), you can use it freely, at no cost, and in any commercial application, or you may redistribute it as is.

Installing the JBoss Application Server

Before going any further, make sure you have the Java SE JDK 5 or higher installed and correctly configured.

To download the JBoss binaries, go to the JBoss web site at *http://www.jboss.com/products/jbossas/downloads*. You should be able to start the installation process directly from this page by clicking the Run Installer link. The first few screens of the installer are self-explanatory. They ask for a license acceptance as well as the installation directory. When you get to the Installation Type screen, make sure that you choose the EJB 3.0 installation option, as shown in Figure W-1.

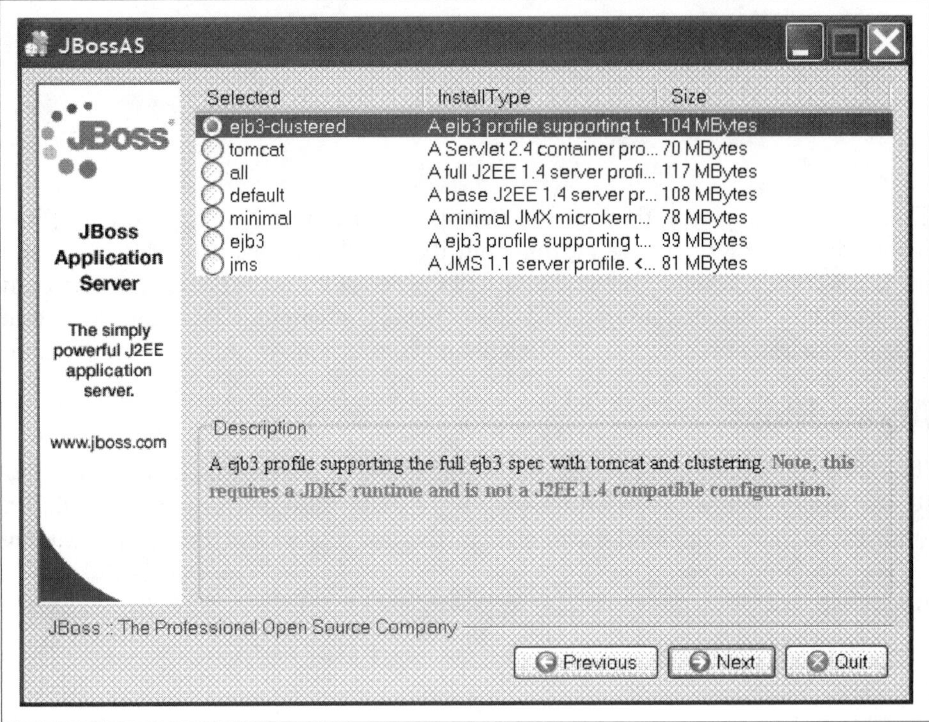

Figure W-1. Installation Type screen

The next screen allows you to choose what packages you want to have installed. For now, click Next and use the default settings. After the Packages screen, you will land on the Configuration Name screen shown in Figure W-2. Make sure you use the default value provided here because all of the workbook examples rely on this relative directory structure.

When the installation completes, you can launch JBoss by executing the *run* script in the *$JBOSS_HOME/bin* directory:

> *Unix:$ run.sh*
> *Windows:C:\jboss-4.0.x\bin>run.bat*

That's it! You now have a fully working JBoss server!

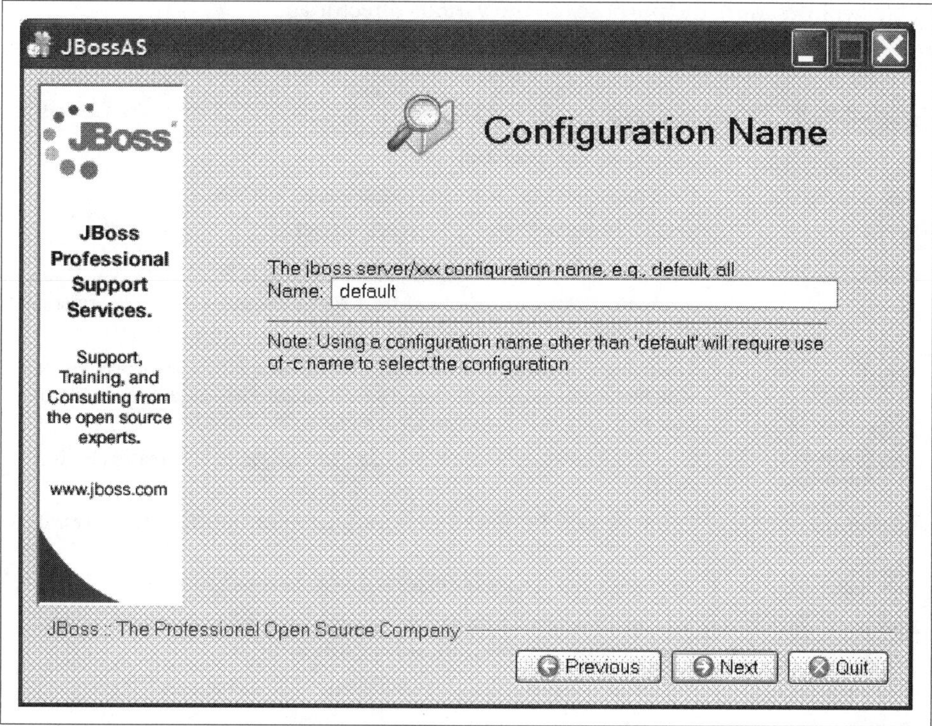

Figure W-2. Configuration Name screen

Discovering the JBoss Directory Structure

Installing JBoss creates the directory structure shown in Figure W-3.

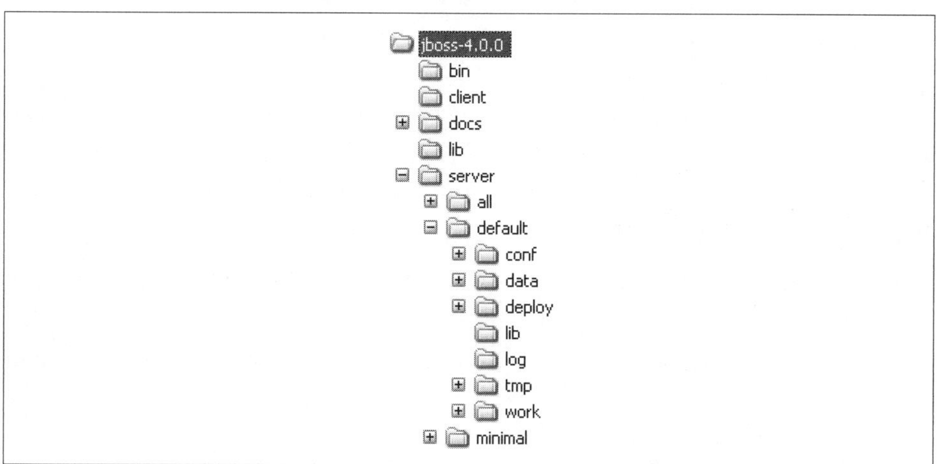

Figure W-3. JBoss directory structure

Table W-1 describes the purposes of the various directories.

Table W-1. JBoss directories

Directory	Description
bin	Scripts to start up and shut down JBoss.
client	Client-side Java libraries (JARs) required to communicate with JBoss.
docs	Sample configuration files (for database configuration, etc.).
docs/dtd	Document Type Definitions (DTDs) for the various XML files used in JBoss.
lib	JARs loaded at startup by JBoss and shared by all JBoss configurations. (You won't put your own libraries here.)
server	Various JBoss configurations. (Each configuration must be in a different subdirectory. The name of the subdirectory represents the name of the configuration. The configuration name will be what you picked in the Configuration Screen when installing JBoss in Figure W-2.)
server/default	JBoss' default configuration; used when no configuration name is specified on the JBoss command line.
server/default/conf	JBoss' configuration files. (You will learn more about the content of this directory in the next section.)
server/default/data	JBoss' database files (embedded database or JBossMQ, for example).
server/default/deploy	JBoss' hot-deployment directory. (Any file or directory dropped in this directory is automatically deployed in JBoss: EJBs, WARs, EARs, and even services.)
server/default/lib	JARs that JBoss loads at startup when starting this particular configuration.
server/default/log	JBoss' logfiles.
server/default/tmp	JBoss' temporary files.

If you want to define your own configuration, you can rerun the installer and choose a different configuration name when you get to the screen shown in Figure W-2. To start JBoss with a given configuration, use the -c parameter on the command line:

```
Windows:C:\jboss-4.0.x\bin> run.bat -c config-name
Unix:$ ./run.sh -c config-name
```

A run script with no parameters defaults to a configuration installed in the *server/default* directory.

JBoss Configuration Files

As the previous section described, JBoss' *server* directory can contain any number of directories, each representing a different JBoss configuration.

The *server/default/conf* directory contains JBoss' configuration files. The purpose of the various files is discussed in Table W-2.

Table W-2. JBoss configuration files

File	Description
jacorb.properties	JBoss IIOP configuration.
jbossmq-state.xml	JBossMQ (JMS implementation) user configuration.
jboss-service.xml	Definition of JBoss' services launched at startup (class loaders, JNDI, deployers, etc.).
log4j.xml	Log4J logging configuration.
login-config.xml	JBoss security configuration (JBossSX).

Deployment in JBoss

The deployment process in JBoss is straightforward. In each configuration, JBoss constantly scans a specific directory, *$JBOSS_HOME/server/default/deploy*, for changes. This directory is generally referred to informally as the *deploy* directory.

You can copy the following to this directory:

- Any JAR library (the classes it contains are automatically added to the JBoss classpath)
- An EJB-JAR
- A Web Application aRchive (WAR)
- An Enterprise Application aRchive (EAR)
- An XML file containing JBoss MBean definitions
- A directory ending in *.jar*, *.war*, or *.ear* and containing the extracted content of an EJB-JAR, a WAR, or an EAR, respectively.

To *redeploy* any of these files (JAR, WAR, EAR, XML, etc.), simply overwrite it with a more recent version. JBoss will detect the change by comparing the files' timestamps, undeploy the previous files, and deploy their replacements. To redeploy a directory, update its modification timestamp by using a command-line utility such as *touch*. To *undeploy* a file, simply remove it from the *deploy* directory.

A Quick Look at JBoss Internals

Since Version 3.0, JBoss has been built around a few very powerful concepts that allow users to customize and fine-tune their servers for specific needs, not limited to Java EE. This flexibility allows JBoss to be used in vastly different environments, ranging from embedded systems to very large server clusters. The next few sections comment briefly on some of these concepts.

Microkernel Architecture

JBoss is based on a microkernel design into which components can be plugged at runtime to extend its behavior.

This design fits particularly well with the Java EE platform, which is essentially a service-based platform. The platform contains services for persistence, transactions, security, naming, messaging, logging, and so on.

Other application servers are generally built as monolithic applications containing all services of the Java EE platform at all times. JBoss takes a radically different approach: each service is hot-deployed as a component running on top of a very compact core, called the *JBoss Server Spine* (see Figure W-4). Furthermore, users are encouraged to implement their own services to run on top of JBoss.

Consequently, the JBoss application server is not limited to Java EE applications and in fact, is frequently used to build any kind of application requiring a strong and reliable base. For this reason, the JBoss core is also known as the *WebOS*.

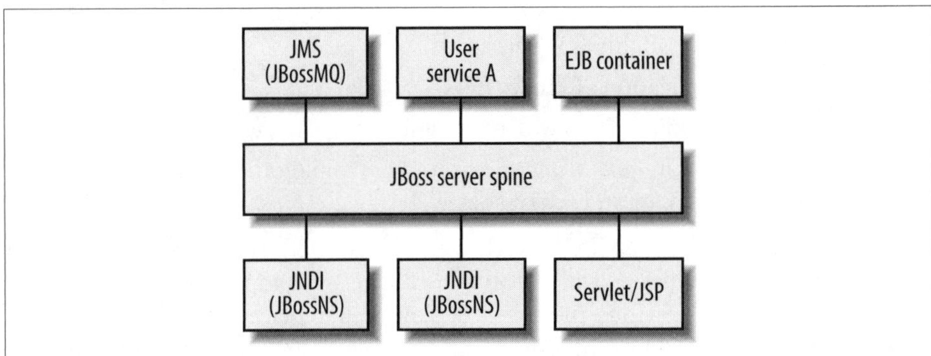

Figure W-4. JBoss Server Spine with some hot-deployed services

The JBoss Server Spine itself is based on Sun's Java Management eXtensions (JMX) specification, making any deployed component automatically manageable in a standard fashion. In the JMX terminology, a service deployed in JBoss is called a *managed bean* (MBean).

You can find more information about the JMX specification at the Sun web site, *http://java.sun.com/products/JavaManagement*.

Hot Deployment

Since Release 2.0, JBoss has been famous for being the first Java EE-based application server to support hot deployment and redeployment of applications (EJB-JAR, WAR, and EAR), while many application servers required a restart to update an application.

Thanks to its microkernel architecture and revolutionary Java class loader, JBoss 3.0 and later releases push this logic further. Not only can they hot-deploy and -redeploy applications, but they also can hot-(re)deploy any service and keep track of dependencies between services. These features make JBoss usable in very demanding environments, such as telecommunications systems.

Net Boot

JBoss is able to boot itself and your applications from any network location just by pointing the JBoss Server Spine to a simple URL. This allows you to manage the entire configuration of a cluster of JBoss nodes from one central web server. This impressive flexibility makes deployment of new servers very easy (see Figure W-5).

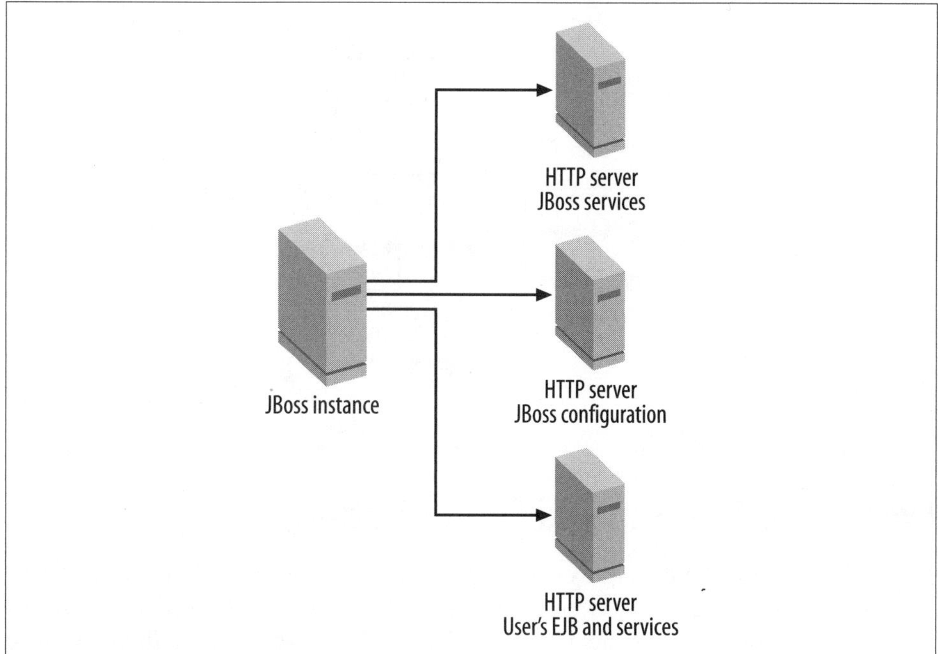

Figure W-5. A JBoss instance bootstrapping from three distinct netboot servers

JBoss' bootstrap code is approximately 50K, which makes it suitable for many embedded systems.

Detached Invokers

JBoss completely detaches the protocol handlers receiving invocations from the target service that eventually serves the requests. Consequently, when a new handler (called an *invoker* in JBoss) for a given protocol is deployed in JBoss, all existing services and applications can be reached automatically through this new invocation transport. Figure W-6 shows detached invokers.

JBoss 4.0 currently supports the following kinds of invokers:

Fast Socket
Fast Socket over HTTP (HTTP tunneling)
IIOP
JMS
SOAP

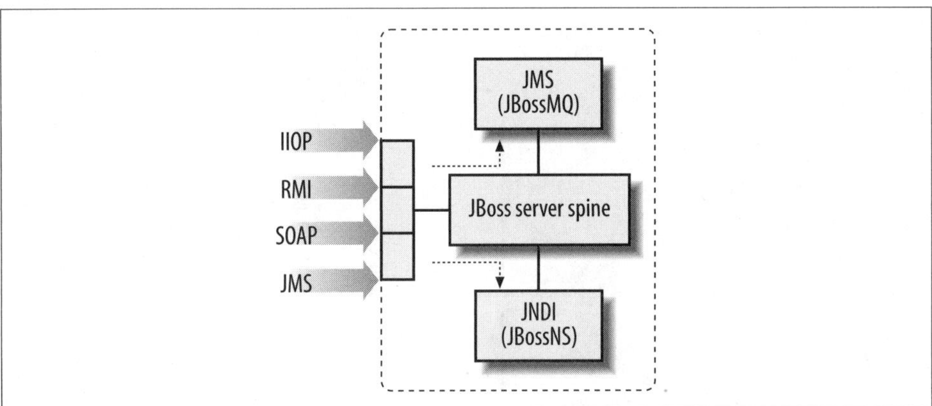

Figure W-6. Detached invokers

Exercise Code Setup and Configuration

You can download the example code for the exercises from *http://www.sourceforge.net/projects/jboss/*.... Exercises that require a database will use JBoss' default embedded database. Consequently, no additional database setup is required. If you want to configure JBoss to use a different database, this workbook includes an appendix that shows you how to do so.

Exercise Directory Structure

The example code is organized as a set of directories, one for each exercise (see Figure W-7). You'll find the code for each exercise in the *src/main* subdirectory and the configuration files in *src/resources*.

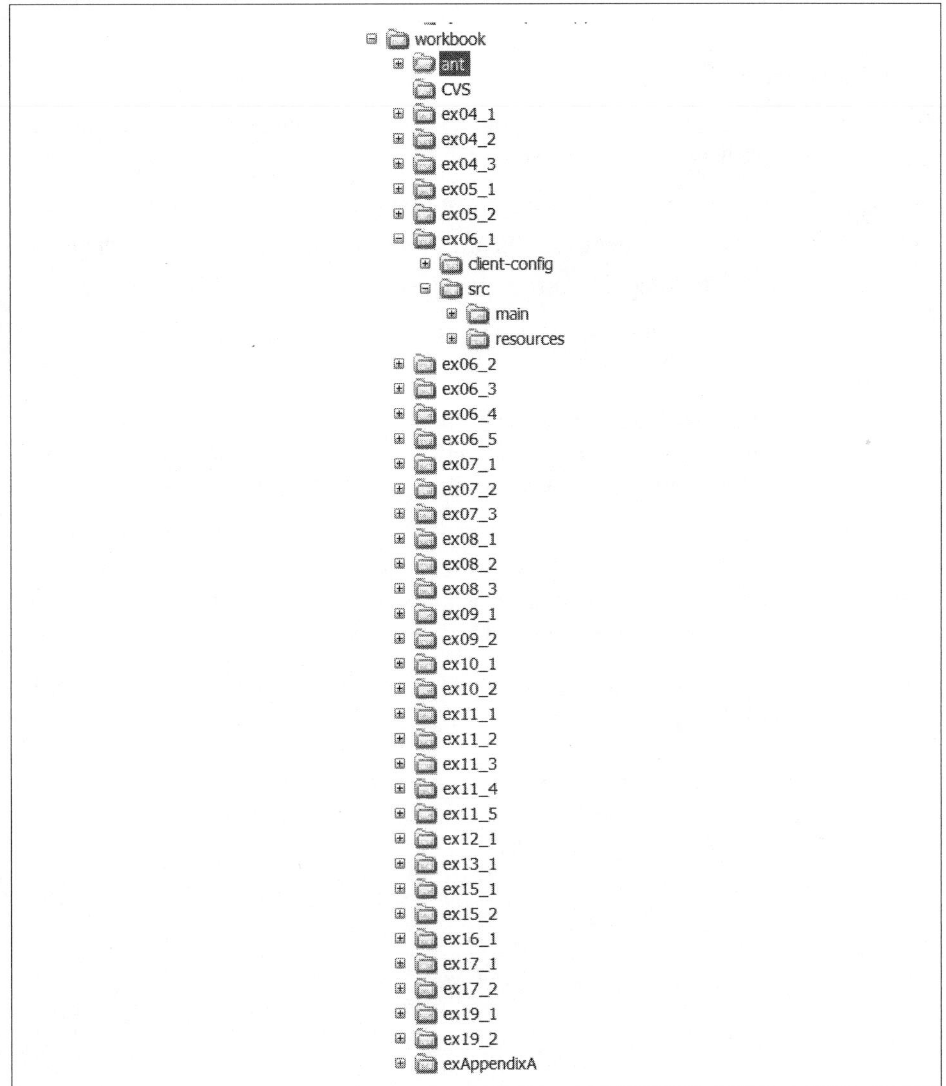

Figure W-7. Exercise directory structure

To build and run the exercises, you'll use the Ant tool. A *build.xml* file is provided for each exercise. It contains the Ant configuration needed to compile the classes, build the EJB-JAR, deploy it to JBoss, and run the client test applications. For this reason, the Ant tool is provided with the exercises and can be found in the *ant* directory.

You can find out more about Ant at the Apache Jakarta web site, *http://jakarta.apache.org/ant*.

Environment Setup

For the Ant scripts to work correctly, you must first set some environment variables in the shells you will use to run the exercises:

- The `JAVA_HOME` environment variable must point to where your JDK is installed.
- The `JBOSS_HOME` environment variable must point to where JBoss is installed.
- The directory containing the Ant scripts must be in your path.

Depending on your platform, you'll have to execute commands like these:

- Windows:

```
C:\workbook\ex04_1>set JAVA_HOME=C:\jdk1.5.0
C:\workbook\ex04_1> set JBOSS_HOME=C:\jboss-4.0.x
C:\workbook\ex04_1> set PATH=..\ant\bin;%PATH%
```

- Unix:

```
$ export JAVA_HOME=/usr/local/jdk1.5.0
$ export JBOSS_HOME=/usr/local/jboss-4.0.x
$ export PATH=../ant/bin:$PATH
```

In each chapter, you'll find detailed instructions on how to build, deploy, and run the exercises using Ant.

WORKBOOK 2

Exercises for Chapter 4

Chapter 4 of the EJB book walked you through a very basic example of creating one entity bean that mapped to one table and a session bean that acted as a façade to this entity bean. The entity bean was a simple Cabin entity that emulates a room on a ship. The session bean was a TravelAgent EJB that acted as the business process for interacting with the Cabin entity.

Exercise 4.1 takes the code from Chapter 4 as is and deploys it on the JBoss application server to use and run. Exercises 4.2 and 4.3 show the use of a couple of JBoss-specific annotations and XML.

Exercise 4.1: Your First Beans with JBoss

This exercise allows you to compile and deploy the code from Chapter 4 almost verbatim. You'll see how you can build and deploy an EJB-JAR with an entity bean on the JBoss application server.

Start Up JBoss

Start up JBoss as described earlier in Workbook 1.

Initialize the Database

JBoss comes with an embedded Java database called Hypersonic SQL. All of the examples in the workbook use this database, so there is no need to install and configure any external server. Also, you do not need to create any database tables because the JBoss Java Persistence implementation can be configured to autogenerate them for you when the EJB-JAR is deployed.

Build and Deploy the Example Programs

Perform the following steps:

1. Open a command prompt or shell terminal and change to the *ex04_1* directory created by the extraction process.
2. Set the `JAVA_HOME` and `JBOSS_HOME` environment variables to point to where your JDK and JBoss 4.0 are installed. Examples:

   Windows:

   ```
   C:\workbook\ex04_1> set JAVA_HOME=C:\jdk1.5.0
   C:\workbook\ex04_1> set JBOSS_HOME=C:\jboss-4.0.x
   ```

   Unix:

   ```
   $ export JAVA_HOME=/usr/local/jdk1.5.0
   $ export JBOSS_HOME=/usr/local/jboss-4.0
   ```

3. Add `ant` to your execution path. Ant is the build utility.

   Windows:

   ```
   C:\workbook\ex04_1> set PATH=..\ant\bin;%PATH%
   ```

   Unix:

   ```
   $ export PATH=../ant/bin:$PATH
   ```

4. Perform the build by typing `ant`. Ant uses *build.xml* to figure out what to compile and how to build your JARs.

Before we examine the build file for this example, you might want to take a quick look at the Ant utility at its Jakarta web site home at *http://jakarta.apache.org/ant/index.html*.

The *build.xml* file provides Ant with the rules for building the example. Ant compiles the Java source code, builds the EJB-JAR, and deploys the JAR simply by copying it to JBoss' *deploy* directory. If you are watching the JBoss console window when you run Ant, you will notice that JBoss automatically discovers the EJB-JAR once it has been copied into the *deploy* directory, and automatically deploys the bean.

Another particularly interesting thing about building EJB-JARs is that there is no special EJB compilation step. Unlike other servers, JBoss does not generate code for client stubs. Instead, it has a lightweight mechanism that creates client proxies when the EJB-JAR is deployed, accelerating the development and deployment cycles.

Deconstructing build.xml

The *build.xml* file provided for each workbook exercise gives the Ant utility information about how to compile and deploy your Java programs and EJBs. The following build tasks can be executed by typing `ant taskname`:

- The default task (typing ant without a task name) compiles the code, builds the EJB-JAR, and deploys the JAR into JBoss. The deployment procedure is a simple copy into the JBoss *deploy* directory.
- ant compile compiles all the Java source files.
- ant clean removes all *.class* and *.jar* files from the working directory and undeploys the JAR from JBoss by deleting the file from JBoss' *deploy* directory.
- ant clean.db provides you with a clean copy of the Hypersonic SQL database used throughout the exercises. This task works only with Hypersonic SQL.
- run.client_*xxx* runs a specific example program. Each exercise in this book will have a run.client rule for each example program.

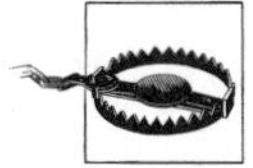

clean.db can be used only when JBoss is not running.

Here's a breakdown of what is contained in *build.xml*.

```
<project name="JBoss" default="ejbjar" basedir=".">
```

The default attribute defines the default target that ant will run if you type only ant on the command line. The basedir attribute tells Ant in what directory to run the build.

```
<property environment="env"/>
<property name="src.dir" value="${basedir}/src/main"/>
<property name="src.resources" value="${basedir}/src/resources"/>
<property name="jboss.home" value="${env.JBOSS_HOME}"/>
<property name="build.dir" value="${basedir}/build"/>
<property name="build.classes.dir" value="${build.dir}/classes"/>
```

All of these defined properties are variables that Ant will use throughout the build process. You can see that the JBOSS_HOME environment variable is pulled from the system environment and other defined directory paths:

```
<path id="classpath">
      <fileset dir="${jboss.home}/client">
          <include name="**/*.jar"/>
      </fileset>
  <pathelement location="${build.classes.dir}"/>
  <pathelement location="${basedir}/client-config"/>
</path>
```

To compile and run the example applications in this workbook, add all the JARs in *$JBOSS_HOME/client* to the Java classpath. Also notice that *build.xml* inserts the *${basedir}/client-config* directory into the classpath. A *jndi.properties* file in this directory enables the example programs to find and connect to JBoss' JNDI server. The *log4j.xml* file in this directory configures the logging system (log4j) that JBoss uses.

```
<property name="build.classpath" refid="classpath"/>

<target name="prepare" >
  <mkdir dir="${build.dir}"/>
```

```
    <mkdir dir="${build.classes.dir}"/>
  </target>
```

The prepare target creates the directories where the Java compiler will place compiled classes.

```
  <target name="compile" depends="prepare">
    <javac srcdir="${src.dir}"
           destdir="${build.classes.dir}"
           debug="on"
           deprecation="on"
           optimize="off"
           includes="**">
            <classpath refid="classpath"/>
    </javac>
  </target>
```

The compile target compiles all the Java files under the *src/main* directory. Notice that it depends on the prepare target; prepare will run before the compile target is executed.

```
<target name="ejbjar" depends="compile">
  <jar jarfile="build/titan.jar">
    <fileset dir="${build.classes.dir}">
          <include name="com/titan/domain/*.class"/>
          <include name="com/titan/travelagent/*.class"/>
    </fileset>
    <fileset dir="${src.resources}/">
        <include name="**/*.xml"/>
    </fileset>
   </jar>
   <copy file="build/titan.jar "
         todir="${jboss.home}/server/default/deploy"/>
</target>
```

The ejbjar target creates the EJB-JAR file and deploys it to JBoss simply by copying it to JBoss' *deploy* directory.

```
<target name="run.client" depends="ejbjar">
  <java classname="com.titan.clients.Client" fork="yes" dir=".">
    <classpath refid="classpath"/>
  </java>
</target>
```

The run.client target is used to run the example program in this chapter.

```
<target name="clean.db">
  <delete dir="${jboss.home}/server/default/db/hypersonic"/>
</target>
```

The clean.db target cleans the default database used by JBoss for the example programs in this book. Remember, you can use it only when JBoss is not running.

```
<target name="clean">
  <delete dir="${build.dir}"/>
  <delete file="${jboss.home}/server/default/deploy/titan.jar"/>
```

```
</target>
</project>
```

The `clean` target removes compiled classes and undeploys the EJB-JAR from JBoss by deleting the JAR file in the *deploy* directory.

JBoss Specifics

No JBoss-specific files are needed in this example. All that is necessary are the JAR'd-up bean classes and interfaces as well as the required *persistence.xml* file.

Remote JNDI binding

Whenever you deploy a session bean with a remote interface, JBoss creates an entry in the global JNDI namespace. The default JNDI binding for a remote interface is obtained by concatenating the EJB-NAME of the bean with */remote*. So, the TravelAgent EJB in this example would be bound to *TravelAgentBean/remote*. Exercises 4.2 and 4.3 show you how to override the base JNDI binding with an annotation or with a JBoss-specific XML deployment descriptor.

persistence.xml

The *persistence.xml* file included with this example is basic:

```
<persistence>
   <persistence-unit>
      <name>titan</name>
      <jta-data-source>java:/DefaultDS</jta-data-source>
      <properties>
         <property name="hibernate.hbm2ddl.auto" value="create-drop"/>
      </properties>
   </persistence-unit>
</persistence>
```

The `<name>` element is described in Chapter 5 of the EJB book.

The `<jta-data-source>` element is required in JBoss and references a data source bound in the global JNDI namespace. Here we specify the default Hypersonic SQL database that is created when JBoss boots up. Check out the Appendix to learn how to configure and deploy your own specific data source.

The `<properties>` element is used to configure JBoss-specific properties. The only property set here is the `hibernate.hbm2ddl.auto` property, which is used to autogenerate database schemas. The two interesting values for this property are `create-drop` and `update`.

The `create-drop` value creates a table for each entity bean class deployed based on the mapping declared in that bean class and any mapping file. The tables are created when the persistence unit is deployed on the application server. The tables are dropped and removed from the database when the persistence unit is undeployed or redeployed on the application server. This value is very useful for tutorials!

The update value checks to see if the tables already exist in the database. If they exist, they are altered with any updates made to the bean class or mapping files.

Usually the hibernate.hbm2ddl.auto property is not used in a production environment because the database schema is usually created and maintained by a DBA.

Examine and Run the Client Applications

The example program creates a single Cabin bean, populates each of its attributes, and then queries the created bean with its primary key.

Client.java

```
package com.titan.clients;

import com.titan.travelagent.TravelAgentRemote;
import com.titan.domain.Cabin;

import javax.naming.InitialContext;
import javax.naming.Context;
import javax.naming.NamingException;

import javax.rmi.PortableRemoteObject;

public class Client
{
    public static void main(String [] args)
    {
        try
        {
            Context jndiContext = getInitialContext( );
            Object ref = jndiContext.lookup("TravelAgentBean/remote");
            TravelAgentRemote dao = (TravelAgentRemote)
                PortableRemoteObject.narrow(ref,TravelAgentRemote.class);

            Cabin cabin_1 = new Cabin( );
            cabin_1.setId(1);
            cabin_1.setName("Master Suite");
            cabin_1.setDeckLevel(1);
            cabin_1.setShipId(1);
            cabin_1.setBedCount(3);

            dao.createCabin(cabin_1);

            Cabin cabin_2 = dao.findCabin(1);
            System.out.println(cabin_2.getName( ));
            System.out.println(cabin_2.getDeckLevel( ));
            System.out.println(cabin_2.getShipId( ));
            System.out.println(cabin_2.getBedCount( ));

        }
        catch (javax.naming.NamingException ne)
        {
```

```
            ne.printStackTrace( );
        }
    }

    public static Context getInitialContext( )
        throws javax.naming.NamingException
    {
        return new javax.naming.InitialContext( );
    }
}
```

The `getInitialContext( )` method creates an `InitialContext` with no properties. Because no properties are set, the Java library that implements `InitialContext` searches the classpath for the file *jndi.properties*. Each example program in this workbook will have a *client-config* directory that contains a *jndi.properties* file. You will be executing all example programs through Ant, and it will set the classpath appropriately to refer to this properties file.

Run the Client application by invoking `ant run.client` at the command prompt. Remember to set your `JBOSS_HOME` and `PATH` environment variables.

The output of the Client application should look something like this:

```
C:\workbook\ex04_1>ant run.client
Buildfile: build.xml

prepare:

compile:

ejbjar:

run.client:
     [java] Master Suite
     [java] 1
     [java] 1
     [java] 3
```

The Client application adds a row to the database representing the Cabin bean and does not delete it at the conclusion of the program. You cannot run this program more than once unless you stop JBoss, clean the database by invoking the Ant task `clean.db`, and restart the application server. Otherwise, you will get the following error:

```
run.client:
     [java] Exception in thread "main" java.lang.RuntimeException: org.jboss.tm.
JBossRollbackException: Unable to commit
, tx=TransactionImpl:XidImpl[FormatId=257, GlobalId=null:1099/7, BranchQual=null:
1099, localId=0:7], status=STATUS_NO_TR
ANSACTION; - nested throwable: (org.hibernate.exception.GenericJDBCException: Could
not execute JDBC batch update)
     [java]     at org.jboss.aspects.tx.TxPolicy.
handleEndTransactionException(TxPolicy.java:198)
     [java]     at org.jboss.aspects.tx.TxPolicy.endTransaction(TxPolicy.java:180)
```

```
     [java]      at org.jboss.aspects.tx.TxPolicy.invokeInOurTx(TxPolicy.java:87)
     [java]      at org.jboss.aspects.tx.TxInterceptor$Required.invoke(TxInterceptor.
java:195)
     [java]      at org.jboss.aop.joinpoint.MethodInvocation.
invokeNext(MethodInvocation.java:103)
     [java]      at org.jboss.aspects.tx.TxPropagationInterceptor.
invoke(TxPropagationInterceptor.java:76)
...
```

This doesn't look like much of an error message, but JBoss is relying on the database and JDBC driver to provide a meaningful message.

Viewing the Database

The embedded Hypersonic SQL database has a GUI management console where you view, alter, and create database tables and their contents. To access this console for the default data source that comes with JBoss, first go to *http://localhost:8080/jmx-console* (see Figure W-8).

Click on the "database=localDB,service=Hypersonic" link shown in Figure W-8. This will bring you to the management page of the database. Scroll down and click on the startDatabaseManager MBean Operation Invoke button shown in Figure W-9.

Click on the Invoke button to bring up the HSQL Database Manager shown in Figure W-10.

When you get to the heavy Java Persistence exercises in Chapters 6–8, you may find it useful to view the database schema generated by these examples in the Database Manager.

Exercise 4.2: JNDI Binding with Annotations

This exercise is the same code as in Exercise 4.1, except it uses a JBoss-specific annotation to override the remote JNDI binding that is used by clients to look up the TravelAgent EJB.

Start Up JBoss

If you already have JBoss running, there is no reason to restart it. Otherwise, start it up as instructed in Workbook 1.

Initialize the Database

If you have problems running this example, shut down JBoss and run the clean.db Ant task.

Figure W-8. JMX console

Build and Deploy the Example Programs

Perform the following steps:

1. Open a command prompt or shell terminal and change to the *ex04_2* directory created by the extraction process.
2. Set the `JAVA_HOME` and `JBOSS_HOME` environment variables to point to where your JDK and JBoss 4.0 are installed. Examples:

   Windows:

   ```
   C:\workbook\ex04_2> set JAVA_HOME=C:\jdk1.5.0
   C:\workbook\ex04_2> set JBOSS_HOME=C:\jboss-4.0.x
   ```

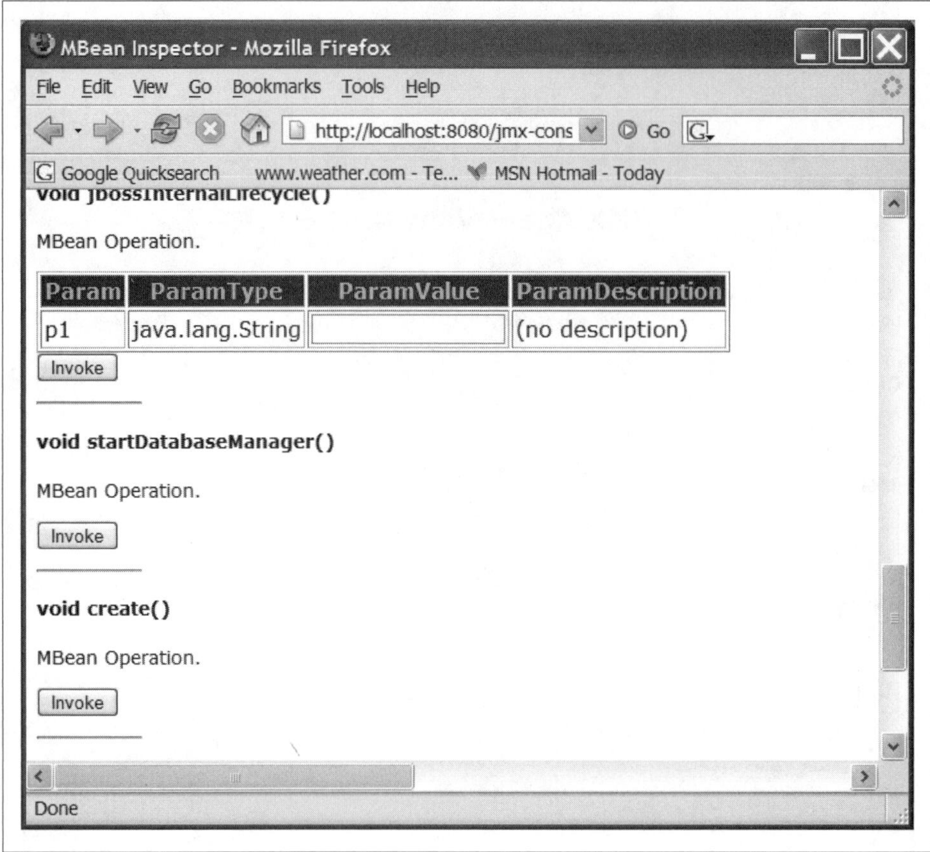

Figure W-9. Hypersonic management page

Unix:

```
$ export JAVA_HOME=/usr/local/jdk1.5.0
$ export JBOSS_HOME=/usr/local/jboss-4.0
```

3. Add ant to your execution path. Ant is the build utility.

   Windows:

   ```
   C:\workbook\ex04_2> set PATH=..\ant\bin;%PATH%
   ```

   Unix:

   ```
   $ export PATH=../ant/bin:$PATH
   ```

4. Perform the build by typing `ant`.

As in the last exercise, *titan.jar* is rebuilt, copied to the JBoss *deploy* directory, and redeployed by the application server.

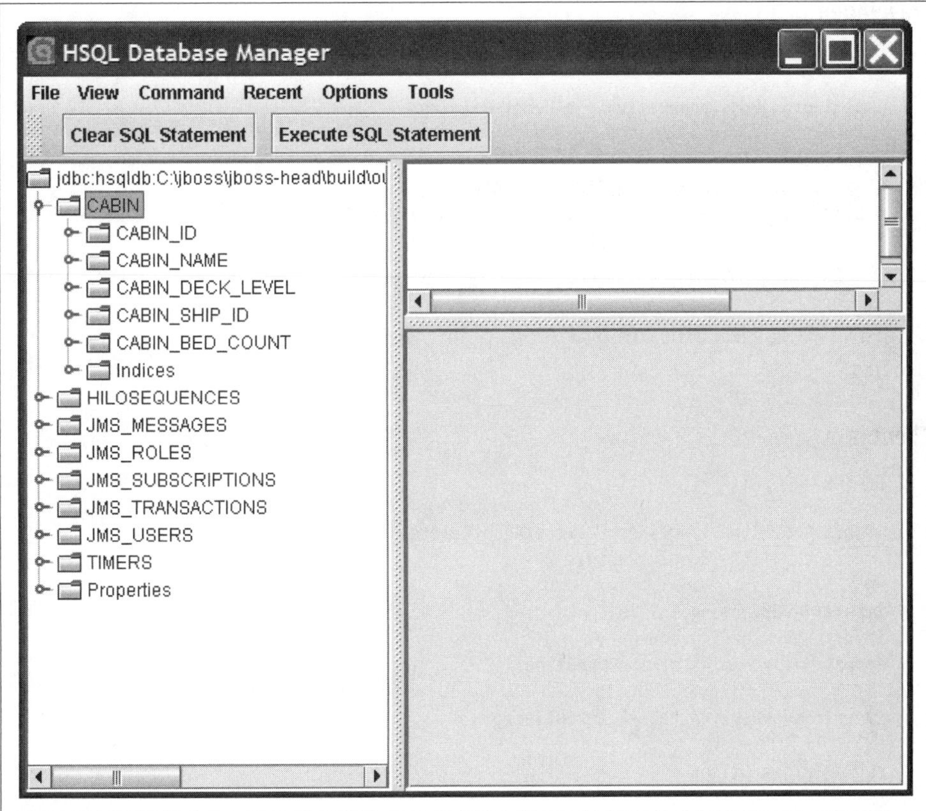

Figure W-10. HSQL Database Manager

Using @RemoteBinding

If you do not like the default remote JNDI binding for the TravelAgent EJB discussed in Exercise 4.1, you can override it with the `@org.jboss.annotation.ejb.RemoteBinding` annotation:

```
package org.jboss.annotation.ejb.RemoteBinding

@Target({TYPE, ANNOTATION_TYPE}) @Retention(RUNTIME)
public @interface RemoteBinding
{
   String jndiBinding( ) default "";
   String interceptorStack( ) default "";
   String clientBindUrl( ) default "socket://0.0.0.0:3873";
   Class factory( ) default org.jboss.ejb3.remoting.RemoteProxyFactory.class;
}
```

The `jndiBinding( )` attribute is used to specify the JNDI binding override. To learn about the other attributes, check out the JBoss EJB 3.0 documentation.

TravelAgentBean.java

```
package com.titan.travelagent;

import org.jboss.annotation.ejb.RemoteBinding;

@Stateless
@RemoteBinding(jndiBinding="TravelAgentRemote")
public class TravelAgentBean implements TravelAgentRemote
{
...
}
```

With the @RemoteBinding annotation in place, the client program can be modified to use it.

Client.java

```
package com.titan.clients;

import com.titan.travelagent.TravelAgentRemote;
import com.titan.domain.Cabin;

import javax.naming.InitialContext;
import javax.naming.Context;
import javax.naming.NamingException;

import javax.rmi.PortableRemoteObject;

public class Client
{
    public static void main(String [] args)
    {
        try
        {
            Context jndiContext = getInitialContext( );
            Object ref = jndiContext.lookup("TravelAgentRemote");
            TravelAgentRemote dao = (TravelAgentRemote)
                PortableRemoteObject.narrow(ref,TravelAgentRemote.class);
...
    }

    public static Context getInitialContext( )
        throws javax.naming.NamingException
    {
        return new javax.naming.InitialContext( );
    }
}
```

Run the client

Run the Client application by invoking ant run.client at the command prompt. Remember to set your JBOSS_HOME and PATH environment variables.

Exercise 4.3: JNDI Binding with XML

This exercise is the same code as in Exercise 4.1, except it uses a JBoss XML deployment descriptor to override the remote JNDI binding that is used by clients to look up the TravelAgent EJB.

Start Up JBoss

If you already have JBoss running, there is no reason to restart it. Otherwise, start it up as instructed in Workbook 1.

Initialize the Database

If you have problems running this example, shut down JBoss and run the clean.db Ant task.

Build and Deploy the Example Programs

Perform the following steps:

1. Open a command prompt or shell terminal and change to the *ex04_3* directory created by the extraction process.
2. Set the `JAVA_HOME` and `JBOSS_HOME` environment variables to point to where your JDK and JBoss 4.0 are installed. Examples:

   Windows:

   ```
   C:\workbook\ex04_3> set JAVA_HOME=C:\jdk1.5.0
   C:\workbook\ex04_3> set JBOSS_HOME=C:\jboss-4.0.x
   ```

   Unix:

   ```
   $ export JAVA_HOME=/usr/local/jdk1.5.0
   $ export JBOSS_HOME=/usr/local/jboss-4.0
   ```

3. Add `ant` to your execution path. Ant is the build utility.

   Windows:

   ```
   C:\workbook\ex04_3> set PATH=..\ant\bin;%PATH%
   ```

   Unix:

   ```
   $ export PATH=../ant/bin:$PATH
   ```

4. Perform the build by typing `ant`.

As in the last exercise, *titan.jar is* rebuilt, copied to the JBoss *deploy* directory, and redeployed by the application server.

The jboss.xml Deployment Descriptor

The JBoss EJB 3.0 implementation has a vendor-specific XML deployment descriptor called `jboss.xml` that is used to configure various JBoss-specific things, such as the JNDI binding of the TravelAgent EJB's remote interface.

jboss.xml

```
<jboss>
   <enterprise-beans>
      <session>
         <ejb-name>TravelAgentBean</ejb-name>
         <jndi-name>TravelAgentRemote</jndi-name>
      </session>
   </enterprise-beans>
</jboss>
```

The <jndi-name> element is used to override the default JNDI binding for the remote interface of the TravelAgent EJB. The client program is unmodified from Exercise 4.2.

Client.java

```
package com.titan.clients;

import com.titan.travelagent.TravelAgentRemote;
import com.titan.domain.Cabin;

import javax.naming.InitialContext;
import javax.naming.Context;
import javax.naming.NamingException;

import javax.rmi.PortableRemoteObject;

public class Client
{
    public static void main(String [] args)
    {
        try
        {
            Context jndiContext = getInitialContext( );
            Object ref = jndiContext.lookup("TravelAgentRemote");
            TravelAgentRemote dao = (TravelAgentRemote)
                PortableRemoteObject.narrow(ref,TravelAgentRemote.class);
...
    }

    public static Context getInitialContext( )
        throws javax.naming.NamingException
    {
        return new javax.naming.InitialContext( );
    }
}
```

Run the Client

Run the Client application by invoking `ant run.client` at the command prompt. Remember to set your `JBOSS_HOME` and `PATH` environment variables.

WORKBOOK 3

Exercises for Chapter 5

Chapter 5 of the EJB book walked you through all of the details for deploying, creating, and interacting with the `EntityManager` interface. This chapter uses the same Cabin entity bean introduced in Chapter 4 to illustrate the concepts and APIs discussed in Chapter 5. You will see examples of:

- The `merge( )`, `flush( )`, and `refresh( )` operations in action
- An explanation of `FlushModeType`
- The differences between a transaction-only and an extended persistence context
- Using Java Persistence in a standalone Java application

Exercise 5.1 walks you through the first three bullets, and Exercise 5.2 shows you how to use persistence outside of the application server.

Exercise 5.1: Interacting with EntityManager

This exercise has four different clients to build and run against the JBoss application server:

Client_1.java
: This client demonstrates what happens when you use the `EntityManager.merge( )` operation. It interacts with the TravelAgent EJB.

Client_2.java
: This client demonstrates the difference between a transaction-only and an extended persistence context. The TransactionPersistenceContext EJB injects and uses a transaction-scoped entity manager. The ExtendedPersistenceContext EJB injects and uses an extended entity manager.

Client_3.java
: This client demonstrates how `FlushModeType` affects your application—specifically, when updates are synchronized with the database.

These clients must be executed in order; Client_1 creates a Cabin entity that is used by the rest of the examples.

Start Up JBoss

If you already have JBoss running, there is no reason to restart it. Otherwise, start it up as instructed in Workbook 1.

Initialize the Database

The database tables will be created when Exercise 5.1 is deployed to JBoss. If you have problems running this example, shut down JBoss and run the clean.db Ant task.

Build and Deploy the Example Programs

Perform the following steps:

1. Open a command prompt or shell terminal and change to the *ex05_1* directory created by the extraction process.
2. Set the `JAVA_HOME` and `JBOSS_HOME` environment variables to point to where your JDK and JBoss 4.0 are installed. Examples:

   Windows:

   ```
   C:\workbook\ex05_1> set JAVA_HOME=C:\jdk1.5.0
   C:\workbook\ex05_1> set JBOSS_HOME=C:\jboss-4.0.x
   ```

   Unix:

   ```
   $ export JAVA_HOME=/usr/local/jdk1.5.0
   $ export JBOSS_HOME=/usr/local/jboss-4.0
   ```

3. Add `ant` to your execution path. Ant is the build utility.

   Windows:

   ```
   C:\workbook\ex05_1> set PATH=..\ant\bin;%PATH%
   ```

   Unix:

   ```
   $ export PATH=../ant/bin:$PATH
   ```

4. Perform the build by typing `ant`.

As in the last exercise, *titan.jar* is rebuilt, copied to the JBoss *deploy* directory, and redeployed by the application server.

Using find( ) and merge( )

Client_1.java interacts with the TravelAgent EJB to create, find, and then update a Cabin entity. Let's break apart Client_1.java to see what is going on in the example:

```
public class Client_1
{
    public static void main(String [] args)
```

```
    {
        try
        {
            Context jndiContext = getInitialContext( );
            Object ref = jndiContext.lookup("TravelAgentBean/remote");
            TravelAgentRemote dao = (TravelAgentRemote)
                PortableRemoteObject.narrow(ref,TravelAgentRemote.class);
```

First, we must obtain a remote reference to the TravelAgent EJB:

```
            Cabin noCabin = dao.findCabin(1);
            System.out.println("no cabin should be null: " + noCabin);
```

This example shows that the `EntityManager.find( )` method returns `null` if it cannot find a Cabin entity in the database.

```
            Cabin cabin_1 = new Cabin( );
            cabin_1.setId(1);
            cabin_1.setName("Master Suite");
            cabin_1.setDeckLevel(1);
            cabin_1.setShipId(1);
            cabin_1.setBedCount(3);

            dao.createCabin(cabin_1);
```

A `Cabin` instance is allocated and initialized locally. Then, it is sent to the TravelAgent EJB to be inserted into the database, which is accomplished by calling the remote `createCabin( )` method and passing the `Cabin` instance to the server.

```
            Cabin cabin_2 = dao.findCabin(1);
            System.out.println(cabin_2.getName( ));
            System.out.println(cabin_2.getDeckLevel( ));
            System.out.println(cabin_2.getShipId( ));
            System.out.println(cabin_2.getBedCount( ));
```

Next, the client asks the TravelAgent EJB to find the Cabin entity based on its primary key to make sure that the Cabin was inserted into the database correctly.

```
            System.out.println("Updating detached cabin instance with new bed count
of 4");
            cabin_2.setBedCount(4);
            dao.updateCabin(cabin_2);
```

The code then takes the local instance of the `Cabin` and sets a new bed count to `4` on the instance. It is important to remember that this `Cabin` instance is local to the client code. When the bed count is set to `4` with the `setBedCount( )` method, only the internal state of the `Cabin` instance is changed. No database interaction happens until we call the `updateCabin( )` method on the TravelAgent EJB passing the `Cabin` as a parameter. Later, on the server, you will see that the `updateCabin( )` method invokes the `merge( )` operation on an `EntityManager` representing the persistence unit to which the Cabin entity belongs.

```
            System.out.println("Finding cabin to see it has been updated with a
merge( ) on server");
            Cabin cabin_3 = dao.findCabin(1);
```

```
            System.out.println("new bed count is: " + cabin_3.getBedCount( ));
        }
        catch (javax.naming.NamingException ne)
        {
            ne.printStackTrace( );
        }
    }
...
}
```

Finally, after performing the merge, check to make sure the changes were made.

TravelAgentBean.java

```
@Stateless
public class TravelAgentBean implements TravelAgentRemote
{
   @PersistenceUnit(unitName="titan") private EntityManagerFactory factory;
   @PersistenceContext(unitName="titan") private EntityManager manager;

   public void createCabin(Cabin cabin)
   {
      manager.persist(cabin);
   }

   public Cabin findCabin(int pKey)
   {
      return manager.find(Cabin.class, pKey);
   }

   public void updateCabin(Cabin cabin)
   {
      manager.merge(cabin);
   }
   ...
}
```

The `createCabin( )`, `findCabin( )`, and `updateCabin( )` methods are the TravelAgent EJB methods used in Client_1. As you can see, they are simply wrappers around the `persist( )`, `find( )`, and `merge( )` methods of the injected `EntityManager`.

Run the client

Run the Client_1 application by invoking `ant run.client_1` at the command prompt. Remember to set your `JBOSS_HOME` and `PATH` environment variables. The output should look like this:

```
run.client_1:
     [java] no cabin should be null: null
     [java] Master Suite
     [java] 1
     [java] 1
     [java] 3
```

```
[java] Updating detached cabin instance with new bed count of 4
[java] Finding cabin to see it has been updated with a merge( ) on server
[java] new bed count is: 4
```

Transaction Versus Extended Persistence Contexts

In Chapter 5, you learned that with a transaction-scoped persistence context, entity bean instances are managed by the entity manager only for the duration of a transaction. When the transaction finishes, the entity instances become detached and are no longer associated with any persistence context.

This behavior is different with extended persistence contexts. With them, even after the transaction ends, the entity instance remains managed by the entity manager until the entity manager is closed or destroyed. In this exercise, we will show you two stateful session beans that are identical in every way except in how they reference their persistence context. They are TransactionPersistenceContextBean and ExtendedPersistenceContextBean.

TransactionPersistenceContextBean.java

```
package com.titan.travelagent;

import javax.ejb.Stateful;
import javax.ejb.Remove;
import javax.persistence.EntityManager;
import javax.persistence.PersistenceContext;
import javax.persistence.PersistenceContextType;

import com.titan.domain.Cabin;

@Stateful
public class TransactionPersistenceContextBean
     implements TransactionPersistenceContextRemote
{
   @PersistenceContext(unitName="titan", type=PersistenceContextType.TRANSACTION)
   private EntityManager manager;

   private Cabin cabin;

   public void setCabin(int pk)
   {
      cabin = manager.find(Cabin.class, pk);
   }

   public void updateBedCount(int newBedCount)
   {
      cabin.setBedCount(newBedCount);
   }

   @Remove
   public void remove( )
```

```
    {
    }
}
```

TransactionPersistenceContextBean is a stateful session bean. It has a field called manager, into which a transaction-scoped persistence context is injected by the container when the bean instance is created. It also has a cabin field that is set via the setCabin( ) method. The updateBedCount( ) method will update the cabin field's bed count. The remove( ) method is simply a way to clean up the stateful session bean when we are finished with it.

ExtendedPersistenceContextBean is identical, except for the type of persistence context that is injected:

```
@Stateful
public class ExtendedPersistenceContextBean implements
ExtendedPersistenceContextRemote
{
    @PersistenceContext(unitName="titan", type=PersistenceContextType.EXTENDED)
    private EntityManager manager;
    private Cabin cabin;

    public void setCabin(int pk)
    {
       cabin = manager.find(Cabin.class, pk);
    }

    public void updateBedCount(int newBedCount)
    {
       cabin.setBedCount(newBedCount);
    }

    @Remove
    public void remove( )
    {
    }
}
```

An extended persistence context is created for the manager field instead of a transaction-scoped persistence context. When the setCabin( ) method is invoked on ExtendedPersistenceContextBean, the cabin field remains managed by the extended entity manager after the method is finished. This extended persistence context remains active for the lifetime of the stateful session bean into which it is injected. See Chapter 11 for more details on this behavior.

Client_2 interacts with both of the stateful session beans to show the difference in behavior between the identical updateBedCount( ) methods of these two EJBs. While the updateBedCount( ) method of ExtendedPersistenceContextBean causes a database update, the one in TransactionPersistenceContextBean does not. This is because when the cabin field is set in the setCabin( ) method, the instance remains managed in ExtendedPersistenceContextBean but not in TransactionPersistenceContextBean. Let's walk through Client_2 to see how it demonstrates this behavior.

Client_2.java

```
public class Client_2
{
    public static void main(String [] args)
    {
        try
        {
            Context jndiContext = getInitialContext( );
            Object ref = jndiContext.lookup("TravelAgentBean/remote");
            TravelAgentRemote dao = (TravelAgentRemote)
                PortableRemoteObject.narrow(ref,TravelAgentRemote.class);
```

This code obtains a reference to the TravelAgent EJB so that we can get a clean copy of what is currently stored in the database for a particular cabin.

```
            ref = jndiContext.lookup("TransactionPersistenceContextBean/remote");
            TransactionPersistenceContextRemote txBean =
                (TransactionPersistenceContextRemote)ref;
```

First, we look up TransactionPersistenceContextBean through JNDI. This act creates a stateful session bean instance that will hold conversational state (see Chapter 11 for more details):

```
            Cabin fetchedCabin = dao.findCabin(1);
            int oldBedCount = fetchedCabin.getBedCount( );
```

The code fetches a clean copy of a `Cabin` and stores its bed count into a local variable. It obtains this `Cabin` instance from the TravelAgent EJB:

```
            System.out.println("Set up transaction persistence context stateful
bean");
            txBean.setCabin(1);
            txBean.updateBedCount(5);

            fetchedCabin = dao.findCabin(1);
            System.out.println("Cabin bed count will still be " + oldBedCount + ": "
+ fetchedCabin.getBedCount( ));
```

Now that the client has a reference to TransactionPersistenceContextBean, the code sets the EJB's `Cabin` instance and then updates the bed count of that instance by calling the `setCabin( )` and `updateBedCount( )` methods, respectively. After doing this, the client fetches a new copy of the `Cabin` instance to show that the bed count has not changed. Why hasn't it changed in the database? If you go back and look at the implementation of TransactionPersistenceContextBean, you will see that the injected entity manager is a transaction-scoped entity manager. When the `setCabin( )` method was invoked, the `cabin` field did not remain managed by the persistence context after the method completed. So, when `updateBedCount( )` was called, the method was modifying a detached entity instance.

```
            System.out.println(
               "Set up extended persistence context stateful bean");

            ref = jndiContext.lookup(
                 "ExtendedPersistenceContextBean/remote");
            ExtendedPersistenceContextRemote extendedBean =
                 (ExtendedPersistenceContextRemote)ref;
```

The second part of Client_2 obtains a session to ExtendedPersistenceContextBean:

```
            extendedBean.setCabin(1);
            extendedBean.updateBedCount(5);

            fetchedCabin = dao.findCabin(1);
            System.out.println("Cabin bed count will be 5: " + fetchedCabin.
getBedCount( ));
```

This calls the same sequence of methods as the one called earlier: `setCabin( )` and `updateBedCount( )`. The difference is that when the `setCabin( )` method is invoked, the `cabin` field remains managed because the stateful bean's entity manager is an extended persistence context.

```
            // cleanup
            txBean.remove( );
            extendedBean.remove( );
         }
         catch (javax.naming.NamingException ne)
         {
            ne.printStackTrace( );
         }
      }
..
}
```

The remaining part of the client is uninteresting; it simply cleans up the stateful session bean sessions we started.

Run the client

Run the Client_2 application by invoking `ant run.client_2` at the command prompt. Remember to set your `JBOSS_HOME` and `PATH` environment variables. The output should look like this:

```
run.client_2:
     [java] Set up transaction persistence context stateful bean
     [java] Cabin bed count will still be 4: 4
     [java] Set up extended persistence context stateful bean
     [java] Cabin bed count will be 5: 5
```

FlushModeType Behavior

This exercise shows you how `javax.persistence.FlushModeType` affects entity updates. The Client_3.java code is very simple, so we will not go over it. It simply obtains a reference to a TravelAgent EJB and calls the TravelAgentBean. flushmodeExample( ) method. The flushModeExample( ) method illustrates how different FlushModeType settings change the synchronization behavior of your entity manager.

TravelAgentBean.java

```
@Stateless
public class TravelAgentBean implements TravelAgentRemote
{
   @PersistenceUnit(unitName="titan") private EntityManagerFactory factory;
   @PersistenceContext(unitName="titan") private EntityManager manager;
...
```

Notice that TravelAgentBean has both an EntityManagerFactory and an EntityManager of the same persistence unit injected into it. Both of these member variables are used in the flushModeExample( ) method.

```
   public void flushModeExample( )
   {
      EntityManager createdManager = factory.createEntityManager( );

      try
      {
         Cabin newCabin2 = new Cabin( );
         newCabin2.setId(2);
         newCabin2.setName("Another Cabin");
         newCabin2.setBedCount(1);
         createdManager.persist(newCabin2);
```

First, an EntityManager is created by calling the injected EntityManagerFactory. createEntityManager( ) method. This gives us a sandbox in which to work so that different FlushModeType behavior can be illustrated.

Next, a brand-new Cabin is allocated and then persisted to the database using the createdManager.persist( ) method. The default FlushModeType of an entity manager is always AUTO. This means that any inserts, updates, and deletes are not done on the database until a query is invoked or the transaction commits.

```
         Cabin cabin2 = manager.find(Cabin.class, 2);
         if (cabin2 != null)
         {
            throw new RuntimeException("newCabin2 should not be flushed yet");
         }
```

To show that the persist( ) operation has not yet been synchronized, the code uses the injected manager field. Because this is an entirely different persistence context than the one used to persist the entity, it does not find the newly created Cabin within its persistence context, nor in the database. The code checks to make sure that this is actually the case.

```
         Cabin cabin1 = (Cabin)createdManager.createQuery(
               "FROM Cabin c WHERE c.id = 1").getSingleResult( );
```

```
            cabin2 = manager.find(Cabin.class, 2);
            if (cabin2 == null)
            {
               throw new RuntimeException("newCabin2 should be flushed now");
            }
```

Next, we invoke a simple query on the factory-created entity manager. Because the FlushModeType is AUTO, the persisted entity will be flushed. This will allow it to be found when the subsequent manager.find( ) method is invoked.

```
            createdManager.setFlushMode(FlushModeType.COMMIT);
            newCabin2.setBedCount(99);

            cabin1 = (Cabin)createdManager.createQuery(
                 "FROM Cabin c WHERE c.id = 1").getSingleResult( );

            manager.refresh(cabin2);
            if (cabin2.getBedCount( ) == 99)
            {
               throw new RuntimeException(
                    "should not be 99 yet with COMMIT and a query");
            }
```

Now let's look at how FlushModeType.COMMIT works. The code sets the FlushModeType to COMMIT and then changes the bed count of the Cabin created by createdManager earlier. After this, a query is invoked. Unlike AUTO's behavior, FlushModeType.COMMIT does not flush changes until the transaction is committed. So, when manager.refresh( ) is called on cabin2, you will not see the changes because the transaction hasn't committed* yet.

```
            createdManager.flush( );

            manager.refresh(cabin2);
            if (cabin2.getBedCount( ) != 99)
            {
               throw new RuntimeException("should be 99 yet with a flush");
            }
```

Finally, flush the bed count update we did by calling createdManager.flush( ). The manager persistence context will now be able to refresh cabin2 with the new bed count since the database has been updated.

```
         }
         finally
         {
            createdManager.close( );
         }
      }
   }
```

* The transaction lasts for the duration of the method call because session beans, by default, have the REQUIRED behavior. See Chapter 16 for more information.

Don't forget to clean up any entity manager that was created by an entity manager factory.

Run the client

Run the Client_3 application by invoking `ant run.client_3` at the command prompt. Remember to set your `JBOSS_HOME` and `PATH` environment variables. There is no interesting output.

Exercise 5.2: Standalone Persistence

You can use Java Persistence in standalone Java applications. This exercise shows you how to do this with JBoss. JBoss is distributed with the Hibernate Entity Manager project separately downloadable at *http://www.hibernate.org*. The Ant build file had to be changed a little bit so that the required Hibernate JARs could be put in the classpath.

build.xml

```
<path id="build.classpath">
      <fileset dir="${jboss.home}/server/default/lib">
          <include name="*.jar"/>
      </fileset>
      <fileset dir="${jboss.home}/server/default/deploy/ejb3.deployer">
          <include name="*.jar"/>
      </fileset>
      <fileset dir="${jboss.home}/server/default/deploy/jboss-aop-jdk50.deployer">
          <include name="*.jar"/>
      </fileset>
      <fileset dir="${jboss.home}/lib">
          <include name="*.jar"/>
      </fileset>
</path>

<path id="run.classpath">
   <path refid="build.classpath"/>
   <fileset dir="${build.dir}">
       <include name="*.jar"/>
   </fileset>
   <pathelement location="${basedir}/client-config"/>
</path>
```

The classpath setup is a bit convoluted for this example because the JAR files necessary to run a standalone Java Persistence application are a bit dispersed. If you want a more compact distribution, go to Hibernate's web site to obtain it.

Initialize the Database

The database tables are created when Exercise 5.2 is executed. The standalone Java Persistence solution also initializes the Hypersonic SQL database and generates the database schema. This is an in-memory database, so you will not see any files created for the database.

Build the Example Program

Perform the following steps:

1. Open a command prompt or shell terminal and change to the *ex05_2* directory created by the extraction process.
2. Set the `JAVA_HOME` and `JBOSS_HOME` environment variables to point to where your JDK and JBoss 4.0 are installed. Examples:

   Windows:

   ```
   C:\workbook\ex05_2> set JAVA_HOME=C:\jdk1.5.0
   C:\workbook\ex05_2> set JBOSS_HOME=C:\jboss-4.0.x
   ```

   Unix:

   ```
   $ export JAVA_HOME=/usr/local/jdk1.5.0
   $ export JBOSS_HOME=/usr/local/jboss-4.0
   ```

3. Add `ant` to your execution path. Ant is the build utility.

   Windows:

   ```
   C:\workbook\ex05_2> set PATH=..\ant\bin;%PATH%
   ```

   Unix:

   ```
   $ export PATH=../ant/bin:$PATH
   ```

4. Perform the build by typing `ant`.

A *titan.jar* will be created in the *build* directory. You run the standalone Java application with this file in your classpath.

Examine the JAR

The *titan.jar* file has three files within it: *Cabin.class*, *StandaloneClient.class*, and a *persistence.xml* file. The *persistence.xml* configuration is very specific to the Hibernate implementation.

persistence.xml

```
<?xml version="1.0" encoding="UTF-8"?>
<persistence>
   <persistence-unit name="titan">
      <properties>
         <property name="hibernate.connection.driver_class" value="org.hsqldb.
jdbcDriver"/>
```

```
            <property name="hibernate.connection.username" value="sa"/>
            <property name="hibernate.connection.password" value=""/>
            <property name="hibernate.connection.url" value="jdbc:hsqldb:."/>
            <property name="hibernate.hbm2ddl.auto" value="create-drop"/>
            <property name="hibernate.cache.provider_class" value="org.hibernate.
cache.HashtableCacheProvider"/>
        </properties>
    </persistence-unit>
</persistence>
```

Because we're not running in an application server, the persistence provider needs to initialize the connection to the database.

The `hibernate.connection.driver_class` property is the driver class for the JDBC driver you are using. In this case, it is the driver for the Hypersonic SQL database.

`hibernate.connection.username` and `hibernate.connection.password` specify the username and password used by the database.

`hibernate.connection.url` is a JDBC-based URL that points to the database instance.

`hibernate.cache.provider_class` specifies the caching implementation that will be used by Hibernate. In this instance, we need to set it to `HashtableCacheProvider` because this is what will be used outside of the application server.

Although the specification says that you must list all classes that belong to a persistence unit within your *persistence.xml* file if you are using Java Persistence in a standalone application, Hibernate will automatically scan the JAR that contains the *persistence.xml* file for any entity classes that need to be added to the persistence unit. In practice, you will find that most vendors will support this feature when running in Java SE.

Examine the Standalone Application

The standalone application is contained in StandaloneClient.java. This application is very similar to Exercise 4.1 of this workbook in that all it does is create a `Cabin` within the database. Let's look at it:

```
package com.titan.clients;

import javax.persistence.EntityManagerFactory;
import javax.persistence.EntityManager;
import javax.persistence.EntityTransaction;
import javax.persistence.Persistence;

import com.titan.domain.Cabin;
public class StandaloneClient
{
   public static void main(String[] args) throws Exception
   {
      EntityManagerFactory factory =
         Persistence.createEntityManagerFactory("titan");
      EntityManager manager = factory.createEntityManager( );
```

Because we are running outside of the application server, you must create the EntityManager via an EntityManagerFactory. To locate the factory, the javax.persistence.Persistence API is used. When you pass in titan to the createEntityManagerFactory( ) method, Hibernate searches for any *META-INF/persistence.xml* files in your classpath that have the titan persistence unit defined. From this, it creates the EntityManagerFactory.

```
         try
         {
            createCabin(manager);
            Cabin cabin_2 = manager.find(Cabin.class, 1);
            System.out.println(cabin_2.getName( ));
            System.out.println(cabin_2.getDeckLevel( ));
            System.out.println(cabin_2.getShipId( ));
            System.out.println(cabin_2.getBedCount( ));
         }
         finally
         {
            manager.close( );
            factory.close( );
         }
      }
```

Next, we simply call the createCabin( ) static method to create the Cabin entity in the database, and locate it with the EntityManager.find( ) method:

```
      public static void createCabin(EntityManager manager)
      {
         Cabin cabin_1 = new Cabin( );
         cabin_1.setId(1);
         cabin_1.setName("Master Suite");
         cabin_1.setDeckLevel(1);
         cabin_1.setShipId(1);
         cabin_1.setBedCount(3);

         EntityTransaction transaction = manager.getTransaction( );
         transaction.begin( );
         manager.persist(cabin_1);
         transaction.commit( );
      }
   }
```

The createCabin( ) method is straightforward. Notice that a javax.persistence.EntityTransaction is needed to persist the new Cabin. When running outside of the application server, you must use resource-local transactions to interact with your EntityManager instances.

Exercises for Chapter 6

Chapter 6 of the EJB book walked you through some basic object-to-relational mappings for the persistent properties of your entity bean classes. The exercises in this chapter use a lot of the example code from Chapter 6 to illustrate basic mapping types. You will see examples of:

- Autogenerated primary keys
- `@IdClass` and `@EmbeddedId` primary key class mappings
- `@Temporal`, `@Transient`, `@Lob`, and `@Enumerated` mappings
- An entity class that maps to multiple tables
- An entity class that has an embedded class as a property

Exercise 6.1: Basic Property Mappings

This exercise shows you an example of the `@Temporal`, `@Lob`, and `@Enumerated` mapping types discussed in Chapter 6, as well as an example of an autogenerated primary key.

Start Up JBoss

If you already have JBoss running, there is no reason to restart it. Otherwise, start it up as instructed in Workbook 1.

Initialize the Database

The database tables will be created when Exercise 6.1 is deployed to JBoss. If you have problems running this example, shut down JBoss and run the clean.db Ant task.

Build and Deploy the Example Programs

Perform the following steps:

1. Open a command prompt or shell terminal and change to the *ex06_1* directory created by the extraction process.
2. Set the `JAVA_HOME` and `JBOSS_HOME` environment variables to point to where your JDK and JBoss 4.0 are installed. Examples:

   Windows:

   ```
   C:\workbook\ex06_1> set JAVA_HOME=C:\jdk1.5.0
   C:\workbook\ex06_1> set JBOSS_HOME=C:\jboss-4.0.x
   ```

   Unix:

   ```
   $ export JAVA_HOME=/usr/local/jdk1.5.0
   $ export JBOSS_HOME=/usr/local/jboss-4.0
   ```

3. Add `ant` to your execution path. Ant is the build utility.

   Windows:

   ```
   C:\workbook\ex06_1> set PATH=..\ant\bin;%PATH%
   ```

   Unix:

   ```
   $ export PATH=../ant/bin:$PATH
   ```

4. Perform the build by typing `ant`.

As in the last exercise, *titan.jar* is rebuilt, copied to the JBoss *deploy* directory, and redeployed by the application server.

Examine the Customer Entity

This exercise maps one Customer entity with some of the basic mapping types shown in Chapter 6 of the EJB book.

Customer.java

```
package com.titan.domain;

import javax.persistence.*;

import java.util.Date;

@Entity
@Table(name="CUSTOMER_TABLE")
public class Customer implements java.io.Serializable
{
```

The `@javax.persistence.Table` annotation is used to set the relational table to which the Customer entity maps.

```
    private int id;
    private String lastName;
    private String firstName;
```

```
    private CustomerType customerType;
    private Date timeCreated = new Date( );
    private JPEG picture;

    @Id
    @GeneratedValue
    @Column(name="CUST_ID")
    public int getId( )
    {
       return id;
    }
    public void setId(int pk)
    {
       id = pk;
    }
```

The `@javax.persistence.GeneratedValue` annotation tells the persistence provider that we want the `id` property of the Customer entity to be autogenerated when `EntityManager.persist( )` is executed. The `@javax.persistence.Column` annotation is used to specify the name of the column to which the `id` property maps in `CUSTOMER_TABLE`.

```
    public String getLastName( ) { return lastName; }
    public void setLastName(String lastName) { this.lastName = lastName; }

    public String getFirstName( ) { return firstName; }
    public void setFirstName(String lastName) { this.firstName = firstName; }
```

Although the `lastName` and `firstName` properties are not annotated, the persistence provider will assume that they are persistent. Use the `@javax.persistence.Transient` annotation if you want to mark a property as nonpersistent.

```
    @Enumerated(EnumType.STRING)
    public CustomerType getCustomerType( ) { return customerType; }
    public void setCustomerType(CustomerType type) { customerType = type; }
```

`com.titan.domain.CustomerType` is a Java `enum`. The `@javax.persistence.Enumerated` annotation is used here to tell the persistence provider that we want to store it as a string in the database.

```
    @Temporal(TemporalType.TIME)
    public Date getTimeCreated( ) { return timeCreated; }
```

A `java.util.Date` can be stored in different ways in the database, so here we specify that we want the database to store it as a time SQL type, using the `@javax.persistence.Temporal` annotation to do this.

```
    @Lob @Basic(fetch=FetchType.LAZY)
    public JPEG getPicture( ) { return picture; }
    public void setPicture(JPEG jpeg) { picture = jpeg; }
}
```

Our last property is of type `com.titan.domain.JPEG`. Let's pretend that this class is actually an in-memory representation of a *.jpeg* image. If you open up the *JPEG.java* implementation, you'll see that it is just a dummy class. By marking the Customer's `picture` property as an `@Lob`, the persistence provider will see that `com.titan.domain.JPEG` is a serializable Java object and will map it to an SQL `Blob` type in the database.

When you have this exercise built and deployed, bring up the Hypersonic SQL Database Manager program, as discussed in Workbook 2.

Figure W-11 shows how the annotation mappings have affected the schema of our autogenerated database.

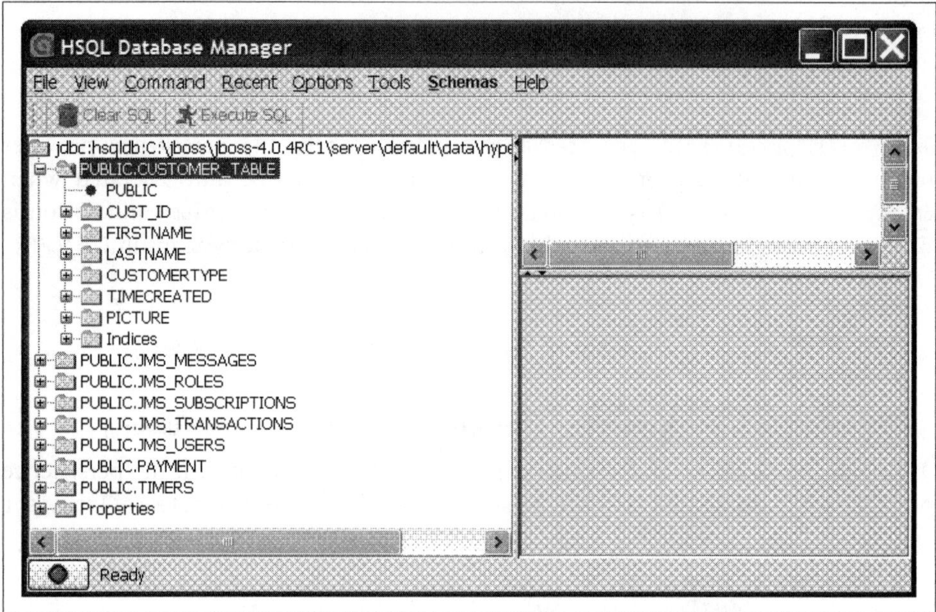

Figure W-11. CUSTOMER_TABLE

Examine TravelAgentBean

`TravelAgentBean` acts as a façade around the persistence unit that holds the Customer entity. Let's take a look at it.

TravelAgentBean.java

```
package com.titan.travelagent;

import javax.ejb.Stateless;
import javax.persistence.EntityManager;
import javax.persistence.PersistenceContext;

import com.titan.domain.Customer;
```

```
@Stateless
public class TravelAgentBean implements TravelAgentRemote
{
   @PersistenceContext(unitName="titan") private EntityManager manager;

   public int createCustomer(Customer cust)
   {
      manager.persist(cust);
      return cust.getId( );
   }

   public Customer findCustomer(int pKey)
   {
      return manager.find(Customer.class, pKey);
   }
}
```

The Customer entity is allocated on the client and is sent via the `createCustomer( )` method to the server. After the `manager.persist( )` method has executed, the primary key for the Customer entity has been generated and is returned by the method invocation. The `findCustomer( )` method simply finds and returns the entity based on its primary key.

Examine the Client

The client's only role is to allocate a `Customer` instance and invoke the `createCustomer( )` and `findCustomer( )` methods of `TravelAgentBean`. There's not much else to add here.

Run the Client

Run the Client application by invoking `ant run.client` at the command prompt. Remember to set your `JBOSS_HOME` and `PATH` environment variables. This is the output:

```
run.client:
     [java] Bill
     [java] Burke
     [java] BIG_SPENDAH
```

Exercise 6.2: @IdClass

This exercise shows you an example of using `@javax.persistence.IdClass` to map a primary key class to the database.

Start Up JBoss

If you already have JBoss running, there is no reason to restart it. Otherwise, start it up as instructed in Workbook 1.

Initialize the Database

The database tables will be created when Exercise 6.2 is deployed to JBoss. If you have problems running this example, shut down JBoss and run the clean.db Ant task.

Build and Deploy the Example Programs

Perform the following steps:

1. Open a command prompt or shell terminal and change to the *ex06_2* directory created by the extraction process.
2. Set the `JAVA_HOME` and `JBOSS_HOME` environment variables to point to where your JDK and JBoss 4.0 are installed. Examples:

   Windows:

   ```
   C:\workbook\ex06_2> set JAVA_HOME=C:\jdk1.5.0
   C:\workbook\ex06_2> set JBOSS_HOME=C:\jboss-4.0.x
   ```

   Unix:

   ```
   $ export JAVA_HOME=/usr/local/jdk1.5.0
   $ export JBOSS_HOME=/usr/local/jboss-4.0
   ```

3. Add `ant` to your execution path. Ant is the build utility.

   Windows:

   ```
   C:\workbook\ex06_2> set PATH=..\ant\bin;%PATH%
   ```

   Unix:

   ```
   $ export PATH=../ant/bin:$PATH
   ```

4. Perform the build by typing `ant`.

As in the last exercise, *titan.jar* is rebuilt, copied to the JBoss *deploy* directory, and redeployed by the application server.

Examine the Example Files

The Customer entity code was a cut-and-paste from the `@IdClass` section of Chapter 6, so it needs no further explanation. `TravelAgentBean` again acts as a simple data access object, wrapping invocations around the `EntityManager` instance injected into this EJB. The Client application simply allocates a Customer entity and then calls `createCustomer( )` and `findCustomer( )` on `TravelAgentBean` to insert and find the Customer in the database.

Run the Client

Run the Client application by invoking `ant run.client` at the command prompt. Remember to set your `JBOSS_HOME` and `PATH` environment variables. This is the output:

```
run.client:
     [java] Bill
```

```
[java] Burke
[java] 9999999
```

Exercise 6.3: @EmbeddedId

This exercise shows you an example of using `@javax.persistence.EmbeddedId` to map a primary key class to the database. It also shows how the `@javax.persistence.Transient` annotation can be used to mark nonpersistent properties.

Start Up JBoss

If you already have JBoss running, there is no reason to restart it. Otherwise, start it up as instructed Workbook 1.

Initialize the Database

The database tables will be created when Exercise 6.3 is deployed to JBoss. If you have problems running this example, shut down JBoss and run the clean.db Ant task.

Build and Deploy the Example Programs

Perform the following steps:

1. Open a command prompt or shell terminal and change to the *ex06_3* directory created by the extraction process.
2. Set the `JAVA_HOME` and `JBOSS_HOME` environment variables to point to where your JDK and JBoss 4.0 are installed. Examples:

   Windows:

   ```
   C:\workbook\ex06_3> set JAVA_HOME=C:\jdk1.5.0
   C:\workbook\ex06_3> set JBOSS_HOME=C:\jboss-4.0.x
   ```

   Unix:

   ```
   $ export JAVA_HOME=/usr/local/jdk1.5.0
   $ export JBOSS_HOME=/usr/local/jboss-4.0
   ```

3. Add `ant` to your execution path. Ant is the build utility.

   Windows:

   ```
   C:\workbook\ex06_3> set PATH=..\ant\bin;%PATH%
   ```

   Unix:

   ```
   $ export PATH=../ant/bin:$PATH
   ```

4. Perform the build by typing `ant`.

As in the last exercise, *titan.jar* is rebuilt, copied to the JBoss *deploy* directory, and redeployed by the application server.

Examine the Customer Entity

The Customer entity in this exercise is pretty close to the `@EmbeddedId` example in Chapter 6, except that an example of `@Transient` properties was added to illustrate this concept.

Customer.java

```
public class Customer implements java.io.Serializable {
   private String firstName;
   private CustomerPK pk;

   public String getFirstName( ) { return firstName; }
   public void setFirstName(String firstName) { this.firstName = firstName; }

   @EmbeddedId
   @AttributeOverrides({
       @AttributeOverride(name="lastName", column=@Column(name="LAST_NAME"),
       @AttributeOverride(name="ssn", column=@Column(name="SSN"))
   })
   public PK getPk( ) { return pk; }
   public void setPk(CustomerPK pk) { this.pk = pk; }

   @Transient
   public String getLastName() { return pk.getLastName( ); }

   @Transient
   public long getSsn() { return pk.getSsn( ); }
}
```

The `getLastName( )` and `getSsn( )` methods are marked as `@Transient` because they are not persistent properties. They are simply convenience methods for accessing the `lastName` and `ssn` properties stored in the `CustomerPK` primary key class.

Examine Other Files

`TravelAgentBean` again acts as a simple data access object, wrapping invocations around the `EntityManager` instance injected into this EJB. The Client application simply allocates a Customer entity and then calls `createCustomer( )` and `findCustomer( )` to insert and find the `Customer` in the database. Because they are so simple and similar to other exercises in this chapter, we won't go over them in detail.

Run the Client

Run the Client application by invoking `ant run.client` at the command prompt. Remember to set your `JBOSS_HOME` and `PATH` environment variables. This is the output:

```
run.client:
     [java] Bill
     [java] Burke
     [java] 9999999
```

Exercise 6.4: Multitable Mappings

This exercise demonstrates how you can use the `@javax.persistence.SecondaryTable` annotation to map one entity class to multiple tables.

Start Up JBoss

If you already have JBoss running, there is no reason to restart it. Otherwise, start it up as instructed in Workbook 1.

Initialize the Database

The database tables will be created when Exercise 6.4 is deployed to JBoss. If you have problems running this example, shut down JBoss and run the clean.db Ant task.

Build and Deploy the Example Programs

Perform the following steps:

1. Open a command prompt or shell terminal and change to the *ex06_4* directory created by the extraction process.
2. Set the `JAVA_HOME` and `JBOSS_HOME` environment variables to point to where your JDK and JBoss 4.0 are installed. Examples:

   Windows:

   ```
   C:\workbook\ex06_4> set JAVA_HOME=C:\jdk1.5.0
   C:\workbook\ex06_4> set JBOSS_HOME=C:\jboss-4.0.x
   ```

   Unix:

   ```
   $ export JAVA_HOME=/usr/local/jdk1.5.0
   $ export JBOSS_HOME=/usr/local/jboss-4.0
   ```

3. Add `ant` to your execution path. Ant is the build utility.

   Windows:

   ```
   C:\workbook\ex06_4 set PATH=..\ant\bin;%PATH%
   ```

   Unix:

   ```
   $ export PATH=../ant/bin:$PATH
   ```

4. Perform the build by typing `ant`.

As in the last exercise, *titan.jar* is rebuilt, copied to the JBoss *deploy* directory, and redeployed by the application server.

Examine the Customer Entity

The Customer entity is mapped to two different tables: CUSTOMER_TABLE and ADDRESS_TABLE. The firstName and lastName properties are stored in CUSTOMER_TABLE, and the street, address, and city properties are stored in ADDRESS_TABLE.

Customer.java

```
package com.titan.domain;

import javax.persistence.*;

package com.titan.domain;

import javax.persistence.*;

@Entity
@Table(name="CUSTOMER_TABLE")
@SecondaryTable(name="ADDRESS_TABLE",
                pkJoinColumns={
                   @PrimaryKeyJoinColumn(name="ADDRESS_ID")})
public class Customer implements java.io.Serializable {
   private long id;
   private String firstName;
   private String lastName;
   private String street;
   private String city;
   private String state;

   @Id @GeneratedValue
   public int getId( ) { return id; }
   public void setId(int id) { this.id = id; }

   public String getFirstName( ) { return firstName; }
   public void setFirstName(String first) { this.firstName = first; }

   public String getLastName( ) { return lastName; }
   public void setLastName(String last) { this.lastName = last; }

   @Column(name="STREET", table="ADDRESS_TABLE")
   public String getStreet( ) { return street; }
   public void setStreet(String street) { this.street = street; }

   @Column(name="CITY", table="ADDRESS_TABLE")
   public String getCity( ) { return city; }
   public void setCity(String city) { this.city = city; }

   @Column(name="STATE", table="ADDRESS_TABLE")
   public String getState( ) { return state; }
   public void setState(String state) { this.state = state; }
}
```

Examine Other Files

`TravelAgentBean` again acts as a simple data access object, wrapping invocations around the `EntityManager` instance injected into this EJB. The Client application simply allocates a Customer entity and then calls `createCustomer( )` and `findCustomer( )` to insert and find the `Customer` in the database. Because they are so simple and similar to other exercises in this chapter, we won't go over them in detail.

Run the Client

Run the Client application by invoking `ant run.client` at the command prompt. Remember to set your `JBOSS_HOME` and `PATH` environment variables. This is the output:

```
run.client:
     [java] Bill
     [java] Burke
     [java] Clarendon Street
     [java] Boston
     [java] MA
```

Exercise 6.5: Embeddable Classes

This exercise demonstrates how you can use the `@javax.persistence.Embedded` annotation to map a persistent property that is a nonentity class.

Start Up JBoss

If you already have JBoss running, there is no reason to restart it. Otherwise, start it up as instructed in Workbook 1.

Initialize the Database

The database tables will be created when Exercise 6.5 is deployed to JBoss. If you have problems running this example, shut down JBoss and run the clean.db Ant task.

Build and Deploy the Example Programs

Perform the following steps:

1. Open a command prompt or shell terminal and change to the *ex06_5* directory created by the extraction process.
2. Set the `JAVA_HOME` and `JBOSS_HOME` environment variables to point to where your JDK and JBoss 4.0 are installed. Examples:

Windows:

C:\workbook\ex06_5> set JAVA_HOME=C:\jdk1.5.0
C:\workbook\ex06_5> set JBOSS_HOME=C:\jboss-4.0.x

Unix:

$ export JAVA_HOME=/usr/local/jdk1.5.0
$ export JBOSS_HOME=/usr/local/jboss-4.0

3. Add ant to your execution path. Ant is the build utility.

Windows:

C:\workbook\ex06_2> set PATH=..\ant\bin;%PATH%

Unix:

$ export PATH=../ant/bin:$PATH

4. Perform the build by typing `ant`.

As in the last exercise, *titan.jar* is rebuilt, copied to the JBoss *deploy* directory, and redeployed by the application server.

Examine the Customer Entity

The `Customer` entity class has an `address` property that maps to the regular Java class `Address`. The `Customer` and `Address` classes are the same in this exercise as described in the `@Embedded` objects section of Chapter 6. Refer to that section for a complete explanation of how these classes are wired together.

Examine Other Files

`TravelAgentBean` again acts as a simple data access object, wrapping invocations around the `EntityManager` instance injected into this EJB. The Client application simply allocates a `Customer` entity and then calls `createCustomer( )` and `findCustomer( )` to insert and find the `Customer` in the database. Because they are so simple and similar to other exercises in this chapter, we won't go over them in detail.

Run the Client

Run the Client application by invoking `ant run.client` at the command prompt. Remember to set your `JBOSS_HOME` and `PATH` environment variables. This is the output:

```
run.client:
     [java] Clarendon Street
     [java] Boston
     [java] MA
```

WORKBOOK 5

Exercises for Chapter 7

Chapter 7 of the EJB book walked you through the seven relationship types. The exercises in this chapter implement all of the entities mentioned in Chapter 7. You will get to see how these entities and their relationships are created and how Hibernate autogenerates the database schema. You will also see how cascading and lazy loading affect your applications.

Exercise 7.1: Cascading

This exercise shows you how cascading affects the operation of entity manager life cycle methods. The examples in this section do not require the JBoss application server to run, and they use the Hibernate standalone persistence implementation of Java Persistence. Two client applications demonstrate the concepts of cascading:

Client1.java
: This client shows how cascading affects the operation of the `persist( )`, `merge( )`, and `remove( )` methods of the `EntityManager` interface.

Client2.java
: This client shows you how the `merge( )` operation can also persist new related entities.

Start Up JBoss

There is no need to start up JBoss in this example because standalone persistence is being used.

Initialize the Database

The database tables will be created when the clients in this exercise run. The database is an in-memory-only database and will not be available when the program completes.

Build the Example Programs

Perform the following steps:

1. Open a command prompt or shell terminal and change to the *ex07_1* directory created by the extraction process.
2. Set the `JAVA_HOME` and `JBOSS_HOME` environment variables to point to where your JDK and JBoss 4.0 are installed. Examples:

   Windows:

   C:\workbook\ex07_1> set JAVA_HOME=C:\jdk1.5.0
   C:\workbook\ex07_1> set JBOSS_HOME=C:\jboss-4.0.x

   Unix:

   $ export JAVA_HOME=/usr/local/jdk1.5.0
   $ export JBOSS_HOME=/usr/local/jboss-4.0

3. Add ant to your execution path. Ant is the build utility.

   Windows:

   C:\workbook\ex07_1> set PATH=..\ant\bin;%PATH%

   Unix:

   $ export PATH=../ant/bin:$PATH

4. Perform the build by typing `ant`.

The *titan.jar* will be built. This JAR contains all the client and entity classes used in this example.

Examine the Entities

This exercise implements all of the entities from Chapter 7. You can find the implementations of the `Ship`, `Cabin`, `Cruise`, `Customer`, `Phone`, `CreditCard`, and `Reservation` classes in the `com.titan.domain` package in the *src* directory of the exercise. Take a moment to browse these files. We will not go into detail on every implementation of these files because this topic is already discussed in detail in Chapter 7.

Examine Client1

Client1 shows an example of manipulating the `@OneToOne` relationship between the Customer and Address entity beans. It illustrates how cascading affects the behavior of the `persist( )`, `merge( )`, and `remove( )` `EntityManager` methods. Let's examine this file.

Client1.java

```
package com.titan.clients;

import javax.persistence.EntityManagerFactory;
import javax.persistence.EntityManager;
```

```
import javax.persistence.EntityTransaction;
import javax.persistence.Persistence;

import com.titan.domain.*;

public class Client1
{
   public static void main(String[] args) throws Exception
   {
```

Because we're using Java Persistence in a standalone application, we first obtain access to an EntityManagerFactory instance so that we can obtain EntityManager instances:

```
      try
      {
         EntityManagerFactory factory =
            Persistence.createEntityManagerFactory("titan");
         Customer cust = createCustomerAddress(factory);
         cascadeMergeAddress(factory, cust);
         cascadeRemoveAddress(factory, cust);
      }
      finally
      {
         factory.close( );
      }
   }
```

The example first calls the createCustomerAddress( ) method to initialize the database. Then, the cascadeMergeAddress( ) method is called to show the effects of cascading and merging. Finally, the cascadeRemoveAddress( ) method is called to display the effects of cascading with the EntityManager.remove( ) operation. Let's examine each method.

createCustomerAddress( )

```
   public static Customer createCustomerAddress(EntityManagerFactory factory)
   {
      Customer cust = new Customer( );
      cust.setFirstName("Bill");
      cust.setLastName("Burke");
      Address address = new Address( );
      address.setStreet("Beacon Street");
      address.setCity("Boston");
      address.setState("MA");
      address.setZip("02115");
      cust.setAddress(address);
```

The method begins by allocating a Customer and Address and then initializing their properties. The Customer-Address relationship is set up as well.

```
      EntityManager manager = factory.createEntityManager( );
      try {
```

```
        manager.getTransaction().begin( );
        manager.persist(cust);
        manager.getTransaction().commit( );
```

Next, the method creates an EntityManager instance and begins a resource-local transaction. The Customer instance is then persisted using EntityManager.persist( ). When the resource-local transaction is committed, a primary key is generated for the Customer and Address instances and both are inserted into the database. Given that the @OneToOne relationship has a CascadeType of ALL, you do not additionally need to persist( ) the Address instance. The entity manager does this operation automatically for you.

```
      } finally {
        manager.close( );
      }

      System.out.println("Address was also persisted with auto-generated key: "
                         + address.getId( ));
      System.out.println("Return detached Customer instance: " + cust.getId( ));
      return cust;
   }
```

The createCustomerAddress( ) method ends by first cleaning up the EntityManager instance and then outputting the generated primary keys of the Customer and Address instances.

cascadeMergeAddress( )

```
   public static void cascadeMergeAddress(EntityManagerFactory factory,
                                          Customer cust)
   {
      System.out.println("Show cascade merge( )");
      cust.getAddress( ).setStreet("1 Yawkey Way");
```

Outside of a transaction, the Customer entity's street address is updated.

```
      EntityManager manager = factory.createEntityManager( );
      try {
        manager.getTransaction().begin( );
        manager.merge(cust);
        manager.getTransaction().commit( );
```

The code then begins a resource-local transaction and merges the Customer instance. Because the CascadeType is ALL for the Customer's address property, the entity manager will traverse the Address relationship and merge the changes to the Address's street. After the merge, the changes are committed to the database.

```
        manager.clear( );
        Customer custCopy = manager.find(Customer.class, cust.getId( ));
        System.out.println(custCopy.getAddress().getStreet( ));
```

To indicate that the customer's street address has actually changed in the database, the code detaches all managed entity instances and queries for the Customer entity again.

```
        } finally {
           manager.close( );
        }
     }
```

Finally, the created EntityManager instance is cleaned up.

cascadeRemoveAddress( )

```
     public static void cascadeRemoveAddress(EntityManagerFactory factory, Customer
  cust)
     {
        System.out.println("Show cascade remove( )");
        EntityManager manager = factory.createEntityManager( );
        try {
           manager.getTransaction().begin( );
           Customer custCopy = manager.find(Customer.class, cust.getId( ));
           manager.remove(custCopy);
           manager.getTransaction().commit( );
```

This part of the method begins a new resource-local transaction and removes the Customer entity from the database. Again, because the Customer's address property has a CascadeType of ALL, the related Address is removed along with the Customer.

```
           Address addressCopy = manager.find(Address.class, cust.getAddress( ).getId(
  ));
           System.out.println("addressCopy is null: " + addressCopy);
        } finally {
           manager.close( );
        }
     }
  }
```

Finally, the code shows that the related Address has been removed from the database by querying for it and showing that the value is null.

Run Client1

Run the Client1 application by invoking ant run.client1 at the command prompt. Remember to set your JBOSS_HOME and PATH environment variables. This is the output:

```
run.client1:
     [java] Create 1st Customer
     [java] Address was also persisted with auto-generated key: 1
     [java] Return detached Customer instance: 1
     [java] Show cascade merge( )
     [java] 1 Yawkey Way
     [java] Show cascade remove( )
     [java] addressCopy is null: null
```

Examine Client2

Client2 shows an example of how a cascaded merge will also create related entities in the database if they do not already exist. Let's examine this file.

Client2.java

```
package com.titan.clients;

import javax.persistence.EntityManagerFactory;
import javax.persistence.EntityManager;
import javax.persistence.EntityTransaction;
import javax.persistence.Persistence;

import com.titan.domain.*;

public class Client2
{
   public static void main(String[] args) throws Exception
   {
      EntityManagerFactory factory =
         Persistence.createEntityManagerFactory("titan");
```

Because this is a standalone Java application, we again need to obtain an `EntityManagerFactory` to create our `EntityManager` instances:

```
      try
      {
         Customer cust = Client1.createCustomerAddress(factory);
         addPhoneNumbers(factory, cust);
      }
      finally
      {
         factory.close( );
      }
   }
```

The example creates the same Customer entity that Client1 does by calling that program's `createCustomerAddress( )` method. This method returns a detached `Customer` instance. It then adds some phone numbers to the detached `Customer` in the `addPhoneNumbers( )` method. Let's look at the implementation of this method:

```
   public static void addPhoneNumbers(EntityManagerFactory factory,
                                      Customer cust)
   {
      Phone phone1 = new Phone( );
      phone1.setNumber("617-666-6666");
      phone1.setType((byte)1);
      cust.getPhoneNumbers( ).add(phone1);
```

Outside of a transaction, the code first allocates a Phone entity and adds it to the detached `Customer`'s set of `phoneNumbers`.

```
        EntityManager manager = factory.createEntityManager( );
        try {
           manager.getTransaction().begin( );
           manager.merge(cust);
           manager.getTransaction().commit( );
     }
```

Next, within a resource-local transaction, the code merges the modified Customer instance. Because the Customer's phoneNumbers property has a CascadeType of ALL, the merge( ) operation sees that the phoneNumbers property has a brand-new Phone instance within it and inserts this new entity into the database.

```
           manager.clear( );
           Customer custCopy = manager.find(Customer.class, cust.getId( ));
           for (Phone phone : custCopy.getPhoneNumbers( ))
           {
              System.out.println("Phone number: " + phone.getNumber( ));
           }
        } finally {
           manager.close( );
        }
     }
  }
```

Finally, the code detaches all entity instances from the entity manager by calling EntityManager.clear( ) and queries for a new copy of the Customer entity. Examining the new copy shows that the phone number was added to the Customer-Phone relationship.

Run Client2

Run the Client2 application by invoking ant run.client2 at the command prompt. Remember to set your JBOSS_HOME and PATH environment variables. This is the output:

```
run.client2:
     [java] Create 1st Customer
     [java] Address was also persisted with auto-generated key: 1
     [java] Return detached Customer instance: 1
     [java] Phone number: 617-666-6666
```

Exercise 7.2: Inverse Relationships

This exercise illustrates what happens when you modify only the inverse side of a relationship.

Start Up JBoss

There is no need to start up JBoss in this example because standalone persistence is being used.

Initialize the Database

The database tables will be created when the clients in this exercise run. The database is an in-memory-only database and will not be available when the program completes.

Build the Example Programs

Perform the following steps:

1. Open a command prompt or shell terminal and change to the *ex07_2* directory created by the extraction process.
2. Set the `JAVA_HOME` and `JBOSS_HOME` environment variables to point to where your JDK and JBoss 4.0 are installed. Examples:

   Windows:

   ```
   C:\workbook\ex07_2> set JAVA_HOME=C:\jdk1.5.0
   C:\workbook\ex07_2> set JBOSS_HOME=C:\jboss-4.0.x
   ```

   Unix:

   ```
   $ export JAVA_HOME=/usr/local/jdk1.5.0
   $ export JBOSS_HOME=/usr/local/jboss-4.0
   ```

3. Add `ant` to your execution path. Ant is the build utility.

   Windows:

   ```
   C:\workbook\ex07_2> set PATH=..\ant\bin;%PATH%
   ```

   Unix:

   ```
   $ export PATH=../ant/bin:$PATH
   ```

4. Perform the build by typing `ant`.

The *titan.jar* will be built. This JAR contains all the client and entity classes used in this example.

Examine the Entities

This exercise implements all of the entities from Chapter 7. You can find the implementations of the `Ship`, `Cabin`, `Cruise`, `Customer`, `Phone`, `CreditCard`, and `Reservation` entity classes in the `com.titan.domain` package in the *src* directory of the exercise. Take a moment to browse these files. We will not go over the implementation of these files because it is already discussed in detail in Chapter 7.

Examine Client1

Client1 illustrates an example of manipulating the inverse side of an `@OneToOne` relationship. It creates a `CreditCard` instance, sets the `customer` property of this relationship, and persists the `CreditCard`. It shows that since the `CreditCard` is the inverse side of the Customer-CreditCard relationship, the relationship is not stored in the database. Let's examine this file.

Client1.java

```
package com.titan.clients;

import javax.persistence.EntityManagerFactory;
import javax.persistence.EntityManager;
import javax.persistence.EntityTransaction;
import javax.persistence.Persistence;

import com.titan.domain.*;

public class Client1
{
   public static void main(String[] args) throws Exception
   {
      EntityManagerFactory factory =
         Persistence.createEntityManagerFactory("titan");
```

Because we're not running this example inside an application server, we need to fetch an `EntityManagerFactory` to obtain `EntityManager` instances with which we can work:

```
      try
      {
         Customer cust = createCustomerAddress(factory);
         createCreditCard(factory, cust);
      }
      finally
      {
         factory.close( );
      }
   }
```

First, we create a `Customer` in the database using the `createCustomerAddress( )` method. We will not go over the details of this method because it is the same as the method in Exercise 7.1. Next, a `CreditCard` is added to the `Customer` within the `createCreditCard( )` method:

```
   public static Customer createCreditCard(
            EntityManagerFactory factory, Customer cust)
   {
      CreditCard card = new CreditCard( );
      card.setExpirationDate(new java.util.Date( ));
      card.setNumber("4444-4444-4444-4444");
      card.setNameOnCard("William Burke");
      card.setCreditOrganization("Capital One");
      card.setCustomer(cust);
```

This method starts by allocating an instance of a `CreditCard` entity. Notice that the `customer` property is set with the detached customer we created earlier in the program.

```
        EntityManager manager = factory.createEntityManager( );
        try {
           manager.getTransaction().begin( );
           manager.persist(card);
           manager.getTransaction().commit( );
```

Next, the CreditCard instance is persisted in the database within a resource-local transaction. Because CreditCard is the inverse side of the @OneToOne relationship between Customer and CreditCard, the relationship will not be wired in the database even though we set CreditCard's customer property.

```
           // Show that card.getCustomer( ) returns null

           manager.clear( );
           CreditCard cardCopy = manager.find(CreditCard.class, card.getId( ));
           System.out.println("should be null: " + cardCopy.getCustomer( ));
```

We begin a new resource-local transaction to retrieve a new copy of the CreditCard. The card's customer property is output to show that the related Customer instance is null.

```
           manager.getTransaction().begin( );
           System.out.println("now set the owning side of the relationship");
           Customer custCopy = manager.find(Customer.class, cust.getId( ));
           custCopy.setCreditCard(cardCopy);
           manager.getTransaction().commit( );
```

The relationship is then set correctly. The code retrieves a managed instance of the Customer and calls its setCreditCard( ) method. Because the Customer entity is the owning side of the relationship, the relationship is persisted when the transaction commits:

```
           manager.clear( );
           cardCopy = manager.find(CreditCard.class, card.getId( ));
           System.out.println("should be set now: " +
                              cardCopy.getCustomer().getFirstName( ));
        } finally {
           manager.close( );
        }
        return cust;
     }
  ...
  }
```

Finally, a new copy of the CreditCard is fetched from the database to show that the Customer relationship is now set.

Run Client1

Run the Client1 application by invoking ant run.client1 at the command prompt. Remember to set your JBOSS_HOME and PATH environment variables. This is the output:

```
run.client1:
     [java] Create 1st Customer
     [java] Address was also persisted with auto-generated key: 1
     [java] Return detached Customer instance: 1
     [java] should be null: null
     [java] now set the owning side of the relationship
     [java] should be set now: Bill
```

Exercise 7.3: Lazy Initialization

This example interacts with the Reservation entity to show the effects of lazy initialization when an entity becomes detached from a persistence context. Unlike the previous exercises in this chapter, this section runs within JBoss, so you will need to start it up.

Start Up JBoss

If you already have JBoss running, there is no reason to restart it. Otherwise, start it up as instructed in Workbook 1.

Build and Deploy the Example Programs

Perform the following steps:

1. Open a command prompt or shell terminal and change to the *ex07_3* directory created by the extraction process.
2. Set the `JAVA_HOME` and `JBOSS_HOME` environment variables to point to where your JDK and JBoss 4.0 are installed. Examples:

   Windows:

   C:\workbook\ex07_3> set JAVA_HOME=C:\jdk1.5.0
   C:\workbook\ex07_3> set JBOSS_HOME=C:\jboss-4.0.x

   Unix:

   $ export JAVA_HOME=/usr/local/jdk1.5.0
   $ export JBOSS_HOME=/usr/local/jboss-4.0

3. Add `ant` to your execution path. Ant is the build utility.

   Windows:

   C:\workbook\ex07_3> set PATH=..\ant\bin;%PATH%

   Unix:

   $ export PATH=../ant/bin:$PATH

4. Perform the build by typing `ant`.

titan.jar is rebuilt, copied to the JBoss *deploy* directory, and redeployed by the application server.

Initialize the Database

The database tables are created when Exercise 7.3 is deployed to JBoss. If you have problems running this example, shut down JBoss and run the `clean.db` Ant task. The database is initialized by invoking `ant run.initialize` at the command prompt:

```
run.initialize:
    [java] added Bill Burke
    [java] added Sacha Labourey
    [java] added Marc Fleury
    [java] added Queen Mary ship
    [java] added Titanic ship
    [java] added Queen Cabin 1 to Queen Mary
    [java] added Queen Cabin 2 to Queen Mary
    [java] Titanic Cabin 1 to Titanic
    [java] Titanic Cabin 2 to Titanic
    [java] Titanic Cabin 3 to Titanic
    [java] added Alaskan Cruise on the Queen Mary
    [java] added Atlantic Cruise on the Titanic
    [java] Booked Bill and Sacha on Alaskan cruise in Cabin 1 and Cabin 2
    [java] Booked Marc in Cabin 1 on the Atlantic Cruise on the Titanic.  Say hi
    to Leo for us!
```

This task calls the DataAccess EJB (shown later) to create a few reservations in the database. Since we're running inside JBoss, take a chance to bring up the Hypersonic SQL Database Manager so that you can review the database schema that was created for the entities in this exercise (see Figure W-12).

If you don't remember how to bring up this tool, refer to Workbook 2.

Examine the DataAccess EJB

The DataAccess EJB sits in the `com.titan.access` package. This stateless session bean has a method that seeds the database with several entity instances of our Titan Reservation system, which we won't go over. It also has some methods to fetch the reservations we've made. One fetch method returns `Reservation` instances that have uninitialized relationship properties. The other data access method traverses these relationships so that they are initialized when the `Reservation` instances are sent back to the client.

DataAccessBean.java

```
@Stateless
public class DataAccessBean implements DataAccess
{
   @PersistenceContext(unitName="titan") EntityManager manager;

   public List fetchReservations( )
   {
      return manager.createQuery("FROM Reservation res").getResultList( );
   }
```

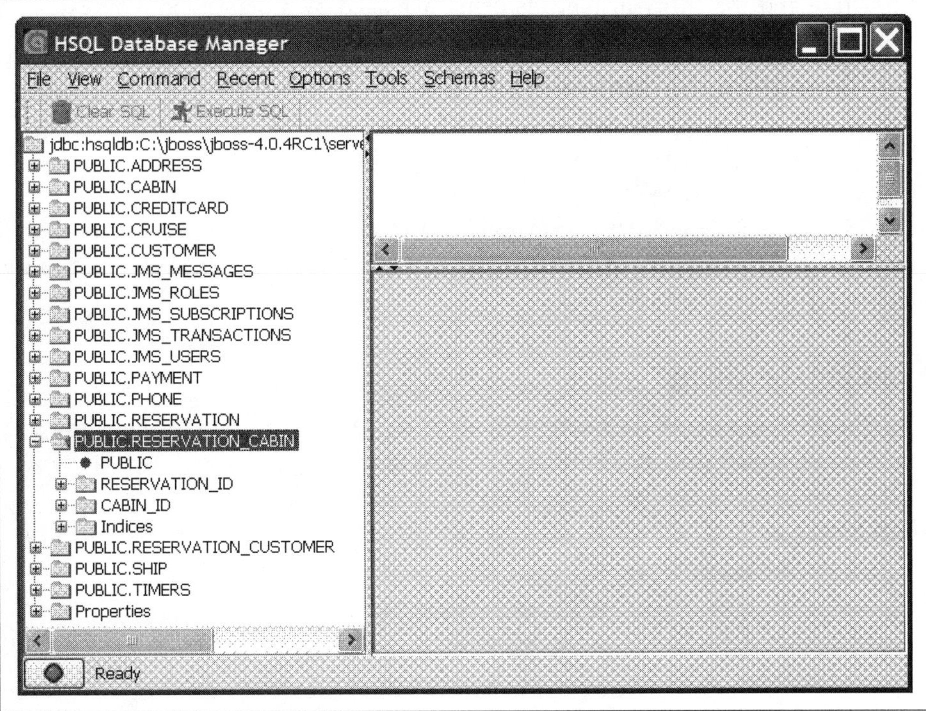

Figure W-12. Database Manager

When this query executes, it pulls all reservations from the database. Because the default `fetch()` attribute for the Reservation's `@ManyToMany` relationships is `LAZY`, the `cabins` and `customers` properties will not be initialized in the `Reservation` instances that are passed back to the client. `@ManyToOne` relationships are eagerly loaded by default, so the cruise property is initialized.

```
public List fetchReservationsWithRelationships( )
{
   List list = manager.createQuery("FROM Reservation res").getResultList( );
   for (Object obj : list)
   {
      Reservation res = (Reservation)obj;
      res.getCabins().size( );
      res.getCustomers().size( );
   }
   return list;
}
```

The `fetchReservationsWithRelationships( )` method queries all the Reservations in the database, but also traverses the `cabins` and `customers` properties within the transaction so that they are fetched and initialized when the `Reservation` instances are returned to the client. When you traverse a lazily loaded relationship within a transaction and the entity instance is being managed by a persistence context, Java Persistence will fetch the relationships.

```
      public String initializeDatabase( )
      {
...
      }
   }
```

We will not discuss the initializeDatabase( ) method because it is pretty boring. If you want to see how all the entities are created and wired together, open up this file and browse it.

Examine the Client

The Client interacts with the fetch methods of the DataAccess EJB to show how lazy initialization affects detached entities. Let's examine it.

Client.java

```
public class Client
{
    public static void main(String [] args)
    {
        try
        {
            Context jndiContext = getInitialContext( );
            Object ref = jndiContext.lookup(DataAccess.class.getName( ));
            DataAccess dao = (DataAccess)
                PortableRemoteObject.narrow(ref,DataAccess.class);
```

We start by obtaining an InitialContext and looking up a remote reference to the DataAccess EJB.

```
            System.out.println("Fetch reservations with loaded relationships");
            System.out.println( );
            List list = dao.fetchReservationsWithRelationships( );
            for (Object obj : list)
            {
               Reservation res = (Reservation)obj;
               System.out.println("Reservation for: " + res.getCruise().getName( ));
               System.out.println("\tNum cabins: " + res.getCabins().size( ));
               System.out.println("\tNum customers: "
                                     + res.getCustomers().size( ));
            }
```

The fetchReservationsWithRelationships( ) method on DataAccess is called, and we iterate through the Relationships to print out the cruise name, the number of cabins reserved, and who reserved them. This loop executes successfully because the fetchReservationsWithRelationships( ) method traverses and loads the relationships on the server.

```
            System.out.println("----------");
            System.out.println("Try to access uninitialized relationships");
            System.out.println("----------");
            list = dao.fetchReservations( );
            for (Object obj : list)
            {
               Reservation res = (Reservation)obj;
               System.out.println("Reservation for: "
                      + res.getCruise().getName( ));
```

Next, we do the same iteration, except we get the list of `Reservation` instances from the `fetchReservations( )` method. As you saw before, this method is different because it only queries for the Reservations and doesn't initialize any of the lazily loaded relationships. When you run this, you will see that the `cruise` property is initialized because `@ManyToOne` relationships are eagerly loaded by default.

```
               try
               {
                  System.out.println("\tNum cabins: " + res.getCabins().size( ));
                  System.out.println("\tNum customers: " + res.getCustomers( ).size(
));
               }
               catch (org.hibernate.LazyInitializationException ex)
               {
                  System.out.println(ex.getMessage( ));
               }
```

However, when the `cabins` property is traversed, `org.hibernate.LazyInitializationException` is thrown. Hibernate does not allow you to traverse an uninitialized relationship and aborts the operation instead.

```
            }
         }
         catch (javax.naming.NamingException ne)
         {
            ne.printStackTrace( );
         }
      }

      public static Context getInitialContext( )
         throws javax.naming.NamingException
      {
         return new javax.naming.InitialContext( );
      }
   }
```

The rest of *Client.java* is pretty uninteresting.

Run the Client

Run the Client application by invoking `ant run.client` at the command prompt. Remember to set your `JBOSS_HOME` and `PATH` environment variables. This is the output:

```
run.client:
     [java] Fetch reservations with loaded relationships

     [java] Reservation for: Alaskan Cruise
     [java]     Num cabins: 2
     [java]     Num customers: 2
     [java] Reservation for: Atlantic Cruise
     [java]     Num cabins: 1
     [java]     Num customers: 1
     [java] ----------
     [java] Try to access uninitialized relationships
     [java] ----------
     [java] Reservation for: Alaskan Cruise
     [java] failed to lazily initialize a collection of role: com.titan.domain.
Reservation.cabins, no session or session
 was closed
     [java] Reservation for: Atlantic Cruise
     [java] failed to lazily initialize a collection of role: com.titan.domain.
Reservation.cabins, no session or session
 was closed
```

WORKBOOK 6

Exercises for Chapter 8

Chapter 8 of the EJB book walked you through some basic examples of mapping inheritance hierarchies. The exercises in this chapter use the code from Chapter 8 to show you each inheritance mapping strategy in action.

Exercise 8.1: Single Table per Hierarchy

This exercise maps the Person-Customer-Employee hierarchy shown in Chapter 8 using the `SINGLE_TABLE` inheritance mapping strategy.

Start Up JBoss

If you already have JBoss running, there is no reason to restart it. Otherwise, start it up as instructed in Workbook 1.

Initialize the Database

The database tables will be created when Exercise 8.1 is deployed to JBoss. If you have problems running this example, shut down JBoss and run the `clean.db` Ant task.

Build and Deploy the Example Programs

Perform the following steps:

1. Open a command prompt or shell terminal and change to the *ex08_1* directory created by the extraction process.
2. Set the `JAVA_HOME` and `JBOSS_HOME` environment variables to point to where your JDK and JBoss 4.0 are installed. Examples:

   Windows:

   ```
   C:\workbook\ex08_1> set JAVA_HOME=C:\jdk1.5.0
   C:\workbook\ex08_1> set JBOSS_HOME=C:\jboss-4.0.x
   ```

Unix:

```
$ export JAVA_HOME=/usr/local/jdk1.5.0
$ export JBOSS_HOME=/usr/local/jboss-4.0
```

3. Add ant to your execution path. Ant is the build utility.

   Windows:

   ```
   C:\workbook\ex08_1> set PATH=..\ant\bin;%PATH%
   ```

   Unix:

   ```
   $ export PATH=../ant/bin:$PATH
   ```

4. Perform the build by typing `ant`.

titan.jar is rebuilt, copied to the JBoss *deploy* directory, and redeployed by the application server.

Examine the Database Schema

Now that you have built the example, look at the database schema by going to the JMX management console and bringing up the Hypersonic Database Manager described in previous chapters. This will allow you to see how the code in Chapter 8 maps to an autogenerated database (see Figure W-13).

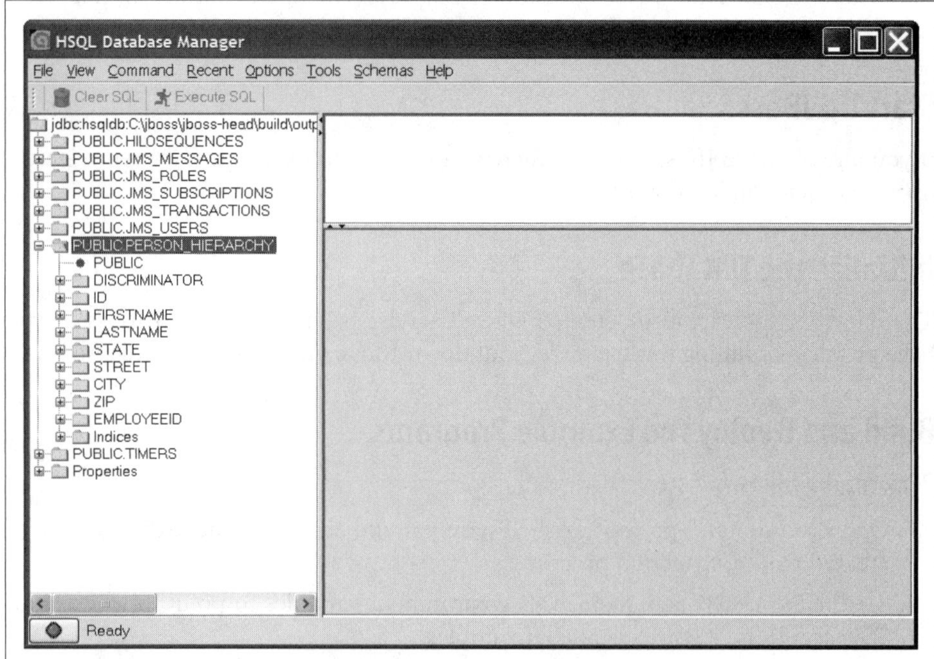

Figure W-13. PERSON_HIERARCHY Table

The Hypersonic Database Manager is particularly useful in the exercises in this chapter because the code is basically the same, but the schema is different for each example.

Examine the Code

We're not going to examine any of the entity classes in this chapter because they are already discussed in detail in Chapter 8. Instead, we will look at the stateless session bean that has business methods to initialize and query the database, as well as the client code.

DataAccessBean.java

```
package com.titan.access;

import javax.ejb.Stateless;
import javax.persistence.EntityManager;
import javax.persistence.PersistenceContext;
import java.util.List;

import com.titan.domain.*;

@Stateless
public class DataAccessBean implements DataAccessRemote
{
   @PersistenceContext private EntityManager manager;

   public void initializeDatabase( )
   {
      Person p = new Person( );
      p.setFirstName("Bill");
      p.setLastName("Burke");
      manager.persist(p);

      Customer cust = new Customer( );
      cust.setFirstName("Sacha");
      cust.setLastName("Labourey");
      cust.setStreet("C'est La Vie");
      cust.setCity("Neuchatel");
      cust.setState("Switzerland");
      cust.setZip("3332002-111");
      manager.persist(cust);

      Employee employee = new Employee( );
      employee.setFirstName("Gavin");
      employee.setLastName("King");
      employee.setStreet("1st Street");
      employee.setCity("Atlanta");
      employee.setState("GA");
      employee.setZip("33320");
```

```
        employee.setEmployeeId(15);
        manager.persist(employee);

    }
```

The initializeDatabase( ) method simply allocates and persists three entity beans. These three beans are of type Person, Customer, and Employee, respectively.

```
    public List findAllPersons( )
    {
        return manager.createQuery("FROM Person p").getResultList( );
    }
}
```

The findAllPersons( ) method creates and executes a query that pulls all Person entities from the database. Because Person is the root of a mapped inheritance hierarchy, this query is polymorphic and returns all Person, Customer, and Employee records.

Client.java

```
package com.titan.clients;

import com.titan.access.DataAccessRemote;
import com.titan.domain.*;

import javax.naming.InitialContext;
import javax.naming.Context;
import javax.naming.NamingException;
import java.util.List;

import javax.rmi.PortableRemoteObject;

public class Client
{
    public static void main(String [] args)
    {
        try
        {
            Context jndiContext = getInitialContext( );
            Object ref = jndiContext.lookup("DataAccessBean/remote");
            DataAccessRemote dao = (DataAccessRemote)
                PortableRemoteObject.narrow(ref,DataAccessRemote.class);
            dao.initializeDatabase( );
            List persons = dao.findAllPersons( );
            System.out.println("persons.size() = " + persons.size( ));
            for (Object obj : persons)
            {
               Person p = (Person)obj;
               System.out.println("\tclass is: " + p.getClass().getName( ));
               System.out.println("\tperson: " + p.getFirstName( ) + " "
                              + p.getLastName( ));
            }
        }
```

```
            catch (javax.naming.NamingException ne)
            {
               ne.printStackTrace( );
            }
        }

        public static Context getInitialContext( )
            throws javax.naming.NamingException
        {
            return new javax.naming.InitialContext( );
        }
    }
```

The client code simply looks up the remote interface of the DataAccess EJB and invokes its two methods. It iterates through the list returned from `findAllPersons( )` and shows that the query returned the entities created earlier.

Run the Client

Run the Client application by invoking `ant run.client` at the command prompt. Remember to set your `JBOSS_HOME` and `PATH` environment variables. This is the output:

```
run.client:
     [java] persons.size( ) = 3
     [java]     class is: com.titan.domain.Person
     [java]     person: Bill Burke
     [java]     class is: com.titan.domain.Customer
     [java]     person: Sacha Labourey
     [java]     class is: com.titan.domain.Employee
     [java]     person: Gavin King
```

Exercise 8.2: Single Table per Hierarchy

This exercise maps the Person-Customer-Employee hierarchy using the `TABLE_PER_CLASS` inheritance mapping strategy.

Start Up JBoss

If you already have JBoss running, there is no reason to restart it. Otherwise, start it up as instructed in Workbook 1.

Initialize the Database

The database tables will be created when Exercise 8.2 is deployed to JBoss. If you have problems running this example, shut down JBoss and run the `clean.db` Ant task.

Build and Deploy the Example Programs

Perform the following steps:

1. Open a command prompt or shell terminal and change to the *ex08_2* directory created by the extraction process.
2. Set the `JAVA_HOME` and `JBOSS_HOME` environment variables to point to where your JDK and JBoss 4.0 are installed. Examples:

   Windows:

   ```
   C:\workbook\ex08_2> set JAVA_HOME=C:\jdk1.5.0
   C:\workbook\ex08_2> set JBOSS_HOME=C:\jboss-4.0.x
   ```

   Unix:

   ```
   $ export JAVA_HOME=/usr/local/jdk1.5.0
   $ export JBOSS_HOME=/usr/local/jboss-4.0
   ```

3. Add `ant` to your execution path. Ant is the build utility.

   Windows:

   ```
   C:\workbook\ex08_2> set PATH=..\ant\bin;%PATH%
   ```

   Unix:

   ```
   $ export PATH=../ant/bin:$PATH
   ```

4. Perform the build by typing `ant`.

As in the last exercise, *titan.jar* is rebuilt, copied to the JBoss *deploy* directory, and redeployed by the application server.

Examine the Database Schema

Now that you have built the example, look at the database schema by going to the JMX management console and bringing up the Hypersonic Database Manager described in previous chapters. This will allow you to see how the code in Chapter 8 maps to an autogenerated database (see Figure W-14).

The Hypersonic Database Manager is particularly useful in the exercises in this chapter because the code is basically the same, but the schema is different for each example.

Examine the Code

The code for this exercise is exactly the same as Exercise 8.1, except that the entity classes are mapped using the `TABLE_PER_CLASS` inheritance strategy and there is one minor change to the `DataAccessBean` class. We do not use auto-primary-key generation for this example. The default generation strategy Hibernate uses for the Hypersonic SQL database engine is the `IDENTITY` strategy. This generation technique is not compatible with the SQL `UNION`s that are needed to perform the mappings internally.

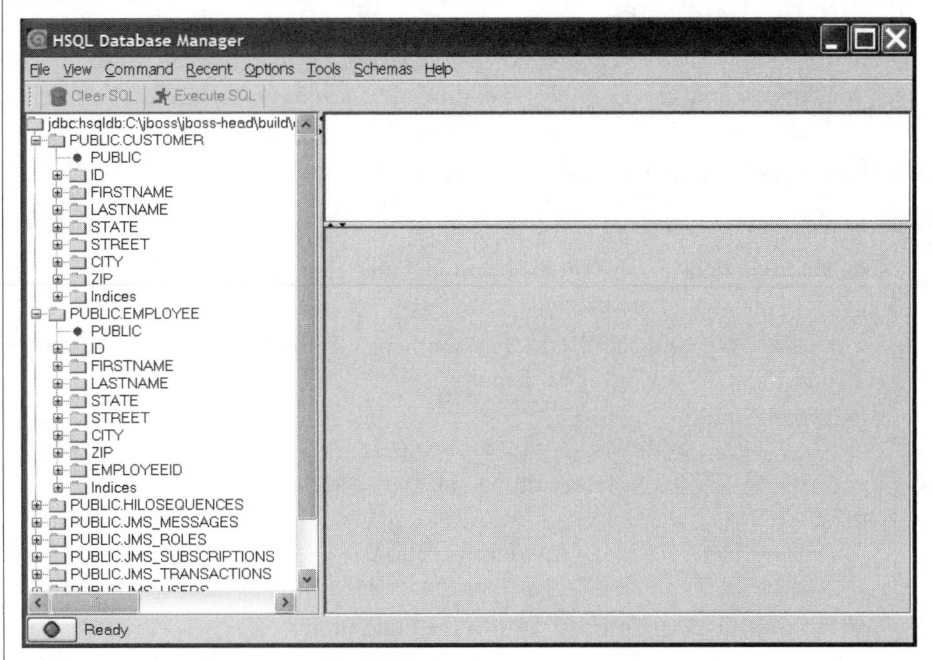

Figure W-14. TABLE_PER_CLASS Schema

Run the Client

Run the Client application by invoking `ant run.client` at the command prompt. Remember to set your `JBOSS_HOME` and `PATH` environment variables. This is the output:

```
run.client:
     [java] persons.size( ) = 3
     [java]      class is: com.titan.domain.Person
     [java]      person: Bill Burke
     [java]      class is: com.titan.domain.Customer
     [java]      person: Sacha Labourey
     [java]      class is: com.titan.domain.Employee
     [java]      person: Gavin King
```

Exercise 8.3: JOINED Inheritance Strategy

This exercise maps the Person-Customer-Employee hierarchy using the `JOINED` inheritance mapping strategy.

Start Up JBoss

If you already have JBoss running, there is no reason to restart it. Otherwise, start it up as instructed in Workbook 1.

Initialize the Database

The database tables will be created when Exercise 8.3 is deployed to JBoss. If you have problems running this example, shut down JBoss and run the `clean.db` Ant task.

Build and Deploy the Example Programs

Perform the following steps:

1. Open a command prompt or shell terminal and change to the *ex08_3* directory created by the extraction process.
2. Set the `JAVA_HOME` and `JBOSS_HOME` environment variables to point to where your JDK and JBoss 4.0 are installed. Examples:

   Windows:

   ```
   C:\workbook\ex08_3> set JAVA_HOME=C:\jdk1.5.0
   C:\workbook\ex08_3> set JBOSS_HOME=C:\jboss-4.0.x
   ```

   Unix:

   ```
   $ export JAVA_HOME=/usr/local/jdk1.5.0
   $ export JBOSS_HOME=/usr/local/jboss-4.0
   ```

3. Add `ant` to your execution path. Ant is the build utility.

   Windows:

   ```
   C:\workbook\ex08_3> set PATH=..\ant\bin;%PATH%
   ```

   Unix:

   ```
   $ export PATH=../ant/bin:$PATH
   ```

4. Perform the build by typing `ant`.

As in the last exercise, *titan.jar* is rebuilt, copied to the JBoss *deploy* directory, and redeployed by the application server.

Examine the Database Schema

Now that you have built the example, look at the database schema by going to the JMX management console and bringing up the Hypersonic Database Manager described in previous chapters. This will allow you to see how the code in Chapter 8 maps to an autogenerated database (see Figure W-15).

The Hypersonic Database Manager is particularly useful in the exercises in this chapter because the code is basically the same, but the schema is different for each example.

Examine the Code

The code for this exercise is exactly the same as Exercise 8.1, except that the entity classes are mapped using the `JOINED` inheritance strategy.

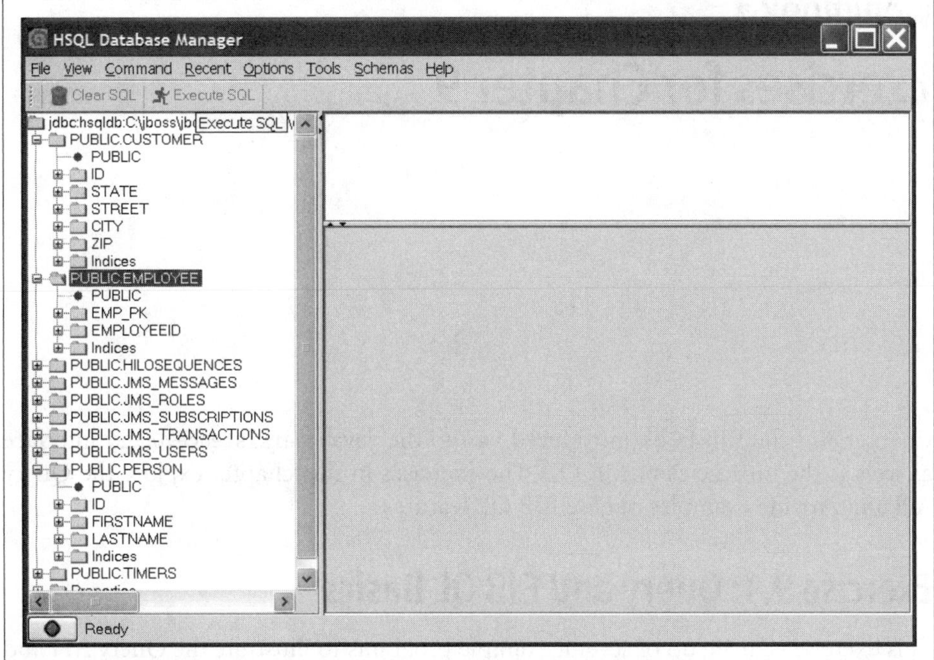

Figure W-15. JOINED Strategy Schema

Run the Client

Run the Client application by invoking ant run.client at the command prompt. Remember to set your JBOSS_HOME and PATH environment variables. This is the output:

```
run.client:
     [java] persons.size() = 3
     [java]     class is: com.titan.domain.Person
     [java]     person: Bill Burke
     [java]     class is: com.titan.domain.Customer
     [java]     person: Sacha Labourey
     [java]     class is: com.titan.domain.Employee
     [java]     person: Gavin King
```

WORKBOOK 7

Exercises for Chapter 9

Chapter 9 of the EJB book introduced you to the `javax.persistence.Query` interface as well as the intricacies of EJB QL. The exercises in this chapter explore the Query API and provide examples of base EJB QL features.

Exercise 9.1: Query and EJB QL Basics

This exercise is made up of several example programs to illustrate the Query API and the basic features of EJB QL. The example programs run outside of the application server, so there is no need to start up JBoss.

Initialize the Database

The standalone Java Persistence solution initializes the Hypersonic SQL database and generates the database schema each time one of the sample programs is run. This is an in-memory database, so you will not see any files created for the database.

Build the Example Programs

Perform the following steps:

1. Open a command prompt or shell terminal and change to the *ex09_1* directory created by the extraction process.
2. Set the `JAVA_HOME` and `JBOSS_HOME` environment variables to point to where your JDK and JBoss 4.0 are installed. Examples:

   Windows:

   ```
   C:\workbook\ex09_1> set JAVA_HOME=C:\jdk1.5.0
   C:\workbook\ex09_1> set JBOSS_HOME=C:\jboss-4.0.x
   ```

   Unix:

   ```
   $ export JAVA_HOME=/usr/local/jdk1.5.0
   $ export JBOSS_HOME=/usr/local/jboss-4.0
   ```

3. Add ant to your execution path. Ant is the build utility.

   Windows:

   C:\workbook\ex09_1> set PATH=..\ant\bin;%PATH%

   Unix:

   $ export PATH=../ant/bin:$PATH

4. Perform the build by typing ant.

Example Basics

Each example program starts off in the same way. It creates an EntityManagerFactory and populates the database with some seed data:

```
public static void main(String[] args) throws Exception
{
   HashMap map = new HashMap( );
   //map.put("hibernate.show_sql", "true");
   EntityManagerFactory factory =
      Persistence.createEntityManagerFactory("titan", map);
   EntityManager entityManager = factory.createEntityManager( );
```

Hibernate Java Persistence implementation allows you to log each SQL query by setting the hibernate.show_sql property within the java.util.Map that is passed to Persistence.createEntityManagerFactory( ). Each example program has this option turned off by default, but you can enable it by uncommenting the map initialization:

```
   entityManager.getTransaction().begin( );
   try
   {
      System.out.println("Initialize DB");
      InitializeDB.initialize(entityManager);
```

The com.titan.clients.InitializeDB class is responsible for populating the database with some initial Customer, Ship, Cabin, Cruise, and Reservation entity data. We will not go over this class, but you might want to browse it to see the basic structure of the initialized database.

Parameters and Paging

The first example illustrates how to pass in parameters to a javax.persistence.Query and how to page the results of a query. The code for this example is in *com/titan/clients/ParametersAndPaging.java*. After creating the EntityManagerFactory and populating the database, the first part of the example calls the findCustomerByNamedParameter( ) method to demonstrate how you can pass named parameters to a Query object:

```
public static Customer findCustomerByNamedParameter(
      EntityManager entityManager, String first, String last)
{
```

```
    Query query = entityManager.createQuery("from Customer c " +
                                            " where c.firstName=:first" +
                                            " and c.lastName=:last");
    query.setParameter("first", first);
    query.setParameter("last", last);
    return (Customer)query.getSingleResult( );
}
```

The EJB QL defines two named parameters for the query: first and last. These parameters are set with the Query.setParameter( ) methods and the query is executed.

The example then shows the same query, except that it uses indexed parameters rather than named parameters. The findCustomerByIndexedParameter( ) method illustrates this:

```
public static Customer findCustomerByIndexedParameter(
        EntityManager entityManager, String first, String last)
{
    Query query = entityManager.createQuery("from Customer c " +
                                            " where c.firstName=?1" +
                                            " and c.lastName=?2");
    query.setParameter(1, first);
    query.setParameter(2, last);
    return (Customer)query.getSingleResult( );
}
```

The EJB QL defines two indexed parameters for the query: ?1 and ?2. These parameters are set with the Query.setParameter( ) method and the query is executed.

The final part of the program shows how you can page results from a query. Paging allows you to control how much data is returned by a query. When a query references thousands of rows in a database, you will want to limit the number of entities that are in memory at one time. Let's look at how the example program uses paging:

```
System.out.println("Output all customers via paging");
List results;
int first = 0;
int max = 2;
do
{
    results = getCustomers(entityManager, max, first);
    Iterator it = results.iterator( );
    while (it.hasNext( ))
    {
        Customer c = (Customer)it.next( );
        System.out.println(c.getFirstName() + " " + c.getLastName( ));
    }
    entityManager.clear( );
    first = first + results.size( );
} while (results.size( ) > 0);
```

The code is a simple example that outputs all Customer entities stored in the database by delegating to the getCustomers( ) method. This method pulls a fixed-size set of Customer entities. The EntityManager.clear( ) method is invoked to release

Customer entities that are no longer being used. Although our example program does not have many customers in the database, this may not be true on a live system. Because a queried entity remains managed until the persistence context is closed, you may run out of memory quickly if you are interacting with thousands of entity objects. Now let's take a look at the getCustomers( ) method:

```
public static List getCustomers(
          EntityManager entityManager, int max, int index)
{
   Query query = entityManager.createQuery("from Customer c");
   return query.setMaxResults(max).
      setFirstResult(index).
      getResultList( );
}
```

The getCustomers( ) method uses the max parameter to set the number of entities that should be returned by the query. The Query.setMaxResults( ) method sets this maximum value. The index parameter sets the first result we want to be returned by the query. The Query.setFirstResult( ) method sets this index.

Run the example

Run the ParametersAndPaging application by invoking ant run.parameters.paging at the command prompt. Remember to set your JBOSS_HOME and PATH environment variables. This is the output:

```
run.parameters.paging:
     [java] Initialize DB

     [java] Find Bill Burke by named parameter
     [java] Bill Burke's cust id: 2

     [java] Find Gavin King by indexed parameter
     [java] Gavin King's cust id: 6

     [java] Output all customers via paging
     [java] Richard Monson-Haefel
     [java] Bill Burke
     [java] Sacha Labourey
     [java] Marc Fleury
     [java] Monica Burke
     [java] Gavin King
```

The SELECT Clause

This example illustrates some basics about the EJB QL SELECT clause. Three separate queries are executed. The first shows how individual properties can be returned by a query. The second pulls entity properties from a nested relationship. The final example shows how you can wrap a result set in a constructed object. The code for this example is in *com/titan/clients/SelectClause.java*.

columnResultSet( )

```
public static void columnResultSet(EntityManager entityManager)
{
   System.out.println("Executing query: ");
   System.out.println("SELECT c.firstName, c.lastName FROM Customer AS c");
   Query query = entityManager.createQuery(
         "SELECT c.firstName, c.lastName FROM Customer AS c");
   List list = query.getResultList( );
   Iterator it = list.iterator( );
   while (it.hasNext( ))
   {
      Object[] result = (Object[])it.next( );
      System.out.println("\t" + result[0] + " " + result[1]);
   }
}
```

This method simply queries for the first name and last name of every customer in the database and outputs it to the screen. Unlike EJB 2.1 EJB QL, Java Persistence allows you to query for multiple entity properties.

nestedRelationshipPropertyResultSet( )

```
   public static void nestedRelationshipPropertyResultSet(EntityManager
entityManager)
   {
      System.out.println("Executing query: ");
      System.out.println("SELECT c.creditCard.creditCompany.address.city FROM
Customer AS c");
      Query query = entityManager.createQuery("SELECT c.creditCard.creditCompany.
address.city FROM Customer AS c");
      List list = query.getResultList( );
      Iterator it = list.iterator( );
      while (it.hasNext( ))
      {
         System.out.println("\t" + it.next( ));
      }
   }
```

This method shows a complex example of outputting all the cities of a customer's credit card company. As you can see, you can traverse a complex set of relationships to query the particular attribute in which you are interested.

constructorExpression( )

```
public static void constructorExpression(EntityManager entityManager)
{
   System.out.println("Executing query: ");
   System.out.println("SELECT " +
           "new com.titan.domain.Name(c.firstName, c.lastName) " +
           " FROM Customer c");
```

```
        Query query = entityManager.createQuery("SELECT new com.titan.domain.Name(c.
firstName, c.lastName) FROM Customer c");
        List list = query.getResultList( );
        Iterator it = list.iterator( );
        while (it.hasNext( ))
        {
           Name result = (Name)it.next( );
           System.out.println("\t" + result.getFirst() + " " + result.getLast( ));
        }
    }
```

This example shows you how you can wrap the result from a query within a plain Java object. It queries the first and last names of each customer and allocates a `com.titan.domain.Name` object for each row. The result set that is returned is a list of `Name` objects. This feature is very powerful for reporting.

Run the example

Run the SelectClause application by invoking `ant run.select.clause` at the command prompt. Remember to set your `JBOSS_HOME` and `PATH` environment variables. This is the output:

```
run.select.clause:
     [java] Initialize DB

     [java] Executing query:
     [java] SELECT c.firstName, c.lastName FROM Customer AS c
     [java]     Richard Monson-Haefel
     [java]     Bill Burke
     [java]     Sacha Labourey
     [java]     Marc Fleury
     [java]     Monica Burke
     [java]     Gavin King

     [java] Executing query:
     [java] SELECT c.creditCard.creditCompany.address.city FROM Customer AS c
     [java]     Richmond
     [java]     Richmond
     [java]     Charlotte
     [java]     Charlotte
     [java]     Charlotte

     [java] Executing query:
     [java] SELECT new com.titan.domain.Name(c.firstName, c.lastName)
            FROM Customer c
     [java]     Richard Monson-Haefel
     [java]     Bill Burke
     [java]     Sacha Labourey
     [java]     Marc Fleury
     [java]     Monica Burke
     [java]     Gavin King
```

The IN Operator and INNER JOIN

This example illustrates some basics about EJB QL inner joins. The queries are taken directly from Chapter 9 of the EJB book—specifically, from the section titled "The IN Operator and INNER JOIN"—so we won't go over the code. You should be able to understand what queries have been executed by looking at the output. The code for this example is in *com/titan/clients/InnerJoin.java*.

Run the example

Run the InnerJoin application by invoking `ant run.inner.join` at the command prompt. Remember to set your `JBOSS_HOME` and `PATH` environment variables. This is the output:

```
run.inner.join:
     [java] Initialize DB

     [java] THE IN OPERATOR and INNER JOIN
     [java] -------------------------------
     [java] SELECT r
     [java] FROM Customer AS c, IN( c.reservations ) r
     [java]    Reservation for Alaskan Cruise
     [java]    Reservation for Atlantic Cruise
     [java]    Reservation for Alaskan Cruise
     [java]    Reservation for Atlantic Cruise

     [java] SELECT r.cruise
     [java] FROM Customer AS c, IN( c.reservations ) r
     [java]    Cruise Alaskan Cruise
     [java]    Cruise Atlantic Cruise
     [java]    Cruise Alaskan Cruise
     [java]    Cruise Atlantic Cruise

     [java] SELECT cbn.ship
     [java] FROM Customer AS c, IN( c.reservations ) r,
     [java] IN( r.cabins ) AS cbn
     [java]    Ship Queen Mary
     [java]    Ship Queen Mary
     [java]    Ship Titanic
     [java]    Ship Queen Mary
     [java]    Ship Queen Mary
     [java]    Ship Titanic

     [java] SELECT cbn.ship
     [java] FROM Customer c INNER JOIN c.reservations r
     [java] INNER JOIN r.cabins cbn
     [java]    Ship Queen Mary
     [java]    Ship Queen Mary
     [java]    Ship Titanic
     [java]    Ship Queen Mary
     [java]    Ship Queen Mary
     [java]    Ship Titanic
```

LEFT JOIN

This example illustrates some basics about EJB QL left joins. The queries are taken directly from Chapter 9 of the EJB book—specifically, from the section titled "LEFT JOIN"—so we won't go over the code. You should be able to understand what queries have been executed by looking at the output. The code for this example is in *com/titan/clients/LeftJoin.java*.

Run the example

Run the LeftJoin application by invoking ant `run.left.join` at the command prompt. Remember to set your `JBOSS_HOME` and `PATH` environment variables. This is the output:

```
run.left.join:
     [java] Initialize DB

     [java] LEFT JOIN
     [java] --------------------------------
     [java] SELECT c.firstName, c.lastName, p.number
     [java] FROM Customer c LEFT JOIN c.phoneNumbers p
     [java]     Richard Monson-Haefel null
     [java]     Bill Burke 978-555-5555
     [java]     Bill Burke 617-555-5555
     [java]     Sacha Labourey null
     [java]     Marc Fleury null
     [java]     Monica Burke 617-555-5555
     [java]     Gavin King null
```

Fetch Joins

This example demonstrates the power of EJB QL fetch joins. For this program, the `hibernate.show_sql` property is turned on so that you can see the difference between using a fetch join and not using one. The example code is extracted from the "Fetch Joins" section of Chapter 9 and is available in *com/titan/clients/FetchJoins.java*. Two methods are invoked to illustrate the example: `noJoin( )` and `joinFetch( )`. They are almost the same, except in how they do the initial query.

noJoin( )

```
public static void noJoin(EntityManager manager)
{
   System.out.println("-----------");
   System.out.println("  NO JOIN  ");
   System.out.println("-----------");
   Query query = manager.createQuery("SELECT c FROM Customer c");
   List results = query.getResultList( );
   System.out.println( );
   Iterator it = results.iterator( );
   while (it.hasNext( )) {
```

```
            Customer c = (Customer)it.next( );
            Collection<Phone> phoneNumbers = c.getPhoneNumbers( );
            // force the query so output looks nice
            phoneNumbers.size( );
            System.out.print(c.getFirstName() + " " + c.getLastName( ));
            for (Phone p : phoneNumbers) {
               System.out.print(" " + p.getNumber( ));
            }
            System.out.println("");
         }
      }
```

The noJoin( ) method queries for all customers and outputs each customer's phone number. When you run the example, you will see that an SQL query is executed each time Customer.getPhoneNumbers( ) is executed in this method. This is because the Customer-Phone relationship is lazily loaded.

joinFetch( )

```
      public static void joinFetch(EntityManager manager)
      {
         System.out.println("------------");
         System.out.println(" JOIN FETCH ");
         System.out.println("------------");
         Query query = manager.createQuery("SELECT c FROM Customer c " +
                              " LEFT JOIN FETCH c.phoneNumbers");
         List results = query.getResultList( );
         HashSet set = new HashSet( );
         set.addAll(results);
         System.out.println( );
         Iterator it = set.iterator( );
         while (it.hasNext( )) {
            Customer c = (Customer)it.next( );
            System.out.print(c.getFirstName() + " " + c.getLastName( ));
            for (Phone p : c.getPhoneNumbers( )) {
               System.out.print(" " + p.getNumber( ));
            }
            System.out.println("");
         }
      }
```

The joinFetch( ) method is almost the same as noJoin( ). The difference is that a LEFT JOIN FETCH is used to preload the Customer-Phone one-to-many relationship. When you run this example, only one SQL query is executed. This is much more efficient than the $N + 1$ queries performed in the noJoin( ) method.

There is a Hibernate peculiarity of which you should be aware. If you executed the raw SQL LEFT JOIN shown in the logging code, you would get duplicate customer entries. This is how LEFT JOINs work in SQL. Hibernate will return a similar duplicated result set even if you use the DISTINCT operator. To remove the duplicate Customer entity instances returned by the EJB QL query, the result set is stuffed into a java.util.HashSet.

Run the example

Run the FetchJoins application by invoking `ant run.fetch.joins` at the command prompt. Remember to set your `JBOSS_HOME` and `PATH` environment variables. Because the application is logging all SQL commands, the output is truncated, skipping the SQL performed in the initialization phase. Here is the output:

```
     [java] -----------
     [java]   NO JOIN
     [java] -----------
     [java] Hibernate: select customer0_.id as id4_, customer0_.firstName as
firstName4_, customer0_.lastName as lastNam
e4_, customer0_.hasGoodCredit as hasGoodC4_4_, customer0_.creditCard_id as
creditCard5_4_, customer0_.ADDRESS_ID as ADDR
ESS6_4_ from Customer customer0_

     [java] Hibernate: select phonenumbe0_.CUSTOMER_ID as CUSTOMER4_1_, phonenumbe0_.
id as id1_, phonenumbe0_.id as id1_
0_, phonenumbe0_.type as type1_0_, phonenumbe0_.number as number1_0_ from Phone
phonenumbe0_ where phonenumbe0_.CUSTOMER
_ID=?
     [java] Richard Monson-Haefel
     [java] Hibernate: select phonenumbe0_.CUSTOMER_ID as CUSTOMER4_1_, phonenumbe0_.
id as id1_, phonenumbe0_.id as id1_
0_, phonenumbe0_.type as type1_0_, phonenumbe0_.number as number1_0_ from Phone
phonenumbe0_ where phonenumbe0_.CUSTOMER
_ID=?
     [java] Bill Burke 978-555-5555 617-555-5555
     [java] Hibernate: select phonenumbe0_.CUSTOMER_ID as CUSTOMER4_1_, phonenumbe0_.
id as id1_, phonenumbe0_.id as id1_
0_, phonenumbe0_.type as type1_0_, phonenumbe0_.number as number1_0_ from Phone
phonenumbe0_ where phonenumbe0_.CUSTOMER
_ID=?
     [java] Sacha Labourey
     [java] Hibernate: select phonenumbe0_.CUSTOMER_ID as CUSTOMER4_1_, phonenumbe0_.
id as id1_, phonenumbe0_.id as id1_
0_, phonenumbe0_.type as type1_0_, phonenumbe0_.number as number1_0_ from Phone
phonenumbe0_ where phonenumbe0_.CUSTOMER
_ID=?
     [java] Marc Fleury
     [java] Hibernate: select phonenumbe0_.CUSTOMER_ID as CUSTOMER4_1_, phonenumbe0_.
id as id1_, phonenumbe0_.id as id1_
0_, phonenumbe0_.type as type1_0_, phonenumbe0_.number as number1_0_ from Phone
phonenumbe0_ where phonenumbe0_.CUSTOMER
_ID=?
     [java] Monica Burke 617-555-5555
     [java] Hibernate: select phonenumbe0_.CUSTOMER_ID as CUSTOMER4_1_, phonenumbe0_.
id as id1_, phonenumbe0_.id as id1_
0_, phonenumbe0_.type as type1_0_, phonenumbe0_.number as number1_0_ from Phone
phonenumbe0_ where phonenumbe0_.CUSTOMER
_ID=?
     [java] Gavin King
```

```
     [java] ------------
     [java]  JOIN FETCH
     [java] ------------
     [java] Hibernate: select customer0_.id as id4_0_, phonenumbe1_.id as id1_1_,
customer0_.firstName as firstName4_0_,
 customer0_.lastName as lastName4_0_, customer0_.hasGoodCredit as hasGoodC4_4_0_,
customer0_.creditCard_id as creditCard
5_4_0_, customer0_.ADDRESS_ID as ADDRESS6_4_0_, phonenumbe1_.type as type1_1_,
phonenumbe1_.number as number1_1_, phonen
umbe1_.CUSTOMER_ID as CUSTOMER4_0__, phonenumbe1_.id as id0__ from Customer
customer0_ left outer join Phone phonenumbe1
_ on customer0_.id=phonenumbe1_.CUSTOMER_ID

     [java] Bill Burke 978-555-5555 617-555-5555
     [java] Gavin King
     [java] Sacha Labourey
     [java] Richard Monson-Haefel
     [java] Monica Burke 617-555-5555
     [java] Marc Fleury
```

As you can see from the output, an additional SQL query is performed whenever the Customer-Phone relationship is traversed in the `noJoin()` method. For the `joinFetch()` method, only one query is executed.

Using DISTINCT

This example illustrates some basics about EJB QL's `DISTINCT` keyword. The queries are taken directly from the "Using DISTINCT section of Chapter 9, so we won't go over the code. You should be able to understand what queries have been executed by looking at the output. The code for this example is in *com/titan/clients/UsingDistinct.java*.

Run the example

Run the UsingDistinct application by invoking `ant run.using.distinct` at the command prompt. Remember to set your `JBOSS_HOME` and `PATH` environment variables. This is the output:

```
run.using.distinct:
     [java] Initialize DB


     [java] USING DISTINCT
     [java] --------------------------------
     [java] Non-distinct:
     [java] SELECT cust
     [java] FROM Reservation res, IN (res.customers) cust
     [java]    Bill has a reservation.
     [java]    Sacha has a reservation.
     [java]    Marc has a reservation.
     [java]    Bill has a reservation.
```

```
[java] Distinct:
[java] SELECT DISTINCT cust
[java] FROM Reservation res, IN (res.customers) cust
[java]    Bill has a reservation.
[java]    Sacha has a reservation.
[java]    Marc has a reservation.
```

The WHERE Clause and Literals

This example illustrates some basics about literals in a `WHERE` clause. The queries are taken directly from the section "The WHERE Clause and Literals," in Chapter 9, so we won't go over the code. You should be able to understand what queries have been executed by looking at the output. The code for this example is in *com/titan/clients/Literals.java*.

Run the example

Run the Literals application by invoking `ant run.literals` at the command prompt. Remember to set your `JBOSS_HOME` and `PATH` environment variables. This is the output:

```
run.literals:
     [java] Initialize DB

     [java] THE WHERE CLAUSE AND LITERALS
     [java] --------------------------------
     [java] SELECT c FROM Customer AS c
     [java] WHERE c.creditCard.creditCompany.name = 'Capital One'
     [java]    Bill has a Capital One card.
     [java]    Sacha has a Capital One card.

     [java] SELECT s FROM Ship AS s
     [java] WHERE s.tonnage = 100000.0
     [java]    Ship Titanic has tonnage 100000.0

     [java] SELECT c FROM Customer AS c
     [java] WHERE c.hasGoodCredit = TRUE
     [java]    Bill has good credit.
     [java]    Marc has good credit.
     [java]    Monica has good credit.
     [java]    Gavin has good credit.
```

The WHERE Clause and BETWEEN

This example illustrates some basics about EJB QL's `BETWEEN` keyword. The queries are taken directly from the section "The WHERE Clause and BETWEEN," in Chapter 9, so we won't go over the code. You should be able to understand what queries have been executed by looking at the output. The code for this example is in *com/titan/clients/Between.java*.

Run the example

Run the Between application by invoking ant `run.between` at the command prompt. Remember to set your `JBOSS_HOME` and `PATH` environment variables. This is the output:

```
run.between:
     [java] Initialize DB

     [java] THE WHERE CLAUSE AND BETWEEN
     [java] --------------------------------
     [java] SELECT s FROM Ship s
     [java] WHERE s.tonnage BETWEEN 80000.00 and 130000.00
     [java]    Titanic has tonnage 100000.0

     [java] SELECT s FROM Ship s
     [java] WHERE s.tonnage NOT BETWEEN 80000.00 and 130000.00
     [java]    Queen Mary has tonnage 40000.0
```

The WHERE Clause and IN

This example illustrates some basics about EJB QL's `IN` keyword. The queries are similar to the queries explained in the section "The WHERE Clause and IN," in Chapter 9, so we won't go over the code. You should be able to understand what queries have been executed by looking at the output. The code for this example is in *com/titan/clients/WhereIn.java*.

Run the example

Run the WhereIn application by invoking ant `run.where.in` at the command prompt. Remember to set your `JBOSS_HOME` and `PATH` environment variables. This is the output:

```
run.where.in:
     [java] Initialize DB


     [java] THE WHERE CLAUSE AND IN
     [java] --------------------------------
     [java] SELECT c FROM Customer c
     [java] WHERE c.address.state IN ('GA', 'MA')
     [java]    Bill
     [java]    Marc
     [java]    Monica
     [java]    Gavin

     [java] SELECT c FROM Customer c
     [java] WHERE c.address.state NOT IN ('GA', 'MA')
     [java]    Sacha
```

The WHERE Clause and IS NULL

This example illustrates some basics about EJB QL's `IS NULL` keywords. The queries are similar to the queries explained in the section "The WHERE Clause and IS NULL," in Chapter 9, so we won't go over the code. You should be able to understand what queries have been executed by looking at the output. The code for this example is in *com/titan/clients/IsNull.java*.

Run the example

Run the IsNull application by invoking `ant run.is.null` at the command prompt. Remember to set your `JBOSS_HOME` and `PATH` environment variables. This is the output:

```
run.is.null:
     [java] Initialize DB

     [java] THE WHERE CLAUSE AND IS NULL
     [java] -------------------------------
     [java] SELECT c FROM Customer c
     [java] WHERE c.address IS NULL
     [java]    Richard

     [java] SELECT c FROM Customer c
     [java] WHERE c.address IS NOT NULL
     [java]    Bill
     [java]    Sacha
     [java]    Marc
     [java]    Monica
     [java]    Gavin
```

The WHERE Clause and IS EMPTY

This example illustrates some basics about EJB QL's `IS EMPTY` keywords. The queries are similar to the queries explained in the section "The WHERE Clause and IS EMPTY," in Chapter 9, so we won't go over the code. You should be able to understand what queries have been executed by looking at the output. The code for this example is in *com/titan/clients/IsEmpty.java*.

Run the example

Run the IsEmpty application by invoking `ant run.is.empty` at the command prompt. Remember to set your `JBOSS_HOME` and `PATH` environment variables. This is the output:

```
run.is.empty:
     [java] Initialize DB

     [java] THE WHERE CLAUSE AND IS EMPTY
     [java] -------------------------------
     [java] SELECT OBJECT( crs ) FROM Cruise crs
     [java] WHERE crs.reservations IS EMPTY
```

```
    [java] SELECT crs FROM Cruise crs
    [java] WHERE crs.reservations IS NOT EMPTY
    [java]    Alaskan Cruise is NOT empty.
    [java]    Atlantic Cruise is NOT empty.
    [java]    Marc
    [java]    Monica
    [java]    Gavin
```

The WHERE Clause and MEMBER OF

This example illustrates some basics about EJB QL's `MEMBER OF` keywords. The queries are similar to the queries explained in the section "The WHERE Clause and MEMBER OF," in Chapter 9, so we won't go over the code. You should be able to understand what queries have been executed by looking at the output. The code for this example is in *com/titan/clients/MemberOf.java*.

Run the example

Run the MemberOf application by invoking `ant run.memberof` at the command prompt. Remember to set your `JBOSS_HOME` and `PATH` environment variables. This is the output:

```
run.memberof:
     [java] Initialize DB

     [java] THE WHERE CLAUSE AND MEMBER OF
     [java] --------------------------------
     [java] SELECT crs FROM Cruise crs,
     [java] IN (crs.reservations) res, Customer cust
     [java] WHERE cust = :c AND cust MEMBER OF res.customers
     [java] Use Bill Burke
     [java]    Bill is member of Alaskan Cruise
     [java]    Bill is member of Atlantic Cruise

     [java] SELECT crs FROM Cruise crs,
     [java] IN (crs.reservations) res, Customer cust
     [java] WHERE cust = :c AND cust NOT MEMBER OF res.customers
     [java] Use Bill again
     [java]    Bill is not member of Atlantic Cruise
```

The WHERE Clause and LIKE

This example illustrates some basics about EJB QL's `LIKE` keyword. The queries are similar to the queries explained in the section "The WHERE Clause and LIKE," in Chapter 9, so we won't go over the code. You should be able to understand what queries have been executed by looking at the output. The code for this example is in *com/titan/clients/Like.java*.

Run the example

Run the Like application by invoking `ant run.like` at the command prompt. Remember to set your `JBOSS_HOME` and `PATH` environment variables. This is the output:

```
run.like:
     [java] Initialize DB

     [java] THE WHERE CLAUSE AND LIKE
     [java] -------------------------------
     [java] SELECT c FROM Customer c
     [java] WHERE c.lastName LIKE '%-%'
     [java]     Monson-Haefel
String Functional Expressions
```

This example illustrates some basic string functional expressions available in EJB QL. The queries are similar to the queries explained in the section "Functional Expressions," in Chapter 9, so we won't go over the code. You should be able to understand what queries have been executed by looking at the output. The code for this example is in *com/titan/clients/FunctionalExpressions.java*.

Run the example

Run the FunctionalExpressions application by invoking `ant run.functional.expressions` at the command prompt. Remember to set your `JBOSS_HOME` and `PATH` environment variables. This is the output:

```
run.functional.expressions:
     [java] 15:20:03,067 FATAL [PersistenceXmlLoader] titan JTA
     [java] Initialize DB


     [java] THE WHERE CLAUSE AND FUNCTIONAL EXPRESSIONS
     [java] -------------------------------
     [java] SELECT c FROM Customer c
     [java] WHERE LENGTH(c.lastName) > 6 AND
     [java] LOCATE('Monson', c.lastName) > 0
     [java]     Monson-Haefel
```

Aggregate Functions

This example illustrates some basic aggregate functional expressions available in EJB QL. The queries are similar to the queries explained in the "Aggregate functions in the SELECT clause" subsection of Chapter 9, so we won't go over the code. You should be able to understand what queries have been executed by looking at the output. The code for this example is in *com/titan/clients/Aggregates.java*.

Run the example

Run the Aggregates application by invoking `ant run.aggregates` at the command prompt. Remember to set your `JBOSS_HOME` and `PATH` environment variables. This is the output:

```
run.aggregates:
     [java] Initialize DB

     [java] Aggregate Functions
     [java] -------------------------------
     [java] SELECT DISTINCT COUNT(c.address.zip)
     [java] FROM Customer AS c
     [java] WHERE c.address.zip LIKE '0%'

     [java] count of zip codes starting with 0: 2
     [java] -------------------------------
     [java] SELECT MAX(r.amountPaid)
     [java] FROM Reservation As r

     [java] max amount paid for a reservation: $500.0
     [java] -------------------------------
     [java] SELECT SUM( r.amountPaid)
     [java] FROM Cruise c, IN( c.reservations) r
     [java] WHERE  c = :cruise

     [java] Sum of Atlantic Cruise reservations: $542.0
     [java] -------------------------------
     [java] SELECT AVG( r.amountPaid)
     [java] FROM Cruise c, IN( c.reservations) r
     [java] WHERE  c = :cruise

     [java] Average of Atlantic Cruise reservations: $271.0
```

The ORDER BY Clause

This example illustrates some basics about EJB QL's `ORDER BY` keywords. The queries are similar to the queries explained in the section "The ORDER BY Clause," in Chapter 9, so we won't go over the code. You should be able to understand what queries have been executed by looking at the output. The code for this example is in *com/titan/clients/OrderBy.java*.

Run the example

Run the OrderBy application by invoking `ant run.orderby` at the command prompt. Remember to set your `JBOSS_HOME` and `PATH` environment variables. This is the output:

```
run.orderby:
     [java] 18:29:09,093 FATAL [PersistenceXmlLoader] titan JTA
     [java] Initialize DB
```

```
[java] ORDER BY Clause
[java] --------------------------------
[java] SELECT c FROM Customer AS c
[java] ORDER BY c.lastName DESC
[java]    Richard Monson-Haefel
[java]    Sacha Labourey
[java]    Gavin King
[java]    Marc Fleury
[java]    Monica Burke
[java]    Bill Burke
```

GROUP BY and HAVING

This example illustrates the same `GROUP BY` example shown in the "GROUP BY and HAVING" section of Chapter 9. It uses the same `ReservationSummary` class to generate a report with the `GROUP BY` and `HAVING` keywords. You should be able to understand what is happening in this example by looking at the output. The code for this example is in *com/titan/clients/GroupByHaving.java*.

Run the example

Run the GroupByHaving application by invoking `ant run.groupby` at the command prompt. Remember to set your `JBOSS_HOME` and `PATH` environment variables. This is the output:

```
run.groupby:
     [java] 15:28:26,895 FATAL [PersistenceXmlLoader] titan JTA
     [java] Initialize DB


     [java] GROUP BY Clause
     [java] --------------------------------
     [java] SELECT new com.titan.clients.ReservationSummary(cr.name, COUNT(res),
SUM(res.amountPaid))
     [java] FROM Cruise cr
     [java] LEFT JOIN cr.reservations res
     [java] GROUP BY cr.name
     [java]    Alaskan Cruise: 1   0.0
     [java]    Atlantic Cruise: 2   542.0
     [java] GROUP BY Clause
     [java] --------------------------------
     [java] SELECT new com.titan.clients.ReservationSummary(cr.name, COUNT(res),
SUM(res.amountPaid))
     [java] FROM Cruise cr
     [java] LEFT JOIN cr.reservations res
     [java] GROUP BY cr.name
     [java] HAVING count(res) > 1
     [java]    Atlantic Cruise: 2   542.0
```

Subqueries

This example illustrates some basics about EJB QL's ORDER BY keywords. The queries are similar to the queries explained in the "Subqueries" section of Chapter 9, so we won't go over the code. You should be able to understand what queries have been executed by looking at the output. The code for this example is in *com/titan/clients/Subqueries.java*.

Run the example

Run the Subqueries application by invoking ant run.subqueries at the command prompt. Remember to set your JBOSS_HOME and PATH environment variables. This is the output:

```
run.subqueries:
     [java] Initialize DB

     [java] Subquery
     [java] -------------------------------
     [java] SELECT COUNT(res) FROM Reservation res
     [java] WHERE res.amountPaid >
     [java] (SELECT AVG(r.amountPaid) FROM Reservation r)
     [java] Number of reservations paid above the average: 1


     [java] Subquery with ALL
     [java] -------------------------------
     [java] FROM Cruise cr
     [java] WHERE 0 < ALL
     [java] (SELECT res.amountPaid from cr.reservations res)
     [java] Cruises where all reservations have down payments:
     [java]     Atlantic Cruise


     [java] Subquery with ANY
     [java] -------------------------------
     [java] FROM Cruise cr
     [java] WHERE 0 = ANY
     [java] (SELECT res.amountPaid from cr.reservations res)
     [java] Cruises where any reservation doesn't have down payments:
     [java]     Alaskan Cruise


     [java] Subquery with EXISTS
     [java] -------------------------------
     [java] FROM Cruise cr
     [java] WHERE NOT EXISTS
     [java] (SELECT res.amountPaid from cr.reservations res WHERE res.amountPaid = 0)
     [java] Cruises that have reservations that don't have a down payment:
     [java]     Atlantic Cruise
```

Exercise 9.2: Native SQL Queries

This exercise executes a few different native SQL queries and shows how you can map them to an entity result set. The example programs run outside of the application server, so there is no need to start up JBoss.

Initialize the Database

The standalone Java Persistence solution initializes the Hypersonic SQL database and generates the database schema each time one of the sample programs is run. This is an in-memory database, so you will not see any files created for the database.

Build the Example Program

Perform the following steps:

1. Open a command prompt or shell terminal and change to the *ex09_2* directory created by the extraction process.
2. Set the `JAVA_HOME` and `JBOSS_HOME` environment variables to point to where your JDK and JBoss 4.0 are installed. Examples:

   Windows:

   C:\workbook\ex09_2> set JAVA_HOME=C:\jdk1.5.0
   C:\workbook\ex09_2> set JBOSS_HOME=C:\jboss-4.0.x

   Unix:

   $ export JAVA_HOME=/usr/local/jdk1.5.0
   $ export JBOSS_HOME=/usr/local/jboss-4.0
3. Add ant to your execution path. Ant is the build utility.

   Windows:

   C:\workbook\ex09_2> set PATH=..\ant\bin;%PATH%

   Unix:

   $ export PATH=../ant/bin:$PATH
4. Perform the build by typing `ant`.

Examine the Example

You can find the example program in *com/titan/clients/NativeQueries.java*. This program has three different methods to illustrate various concepts for mapping native queries. Let's look at each of them.

nativeSql( )

```
public static void nativeSql(EntityManager manager)
{
   System.out.println("Named Native Query, implicit mapping");
```

```
        System.out.println("-----------------------------------");
        System.out.println("Executing @NamedNativeQuery(name=\"NativePhone\")");
        Query query;
        query = manager.createNamedQuery("NativePhone");
        List phones = query.getResultList( );
        Iterator it = phones.iterator( );
        while (it.hasNext( ))
        {
           Phone phone = (Phone)it.next( );
           System.out.println("Phone Number: " + phone.getNumber( ));
        }
    }
```

This code executes a native named query that is declared on the `com.titan.domain.Phone` class.

```
package com.titan.domain;

import javax.persistence.*;

@Entity
@NamedNativeQuery(name="NativePhone",
                  query="SELECT p.phone_PK, p.phone_number, p.type FROM PHONE AS p",
                  resultClass=Phone.class)
public class Phone implements java.io.Serializable
{
...
}
```

This native query returns a result set of Phone entities. It needs no special mapping because the columns match the property mappings of the Phone entity.

nativeWithMultipleEntities( )

```
    public static void nativeWithMultipleEntities(EntityManager manager)
    {
        System.out.println("Complex Native queries");
        System.out.println("-----------------------------------");
        System.out.println("SELECT c.id, c.firstName, c.lastName, ");
        System.out.println(" cc.id AS CC_ID, cc.number, ");
        System.out.println("FROM CUST_TABLE c, CREDIT_CARD_TABLE cc ");
        System.out.println("WHERE c.credit_card_id = cc.id");


        Query query = manager.createNativeQuery("SELECT c.id, c.firstName, " +
                           "              c.lastName, cc.id As CC_ID, cc.number " +
                                          "FROM CUST_TABLE c, CREDIT_CARD_TABLE cc " +
                                          "WHERE c.credit_card_id = cc.id",
                                                 "customerAndCreditCardMapping");
        List phones = query.getResultList( );
        Iterator it = phones.iterator( );
        while (it.hasNext( ))
        {
           Object[] result = (Object[])it.next( );
```

```
            Customer cust = (Customer)result[0];
            CreditCard cc = (CreditCard)result[1];
            System.out.println(cust.getFirstName() + " " + cc.getNumber( ));
        }
    }
```

The nativeWithMultipleEntities( ) method performs a native SQL query that returns a result set containing two entities: Customer and Phone. Because this is a complex native query, an @javax.persistence.SqlResultSetMapping named customerAndCreditCardMapping is declared on the com.titan.domain.Customer class and is referenced in the EntityManager.createNativeQuery( ) execution:

```
package com.titan.domain;

import javax.persistence.*;
import java.util.*;


@Entity
@Table(name="CUST_TABLE")
@SqlResultSetMapping(name="customerAndCreditCardMapping",
      entities={@EntityResult(entityClass=Customer.class),
                @EntityResult(entityClass=CreditCard.class,
                              fields={@FieldResult(name="id", column="CC_ID"),
                                    @FieldResult(name="number", column="number")}
                              )})
public class Customer implements java.io.Serializable
{
...
}
```

Because both the Customer and CreditCard entities have the same column name for their primary key columns, we must modify our SQL code and result set mapping to distinguish between them. If you look at the native SQL, you will see that the AS operator is used to provide an alias for the CreditCard's id column. This alias is referenced in the @javax.persistence.FieldResult mapping, thus alleviating the ambiguity.

mixedNative( )

```
public static void mixedNative(EntityManager manager)
{
   System.out.println("Complex Native queries");
   System.out.println("-------------------------------");
   System.out.println("SELECT c.id, count(Reservation.id) as resCount");
   System.out.println("FROM Cruise c ");
   System.out.println("LEFT JOIN Reservation ON c.id =Reservation.CRUISE_ID");
   System.out.println("GROUP BY c.id");

   Query query = manager.createNativeQuery("SELECT c.id, " +
                                           " count(Reservation.id) " +
                                           " as resCount " +
```

```
                                         "FROM Cruise c " +
                                         "LEFT JOIN Reservation " +
                                         "ON c.id = Reservation.CRUISE_ID " +
                                           "GROUP BY c.id",
                                           "reservationCount");
      List phones = query.getResultList( );
      Iterator it = phones.iterator( );
      while (it.hasNext( ))
      {
         Object[] result = (Object[])it.next( );
         Cruise cruise = (Cruise)result[1];
         int count = (Integer)result[0];
         System.out.println(cruise.getName( ) + " " + count);
      }
   }
```

This example executes a native query that returns both an entity result and a scalar value. The result is a report of the reservations made on each cruise. Because this is a complex query, an `@SqlResultSetMapping` named `reservationCount` is declared on the `com.titan.domain.Cruise` class:

```
package com.titan.domain;

import java.util.*;
import javax.persistence.*;

@Entity
@SqlResultSetMapping(name="reservationCount",
        entities=@EntityResult(entityClass=Cruise.class,
                        fields=@FieldResult(name="id", column="id")),
        columns=@ColumnResult(name="resCount"))
public class Cruise implements java.io.Serializable
{
...
}
```

For `@SqlResultSetMapping`, both `@EntityResult` and `@ColumnResult` are declared to map the two items returned by the query.

Run the Example

Run the NativeQueries application by invoking ant `run.native.queries` at the command prompt. Remember to set your `JBOSS_HOME` and `PATH` environment variables. This is the output:

```
run.native.queries:
     [java] Initialize DB

     [java] Named Native Query, implicit mapping
     [java] --------------------------------
     [java] Executing @NamedNativeQuery(name="NativePhone")
     [java] Phone Number: 978-555-5555
     [java] Phone Number: 617-555-5555
     [java] Phone Number: 617-555-5555
```

```
[java] Complex Native queries
[java] -------------------------------
[java] SELECT c.id, c.firstName, c.lastName,
[java]  cc.id AS CC_ID, cc.number,
[java] FROM CUST_TABLE c, CREDIT_CARD_TABLE cc
[java] WHERE c.credit_card_id = cc.id
[java] Bill 5324 9393 1010 2929
[java] Sacha 3311 5000 1011 2333
[java] Marc 4310 5131 7711 2663
[java] Monica 4310 5144 7711 2663
[java] Gavin 5310 5144 7711 2663

[java] Complex Native queries
[java] -------------------------------
[java] SELECT c.id, count(Reservation.id) as resCount
[java] FROM Cruise c
[java] LEFT JOIN Reservation ON c.id = Reservation.CRUISE_ID
[java] GROUP BY c.id
[java] Alaskan Cruise 1
[java] Atlantic Cruise 2
```

WORKBOOK 8

Exercises for Chapter 10

This chapter focuses on exercises that illustrate the entity callback annotations and entity listener constructs discussed in Chapter 10 of the EJB book.

Exercise 10.1: Entity Callbacks

This exercise shows you a simple example of applying the entity callback annotations to an entity bean class. You will see the full life cycle of an entity bean as it is created, loaded, updated, and deleted. Of particular interest is when the Hibernate Entity Manager performs these callbacks. The example makes it clearer when Hibernate performs interactions with the database.

Start Up JBoss

If you already have JBoss running, there is no reason to restart it. Otherwise, start it up as instructed in Workbook 1.

Initialize the Database

The database tables will be created when Exercise 10.1 is deployed to JBoss. If you have problems running this example, shut down JBoss and run the `clean.db` Ant task.

Build and Deploy the Example Programs

Perform the following steps:

1. Open a command prompt or shell terminal and change to the *ex10_1* directory created by the extraction process.
2. Set the `JAVA_HOME` and `JBOSS_HOME` environment variables to point to where your JDK and JBoss 4.0 are installed. Examples:

Windows:

```
C:\workbook\ex10_1> set JAVA_HOME=C:\jdk1.5.0
C:\workbook\ex10_1> set JBOSS_HOME=C:\jboss-4.0.x
```

Unix:

```
$ export JAVA_HOME=/usr/local/jdk1.5.0
$ export JBOSS_HOME=/usr/local/jboss-4.0
```

3. Add `ant` to your execution path. Ant is the build utility.

   Windows:

   ```
   C:\workbook\ex10_1> set PATH=..\ant\bin;%PATH%
   ```

   Unix:

   ```
   $ export PATH=../ant/bin:$PATH
   ```

4. Perform the build by typing `ant`.

As in earlier exercises in other chapters, *titan.jar* is rebuilt, copied to the JBoss *deploy* directory, and redeployed by the application server.

Examine the Customer Entity

This exercise interacts with the Customer entity you saw in previous chapters. The `Customer` class has been augmented with the full suite of entity callback annotations.

Customer.java

```
package com.titan.domain;

import javax.persistence.*;

import java.util.Date;

@Entity
public class Customer implements java.io.Serializable
{
   private int id;
   private String lastName;
   private String firstName;

   @Id
   @GeneratedValue
   public int getId( )
   {
      return id;
   }
   public void setId(int pk)
   {
      id = pk;
   }
```

```
    public String getLastName( ) { return lastName; }
    public void setLastName(String lastName) { this.lastName = lastName; }

    public String getFirstName( ) { return firstName; }
    public void setFirstName(String firstName) { this.firstName = firstName; }

    @PrePersist
    public void prePersist( )
    {
       System.out.println("@PrePersist");
    }

    @PostPersist
    public void postPersist( )
    {
       System.out.println("@PostPersist");
    }

    @PostLoad
    public void postLoad( )
    {
       System.out.println("@PostLoad");
    }

    @PreUpdate
    public void preUpdate( )
    {
       System.out.println("@PreUpdate");
    }

    @PostUpdate
    public void postUpdate( )
    {
       System.out.println("@PostUpdate");
    }

    @PreRemove
    public void preRemove( )
    {
       System.out.println("@PreRemove");
    }

    @PostRemove
    public void postRemove( )
    {
       System.out.println("@PostRemove");
    }

}
```

Each callback annotation simply outputs a message to `System.out`.

Examine TravelAgentBean

TravelAgentBean acts as a façade around the persistence unit that holds the Customer entity. It has simple operations that create, load, update, and remove a Customer instance. Let's take a look at it.

TravelAgentBean.java

```
package com.titan.travelagent;

import javax.ejb.Stateless;
import javax.persistence.EntityManager;
import javax.persistence.PersistenceContext;

import com.titan.domain.Customer;

@Stateless
public class TravelAgentBean implements TravelAgentRemote
{
   @PersistenceContext(unitName="titan") private EntityManager manager;

   public int createCustomer(Customer cust)
   {
      System.out.println("--------------------------------------");
      System.out.println("Calling createCustomer():" + cust.getFirstName( ));
      System.out.println("Calling manager.persist( )");
      manager.persist(cust);
      System.out.println("Ending createCustomer.");
      return cust.getId( );
   }

   public Customer findCustomer(int pKey)
   {
      System.out.println("--------------------------------------");
      System.out.println("Calling findCustomer( )");
      System.out.println("manager.find( )");
      Customer cust = manager.find(Customer.class, pKey);
      System.out.println("Returning from findCustomer(): " + cust.getFirstName( ));
      return cust;
   }

   public void doMerge(Customer cust)
   {
      System.out.println("--------------------------------------");
      System.out.println("Calling doMerge( )");
      manager.merge(cust);
      System.out.println("Returning from doMerge( )");
   }

   public void doFlush(int pKey)
   {
      System.out.println("--------------------------------------");
      System.out.println("Calling doFlush( )");
```

```
        System.out.println("manager.find( )");
        Customer cust = manager.find(Customer.class, pKey);
        System.out.println("cust.setName( )");
        cust.setFirstName("doFlush");
        System.out.println("calling manager.flush( )");
        manager.flush( );
        System.out.println("returning from doFlush( )");
    }

    public void doRemove(int pKey)
    {
        System.out.println("--------------------------------------");
        System.out.println("Calling doRemove( )");
        System.out.println("manager.find( )");
        Customer cust = manager.find(Customer.class, pKey);
        System.out.println("calling manager.remove( )");
        manager.remove(cust);
        System.out.println("returning from doRemove( )");
    }

}
```

Each of the TravelAgentBean's methods interacts with the entity bean in different situations so that you can see when the Customer class's callback methods are executed. EntityManager methods such as persist( ), find( ), merge( ), flush( ), and remove( ) are invoked so that you can see their effect on a Customer entity.

Examine the Client

The client's only role is to allocate a Customer instance and invoke each of the TravelAgentBean's methods in sequence. It is not very interesting, so we won't go over it.

Run the Client

Run the Client application by invoking ant run.client at the command prompt. Remember to set your JBOSS_HOME and PATH environment variables. The client program has no interesting output. You will need to view the JBoss console window to see the output from the Customer's callback methods. After running the example, notice that the update from the merge( ) operation is queued until the transaction commits. The same is true of the remove( ) operation. This is the console output:

```
18:39:35,973 INFO  [EJB3Deployer] Deployed: file:/C:/jboss/jboss-4.0.4RC1/server/
default/deploy/titan.jar
18:39:44,567 INFO  [STDOUT] --------------------------------------
18:39:44,567 INFO  [STDOUT] Calling createCustomer( ):Bill
18:39:44,567 INFO  [STDOUT] Calling manager.persist( )
18:39:44,770 INFO  [STDOUT] @PrePersist
18:39:44,817 INFO  [STDOUT] @PostPersist
```

```
18:39:44,817 INFO  [STDOUT] Ending createCustomer.
18:39:44,864 INFO  [STDOUT] --------------------------------------
18:39:44,864 INFO  [STDOUT] Calling findCustomer( )
18:39:44,864 INFO  [STDOUT] manager.find( )
18:39:44,895 INFO  [STDOUT] @PostLoad
18:39:44,895 INFO  [STDOUT] Returning from findCustomer( ): Bill
18:39:44,910 INFO  [STDOUT] --------------------------------------
18:39:44,910 INFO  [STDOUT] Calling doMerge( )
18:39:44,910 INFO  [STDOUT] @PostLoad
18:39:44,926 INFO  [STDOUT] Returning from doMerge( )
18:39:44,926 INFO  [STDOUT] @PreUpdate
18:39:44,926 INFO  [STDOUT] @PostUpdate
18:39:44,942 INFO  [STDOUT] --------------------------------------
18:39:44,942 INFO  [STDOUT] Calling doFlush( )
18:39:44,942 INFO  [STDOUT] manager.find( )
18:39:44,942 INFO  [STDOUT] @PostLoad
18:39:44,942 INFO  [STDOUT] cust.setName( )
18:39:44,942 INFO  [STDOUT] calling manager.flush( )
18:39:44,942 INFO  [STDOUT] @PreUpdate
18:39:44,957 INFO  [STDOUT] @PostUpdate
18:39:44,957 INFO  [STDOUT] returning from doFlush( )
18:39:44,957 INFO  [STDOUT] --------------------------------------
18:39:44,957 INFO  [STDOUT] Calling doRemove( )
18:39:44,957 INFO  [STDOUT] manager.find( )
18:39:44,973 INFO  [STDOUT] @PostLoad
18:39:44,973 INFO  [STDOUT] calling manager.remove( )
18:39:44,973 INFO  [STDOUT] @PreRemove
18:39:44,973 INFO  [STDOUT] returning from doRemove( )
18:39:44,989 INFO  [STDOUT] @PostRemove
```

Exercise 10.2: Entity Listeners

This exercise shows you how to write an entity listener. The entity listener in this example gathers life cycle stats for every entity class to which it is applied. A JMX MBean is also implemented so that you can view these stats in the JBoss JMX Management Console. The rest of the code is the same as in Exercise 10.1.

Start Up JBoss

If you already have JBoss running, there is no reason to restart it. Otherwise, start it up as instructed in Workbook 1.

Initialize the Database

The database tables will be created when Exercise 10.2 is deployed to JBoss. If you have problems running this example, shut down JBoss and run the `clean.db` Ant task.

Build and Deploy the Example Programs

Perform the following steps:

1. Open a command prompt or shell terminal and change to the *ex10_2* directory created by the extraction process.
2. Set the `JAVA_HOME` and `JBOSS_HOME` environment variables to point to where your JDK and JBoss 4.0 are installed. Examples:

   Windows:

   C:\workbook\ex10_2> set JAVA_HOME=C:\jdk1.5.0
   C:\workbook\ex10_2> set JBOSS_HOME=C:\jboss-4.0.x

   Unix:

   $ export JAVA_HOME=/usr/local/jdk1.5.0
   $ export JBOSS_HOME=/usr/local/jboss-4.0
3. Add `ant` to your execution path. Ant is the build utility.

   Windows:

   C:\workbook\ex10_2> set PATH=..\ant\bin;%PATH%

   Unix:

   $ export PATH=../ant/bin:$PATH
4. Perform the build by typing `ant`.

As in earlier exercises, *titan.jar* is built, copied to the JBoss *deploy* directory, and redeployed by the application server. Additionally, a *titan-mbeans.sar* file is created for the deployed JMX MBean.

Examine the Entity Listener

```
package com.titan.stats;

import javax.persistence.*;
import java.util.concurrent.ConcurrentHashMap;

public class EntityListener
{
   public static class Stats
   {
      public String entity;
      public int updates;
      public int loads;
      public int inserts;
      public int removes;
   }

   public static ConcurrentHashMap<String, Stats> map =
                       new ConcurrentHashMap<String, Stats>( );
```

```
    private static Stats getStats(Object entity)
    {
       String name = entity.getClass().getName( );
       Stats stats = map.get(name);
       if (stats == null)
       {
          stats = new Stats( );
          map.put(name, stats);
          stats.entity = name;
       }
       return stats;
    }

    @PostUpdate
    public void update(Object entity)
    {
       System.out.println("@PostUpdate: " + entity.getClass().getName( ));
       Stats stats = getStats(entity);
       synchronized(stats) {stats.updates++;}
    }

    @PostPersist
    public void persist(Object entity)
    {
       System.out.println("@PostPersist: " + entity.getClass().getName( ));
       Stats stats = getStats(entity);
       synchronized(stats) {stats.inserts++;}
    }

    @PostLoad
    public void load(Object entity)
    {
       System.out.println("@PostLoad: " + entity.getClass().getName( ));
       Stats stats = getStats(entity);
       synchronized(stats) {stats.loads++;}
    }

    @PostRemove
    public void remove(Object entity)
    {
       System.out.println("@PostRemove: " + entity.getClass().getName( ));
       Stats stats = getStats(entity);
       synchronized(stats) {stats.removes++;}
    }

}
```

The com.titan.stats.EntityListener class intercepts all entity callback events. It has a static ConcurrentHashMap that is keyed by the class name of the entity. The stats are stored in the inner Stats class. Every time an entity callback event is intercepted, it looks up a Stats object within the static map and increments the appropriate event count.

Examine the JMX MBean

The JMX MBean consists of two separate files: *EntityStats.java* and *EntityStatsMBean.java*.

EntityStats.java

```
package com.titan.stats;

import java.util.concurrent.ConcurrentHashMap;

public class EntityStats implements EntityStatsMBean
{
   public String output( )
   {
      StringBuffer buf = new StringBuffer("<table><tr><td>Entity Name</td><td>Loads</
td><td>Inserts</td><td>Updates</td><td>Deletes</td></tr>");
      for (EntityListener.Stats stats : EntityListener.map.values( ))
      {
         buf.append("<tr><td>" + stats.entity).append("</td>");
         buf.append("<td>" + stats.loads).append("</td>");
         buf.append("<td>" + stats.inserts).append("</td>");
         buf.append("<td>" + stats.updates).append("</td>");
         buf.append("<td>" + stats.removes).append("</td></tr>");
      }
      buf.append("</table>");
      return buf.toString( );
   }


}
```

The `EntityStats` class has one `output( )` method that generates some HTML by browsing the `EntityListener`'s map of entity stats. Writing an MBean is as simple as writing a Java class that implements a Java interface whose name ends in *MBean*.

EntityStatsMBean.java

```
package com.titan.stats;

public interface EntityStatsMBean
{
   public String output( );
}
```

MBeans are very analogous to session beans. They implement the interface that they publish to the world. The EntityStats MBean publishes one `output( )` method. Later, you will invoke this method through JBoss's JMX Management Console.

jboss-service.xml

```
<?xml version="1.0" encoding="UTF-8"?>

<server>

   <mbean code="com.titan.stats.EntityStats"
          name="oreilly-workbook:service=entity-stats"/>
</server>
```

The JMX specification does not define a deployment descriptor mechanism for JMX MBeans. This is where JBoss comes in. The descriptor simply tells JBoss to create an `EntityStats` instance and register it under the name `oreilly-workbook:service=entity-stats`. You will reference this MBean under this name when you browse the JMX Management Console. This file is JAR'd into the *META-INF* directory of the *titan-mbeans.sar* file along with the other two classes just mentioned.

Examine the Customer Entity

```
package com.titan.domain;

import javax.persistence.*;

import java.util.Date;

@Entity
@EntityListeners(com.titan.stats.EntityListener.class)
public class Customer implements java.io.Serializable
{
...
}
```

The `Customer` class applies `com.titan.stats.EntityListener` using the `@javax.persistence.EntityListeners` annotation.

Run the Client

Run the Client application by invoking `ant run.client` at the command prompt. Remember to set your `JBOSS_HOME` and `PATH` environment variables. The client program has no interesting output. You will need to view the JBoss console window to see the output from the `EntityListener` class applied to the Customer entity.

```
18:50:24,489 INFO  [EJB3Deployer] Deployed: file:/C:/jboss/jboss-4.0.4RC1/server/
default/deploy/titan.jar
19:15:09,879 INFO  [STDOUT] --------------------------------------
19:15:09,879 INFO  [STDOUT] Calling createCustomer():Bill
19:15:09,879 INFO  [STDOUT] Calling manager.persist()
19:15:09,879 INFO  [STDOUT] @PostPersist: com.titan.domain.Customer
19:15:09,879 INFO  [STDOUT] Ending createCustomer.
19:15:09,910 INFO  [STDOUT] --------------------------------------
19:15:09,910 INFO  [STDOUT] Calling findCustomer()
19:15:09,910 INFO  [STDOUT] manager.find()
19:15:09,910 INFO  [STDOUT] @PostLoad: com.titan.domain.Customer
```

```
19:15:09,910 INFO  [STDOUT] Returning from findCustomer(): Bill
19:15:09,910 INFO  [STDOUT] -------------------------------------
19:15:09,910 INFO  [STDOUT] Calling doMerge()
19:15:09,926 INFO  [STDOUT] @PostLoad: com.titan.domain.Customer
19:15:09,926 INFO  [STDOUT] Returning from doMerge()
19:15:09,926 INFO  [STDOUT] @PostUpdate: com.titan.domain.Customer
19:15:09,926 INFO  [STDOUT] -------------------------------------
19:15:09,926 INFO  [STDOUT] Calling doFlush()
19:15:09,926 INFO  [STDOUT] manager.find()
19:15:09,942 INFO  [STDOUT] @PostLoad: com.titan.domain.Customer
19:15:09,942 INFO  [STDOUT] cust.setName()
19:15:09,942 INFO  [STDOUT] calling manager.flush()
19:15:09,942 INFO  [STDOUT] @PostUpdate: com.titan.domain.Customer
19:15:09,942 INFO  [STDOUT] returning from doFlush()
19:15:09,957 INFO  [STDOUT] -------------------------------------
19:15:09,957 INFO  [STDOUT] Calling doRemove()
19:15:09,957 INFO  [STDOUT] manager.find()
19:15:09,957 INFO  [STDOUT] @PostLoad: com.titan.domain.Customer
19:15:09,957 INFO  [STDOUT] calling manager.remove()
19:15:09,957 INFO  [STDOUT] returning from doRemove()
19:15:09,957 INFO  [STDOUT] @PostRemove: com.titan.domain.Customer
```

Examine the JMX Management Console

You can view the stats gathered by the JBoss JMX Management Console by pointing your browser to *http://localhost:8080/jmx-console*. Scroll down to the end of this page until you see the EntityStats JMX MBean you deployed. Figure W-16 shows what this page looks like.

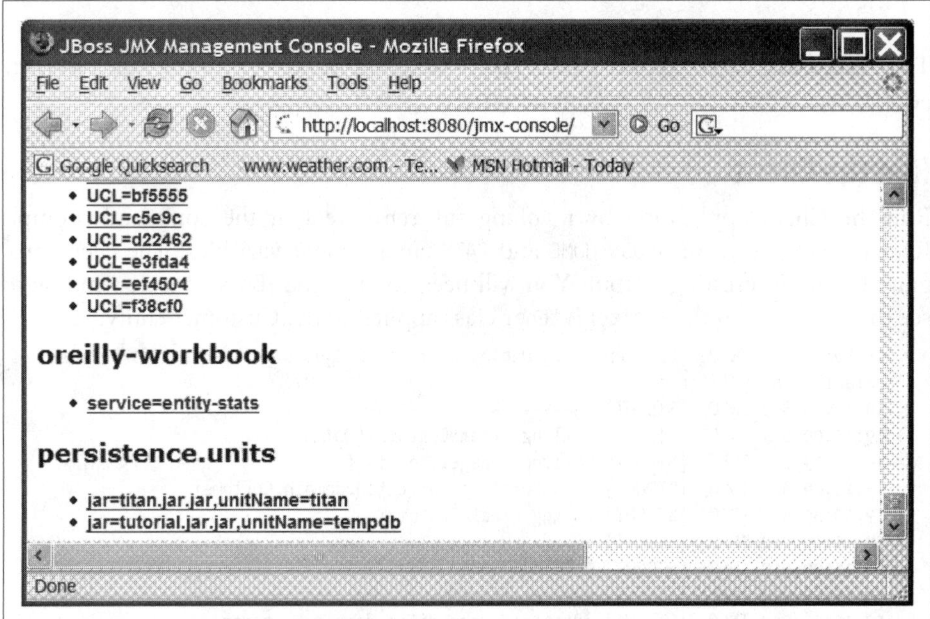

Figure W-16. Main JMX console page

Click on the service=entity-stats link. It brings you to the page shown in Figure W-17.

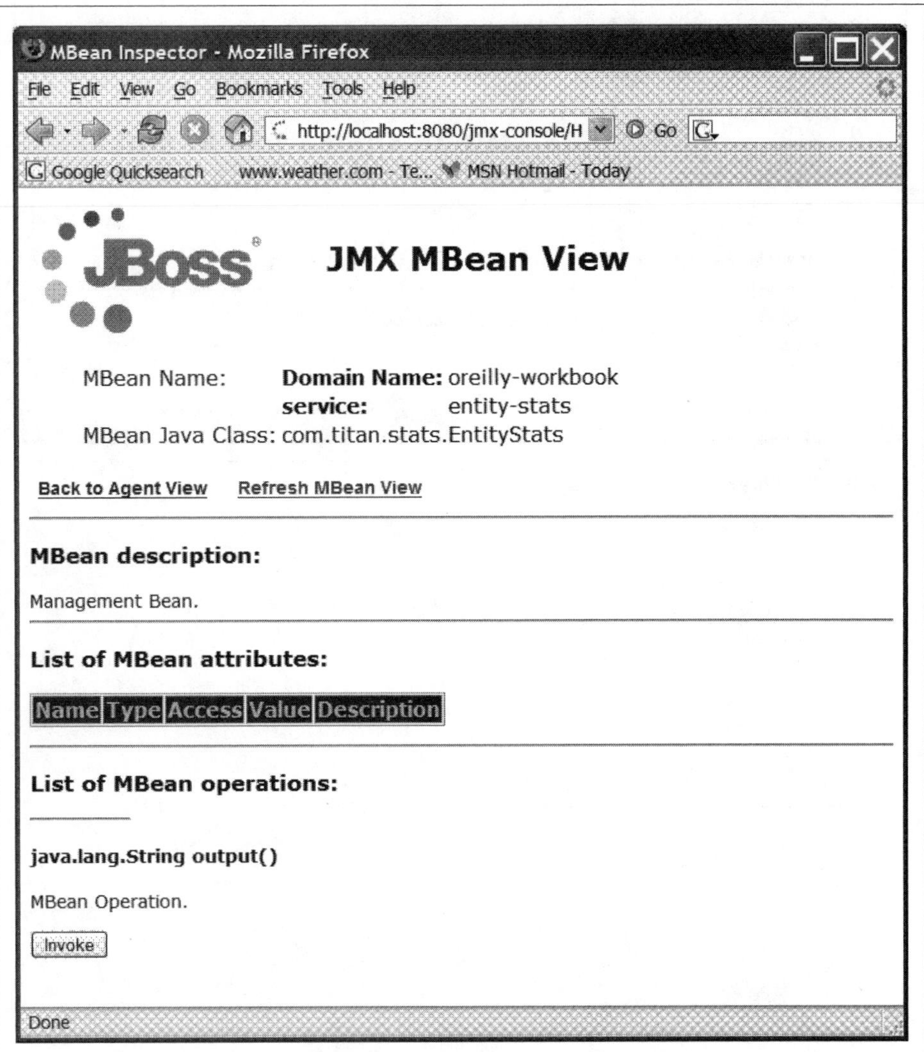

Figure W-17. EntityStats MBean GUI

Click on the Invoke button under the `output()` operation. This action will cause the `output()` method to be invoked on the `EntityStats` class. Figure W-18 shows the output of this management operation. All of the life cycle event counts performed on each entity class are listed.

The entity listener and JMX MBean demonstrated in this example are simple, but you can reuse them in any application you write.

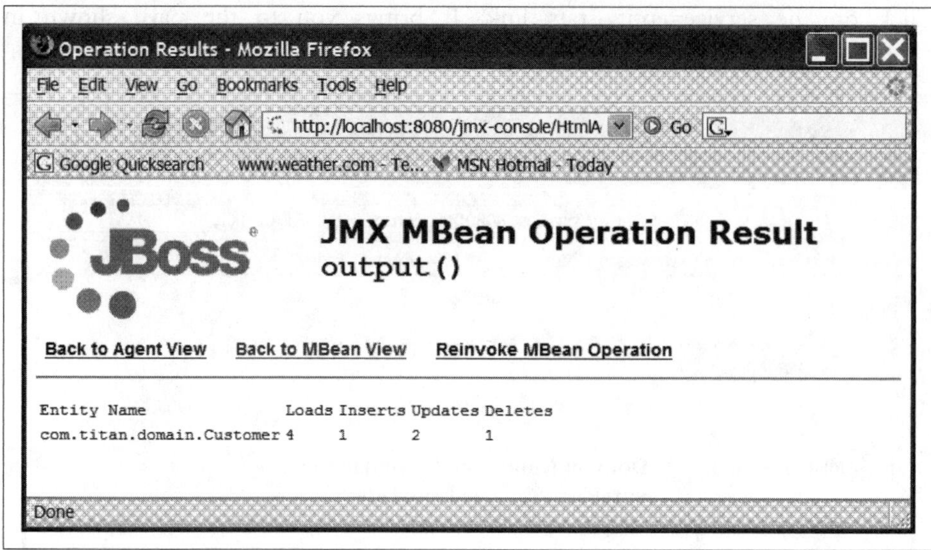

Figure W-18. Entity life cycle stats

Exercises for Chapter 11

This chapter implements exercises that illustrate the concepts introduced in Chapter 11 of the EJB book.

Exercise 11.1: Stateless Session Bean

This exercise utilizes the ProcessPayment EJB described in Chapter 11 of the EJB book. The code for this stateless bean is copied as is from Chapter 11, but a few additional classes are implemented to facilitate the example.

Start Up JBoss

If you already have JBoss running, there is no reason to restart it. Otherwise, start it up as instructed in Workbook 1.

Initialize the Database

The database tables will be created when Exercise 11.1 is deployed to JBoss. If you have problems running this example, shut down JBoss and run the `clean.db` Ant task.

Build and Deploy the Example Programs

Perform the following steps:

1. Open a command prompt or shell terminal and change to the *ex11_1* directory created by the extraction process.
2. Set the `JAVA_HOME` and `JBOSS_HOME` environment variables to point to where your JDK and JBoss 4.0 are installed. Examples:

   Windows:

   ```
   C:\workbook\ex11_1> set JAVA_HOME=C:\jdk1.5.0
   C:\workbook\ex11_1> set JBOSS_HOME=C:\jboss-4.0.x
   ```

Unix:

    $ export JAVA_HOME=/usr/local/jdk1.5.0
    $ export JBOSS_HOME=/usr/local/jboss-4.0

3. Add ant to your execution path. Ant is the build utility.

   Windows:

       C:\workbook\ex11_1> set PATH=..\ant\bin;%PATH%

   Unix:

       $ export PATH=../ant/bin:$PATH

4. Perform the build by typing ant.

As in the exercises in earlier chapters of this workbook, *titan.jar* is rebuilt, copied to the JBoss *deploy* directory, and redeployed by the application server.

Examine ProcessPaymentBean

`com.titan.processpayment.ProcessPaymentBean` is copied as is from Chapter 11. `@Resource` injection is very vendor-specific. Let's look at how JBoss supports this annotation:

```
package com.titan.processpayment;

import com.titan.domain.*;

import java.sql.*;

import javax.ejb.*;
import javax.annotation.Resource;
import javax.sql.DataSource;
import javax.ejb.EJBException;

@Stateless
public class ProcessPaymentBean implements ProcessPaymentRemote,
                                           ProcessPaymentLocal
{

   final public static String CASH = "CASH";
   final public static String CREDIT = "CREDIT";
   final public static String CHECK = "CHECK";

   @Resource(mappedName="java:/DefaultDS") DataSource dataSource;
```

When you use the `@javax.annotation.Resource` annotation or its XML equivalent, `<resource-ref>`, JBoss requires that you specify the `mappedName()` attribute. JBoss stores all resources in its global JNDI tree. The `mappedName()` attribute expects a global JNDI name string. The `java:/DefaultDS` value references JBoss's default data source. Appendix A provides more detail on how to deploy your own data sources. The `mappedName()` attribute is used in the same way to inject JMS destinations and connection factories.

Examine DataAccessBean

com.titan.access.DataAccessBean is a simple stateless session bean that is used to find and create Customer entities. It also has methods to create and destroy the tables that are needed by the ProcessPayment EJB. We won't go over these because they are quite simple.

Examine the Client

The main client is the com.titan.clients.MakePayment class:

```
package com.titan.clients;

import com.titan.processpayment.*;
import com.titan.domain.Customer;
import com.titan.access.DataAccess;

import java.util.Calendar;
import javax.naming.InitialContext;
import javax.naming.Context;
import javax.naming.NamingException;

/**
 * Example demonstrating use of ProcessPayment EJB directly
 *
 */

public class MakePayment
{

   public static void main(String [] args)
   {
      try
      {
         // obtain CustomerHome
         Context jndiContext = getInitialContext( );
         DataAccess access = (DataAccess)jndiContext.lookup("DataAccessBean/remote");

         access.makePaymentDbTable( );
         Customer cust = new Customer( );
         cust.setFirstName("Bill");
         cust.setLastName("Burke");
         access.createCustomer(cust);
```

The client starts by getting a reference to the DataAccessBean's remote interface. It initializes the payment tables by calling the DataAccess.makePaymentDbTable( ) method and then creates a Customer entity:

```
         ProcessPaymentRemote procpay = (ProcessPaymentRemote)jndiContext.
lookup("ProcessPaymentBean/remote");
```

After obtaining a reference to the ProcessPayment EJB's remote interface, three separate payments are made by cash, check, and credit card for the Customer entity that was created:

```
            System.out.println("Making a payment using byCash()..");
            procpay.byCash(cust,1000.0);

            System.out.println("Making a payment using byCheck()..");
            CheckDO check = new CheckDO("010010101101010100011", 3001);
            procpay.byCheck(cust,check,2000.0);

            System.out.println("Making a payment using byCredit()..");
            Calendar expdate = Calendar.getInstance();
            expdate.set(2025,1,28); // month=1 is January
            CreditCardDO credit = new CreditCardDO("370000000000002",
                     expdate.getTime(),"AMERICAN_EXPRESS");
            procpay.byCredit(cust,credit,3000.0);

            System.out.println("Making a payment using byCheck() with a low check
number..");
            CheckDO check2 = new CheckDO("111000100111010110101", 50);
            try
            {
               procpay.byCheck(cust,check2,9000.0);
               System.out.println("Problem! The PaymentException has not been raised!");
            }
            catch(PaymentException pe)
            {
               System.out.println("Caught PaymentException: "+pe.getMessage());
            }
```

The last bit of code tries to make a check payment with a check number that is too low. A payment exception is thrown in this instance.

```
            access.dropPaymentDbTable();
         }
         catch(Throwable t)
         {
            t.printStackTrace();
         }

      }

      static public Context getInitialContext() throws Exception
      {
         return new InitialContext();
      }

   }
```

The client finishes by dropping the payment table.

Run the Client Application

Run the MakePayment application by invoking ant run.payment at the command prompt. Remember to set your JBOSS_HOME and PATH environment variables. This is the output:

```
run.payment:
     [java] Making a payment using byCash()..
     [java] Making a payment using byCheck()..
     [java] Making a payment using byCredit()..
     [java] Making a payment using byCheck() with a low check number..
     [java] Caught PaymentException: Check number is too low. Must be at least 100
```

Exercise 11.2: XML Override

This exercise is a duplicate of Exercise 11.1, except that the minimum check number required to make a check payment has been overridden in the ejb-jar.xml deployment descriptor.

Start Up JBoss

If you already have JBoss running, there is no reason to restart it. Otherwise, start it up as instructed in Workbook 1.

Initialize the Database

The database tables will be created when Exercise 11.2 is deployed to JBoss. If you have problems running this example, shut down JBoss and run the clean.db Ant task.

Build and Deploy the Example Programs

Perform the following steps:

1. Open a command prompt or shell terminal and change to the *ex11_2* directory created by the extraction process.
2. Set the JAVA_HOME and JBOSS_HOME environment variables to point to where your JDK and JBoss 4.0 are installed. Examples:

   Windows:

   ```
   C:\workbook\ex11_2> set JAVA_HOME=C:\jdk1.5.0
   C:\workbook\ex11_2> set JBOSS_HOME=C:\jboss-4.0.x
   ```

   Unix:

   ```
   $ export JAVA_HOME=/usr/local/jdk1.5.0
   $ export JBOSS_HOME=/usr/local/jboss-4.0
   ```

3. Add ant to your execution path. Ant is the build utility.

Windows:

```
C:\workbook\ex11_2> set PATH=..\ant\bin;%PATH%
```

Unix:

```
$ export PATH=../ant/bin:$PATH
```

4. Perform the build by typing ant.

As in the earlier exercise, *titan.jar* is rebuilt, copied to the JBoss *deploy* directory, and redeployed by the application server.

Examine ProcessPaymentBean

In the ProcessPaymentBean implementation, we defined a minCheckNumber constant that was used to verify that a customer's check number was above a certain number. Otherwise, the payment was not allowed to be processed:

```
package com.titan.processpayment;

import com.titan.domain.*;

import java.sql.*;

import javax.ejb.*;
import javax.annotation.Resource;
import javax.sql.DataSource;
import javax.ejb.EJBException;

@Stateless
public class ProcessPaymentBean implements ProcessPaymentRemote,
                                           ProcessPaymentLocal
{

   final public static String CASH = "CASH";
   final public static String CREDIT = "CREDIT";
   final public static String CHECK = "CHECK";

   @Resource(mappedName="java:/DefaultDS") DataSource dataSource;

   @Resource(name="min") int minCheckNumber = 100;
```

In Exercise 11.1, the minCheckNumber field's @Resource annotation was really more for documentation purposes than to provide any functionality for the application. In Exercise 11.2, however, we override this constant as an <env-entry> with *ejb-jar.xml*.

ejb-jar.xml

```
<ejb-jar
       xmlns="http://java.sun.com/xml/ns/javaee"
       xmlns:xsi="http://www.w3.org/2001/XMLSchema-instance"
       xsi:schemaLocation="http://java.sun.com/xml/ns/javaee
                           http://java.sun.com/xml/ns/javaee/ejb-jar_3_0.xsd"
       version="3.0">
```

```
   <enterprise-beans>
      <session>
         <ejb-name>ProcessPaymentBean</ejb-name>
         <env-entry>
            <env-entry-name>min</env-entry-name>
            <env-entry-type>java.lang.Integer</env-entry-type>
            <env-entry-value>10</env-entry-value>
         </env-entry>
      </session>
   </enterprise-beans>
</ejb-jar>
```

`<env-entry-name>` matches `@Resource`'s `name( )` attribute and `minCheckNumber` is overridden with the value of 10.

Examine the Client

The main client is the `com.titan.clients.MakePayment` class:

```
package com.titan.clients;

import com.titan.processpayment.*;
import com.titan.domain.Customer;
import com.titan.access.DataAccess;

import java.util.Calendar;
import javax.naming.InitialContext;
import javax.naming.Context;
import javax.naming.NamingException;

/**
 * Example demonstrating use of ProcessPayment EJB directly
 *
 */

public class MakePayment
{

   public static void main(String [] args)
   {
...

         System.out.println("Making a payment using byCheck( ) with a low check
number..");
         CheckDO check2 = new CheckDO("111000100111010110101", 50);
         try
         {
            procpay.byCheck(cust,check2,9000.0);
            System.out.println("The PaymentException has not been raised because the
min check number has been overridden in ejb-jar.xml");
         }
         catch(PaymentException pe)
         {
```

```
        System.out.println("Caught PaymentException: "+pe.getMessage( ));
    }
```

In Exercise 11.1, this bit of code aborted with a `PaymentException` because the check number was too low. Because the `minCheckNumber` field in `ProcessPaymentBean` has been overridden with XML, this check payment is now successful.

Run the Client Application

Run the MakePayment application by invoking `ant run.payment` at the command prompt. Remember to set your `JBOSS_HOME` and `PATH` environment variables. This is the output:

```
run.payment:
     [java] Making a payment using byCash( )..
     [java] Making a payment using byCheck( )..
     [java] Making a payment using byCredit( )..
     [java] Making a payment using byCheck( ) with a low check number..
     [java] The PaymentException has not been raised because the min check number
            has been overridden in ejb-jar.xml
```

Exercise 11.3: Annotationless Stateless Session Bean

This exercise is a duplicate of Exercise 11.2, except that all annotations on the ProcessPayment EJB's bean and interface classes have been removed. All metadata is expressed in the `ejb-jar.xml` deployment descriptor.

Start Up JBoss

If you already have JBoss running, there is no reason to restart it. Otherwise, start it up as instructed in Workbook 1.

Initialize the Database

The database tables will be created when Exercise 11.3 is deployed to JBoss. If you have problems running this example, shut down JBoss and run the `clean.db` Ant task.

Build and Deploy the Example Programs

Perform the following steps:

1. Open a command prompt or shell terminal and change to the *ex11_3* directory created by the extraction process.
2. Set the `JAVA_HOME` and `JBOSS_HOME` environment variables to point to where your JDK and JBoss 4.0 are installed. Examples:

Windows:

C:\workbook\ex11_3> set JAVA_HOME=C:\jdk1.5.0
C:\workbook\ex11_3> set JBOSS_HOME=C:\jboss-4.0.x

Unix:

$ export JAVA_HOME=/usr/local/jdk1.5.0
$ export JBOSS_HOME=/usr/local/jboss-4.0

3. Add `ant` to your execution path. Ant is the build utility.

   Windows:

   C:\workbook\ex11_3> set PATH=..\ant\bin;%PATH%

   Unix:

   $ export PATH=../ant/bin:$PATH

4. Perform the build by typing `ant`.

As in the earlier exercises, *titan.jar* is rebuilt, copied to the JBoss *deploy* directory, and redeployed by the application server.

Run the Client

Run the MakePayment application by invoking `ant run.payment` at the command prompt. Remember to set your `JBOSS_HOME` and `PATH` environment variables. This is the output:

```
run.payment:
     [java] Making a payment using byCash()..
     [java] Making a payment using byCheck()..
     [java] Making a payment using byCredit()..
     [java] Making a payment using byCheck() with a low check number..
     [java] The PaymentException has not been raised because the min check number
            has been overridden in ejb-jar.xml
```

Exercise 11.4: Stateful Session Bean

This exercise uses the stateful session TravelAgent EJB introduced in Chapter 11 to implement a crude command-line-driven reservation system. Through this reservation system, you can book a cruise for a customer and pay for it with their credit card.

Start Up JBoss

If you already have JBoss running, there is no reason to restart it. Otherwise, start it up as instructed in Workbook 1.

Initialize the Database

The database tables will be created when Exercise 11.4 is deployed to JBoss. If you have problems running this example, shut down JBoss and run the `clean.db` Ant task.

Build and Deploy the Example Programs

Perform the following steps:

1. Open a command prompt or shell terminal and change to the *ex11_4* directory created by the extraction process.
2. Set the `JAVA_HOME` and `JBOSS_HOME` environment variables to point to where your JDK and JBoss 4.0 are installed. Examples:

   Windows:

   C:\workbook\ex11_4> set JAVA_HOME=C:\jdk1.5.0
   C:\workbook\ex11_4> set JBOSS_HOME=C:\jboss-4.0.x

   Unix:

   $ export JAVA_HOME=/usr/local/jdk1.5.0
   $ export JBOSS_HOME=/usr/local/jboss-4.0
3. Add `ant` to your execution path. Ant is the build utility.

   Windows:

   C:\workbook\ex11_4> set PATH=..\ant\bin;%PATH%

   Unix:

   $ export PATH=../ant/bin:$PATH
4. Perform the build by typing `ant`.

As in the earlier exercises, *titan.jar* is rebuilt, copied to the JBoss *deploy* directory, and redeployed by the application server.

Examine ProcessPaymentBean and TravelAgentBean

These two EJBs are taken directly from Chapter 11, so there is no need to go over their code.

Examine DataAccessBean

The `com.titan.access.DataAccessBean` class was expanded from the previous example to completely initialize the database with a set of Ship, Cruise, and Cabin entities. This initialization is done in the `DataAccessBean.initializeDB( )` method. We won't go over this code because it isn't that interesting.

Examine the Client

The main client is the `com.titan.clients.TravelAgentShell` class. It implements a command-line console that allows you to view cruises and book reservations interactively. The heart of this class is the `shell( )` method:

```
public void shell( ) throws Exception
{
   access = (DataAccess)getInitialContext( ).lookup("DataAccessBean/remote");
   access.initializeDB( );
```

```
        try
        {
           access.makePaymentDbTable( );
        }
        catch (Exception ignored) {}
        while (true)
        {
           System.out.println( );
           System.out.print("> ");

           String command = "";
           char read = '\0';

           while (read != '\r' && read != '\n')
           {
              read = (char)System.in.read( );
              command = command + read;
           }
           // clear out newlines from system input
           int available = System.in.available( );
           for (int i = 0; i < available; i++) System.in.read( );

           command = command.trim( );
           if (command.equals(""))
           {
              continue;
           }
           processCommand(command);
        }
     }
```

The `shell( )` method starts by getting a reference to `DataAccessBean` and initializing the database. It then goes into an infinite loop that accepts command-line input. When it receives user input, it calls the `processCommand( )` method to execute the command. The `processCommand( )` method simply does a series of *if-else-if* blocks to determine the user command entered. We won't go over this code because it is pretty straightforward. Instead, let's look at each method that implements the commands of our console:

```
     public void cruises( )
     {
        System.out.println( );
        List list = access.getCruises( );
        for (Object obj : list)
        {
           Cruise cruise = (Cruise)obj;
           System.out.println(cruise.getId() + "     " + cruise.getName( ));
        }
     }

     public void cabins(String command)
     {
        StringTokenizer tokens = new StringTokenizer(command);
```

```
        tokens.nextToken( );
        int cruiseId = Integer.parseInt(tokens.nextToken().trim( ));

        System.out.println( );
        List list = access.getCabins(cruiseId);
        for (Object obj : list)
        {
           Cabin cabin = (Cabin)obj;
           System.out.println(cabin.getId() + "    " + cabin.getName( ));
        }
        System.out.println( );
     }
```

The cruises( ) and cabins( ) methods interact with DataAccessBean to list possible cruises and cabins the travel agent might want to book. The cabins( ) method requires an integer parameter for the Cruise's primary key so that it can query all cabins that belong to that cruise:

```
     private TravelAgentRemote agent;
     private DataAccess access;

     private TravelAgentRemote getAgent( )
     {
        try
        {
           if (agent == null) agent = (TravelAgentRemote)getInitialContext( ).
   lookup("TravelAgentBean/remote");
        }
        catch (Exception ex){ throw new RuntimeException(ex);}
        return agent;
     }

     public void customer(String command)
     {
        StringTokenizer tokens = new StringTokenizer(command);
        tokens.nextToken( );
        String first = tokens.nextToken().trim( );
        String last = tokens.nextToken().trim( );
        getAgent( ).findOrCreateCustomer(first, last);
        System.out.println("set customer: " + first + " " + last);
     }
```

The customer( ) method finds or creates an existing customer with a given first and last name. It obtains a TravelAgentBean session by calling the getAgent( ) method. The getAgent( ) method determines if the shell program has already created an existing TravelAgent EJB session, and if not, it does a JNDI lookup to create one. Once the customer( ) method has the TravelAgent EJB reference, it invokes the findOrCreateCustomer( ) method to initialize the session's customer:

```
     public void cruise(String command)
     {
        StringTokenizer tokens = new StringTokenizer(command);
        tokens.nextToken( );
```

```
        String id = tokens.nextToken().trim( );
        int cruiseId = Integer.parseInt(id);
        getAgent( ).setCruiseID(cruiseId);
        System.out.println("set cruise: " + id);
    }

    public void cabin(String command)
    {
        StringTokenizer tokens = new StringTokenizer(command);
        tokens.nextToken( );
        String id = tokens.nextToken().trim( );
        int cabinId = Integer.parseInt(id);
        getAgent( ).setCabinID(cabinId);
        System.out.println("set cabin");
    }
```

The `cruise( )` and `cabin( )` methods set the cruise and cabin for which the TravelAgent EJB will book a reservation. They expect an integer ID of the Cabin and Cruise entities:

```
    public void book(String command)
    {
        StringTokenizer tokens = new StringTokenizer(command);
        tokens.nextToken( );
        String number = tokens.nextToken().trim( );
        String exp = tokens.nextToken().trim( );
        String dollars = tokens.nextToken().trim( );
```

The `book( )` method is responsible for booking the reservation. It takes a credit card number, an expiration date, and the dollar amount of the purchase:

```
        Date expDate = null;
        try
        {
            expDate = DateFormat.getDateInstance(DateFormat.SHORT).parse(exp);
        }
        catch (ParseException ex)
        {
            System.out.println("Illegal date format for expiration date! Format is MM/
DD/YY");
            return;
        }
```

The expiration date is parsed from the command line by the `java.text.DateFormat` class, which throws an exception if an illegal date is entered.

```
        if (expDate.before(new java.util.Date( )))
        {
            System.out.println("Credit Card expired: " + expDate.toString( )
                        + " today: " + (new java.util.Date()).toString( ));
            return;
        }
        double amount = Double.parseDouble(dollars);

        String type = "";
```

```
// bet you didn't know that first digit determines type?
if (number.startsWith("5")) type = CreditCardDO.MASTER_CARD;
else if (number.startsWith("4")) type = CreditCardDO.VISA;
else if (number.startsWith("3")) type = CreditCardDO.AMERICAN_EXPRESS;
else type = "UNKNOWN";
```

The code checks to see if the expiration date has passed and converts the command-line dollar amount from a string to a numeric value. The credit card type can be determined from the credit card number. This is an industry standard.

```
CreditCardDO card = new CreditCardDO(number, expDate, type);
try
{
   TicketDO ticket = getAgent( ).bookPassage(card, amount);
   System.out.println(ticket.toString( ));
   System.out.println( );
}
catch (IncompleteConversationalState ex)
{
   System.out.println("You have not set either customer, cruise, or cabin yet.
");
}
```

The code books the reservation by calling the `TravelAgentRemote.bookPassage( )` method. Because this bean class method is annotated with `@javax.ejb.Remove`, the session is destroyed when the method completes.

```
      // agent was removed
      agent = null;
   }
```

Finally, the code nulls out the agent member variable because the stateful TravelAgent EJB session is no longer valid.

Run the Application

Run the TravelAgentShell application by invoking *Shell.bat* or the *Shell.sh* script at the command prompt. Remember to set your `JBOSS_HOME` and `PATH` environment variables. The program starts up with the following prompt:

```
C:\jboss\oreilly-ejb3\workbook\ex11_4>shell

********************
    Titan Cruises
********************



>
```

Type `help` to see the list of commands available from the Titan Cruises reservation system:

```
> help

Titan Cruises Commands
```

```
cruises - list all cruises
cabins {cruiseId} - list all cabins
customer {first} {last} - find or create a customer
cabin {id} - set cabin
cruise {id} - set cruise
book {credit, MM/DD/YY, amount} - book a cruise

>
```

Type cruises to see the list of cruises in the database. This will output the primary key first, and then the name of the cruise. You will need the primary key when booking a reservation.

```
> cruises

1   Alaskan Cruise
2   Atlantic Cruise
```

Type cabins followed by the primary key of a cruise. This will list all the cabins available for that cruise.

```
> cabins 1

1   Queen Cabin 1
2   Queen Cabin 2
```

Type customer followed by any first and last name. This will locate a customer in the database or create one for you by interacting with a TravelAgent EJB session.

```
> customer Bill Burke
set customer: Bill Burke
```

Execute the cruise command, passing in the primary key of the cruise for which you want to make a reservation:

```
> cruise 1
set cruise: 1
```

Execute the cabin command, passing in the primary key of the cabin you want to reserve for that cruise:

```
> cabin 1
set cabin
```

Finally, book a reservation by executing the book command. You need to specify a credit card number (any number beginning with a 3, 4, or 5), as well as an expiration date and the amount of the purchase.

```
> book 4444444444444444 11/1/06 550.0
Bill Burke has been booked for the Alaskan Cruise cruise on ship Queen Mary.
 Your accommodations include Queen Cabin 1 a 1 bed cabin on deck level 1.
 Total charge = 550.0
```

That's it. You have booked a reservation. You can continue to book more reservations if you desire.

Exercise 11.5: Annotationless Stateful Session Bean

This exercise is a duplicate of Exercise 11.4, except that all annotations on the TravelAgent EJB's bean and interface classes have been removed. All metadata is expressed in the `ejb-jar.xml` deployment descriptor.

Start Up JBoss

If you already have JBoss running, there is no reason to restart it. Otherwise, start it up as instructed in Workbook 1.

Initialize the Database

The database tables will be created when Exercise 11.5 is deployed to JBoss. If you have problems running this example, shut down JBoss and run the `clean.db` Ant task.

Build and Deploy the Example Programs

Perform the following steps:

1. Open a command prompt or shell terminal and change to the *ex11_5* directory created by the extraction process.
2. Set the `JAVA_HOME` and `JBOSS_HOME` environment variables to point to where your JDK and JBoss 4.0 are installed. Examples:

   Windows:

   ```
   C:\workbook\ex11_5> set JAVA_HOME=C:\jdk1.5.0
   C:\workbook\ex11_5> set JBOSS_HOME=C:\jboss-4.0.x
   ```

   Unix:

   ```
   $ export JAVA_HOME=/usr/local/jdk1.5.0
   $ export JBOSS_HOME=/usr/local/jboss-4.0
   ```

3. Add `ant` to your execution path. Ant is the build utility.

   Windows:

   ```
   C:\workbook\ex11_5> set PATH=..\ant\bin;%PATH%
   ```

   Unix:

   ```
   $ export PATH=../ant/bin:$PATH
   ```

4. Perform the build by typing `ant`.

As in the earlier exercises, *titan.jar* is rebuilt, copied to the JBoss *deploy* directory, and redeployed by the application server.

Run the Application

Run the TravelAgentShell application by invoking *Shell.bat* or the *Shell.sh* script at the command prompt. Remember to set your `JBOSS_HOME` and `PATH` environment variables. Interaction with this program is described in Exercise 11.4.

WORKBOOK 10

Exercises for Chapter 12

Exercise 12.1: The Message-Driven Bean

In this exercise, we will build the same ReservationProcessor MDB described in Chapter 12. The ReservationProcessor MDB plays the same role as the TravelAgent EJB, but it receives its booking orders through a JMS queue rather than a synchronous remote interface.

To test the MDB, a new client application makes multiple reservations in batch mode, using a JMS queue that's bound to the MDB. A second client application listens on another queue to receive booking confirmation messages.

Along the way, you'll learn how to create a new JMS queue in JBoss and configure a message-driven bean.

Start Up JBoss

If you already have JBoss running, there is no reason to restart it. Otherwise, start it up as instructed in Workbook 1.

Initialize the Database

The database tables will be created when Exercise 12.1 is deployed to JBoss. If you have problems running this example, shut down JBoss and run the `clean.db` Ant task.

Create a New JMS Queue

This exercise requires two different JMS queues: one for the ReservationProcessor MDB and one to receive booking confirmations.

Adding new JMS queues to JBoss is much like adding new JMS topics. As in the exercises in earlier chapters of this workbook, you have two options: one involving a configuration file, the other involving the JMX HTTP connector.

Adding a JMS queue through a configuration file

Adding new JMS queues to JBoss is much like adding new JMS topics. The most common way to set up a JMS queue is to use an XML configuration file. As you learned in Workbook 1, every component in JBoss is a JMX MBean that can be hot-deployed. This part of the exercise shows you how to write a JMX MBean definition for a new JMS queue. You can find the JMX configuration file in the *ex12_1* directory.

jbossmq-titanqueues-service.xml

```
<server>
  <mbean code="org.jboss.mq.server.jmx.Queue"
         name="jboss.mq.destination:service=Queue,
               name=titan-ReservationQueue">
    <depends optional-attribute-name="DestinationManager"
     >jboss.mq:service=DestinationManager</depends>
  </mbean>

  <mbean code="org.jboss.mq.server.jmx.Queue"
         name="jboss.mq.destination:service=Queue,
               name=titan-TicketQueue">
    <depends optional-attribute-name="DestinationManager"
     >jboss.mq:service=DestinationManager</depends>
  </mbean>
</server>
```

Each set of MBeans in a JMX configuration file must be defined within a `<server>` tag. An MBean itself is declared in an `<mbean>` tag. The MBean declarations in this file define the JMS queues you'll use for the example code in this chapter. Each MBean is uniquely identified by its name, called an *ObjectName*. JMX ObjectNames can include any number of key-value parameters to describe the MBean further. In our case, the MBean class representing the JMS topic is declared first (`org.jboss.mq.server.jmx.Queue`), along with its JMX ObjectNames (`jboss.mq.destination:service=Queue, name=titan-ReservationQueue` and `jboss.mq.destination:service=Queue, name=titan-TicketQueue`). For JMS queue MBeans, the `name` attribute of the ObjectName defines how the destination is referenced.

One thing to note is that the application server must deploy the DestinationManager MBean before any queue or topic is deployed. This dependency is declared in *jbossmq-titanqueues-service.xml*'s `depends` tag. JBoss will take care of satisfying this dependency and make sure the `titan-TicketTopic` isn't started until the DestinationManager MBean has finished initializing and is ready to provide services to new queues and topics. Copying this file into the JBoss *deploy* directory will hot-deploy the JMS topic and make it ready for use.

To deploy *jbossmq-titanqueues-service.xml*, run the `make-queues` Ant target:

```
C:\workbook\ex12_2>ant make-queues
Buildfile: build.xml
```

```
make-queues:
     [copy] Copying 1 file to C:\jboss-4.0\server\default\deploy
```

On the server side, the following lines are displayed:

```
[titan-ReservationQueue] Bound to JNDI name: queue/titan-ReservationQueue
[titan-TicketQueue] Bound to JNDI name: queue/titan-TicketQueue
```

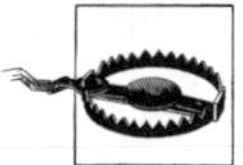

You must deploy the XML file containing the queues *before* you deploy the JAR containing your beans (explained shortly). If you deploy your EJB-JAR first, JBoss detects that the MDB's expected queue does not exist and creates it dynamically. Then, when you try to deploy the XML file that contains the queues, an exception arises, stating that you're trying to create a queue that already exists.

Build and Deploy the Example Programs

Perform the following steps:

1. Open a command prompt or shell terminal and change to the *ex12_1* directory created by the extraction process.
2. Set the `JAVA_HOME` and `JBOSS_HOME` environment variables to point to where your JDK and JBoss 4.0 are installed. Examples:

   Windows:

   ```
   C:\workbook\ex12_1> set JAVA_HOME=C:\jdk1.5.0
   C:\workbook\ex12_1> set JBOSS_HOME=C:\jboss-4.0.x
   ```

   Unix:

   ```
   $ export JAVA_HOME=/usr/local/jdk1.5.0
   $ export JBOSS_HOME=/usr/local/jboss-4.0
   ```

3. Add `ant` to your execution path. Ant is the build utility.

   Windows:

   ```
   C:\workbook\ex12_1> set PATH=..\ant\bin;%PATH%
   ```

   Unix:

   ```
   $ export PATH=../ant/bin:$PATH
   ```

4. Perform the build by typing `ant`.

As in the exercises in earlier chapters of this workbook, *titan.jar* is rebuilt, copied to the JBoss *deploy* directory, and redeployed by the application server.

Examine ProcessPaymentBean and DataAccessBean

The ProcessPayment and DataAccess EJBs are copied directly from Exercise 11.4 in Workbook 9. We won't go over these files again.

Examine the Client Applications

In this exercise, you run two client applications at the same time. The producer generates large numbers of JMS messages destined for the ReservationProcessor MDB. The consumer listens to a JMS queue for messages confirming the bookings and displays them as they come in.

First, the producer gets the cruise ID and the number of bookings from the command line.

JmsClient_ReservationProducer.java

```
public static void main (String [] args) throws Exception
{
   if (args.length != 2)
      throw new Exception
   ("Usage: java JmsClient_ReservationProducer <CruiseID> <count>");

   Integer cruiseID = new Integer (args[0]);
   int count = new Integer (args[1]).intValue ( );
```

The producer then obtains a reference to the DataAccess EJB so that it can initialize all the entities and tables used in the example:

```
Context jndiContext = getInitialContext( );

DataAccess access =(DataAccess)jndiContext.lookup("DataAccessBean/remote");

access.initializeDB( );
try
{
   access.makePaymentDbTable( );
}
catch (Exception ignored) {}
```

Then, the code looks up a `ConnectionFactory` and two JMS queues from the JBoss naming service. The first queue is the one bound to the ReservationProcessor MDB, to which passage booking messages will be sent. The second is the queue that the ReservationProcessor MDB will use to send confirmation messages.

```
ConnectionFactory factory =(ConnectionFactory)
      jndiContext.lookup("ConnectionFactory");

Queue reservationQueue =(Queue)
     jndiContext.lookup("queue/titan-ReservationQueue");
Queue ticketQueue =(Queue)jndiContext.lookup("queue/titan-TicketQueue");

Connection connect = factory.createConnection( );
Session session = connect.createSession(false, Session.AUTO_ACKNOWLEDGE);
MessageProducer sender = session.createProducer(reservationQueue);
```

The client application is now ready to send count booking messages in batch.

For each booking, it then creates a JMS `MapMessage`, assigns the ticket queue into the message's `JMSReplyTo` property, and sets the booking data: Cruise ID, Customer ID, Cabin ID, price, credit card number, expiration date, and so on. Note that only basic data types such as `String` and `int` can be stored in a `MapMessage`:

```
      for(int i = 0; i < count; i++)
      {
         MapMessage message = session.createMapMessage( );

         message.setJMSReplyTo(ticketQueue);  // Used in ReservationProcessor to send
Tickets back out

         message.setStringProperty("MessageFormat", "Version 3.4");

         message.setInt("CruiseID", cruiseID);
         message.setInt("CustomerID", i%2 + 1);  // either Customer 1 or 2, all we've
got in database
         message.setInt("CabinID", i%5 + 1);  // cabins 100-109 only
         message.setDouble("Price",(double)1000 + i);

         // the card expires in about 30 days
         //
         Date expDate = new Date(System.currentTimeMillis( ) + 30*24*60*60*1000L);

         message.setString("CreditCardNum", "5549861006051975");
         message.setLong("CreditCardExpDate", expDate.getTime( ));
         message.setString("CreditCardType", CreditCardDO.MASTER_CARD);

         System.out.println("Sending reservation message #"+i);
         sender.send(message);
      }

      connect.close( );
   }
```

Once all messages are sent, the application closes the connection and terminates. Because messages are sent asynchronously, the application may terminate before the ReservationProcessor EJB has processed all of the messages in the batch.

The consumer application is very similar to the client application in Exercise 12.1. This time, though, it will subscribe not to a topic, but to a queue.

JmsClient_TicketConsumer.java

The consumer application listens for reservation confirmation messages. To receive JMS messages, the client application class implements the `javax.jms.MessageListener` interface, which defines the `onMessage( )` method. The main method simply creates an instance of the class and makes the main thread wait indefinitely:

```
package com.titan.clients;

import javax.jms.Message;
import javax.jms.ObjectMessage;
```

```
import javax.jms.ConnectionFactory;
import javax.jms.Connection;
import javax.jms.Session;
import javax.jms.Queue;
import javax.jms.MessageConsumer;
import javax.jms.JMSException;

import javax.naming.Context;
import javax.naming.InitialContext;

import com.titan.travelagent.TicketDO;

public class JmsClient_TicketConsumer
   implements javax.jms.MessageListener
{

   public static void main(String [] args) throws Exception
   {
      new JmsClient_TicketConsumer( );

      while(true) { Thread.sleep (10000); }
   }
```

The constructor is very simple JMS code that subscribes the client application to the JMS queue and waits for incoming messages:

```
   public JmsClient_TicketConsumer ( ) throws Exception
   {
      Context jndiContext = getInitialContext ( );

      ConnectionFactory factory = (ConnectionFactory)
      jndiContext.lookup ("ConnectionFactory");

      Queue ticketQueue = (Queue)
      jndiContext.lookup ("queue/titan-TicketQueue");

      Connection connect = factory.createConnection( );
      Session session =
         connect.createSession(false,Session.AUTO_ACKNOWLEDGE);
      MessageConsumer receiver = session.createConsumer(ticketQueue);
      receiver.setMessageListener(this);

      System.out.println ("Listening for messages on titan-TicketQueue...");
      connect.start ( );
   }
```

When a message arrives in the queue, the consumer's onMessage( ) method is called. The method simply displays the content of the ticket:

```
   public void onMessage (Message message)
   {
      try
      {
         ObjectMessage objMsg = (ObjectMessage)message;
         TicketDO ticket = (TicketDO)objMsg.getObject ( );
```

```
            System.out.println ("********************************");
            System.out.println (ticket);
            System.out.println ("********************************");

        }
        catch (JMSException displayed)
        {
            displayed.printStackTrace ( );
        }
    }
```

Examine ReservationProcessorBean

`com.titan.reservationprocessor.ReservationProcessorBean` is the MDB that will receive requests from our client application. The code is copied from Chapter 12 of the EJB book. Reference that chapter for an explanation of this code.

Run the Client Applications

You will need two command windows to run this example. In the first console window, launch the consumer application by running `ant run.consumer`. The application waits for reservation confirmation messages:

```
C:\jboss\oreilly-ejb3\workbook\ex12_1>ant run.consumer
Buildfile: build.xml

prepare:

compile:

jar:

run.consumer:
     [java] Listening for messages on titan-TicketQueue...
```

Start the reservation producer with either *BookInBatch.bat* or the *BookInBatch* script, depending on whether you are using Windows or Unix. Adhere to the following usage:

```
BookInBatch <cruiseID> <count>
```

where `cruiseID` is the ID of a cruise in the database and `count` is the number of passages to book.

Book five passages on the Alaskan Cruise:

```
C:\jboss\oreilly-ejb3\workbook\ex12_1>BookInBatch 1 5
Buildfile: build.xml

prepare:

compile:
```

```
jar:

run.bookinbatch:
     [java] Sending reservation message #0
     [java] Sending reservation message #1
     [java] Sending reservation message #2
     [java] Sending reservation message #3
     [java] Sending reservation message #4
```

Shortly after the producer starts, the consumer—which has been patiently listening to its JMS queue for booking confirmations—will display the following:

```
run.consumer:
     [java] Listening for messages on titan-TicketQueue...
     [java] ********************************
     [java] Richard Monson-Haefel has been booked for the Alaskan Cruise cruise on
ship Queen Mary.
     [java]  Your accommodations include Titanic Cabin 1 a 2 bed cabin on deck level
1.
     [java]  Total charge = 1002.0
     [java] ********************************
     [java] ********************************
     [java] Richard Monson-Haefel has been booked for the Alaskan Cruise cruise on
ship Queen Mary.
     [java]  Your accommodations include Queen Cabin 1 a 1 bed cabin on deck level 1.
     [java]  Total charge = 1000.0
     [java] ********************************
     [java] ********************************
     [java] Bill Burke has been booked for the Alaskan Cruise cruise on ship Queen
Mary.
     [java]  Your accommodations include Titanic Cabin 2 a 2 bed cabin on deck level
1.
     [java]  Total charge = 1003.0
     [java] ********************************
     [java] ********************************
     [java] Bill Burke has been booked for the Alaskan Cruise cruise on ship Queen
Mary.
     [java]  Your accommodations include Queen Cabin 2 a 1 bed cabin on deck level 1.
     [java]  Total charge = 1001.0
     [java] ********************************
     [java] ********************************
     [java] Richard Monson-Haefel has been booked for the Alaskan Cruise cruise on
ship Queen Mary.
     [java]  Your accommodations include Titanic Cabin 3 a 2 bed cabin on deck level
1.
     [java]  Total charge = 1004.0
     [java] ********************************
```

Note that because the booking confirmation messages are queued, you could start the consumer much later than the producer, rather than before. The confirmation messages sent by the ReservationProcessor MDB would then be stored on the server until the client application starts and begins to listen to the queue.

WORKBOOK 11

Exercises for Chapter 13

Exercise 13.1: EJB Timer Service

In this exercise, you will learn how to work with the EJB Timer Service. The example in this chapter matches the stateless session bean, ShipMaintenanceBean, that was defined in Chapter 13.

Start Up JBoss

If you already have JBoss running, there is no reason to restart it. Otherwise, start it up as instructed in the Workbook 1.

Initialize the Database

No database is used in this example.

Build and Deploy the Example Programs

Perform the following steps:

1. Open a command prompt or shell terminal and change to the *ex13_1* directory created by the extraction process.
2. Set the `JAVA_HOME` and `JBOSS_HOME` environment variables to point to where your JDK and JBoss 4.0 are installed. Examples:

   Windows:

   ```
   C:\workbook\ex13_1> set JAVA_HOME=C:\jdk1.5.0
   C:\workbook\ex13_1> set JBOSS_HOME=C:\jboss-4.0.x
   ```

   Unix:

   ```
   $ export JAVA_HOME=/usr/local/jdk1.5.0
   $ export JBOSS_HOME=/usr/local/jboss-4.0
   ```

3. Add ant to your execution path. Ant is the build utility.

   Windows:

   C:\workbook\ex13_1> set PATH=..\ant\bin;%PATH%

   Unix:

   $ export PATH=../ant/bin:$PATH

4. Perform the build by typing ant.

As in the exercises in earlier chapters of this workbook, *titan.jar* is rebuilt, copied to the JBoss *deploy* directory, and redeployed by the application server.

Examine ShipMaintenanceBean

com.titan.processpayment.ShipMaintenanceBean is copied as is from Chapter 13, so we won't go over it here.

Examine the Client

The client is the com.titan.clients.ScheduleMaintenace class:

```
package com.titan.clients;

import com.titan.maintenance.ShipMaintenanceRemote;

import java.util.Date;
import java.text.DateFormat;
import java.text.ParseException;

import javax.naming.InitialContext;
import javax.naming.Context;
import javax.naming.NamingException;

/**
 * Example demonstrating use of ProcessPayment EJB directly
 *
 */

public class ScheduleMaintenance
{

   public static void main(String [] args)
   {
      try
      {
         if (args.length < 2)
         {
            System.err.println("usage: ScheduleMaintenance <ship-name> <description>
");
            return;
         }
```

This client expects two parameters that are passed to it from the command line: a ship name and the description of the maintenance you are performing on the ship.

```
         // obtain CustomerHome
         Context jndiContext = getInitialContext( );
         ShipMaintenanceRemote access = (ShipMaintenanceRemote)jndiContext.
lookup("ShipMaintenanceBean/remote");

         String ship = args[0];
         Date date = new Date(System.currentTimeMillis( ) + 5000);
         String desc = args[1];

         access.scheduleMaintenance(ship, desc, date);
```

A reference to the ShipMaintenanceBean is obtained. The date of the maintenance is set to five seconds in the future so that you can see the timeout callback made to the stateless session bean.

Run the Application

Run the ScheduleMaintenance application by invoking *ScheduleMaintenance.bat* or the *ScheduleMaintenance* script at the command prompt, depending on whether you are running on Windows or Unix. Remember to set your JBOSS_HOME and PATH environment variables. You must specify a ship name and a description of the maintenance. There is no interesting output from the client application:

```
C:\jboss\oreilly-ejb3\workbook\ex13_1>ScheduleMaintenance Alaskan Lightbulbs
Buildfile: build.xml

prepare:

compile:

jar:

run.maintenance:

BUILD SUCCESSFUL
```

Look at the JBoss console window. After five seconds or so, the ShipMaintenance-Bean's timer will trigger and you will see the following output:

```
23:07:22,625 INFO  [EJB3Deployer] Deployed: file:/C:/jboss/jboss-4.0.4RC1/server/
default/deploy/titan.jar
23:07:44,546 INFO  [STDOUT] TIMEOUT METHOD CALLED
23:07:44,546 INFO  [STDOUT] Alaskan is scheduling maintenance of Lightbulbs
```

WORKBOOK 12

Exercises for Chapter 15

This chapter implements the interceptor examples shown in Chapter 15 of the EJB book.

Exercise 15.1: EJB Interceptors

This exercise implements the profiling interceptor shown in Chapter 15. The `@javax.interceptor.Interceptors` annotation is applied to the TravelAgent EJB's `bookPassage()` method to show method-level interception.

Start Up JBoss

If you already have JBoss running, there is no reason to restart it. Otherwise, start it up as instructed in Chapter 15.

Initialize the Database

The database tables will be created when Exercise 15.1 is deployed to JBoss. If you have problems running this example, shut down JBoss and run the `clean.db` Ant task.

Build and Deploy the Example Programs

Perform the following steps:

1. Open a command prompt or shell terminal and change to the *ex15_1* directory created by the extraction process.
2. Set the `JAVA_HOME` and `JBOSS_HOME` environment variables to point to where your JDK and JBoss 4.0 are installed. Examples:

   Windows:

   ```
   C:\workbook\ex15_1> set JAVA_HOME=C:\jdk1.5.0
   C:\workbook\ex15_1> set JBOSS_HOME=C:\jboss-4.0.x
   ```

Unix:

$ export JAVA_HOME=/usr/local/jdk1.5.0
$ export JBOSS_HOME=/usr/local/jboss-4.0

3. Add ant to your execution path. Ant is the build utility.

   Windows:

   C:\workbook\ex15_1> set PATH=..\ant\bin;%PATH%

   Unix:

   $ export PATH=../ant/bin:$PATH

4. Perform the build by typing ant.

As in the exercises in earlier chapters of this workbook, *titan.jar* is rebuilt, copied to the JBoss *deploy* directory, and redeployed by the application server.

Examine the Code

This example extends the command-line-driven Titan Reservation console application in Exercise 11.4 in Workbook 9. The interceptor class we will apply to the TravelAgent EJB is an exact copy of the `Profiler` interceptor class described in Chapter 15 of the EJB book. We will not cover this code. The `TravelAgentBean` class has been modified to apply the `Profiler` interceptor to the `bookPassage( )` method:

```
package com.titan.travelagent;

import com.titan.processpayment.*;
import com.titan.domain.*;
import javax.ejb.*;
import javax.persistence.*;
import javax.annotation.EJB;
import java.util.Date;

@Stateful
public class TravelAgentBean implements TravelAgentRemote {
...

    @Remove
    @Interceptors(com.titan.interceptors.Profiler.class)
    public TicketDO bookPassage(CreditCardDO card, double price)
        throws IncompleteConversationalState {

        if (customer == null || cruise == null || cabin == null)
        {
            throw new IncompleteConversationalState( );
        }
        try {
            Reservation reservation = new Reservation(
                                  customer, cruise, cabin, price, new Date( ));
            entityManager.persist(reservation);

            processPayment.byCredit(customer, card, price);
```

```
            TicketDO ticket = new TicketDO(customer, cruise, cabin, price);
            return ticket;
        } catch(Exception e) {
            throw new EJBException(e);
        }
    }
```

Run the Application

Run the TravelAgentShell application by invoking *Shell.bat* or the *Shell.sh* script at the command prompt. Remember to set your JBOSS_HOME and PATH environment variables. Interact with the Titan Cruises reservation system as you did in Exercise 11.4 in Workbook 9:

```
> book 4444444444444444 11/1/06 550.0
Bill Burke has been booked for the Alaskan Cruise cruise on ship Queen Mary.
 Your accommodations include Queen Cabin 1 a 1 bed cabin on deck level 1.
 Total charge = 550.0
```

After you have booked a reservation, look at the JBoss console. You will see that the Profiler interceptor has timed the bookPassage( ) method and output it to the screen:

```
12:27:29,750 INFO  [STDOUT] Method public com.titan.travelagent.TicketDO com.titan.
travelagent.TravelAgentBean.bookPassa
ge(com.titan.processpayment.CreditCardDO,double) throws com.titan.travelagent.
IncompleteConversationalState took 16 (ms)
```

Exercise 15.2: Intercepting EJB Callbacks

This exercise implements the @JndiInjected custom injection annotation discussed in Chapter 15. A simple stateless session bean uses this annotation to inject JBoss's transaction manager, which is available in the global JNDI.

Start Up JBoss

If you already have JBoss running, there is no reason to restart it. Otherwise, start it up as instructed in Workbook 1.

Initialize the Database

There is no database in this example.

Build and Deploy the Example Programs

Perform the following steps:

1. Open a command prompt or shell terminal and change to the *ex15_2* directory created by the extraction process.

2. Set the `JAVA_HOME` and `JBOSS_HOME` environment variables to point to where your JDK and JBoss 4.0 are installed. Examples:

   Windows:

   ```
   C:\workbook\ex15_2> set JAVA_HOME=C:\jdk1.5.0
   C:\workbook\ex15_2> set JBOSS_HOME=C:\jboss-4.0.x
   ```

   Unix:

   ```
   $ export JAVA_HOME=/usr/local/jdk1.5.0
   $ export JBOSS_HOME=/usr/local/jboss-4.0
   ```

3. Add `ant` to your execution path. Ant is the build utility.

   Windows:

   ```
   C:\workbook\ex15_2> set PATH=..\ant\bin;%PATH%
   ```

   Unix:

   ```
   $ export PATH=../ant/bin:$PATH
   ```

4. Perform the build by typing `ant`.

As in earlier exercises, *titan.jar* is rebuilt, copied to the JBoss *deploy* directory, and redeployed by the application server.

Examine the Code

The `@JndiInjected` annotation and the `JndiInjector` interceptor are taken directly from Chapter 15, so no further explanation is required. The `@JndiInjected` annotation is used on a simple stateless session bean that uses the injected `javax.transaction.TransactionManager` to see if there is a current transaction:

```
package com.titan.simple;

import com.titan.annotations.JndiInjected;
import javax.ejb.*;
import javax.transaction.TransactionManager;


@Stateless
public class SimpleBean implements SimpleRemote
{

   @JndiInjected("java:/TransactionManager")
   TransactionManager tm;

   public void echo(String message) throws Exception
   {
      System.out.print(message);

      System.out.println("Is there a transaction: " + (tm.getTransaction( ) != null));
   }

}
```

The client application simply obtains a reference to SimpleBean and invokes the echo( ) method. The JndiInjector interceptor is applied using the *ejb-jar.xml* deployment descriptor:

```
<?xml version="1.0" encoding="UTF-8"?>
<ejb-jar
       xmlns="http://java.sun.com/xml/ns/javaee"
       xmlns:xsi="http://www.w3.org/2001/XMLSchema-instance"
       xsi:schemaLocation="http://java.sun.com/xml/ns/javaee
                           http://java.sun.com/xml/ns/javaee/ejb-jar_3_0.xsd"
       version="3.0">
   <assembly-descriptor>
      <interceptor-binding>
         <ejb-name>*</ejb-name>
         <interceptor-class>
            com.titan.interceptors.JndiInjector
         </interceptor-class>
      </interceptor-binding>
   </assembly-descriptor>
</ejb-jar>
```

A default interceptor binding is used to apply the JndiInjector interceptor.

Run the Client

Run the Client application by invoking ant run.client. Remember to set your JBOSS_HOME and PATH environment variables. The client has no interesting output, but JBoss will output an echo message on the JBoss console window:

```
13:30:03,359 INFO  [EJB3Deployer] Deployed: file:/C:/jboss/jboss-4.0.4RC1/server/
default/deploy/titan.jar
13:30:07,578 INFO  [STDOUT] hello world
13:30:07,578 INFO  [STDOUT] Is there a transaction: true
```

WORKBOOK 13

Exercises for Chapter 16

This chapter's exercises illustrate the conversational persistence context behavior discussed in Chapter 16.

Exercise 16.1: Conversational Persistence Contexts

This exercise implements the modifications we made to the TravelAgent and ProcessPayment EJBs to illustrate queuing behavior when extended persistence contexts are invoked upon outside of a transaction. The Titan Cruises reservation system from Exercise 11.4 in Workbook 9 has been modified so that you can book multiple reservations with the same TravelAgent EJB in one large, distributed conversation.

Start Up JBoss

If you already have JBoss running, there is no reason to restart it. Otherwise, start it up as instructed in Workbook 1.

Initialize the Database

The database tables will be created when Exercise 16.1 is deployed to JBoss. If you have problems running this example, shut down JBoss and run the `clean.db` Ant task.

Build and Deploy the Example Programs

Perform the following steps:

1. Open a command prompt or shell terminal and change to the *ex16_1* directory created by the extraction process.
2. Set the `JAVA_HOME` and `JBOSS_HOME` environment variables to point to where your JDK and JBoss 4.0 are installed. Examples:

   Windows:

   ```
   C:\workbook\ex16_1> set JAVA_HOME=C:\jdk1.5.0
   C:\workbook\ex16_1> set JBOSS_HOME=C:\jboss-4.0.x
   ```

Unix:

```
$ export JAVA_HOME=/usr/local/jdk1.5.0
$ export JBOSS_HOME=/usr/local/jboss-4.0
```

3. Add ant to your execution path. Ant is the build utility.

   Windows:

   ```
   C:\workbook\ex16_1> set PATH=..\ant\bin;%PATH%
   ```

   Unix:

   ```
   $ export PATH=../ant/bin:$PATH
   ```

4. Perform the build by typing `ant`.

As in the exercises in earlier chapters of this workbook, *titan.jar* is rebuilt, copied to the JBoss *deploy* directory, and redeployed by the application server.

Examine the Server Code

The changes made to the TravelAgent and ProcessPayment EJBs have been taken directly from the "Conversational Persistence Contexts" section of Chapter 16. That chapter adequately describes the class changes, so we won't go over them here. The CruiseCabin entity described in the "Optimistic Locking" section is incorporated into the example, along with the Payment entity defined in the "Conversational Persistence Contexts" section.

The primary key generation mechanism had to be changed for this example. The purpose of this exercise is to show how entity manager operations are queued until the persistence context becomes associated with a transaction. The Hibernate Entity Manager implementation uses an identity column by default for its primary key generation. This requires a database insert immediately when the `EntityManager.persist( )` method is executed. Because the whole point of this exercise is to queue inserts, an `@TableGenerator` primary key generation strategy was necessary for all entities in this example.

Examine the Client

The `TravelAgentShell` class has been modified a little bit to support multiple reservations per TravelAgent EJB. The `book( )` method no longer nulls out the agent member variable because `TravelAgentBean.bookPassage( )` doesn't end the session. A new `checkout` command was also added:

```
public void checkout( )
{
   getAgent().checkout( );
   agent = null;
}
```

The TravelAgentBean.checkout( ) method is annotated with @Remove. When this method is invoked, all booked reservations are added to the database and the TravelAgent session is completed and removed.

Run the Application

Run the TravelAgentShell application by invoking *Shell.bat* or the *Shell.sh* script at the command prompt. Remember to set your JBOSS_HOME and PATH environment variables. This program works as it does in Exercise 11.4, except that reservations are not created in the database until you execute the checkout command:

```
C:\jboss\oreilly-ejb3\workbook\ex16_1>shell

********************
    Titan Cruises
********************


> cruise 1
set cruise: 1

> cabin 1
set cabin

> customer Bill Burke
set customer: Bill Burke

> book 4444444444444444 10/1/06 550.0
Bill Burke has been booked for the Alaskan Cruise cruise on ship Queen Mary.
 Your accommodations include Queen Cabin 1 a 1 bed cabin on deck level 1.
 Total charge = 550.0


> cabin 2
set cabin

> book 4444444444444444 10/1/06 750.0
Bill Burke has been booked for the Alaskan Cruise cruise on ship Queen Mary.
 Your accommodations include Queen Cabin 2 a 1 bed cabin on deck level 1.
 Total charge = 750.0

> checkout
```

For this example, the hibernate.show_sql property has been set so that you can see all the SQL executed in the JBoss console window. If you watch the console as you interact with the reservation system, you will see that no inserts or updates are executed until the checkout command is issued.

WORKBOOK 14

Exercises for Chapter 17

This chapter implements the security changes to the EJBs discussed in Chapter 17 of the EJB book.

Exercise 17.1: Security

This exercise secures the Titan Cruises Reservation system introduced in Exercise 11. 4 in Workbook 9. It modifies the ProcessPayment EJB so that only authorized merchant users can invoke payment operations.

Configure JBoss Security

If JBoss is running, shut it down. You will need to make some configuration modifications to enable security for this exercise.

To enable security in the JBoss application server, you need to create a *security domain*. A security domain is a repository for users, passwords, and the roles with which each user is associated. The EJB container delegates to the security domain when performing authentication and authorization. Each container can be associated with a different domain.

Out of the box, JBoss supports three types of domains: relational databases, LDAP, and a flat file. For this example, we will use a clear-text flat file to store our users, passwords, and role associations. Security domains are configured in the *jboss-4.0.x/server/default/conf/login-config.xml* file. Open this file in your favorite editor and add the following XML within the <policy> element:

```
<application-policy name="TitanIdentityDB">
  <authentication>
      <login-module code="org.jboss.security.auth.spi.UsersRolesLoginModule"
                   flag = "required">
         <module-option name="usersProperties">
                  users-titan.properties
         </module-option>
```

```
            <module-option name="rolesProperties">
                    roles-titan.properties
            </module-option>
        </login-module>
    </authentication>
</application-policy>
```

The name attribute of the <application-policy> element is the name of your security domain. You will reference this name when you configure your EJBs for security. Two files are used to store security information; they are defined by the usersProperties and rolesProperties module options. The values reference a file that should be available as a resource in your Java classpath. For this exercise, these files are located in the *src/resources* directory. They are stored in the EJB-JAR file created by the Ant build script for this exercise. Let's look at each of them.

users-titan.properties

```
wburke=password
richard=password
```

The *users-titan.properties* file is a set of name value pairs, where the name represents a user in our Titan Cruises reservation system and the value is the user's clear-text password. We have two users defined: wburke and richard.

roles-titan.properties

```
wburke=AUTHORIZED_MERCHANT
richard=UNAUTHORIZED_MERCHANT
```

The *roles-titan.properties* file defines which roles are associated with each user. It is a set of name value pairs, where the name is the user and the value is a comma-delimited list of roles with which the user is associated.

Start Up JBoss

After you have modified *login-config.xml,* restart it as instructed in Workbook 1.

Initialize the Database

The database tables will be created when Exercise 17.1 is deployed to JBoss. If you have problems running this example, shut down JBoss and run the clean.db Ant task.

Build and Deploy the Example Programs

Perform the following steps:

1. Open a command prompt or shell terminal and change to the *ex17_1* directory created by the extraction process.

2. Set the JAVA_HOME and JBOSS_HOME environment variables to point to where your JDK and JBoss 4.0 are installed. Examples:

   Windows:

   C:\workbook\ex17_1> set JAVA_HOME=C:\jdk1.5.0
   C:\workbook\ex17_1> set JBOSS_HOME=C:\jboss-4.0.x

   Unix:

   $ export JAVA_HOME=/usr/local/jdk1.5.0
   $ export JBOSS_HOME=/usr/local/jboss-4.0

3. Add ant to your execution path. Ant is the build utility.

   Windows:

   C:\workbook\ex17_1> set PATH=..\ant\bin;%PATH%

   Unix:

   $ export PATH=../ant/bin:$PATH

4. Perform the build by typing ant.

As in the exercises in earlier chapters of this workbook, *titan.jar* is rebuilt, copied to the JBoss *deploy* directory, and redeployed by the application server.

Examine the ProcessPaymentBean Class

To enable security for the ProcessPayment EJB, we must apply the @org.jboss.annotation.security.SecurityDomain annotation to the com.titan.processpayment.ProcessPaymentBean class:

```
package com.titan.processpayment;

import com.titan.domain.*;

import java.sql.*;

import javax.ejb.*;
import javax.annotation.Resource;
import javax.sql.DataSource;
import javax.ejb.EJBException;
import org.jboss.annotation.security.SecurityDomain;
import javax.annotation.security.PermitAll;
import javax.annotation.security.RolesAllowed;

@Stateless
@SecurityDomain("TitanIdentityDB")
@RolesAllowed("AUTHORIZED_MERCHANT")
public class ProcessPaymentBean implements ProcessPaymentRemote,
                                           ProcessPaymentLocal
{
```

The value you specify for the @SecurityDomain annotation must match the security domain you configured earlier in *login-config.xml*. The bean class is also annotated with the default roles allowed for each method of this EJB:

```
final public static String CASH = "CASH";
final public static String CREDIT = "CREDIT";
final public static String CHECK = "CHECK";

@Resource(mappedName="java:/DefaultDS") DataSource dataSource;

@Resource(name="min") int minCheckNumber = 100;

@PermitAll
public boolean byCash(Customer customer, double amount)
   throws PaymentException
{
   return process(customer.getId( ), amount, CASH, null, -1, null, null);
}

@RolesAllowed({"AUTHORIZED_MERCHANT", "CHECK_FRAUD_ENABLED"})
public boolean byCheck(Customer customer, CheckDO check, double amount)
   throws PaymentException
{
   if (check.checkNumber > minCheckNumber)
   {
      return process(customer.getId( ), amount, CHECK,
                     check.checkBarCode, check.checkNumber, null, null);
   }
   else
   {
      throw new PaymentException("Check number is too low. Must be at least
"+minCheckNumber);
   }
}
public boolean byCredit(Customer customer, CreditCardDO card,
                        double amount) throws PaymentException
{
```

The rest of the bean methods are annotated the same way as the example in Chapter 17.

Examine the Client

The `TravelAgentShell` class has been modified a little bit to support a login. The `shell( )` method calls the `login( )` method before it starts to receive commands:

```
public void login( ) throws Exception
{
   String prompt = "user: ";
   boolean hasUser = false;
   boolean hasPassword = false;
   System.out.println( );
   while (!hasPassword)
   {
      System.out.print(prompt);

      String command = "";
      char read = '\0';
```

```
            while (read != '\r' && read != '\n')
            {
               read = (char)System.in.read( );
               command = command + read;
            }
            // clear out newlines from system input
            int available = System.in.available( );
            for (int i = 0; i < available; i++) System.in.read( );

            command = command.trim( );
            if (command.equals(""))
            {
               continue;
            }
            if (!hasUser)
            {
               user = command;
               hasUser = true;
               prompt = "password: ";
            }
            else
            {
               password = command;
               hasPassword = true;
            }
         }
      }
```

The `login( )` method retrieves the username and password from the command line and stores them in two member variables.

JBoss associates the username and password through the JNDI API. The `getInitialContext( )` method performs this association:

```
      public Context getInitialContext( ) throws Exception
      {
         Properties env = new Properties( );
         env.setProperty(Context.SECURITY_PRINCIPAL, user);
         env.setProperty(Context.SECURITY_CREDENTIALS, password);
         env.setProperty(Context.INITIAL_CONTEXT_FACTORY, "org.jboss.security.jndi.
   JndiLoginInitialContextFactory");
         return new InitialContext(env);
      }
```

Authentication does not take place when `InitialContext` is created; the EJB container is responsible for starting that process. We have not associated a security domain with the TravelAgent EJB. Authentication and authorization do not take place until the `TravelAgentBean.bookPassage( )` method invokes on the ProcessPayment EJB. In a real system, you probably would want to secure the TravelAgent EJB as well. The exercise was implemented in this way to show you that the security principal and credentials are propagated to nested EJB calls.

Run the Application

Run the TravelAgentShell application by invoking *Shell.bat* or the *Shell.sh* script at the command prompt. Remember to set your JBOSS_HOME and PATH environment variables. When you start up this program, it asks you for a username and a password. Specify one of the users defined in the *users-titan.properties* file. Only wburke will work:

```
C:\jboss\oreilly-ejb3\workbook\ex17_1>shell

********************
    Titan Cruises
********************


user: wburke
password: password

>
```

Interact with the Titan Cruises Reservation system the same way you did in Exercise 11.4 in Workbook 9. If you have entered a wrong username or password, the book command will fail with a javax.ejb.EJBAccessException thrown.

Exercise 17.2: Securing Through XML

This exercise uses the same code as that in Exercise 17.1, except that we do not use the @SecurityDomain annotation to secure the ProcessPayment EJB.

Configure JBoss Security

If you haven't already, configure the security domain described in Exercise 17.1.

Start Up JBoss

After you have modified *login-config.xml,* restart it as instructed in Workbook 1.

Initialize the Database

The database tables will be created when Exercise 17.2 is deployed to JBoss. If you have problems running this example, shut down JBoss and run the clean.db Ant task.

Build and Deploy the Example Programs

Perform the following steps:

1. Open a command prompt or shell terminal and change to the *ex17_2* directory created by the extraction process.

2. Set the JAVA_HOME and JBOSS_HOME environment variables to point to where your JDK and JBoss 4.0 are installed. Examples:

   Windows:

   C:\workbook\ex17_2> set JAVA_HOME=C:\jdk1.5.0
   C:\workbook\ex17_2> set JBOSS_HOME=C:\jboss-4.0.x

   Unix:

   $ export JAVA_HOME=/usr/local/jdk1.5.0
   $ export JBOSS_HOME=/usr/local/jboss-4.0

3. Add ant to your execution path. Ant is the build utility.

   Windows:

   C:\workbook\ex17_2> set PATH=..\ant\bin;%PATH%

   Unix:

   $ export PATH=../ant/bin:$PATH

4. Perform the build by typing ant.

As in the exercises in earlier chapters of this workbook, *titan.jar* is rebuilt, copied to the JBoss *deploy* directory, and redeployed by the application server.

Examine the JBoss Configuration Files

Instead of using the @SecurityDomain annotation, we will secure both the TravelAgent and ProcessPayment EJBs using the jboss.xml deployment descriptor:

```
<?xml version="1.0" encoding="UTF-8"?>
<jboss>
   <security-domain>TitanIdentityDB</security-domain>
</jboss>
```

The <security-domain> element defines a security domain that will be associated with each EJB in the deployment.

Run the Application

Run the TravelAgentShell application by invoking *Shell.bat* or the *Shell.sh* script at the command prompt, just as you did in Exercise 17.1. Remember to set your JBOSS_HOME and PATH environment variables. When you start up this program, it will ask you for a username and a password. This time, enter a bad username or a bad password. Because the TravelAgent EJB is now secured, a javax.ejb.EJBAccessException is thrown:

```
C:\jboss\oreilly-ejb3\workbook\ex17_2>shell

********************
    Titan Cruises
********************


user: baduser
password: badpass
Exception in thread "main" javax.ejb.EJBAccessException: Authentication failure
       at ...
```

WORKBOOK 15

Exercises for Chapter 19

Chapter 19 of the EJB book explained the web services APIs available in EJB 3.0. The exercises in this chapter walk you through exposing and using an EJB as a web service.

Exercise 19.1: Exposing a Stateless Bean

This exercise exposes `TravelAgentBean`, which was developed in Chapter 4, as a web service using JAX-WS. To demonstrate interoperability, and to provide example material for the JAX-RPC sections, the client that calls `TravelAgentBean` will use the JAX-RPC API. We will begin by building and deploying the EJB-JAR and the Java EE application client JAR.

Start Up JBoss

Start up JBoss as described in Workbook 1.

Initialize the Database

You do not need to create any database tables because we will use the same persistence configuration in the exercises for Chapter 4, which will generate the tables automatically.

Build and Deploy the Example Programs

Perform the following steps:

1. Open a command prompt or shell terminal and change to the *ex19_1* directory created by the extraction process.
2. Set the `JAVA_HOME` and `JBOSS_HOME` environment variables to point to where your JDK and JBoss 4.0 are installed. Examples:

Windows:

C:\workbook\ex19_1> set JAVA_HOME=C:\jdk1.5.0
C:\workbook\ex19_1> set JBOSS_HOME=C:\jboss-4.0.x

Unix:

$ export JAVA_HOME=/usr/local/jdk1.5.0
$ export JBOSS_HOME=/usr/local/jboss-4.0

3. Add ant to your execution path. Ant is the build utility.

   Windows:

   C:\workbook\ex19_1> set PATH=..\ant\bin;%PATH%

   Unix:

   $ export PATH=../ant/bin:$PATH

4. Perform the build by typing `ant`. Ant uses *build.xml* to figure out what to compile and how to build your JARs.

This will build and deploy two JARs: *titan.jar* and *titan-client.jar*. The former contains the stateless `TravelAgentBean` and the `Cabin` entity bean; the latter contains deployment descriptors, which are necessary for a Java EE application client.

Examining TravelAgentBean

We start by looking at the `TravelAgentBean` source code. As you can see, the implementation is nearly identical to the one in Chapter 4; only a few JAX-WS annotations have been added:

```
@WebService(name = "TravelAgent", serviceName="TravelAgentService")
@Stateless
public class TravelAgentBean implements TravelAgentRemote
{
    @PersistenceContext(unitName="titan") private EntityManager manager;

    @WebMethod
    public void createCabin(
       @WebParam(name = "Cabin")
       Cabin cabin
    )
    {
        manager.persist(cabin);
    }

    @WebMethod
    @WebResult(name = "Cabin")
    public Cabin findCabin(
       @WebParam(name = "ID")
       int pKey
    )
    {
        return manager.find(Cabin.class, pKey);
    }
}
```

Both createCabin( ) and findCabin( ) are exposed as web services operations, and their corresponding parameters and return values are assigned capitalized names. Just as in Chapter 4, the Cabin entity bean is reused as a Data Transfer Object. This object will automatically be mapped to schema that describes its *getter/setter* methods. Because we have not declared a style, we know that the default Document/Literal Wrapped style will be used.

Examining the Generated WSDL

At this point, the TravelAgentBean has already been deployed, so the WSDL from the service can be retrieved by adding ?wsdl to the TravelAgentBean's endpoint address. Open your favorite web browser and enter the following URL:

http://localhost:8080/titan/TravelAgentBean?wsdl

If you look at the generated schema, you will see that the request and response messages contain the names assigned with the @WebParam and @WebResult annotations:

```
<complexType name="createCabin">
  <sequence>http://localhost:8080/titan/TravelAgentBean?wsdl
    <element name="Cabin" nillable="true" type="ns2:Cabin" />
  </sequence>
</complexType>
<complexType name="createCabinResponse">
  <sequence />
</complexType>
<complexType name="findCabin">
  <sequence>
    <element name="ID" type="int" />
  </sequence>
</complexType>
<complexType name="findCabinResponse">
  <sequence>
    <element name="Cabin" nillable="true" type="ns2:Cabin" />
  </sequence>
</complexType>
<element name="createCabin" type="tns:createCabin" />
<element name="createCabinResponse" type="tns:createCabinResponse" />
<element name="findCabin" type="tns:findCabin" />
<element name="findCabinResponse" type="tns:findCabinResponse" />
```

Also, a schema type will describe the Cabin entity bean:

```
<complexType name="Cabin">
  <sequence>
    <element name="bedCount" type="int" />
    <element name="deckLevel" type="int" />
    <element name="id" type="int" />
    <element name="name" nillable="true" type="string" />
    <element name="shipId" type="int" />
  </sequence>
</complexType>
```

Examining the Client

The Client is very similar to the RMI client developed in Chapter 4. There are only two differences. The first is the use of a Data Transfer Object. In order to have greater separation between the client and the server, we created a duplicate class for `Cabin`. The class is nearly identical to the Cabin entity bean, except that it has no annotations. However, we did not have to do this; we could have just reused the entity bean on the client side as well. The other difference is the process for obtaining the bean reference. With RMI, we simply had to look up the remote interface. With our JAX-RPC client, we need to look up the service interface and then call `getTravelAgentPort( )` to get our endpoint interface. Beyond that point, the client is identical:

```
Context jndiContext = getInitialContext( );
TravelAgentService service =
    (TravelAgentService) jndiContext.lookup(
       "java:comp/env/service/TravelAgentService");
TravelAgent agent = service.getTravelAgentPort( );

Cabin cabin_1 = new Cabin( );
cabin_1.setId(1);
cabin_1.setName("Master Suite");
cabin_1.setDeckLevel(1);
cabin_1.setShipId(1);
cabin_1.setBedCount(3);

agent.createCabin(cabin_1);

Cabin cabin_2 = agent.findCabin(1);
System.out.println(cabin_2.getName( ));
System.out.println(cabin_2.getDeckLevel( ));
System.out.println(cabin_2.getShipId( ));
System.out.println(cabin_2.getBedCount( ));
```

The Java EE Application Client Deployment Descriptor

The preceding client code performed a lookup on the name `java:comp/env/service/TravelAgentService`. This name refers to a service called `service/TravelAgentService` that is within the Environment Naming Context (ENC) of the Java EE application client. This value is pulled from the `application-client.xml` deployment descriptor:

```
<application-client xmlns="http://java.sun.com/xml/ns/j2ee"
  xmlns:xsi="http://www.w3.org/2001/XMLSchema-instance"
  xsi:schemaLocation="http://java.sun.com/xml/ns/j2ee http://java.sun.com/xml/ns/
j2ee/application-client_1_4.xsd"
  version="1.4">

  <display-name>TravelAgent Client</display-name>

  <service-ref>
    <service-ref-name>service/TravelAgentService</service-ref-name>
```

```
    <service-interface>com.titan.clients.TravelAgentService</service-interface>
    <wsdl-file>META-INF/wsdl/TravelAgentBean.wsdl</wsdl-file>
    <jaxrpc-mapping-file>META-INF/jaxrpc-mapping.xml</jaxrpc-mapping-file>
    <port-component-ref>
      <service-endpoint-interface>com.titan.clients.TravelAgent</service-endpoint-
interface>
    </port-component-ref>
  </service-ref>

</application-client>
```

As in the preceding code, `service/TravelAgentService` is mapped to the `TravelAgentService` service interface, as well as the `TravelAgent` service endpoint interface. The location of the JAX-RPC mapping file within the `titan-`*client.jar* file is also specified.

The JBoss Application Client Deployment Descriptor

The astute reader may have noticed that the `<wsdl-file>` tag specifies a file that does not exist in the client deployment. This is intentional, because in this example, we wish to pull the file dynamically from a URL. Because the specification only allows for files, a proprietary configuration element is needed. It is specified using the `<wsdl-override>` tag in the *jboss-client.xml* file:

```
<!DOCTYPE jboss-client PUBLIC
   "-//JBoss//DTD Application Client 4.0//EN"
   "http://www.jboss.org/j2ee/dtd/jboss-client_4_0.dtd">

<jboss-client>
  <jndi-name>titan-client</jndi-name>

  <service-ref>
    <service-ref-name>service/TravelAgentService</service-ref-name>
    <wsdl-override>http://localhost:8080/titan/TravelAgentBean?wsdl</wsdl-override>
  </service-ref>

</jboss-client>
```

Examining the Service Endpoint Interface

The service endpoint interface used by our JAX-RPC client looks identical to the contract provided by the JAX-WS service we reviewed earlier:

```
package com.titan.clients;

/**
 * JAX-RPC Service Endpoint Interface
 */
public interface TravelAgent extends java.rmi.Remote
{
```

```
    public CreateCabinResponse createCabin(Cabin cabin) throws java.rmi.
RemoteException;
    public Cabin findCabin(int ID) throws java.rmi.RemoteException;
}
```

Examining the JAX-RPC Mapping File

The JAX-RPC mapping file must specify how the custom types defined in the TravelAgentBean WSDL are represented in Java. The Cabin schema type is mapped to the Cabin Data Transfer Object as follows:

```
<java-type>com.titan.clients.Cabin</java-type>
<root-type-qname xmlns:typeNS="http://domain.titan.com/jaws">typeNS:Cabin</root-type-
qname>
  <qname-scope>complexType</qname-scope>
  <variable-mapping>
    <java-variable-name>bedCount</java-variable-name>
    <xml-element-name>bedCount</xml-element-name>
  </variable-mapping>
  <variable-mapping>
    <java-variable-name>deckLevel</java-variable-name>
    <xml-element-name>deckLevel</xml-element-name>
  </variable-mapping>
  <variable-mapping>
    <java-variable-name>id</java-variable-name>
    <xml-element-name>id</xml-element-name>
  </variable-mapping>
  <variable-mapping>
    <java-variable-name>name</java-variable-name>
    <xml-element-name>name</xml-element-name>
  </variable-mapping>
  <variable-mapping>
    <java-variable-name>shipId</java-variable-name>
    <xml-element-name>shipId</xml-element-name>
  </variable-mapping>
</java-xml-type-mapping>
```

It must also define how the service endpoint interface maps to the TravelAgentBean WSDL:

```
<service-endpoint-interface>
  com.titan.clients.TravelAgent
</service-endpoint-interface>
<wsdl-port-type xmlns:portTypeNS="http://travelagent.titan.com/jaws">
  portTypeNS:TravelAgent
</wsdl-port-type>
<wsdl-binding xmlns:bindingNS="http://travelagent.titan.com/jaws">
  bindingNS:TravelAgentBinding
</wsdl-binding>
<service-endpoint-method-mapping>
  <java-method-name>createCabin</java-method-name>
  <wsdl-operation>createCabin</wsdl-operation>
  <wrapped-element/>
```

```
    <method-param-parts-mapping>
      <param-position>0</param-position>
      <param-type>com.titan.clients.Cabin</param-type>
      <wsdl-message-mapping>
        <wsdl-message xmlns:wsdlMsgNS="http://travelagent.titan.com/jaws">
          wsdlMsgNS:TravelAgent_createCabin</wsdl-message>
        <wsdl-message-part-name>Cabin</wsdl-message-part-name>
        <parameter-mode>IN</parameter-mode>
      </wsdl-message-mapping>
    </method-param-parts-mapping>
  </service-endpoint-method-mapping>
    <service-endpoint-method-mapping>
      <java-method-name>findCabin</java-method-name>
      <wsdl-operation>findCabin</wsdl-operation>
      <wrapped-element/>
      <method-param-parts-mapping>
        <param-position>0</param-position>
        <param-type>int</param-type>
        <wsdl-message-mapping>
          <wsdl-message xmlns:wsdlMsgNS="http://travelagent.titan.com/jaws">
            wsdlMsgNS:TravelAgent_findCabin
          </wsdl-message>
          <wsdl-message-part-name>ID</wsdl-message-part-name>
          <parameter-mode>IN</parameter-mode>
        </wsdl-message-mapping>
      </method-param-parts-mapping>
      <wsdl-return-value-mapping>
        <method-return-value>com.titan.clients.Cabin</method-return-value>
        <wsdl-message xmlns:wsdlMsgNS="http://travelagent.titan.com/jaws">
          wsdlMsgNS:TravelAgent_findCabinResponse
        </wsdl-message>
        <wsdl-message-part-name>Cabin</wsdl-message-part-name>
      </wsdl-return-value-mapping>
    </service-endpoint-method-mapping>
  </service-endpoint-interface-mapping>
```

Running the Client

After executing the run.client task, the output of Client should look something like this:

```
C:\workbook\ex04_1>ant run.client
Buildfile: build.xml

prepare:

compile:

ejbjar:

clientjar:

run.client:
```

```
     [java] Master Suite
     [java] 1
     [java] 1
     [java] 3
```

Client adds a row to the database representing the Cabin bean and does not delete it at the conclusion of the program. You cannot run this program more than once unless you stop JBoss, clean the database by invoking the Ant task `clean.db`, and restart the application server. Otherwise, you will get the following error:

```
run.client:
     [java] java.rmi.RemoteException: Call invocation failed with code
          [Client] because of: java.lang.RuntimeException:
            org.jboss.tm.JBossRollbackException: Unable
            to commit, tx=TransactionImpl:XidImpl[FormatId=257,
            GlobalId=null:1099/3, BranchQual=null:1099, localId=0:3],
            status=STATUS_NO_TRANSACTION; - nested throwable:
            (org.hibernate.exception.GenericJDBCException:
               Could not execute JDBC batch update); nested exception is:
     [java]      javax.xml.rpc.soap.SOAPFaultException: java.lang.RuntimeException:
                 org.jboss.tm.JBossRollbackException: Unable to commit,
                tx=TransactionImpl:XidImpl[FormatId=257, GlobalId=null:1099/3,
                BranchQual=null:1099, localId=0:3], status=STATUS_NO_TRANSACTION; -
                nested throwable: (org.hibernate.exception.GenericJDBCException:
                Could not execute JDBC batch update)
     [java]     at org.jboss.ws.jaxrpc.CallImpl.invokeInternal(CallImpl.java:699)
     [java]     at org.jboss.ws.jaxrpc.CallImpl.invoke(CallImpl.java:408)
     [java]     at org.jboss.ws.jaxrpc.CallProxy.invoke(CallProxy.java:116)
     [java]     at $Proxy2.createCabin(Unknown Source)
     [java]     at com.titan.clients.Client.main(Client.java:25)
     [java] Caused by: javax.xml.rpc.soap.SOAPFaultException: java.lang.
RuntimeException: org.jboss.tm.JBossRollbackException: Unable to commit,
tx=TransactionImpl:XidImpl[FormatId=257, GlobalId=null:1099/3, BranchQual=null:1099,
localId=0:3], status=STATUS_NO_TRANSACTION; - nested throwable: (org.hibernate.
exception.GenericJDBCException: Could not execute JDBC batch update)
     [java]     at
          org.jboss.ws.jaxrpc.SOAPFaultExceptionHelper.getSOAPFaultException(
          SOAPFaultExceptionHelper.java:100)
     [java]     at
          org.jboss.ws.binding.soap.SOAPBindingProvider.unbindResponseMessage(
          SOAPBindingProvider.java:505)
     [java]     at org.jboss.ws.jaxrpc.CallImpl.invokeInternal(CallImpl.java:689)
     [java]     ... 4 more
```

This doesn't look like much of an error message, but JBoss is relying on the database and JDBC driver to provide a meaningful message.

Viewing the Database

Follow the steps outlined in the exercise for Chapter 4 to view the database. You should see identical data.

Exercise 19.2: Using a .NET Client

This exercise reuses the JAX-WS EJB endpoint defined in Exercise 19.1, but communicates to it using a .NET client rather than a Java-based JAX-RPC client. This demonstrates the powerful level of interoperability that can come from using web services.

Installing the Necessary Software

To build the .NET client, you are going to need the proper SDK and tools for your OS.

Windows

If you are running Windows, you will need to install the Microsoft .NET Framework and the .NET Framework SDK (separate downloads).

Unix

Download and install Mono.

Start Up JBoss

If you already have JBoss running, there is no reason to restart it. Otherwise, start it up as instructed in Workbook 1.

Initialize the Database

If you have problems running this example, shut down JBoss and run the `clean.db` Ant task.

Build and Deploy the Titan JAR

Perform the following steps:

1. Open a command prompt or shell terminal and change to the *ex19_2* directory created by the extraction process.
2. Set the `JAVA_HOME` and `JBOSS_HOME` environment variables to point to where your JDK and JBoss 4.0 are installed. Examples:

   Windows:

   ```
   C:\workbook\ex19_2> set JAVA_HOME=C:\jdk1.5.0
   C:\workbook\ex19_2> set JBOSS_HOME=C:\jboss-4.0.x
   ```

   Unix:

   ```
   $ export JAVA_HOME=/usr/local/jdk1.5.0
   $ export JBOSS_HOME=/usr/local/jboss-4.0
   ```

3. Add ant to your execution path. Ant is the build utility.

   Windows:

   C:\workbook\ex19_2> set PATH=..\ant\bin;%PATH%

   Unix:

   $ export PATH=../ant/bin:$PATH
4. Perform the build by typing ant.

As in the last exercise, *titan.jar* is rebuilt, copied to the JBoss *deploy* directory, and redeployed by the application server.

Examine the Client

Notice that the C# version of this client is strikingly similar to the Java client:

```
public class Client {
    public static void Main( ) {

       Cabin cabin_1 = new Cabin( );
       cabin_1.id = 2;
       cabin_1.name = "Jumbo Suite";
       cabin_1.deckLevel = 1;
       cabin_1.shipId = 1;
       cabin_1.bedCount = 2;

       TravelAgentService agent = new TravelAgentService( );

       agent.createCabin(cabin_1);

       Cabin cabin_2 = agent.findCabin(2);
       Console.WriteLine(cabin_2.name);
       Console.WriteLine(cabin_2.deckLevel);
       Console.WriteLine(cabin_2.shipId);
       Console.WriteLine(cabin_2.bedCount);
    }
}
```

Compile the Client

Windows

On Windows, the easiest way to set the proper system path and environmental variables is to run the .NET SDK Command Prompt, which should be in your menu after installing. After pulling up the prompt, follow these directions:

1. Change to the *ex19_2\dotnet* directory created by the extraction process.
2. Compile all files:

   csc TravelAgentService.cs Client.cs

Unix

On Unix, make sure that the Mono C# compiler (`mcs`) is in your path:

1. Open a terminal window and change to the *ex19_2/dotnet* directory created by the extraction process.
2. Compile all files:

   mcs TravelAgentService.cs Client.cs /r:System.Web.Services.dll

Run the Client

Run the Client application by invoking `Client`.exe. The following output should occur.

Windows:

```
.\Client.exe
Jumbo Suite
1
1
2
```

Unix:

```
mono Client.exe
Jumbo Suite
1
1
2
```

As before, rerunning the program will cause another insert of the same row, which should lead to the same JDBC error:

```
Unhandled Exception: System.Web.Services.Protocols.SoapException:
java.lang.RuntimeException:
      org.jboss.tm.JBossRollbackException: Unable to commit,
 tx=TransactionImpl:XidImpl[FormatId=257, GlobalId=null:1099/3, BranchQual=null:1099,
localId=0:3], status=STATUS_NO_TRANSACTION; - nested throwable: (org.hibernate.
exception.GenericJDBCException: Could not execute JDBC batch update)
in <0x00469> System.Web.Services.Protocols.SoapHttpClientProtocol:ReceiveResponse
(System.Net.WebResponse response, System.Web.Services.Protocols.SoapClientMessage
message, System.Web.Services.Protocols.SoapExtension[] extensions)
in (wrapper remoting-invoke-with-check) System.Web.Services.Protocols.
SoapHttpClientProtocol:ReceiveResponse (System.Net.WebResponse,System.Web.Services.
Protocols.SoapClientMessage,
     System.Web.Services.Protocols.SoapExtension[])
in <0x0026d> System.Web.Services.Protocols.SoapHttpClientProtocol:Invoke
 (System.String method_name, System.Object[] parameters)
in (wrapper remoting-invoke-with-check)
System.Web.Services.Protocols.SoapHttpClientProtocol:Invoke (string,object[])
in <0x0003e> TravelAgentService:createCabin (.Cabin Cabin)
in (wrapper remoting-invoke-with-check) TravelAgentService:createCabin (Cabin)
in <0x0006e> Client:Main ()
```

PART III

Appendix

APPENDIX

JBoss Database Configuration

This appendix describes how to set up database pools for data sources other than the default database embedded in JBoss, Hypersonic SQL. It also shows you how to set up your EJBs and entity beans to use these database pools. For illustration purposes, we've modified Exercise 4.1 in Workbook 2 to configure and use an Oracle connection pool with JBoss.

Set Up the Database

To deploy a database connection pool, JBoss requires a data pool configuration file. The configuration file is very simple, yet you can use it for almost all standard data pool setups.

Basic Setup

The first step is to download the JDBC driver classes for your database. Copy your database's JDBC JAR file to *$JBOSS_HOME/server/default/lib*. For example, the Oracle JDBC class files are contained in *classes12.zip*.

The JBoss distribution includes example database connection-pool files in the directory *$JBOSS_HOME/docs/examples/jca*. The name of each file ends in *-ds.xml*. For this exercise, we've copied the *oracle-ds.xml* configuration file to *exAppendixA/titandb-ds.xml* and modified it accordingly.

To deploy this connection pool, you must copy *titandb-ds.xml* to the *$JBOSS_HOME/service/default/deploy* directory. Note that the name of this config file must end with *-ds.xml*, or JBoss will not deploy it.

Database connection pools are among the many things that can be hot-deployed in JBoss, simply by dropping the pool's XML configuration file into the *deploy* directory.

Examine some of the configuration parameters defined by this file.

titandb-ds.xml

```
<datasources>
  <local-tx-datasource>
    <jndi-name>OracleDS</jndi-name>
```

The <jndi-name> tag identifies the connection pool within JNDI. You can look up this pool in JNDI with the java:/OracleDS string. The class of this bound object is javax.sql.DataSource.

```
    <connection-url>jdbc:oracle:thin:@localhost:1521:JBOSSDB</connection-url>
```

The <connection-url> tag tells the Oracle JDBC driver how to connect to the database. The URL varies depending on the database you use, so consult your database JDBC manuals to find out how to obtain the appropriate address.

```
    <driver-class>oracle.jdbc.driver.OracleDriver</driver-class>
```

The <driver-class> tag tells JBoss and the base JDBC classes the name of the Oracle JDBC driver class that they need to instantiate and use.

```
    <user-name>scott</user-name>
    <password>tiger</password>
  </local-tx-datasource>
</datasources>
```

Finally, the <user-name> and <password> tags are used when you are connecting to the Oracle database.

Examine the persistence.xml File

To use this Oracle data source, modify the *persistence.xml* file described in Exercise 4.1 to point to this file.

persistence.xml

```
<persistence>
   <persistence-unit>
      <name>titan</name>
      <jta-data-source>java:/OracleDS</jta-data-source>
      <properties>
         <property name="hibernate.hbm2ddl.auto" value="create-drop"/>
      </properties>
   </persistence-unit>
</persistence>
```

Notice that the java:/ string prefixes the <jndi-name> data source that you defined in the *titandb-ds.xml* file.

Start Up JBoss

In this variation of Exercise 4.1, you must restart JBoss so that it recognizes the JDBC JAR file you copied into the *lib* directory. Review Workbook 1 at the beginning of this workbook if you don't remember how to start JBoss.

Build and Deploy the Example Programs

Perform the following steps:

1. Open a command prompt or shell terminal and change to the *exAppendixA* directory created by the extraction process.
2. Set the `JAVA_HOME` and `JBOSS_HOME` environment variables to point to where your JDK and JBoss 4.0 are installed. Examples:

   Windows:

   ```
   C:\workbook\exAppendixA> set JAVA_HOME=C:\jdk1.5.0
   C:\workbook\exAppendixA> set JBOSS_HOME=C:\jboss-4.0.x
   ```

   Unix:

   ```
   $ export JAVA_HOME=/usr/local/jdk1.5.0
   $ export JBOSS_HOME=/usr/local/jboss-4.0
   ```

3. Add `ant` to your execution path. Ant is the build utility.

   Windows:

   ```
   C:\workbook\exAppendixA> set PATH=..\ant\bin;%PATH%
   ```

   Unix:

   ```
   $ export PATH=../ant/bin:$PATH
   ```

4. Perform the build by typing `ant`.

As in the exercise in the workbook chapters, *titan.jar* is rebuilt, copied to the JBoss *deploy* directory, and redeployed by the application server. The build script copies *titandb-ds.xml* to the *deploy* directory as well, which triggers deployment of the customer database pool.

Examine and Run the Client Applications

As in Exercise 4.1, the example program creates a single Cabin bean, populates each of its attributes, and then queries the created bean with its primary key.

Run the Client application by invoking `ant run.client` at the command prompt. Remember to set your `JBOSS_HOME` and `PATH` environment variables.

The output of Client should look something like this:

```
C:\workbook\exAppendixA>ant run.client
Buildfile: build.xml
```

```
prepare:

compile:

ejbjar:

run.client:
     [java] Master Suite
     [java] 1
     [java] 1
     [java] 3
```

Index

A

We'd like to hear your suggestions for improving our indexes. Send email to *index@oreilly.com*.

B

C

D

E

F

G

J

K

L

M

N

O

P

Q

R

S

T

U

V

W

X

Z

About the Authors

Bill Burke is chief architect at JBoss, Inc. Besides coleading the EJB 3.0 and AOP projects at JBoss, he represents JBoss as an expert on the EJB 3.0 and Java EE 5 specification committees. Bill was the co-author of the JBoss workbook included with *Enterprise JavaBeans*, Fourth Edition, and has published numerous articles in various print and online magazines.

Richard Monson-Haefel is the award-winning author of three best-selling editions of *Enterprise JavaBeans* (O'Reilly), *J2EE Web Services* (Addison-Wesley), and the coauthor of *Java Message Service* (O'Reilly). He is one of the world's leading experts and book authors on Enterprise Java. He is the lead architect of OpenEJB, an open source EJB container used in Apple Computer's WebObjects platform, and has consulted as an architect on J2EE, CORBA, Java RMI, and other distributed computing projects over the past several years. You can learn more about Richard at his web site, *http://www.monson-haefel.com*.

Colophon

The animals on the cover of *Enterprise JavaBeans*, Fifth Edition, are a wallaby and her joey. Wallabies are middle-sized marsupials belonging to the kangaroo family (*Macropodidae*, the second-largest marsupial family). They are grazers and browsers, native to Australia and found in a variety of habitats on that continent. Female wallabies have a well-developed anterior pouch in which they hold their young. When they are born, the tiny, still-blind joeys instinctively crawl up into their mothers' pouches and begin to nurse. They stay in the pouch until they are fairly well-grown. A female wallaby can support joeys from up to three litters at once: one in her uterus, one in her pouch, and one that has graduated from the pouch but still returns to nurse.

Like all *Macropodidae*, wallabies have long, narrow hind feet and powerful hind limbs. Their long, heavy tails are used primarily for balance and stability and are not prehensile. Wallabies resemble kangaroos, but are smaller: they can measure anywhere from less than two feet to over five feet long, with the tail accounting for nearly half of their total length. Oddly enough, although they can hop along quite quickly (reaching speeds of up to 50 km/h), it is physically impossible for wallabies to walk backward!

The three main types of wallaby are brush, rock, and nail-tailed. There are 11 species of brush wallaby (genus *Macropus*), including the red-necked and pretty-faced wallabies, and 6 named species of rock wallaby (*Petrogale*). Brush wallabies usually live in brushland or open woods. Rock wallabies, which are notable for their extreme agility, are usually found among rocks and near water. There are only three species of nail-tailed wallaby (*Onychogalea*), which are so named because of the horny growth that appears on the tip of their tails. Two of these species are endangered—although they were once the most numerous type of wallaby, their numbers have been seriously depleted by foxes and feral cats. Aside from hunting and habitat destruction, predation and competition by introduced species such as these are what threaten wallabies today.

The cover image is an original engraving from *The Illustrated Natural History: Mammalia*, by J.G. Wood, published in 1865. The cover font is Adobe ITC Garamond. The text font is Linotype Birka; the heading font is Adobe Myriad Condensed; and the code font is LucasFont's TheSans Mono Condensed.

Related Titles from O'Reilly

Java

Ant: The Definitive Guide, *2nd Edition*

Better, Faster, Lighter Java

Beyond Java

Eclipse

Eclipse Cookbook

Eclipse IDE Pocket Guide

Enterprise JavaBeans 3.0, *5th Edition*

Hardcore Java

Head First Design Patterns

Head First Design Patterns Poster

Head First Java, *2nd Edition*

Head First Servlets & JSP

Head First EJB

Hibernate: A Developer's Notebook

J2EE Design Patterns

Java 5.0 Tiger: A Developer's Notebook

Java & XML Data Binding

Java & XML

Java Cookbook, *2nd Edition*

Java Data Objects

Java Database Best Practices

Java Enterprise Best Practices

Java Enterprise in a Nutshell, *3nd Edition*

Java Examples in a Nutshell, *3rd Edition*

Java Extreme Programming Cookbook

Java Generics and Collections

Java in a Nutshell, *5th Edition*

Java Management Extensions

Java Message Service

Java Network Programming, *2nd Edition*

Java NIO

Java Performance Tuning, *2nd Edition*

Java RMI

Java Security, *2nd Edition*

JavaServer Faces

JavaServer Pages, *2nd Edition*

Java Servlet & JSP Cookbook

Java Servlet Programming, *2nd Edition*

Java Swing, *2nd Edition*

Java Web Services in a Nutshell

JBoss: A Developer's Notebook

JBoss at Work: A Practical Guide

Learning Java, *2nd Edition*

Mac OS X for Java Geeks

Maven: A Developer's Notebook

Programming Jakarta Struts, *2nd Edition*

QuickTime for Java: A Developer's Notebook

Spring: A Developer's Notebook

Swing Hacks

Tomcat: The Definitive Guide

WebLogic: The Definitive Guide

O'REILLY®